Contents

KV-577-379

Notes on contributors

Anne Alexander has written most recently in this journal on the Iraqi resistance and is the author of *Nasser* (2005).

Paul Blackledge is author of *Perry Anderson, Marxism and the New Left* and *Reflections on the Marxist Theory of History*.

Andy Brown teaches at a secondary school in east London.

Choi Il-bung is a leading member of All Together in South Korea.

Judy Cox is active in Respect in east London.

Panos Garganas is a member of the Greek party Sosialistiko Ergatiko Komma, and edits their paper.

Mike Gonzalez was a member of the executive of the Scottish Socialist Party and has written in this journal on Latin America.

Mike Haynes is author of *Russia: Class and Power in the Twentieth Century* and *A Century of State Murder?*

Christian Høgsbjerg is doing research in Leeds on the life of C L R James.

Kim Ha-young's book on North Korea was reviewed in *IS* 109 and translations from it are on our website.

Michael Löwy is a member of the LCR in France and author of *George Lukács, from Romanticism to Bolshevism*.

John Molyneux is author of *Marxism and the Party*, *Leon Trotsky's Theory of Revolution*, and *Rembrandt*.

Stan Newens was a member of the Socialist Review Group (the distant forerunner of the Socialist Workers Party) in the 1950s. He became a Labour MP in 1964 and then an MEP.

John Newsinger is the author, most recently, of *The Blood Never Dried: A People's History of the British Empire*.

Chris Nineham is active in the Stop the War Coalition.

Mark Shenkin is researching social movements in Latin America, and is a founding member of Documentalistas Sin Tierra.

Crawford Spence teaches in the School of Management at St Andrews University in Scotland.

The painful passing of Tony Blair

The political crisis in the New Labour government was coming to a head as we went to press. Arguments over exactly when Tony Blair would enable Gordon Brown to attempt to succeed him as prime minister were leading to incredible levels of vitriolic abuse between the rival New Labour camps, with shouting matches in Downing Street, ex-ministers and ministers denouncing each other, and MPs circulating rival petitions. Most bewildering for many people was the complete lack of political difference between the two sides. Brown has enthusiastically pushed through Blair's policies over privatisation, public private partnerships, cuts in pension entitlement and finance for the wars in Iraq and the Middle East. Just in case anyone had any doubts, he has came out over the summer in full support for nuclear power, for upgrading Britain's nuclear submarine missiles and for being a junior partner in Bush's wars.

On the face of it, then, there is no politics involved in the war between two egos. Hence the obscenity of various trade unions telling people that a Brown government would somehow how be a victory for their members.

Yet this non-political fight has significant political roots and can have important political consequences. The roots lie in the very character of New Labour politics. For Blair and Brown alike, politics consists of using a mixture of public relations spin and fashionable management techniques to impose, in a top-down way, neo-liberal policies in the name of reform. The hope is to keep the Murdoch, Rothermere and Desmond media corporations happy, and so, supposedly, win over 'middle England' voters. 'Old fashioned' Labour politics, with its meetings and resolutions and debates, is replaced by 'modern' rallies where people have to do no more than stand up and applaud those the media decide are their best leaders.

The result inevitably has been the haemorrhaging of party membership under the impact of the policies pursued. In the first term these were a pursuance of Tory cutbacks in public sector expenditure. In the second term they were the wars against Afghanistan and Iraq, and repeated verbal attacks on public sector workers. Now, in the third term, they are the open support for the Israeli onslaught on Lebanon and a new batch of privatisation measures, particularly in the health service. Today the party membership is a good deal less than half what it was when New Labour was elected nine years ago.

The political machines built round Blair and Brown to impose their shared policies now have no way of resolving a clash of personalities between their leaders other than to turn their spin and their bullying against each other. Political debate is replaced by tit for tat character assassination, creating a bitterness that is going to make life difficult for whichever machine finally wins. If Brown wins, he risks facing the animosity of all those who blame him for ruining what was meant to be Blair's triumphant final year; if the Blairites prevent Brown from winning, his shadow will stalk them at every turn. They will be stalked by something else as well.

It was support for Bush's war—and the impact of the enormous anti-war movement—that made Blair so weak that he finally had to concede some ground to the Brownites over when he was going to resign. Particularly important was the way opposition to Blair's support for the Israeli onslaught on Lebanon shook the loyalty even of many MPs who had voted for the Afghan and Iraq wars. But Blair has left two poisoned chalices for his successor—a war in Iraq that cannot be won, and a war in Afghanistan which could well end in an old fashioned defeat. Iraq cannot be controlled with only a quarter of the number of troops the Russians used in their war on Afghanistan, and to attempt to control Afghanistan with a fifth of the number of troops in Iraq is almost to guarantee disaster. Brown has no easier answer to that than Blair.

But the real importance of the leadership crisis is its impact on the rather meagre ranks of New Labour enthusiasts. This has major implications for all the activists who hold the wider labour movement together—the men and women who run union branches, sit on shop stewards committees and act as workplace reps. There are hundreds of thousands of them.

For the best part of a century their politics has been Labour politics in the widest sense of the term, with no more than one in ten of the activists ever accepting the alternative politics once provided by the Communist Party. There has been a clean break with New Labour by some activists in the last few years, as is shown by the disaffiliation of the firefighters' FBU and the rail workers' RMT from the Labour Party, but the majority still retain a residual loyalty, however strained, to the party. The big guns of the trade union bureaucracy are trying to divert disaffection with Blair into support for Brown. But he makes it more difficult for them every time he opens his mouth to address the City of London or the Murdoch press.

There was a time when the traditional Labour left believed it and it alone could provide an alternative to the Labour right. So in 1931, 1951, 1970 and 1979, it grew in strength with the demise of Labour governments, even if its illusory hopes that it could change capitalism through the Labour Party never came to fruition. The pattern was already sufficiently established 40 years ago to be one of the themes of Ralph Miliband's classic history of labourism, *Parliamentary Socialism*.

This time round the Labour left is in a very weak position with the collapse of Labour's membership and the concentration of power in the apparatus. Left MP John McDonnell has declared himself as a candidate whenever the leadership election finally takes place. But it is a challenge that even many of those who support him do not place much hope in. The leaders of the big unions will not back him—the exception, Mark Serwotka of the civil service PCS, leads a non-affiliated union. The centre-left 'Grass Roots Alliance' has just won the four local constituency seats on the party's national executive but its top vote was only 19,000 (out of 36,313 returned ballot papers from a total claimed membership of 178,889). And the parliamentary left organised in the Campaign Group are divided over whether to back McDonnell. This is all a very far cry from when Tony Benn stood for deputy leader in 1981 and took 49.5 percent of the votes.

John McDonnell's candidacy has the potential to make some activists see through the pretensions of the Blairites and Brownites alike. For this reason, it should have the sympathy of everyone who is hostile to New Labour, its wars and its neo-liberalism. But it is not going break the hold of

New Labour, still less turn the Labour Party into an instrument for achieving decisive social change. The Labour left deserve our solidarity in their efforts to confront the right. But with solidarity should go fraternal debate over the incapacity of the means they have chosen to achieve the transformation of society they desire—a lesson which the leadership contest itself can only confirm.

There is unease among hundreds of thousands of activists with Brown, which the established Labour left is unable to capitalise on. This provides the anti-capitalist left outside the Labour Party with both an opportunity and a challenge. The opportunity is to seize on the disarray in New Labour ranks to begin to break the century-old hold of labourism on the movement's activists. The challenge is to find the means to do this.

It is not going to be achieved by mere propaganda about the past as well as present failings of Labour, however useful that it is. Still less will it come about by an 'I told you so' approach. What is required is a two-pronged strategy that reaches out to those people who are unclear as to which way to turn.

The first element is what Respect has been trying to do—to build unity for an electoral challenge to New Labour around a set of minimal demands against war and neo-liberalism. Such a challenge is needed to provide a national left political focus for people who might otherwise react to New Labour's behaviour by dropping into apathy or even looking to the right.

But building the electoral focus by itself is not enough.

There is the potential to draw many people not yet prepared to break electorally with Labour into fightbacks over particular issues—above all over opposition to Bush's wars, but also against neo-liberal measures like health cuts or in support of important strikes. Such fightbacks cannot be organised on a sufficiently large scale simply by relying on the forces of the established far left. United platforms involving left MPs and left union leaders are needed to draw in those who have traditionally looked to such people.

Fortunately, the cracks in New Labour at the top are creating the conditions which make it easier to establish such united platforms. Even union leaders who are coming out for Brown are voicing some verbal opposition to the wars and to the latest raft of privatisations and cutbacks. And a number of Labour MPs regarded as 'loyal' in the past are making at least occasional noises of discontent. The most extreme instance is that of

Clare Short, moving in three and a half years from voting for the war so as to keep her cabinet position to a complete, if confused, break with the Labour Party. But there are quite a few others who feel they have little to show for compromising their beliefs in the past. Their motives will often be mixed: it has always been amazing how many Labour MPs remember near-forgotten political principles when their ministerial hopes are thwarted or when party policies seem to pose the risk of electoral defeat. But regardless of their motives, their voicing of discontent can act as a focus to draw very many other people into struggle. And while the experience of successful united struggle is unlikely to convince many of the leaders to look to an alternative politics to those of labourism, it can have that effect on many of the rank and file.

Hopefully, we will have enjoyed one example of a united front mobilisation by the time readers get this journal—the 'Time To Go' anti-war demonstration called outside Tony Blair's final Labour Party conference in Manchester. This should make it possible to build towards making a success of November's Organising for Fighting Unions conference, which Respect has sponsored but which also includes figures from the Labour and trade union left. In such ways the dynamism of the anti-war movement can fuse with the anger at domestic policies to beak the grip of New Labour on the wider working class movement.

Hizbollah and the war Israel lost[1]
Chris Harman

For the first time, the Israel Defence Forces were unable to prevail in an all-out war—*Olivier Roy,* **Financial Times**

What is new—and dramatically so—about this campaign is its outcome. Arabs soon dubbed this the sixth Arab-Israeli war, and for some of them—and indeed for some Israelis—it already ranks, in its strategic, psychological and political consequences, as perhaps the most significant since Israel's 'war of independence' in 1948... A small band of irregulars kept at bay one of the world's most powerful armies for over a month, and inflicted remarkable losses on it—*David Hirst, the* **Guardian**'s *veteran Middle East correspondent*

Israeli military authorities talked of 'cleaning' and 'mopping up' operations by their soldiers south of the Litany river but, to the Lebanese, it seems as if it is the Hizbollah that have been doing the 'mopping up'. By last night, the Israelis had not even been able to reach the dead crew of a helicopter—shot down on Saturday night—which crashed into a Lebanese valley—*Robert Fisk, of the* **Independent**, *on the last day of the war*

Hizbollah could not inflict a major military defeat on Israel, a possibility that was always excluded by the utterly disproportionate balance of forces in the same way that it was impossible for the Vietnamese resistance to inflict a major military defeat on the US; but neither could Israel inflict any defeat on

Hizbollah. In this sense, Hizbollah is undoubtedly the real political victor and Israel the real loser in the 33-day war—*Gilbert Achcar, Lebanese Marxist living in France*

Hizbollah has remained as it was. It has not been destroyed, nor disarmed, nor even removed from where it was. Its fighters have proved themselves in battle and have even garnered compliments from Israeli soldiers… In Israel, there is now a general atmosphere of disappointment and despondency—*Uri Avnery, Israeli writer*

The same conclusion came from all sides after the summer's 33-day war of Israel against Hizbollah and Lebanon. What began as a long planned Israeli attack aimed at destroying Hizbollah ended in a humiliation for Israel.

This outcome was not only a shock to the Israeli military. It was also a devastating blow to George Bush and his junior partner Tony Blair in their attempt to rescue US global hegemony from the debacle of their Iraq adventure. The US administration gave at least a nod and a wink to the Israeli military and may well have been involved in planning the onslaught unleashed on 12 July, as US journalist Seymour Hersh has claimed.[2] Their aim was simple. The Israelis were to deal a devastating blow to Iranian influence in Lebanon—and hopefully to Iranian influence over the Shias in Iraq—as part of the offensive against Iran itself.

As Charles Krauthammer put it in the *Washington Post*:

The defeat of Hizbollah would be a huge loss for Iran, both psychologically and strategically. Iran would lose its foothold in Lebanon. It would lose its major means to destabilise and inject itself into the heart of the Middle East. It would be shown to have vastly overreached in trying to establish itself as the regional superpower.[3]

The assumption of the Israeli and American governments was that victory would be easy.

Hani Shukrallah (managing editor of the influential Cairo-based *Al-Ahram Weekly*) has spelt out how they saw it:

Hizbollah's head seemed 'ripe for the picking'. A year before, a great section of the Lebanese people had risen up in rebellion against Syria's political and military sway over their country… Washington had found a willing, if uncommon ally in Paris, the erstwhile 'old Europe's' supreme representative… The Arab regimes had reasons of their own for wishing Hizbollah to simply go away…muttering darkly about the growing threat of a 'Shiite arc' in their midst… So confident were the Americans and Israelis of the success of this strategy, they initially gave it a week to work.[4]

But things turned out very differently:

Week one passed into week two, into week three, Lebanon did not fracture… Seventeen days after the start of the Israeli attack on Lebanon, Israel was withdrawing its elite Golani Brigade from the southern Lebanese town of Bint Jbeil, which they had claimed to have taken a week earlier.[5]

What was meant to be a great military and poltical advance for Israel and the US turned into its opposite:

Everybody was changing their tune. The Israelis, who initially had spoken of crushing Hizbollah, were now talking of keeping Hizbollah's rockets out of range of northern Israeli towns. US state secretary Condoleezza Rice, who had been literally sticking her tongue out at world public opinion as Washington continued to veto a ceasefire call a mere week before, was heading back to the region and speaking of the 'great sacrifices' both sides had to make. The Europeans, who had been happy to look the other way, mumbling about 'disproportionate' response, were now…willing to actually come out in condemnation of Israel's brutality and slaughter of civilians… And the 'Arab friends' were in a fix—yet again. Faced with the intensifying rage of their peoples, they were now scrambling over each other in their rush to find suitably heated and flowery rhetoric with which to express their condemnation of Israel.[6]

There could hardly be a greater contrast with previous Arab-Israeli wars. They saw very quick victories for the Israeli armies, the Arab armies very quickly suing for peace. The 1967 war was the most graphic example, with the Israeli force smashing three Arab armies in six days, taking control of the West Bank, Gaza, Golan Heights (which they still hold 39 years later) and the Sinai Peninsula (which they returned to Egypt after the peace treaty of 1977).

For a whole generation of Arab nationalists the 1967 defeat was the death of their project of achieving independence from imperialism and liberating Palestine. Now it is an Arab army which has been victorious.[7] The consequences for the Middle East as a whole can be immense.

Behind the Hizbollah victory

There were two main reasons for the ease of past Israeli victories, besides the general superiority of their armaments (because of massive US military aid since the early 1950s):[8]

● The soldiers of the Israeli army were much more dedicated fighters than their Arab opponents. They had seized another people's land and were convinced they had no choice but to fight to hold it. To this degree they had some of the characteristics of a citizens' or a people's army, despite their privileged situation vis a vis the Arabs. By contrast, the armies of the various Arab nations were made up of two groups which had little interest in fighting seriously, as Tony Cliff pointed out at the time of the 1967 war.[9] The officer corps were more concerned with maintaining their socially privileged positions in their own states than with making sacrifices on behalf of the Palestinians. And the mass of the peasant conscripts could hardly be expected to fight to the death in defence of the Palestinians' right to land when they barely had that right in their own countries.

● The Israeli army, made up in the main of educated settlers, was much more adept at using modern sophisticated weaponry than Arab armies mainly composed of poorly educated peasant conscripts

Things were different on both sides in this summer's war.

● Hizbollah was not formed by an established government and officered by members of a privileged group concerned mainly with advancing their social position. Rather, it was formed from below, by people reacting to the experience of oppression by other groups in Lebanese society and of military occupation by Israeli forces in 1982 and after. It was forged in struggles by people who know they are fighting to hold on to what they have, however little that may be in some cases.

● At the same time, decades of slow educational advance mean that today Arab universities turn out thousands of people every year with the technical skills to handle sophisticated weaponry. As a book by a member of Hizbollah points out: 'With an increasing presence of educated and cultured members it became possible to employ the benefits from modern computers, communications and various engineering technologies'.[10]

This has enabled Hizbollah to combine 'a guerrilla force's decentralised flexibility and a national military's sophistication, fielding weapons like the C-802 Noor radar-guided anti-ship missile (an Iranian-made knockoff of the Chinese "Silkworm" C-802) that struck an Israeli warship on 14 July'.[11]

While an Arab force has finally emerged with these characteristics, the Israeli army has lost some of its old winning points. The early settler society, with its commitment to creating a new society on another people's land, has given way to one dominated by second and third generations who have not experienced any sense of threat to their own well-being for four decades. The new settlers (like the million Russians, many of whom have only dubious claims to be Jewish[12]) come to enjoy the benefits of this established society, not to fight to build it. They have been conscripted to take part in the occupation of the West Bank. But that has involved bombarding civilians from the security of fortified posts and heavily armoured tanks, not real fighting.

The former Israeli minister Yossi Sarid has argued:

> The IDF was not properly prepared for this new war in Lebanon... Instead of functioning and preparing like an army, the IDF has been deployed and has been behaving like a foreign legion or quasi-police force... The young soldiers and officers were told during the intifada years that they were at war... But any similarity between the fighting in the territories and war is vague at best... Attempts to apprehend wanted terrorists by surrounding a house—that is not war; targeted assassination—that is not war; raiding factories—that is not war; even the siege placed on Yasser Arafat's headquarters in Ramallah is not a military campaign about which books will be written. Almost everything that happens in the occupied territories, from the day the IDF occupied them, has really only been a deluxe form of war.[13]

The result was that after failing to subdue Hizbollah by creating terror through aerial bombardment of civilian targets the Israeli forces pushed into Lebanon with their tanks—and their soldiers found themselves sitting targets for the Hizbollah anti-tank guns. From working with the US and Britain to avoid at all costs a UN call for a ceasefire in the first days of the war, Israel ended up a month later heaving a sigh of relief at the US-French agreement to push for UN resolution 1701 with its promise of an international force to try to do what the Israelis had failed to do—stop Hizbollah activity in the area between the Israeli border and the Litany river.

The reasons for Hizbollah's success

An account of Hizbollah by one of its members explains its greater military successes compared with previous Arab resistance to Israel as based on two things: 'the fighters' belief in the cause'[14] and stress within Hizbollah of not getting 'trapped' by 'subordination' to politics of regimes.[15]

But it was not just because they were run by governments that previous Arab armies were so unsuccessful in resisting Israeli aggression. It was that the governments and their armies reflected the class character of the societies. The armies which fought so unsuccessfully in 1948 were those of regimes representing the interests of the old 'feudal' landowning classes and imposed by the Western colonial powers—with the most effective army, that of Jordan, getting its orders from British officers (see Anne Alexander's article later in this issue). The divergent interests between the different ruling classes meant there was no strategic or military coordination and the war was as much a scramble between them to grab Palestinian land for themselves as a battle against the Israelis.

By the time of the 1967 war revolutionary movements and military coups had replaced these regimes with ones who were verbally committed to Arab nationalism, with talk of a single Arab nation 'from the Atlantic to the Gulf' standing in the interests of the mass of the population. There had been substantial reform, with a break up of the big landed estates and nationalisation of much industry. But it was reform in the interests of the class from which the army officers who oversaw it came—a section of the middle class who aspired to upward mobility by using the state to advance its own interests. This was reflected in the behaviour of the bulk of the officer corps itself, which showed little more dedication, courage or competence than in 1948. And however much they used rhetoric about 'the Arab nation', their priorities lay with their own class interests, bound up as they were with the advance of their own particular state and not with a united, coordinated struggle against Israel. This was reflected in strategic and tactical ineptness, and an unwillingness to draw the Israeli army into forms of guerrilla struggle that might damage their own material interests.

Writing immediately after the 1967 defeat, Tony Cliff contrasted the disastrous approach of the most significant of the Arab nationalist regimes, Nasser's in Egypt, with that used by the National Liberation Front against the US in Vietnam:

> The strength of any anti-imperialist liberation movement is in the masses of workers and peasants mobilised, in their self-activity on the one hand, and the correct choice of the weakest link in the imperialist chain on the other. Hence the National Liberation Front (NLF) in Vietnam is absolutely right in relying on mass guerrilla bands and armies, and harassing the US army and its hangers-on. The potential strength of the Arab anti-imperialist movement lies in the mass of workers and peasants. The targets of attack should be the oilfields, the oil pipelines and refineries. The peasants should carry out revolutionary land reform, thus creating the base for a guerilla war. Nasser's military confrontation with Israel is exactly the opposite of the policy and tactics of the NLF.[16]

The Arab nationalist regimes as class regimes tied into capitalism were incapable of the sort of warfare needed to defeat Israel and its imperialist backers. And once they had failed to defeat Israel a third time in the 1973 'Yom Kippur War', despite some initial succcses, they drew the logic and one after another did deals with imperialism and even, in the case of Nasser's successors in Egypt, with Israel.

Hizbollah's record has been different, not because it is not a state, but because it originated out of an organisation of struggle from below.

The Shias of Lebanon were historically the most opprssed section of the country's people. This did not mean they were all peasants or workers. There was always a handful of very wealthy families, and a layer of shopkeepers, traders and middle class professionals. But a much greater proportion of the Shias belonged to the lower classes than was the case with the country's other religious groups—they were 'over-represented among working classes in the under-developed sectors of industry and agriculture'.[17] Even the middle classes were squeezed by the state structure bequeathed by French imperialism, which divided political power between the leaders of the Maronite Christians, the Sunni Muslims and the Druze. At the time of independence from the French 40 percent of the highest posts in the civil service were Maronite, 27 percent Sunni, only 3.2 percent

Shia,[18] and such discrimination remained fundamentally in place, though in less blatant proportions, until the Taif agreement that ended the country's civil war in 1989.

Two things interacted to give rise to Hizbollah as a movement. The first was the way the Iranian Revolution of 1979 brought to power a regime led by Shia clerics. Some of the Shia clergy in Lebanon had close educational and family ties to the victors in Iran and were inspired by their ideology of overcoming oppression and poverty through the creation of an Islamic 'community' that united rich and poor, doing away with the greed and atomisation resulting from 'Western influences'. They sought to bring about change by combining religious preaching with the establishment of 'a socio-political movement with the primary mission of alleviating poverty', especially in South Lebanon, the Eastern Beka, and 'boroughs of misery around Beirut'.[19]

The second was the Israeli invasions of Lebanon in 1978 and 1982 aimed at smashing the Palestinians. It soon became clear that the local Lebanese population, mainly Shia in composition, was bearing the brunt of the Israeli occupation. The radical Shia clergy began working in the Beka valley with a big detachment of Revolutionary Guards from Iran to create a guerrilla organisation capable of putting up resistance to the Israeli occupation. The training was not just military. It involved a very high religious content, aimed at creating an intense dedication to the struggle. As one account puts it:

> Hizbollah's fighters have to undergo the greater jihad, that is, spiritual religious transformation, if they are to master the smaller jihad, that is, armed struggle that requires martyrdom. By overcoming one's self and earthly desires, through acceptance of the virtues of martyrdom, Hizbollah's fighters have been able to evoke fear and alarm among their enemies.[20]

A willingness to accept martyrdom was seen as essential to the struggle—'the power imbalance' caused by the much greater armoury available to Israelis 'could only be equalised through martyrdom'.[21] And a very deep Shia religious commitment was necessary to establish the required frame of mind. But suicide attacks were by no means the usual predominant form of struggle.

'Priority is with methods that do not necessitate martyrdom… Only twelve operations executed with car bombs were recorded.' Most martyrdom was through 'atypical' operations where death was 'an expected result'.[22]

The key to Hizbollah's strategy against the Israeli army's occupation of South Lebanon from 1982 to 2000 was to hit the enemy unexpectedly and not to engage in supposedly heroic but in reality disastrous fights on the enemy's terms. In this way, the number of operations grew from 100 in 1985–89 to 1,030 in 1990–95 to 4,928 in 1996–2000,[23] when the disarray in which the Israeli forces finally withdrew gave an enormous boost to Hizbollah's popularity. Sources say that three years ago Hizbollah had '20,000 fighters and 5,000 security personnel'.[24]

Such has been its popularity, that it has had non-Shias wanting to join in its resistance activities, and has set up special guerrilla units for them—although it ensures that overall control is in the hands of the 'devout'. According to Hamzeh, Hizbollah's Islamic Current includes Sunni groups that coordinate their activities with Hizbollah, plus Lebanese Resistance Brigades that include Islamists and non-Islamists.[25] In the 33-day war it also coordinated its activities with independent resistance groups, for instance those run by the Lebanese Communist Party.

If Hizbollah did not begin just as a military organisation, it is much more than that today. Its welfare network of clinics, hospital, schools, community and educational scholarships has expanded massively, until according to some accounts it is greater than that of the Lebanese state in the southern suburbs of Beirut, in the Beka valley and in southern Lebanon.[26] Its medical units, for instance, are said to deal with half a million people a year. And in order to solidify support, it has branched out from providing services to Shias to also cater for some Sunnis, Christians and Druze in its localities.

It runs a fully equipped TV channel, al-Manar, which 'has a corporate atmosphere with several hundred employees'[27] and its 'syndicate unit has representatives in the Lebanese Labour Federation, the Lebanese trade unions, the Lebanese Farmers' Union, the Lebanese University Faculty Association, the Engineers Syndicate Association, and the Lebanese University Student Association'.[28]

It is this network of popular activities and organisations that explains the degree of popular support it has built up and which enabled it to operate under the very turrets of the Israeli tanks. The network has also enabled it to insert itself into the very centre of Lebanon's public institutions, with influence over local authorities, MPs and, since last year, two members of the cabinet.

Yet this involves it in two different sorts of compromises.

The first are with its religious basis. The Shias are a minority in Lebanese society, although today the biggest single minority, and there are other political forces among the Shias besides Hizbollah. In order to build the influence of their organisation in such a situation—and to avoid plunging the country into another sectarian civil war—the Hizbollah leadership have effectively dropped the demand for a Shia Islamic state on which they were originally founded under Khomeini's influence.[29]

The Hizbollah historian of the organisation, Qassem, quotes the Quran as opposing compulsion in religion and argues that, therefore, 'the creation of an Islamic state is not a function of adoption by one group or branch and a subsequent imposition on other groups'. Hizbollah, he writes, calls for 'implementation of the Islamic system based on direct and free choice by the people and not through forceful imposition...' and that 'We believe that our political experience in Lebanon has proved a pattern that is harmonious with an Islamic vision within a mixed society—a country not following an Islamic mode of thinking'.[30] In municipal elections Hizbollah placed great emphasise on economic and social issues and 'introduced its candidates on a non-sectarian basis, emphasising honesty and seriousness in municipal work'.[31]

This does not mean that Hizbollah has transformed itself into a free thinking liberal organisation. In the past it has used its weapons to deal with those who opposed it—in the early 1980s against some Communist resistance fighters and against its Shia rival Amal (although many Communist activists joined its ranks soon after and today it collaborates both with the Communist Party and Amal), and its leaders are still committed to a religious vision and do their best to get acceptance of their notions (like the veiling of women) in the areas they control. They attempt to administer them using their version of the sharia (which puts enormous stress on the role of Islamic judges in mediating conflicts in order to break old vendetta traditions between families).[32] But the fact that its leaders reach out to non-Shias, and even non-religious forces in order to confront the 'Great Satan' of the United States and the 'little Satan' of Israel is an element in contradiction to the narrow religious standpoint from which they started, and has been one of the factors behind past splits within the Hizbollah leadership.[33] It is a contradiction that will grow greater in so far as the non-Shia and non-Muslim resistance to imperialism internationally grows.

However, this contradiction is interwoven with compromises of a different order—towards the Lebanese state, the country's other political parties, including those aligned with imperialism, and the other Arab states. The Lebanese political system rests upon deals in which political leaders within each religious group do deals with the leaders of other groups in order to get their hands on sufficient state patronage to maintain the allegiance of their followers. In such a system there can be enormous conflict between different parties, including armed conflict, without the essentials of the political and economic system ever being brought into question. After denouncing this system in its early days Hizbollah has chosen to join it. This has meant electoral agreements not only with the anti-imperialist left, but also with the pro-imperialist right. In elections it had joint lists with the Communist Party in Nabatiyyah and Tyre—but in Beirut joined a list formed by Saad Hariri, the Saudi-connected billionaire son of the assassinated prime minister Rafic Hariri. It justified the deal with ideological and political opponents 'so as to maintain sectarian balance'.[34] The most recent deals have been with the Maronite general and prime minister in the last phase of the civil war in the 1980s, Michel Aoun.

It is claimed that such deals protected Hizbollah a little during the confrontation with Israel. Aoun, in order to advance his own presidential ambitions after 15 years of exile, did provide some support for Hizbollah, for instance, organising the hosting of thousands of refugees in Christian villages in Mount Lebanon. But the pro-Western Hariri bloc that dominates the government placed its hopes in Israel smashing Hizbollah so that it itself could take control of the south of the country.[35] Hizbollah's real protection came from its wide social base and its fighting ability —if that had flagged at any point, most of the 'allies' would have put the knife in its back on behalf of their friends in Washington, Paris or Riyadh. What those deals certainly do is constrain its ability to act.

It used to vote no to Rafic Hariri's budgets because it said he saw Lebanese cabinets as acting as 'boards of directors'—with Hariri treating the country as one of his businesses.[36] By joining the government last year, it opted to accept that way of running things. This must weaken its ability to deliver the improvements in conditions of the poor that it has built its base on and to undercut the hold which the various sectarian politicians exercise over their followers. Hizbollah may be able to deliver certain welfare services through its own charitable networks. But they cannot be a substitute for the sorts of services which should be and could be provided by the state if it were not for its entanglement in neo-liberal capitalism.

Such political deals also cut Hizbollah's capacity to wage the struggle against imperialism and capitalism as it might like. In the closing stages of the 33-day war there was enormous pressure on Hizbollah to sign the final truce agreement, to which it eventually conceded. But this left Israeli forces in Lebanon, an Israeli blockade intact, and provided for the entry into the country of forces from France—even though the French government had agreed with the US that Hizbollah should be disarmed. The Hizbollah leader Nasrallah explained, 'We face the reasonable and possible natural results of the great steadfastness that the Lebanese expressed from their various positions'.[37]

The pro-American government was 'in danger of collapse' when its hopes in a quick Israeli victory fell apart. Its 'very survival was down to Hizbollah. The party sees no alternative to "broad consensus".' Yet since the Hizbollah victory 'the Sinhora government has been working hard to block and undermine the rebuilding effort while accepting US money... The most recent example is the government veto on aid payments to those made unemployed by the war—a measure proposed by the minister of labour, Hizbollah's representative in the government'.[38]

It is not only domestic compromises that are involved. Hizbollah has long relied on its alliance with Syria. Naim Qassem, reflecting official Hizbollah thinking, argues that 'it is only natural that Hizbollah's views coincide with those of Syria, for no one is safe from Israel's ambitions'; that it believes in 'the existence of strategic Syrian-Iranian relations' since the Islamic revolution, and that 'the relationship with Syria' is 'the cornerstone for facing major regional obligations'.[39] But the Syrian regime is certainly not motivated by any anti-imperialist—or even anti-Zionist—principles. It willingly worked to help the US at the time of the first US war against Iraq. Before that, in 1976, it intervened in Lebanon in order to prevent the alliance of the left and the Palestinians achieving victory in the first stage of the civil war and then, in the mid-1980s, followed a policy of preventing the Palestinians re-establishing armed bases in the south. Qassem admits, 'Syria massacred 27 [Hizbollah] party members when it entered Beirut to stop the civil war in 1987'.[40] It is an open secret that Syria would do a deal with Israel (and the US) tomorrow if it could get back the Golan Heights, occupied by Israel since 1967.

But it is not only Syria that Hizbollah considers looking to. Qassem is adamant that none of the Arab states, however compromised with imperialism and Zionism, needs to be overthrown. They 'need to adopt a series of changes aimed at achieving reconciliation with their peoples'[41] and 'active social forces need to work diligently and contribute to positive transformation through political means, away from armed conflict'.[42] But 'whoever takes up the slogan of liberating Arab regimes as a prerequisite for liberating Palestine is on an erroneous track and only complicating the task of liberation'.[43]

In line with this approach:

> Hizbollah has welcomed involvement by Qatar in the south. The Quataris, despite close relations with the US and Israel, are being given the green light to rebuild the south. This will come with a political price tag. There has been little condemnation of Egypt, Jordan or Saudi Arabia from with the ranks of the party—though lots from people close to it.[44]

A lesson from the past

No Arab army has achieved as much as Hizbollah did during the 33-day war. But this is not the first time a guerrilla force has arisen that seemed able to fight in the way that the Arab states could not. Such a movement emerged in the shape of the PLO in the wake of the 1967 defeat,[45] with not only Palestinians, but activists thoughout the Middle East, looking on it as pole of attraction after the failure of the Arab regimes, whether of the old or the new, nationalist sort. A Palestinian student using the name Ibrahim Ali wrote in this journal early in 1969:

> The June War, exposing to a certain extent the corruption and bankruptcy of these regimes, has forced the Palestinians towards a revaluation of their position vis a vis these states… This has manifested itself in massive popular support for the guerrilla organisations, who operate independently of the Arab governments.[46]

Fatah was able to channel this feeling and take the leadership of the Palestine movement by achieving a remarkable victory over the Israeli forces in March 1968, only nine mnths after the 1967 defeat. The Israelis launched a big attack on the Jordanian village of Karameh, whiere Fatah had its headquarters. Resistance by the guerrillas held off the Israeli attack long enough to draw the Jordanian army into the battle, leading to 28 Israeli deaths, 80 wounded and the loss of four tanks.[47]

But Karameh proved a flash in the pan. The victory depended on the Israelis advancing into an area where Palestinians were already armed and on the involvement of the regular Jordanian army. It did not provide an approach capable of taking on the Israeli army across the Jordan in Palestine itself. As Ibrahim Ali correctly noted:

> Guerrilla attacks…have not been accompanied by the establishment of guerrilla bases in Israeli-occupied territories. This cannot only be explained on the basis of Israeli vigilance and their policy of massive retaliations. Most West Bank civil servants receive double salaries—from the Jordanians and the Israelis. Regular commercial traffic between the East and West Bank continues while Israeli aircraft napalm Arab villages. The Israelis are using the double-edged policy—massive reprisals on the one hand and concessions on the other. No guerrilla organisation has put forward a programme, although all call for armed struggle leading to a de-Zionised, democratic bi-national Palestine.[48]

There would have been only one way for the Palestinian guerrilla organisations to shift the balance of forces sharply in their own favour. That was to help bring about revolutionary change in one or other of the Arab countries bordering Israel. There were strong possibilities in this direction, especially in Jordan. The monarchy was increasingly unstable, its army having lost half its fertile land to Israel (the West Bank was part of the Jordanian kingdom in 1967) and more than half the population in the area still under Jordanian control was Palestinian. Its weakness was shown by the way it was forced to allow the Fatah-led PLO to operate virtually as a state within the state. But instead of organising for a revolutionary overthrow of a monarchy that had been installed by the British and had done secret deals to partition Palestine with the Israelis in 1947-48, the Fatah leadership followed a policy of 'non-interference' in Jordan. Faced with questions about what to do about the reactionary Arab states, even left-inclined figures in

Fatah used an Arab saying to the effect that there was no need to pick the fruit from a tree when a storm was going to shake it—and the storm would be the defeat of Zionism.[49] In the meantime the PLO looked upon the various Arab states, including the most reactionary monarchies in the Gulf, for funds—and tailored its policies accordingly.

The consequences were to be seen when the Jordanian monarchy decided to drive the PLO from the country in Black September 1970. Even in the midst of the attacks on it, instead of following a revolutionary strategy designed to break the allegiance of Jordanian soldiers to their monarchy, the Fatah leadership agreed to temporary truces that allowed the monarchy to reinforce discipline over its forces before moving on to the next attack. In the midst of the catastrophe the Fatah leader, Arafat, was photographed embracing the Jordanian king, Hussein, as an 'Arab brother'.[50] Hussein reciprocated by forcing Arafat and his forces to leave the country best placed for organising guerrilla warfare in Israel.

The behaviour of Fatah can only be understood by understanding *its* class basis. Although there was enormous identification with it by the great mass of Palestinian peasants, workers and refugees, it was run politically and militarily by members of the middle class, very similar in their attitudes to those who dominated the Arab nationalist governments. Arafat and the other guerrilla leaders were typically Palestinian professionals—civil engineers and the like—who had begun careers in the oil-rich Gulf States. The Fatah organisation was organised hierarchically, with people from a similar background holding the commanding posts—and receiving salaries several times higher than the ordinary fighters. And people from such a class background took it for granted that they had to appeal to the Palestinian middle and upper classes politically, opposing the Israeli occupation but not challenging the class basis of their own privileges either in Palestine or in exile.

A similar logic worked itself out after Black September, when the PLO established a base for itself in South Lebanon. The possibility for revolutionary action was shown in 1975, when Palestinian forces united with the Lebanese left joined together in a movement based on a struggle against social and economic deprivation which came close to overthrowing the regime. Syrian intervention, backed by the US, was necessary to defeat the movement. After that, however, PLO control of Southern Lebanon took on some of the characteristics of a foreign occupation, with allegations of repression, harassment of the local population and banditry. A top-down middle class run military organisation of the Palestinians could not rule in a way that did not trample on the interests of those beneath it.

Finally, when the first Intifada of 1987-90 did force the Israelis to negotiate seriously, it was prepared to settle for a fragment of power in isolated islands of land in the West Bank and Gaza. It hopes that it might find on a microscale the possibilities of using the state to advance its interests that it could not achieve on a large scale without a revolutionary challenge across the Arab world as a whole. Its attempt not only left Israel with a free hand to expand its settlements, but also led to the setting up of Palestinians quasi-state institutions that became notorious for their corruption, incompetence and repression, as if all the faults of the Arab regime had been concentrated with the attempt to imitate them in the small enclaves in which the PLO was allowed to operate.

The class base of Hizbollah

Hizbollah, by relying on deals with its own state and by rejecting a revolutionary approach to the other states, is in danger of going along the path travelled over so many years by the PLO. If it does so, its victory in the summer will not translate into an active strategy for confronting the Israeli state's domination of the Palestinians or imperialist schemes for the region as a whole.

Yet Hizbollah's way of operating ties it into the deals and the compromises. The network of welfare organisations which are so important in cementing its popular base have not arisen out of thin air. They have to be financed. The finance comes mainly from two sources: from an Iranian state within which there are influential political forces who would deal with the US if Iran was accepted as a significant regional power, and from the Shia middle class and business interests in Lebanon and abroad. According to Hamzah, it relies on 'donations from individuals, groups, shops, companies, and banks as well as their counterparts in countries such as the US, Canada, Latin America, Europe and Australia', and on Hizbollah's business investments which take 'advantage of Lebanon's free market economy' with 'dozens of supermarkets, gas stations, department stores, restaurants, construction companies and travel agents'.[51]

It is hardly surprising that an organisation so dependent on functioning within capitalism in reality accepts a 'conservative' economic programme[52] at home and rejects the overthrow of the neighbouring Arab governments. One is reminded of the degree to which the social radicalism of the IRA/Sinn Fein was moderated by its dependence on money from prosperous supporters in the US even while it waged a guerrilla war in the North of Ireland.

But working within the system risks having other effects on Hizbollah, as it did on the PLO. Its compromises involve the radical anti-imperialist and anti–Zionist clerics at the top of the organisation relying on a layer of upwardly mobile middle class professionals to sustain its political networks. 'The candidates or lists backed by Hizbollah in 2004 consisted mainly of individuals from professions—engineers, doctors, lawyers and businessmen'.[53] With such people dominating the practical implementation of its politics, it is perhaps not surprising that the social and economic demands in its programme of action for the local elections were hardly more radical than New Labour's:

> Encourage the citizen to play a more active role in the selection process of development projects.
> Increase the functions and powers of municipalities in the provision of education, healthcare and socioeconomic affairs.
> Involve qualified people in development projects.
> Finance development projects from both municipal revenues and donations.
> Exercise control over public works and prevent embezzlement.
> Renovate the physical and administrative structures of municipalities and provide them with computer facilities.[54]

Hizbollah has become reliant on forces in Lebanon that will support its guerrilla activities in so far as they deter Israeli forces from attacking and occupying the country. But these forces will act as a brake on any notion of offensive actions against Israel—or even provocations on the border designed to draw Israeli troops into traps inside Lebanon. To that extent they will thwart any ambition of direct aid to the Palestinians against the Israeli state.

Response of the left

The Lebanon War produced an enormous wave of opposition, not only in Muslim countries, but in Europe and Latin America. These not only saw demonstrations in some countries bigger than any since the first year of the Iraq war, but there was also an unprecedented willingness to stand up against Israeli aggression. This was in marked contrast to the reaction of most left wing opinion to the 1967 and 1973 wars or even the invasion of Lebanon in 1982 with its massive Lebanese and Palestinian death toll.

But there was still a weakness in some of the arguments and the slogans of many sections of the left. These gravitated around the linked questions of the 'ceasefire' and of 'the Israeli state's right to defend itself'.

Take, for instance, the approach of one of the few principled left wing columnists to write for the *Guardian* newspaper, George Monbiot. He had no hesitation in opposing the Israeli aggression. But he also felt compelled to criticise Hizbollah for taking action against the Israeli state, even though the Israeli state had in the previous weeks been launching repeated onslaughts on Palestinians in Gaza. So he wrote:

> Yes, Hizbollah should have been pulled back from the Israeli border by the Lebanese government and disarmed. Yes, the raid and the rocket attack on 12 July were unjustified, stupid and provocative, like just about everything that has taken place around the border for the past six years.

And then, after arguing for 'withdrawing from the occupied territories in Palestine and Syria', he also called 'to defend the border, while maintaining the diplomatic pressure on Lebanon to disarm Hizbollah (as anyone can see, this would be much more feasible if the occupations were to end)'.[55]

Such arguments were prevalent on many sections of the liberal and social democratic left. So, for instance, some supporters of the Stop the War Coalition in Britain were not happy with Lebanese carrying pro-Hizbollah placards and flags, as if a purely pacifist approach was the only permissible one. And even on the far left there were people who took a 'neither nor' stance on the war—neither for the Israeli aggressor, not for the Hizbollah-led resistance in Lebanon. So, for instance, the Socialist Party/CWI wrote in their paper, the *Socialist*:

> It is the ordinary people of Lebanon, Israel and Gaza who are paying a terrible price. Neither side can win. Hizbollah can never defeat the might of the Israeli state and liberate the Palestinian people from occupation. And the latest conflict can only deepen the divisions between working people in Israel, Lebanon and the Palestinian areas.

It quoted an 'Israeli socialist' as saying that 'this current conflict is about who wins most in terms of prestige and political kudos. The people who lose out in all this will be the working class on both sides... At the root of these national conflicts is a power struggle between the different ruling classes in the region backed by different imperialist powers.'

It handed out a leaflet arguing:

> Hizbollah with its aim of destroying Israel and creating an Islamic state like the reactionary regime in Iran cannot succeed. It can only further divide the multiethnic/religious populations of Lebanon and the Middle East.

Its slogan was not 'Solidarity with the resistance' but an abstract call 'for a socialist Palestine and a socialist Israel as part of a socialist confederation of the Middle East'.

Similarly, the leadership of the now virtually defunct Scottish Socialist Party qualified their opposition to the war with denunciation of Hizbollah as 'one of the most ferocious terrorist organisations in the world' and criticism of it for 'an illegal and ruthless raid across the border'.[56]

The problems of all such arguments were shown once the ceasefire had taken effect. The US, Israeli and British propaganda machines went into top gear demanding the rapid forming of the UN force under resolution 1701 to work with the Lebanese army to disarm Hizbollah and to seal Lebanon's borders so as to provide Israel with an alternative means of 'defence' other than disarming Hizbollah itself. In effect, they were demanding foreign military occupation of Lebanon. There was, of course, no talk of foreign military occupation of Israel to prevent the daily attacks on the Palestinians in Gaza and the West Bank. All those on the left who opposed military action by both sides in the war and simply demanded a ceasefire opened the door to these arguments.

Such confusions bring out two questions of importance for the whole left internationally—the analysis of the state of Israel and the attitude to those Islamist organisations that confront imperialism and Zionism.

The character of the Israeli state[57]

Liberal-left commentators and the pro-US and pro-Israeli right repeat a single theme over and over again—'The Israeli state has the right to exist.' Anyone who questions this is accused of anti-Semitism and of wanting a new holocaust, this time in the Middle East.

But the 'right to exist' of a state is not at all the same as the 'right of its people to continue to live'. The first half of the 20th century saw the destruction or disintegration of numerous states—the Austro-Hungarian Empire and the Ottoman Empire for example. No one on the liberal left lamented the demise of these states, or complained of genocide when it happened. Similarly the last 17 years have seen the disappearance of the USSR, Czechoslovakia and Yugoslavia without anyone screaming about the 'right of states to exist'.

Whether you support or oppose the continued existence of a certain state does not depend on any abstract 'right to exist' but on its character and on what the alternatives to its existence are.

The most important feature to understand in the case of the Israeli state is that it is a *settler* state—that is, one of those states formed by European settlers that accompanied the growth of the European empires. Some 120 years ago the Jewish population of historic Palestine (ie what is now Israel, the West Bank and Gaza) was just a few thousand, the Arab population hundreds of thousands. The Ottoman census for 1893 gave the Jewish population as a mere 9,817;[58] estimates including then-recent immigrants put the figure at about 25,000 as against an Arab population of between 400,000 and 600,000.[59] The growth of the Jewish population until it amounts to 55 percent of the area's population is a result of massive settlement since. This is shown by the fact that in the late 1960s only 24 percent of the adult Israeli population were born in historic Palestine—and only 4 percent of Palestinian-born parents.[60]

Such a population could only expand and eventually, in 1948-49, establish a state encompassing three quarters of the area, by dispossessing the existing inhabitants. As the Israeli general and politician Dayan put it in a speech in 1956:

We are a settler generation, and without the steel helmet and cannon we cannot plant a tree or build a house. Let us not flinch from the hatred enflaming hundreds of thousands of Arabs around us.[61]

In this it was like other settler states established by European colonists at the expense of the local population in North America, Australia, French-ruled Algeria, white-ruled Rhodesia or apartheid South Africa. The fact that in the forefront of settlement were people fleeing oppression in Europe, especially in the aftermath of the Holocaust, did not alter the basic fact that settlement took place at the expense of the indigenous population. Many of the North American settlers were fleeing religious persecution or poverty, many of the Australian settlers arrived as a result of transportation by the British state and many of the Algerian settlers arrived there as deportees punished for participation in the revolution of 1848 or the Paris Commune just as the Jewish settlement was by people who had suffered acute oppression in Europe. But having arrived, they could only maintain themselves by actions against the existing population. The logic of colonial settlement is that those who have been the oppressed become the oppressors.

There were different models of colonisation. The North American and Australian model involved the near and sometimes complete extermination of the local population, so that eventually it represented no threat to the settler population and their descendants and had little or no impact on the character of the state. The model in French Algeria, white Rhodesia and apartheid South Africa involved using the indigenous population as cheap labour for white owned farms and businesses, so that virtually the whole white population identified with the repressive functions of the state as a way of holding on to their own privileges—to such an extent that a million French Algerians migrated to France when Algeria became independent in 1963. The Zionist model in Palestine involved the settlers driving the indigenous population out of the areas of settlement in order to establish wholly Jewish settlements and businesses.

As Tony Cliff, who was brought up in Palestine in the 1920s and 1930s, explained:

A series of human tragedies brought the Jews to Palestine—pogroms in Tsarist Russia, persecution in Eastern Europe and the Holocaust of Nazism. When they reached Palestine they found it was inhabited by Arabs. Whatever the motivation that brought the Jews in, an increasing conflict between Zionist settlers and the Arabs was unavoidable. The colonists would buy land from the Arab landowners and then drive the Arab peasants from it, and they would exclude Arabs from the businesses they set up.

The Arab peasant offered labour and produce at a very low price. How could a European worker find a job under such conditions? The only way was to block the employment of any Arab workers by Jewish employers. In Tel

Aviv, which on the eve of the founding of the state of Israel had barely 300,000 inhabitants, there was not one Arab worker nor one Arab inhabitant.

The Zionists prevented the fellahs [peasants] from selling their produce in the Jewish market. And when, under pressure of hunger, a fellah dared to break the boycott, he was beaten.

Every member of the Zionist trade union federation, the Histadrut, had to pay two special compulsory levies: (1) 'For Jewish Labour'—funds for organising pickets, etc, against the employment of Arab workers; and (2) 'For Jewish Produce', for organising the boycott of Arab produce. Not one Zionist party, not even the most extreme 'left' of Hashomer Hatzair, now Mapam, opposed the boycott of the Arab workers and peasants. The boycott of the Arabs was inherent in Zionism: without the boycott no European worker or farmer would have survived economically.[62]

Such actions necessarily aroused the ire of the Arab masses. There was only one way the settlers could protect themselves against such anger. It was to do a deal with one or other of the imperalist countries. So in the 1920s, 1930s and early 1940s they collaborated with the British—for instance, providing them with armed assistance in smashing the Palestinian uprisng of 1936-39. The military training they received under British rule then enabled them, using US diplomatic backing and East European arms, to seize most of historic Palestine through three military offensives (interspersed with two truces) when the British left in 1948—and to use terror to drive most of the Palestnian population out of the areas they took control of. In the decades that followed, British imperialist interests were increasingly overshadowed by those of the US—and it was to the US that Israel turned.

The liberal Israeli newspaper *Ha'aretz* summed up the relation of Israel to imperialism on 30 September 1951:

Israel has been given a role not unlike that of a watchdog… Should the West prefer for one reason or another to close its eyes it can rely on Israel punishing severely those of the neighbouring states whose lack of manners towards the West has exceeded the proper limits.[63]

In return for playing this role Israel, despite its relatively small size, receives a third of all US overseas aid, much more than any other country. One estimate is that total US aid to the country amounted to over $84 billion between 1949 and 1997. That works out at over $14,000 for each Israeli citizen.[64] A lot of this aid goes on providing Israel with the most up to date military technology for intimidating and, if necessary, attacking other Middle Eastern states. So for 2003 Israel was promised $720 million in economic aid as well as $2.04 billion in military assistance.[65]

A classic Marxist analysis of the Israeli state by Haim Hanegbi, Moshe Machover and Akiva Orr has pointed out that such aid has also allowed Israel to enjoy economic expansion on the cheap:

> In the years 1949-65 Israel received $6 billion more of imports of goods and services than it exported, ie $2,650 per person in the 21 years… In 1949-65 period net saving in Israel averaged zero—but investment was equal to 20 percent of GNP.
>
> Israeli society is not only a settler society… It is also a society which benefits from unique privileges. It enjoys an influx of material resources from the outside of unparalleled quantity and quality… Israel is a unique case in the Middle East. It is financed by imperialism without being economically exploited by it.[66]

They argue that among the beneficiaries has been the Jewish working class:

> The Jewish worker does not get his share in cash, but in terms of new and relatively inexpensive housing; in industrial employment which could not have been started or kept going without external subsidies; in terms of a general standard of living which does not correspond to the output of society.[67]

Certainly, US aid has been used to blunt, although not stop, the impact of economic crises. So, as the *American Jewish Yearbook 1990* says, 'during Israel's economic crisis of 1984-85, emergency US aid…helped Israel,[68] while at the beginning of 2003, when Israel's economy was 'suffering from one of the worst crises in the country's history', an Israeli delegation went to the US to ask for 'an emergency aid package worth $12 billion.[69]

The aid was not expected to be for free. What Israel offered in return was, as the *Year Book* explained, 'US-Israeli strategic cooperation' which survived because 'of the perception that ties with Israel were in America's interest'.[70] In line with this approach, part of the aid Israel wanted in 2003 was to 'boost its defence preparations'[71] for the subsequent US-led war against Iraq.

The Israeli state could not have been established without and can only maintain itself because of such deals. Without the subsidies they provide, there would be no incentive for Jewish people from elsewhere in the world to migrate to Israel. And many existing Israelis, accustomed to European or North American living standards, would migrate to Europe or North America in order to try and get them.

But faced with the possibility of economic crises causing dissension at home and undermining the whole rationale of an exclusively Jewish state, Zionist politicians do not sit passively and wait for the subsidies. They have an interest in encouraging the US to take an aggressive stance in the region, so destabilising existing regimes and making it look even more to its watchdog. That is why there is a natural affinity between the Zionist politicians and the neocons in the US, and why even the more peace inclined section of the Israeli Labour Party always ends up going along with such policies. The more disorder there is in the region, the more important the role of Israeli military might in helping to subdue it and the more likely the state is to receive more subsidies and more possibilities of fulfilling the Zionist aim of further Israeli expansion. Instability in the region is also a precondition for presenting themselves to Jewish people elsewhere in the world as continually under threat and therefore needing continual succour.

This has an inevitable impact in shaping the attitudes of the Israeli working class. The mass of the population of Israel, as in other advanced industrial countries, work and are exploited by their employers. But in the Israeli case, the subsidies which pass to them via the state from US imperialism mean that they are cushioned against part of the impact of this exploitation. They identify with the state and with its collaborating with imperialism, since without this collaboration they would have to suffer the much worse living standards of other workers in the Middle East. Their identification with the state against Palestinians has material roots. Even those whose conditions are very bad tend to see the answer in more identification with the state, not less. So the Jews who migrated to Israel from elsewhere in the Middle East in the 1950s and 1960s have tended to support the more right wing Zionist parties, despite the fact that they are usually worse off than those from Europe.

In this sense they are like white South African workers—even the poorest white South African workers—were before the fall of apartheid.

Haim Hanegbi, Moshe Machover and Akiva Orr noted the 1970s: 'The experience of 50 years does not contain a single example of Israeli workers being mobilised on material or trade union issues to challenge the Israeli regime itself'.[72]

Developments since have not challenged this conclusion. There has been a whittling away of the welfare state and an adoption under Likud-led governments of neo-liberal policies which have produced unemployment levels of up to 11 percent and cuts on dole payments. But the cumulative effect of the subsidies from imperialism still means Israeli workers enjoy living standards way above those of those in Palestine or the neighbouring Arab countries. So the minimum wage at the beginning of 2004 was 3,335 New Shekels (around $700 a month), while the minimum wage in neighbouring Egypt is $28.40 a month. Detailed analyses show welfare benefits to be the middle range of those available in Europe.[73] They are under attack, but the subsidies mean they are still at Western levels, not at the Third World levels available to the Palestinians driven out in 1948 and their descendants. But they only get these subsidies because of the deals the Israeli government does with imperialism. And so their struggles against these attacks on their wages, working conditions or welfare benefits can always be contained by the state, whose easy response to economic crisis is to turn to the US.

There are contradictions. There are big business interests in Israel—interests increasingly linked with North American or sometimes European multinational capital—who see the future in market penetration of the rest of the Middle East and who therefore have a certain interest in peace. But these pressures in themselves have not been sufficient to stop the state adopting an aggressive stance to the Palestinians in the occupied territories or to one or other of the other Middle Eastern states. They will not do so in future either. Multinational capital invests in Israel because it looks to Israeli hegemony in the region (and, it should be added, to profitable military contracts). It shares with Israeli capital an interest in an Israeli state that has the military power to intimidate its neighbours through an armed peace—and that requires a sufficiently aggressive posture to mobilise the mass of the population behind the state as necessary.

Under these circumstance, those who assert 'the right of the Israeli state to exist' are defending a state which necessarily acts as a willing tool of imperialism and behaves aggressively towards its neighbours.

Opposing the Israeli state, it must be repeated, is not the same as wanting to see the Jewish population 'driven into the sea', any more than opposing the apartheid state meant wanting to see the eradication of an Afrikaner population who had lived in the country for 350 years with some elements of a national identity of their own (language, literature, religious institutions and so on). It meant in South Africa the dismantling of a state based upon discrimination by the descendants of settlers against the indigenous population. In the case of Israel, it means dismantling a state based upon forcible removal of the indigenous population from its territory, continual expansion into the 'occupied territories', and massive and bloody military repression of those who fight the occupation and the expansion of the settlement or who fight to return to the land from which their families were expelled.

There are two hypothetical ways of dismantling the settler state. The first would be for the Israeli population to accept the right of return of the Palestinians driven out in 1948, and an end to the occupation and settlements in the West Bank. The second would be the dissolution of Israel into a united, secular democratic state across the whole area of historical Palestine, in which all the inhabitants would enjoy equal citizenship rights. In practice the two roads would end up at the same destination. As the Zionists continually insist, the 'right of return' for the Palestinians would destroy the whole rationale of the settler state by doing away with the privileges for those of Jewish origin, and open the door to a unified secular state. That is why a small minority of Israeli activists and intellectuals are beginning to accept that the only real alternative to the pattern of repression, settlement and war is the path of the secular state.

What force can bring this about? The whole burden of the argument above is that the key to bringing it about does not lie within Israel. So long as the Zionist state seems strong enough to continue to get the subsidies from imperialism to provide even the poorest of its Jewish inhabitants with privileges compared to the Palestinians in Gaza, the West Bank and the refugee camps of Jordan and Lebanon, the majority of them will turn to it. The state can be weakened by class struggle inside Israel, but that will never be enough by itself to break the state, its aggressive policies and its eagerness to work for imperialism. It is weakened when sections of young Israelis rebel against military service in continual occupation and repeated wars. In the process, some at least can come to see the reality of what the Zionist dream has led to.

But for this to develop on any scale depends on the Israeli state losing its capacity to wage war that is virtually cost free, both in financial terms (because of US subsidies) and in terms of Israeli lives. In other words, it depends on Israel suffering a very serious military defeat. Only such a defeat can cause such a shock inside Israel as to lead large numbers of people to see that there is only one secure way forward for them—to break with the whole Zionist vision of building an ethnically pure state—and to make the US ruling class wonder whether their subsidies to Israel are worth maintaining.

As Hanegbi, Machover and Orr argued 30 years ago, participation in the internal struggles in Israeli society, including the struggle of the workers, 'must be subordinated to the general strategy of the struggle against Zionism'.[74] The conclusion remains valid today. Those who fail to see this and take a 'neither nor' attitude to wars like that in Lebanon, accepting the sanctity of Israel's borders, weaken the struggle against imperialism and Zionism, however well intentioned their motives.

Breaking the hold of Zionism on the great majority of the Israeli population remains a very distant prospect. The defeat in Lebanon was only a partial defeat, which not only Israeli leaders but the great bulk of the Israeli population expect to be able to reverse. It is wishful thinking to pretend otherwise, to believe that:

> All this has blown open a window in which it is possible to glimpse the possibility of a comprehensive settlement of the near century old conflicts which lie behind the recent war. Now that the status quo ante has been swept away, we may even see an F W de Klerk moment emerge in Israel (and among its indispensable international backers).[75]

A 'revolutionary breakthrough in the Arab world'[76] remains the precondition for creating the sort of challenge to the Israeli state which could make Zionism buckle. It has not happened yet.

The impact of the victory

Hizbollah achieved a notable victory in the summer, which has cut Israel's pretensions down to size and so has given a boost to all those forces pushing for fundamental change across the Middle East. But Hizbollah cannot be the political tool for achieving that change. This is not mainly because of its religious conceptions, but because beneath them lies reliance upon class forces that cannot go beyond a certain point in confrontation with either Israel or imperialism. It needs to be repeated again and again: victory against imperialism in any country cannot be achieved simply by a struggle confined to that country or victory over Zionism by a struggle confined simply to Palestine. What is needed is a breakthrough in one country which can unleash a revolutionary process across the whole region. The Hizbollah victory will contribute to this insofar as it opens up optimistic visions of what is possible, just as the defeat of 1967 plunged the region's activists into depressive pessimism.

It will probably, in the short term, increase the attraction of forms of Islamism. But there can also be an important shift in the versions of Islam that are popular. The defeats of the past encouraged narrow versions of Islam, which stressed religious purity on the one hand and elitist forms of individualist direct action of the jihadis type on the other. Where these failed miserably, as they did in the contests with the Egyptian and Algerian states, many activists fell back into mild forms of religious reformism. The stress on religious purism also tended to set those with one religious interpretation against those with other forms—not just Islam against other religions, but Sunni against Shia. Such divisions could then be manipulated both by imperialism and its agents, as in Pakistan or much more bloodily in Iraq, and by opportunist careerists out to establish a political base for themselves.

The Hizbollah victory will work against these trends. Hizbollah's own example will be taken as showing that alliances that cross over religious boundaries can be established. The Arab regimes are already worried about the appeal of its victory to their own Sunni majorities. But more is involved than just this. Victories widen people's horizons. They see possibilities they never did before. And examples of anti-imperialist action elsewhere in the world—like anti-war demonstrations in Europe and the US, or Hugo Chavez's withdrawal of the Venezuelan ambassador to Israel—can open people's ideas to see that they have non-Muslim allies just as they have, in the existing Arab regimes, Muslim enemies.

In all this, it is worth repeating a thousand times that Hizbollah's methods are the opposite of Al Qaida's. It is not only that in words Hizbollah rejects the methods of planting bombs to kill civilians in the West or the

Third World, but that its own military success has been dependent on its mass work. Its limitation is that it does not see that mass work is needed among those suffering from imperialism and its local capitalist allies elsewhere in the Arab world—the workers and peasants of Egypt, Syria, Jordan and elsewhere. Its victory will, however, make it easier for those who see this to find an audience, including among some of those with certain Islamist conceptions.

What next for the US?

The situation for US imperialism in general and for the Bush administration in particular is serious. The blow which was meant to destroy Hizbollah and weaken Syria and Iran has had the opposite effect. Even before the results of the 33-day war were clear the prestigious Royal Institute for International Affairs was warning that Iran was the great gainer from the Iraq debacle:

> There is little doubt that Iran has been the chief beneficiary of the war on terror in the Middle East. The United States, with Coalition support, has eliminated two of Iran's regional rival governments—the Taliban in Afghanistan in November 2001 and Saddam Hussein's regime in Iraq in April 2003—but has failed to replace either with coherent and stable political structures.[77]

> Iran views Iraq as its own backyard and has now superseded the US as the most influential power there; this affords it a key role in Iraq's future. Iran is also a prominent presence in its other war-torn neighbour with close social ties, Afghanistan.[78]

Now Hizbollah has increased its prestige massively and in effect forced Arab regimes that would have loved to see it defeated to do a U-turn, at least verbally, and praise its ability to fight the Israelis.

How will the US react now?

The most unlikely reaction is to accept the logic of defeat and to follow the advice of those like the Royal Institute of International Affairs who are effectively urging the US to accept Iran's strength and to do a deal with it:

> Iran is in a powerful regional position and its cooperation and positive influence are needed to help douse the many fires currently alight... The

resolution of the many crises afflicting Iran's region will partly require an improvement in Iran's relations with the West through careful and patient diplomacy on both sides… Iran is frequently depicted as a manipulator and instigator of violence in the broader Middle East; the Iranian regime is wary of provoking generalised chaos in the region because it is essentially conservative and seeks to maintain the status quo.[79]

Effectively this is to argue that Bush should follow the precedent of Richard Nixon's visit to China in 1972 after it had become clear that victory was impossible for the US in Vietnam—to do a deal with the regional power previously painted as the source of all evil.

There is no sign of that. The Bush administration has bet heavily on being able to so strengthen US global hegemony as to maintain it through the 'new century'. It fears that any deal with Iran would not only jeopardise that ambition, but go further and reduce US influence. The success of a fairly weak medium power like Iran in forcing the US to do a U-turn would encourage others to follow the same path of defiance. The only difference between the Bush camp and their mainstream critics is that these believe the US has to mend its fences with 'old Europe' and Russia in order to put pressure on Iran to capitulate symbolically by abandoning its nuclear programme. As that influential journalistic apologist for imperialism Thomas (McDonald's and McDonnell Douglas) Friedman put it at the height of the Lebanon War:

> But the administration now has to admit what anyone—including myself— who believed in the importance of getting Iraq right has to admit: it is not happening, and we can't throw more good lives after good lives… But second best is leaving Iraq. Because the worst option—the one Iran loves— is for us to stay in Iraq, bleeding, and in easy range to be hit by Iran if we strike its nukes… We need to deal with Iran and Syria, but from a position of strength—and that requires a broad coalition. The longer we maintain a unilateral failing strategy in Iraq, the harder it will be to build such a coalition.[80]

But a thoroughgoing compromise with Old Europe and Russia (let alone China) is difficult. The motive of war against Iraq was not merely to seize control of the country's oil for US corporate interests. It was, above all, to end what the neocons saw as the dilly dallying of US global strategy in the 1990s, to gain such a dominant control over the world's most important raw material, oil, as to be able to exercise dominating influence over the other great powers so as to ensure 'a new American century'.[81]

Even if a US administration is eventually forced to compromise fully with Europe, Russia and China, it will first try to reassert its power. This makes a renewed military offensive in the Middle East not only possible, but likely.

Israel's Lebanon war was, from the point of view of the US administration, a detour intended to make it easier to humiliate Iran. The detour turned out to be a dead end. The instincts of the Bush administration will now be to proceed down the main road to some sort of attack on Iran. Its problem is that that road is a very bumpy one, with huge potholes that could derail its efforts—potholes called Shia dominance of southern Iraq, the increased confidence and strength of Iran's allies in Lebanon, and the massive sympathy across the whole Islamic world for those allies as the only force to beat back an Israeli army in 58 years.

The Royal Institute for International Affairs report warns:

> There exists a very real possibility that, if the US attacks Iran, then Iran will inflict a devastating defeat upon the US in Iraq, and also take the fight to the US across the Middle East. Even now the Multinational Force is struggling to influence political developments in the south and central Euphrates regions of Iraq, where there is a predominantly Shia population, and the Arab Sunni insurgency continues to be a deadly presence inflicting catastrophic losses upon the nascent Iraqi security forces and their US backers. These situations could be magnified by Iranian intervention, to the point that the coalition might conceivably be forced to evacuate Iraq, leaving Iran not only as the undeniable formative force in Iraq, but also as the undisputed hegemon in the Gulf.[82]

What we are witnessing is an acute crisis for US imperialism, in which it faces two unpalatable options. One is to retreat after the Iraq and Lebanon debacles. But that means the Bush adminstration admitting that its 'war without end' drive for unchallengeable global hegemony has been a failure and to suffer the consequences, in term of a loss of neocon influence at home and of the US's ability to get its way abroad. The other option is to gamble heavily on an attack on Iran, or at least a further Israeli offensive into Lebanon. Despite the immense dangers of this course, this is the one it is most likely to take.

A wounded beast is a dangerous beast, and it is even possible that before people read these words a new war will be upon us with further large scale fighting in Lebanon or with an attack upon Iran. There are also very real prospects of attempts by the French and Italian troops, under US and Israeli pressure, to disarm Hizbollah.

The 33-day war emphasised the unpredictable nature of Bush's 'war without end', the way its slowly spluttering fuse can suddenly ignite explosively, throwing whole states into crisis and shaking people's ideas elsewhere. It is not the last time this will happen. Nor is it the last time that we will see massive resistance —resistance that can destabilise imperialism's client governments in the Middle East and advance the anti-capitalist movements in its heartlands.

NOTES

1: Thanks are due to Gilbert Achcar, Anne Alexander, Simon Assaf, Lindsey German, Ghassan Makarem, John Rose and Sabby Sagall for comments on and factual corrections to the draft of this article.

2: S Hersh , 'Watching Lebanon', *New Yorker*, 21 August 2006.

3: *Washington Post*, 4 August 2006.

4: H Shukrallah, 'It Didn't Work', August 2006, available on http://www.indy-media.ie/article/77854

5: As above.

6: As above.

7: Hizbollah's first victory was, of course, in forcing Israel to leave Lebanon in 1990; but it was not nearly as dramatic in terms of its effects on people's perceptions as their beating back the onslaught of the Israeli army in front of the whole of the world's media this time round.

8: US and Soviet support (with Czech weaponry) ensured their victory in 1948-

49, but it was in the late 1950s that massive US aid became a permanent feature.

9: Tony Cliff's written analysis at the time exists on the website of this journal at http:// www.isj.org.uk/index.php4?id=230 but he made many pertinent points at meetings which are not contained in any printed text.

10: N Qassem, *Hizbullah: The Story from Within* (London, 2005), p68.

11: M Williams, *Counterpunch*, 14 August 2006.

12: The Israeli state has encouraged immigration from the former USSR of anyone with even the vaguest claim to have 'Jewish' connections. The aim has been to keep the 'Jewish' population of Israel expanding more rapidly than the Palestinian population in Israel and the occupied territories. See, for example, Mark Reutter on www.news.uiuc.edu/gentips/03/07israel. html; Lucy Ash on the BBC website, at news.bbc.co.uk/1/hi/programmes/crossin g_continents/4038859.stm. The policy is at one with substituting a quarter of a million temporary workers from places like the Philippines for Arab workers from the West Bank and Gaza.

13: From the Israeli paper *Ha'aretz*, http://www.haaretz.com/hasen/spages/743767.html

14: N Qassem, as above, p69.

15: As above, pp72-73.

16: Tony Cliff on the 1967 Israeli-Arab War, as above.

17: A N Hamzeh, *In the Path of the Hizbullah* (Syracuse University Press, 2004), p13.

18: As above, p11.

19: As above, p13. The first efforts to build a 'Movement of the Deprived' were begun in 1974 by Musa al-Sadr (who disappeared during a trip to Libya in 1978), but its early development was soon overshadowed by the outbreak of civil war in Lebanon.

20: As above, p87.

21: N Qassem, as above, p74.

22: As above, pp74-75.

23: A N Hamzeh, as above, p89.

24: As above, p75.

25: As above, p77.

26: As above, pp50-55, gives figures for its various sorts of expenditure—but an examination of them makes me suspect he (or the typesetter) had put a few noughts in the wrong place.

27: As above, p59.

28: As above, p67.

29: For a long discussion on the shift in Hizbollah's approach to this issue, see A Saad-Ghorayeb, *Hizbu'llah, Politics and Religion* (London, 2002), pp34-59.

30: N Qassem, as above, p31.

31: A N Hamzeh, as above, p 123.

32: According to the account by A N Hamzeh, as above, pp105-108.

33: Both Hamzeh and Qassem discuss these splits, although from different standpoints.

34: A N Hamzeh, as above, p126.

35: According to private correspondence from Simon Assaf in Beirut, 6 September 2006.

36: Quoted in A N Hamzeh, as above, p121.

37: Quoted by G Achcar in 'Lebanon: The 33-Day War and UNSC Resolution 1701', www.zmag.org/content/showarticle.cfm?ItemID=10767 This article provides an excellent account of the manoeuvring over the wording of the resolution.

38: Correspondence from Simon Assaf in Beirut, 6 September 2006.

39: N Qassem, as above, p243.

40: As above, p240.

41: As above, p243.

42: As above, p244.

43: As above, p245.

44: Correspondence from Simon Assaf in Beirut, 6 September 2006.

45: The PLO and Fatah were founded in the mid-1950s, but it was not until after the 1967 war that they came to hegemonise the Palestinian struggle.

46: I Ali, 'Palestine: Guerrilla Organisations', *International Socialism*, first series, 36 (April-May 1969).

47: See, for instance, the brief account in en.wikipedia.org/wiki/Karameh

48: I Ali, as above.

49: This is based on my personal recollection of discussions in Amman in August 1969.

50: Again my own recollections, from attendance at a PLO conference in Amman during the first phase of the Black September civil war in 1970.

51: N Qassem, as above, p64.

52: The description is from Gilbert Achcar

in conversation.

53: A N Hamzeh, as above, p135.

54: As above, p123.

55: G Monbiot, *Guardian*, 8 August 2006.

56: Centre pages, *Scottish Socialist Voice*, 21 July 2006

57: For a fuller elaboration of the history of Zionism and of the character of the Israeli state, see John Rose's excellent little book, *Israel: The Hijack State*, available from Bookmarks, London, and also in a digital form on www.marxists.de/middleast/rose/4-origin.htm

58: See the discussion over the validity of the census results between Ronald Sander and Yehoshua Porath in the *New York Review of Books*, 16 January 1986.

59: Y Porath, *New York Review of Books*, as above.

60: Figures for 1968 given in H Hanegbi, M Machover, A Orr, 'The Class Nature of Israeli Society', *New Left Review* 65, January-February 1971, p4.

61: Quoted in above, p5.

62: Tony Cliff on the 1967 Israeli-Arab War, as above.

63: *Ha'aretz*, 30 September 1951, quoted in H Hanegbi, M Machover, A Orr, as above, p11.

64: These figures are from the *Washington Report on Middle East Affairs*, see http://www.washington-report.org/html/us_aid_to_israel.htm

65: 'Economist Tallies Swelling Cost of Israel to US', *Christian Science Monitor*, 9 December 2002, on http://www.csmonitor.com/2002/1209/p16s01-wmgn.html

66: H Hanegbi, M Machover, A Orr, as above, p9.

67: As above, p10.

68: *American Jewish Yearbook*, 1990, p270.

69: BBC News, Sunday 5 January 2003, 02:23 GMT http://news.bbc.co.uk/2/hi/business/2627561.stm

70: *American Jewish Yearbook*, 1990, p270.

71: BBC News, Sunday 5 January 2003, 02:23 GMT http://news.bbc.co.uk/2/hi/business/2627561.stm

72: H Hanegbi, M Machover, A Orr, as above, p6.

73: See, for instance, R Cohen and Y Shaul, *Social Protection in Israel and Sixteen European Countries* (Jerusalem, 1998), http://www.issa.int/pdf/jeru98/theme3/3-6d.pdf. They conclude that, compared with the countires of the EU before its recent expansion, 'Israel lies in the middle of scale with respect to maternity allowances and work-injury benefits, but ranks relatively low in terms of unemployment', with overall unemployment benefits worse than those in countries like France and Germany, but about the same as in Britain.

74: H Hanegbi, M Machover, A Orr, as above, p11.

75: George Galloway's claim in 'Hizbullah's Victory has Transformed the Middle East', *Guardian*, 31 August 2006.

76: H Hanegbi, M Machover, A Orr, as above, p11.

77: R Lowe and C Spencer, *Iran, Its Neighbours and the Regional Crises* (Chatham House, August 2006), p6. Available at http://www.chathamhouse.org.uk/pdf/research/mep/Iran0806.pdf

78: As above.

79: As above.

80: *New York Times*, 4 August 2006.

81: For my version of this argument, see my article, 'Analysing Imperialism', in *International Socialism* 99 (Summer 2003).

82: R Lowe and C Spencer, as above.

Remembering 1956
Revolutionary History volume 9, no 3

Edition editor: John McIlroy

John McIlroy, On the Fiftieth Anniversary of 1956; Paul Flewers, The Unexpected Denunciation: The Reception of Khrushchev's 'Secret Speech' in Britain; Steve Parsons, Nineteen Fifty-Six: What Happened in the Communist Party of Great Britain?; John McIlroy, A Communist Historian in 1956: Brian Pearce and the Crisis of British Stalinism; Christian Høgsbjerg, Beyond the Boundary of Leninism? C L R James and 1956; Ian Birchall, Nineteen Fifty-Six and the French Left; Tobias Abse, Palmiro Togliatti and the Italian Communist Party in 1956; Harry Ratner, Remembering 1956

Documents from 1956:
Ernest Mandel, Poznan and its Aftermath (an analysis of the Polish events); Shane Mage, The Discussion of the Crisis of Stalinism at the Recent NEC Meeting (a comment on the US left and 1956); The Marxist-Leninist's Song (a hilarious song about the problems facing Communist Party cadres in the light of 1956); Obituary—Rudolf Segall

Reviews:
● Pierre Broue, *The German Revolution, 1917-1923* (Mike Jones)
● Patrick Hutt, *Confronting an Ill Society: David Widgery, General Practice, Idealism and the Chase for Change* (David Renton)
● Adam Hochschild, *Bury the Chains: The British Struggle to Abolish Slavery* (Harry Ratner)
● Bettany Hughes, *Helen of Troy: Goddess, Princess, Whore* (Chris Gray)
● Loren Goldner, *Herman Melville: Between Charlemagne and the Antemosaic Cosmic Man: Race, Class and the Crisis of Bourgeois Ideology in an American Renaissance Writer* (Christian Høgsbjerg)
● Barry Sheppard, *The Sixties: A Political Memoir* (Louis Proyect)

Price: £9.95; postage UK £1.00, Europe £2.50, anywhere else £4.50
To order, contact us at Barry.Buitekant@tesco.net

www.revolutionary–history.co.uk

Greece's student movement

Panos Garganas

The new academic year started with a bang in Greece. Saturday 9 September saw a mass demonstration from all over the country in Salonica. Twenty thousand people, a mixture of trade unionists and students, converged on the Vellidion Conference Centre where prime minister Costas Karamanlis was presenting his policies for 2006-2007 to an elite audience of businessmen, bankers and top state officials. The police had already had a hard time controlling the area outside the Vellidion because the previous day some 3,000 angry young people, fans of the local football club PAOK, attempted to storm the conference centre in protest against the government.

On Monday 18 September primary school teachers started a five-day strike that is set to be repeated every week throughout the autumn term.

These are the after-effects of a movement that rocked the universities in Greece during May and June this year—the primary school teachers' union took the decision for this strike in June after delegates from their annual conference joined en masse a national demonstration of university students occupying their colleges.

At the height of the movement nearly 420 out of 450 colleges were occupied. Lecturers were on all out strike and students organised the occupations with massive assemblies in every college and city-wide coordinating committees. There were mass demonstrations every week, one week locally, the next week nationally in Athens. Politically, the movement was dominated by the openly anti-capitalist far left. The main demand was for the government to drop its plans for neo-liberal reform in education.

Having failed to break the momentum of the movement with a brutal police attack on a national demo, and confronted with escalating joint action between the students and the trade unions, the government was forced to retreat. Education minister Marietta Yannakou pledged that no legislation would be rushed through parliament during the summer and a long period of public debate ('for as long as it takes') would follow. It was a humiliating U-turn. The students celebrated this as a 'first victory', kept up the occupations for another couple of weeks and promised to be back in the autumn.

Back in March, when the French students were engaged in their struggle against the CPE, there was an open debate in Greece—could it happen here too?

The Greek Tory government said no and tried to present themselves as to the left of their French counterparts. They argued that PASOK, the New Labour type opposition in Greece, was much closer to the Villepin CPE plan. Yet opinion polls at that time showed that a massive 72 percent said yes, the French example could be repeated in Greece. The debate moved on to discuss the character of the new student movement in France. Papers with the highest circulation like *Ta Nea* and *Eleftherotypia* carried articles by academics and intellectuals, veterans of 1968, who compared the new movement to May 1968. The verdict, more or less unanimous, was that this was different: May 1968 was radical; young people then wanted to change the world. The new movement was 'conservative'; it tried to preserve 'privileges' secured in the past. At best, it could be called a defensive movement, and this was 'understandable' in view of the high level of youth unemployment and the insecurity felt by young people.

It was a patronising attitude, using a wrong, crude psychological and sociological approach. It is a mistake to try to explain and characterise a movement with abstract social blueprints. It is politics that shapes movements; it is radicalised people that take initiatives, not some automatic 'social factors'.

Fortunately, this debate was cut short as young people in Greece inspired by the French example put their stamp on events much more forcefully than those of us who argued against the smear of 'conservatism'.

One very visible source of radicalisation was the anti-war movement. Most of the young people going through university studies now were school students in 2003. In March of that year, as the first bombs fell in Iraq, almost every Greek city was shaken by mass demonstrations against Bush's war. They were the biggest demos since the collapse of the junta back in 1974. School students were at the heart of the anti-war explosion, shutting down schools and converging on the city centres in their thousands. The Greek Stop The War Coalition lost count of how many schools marched with their own banners on 21 March 2003 in Athens, Salonica, Yannena and other cities.

As the occupations spread almost three years to the date, we at Workers Solidarity made a point of asking students that we interviewed what they were doing back in 2003. A huge proportion of those involved in the coordinating committees of the occupations now said they were involved in anti-war walkouts back then.

The international movement against capitalist globalisation has been another factor in the student occupations in Greece. At the European Social Forum that took place in Athens in early May one of the biggest seminars brought together students from France, Italy and Greece to discuss the way forward. Before that students from the Greek Genoa 2001 Campaign had organised a speaking tour for a student from the occupied Tobbiac University in Paris. They estimated that around 1,000 students attended those meetings, where people had the opportunity to hear first hand how the French occupations were organised. They very quickly put these lessons into practice. Almost all of them played a key role in the general assemblies that spread the Greek occupations.

One concrete example of this influence came at the Philosophy School in Athens. There a student union executive committee dominated by Tories and CP Youth members refused to call a general assembly. An Ad Hoc Committee of Genoa 2001, the main far left student group EAAK and PASOK Youth members took the initiative in calling a mass meeting. They organised a 'flying picket' of lecture halls and got together a meeting of 1,500 people, the biggest student union assembly in 15 years. That got the occupation started in the Philosophy School. The idea of a 'flying picket' was directly copied from the French experience.

The most immediate factor leading to the student occupations in Greece, however, was the lecturers' strike. The Federation of Teaching and Research Staff (POSDEP) has a radical background. Back in the 1970s assistants in the universities had to organise a 100-day strike to win democratic reform of a system dominated by professional prerogatives. Now these gains are under attack as neo-liberal 'reforms' try to 'free' universities from too much influence by students and staff and open them up to private 'sponsors'. POSDEP is opposing these plans with a series of strikes.

At first the student left was suspicious of lecturers' actions, if not openly hostile. There was a lot of government propaganda about 'irresponsible' staff using students as 'hostages' with their strikes to defend 'privileged positions'. But there was also a lot of ultra-left rhetoric about lecturers having separate 'class interests' from the students. When the first POSDEP strikes began three years ago, the students of 'Genoa 2001' were alone in organising solidarity and joining the strikers' demos.

Things have moved on since then. Other unions have led important struggles, particularly in the last year. Bank workers were on strike for a month in June 2005 fighting against neo-liberal 'reform' of their pension funds. It was a strike that won solidarity action from other unions and obviously had an influence on the students. It was a blow to sectarian ideas that students were on their own, isolated from 'privileged' groups like bank employees and lecturers, not interested in trade unions and joint action. The French example of common demonstrations organised by student occupations and trade unions fell on fertile ground. So when the students of Genoa 2001 proposed that the days of POSDEP strikes should be seen as an opportunity to start occupations in the universities, this time the idea caught on, despite opposition from the CP Youth in the colleges.

Ideas had changed, not just among the students but in the trade union movement too. With the occupations spreading in the universities and the government using the police to attack student demos, the question of trade union action became very pressing. We launched an appeal that was headed by the president of the Fertiliser Workers Union in Salonica. They have been occupying their factory against closure since the beginning of 2006. It proved a strong link, and on 21 June there was a day of joint action. By then the government had retreated, and both the Greek TUC (GSEE) and the students set their eyes on the next date: 9 September in Salonica.

At this stage it is not clear how powerful the emergence of the new student movement will be in the next academic year. But the French and Greek occupations have set a strong example. The neo-liberal attack on education is similar across Europe. Students everywhere have the same reasons to oppose these 'reforms'. Now they have the same sources of inspiration too.

A new radical organised student movement can be a step forward for the broader anti-capitalist movement. For years we have had to face accusations of being 'revolutionary tourists' as we demonstrated in Prague, Genoa, Seville or Edinburgh. Many European governments have tried to drive a wedge between the trade unions and the youth element of the big international demonstrations. The radicalisation of the youth was only visible in the streets and the dominance of autonomist politics seemed to perpetuate this state of affairs. Now the students in their colleges are emerging as a new element, more collective, with their own space where they organise and take initiatives that can inspire broader layers of radicalised youth. This can add greater weight to the movement against capitalist globalisation and imperialist war. It is a perspective that seems within reach and is certainly worth fighting for.

South Korea: the view from the left

Choi Il-bung and Kim Ha-young of the International Socialists of South Korea spoke to **International Socialism** *about the political situation in South Korea and the possibility for the left to build today.*

People in Britain are almost completely ignorant of the situation in South Korea. Could you give a brief account of development over the last 20 years?

Il-bung: In the summer of 1987 we had a huge mass strike and since then the transition to bourgeois democracy has been in progress. It was not until 1993 that a real civilian government, that of Kim Young-sam, took office. One year before the end of his term, on Boxing Day of 1996, he railroaded through a neo-liberal labour law which was faced by another big wave of mass strikes by the workers. There was a key struggle to defeat this new labour law in the early part of 1997.

And at the end of 1997 South Korea, like the other East Asian countries, fell into what Koreans call 'the IMF economic crisis'. Because of this Kim Dae-jung was able to get elected president. He had been arrested and tortured by the former Park Chung-hee military government, and when he was elected the South Korean masses had great expectations of him because he had fought against the dictatorship. But he came to office in the middle of the economic crisis and began to implement neo-liberal policies in an attempt to restructure the South Korean economy. So workers and students got disillusioned and began to fight back against this new government. This was met by an offensive from the ruling class, with the right wing going on the attack. It was a fierce battle and the tension persisted until 2002, the end of Kim Dae-jung's term, when there was a movement against the death of two female teenagers who were killed by US armoured cars. A new generation of youth came into the movement—hundreds of thousands of people came into the streets of Seoul for a candlelight vigil. It was a very energetic movement.

The effect of this movement was that a new government came in, that of Roh Moo-hyun, who was a liberal populist. The oppressed people had very high expectations of him when he became president. But he has failed to carry out the reforms people expected. An example is the issue of the Iraq war. In its first year in office the government announced it was going to deploy troops to Iraq, and there was huge opposition, with a series of big demonstrations. But in August 2004 the law was passed sending troops to Iraq and people became disappointed and demoralised. Then Roh Moo-hyun said he would get rid of the notorious National Security Act, and the disappointed people thought, 'Let's expect from him again.' But in the end he failed to get rid of the act. This blow made people even more demoralised.

When people build a big movement to achieve something but don't get the concrete results they wanted, they begin to look for a political alternative—and often it is reformist politics. So they looked to the parliament (the National Assembly). In fact, president Roh Moo-hyun's Uri Party had become a parliamentary majority since the April 2004 general election. On top of this the Democratic Labour Party (DLP), a left reformist party formed in 1999, had held ten seats. The landslide of the Uri Party and the DLP in the general elections was made possible by the fact that a large majority of people didn't want Roh Moo-hyun to be impeached by the right despite repeated disappointments with him.

Today, however, Roh Moo-Hyun supports the massive enlargement and modernisation of the US military base in Pyoung-taek, a town one and a half hours drive to the south of Seoul, on the basis of the Bush administration's concept of 'strategic flexibility'. He is also going to sign the Korea-US Free Trade Agreement. People have reacted strongly to this. Five thousand people demonstrated in front of the military base despite a serious threat from the government, and were met with violent repression from the South Korean army.

These kinds of betrayals were the reason why in the recent local elections in May Roh Moo-hyun's ruling Uri Party was defeated. This was interpreted as a landslide victory for the right wing Grand National Party, which then gained a lot of confidence. But if you look at the voting figures, their vote only went up by 1 percent compared to the last elections. What happened was the support for Roh Moo-hyun's party slumped (because of a large rate of abstention). The DLP also did not do as well as they expected. We saw it as a very small defeat, but most of the left saw it as a major defeat and got very demoralised.

Because the right have gained confidence the government, under pressure from them, is going on the offensive against the left, with a return to using the National Security Act. Recently a Stalinist scholar was subject to a very heated attack by the right wing press simply for saying the Korean War was an attempt by North Korea to bring about Korean unity. He was put on trial and sentenced to four years in prison albeit with a suspension of sentence. My organisation (All Together) and the Stalinists defended this scholar together. When we went to the courts to demonstrate there was a right wing group having a counter-demonstration and there were scuffles. I think we will see more heated confrontations.

Next year we have the presidential election, and the confrontation between right and left will become more intense.

A question about the working class movement. Until 1987 most unions were illegal or controlled by the state. Since then you have seen the development of a very powerful trade union movement with some of the biggest strikes in the world.
Il-bung: Until 1987 South Korea was under military dictatorship and we had the Federation of Korean Trade Unions (FKTU) which was controlled by the state. The mass strike in July through to August 1987 was basically a rank and file movement. Immediately there was struggle to build independent unions which went on until 1995, when a more left wing Korean Confederation of Trade Unions (KCTU) was founded. We saw a bureaucratisation of the union leaders in this process, but as I said before, when the Kim Young-sam government wanted to pass the neo-liberal labour law at the end of 1996 there was a huge reaction from the working class, and the mass strike also served to strengthen the KCTU trade union leadership as well as the rank and file because Kim Young-sam backed off, apologising to the public. A year later in November 1997 the huge financial crash, the so-called 'IMF crisis', became a litmus test for the bureaucracy. And the economic depression in 1998—the worst South Korea has ever seen—damaged the confidence of the rank and file. Workers said, 'Previously we said, "If we unite in the unions we will be victorious." Now we say it's

wrong.' They were also shocked by what their leaders were doing—the betrayal—in 1998. Subsequently, the need for a political expression of the working class movement led to the creation of the Democratic Labour Party in 1999. The workers' political consciousness that emerged in this period showed that trade union consciousness does not easily leap automatically to socialist consciousness.

The very courageous rank and file activists who led the mass strikes of 1987 became the leadership of the Korean Confederation of Trade Unions. But recently the deputy chairman of the KCTU and the leaders of the Hyundai Auto union and the KIA Auto union, both being key components of the KCTU, were all arrested for bribery and corruption. Apart from that, many of the leaders of the KCTU, let alone right wing FKTU leaders, openly display their reformist approach—for instance, refusing to defend the rights of irregular (casual and temporary) workers. So there is a strong distrust of leaders by the rank and file now. But they do not have enough confidence to act independently of the leadership. In a sense we are in a transitory period.

After 1987 Korean workers' living standards rose until they were nearly at the European level. What was the impact of the crisis of the late 1990s?

Il-bung: During the economic slump of 1998 South Korea's economic growth hit minus and so did real wages. In 1999 the economy started to recover but real wages were still minus. By 2000 organised workers began to fight back and were able to stop the decline in living standards. In 2004 they and regular workers were able to recover to the level before the 1997 crash. But most of the temporary, irregular workers are not unionised, and their living standards remained some 10 percent below the 1997 level. Sixty percent of the Korean labour force are irregular workers and their wages are slightly over half those of organised workers. So the living standard of ordinary Koreans as a whole is slightly less than it was ten years ago, before the 1997 crisis.

What is the attitude of ordinary Korean people today towards North Korea and the threats of war against North Korea?

Ha-young: There was a public opinion poll asking South Korean young people whether they thought North Korea was a threat to South Korea. The majority said no. They believe the Cold War has ended and even though there is still a Cold War atmosphere in the Korean Peninsula, they think that because it has disappeared at the world scale it should also disappear in the Korean Peninsula. What is more, in the Cold War period they were constantly bombarded with the idea that North Korea is a threat, it wants to be hegemonic and all that. But from 1995 and 1996 they could see the serious crisis in North Korea with their own eyes, through the reports in the press and by North Korean refugees. They now realise that North Korea is a very weak state and in need of help. They now see the US as the biggest threat to Korean society because its hostility to North Korea will create more instability.

There was a question to the young people about their attitude if the US attacks North Korea. Almost 90 percent said they would oppose a US attack on North Korea. But when asked if they would like to live in North Korea, they said no; only 3 percent said yes.

The attitude of the South Korean government has also changed, in that it is no longer completely with the US?
Ha-young: Partly, yes. On inauguration Roh Moo-hyun said, 'I will be a president who says no to the US.' He also said, 'I do not speak English. I've never been to the US. I want to create an equal relationship when we are dealing with the US.' So in a sense there is a different attitude than that of the previous presidents. His expressions reflect the wishes of the ordinary people, who want the South Korea-US relationship to be 'normalised'.

The US got angry when he said such things. He was, at that stage, also expressing the feelings of sections of the South Korean ruling class, who could see the potential of Chinese economic growth and military power. They felt it would be a disadvantage to them to depend only on the US. They have one leg in China and the other in the US. The question of the attitude to the US is now a very controversial issue within the ruling class. The majority of the ruling class believes the South Korea-US alliance needs to be maintained in the way it has been.

Right now it seems that Roh Moo-hyun has chosen tradition: for him the South Korea-US alliance is more important than the South Korea-China alliance. On the issue of Iraq he has chosen to support the US and when people oppose him sending the troops he says, 'I am pro-American and at the same time for self-reliance.'

Economic and military competition builds up around the Korean Peninsula, and South Korea is under pressure. And the ruling class wish to find their own right position and are reaching in different directions while trying to maintain what they had before, the South Korea-US alliance.

Some South Korean firms are operating in North Korea, aren't they?
Ha-young: Today investment in North Korea is mainly concentrated on tourism and one industrial complex, Kaesong, about an hour and a half drive from Seoul by bus across the military demarcation line. The Kaesong industrial complex is a solution to the problems of small and middle size enterprises in South Korea because the wages are so low—$57 a month, less than is paid in Vietnam or China. And one of the attractive selling points is that there are no trade unions in North Korea.

There are difficulties. Sections of the ruling class are afraid there are a lot of limitations for South Korean companies to go into North Korea. Meanwhile China's investment in and trade with North Korea have grown much more rapidly than that of South Korea. Sections of the South Korean ruling class are worried about this. They think that the US's hostile policy to North Korea is creating this mood and that they might lose to China the opportunity to develop North Korea.

This is a contradiction for left nationalists. They say that North Korea, especially the Kaesong industrial complex, is the answer to the problems of the 'national economy' of the two Koreas combined—but an article in the *Financial Times* calls it 'a haven for the capitalists, not the workers', not the nation either.

What is the situation of the left? Until 1989 there was a very strong Stalinist, Kim Il-sungist left in South Korea. How has that changed?
Il-bung: Until 1991, when the former USSR collapsed, the great majority of the left was Stalinist. Then we had two varieties of Stalinism. One, called 'NL' (National Liberation currents), was pro North Korea, following Kim Il-sung's 'Jucheist' thought ('Juche' means 'self-reliance'). The other strand called itself PD (People's Democracy currents) and looked towards the USSR and Eastern Europe.

When Eastern Europe and the USSR collapsed, it was a tremendous shock, a total defeat for PD, and they just dissolved, some having an interest in some forms of post-modernism until the late 1990s.

NL, the Jucheists, survived the PD because North Korea survived. But from 1994 to 1998 they went through a deep crisis. First the death of Kim Il-sung in 1994 and then the famine from 1995 onwards, as well as the economic crisis, meant there was widespread feeling among South Koreans that the North Korean regime would collapse at any moment.

1998 was a turning point for NL because South Korea was also involved in a serious economic crisis. The Jucheists felt able to hold that North Korea was better than South Korea. And in the summer of 1998 they saw the launch of the supposedly continental ballistic missiles as showing the advance of technology in North Korea while the Kim Jong-il regime seemed to be stabilising.

The Inter-Korean Summit in 2000 really boosted the confidence of the Jucheists. But immediately afterwards the Jucheists more or less became reformists. Today Jucheists are acting as reformists—as are the bulk of the PD currents. PD has now differentiated into various widely different currents, and you can see all kinds of mishmashes: from die-hard traditional Stalinism, through modern versions of Maoism, through various kinds of social democracy and autonomism, to ultra-left workerism or council communism, as well as an inner DLP faction identifying itself with the Scottish Socialist Party. What binds together these wide varieties of PD, except for autonomist brands, is their workerist legacy and the sectarian attitude towards NL-led anti-imperialist struggles.

The International Socialists of South Korea (ISSK) is the other element in the Korean left. It began in 1990. On the eve of the collapse of the former USSR in August 1991 we had 29 members. In three months we grew to 170. But three months later there was a police raid and many of our members were arrested and went to prison. All through the 1990s, until December 1999 when we joined the DLP, we were underground as being some 150 strong, and regularly assaulted by the police—especially whenever we showed a sign of growth. During the whole decade more than 200 of our members were arrested, some comrades twice or even three times. We were sentenced to between six months and two years in prison. Being underground really had a negative effect (like passivity, temptations towards sectarianism, and so on) on both the group as a whole and its individual members, at a time when the movement was rising—since 1996.

But in late 2002, as I said before, there was a mass movement of young people against the threat of war and military aggression by the US.

This immediately led to the anti-war movement and we started to grow from some 300 in early 2003 to slightly less than 1,200 in 2005. We are part of the DLP and in the recent party election we put up a candidate for policy director, one of the three major national posts, and we received 18 percent of the votes nationally and more than 30 percent in Seoul.

Korea historically had very big students' movements. Is this still true?
Il-bung: Historically, from the 1960s to the 1980s we had a strong tradition of a militant student movement against dictatorship and authoritarian government. Most of the leadership of the left today are from that student movement. But recently there has been a change in the student movement. There is no longer a dictatorship or an authoritarian government and they need to fight against neo-liberalism. But because the movement is influenced by reformists, it is very disoriented. They do not know how to organise and mobilise resistance. Many of them are demoralised.

Nevertheless we have student councils controlled by the various kinds of left nationalists including Jucheists. When there is an issue they think important they can mobilise several thousand students. A prime case was the struggle against the enlargement of the US base in Pyoung-taek town.

Ha-young: Today the students and young people have so much anger, so we have the possibility of highly explosive activism, as was shown in the reaction to the two deaths of female teenagers in 2002. But that was a spontaneous explosion, not linked to the old student movement leadership. One of the Jucheist student leaders told us that when the hundreds of thousands of young people were protesting then, and the Jucheist students turned up with their banner, no one showed any interest. This is because they continue with their old Stalinist ideas which young people and students are not interested in. We find that when we raise internationalist issues like Bush's wars in the Middle East, a lot of young people are attracted to those issues. We find they have a great interest in politics—lots of questions about radical left politics. Many young people and students come to the Marxist Forums we organise around basic or applied ideas of Marxism.

Morales and the Bolivian state

Crawford Spence and Mark Shenkin

The following article explores the tentative development of a new form of political organisation in Bolivia, as it emerged after Evo Morales's victory in the presidential elections of December 2005. Drawing on existing research and extensive interviews conducted in Bolivia over the period July–September 2006, it theorises the underlying conception of the state that exists in the new administration, including the various dynamic relations between the state apparatus and the large body of social and indigenous movements. It questions whether what is developing in Bolivia truly holds the potential to result in a radically new form of grassroots governance or whether the rhetoric of the government only serves to conceal what is really just another brand of centralised and authoritarian political decision-making.

A 'revolutionary epoch'

For little over 20 years following the passing of Decreto Supremo 21060,[1] representative democracy in Bolivia was dominated by the Washington Consensus. By the turn of the century this grand policy of market liberalisation was culminating in crisis after crisis. The frequent replacement of government administrations did little to placate an increasingly mobile and organised populace. What was being called into crisis was not just the neo-liberal orientation of the various administrations, but the very function of the republican state itself. On 18 December 2005 the election of Evo

Morales's Movimiento al Socialismo (MAS) signalled an end to the neo-liberal orientation. His vice-president, Àlvaro García Linera, sociologist, suggests that what Bolivia has been experiencing is what Marx termed a 'revolutionary epoch'—a concept used to understand:

> historical periods of dizzying political change—abrupt shifts in the position and power of social forces, repeated state crises, recomposition of collective identities, repeated waves of social rebellion—separated by periods of relative stability during which the modification, partial or total, of the general structures of political domination nevertheless remain in question.[2]

It is only now, after more than six months in office and with the contours of Evo Morales's presidency defined in more concrete terms, that one can begin to make inferences as to the real characteristics of this period of change. The tsunami-like rise to power of Evo Morales since 2002 is both complex and contingent on a number of specific historical events; not only the intense mobilisation of the people (among whom Morales only relatively recently emerged as the obvious leader), but also the crises in the traditional political parties who increasingly failed to encounter ideological influence among the people.[3] Throughout the period of Morales's rise to power, his political discourse moved beyond that of 'coca' and quickly came to incorporate the diversity of demands of the social movements: the nationalisation of hydrocarbon resources, the rejection of neo-liberalism and, most importantly, the creation of a prominent indigenous platform.

There is no doubt that this government is radically different from anything that Bolivia has ever seen. MAS itself has never been a traditional political party, but a coalition of social movements. Now that they are in power, the relations between the government and the social movements remain strong. As Isaac Avaloz, head of the Confederación Sindical Unica de Trabajadores Campesinos de Bolivia (Bolivian Union of Rural Workers), points out, 'Never before have previous governments consulted us. Now we have meetings with ministers all the time'.[4] This could be explained by the fact that the government itself is populated by ex-union and campesino leaders, former guerrillas and activists. There are few traces of career politicians. Yet the appointment of such personalities was arguably an example of political opportunism. Many ministers continue to operate as technical advisers rather than conforming to the Gramscian concept of 'organic intellectual'.[5]

Regardless of the individuals who constitute its workings, the bounds of the republican state can only be pushed so far. As Mike Gonzalez predicted (in issue 108 of this journal), the election of Morales would result in a protection of the structures and functions of the state at the expense of more revolutionary forms of government. This is indeed the scenario which appears to be developing. The government routinely consults and listens to the demands of the social movements, sometimes with an almost obsessive fervour. Yet while this demonstration of institutional accountability is refreshing in comparison to the traditional bourgeois model of the state (as an entity accountable primarily to capital), it is also limited in its outlook. In the absence of a direct relation between the government and the people, the social movements serve as a mediator. Decisions continue to be made centrally. It could be argued that what is being created is a form of syndicalist corporatism rather than a self-determining mass movement from below.

The contrast lies in the rhetoric of the Bolivian government, a rhetoric that routinely points to the need to redefine and decentralise the colonial state. A far cry from the self-loathing of neo-liberal governments determined to pass all power to the market, the Bolivian administration claims that it wants to pass power to the people. Its primary means of doing this is through the new constitutional assembly, inaugurated on 6 August 2006. This assembly was a cornerstone of MAS's electoral campaign and a clear demand of indigenous organisations since the early 1990s. The people have elected 255 *asambleistas* who will spend the next year and a half rewriting the constitution. MAS sees this, among other things, as the means to transcend the limitations of the colonial state. What could be implied is that MAS's electoral victory, while itself to an extent indicative of their acceptance of existing institutional structures, was merely a step on the way to the initiation of a process that could well result in the spectacular self-destruction of the colonial state and its replacement with more endogenous forms of governance.

If the assembly remains truly an open process, this possibility certainly presents itself. However, one of the concessions made by the government to the traditional political parties was to ensure that each asambleista defined their allegiance to a specific political party. The existence of party lines may serve to temper the radicalism of the new constitution.

Indeed, in spite of MAS's strong rhetoric against the colonial state, it would appear that they do not wish the power of decision-making to be taken away from the executive, but simply would like to ensure that centralised decisions continue to be influenced by a sufficient dynamism from the social movements.[6] Indeed, the ideology of MAS has never been primarily socialist, in spite of what their name may suggest.

Indigenista ideology

Before analysing the most prominent of the government's reforms, the ideological context within which these reforms have been formulated must be understood. 'Movimiento al Socialismo' would appear to be a fairly large misnomer. The social movements at the forefront of the mobilisations of recent years have been those constructed around campesino (indigenous rural workers) organisations and the indigenous populations of the Altiplano.[7] The industrial workers' movement in Bolivia lacks organisation and direction and is nothing like as strong as it was in the early 1950s. This could explain why the government's main focus is on the historically marginalised and oppressed indigenous population rather than traditional working class or proletariat structures. In a recent interview in *La Razòn* the vice-president and theoretical spokesperson of the government pointed this out quite clearly:

> MAS holds an ideology composed of various sources the central one of which, without doubt, is indianismo, defending the right to self-determination of the indigenous peoples… Marxism is not a source but more of a reference point for some people and inside the structure of the government it is a strong tool of understanding and ordering reality… It is a small current but it is present.[8]

The criterion for where to direct government policy is driven less by a traditional notion of class and more by a diverse notion of ethnicity. What we are seeing is the organised construction of a popular-indigenista hegemony. The populist nature of this hegemony is evidenced in the fact that the demands of the Aymara and Quechua indigenous peoples are regularly addressed in government rhetoric. Although there are 36 different peoples and languages in Bolivia, it is these two majority indigenous groups that have been at the forefront of the mobilisations of recent years. The less vocal minority indigenous groups receive less attention, if any, from the Aymaran president.

In one respect, the president has made much out of comparisons with the apartheid era in South Africa, pointing out that only 50 years in the past indigenous peoples were not allowed in government buildings. While this policy of systematic discrimination is now being dramatically changed, the indigenista ideology in itself is limited. As with South Africa and other nationalist revolutions, there is the danger that the changes taking place will be of form rather than content. That is, the current elite in the country may now be permeated by those with a different skin colour and cultural background but the centralisation of power and the economic stratification of society will continue largely unimpeded.

There are therefore broadly two paths open to Bolivia at the moment. The first is an increasing dialectic between the government and the (mostly indigenous) social movements, further grounding the corporatist structures that have begun to emerge. The second is that this corporatism is merely a staging post on the way to a more revolutionary dialectic between the state and the multitude. While the latter option is questionable as a delineation of the government's primary intentions, their attempts to reconstruct the state do not lie entirely in their own hands. The social movements and the people generally have given Morales some time and breathing space to deliver a 'government of the people', yet many of them are mindful of the need to control this government and ensure that their demands are dealt with. The increased democratisation that is taking place in Bolivia offers opportunities to the Bolivian people to go beyond the government's own vision of a more accountable, yet still centralised state.

The actions of MAS since coming to power have gone some way to re-establish the legitimacy of the republican state and therefore have worked counter to more revolutionary processes. Yet the new constitutional assembly, along with the increased participation of the social movements, albeit in a corporatist fashion, has created fissures in the historic bloc. These fissures could be exploited by those with a more profound vision of how to reconstruct society. Thus, whether MAS intends it or not, the conditions for a more revolutionary form of government may well be under construction. These changes depend on the organisation and consciousness of the people and their ability to mobilise themselves around a common ideology that is not handed down by the government. Indeed, the government's grounding of this so-called 'revolutionary epoch' and its potential effect on the consciousness and political will of the people can be inferred from two simultaneous forms of analysis: analysis of the reforms that have actually taken place; and analysis of the rhetorical way in which these reforms are projected by the government. Two of the most important threads of reform are those that relate, respectively, to the nationalisation of the oil and gas industry and the start of a radical process of agrarian reform.

Nationalisation

The pervasive role of the Bolivian state is evident in its proposed nationalisation of the hydrocarbon industry. Nationalisation itself is a misnomer given that the government rhetoric surrounding sovereignty and control of natural resources is at odds with what is actually taking place (see also issue 111 of this journal), which amounts to a renegotiation of contracts rather than full nationalisation. Fifty one percent of the assets will be owned and controlled by YPFB[9] and the Bolivian share of revenues will increase. The international hydrocarbons community is not quaking in its boots, and no multinational corporation appears to be making plans to leave Bolivia. Indeed, the government is actively encouraging inward investment from foreign companies and has upwardly renegotiated export prices with countries such as Argentina and Brazil, tempering any potentially negative impact on company profits that might result from the nationalisation.

The nationalisation of hydrocarbons exemplifies well the government's long term plan for the country, and the role of the state in particular. The particulars of the nationalisation programme (as far as one can make out—the government has been heavy on rhetoric and frustratingly short on detail) give a strong indication of state capitalism. What is implied is that a strengthened state will be the main arbiter and controller of productive resources. At the same time, a strong state, with control over resources, is seen as the means to develop communitarianism. For example, the economic benefits of the industrialisation of gas[10] are to be fed into communities whose own forms of mercantilism will supposedly be sustained and developed endogenously by this new economic boom. Such policies form the backbone of what the government has routinely referred to as 'Andean-Amazonian capitalism'—an attempt to control the financial power of capital in ways which permit community self-determination.

Whether capitalism can be controlled in order to respect the diversity of communities in Bolivia or whether it will homogenise all in its path will only become apparent in time. Such a strategy appears both risky and contradictory, given that it entails making compromises and giving concessions to established economic elites.

Nevertheless, the nationalisation is not countering significant opposition from among the social movements. They appear to have accepted the government line that Bolivia has indeed recuperated sovereignty over its natural resources. This could possibly be explained by the fact that the majority of social movements in Bolivia have a reformist orientation. Given the fragmentary and marginalised position of the traditional Bolivian workers' movement, the difference between 'radicals' and 'moderates' in Bolivia no longer marks a battle between socialism and capitalism. Rather, the difference between moderates and radicals is best understood by reference to how radical the nationalisation of hydrocarbons should be.[11] The demands of more radical groups still culminate in a version of state capitalism where the state is the main conduit of resource allocation and the controller of production. As such, the government's rhetoric has found broad ideological consent. The curious marriage between communitarianism and global capital seems to be one that will proceed for the foreseeable future.

The land question and regional autonomy

The communitarianism element of government discourse is fused with notions of indigenous self-identity and self-determination, with respect being given to the habits and customs of the different communities that exist in Bolivia. Recently, this historical discourse on 'autonomy' has been met by another, more modern form of autonomy that is not based around habits and customs but on the decentralisation of power to each of the nine regions of the country. The modern discourse has been driven largely by the elite of Santa Cruz and Tarija, who see their vast economic resources as under threat from the current government. A referendum in July—a government concession to the latifundistas—saw four of the nine departments vote for regional autonomy in principle. While the details of this autonomy have yet to be worked out, the stage has been set for a conflict between central government and the department of Santa Cruz, in particular around the issue of land.

The recent agrarian reform, actually dubbed the 'agrarian revolution', sets out the government plan to redistribute primarily government lands to landless peasants, and to those with insufficient land. Beyond this, there is also a proposed modification to the existing INRA[12] law which would open the door to expropriation of private land that is currently economically unproductive. It is this modification that is seen as the biggest threat to the latifundistas. Morales considers land redistribution to be a moral right of the Bolivian people and has called on the social movements to force the closure of parliament if this law is not passed.

Notwithstanding the fact that this whole process is being painstakingly fed through current institutions before it is enacted, the proposal is actually a modest one. By focusing only on economically unproductive land, it does not directly challenge the power of the agribusiness elements of the latifundistas, only the large swathes of land that they have historically accumulated and which they hold in reserve. Indeed, the proposal is only a slight modification of that which was proposed by the previous decrees of the Sanchez de Lozada and Carlos Mesa governments. It also follows World Bank logic in that the land will be purchased and made available to indigenous groups through credit, who will then be under pressure to present economically viable projects. This would hardly respect the habits and customs of the Andean and Amazonian communities in Bolivia so much as it would bring more elements of Bolivian society under the shadow of the market.

Similar types of land projects have been undertaken in Colombia, Guatemala and Brazil. The results were painful; many peasants became so indebted that they had to give up their land at the same time as the landowners made good business by selling off their poorest parcels.[13] Thus the 'agrarian revolution' represents another example of a government reform strangled by the constraints of a republican state which demands continuity with previous decrees and adherence to time-consuming and cumbersome legislative processes. As with the nationalisation, the masses appear to be riding on the wave of euphoria that accompanies government rhetoric. There is a limited counter-discourse to the 'agrarian revolution' from below. Rather, the social movements are leading the way in supporting Morales in his quest to push through the modification to the existing INRA law.

Conclusions

On the whole it appears that the Bolivian government to this day maintains a conception of a centralised state, albeit a state now accountable to the social movements and with potentially more flexibility and access by way of a rewritten constitution. The reforms enacted by Morales's Movimiento al Socialismo in the first six months of its presidency represent, on the whole, a 'democratisation' of the structure of the state. Many of the government reforms represent increased access to wealth, land and education for historically marginalised peoples. They reflect and promote increased participation in political affairs. They potentialise a growth in political consciousness and an increase in the capacity for accountability. However, while what has been produced is arguably 'better' than what was before, what we are not seeing is an altogether different structure of power.

Likewise the economic reforms taking place in Bolivia reflect more of a democratisation of capitalism and less of a strong movement towards socialism. Whether or not this 'Andean-Amazonian capitalism' is really a staging post towards socialism will depend more on the people than it will on a government currently increasing its role as arbiter and controller of productive processes. With baited breath the people support Morales. There are general expectations that his rhetoric around a society characterised by equality and justice will indeed materialise, that people will be lifted out of poverty and that development will ensue. It is this rhetoric that has succeeded in displacing, for the time being, the more profound ideological questioning of the very concept of the state in Bolivia.

What is worrying is that as the government continues on this divided path, with its feet between the camps of global capital and indigenous communitarianism, the expectations of the people may never be fully met. It is crucial to note that the proposal of a new ideological route, if it continues to be articulated and effected by way of a republican state, will always be limited in its ability to respond to the demands of the people. Neither is it a historical inevitability that the people will recognise the limitations of the republican state. The danger is that the next crisis in Bolivian politics, like many previous ones, will simply be mystified into inexistence by another change in personnel. The challenge that remains is for the fragmented left of Bolivia to articulate the need for a change in the very form of politics and not merely in their content.

NOTES

1: The now infamous government decree which signalled Bolivia's embrace of neo-liberalism.

2: A Garcia Linera, *New Left Review* 37, January/February 2006.

3: P Stefanoni and H Do Alto, *Evo Morales, de la Coca al Palacio: Una Oportunidad para la Izquierda Indígena* (Malatesta, 2006).

4: Personal interview, 24 July 2006.

5: P Stefanoni and H Do Alto, as above, p90.

6: A Garcìa Linera, *Pagina/12*, 23 February 2006 (in P Stefanoni and H Do Alto, as above, p91).

7: The Andean region in the west of Bolivia which is populated predominantly by Aymara and Quechua peoples.

8: *La Razòn*, 7 August 2006.

9: Yacimientos Petroliferos Fiscales Bolivianos is the state hydrocarbon company which was capitalised in 1996, placing sovereignty of all of Bolivia's hydrocarbons in the hands of just 12 multinational corporations. It is now being reinvigorated as part of the nationalisation.

10: Hydrocarbons have long been exploited in Bolivia but not industrialised. This has meant that much of the value of Bolivia's hydrocarbon wealth has been enjoyed by other countries who have developed the means of processing gas and petrol. It has also increased Bolivia's economic dependency on other nations (see, for example, R Gonzalez Pelaez, *Renacionalización: Travesía hacia la Era Boliviana de los Hidrocarburos* (Santa Cruz, 2005)).

11: P Stefanoni and H Do Alto, as above.

12: Neo-liberal land law elaborated and developed by the Sanchez de Lozada government which, among other things, further entrenched the property rights of latifundistas.

13: *Alerta Laboral* 45 (July 2006), Centro de estudios para el desarrollo laboral y agrario (CEDLA).

The split in the Scottish Socialist Party

Mike Gonzalez

Since Seattle in 1999, and the explosive growth of the anti-capitalist movement, all of us in the international socialist movement have been sailing in uncharted waters. The one thing that we have almost all agreed on is that the left must develop new forms of organisation that can both reflect and engage with this new and growing radical shift. After 9/11 the explosion of anti-war protests opened new directions and possibilities. For the revolutionary left, the potential was enormous provided that we were governed above all by the commitment to become socialists within the movement, working with a broader spectrum of forces than we had perhaps been used to in the previous two decades. That was the challenge.

In Scotland the Scottish Socialist Party offered an exciting possibility of responding to that challenge. Founded in 1998, with comrades from the Militant Tendency playing a central role, it was committed to a project of left unity expressed in a party which could act in an agreed and united way while acknowledging that political debate was the lifeblood of any socialist organisation. In that spirit, the Socialist Workers Party in Scotland was invited to join the SSP as a platform—an opportunity we grasped with the overwhelming agreement of our membership.

The signs were extremely promising, and the party's electoral success in 2003 confirmed that there was widespread support for a principled socialist anti-war party. It is a matter of great regret, therefore, that just three years after that major electoral advance the Scottish Socialist Party has reached a point of insoluble crisis. The project, however, remains as urgent and as hopeful as it was when we joined just five years ago. The deepening crisis of New Labour, the public revulsion against the war in Iraq and Afghanistan and the assault on Lebanon, the aggressive privatisation of public services confirm the objective necessity for an open, democratic, mass-based socialist party. It will not now be the SSP; but it is our hope that the new formation that we have helped to found, provisionally called Solidarity, and which includes Tommy Sheridan, perhaps the key individual on the left of Scottish politics, the majority of previous members of the SSP, and a number of other elements of the wider social movement, will draw towards it the widest range of anti-capitalists.

What follows is an account of the crisis and collapse of the SSP. Its purpose is not to win some abstract moral contest, but to show that the events which brought about the crisis, while apparently personal, were in fact profoundly political. They demonstrate that what was exposed in the course of recent months was a faultline in a particular model of socialist organisation. The point of this narrative, therefore, is to identify that weakness as a warning and a lesson for the next chapter.

1: The catalyst

The immediate cause of the collapse of the SSP was a consequence of a decision by perhaps its best known leading member, Tommy Sheridan, to sue the *News of the World*, owned by Rupert Murdoch's News International corporation, over a story concerning his private life. For socialists, matters of private morality are not our concern; consensual sexual relations concern only those engaged in them. We judge our comrades by their political conduct, not their personal life. The *News of the World* is a newspaper which publishes scandalous reports of sexual behaviour—but more importantly, it is a consistent enemy of the working class movement, using its pages and those of its sister papers to systematically attack trade unionists, socialists, and all those who fight oppression, whether their own or that of others. This is common knowledge, even among many of those who buy the paper for its titillating content. And that is why Sheridan's victory, when a jury found by a majority against the paper, was widely celebrated by working class people in Scotland and beyond.

What caused the internal crisis within the SSP, however, was the astonishing fact that a number of members of the Executive Committee[a] of the SSP came to court to testify for the *News of the World*. Their presence in the court was not just the result of legal compulsion, as they claimed: it was a consequence of a series of actions and decisions taken over previous months which were not only wrong in themselves, but which revealed a much deeper malaise within the party. When the newspaper reports originally emerged, Sheridan asked the executive at a long, fraught meeting to recognise his right to individually pursue his libel case; instead he was pressured to resign. An extremely detailed account of that critical meeting was kept, without informing other executive committee members (including myself) of its content—and this account later became the substance of the *News of the World*'s case. In the days that followed several executive committee members distanced the party from him in a very public way, and leaked rumours and suggestions about him to the press.

The position of the Socialist Worker Platform at the time was well known and repeated on a number of occasions—that we supported Sheridan's right to pursue the case and condemned the mounting campaign against him. For it seemed to us very clear from the outset that there *was* a coordinated and consistent campaign to remove Sheridan from his leading position in the SSP. The extraordinary bitterness and ferocity of the continuing attacks on him and all of those who supported him from within the SSP after the conclusion of the court case have shocked even the most seasoned socialists—and ensured the collapse of the SSP as we knew it.

What matters here, of course, is not anecdotal accounts—though the response of the SSP executive committee immediately after the trial ended was to produce a 12-page document consisting entirely of personal vituperation and accusations against Sheridan. Its effect was to convince the majority of party activists that they could no longer work in a party led by people who could produce such a document.

The question that will be asked is why this happened.

It is my view that the crisis in the SSP has its origins in the central question of the relationship between socialists and the movement. Our original optimistic assessment of the SSP, and our decision to join, reflected

---

a: The overwhelming majority of the EC had been members of the Militant Tendency. Three were members of the Socialist Worker platform, including myself. The one member of our platform present at the meeting in November 2004 voted for the decision calling on Sheridan to resign but immediately and publicly acknowledged that she had been wrong.

its declared commitment to building a broad, open, mass socialist party. The authority and recognition that had been won by Tommy Sheridan in the campaign against the poll tax and his subsequent actions as the sole SSP member of the Scottish Parliament, were a key contributor to that assessment. And the most resounding confirmation of the SSP's potential came with the Scottish parliamentary elections in May 2003, when the party won 6 percent of the national vote, a total of 130,000, and sent six members to the Scottish Parliament.

It was a historic moment—and it was a victory, in our view, that arose directly out of the public perception of the party's leading role in the anti-war movement: 100,000 marched through Glasgow on 15 February that year. It is no coincidence that that figure so closely reflected the numbers in the election.

The conflicts within the party, although as yet unstated, began at that very moment of success. The large numbers voting for the SSP suggested a real possibility of 'opening the gates of the party' to them, laying the foundations for a genuine mass organisation. Yet it was clear even then that there was resistance to embracing the wider movement, and a continuing insistence on SSP-led and SSP-controlled campaigns. There had already been considerable debate between the Socialist Worker Platform and the executive committee majority regarding the anti-war movement. While we had argued that we should set out to replicate the best experiences of the Stop the War campaign and build a broad anti-war movement in alliance with Muslim organisations, the majority of the leadership rejected that view and insisted instead on allying with some very backward Stalinist elements in a recently created bureaucracy which consistently blocked any grassroots activity from that point on.

That suspicion of the wider forces that had entered the historical scene after Seattle reflected a sectarian response which was to characterise the relationship between the SSP and every and any social movement. Curiously, the election result led not, as we had argued, to a more open and dynamic relationship with the wider movement, but to its opposite—an over-emphasis on parliamentary activity at the expense of grassroots activity. Parliaments can be a useful propaganda platform in the building of socialist organisation—as Tommy Sheridan had shown so emphatically when he was the sole member between 1999 and 2003. With six members in the parliament the party became entitled to a number of full-time research and case workers, and the commitment to the MSPs remitting half their parliamentary salary to the party added to the party's resources. But it also reinforced the party's bureaucratic character, and focused its attention on a parliamentary role which could not but be limited and constrained.

The rhetoric, of course, endlessly reasserted the party's commitment to the working class and the purity of its socialist credentials. But it was a serious misrepresentation if this was intended to indicate a concentration on issues in the trade union movement, for example, or a commitment to building the resistance in working class areas around issues like health or housing. Trade union work was limited in reality to seeking relationships with leading trade union officials with a view to affiliation. The Socialist Worker Platform has always argued that we should build links with and between the rank and file; this was questioned time and again because it threatened an often asserted but rarely visible sympathetic relationship with union officials. When the party did move on trade union questions, it was invariably at the last moment, generally tokenistic, and often sectarian in the tone of its interventions.

One consequence of what we regard as a squandered opportunity was that party membership began to decline, as did sales of the party's newspaper *Scottish Socialist Voice*. The paper itself was weak and inward looking and very consciously controlled by the executive committee majority faction. While occasional articles were printed from other positions within the party, they were few and did not reflect any opening of the paper to debate—still less any attempt to make it reflect the wider movement that had carried six comrades into the parliament. The internal atmosphere grew increasingly fractious, and criticisms of Sheridan from a supposedly feminist perspective became increasingly vocal at executive meetings. This was the background to the events of the executive committee meeting November 9th 2004 which forced Sheridan's resignation.

But it was the G8 meeting at Gleneagles in Scotland in July 2005 which would provide the proof of the two perspectives that were in a bitter but undeclared conflict within the SSP. In January 2005, at the regular executive meeting, Socialist Worker Platform members called for a discussion of our preparations for G8. At that meeting and at every subsequent one the SSP's leadership refused to address the question. The people who would attend the Make Poverty History demonstration, it was argued, were middle class liberals; working class people were not interested in such issues, any more than they were concerned with the war in Iraq. Workers were interested only in 'bread and butter questions'.

In the meantime Socialist Worker Platform members within the SSP together with a broad range of other groups and organisations had taken the initiative in setting up a committee to prepare for the Gleneagles protest on the first day of the G8, and the organisation of a counter-conference in Edinburgh on the previous Sunday. The meetings were regular, large and enthusiastic as well as very broad in character. One MSP, Frances Curran, was assigned to link up with that organising group, together with a platform member who had been deeply involved from the outset. The role of the SSP leadership in that activity was a disgrace: time and again their interventions were simply designed to block or spoil what was a broad and democratic initiative, while offering no real practical or political support to the organisers. Refusing to contribute to the Alternative Summit, beyond accepting the opportunity to speak on its platforms, those comrades stuck to the tried and well-worn formula that this was not of interest to workers and the abstention continued. On the Friday before the demonstration four of the six MSPs staged an absurd and pointless stunt in the parliament to veil their ineffectiveness and distance from the movement. The cost was £30,000 in fines and other expenses and the general scorn of the public.

As we expected, the Make Poverty History demonstration was enormous (around 300,000) and as varied, diverse and dynamic as such demonstrations always are. The SSP leadership's main concern, however, was not how party members could best connect with this new movement but rather how we could differentiate ourselves from other marchers. Thus SSP members wore red T-shirts (not white, like everyone else) and organised a tight, closed contingent rather than participating throughout the march in the delegations of trade unionists, students, anti-capitalist protesters and the like.

The Sunday Alternatives Summit was an extraordinary success, with 5,000 people attending a vibrant, open and exciting event full of political ideas and debate. It was sad, then, to see the SSP leadership standing outside the main hall throughout the day collecting signatures for a petition to defend the MSPs who had been expelled from the parliament. Most significantly, Frances Curran speaking at the final rally went to considerable pains to emphasise the *differences* between the SSP and the movement, and the distance separating the SSP from the major international figures with whom she was sharing a platform, including Trevor Ngwane from South Africa, Susan George, Caroline Lucas and George Galloway.

Several members of the executive committee complained bitterly in the subsequent meeting about the conduct of the SSP at this great event, with a supporter of the leadership group publishing a frank and withering assessment of the party's performance in the next issue of *Frontline*, the magazine of the leadership's ISM platform within the SSP. As a party, the SSP had deliberately and explicitly refused to engage with the movement, though the Socialist Worker Platform together with other rank and file members of the SSP, as well as many others outside the party, had worked tirelessly for months to build the event.

It might have been asserted, of course, that this was a political error and lessons could be drawn from it. Instead it was argued in the immediate aftermath that this was an event somehow 'staged' by the SWP. What was not addressed was the paradox that, at a time of intense political debate among growing numbers of working class people, not only had the SSP abstained as an organisation, but its numbers were continuing to decline, as were the sales of its paper, in what was an extraordinarily favourable atmosphere.

Two months after these massive events, the policy coordinator of the party, Alan McCombes, presented a paper to the executive committee which argued that the party's main audience lay not in those who were disaffected by New Labour or those involved in the anti-war or anti-capitalist movement but rather in the poor and dispossessed in the housing schemes:

> The biggest potential reservoir of support for the SSP is not to be found among Labour voters, SNP voters, Lib Dem voters or even Green Party voters, but among the 50 percent of the population who do not participate in elections. Well over 1 million people did not bother to vote in the 2003 Scottish election or in the 2005 general election.

Of course the poor and dispossessed must be *part* of the SSP's potential audience and it is right that a socialist party should be trying to encourage their entry into political life, while recognising the difficulties involved in doing so. McCombes's mistake, however, is to imagine that the dispossessed can be the *main* or *leading* component in our social base (one reason, along with his suggestion that party organisation in future be based on a series of interest groups or 'networks' rather than geographical branches, that his paper was not supported by the executive committee).

2: The parting of the ways

If much of the leadership seemed unaffected by the events at Gleneagles, the same cannot be said of the membership of the SSP. The national conference of the SSP in March of this year (2006) was notable for its changed atmosphere. Around issues of war, racism and climate change, delegates consistently rejected sectarian motions which argued for an 'ourselves alone' approach, in favour of working with other activist and campaigners. When Rosie Kane MSP, for example, spoke in a debate on environmental issues (she is, it should be remembered, the party's most prominent environmental spokesperson) on behalf of the executive committee, she specifically rejected the motion that the party should become involved in the broad Campaign Against Climate Change, arguing instead that 'we don't need to work with anyone else—we can do it by ourselves'. Her position was decisively rejected by the delegates.

The conference delegations included a number of new people who had come towards the SSP through the work around G8 and anti-war activities—the very activities that had been repeatedly rejected as irrelevant and marginal by the leadership of the organisation. It was largely through contact with members of the Socialist Worker Platform that they had joined the SSP; they were mostly young and non-sectarian. But they saw little of their spirit reflected in the party's paper or in the branch meetings. Indeed what they had entered felt like a party in decline, controlled by a bureaucratic layer which saw growth through the movement as a 'dilution'.

The spirit of the conference made no impact on the executive committee. The reality was that our support in the country was ebbing away—a series of local and parliamentary by-elections in 2006 had shown how slender that support now was, slipping in some cases below 2 percent of the votes cast. The process of preparing for the Scottish elections in May 2007 should already have begun, with candidates being selected and campaigns begun at a local level. Instead the party leadership remained totally absorbed in the continuing question of Tommy Sheridan's libel action, and intensified its factional activity, continuing the arguments which had first surfaced nearly two years earlier. Sheridan had been elected chair of the party by conference. But the party's leadership was not prepared to accept the declared will of the party. Instead it counter-attacked, launching yet another whispering campaign intended to force Sheridan to drop the case, and effectively withdrawing the political support of the party from him at a critical moment.

There is a clear pattern of behaviour on the part of the SSP leadership throughout the last three years, whose roots lie still further back in the SSP's history. When put to the test, on every occasion those in control of the party have shown that the declared intention to move towards a new kind of open, mass-based political formation was worth little more than the paper it was written on. The existing membership of the party, declining day by day, neither controlled nor understood what was happening at the top. The prevailing method remained sectarian in relation to the class and bureaucratic in relation to the membership. Far from engaging with and winning the leadership of the movement in Scotland, the SSP stood back from the movement, refused to work to win the leadership of it, and more often than not condemned it for its political limitations.

Sheridan himself was a member of the ISM platform; those who turned against him were almost all his close political allies until very recently. They have now turned against him for reasons that are far more profoundly political than personal. While Sheridan shares his political roots with the SSP leadership, he has had a major influence in winning support for the party in the class with his consistent record of political activism around war, asylum seekers and anti-capitalism. In 2003 his name was on the ballot paper beside the party logo. The project for which people voted was inescapably associated in the public mind with Tommy Sheridan. That is why the majority of party members represented at a party national council in June gave their full support to Sheridan and rejected the convoluted arguments presented by the executive committee majority to justify what was seen as a public betrayal of a leading socialist and the project he represented.

One argument offered by the leadership was that the principal issue was gender rather than class. Sheridan himself has suggested that the conflict is between what he characterises as 'gender politics' and 'class politics'. This is not necessarily a characterisation that we would accept, not least since we see the struggle against class exploitation and for women's liberation as intimately linked. Nevertheless, the dominance of feminist ideas among a section of the party has led them to see the central issue as being Sheridan's alleged personal behaviour rather than News International's attacks on a leading socialist.

The SWP was able to clarify its understanding of the real Marxist tradition on women's liberation through a lengthy and sometimes bitter faction fight in the early 1980s around the question of 'autonomous' women's organisation. By contrast no such debate took place within Militant, which was in fact notorious on the left in the 1970s and 1980s for its denunciation of the women's liberation movement as 'petty bourgeois'. Perhaps as a consequence of that experience, leading SSP members who are former Militant supporters have now 'flip-flopped' into an uncritical acceptance of many feminist ideas. As an example of where such positions can lead, in an article in the *Sunday Herald* MSP Carolyn Leckie (who was not previously in Militant) claimed that the SSP took the nursery nurses' dispute less seriously than other disputes because it involved women workers. This was an outrageous slander against the many SSP comrades, male and female, who visited picket lines on a daily basis but is particularly inaccurate in that an important source of support for Sheridan comes from nursery nurses who joined the party because of his support for their strike!

For the majority of party members it was clear that the court case would never have gone ahead had some executive committee members not attempted to use the case to oust Sheridan from his leadership role. The reasons were always political—at root, a conflict between two different visions of the party. Tommy Sheridan did not argue the case for a wider involvement in the movement against his own colleagues, and until relatively recently he did not openly criticise the intensifying sectarianism within the party. Yet for significant numbers of party members, and many more outside the party, because of his consistent activity and his public association with the anti-war campaign at several levels he has come to *represent* the kind of broad, activist party the SSP should have become.

The decision by party members at a further delegate meeting was that a national conference of the SSP should be held as soon as possible after the ending of the libel case. Motions proposed for that meeting made it very clear that the purpose of that conference would be to force out the old leadership and elect a new and different one. We in the Socialist Worker Platform began to prepare actively for what could have been an important opportunity to change the direction of the party.

In the weeks that followed, however, it became obvious to us all that those controlling the SSP would never allow the change to happen. The campaign of vilification was conducted through the press and the media; so poisonous was it that a number of normally unsympathetic commentators began to offer support to Sheridan. Party members opposed to the present leadership were sent anonymous notes in their party mailing, while others were physically assaulted during branch meetings. It was a clear indication that the sectarian faction still controlling the party would destroy it rather than release their control.

There was still a clear majority of SSP members committed to the project that had brought us together five years ago; our loyalty was to that project, and not to a party which now offered only a sectarian model isolated from the movements and buried in abstraction, a party which continued its slanders against Tommy Sheridan throughout the period when Lebanon was being destroyed by Israeli arms. This was not a minor dispute but a fundamental parting of the ways.

We hope that those forces committed to building a mass-based socialist alternative to New Labour, an anti-capitalist formation open to all those opposed to global capital and war, can now work together to build the newly formed Solidarity organisation. This was the basis of the decision of the members of the Socialist Worker Platform to throw our weight and our commitment behind this new organisation:

> The Socialist Worker Platform recognises with some sadness that the SSP is no longer the broad and open mass party of the left we committed ourselves to building when we joined it some five years ago. While the imperialist war intensifies and spreads into Lebanon, and the level of public anger and opposition grows, the SSP has proved unable to respond to that anger or provide any direction for it.
>
> The potential for building a broad and inclusive organisation of the Scottish left is as great as ever. It is the duty of socialists to respond to and build on that potential. We welcome the initiative of calling an open public meeting of the Scottish left on 3 September in Glasgow to launch Solidarity and will actively work to build it, in the belief that it could represent the first stage in building a new political formation that can answer the needs of the many socialists and activists in Scotland, a launching pad for a new Scottish left that will be open, democratic, internationalist and committed to the building of a new and better world.

1956 and the rebirth of socialism from below

Why commemorate 1956? The answer, in short, is that Sunday 4 November 1956 was one of the major ideological turning points for socialists in the 20th century. On that day Russian tanks moved in to crush workers' councils in Hungary and did so just as the left across the world was mobilising hundreds of thousands of people on the streets in protest at the joint British, French and Israeli military attack on Egypt.

The coincidence brought to a head a ferment that had been brewing all year.

The Russian leader Nikita Khrushchev had stunned the world in February by denouncing the murder of many thousands of committed Communists by his predecessor Joseph Stalin. The impact was enormous for millions of militant fighters against capitalism and imperialism who had been taught for nearly three decades to regard Stalin as infallible.

The shock increased in summer and early autumn when the political crisis caused by strikes and riots in the Polish city of Poznan brought Wladyslaw Gomulka to power as the country's prime minister only two years after his release from a Stalinist prison. Communist leaders who had justified not only the imprisonment of Gomulka but the jailing or execution of scores of leading East European Communists in the late 1940s and early 1950s now had to admit they were wrong—and many activists demanded to know why these leaders had not told the truth in the past.

And then on 23 October full blown revolution erupted in Hungary with all the classic features of mass demonstrations, a general strike, street fighting, barricades, police and army units going over to the revolution, the collapse of the old state machine and, in the midst of all this, the emergence of workers' councils. It was this movement that the Russian army set about crushing systematically. The impact on very many of the best militants was to shatter unbridled faith in the Stalinist message that identified revolutionary socialism with one-party top-down dictatorship. It broke the mental shackles that led those fighting oppression in one part of the world to line up with those imposing it in another part.

There had been shocks to the Stalinist message before, especially in 1939, when the Stalin-Hitler pact betrayed the anti-fascist line that Communist Parties had proclaimed as all-important for the previous five years. But on such previous occasions those who turned against the 'god that failed' moved, in 99.9 percent of cases, towards social democracy or liberalism. And in the late 1940s and early 1950s this meant accepting the claim of US imperialism to stand for 'freedom' and 'democracy'. In Britain many of the novelists and critics who had written for the Communist-run *Left Review* in 1935 were writing for the CIA-financed *Encounter* by 1955.

In 1956 it was different. The claims of the western states to stand for freedom and democracy clashed with the reality of continuing colonial rule in Asia and Africa, and nowhere more so than in the Arab lands of North Africa and the Middle East. France's social democratic government, brought to office at the beginning of 1956 (with Communist Party parliamentary support), was pouring troops into Algeria in a desperate, and unsuccessful, effort to crush the independence movement of the *Front de Libération Nationale* (FLN). And the British government was determined to restore ownership of the Suez Canal—the lifeline through which the oil of the Gulf made its way to Europe—after the Egyptian leader Gamal Abdel Nasser nationalised it in July 1956. The bombing of Egyptian cities by British planes was living proof to many of those who broke with Stalinism that the Western system was no better. And the centrality of the workers' councils of the Hungarian Revolution prompted them to begin to see an alternative to both Cold War blocs.

The historian Edward Thompson, then a young Workers' Education Association lecturer in Yorkshire, gave expression to the new feeling:

Stalinism has sown the wind and now the whirlwind centres on Hungary. As I write the smoke is still rising above Budapest… It is true that dollars have also been sown in this embittered soil. But the crop that is rising will surely not turn out to be the one which [US secretary of state] Mr Dulles expected… By an angry twist of history, it seems that the crop is coming up in students', workers' and soldiers' councils, as 'anti-Soviet' soviets.[1]

It was a feeling that created a 'new left' out of the ideological crisis—and with it the rebirth of Marxism as a living, creative force. Where before Marxism had been identified with a monolithic, stifling, mechanical dogmatism, now there was debate between different schools and different interpretations. Significantly, *New Left Review* and the *International Socialism* journal were both born in the aftermath of 1956.[2]

The impact on the wider class struggle was not immediate. The 1950s were a decade in which workers' living standards rose in an economy kept in permanent boom by a high level of arms spending. Under such circumstances, the great mass of workers did not see a need for a thoroughgoing alternative to capitalism. Working class teenagers expressed rebelliousness against their place in the world through the explosion of rock and roll: 1956 saw the police called to deal with disturbances in cinemas where the film *Rock Around the Clock* was shown. But there was no politics to the rebellion. It was to be another decade before performers like Bob Dylan broke out of the folk music ghetto to find a mass audience for political lyrics.

Nor did 1956 end the pretensions of the different imperialisms. The USSR recovered from the crisis of the mid-1950s to impose its will over Eastern Europe for another generation, crushing revolt in Czechoslovakia a dozen years later with as many troops as in Hungary, but with less bloodshed. And British imperialism, unable any more to play an independent role, now looked to defend its worldwide interests by being the loyal junior partner to the US, a role it is still attempting to play in Iraq and Afghanistan today. In the Middle East the Arab nationalist challenge to imperialism that received such a boost from Suez in 1956 went into near-terminal decline with the debacle of the June 1967 war with Israel only 11 years later.

But none of this diminishes the vital ideological importance of 1956. As the introduction to David Widgery's *The Left in Britain 1956-68* tells us:

In Hungary in 1956 Stalin's tanks blew apart the left in the rest of the world. Old complacencies were shattered and new parties, new ideas and events brought a new militancy. The ferment continued for a decade and burst out in 1968 in Paris and across much of the world.

That is why the excitement of 1956 is still relevant today.

NOTES

1: E Thompson, 'Through the Smoke of Budapest', *Reasoner*, November 1956.

2: *New Left Review* came about through the merger in 1960 of two magazines that both started life in 1957; *International Socialism* began life in a duplicated form.

Hungary: workers' councils against Russian tanks

Mike Haynes

'Tell me what you think about Hungary and I will tell you who you are,' said a Polish writer in late November 1956. So in this spirit let us make a declaration. The Hungarian Revolution of 1956 was an authentic working class revolution. Other factors were involved; revolutions are complex things. But the driving forces of the Hungarian Revolution were the efforts of the workers. First they established organs of popular power. Then they fought to extend them to defend Hungary against the invading Soviet forces that eventually allowed the puppet government of János Kádár to crush the revolt:

> Most of the provincial councils and workers' councils in the capital became, to an ever increasing degree, representative of an attitude unknown in Hungary: the belief in self-government, or to put it in other words, government by soviets, in the original sense of the term—people's councils, organs of local power.[1]

Neither then nor now did the revolt fit into a conflict between Washington and Moscow, between West and East. On 7 November, as Russian forces fought Hungarian workers in Budapest, a group of fighters in Tüzoltó Street ran up a red flag in honour of the October Revolution, the fortieth anniversary of which fell that day. The fluttering flag, like others in those desperate days, signalled a different version of socialism not only in Hungary but the world over. The flag was a rebuke to a Soviet imperialism that had grown upon the ashes of the real October Revolution. For this reason such flags also found little favour in the West. 'We wish for neither capitalism nor Stalinism,' said the Revolutionary Council of Budapest University. And this is the problem. With Stalinism and the USSR gone, the pressure everywhere is to reinterpret the past as a march to Western capitalism. So the role of the workers in the Hungarian Revolution remains an embarrassment.[2]

The Hungarian Revolution

Hungary in 1956 was a small European country of some 10 million people. Once a central part of the Austro-Hungarian Empire, it was now reduced in size and status by two world wars and the unhappy period between them of authoritarian rule, repression and failed development. It was occupied by the Soviet army at the end of the Second World War and incorporated into the Soviet bloc as the Cold War developed. For Moscow, Hungary was in the front line against NATO to the West. For Washington, the Hungarians were another of Moscow's 'captive peoples', a bargaining chip in the jousting for position that characterised the whole Cold War era.

The events of 1956, however, did not derive directly from geopolitical competition. They were a product of the way in which Cold War pressures manifested themselves internally as economic, social and political contradictions. The Eastern European regimes claimed to be socialist but they were driven forward by a competitive industrialisation in which the resources for accumulation were squeezed from the mass of the population using whatever repression was necessary.[5] But on the mass of people pressure was so intense as to become counter-productive, and after Stalin's death in 1953 his successors signalled a degree of relaxation. However, contradictory messages, policy changes, and admissions of the monstrous levels of repression in the past—culminating in the denunciation of Stalin's behaviour by the new Russian leader Nikita Khrushchev in his 'secret speech' of February 1956—opened up a space for the open, if still cautious, articulation of discontent.

In Hungary Mátyás Rákosi, 'Stalin's best Hungarian disciple', was sidelined from Moscow in favour of Imre Nagy, a loyal but reform minded 'Stalinist', in 1953. But Nagy could not consolidate his grip and a change in the balance of power in Moscow enabled Rákosi to come back in 1955 and expel Nagy from the Communist Party.[6] Blind to the pressure for change, Rákosi's triumph was short-lived. After Khrushchev's secret speech Rákosi again found support draining in Moscow—Khrushchev later talked of 'that idiot Rákosi'. At home the growing ferment in the Hungarian Communist Party was reflected in huge popular debates held by the Petöfi Circle—initially a forum for party youth. Critics of the regime were emboldened by events in Poland where June 1956 saw a near-rising of workers against the regime in Poznan.[7] Moscow removed Rákosi (he now thought of himself as 'the last Mohican of the Stalinist era in Eastern Europe') on 18 July, and replaced him, not with a reformer like Nagy, but another man identified with the old Stalinist era—Ernö Gerö.[8] Meanwhile growing revelations about the many victims of Stalinism in Hungary, most notably László Rajk, a leading Communist minister executed as a traitor and spy in the paranoia of 1949-50, stimulated further defiance. The new prime minister, Hegedüs, said that 'by now a big part of the media is not controlled by the party any more'.[9] The Hungarian leadership was forced to allow the ceremonial reburial of the body of Rajk on 6 October and this led to a spontaneous demonstration of support for change. 'The reburial of Rajk's remains dealt a massive blow to the party leadership, whose authority was not all that high to begin with,' Gerö told the Soviet ambassador, Yuri Andropov.[10]

The real explosion came just over a fortnight later on 23 October. Students had called a demonstration in support of Poland, where a reformist government seemed to be standing up to severe political and military pressure from Moscow. But the demonstration immediately brought tens of thousands on to the streets . The regime felt the full force of popular anger when the hated state security secret police—the 50,000-strong AVH —fired upon crowds.

The revolt went through three stages.

From 23 to 28 October there was disorder as protests spread and the old order began to disintegrate. 'The democratic storm…is…raging in full force,' said one Hungarian newspaper at this time.[11] In this storm the initiative passed to the streets and the factories. 'It was the (inner party) opposition who 'prepared' the revolution and yet no one was so dumbfounded by the outbreak as they', wrote Sándor Fekete in an early participant account.[12] Russian forces initially attempted to come to the aid of the Hungarian leadership but were then withdrawn as the revolt gathered

Table 1: Hungary in the 1950s[3]

	Population (in millions)	urban	in Budapest	in provincial towns
1930	8.68	36.2%	16.6%	19.6%
1941	9.31	38.3%	18.4%	19.9%
1949	9.29	36.5%	17.3%	19.2%
1957	9.80	40.3%	18.9%	21.4%
1960	9.98	39.8%	18.2%	21.6%

Figure 1: The main centres of action in 1956

Table 2: Dead and wounded in 1956[4]

	Hungarians		Soviet Forces		
	Wounded	Dead	Wounded	Dead	Missing
Fighting	19,226	2,502	1,540	669	51

force. Nagy was made prime minister but immediately found himself overtaken by the popular mood.

From 29 October to 3 November a degree of order driven from below was established. Nagy, at last, responded to popular demands with announcements of policy changes aimed at democratisation and the weakening of Moscow's grip. But neither he nor anyone in the Hungarian leadership could offer Moscow the prospect of containing the ferment from below. For the Russian leadership fear of the strategic implications of the loss of Hungary and the way revolt was erupting from the bottom up was too much.

On 4 November the revolution entered its third and longest stage. Moscow had already decided that it had been a mistake to withdraw Russian troops and new units had begun to enter Hungary on 1 November. But it was on 4 November that they attacked Budapest and other centres. There were several days of armed resistance, but the odds were in favour of the well armed Russian forces. Nagy fled to the Yugoslav embassy and was later betrayed and executed. Other leaders were rounded up and arrested; still others fled across the border to the West along with some 200,000 others (2 percent of the population). Those who had died fighting the Russians and the old Hungarian regime were buried in unmarked graves. Since 1989 there has been a huge effort in Hungary to uncover their fate, but putting a name on a headstone is a poor memorial if in the process what a person died for remains hidden from history.

Workers' councils, formed from 23 October, now continued to oppose the occupation until December when widespread arrests and repression finally overcame resistance. It is here, in the role of these councils, that we see the real nature of 1956 as a social revolution, and it is exactly this that current accounts are anxious to bury.[13] But before we examine the workers' councils in some detail it is worth pausing a little to say something about the street fighting in 1956.

Street fighting people: round one

On 23 October and in the days following the most visible aspect of the Hungarian Revolution was the street fighting. For a revolution to occur state authority must weaken sufficiently to disorient the forces of repression. This had happened in Hungary. On 23-24 October the panic in the Budapest leadership was such that some fled 'into underground bunkers that were unsuitable for any work', according to Soviet politburo members who were there.[14] The regular police proved powerless, and in Budapest a significant number of the 1,200 officers, led by Sándor Kopácsi, the Budapest police chief, defected to the demonstrators.[15] The army too was disorientated. The only major unit to initially obey orders to repress protests was the Third Army Corps whose commander forced his men into action and even bombed demonstrators in Tiszakeske and Kecskemet from the air before he thought better of it and fled to Russian protection. Most army units took a position of benign neutrality. Sometimes they intervened to enforce ceasefires on the state security forces. Occasionally units, as well as individual soldiers, went directly over to the protesters. The main group defending the state was therefore the hated state security AVH. It was because they appeared so isolated that Gerö called on Soviet forces for support late on 23 October. With some 31,000 troops immediately at hand, and some 1,100 tanks and air power, this was a formidable force.

In most of the provinces, where there was also a limited presence of Russian forces, the Hungarian security forces were soon overwhelmed, despite the shooting of protesters. Conflict in Budapest was more costly. At the peak perhaps 15,000 demonstrators, armed with weapons seized or donated from the civil defence, police and army, faced the disintegrating AVH and the Russian army. The fighting was serious at a small number of key points, but both the AVH and Russians were uncertain of what to do. The Russians had confused orders. Ordinary troops were quickly disconcerted when they found that they were facing ordinary Hungarians. There was some fraternisation. Tensions rose high on 25 October when indiscriminate shooting led to many deaths outside the Hungarian parliament. On 26-28 October the radicalisation and polarisation continued, as did the brutal Russian response—'To solitary shots we replied with salvos,' said one Soviet commander.[16] It was at this point that Nagy managed to establish a ceasefire and announce that Soviet troops would withdraw from Budapest—the start, many hoped, of a negotiated withdrawal from the whole of Hungary.

The evidence from Budapest is that much of the street fighting was done by young people, including even schoolchildren. The fighters tended to form self-organised groups, often around key individuals, some of whom may have had a murky past, though it is difficult to separate claim and counter-claim. But it would be wrong to make too much of this. 'It is touching that it was the hooligans of Ferencváros who created ethics out of nothing during the revolution,' said a student at the time.[17] It is clear that a broad process of radicalisation was occurring. Not the least example of this was the role of Colonel Pál Maléter who became 'the most popular hero of the revolution', for which he would pay with his life, executed by the Kádár regime. Maléter had had an erratic career which ran from being a bodyguard of the pre-war dictator Horthy, to a Russian trained partisan fighting the Nazis and then a senior figure in the new army. He at first tried to play a neutral role when he was sent to try to relieve the Kilián Barracks but then appealed to the ministry of defence to have Soviet forces withdrawn to reduce the tension and loss of life. When this was refused he famously cast his lot with the revolutionaries: 'I must inform you that I will fire on the first Soviet tank to approach the Kilián barracks'.[18]

The rise of the workers' councils

Most of Budapest had stopped work, supported by growing strikes in the rest of the country, while these struggles were taking place. A new network of committees and councils began to emerge. The echoes of 1917 are obvious. Some of these new forms were factory committees. These would then link into revolutionary (sometimes called national) councils or committees. But in smaller places local area-based councils were formed straight away. The pattern and the names are often confusing because, unlike in Russia in 1917, there was not time for more sophisticated forms of organisation to be worked out. But this does not diminish the central role of these councils or what they achieved in a short time. 'Without their political pressure,' say the authors of the standard Hungarian account edited by György Litván, 'the Nagy government would probably have stopped halfway'.[19] But the significance goes beyond this immediate political dynamic, which is why they remain so controversial and why they are so difficult for more conservative accounts to digest.

Budapest was the centre of the workers' council movement. Once the second city of a great empire, it was now the overblown head of a small country and contained nearly a fifth of Hungary's population. Over half of the country's industrial output was produced there by 46 percent of its industrial workers. They were concentrated in engineering works, chemical plants, consumer and food industries. Here too were a significant part of Hungary's building and transport workers. Industry was not evenly spread within the city. Two of the most concentrated areas were the Újpest district to the north and the Csepel island in the Danube to the south, long an industrial area based around iron, engineering, paper and oil. The city, split by the Danube, tended to be more industrial on the Pest side than the Buda, the area developed for the imperial middle class and now the site of the residences of many of the people who had done well under Rákosi.

The first Budapest workers' council was established on 23 October in the Újpest district at the huge Egyesült Izzó (United Lamp) Factory which employed around 10,000 people.[20] A day later factory committees and workers' councils were spreading to most of the city's plants and districts. On 29 and 30 October district workers' councils began to be created in the areas where the bigger plants were concentrated—Újpest, Obuda, Angyalföld, Csepel. Then on 31 October a parliament of workers' councils for Budapest was convened with delegates from 24 factories and looked to establish a new order within them. Many elements of this order remained unclear but most commentators have been struck by the sophistication of the demands. The delegates declared:

> The supreme controlling body of the factory is the workers' council democratically elected by the workers… The director is employed by the factory. The director and highest employees are to be elected by the workers' council…the director is responsible to the workers' council in every matter which concerns the factory.[21]

The councils also looked to the political situation, demanding a whole range of measures of democratisation and, above all, the withdrawal of Russian troops. In this process the old instruments of Stalinist rule were simply pushed aside. The Communist Party and the official trade unions, two of the means of repressing the working class and driving forward accumulation, were marginalised. As Lomax writes, 'When a few days later the government, the Communist Party and the Central Council of Trade Unions called in turn for the creation of workers' councils [in a failed attempt to direct them—MH] they were merely giving official recognition to an already accomplished fact'.[22]

Inevitably the geography of workers' councils outside of Budapest reflected the industrial geography of Hungary, with the strongest ones in the north and the weaker ones in the towns of the southern agricultural plains. But, as Peter Fryer, the shocked but honest reporter for the British Communist Party's *Daily Worker*, put it:

> these committees, a network of which now extended across the whole of Hungary, were remarkably uniform. They were at the same time organs of insurrection—the coming together of delegates elected by factories and universities, mines and army units—and organs of popular self-government which the armed people trusted. As such they enjoyed tremendous authority, and it is no exaggeration to say that until the Soviet attack of 4 November the real power in the country lay in their hands.[23]

Listeners to a radio broadcast from Miskolc heard the following declaration on 25 October: 'We have had enough! Enough of the autonomy of certain leaders! We too want socialism, but according to our special Hungarian conditions, reflecting the interests of the Hungarian working class and the Hungarian nation'.[24] Miskolc was the second largest town in Hungary. It had a population of some 140,000 in 1956 and was situated to the north east of Budapest in Borsod county, 'the largest unbroken industrial area in Hungary'.[25] The whole area had been a centre of rapid expansion in the post-1948 industrialisation drive, based on concentrated investment in heavy industry, cement and brickworks, as well as a textile mill. As Miskolc expanded so it merged with Diósgyör, the site of Hungary's first iron foundry and now the main iron and steel centre as well as the location of a large machine works making rolling stock and turbines.

It is here that we find the second great centre of the workers' councils of 1956. While local students formed a student parliament, committees were formed in the factories and then workers' councils. Things began to move on 22 October with the formation of various committees and then, on 24 October, a 'labour council'. Organisation spread within and between plants in the neighbouring towns. Government authority collapsed locally in the face of a mass demonstration in Miskolc on 26 October when 38 people are thought to have died as state security forces opened fire and the crowd took its revenge. The workers and students and existing forces which defected to them quickly restored order and Radio Miskolc could announce on 27 October that 'for two days the town of Miskolc has been under the leadership of the workers' council and student parliament.' The new councils of the industrial belt linked up to form a countywide Borsod

Workers' Council. When the claim was later made in Budapest that what was at stake was a counter-revolution, the Borsod County Workers' Council simply said, 'You have only to pick up the telephone, and in three hours we will be there, the workers of Ozd, Diosgyör, Miskolc, all 20,000 and armed'.[26]

To the north of Budapest was the smaller town of Salgotarjan. Here industry was based on coal, iron and steel and there was no university. Anyone stopping there in late October would have found a town in which the radicalisation appeared to have involved one of the most peaceful power shifts. On 25 October a strike became general and on 27 October there was a march to the town centre. The local Communist Party attempted to lead the workers' council movement but it was pushed aside. But the relative calm of this period would be deceptive, for in the next phase Salgotarjan would become a major centre of resistance to Russian invasion and the Kádár government.

Györ had a population of around 70,000 in 1956. Situated on the Danube, 80 miles north west of Budapest and on the main Budapest to Vienna route, the town had grown on the basis of the expansion of its pre-war wagon building works, textiles and consumer goods industries. Nearby were the coal mining town of Tatabánya and smaller towns based on open-cast coal and bauxite mining. Some discontent appeared before 23 October but news of the events in Budapest led to a small demonstration on 24 October, which quickly snowballed. In the evening state security forces again opened fire. The next day thousands came out. Strikes were generalised and local authority collapsed. On 26 October a town–wide National Revolutionary Committee was formed and the next day Radio Free Györ announced that 'national committees and workers' councils were being formed everywhere between Györ and Tatabánya'. The Györ council became the core of the Transdanubian National Council formed to represent the western half of Hungary.

While this was happening the state security forces had acted out another massacre at nearby Mosonmagyaróvár in which 52 had died. Order was only restored when the state security police were disarmed by local troops under the control of the Györ council.[27] The strength of the workers' councils here was based on the Györ factories and nearby mines at Tatabánya and Balinka. The Györ National Council not only issued a programme, but also ran the town and even negotiated for a time with local

Soviet military leaders. But its most demanding task was trying to cope with the political cross currents in Győr. The mood in the town was heated and, especially early on, there was frustration with the timidity of Nagy in Budapest. Some right wing forces tried to take advantage of this, as did adventurers, some from within Hungary, others from across the border. There were several tense episodes before the leaders of the local council were able to encourage a focus on building a base through the development of the workers' council movement in the wider Transdanubian area.

Further south on the Danube, some 40 miles from Budapest, was Sztálinváros (now Dunaújváros). This was intended as the centrepiece of Hungary's new industrial development. In the late 1940s it had only been an overgrown village but in the spring of 1950 the building of the Stalin iron and steel works began under the supervision of Soviet engineers with ostensibly a model 'socialist' community—the biggest investment project of Hungary's first five year plan. By 1956 Sztálinváros had a population of 30,000 and, as in Russia, welfare there very much took second place to demands of steel output.[28]

Agriculture still dominated much of the south of the country. Here the major towns had been trading, administrative and educational centres, with their social structure less intensively affected by Stalinist industrialisation. Debrecen is Hungary's third largest town with a population of some 130,000 in 1956. It had been the scene of Kossuth's short-lived declaration of independence from the Austrian Empire in 1849 and the base for the Soviet-backed liberation government in 1944. On 23 October demonstrating students were joined by workers. Local party leaders ordered forces to open fire, killing three people. Over the next days talks between representatives of the local soldiers, students and workers led to the formation of the Debrecen Socialist Revolutionary Committee which soon became the effective power in the town until the second Soviet onslaught on 4 November. A second southern town, Szeged, with a population of just under 100,000, was the place where the first independent student organisations had been created before 23 October. After the 23 October events in Budapest, students in Szeged were involved in local protests and occasional clashes until 26 October when security forces withdrew. Workers' councils in the local factories were set up which then linked with student groups to form a People's Revolutionary Council on 30 October. This then began to organise a local national guard.

Pecs had been the site of Hungary's first university and was also a major trading and agricultural processing centre. In 1956 it had a population of 110,000. Its post-1948 growth had been affected by the development of coal mining nearby and uranium mining. Here, however, the old order held together better in the first days. Local bosses encouraged factory committees in the belief that they could put their own people at the head of them but they were pushed aside. Then, as news spread of events elsewhere, the local state security police began to crumble. On 28 and 29 October councils were elected and a national guard created. The Pecs councils were less impressive in depth than those in the north, but the town would be a major centre of resistance to Russian forces in the next phase.

It was, however, not just the towns that were affected by the revolution. As Table 1 shows, Hungary was still a predominantly agricultural country. Authority began to collapse in the rural areas on the Saturday and Sunday of 27-28 October. The process had echoes of traditional peasant revolt. News arrived of the urban protests, sometimes brought directly by migrant workers returning from the factories. Discussions took place in village centres and pubs, and on the Sunday around and in churches. Fearful of a state which they saw as both oppressive and exploitative, the peasants, reflecting an older moral economy, sought to legitimise their revolt symbolically. Village national committees were elected in many places. While some of the old, imposed rural leaders fled and others were offered some kind of protective security, less hated figures might symbolically hand over village centre keys to the new committees. The state campaign against religion had been especially resented and therefore dressing in one's Sunday best to go to church had a special resonance that weekend. Sometimes local Stalinist party secretaries were made to carry the crosses. Tax records were seen as an instrument of the power of the state and burned in some places.[29] Some villagers also loaded carts with food to take to towns both as a gesture of solidarity and as an assertion of the superior morality of the gift over the past history of forced deliveries to the state.

The level of politicisation in the countryside was much lower than in the towns. But, with the power of the state gone, many peasants took the opportunity to leave what they saw as state organised agriculture. By early 1957 only around 6 percent of peasants were left in state cooperatives which now had some 10 to 12 percent of arable land.[30]

The question arose of how far the workers' councils should sustain the strike and cooperate with the Nagy government as it began to broaden the agenda of change under the pressure of the councils. Almost from the outset delegations had gone to Nagy to influence him. Then on 1 November, with the Russian forces seemingly withdrawn and Nagy radicalising his position, delegates from the councils argued that the strike should be called off while maintaining the general role of the councils. This produced some sharp local debates but when the district councils in Csepel and Újpest agreed to support a return to work the position was endorsed and the date set for Monday 5 November. But the agreement would be rendered redundant by the second Soviet military assault.

The significance of the workers' councils

What was the significance of the workers' councils? The fact that they were set up against a so-called 'socialist state' and then destroyed by it should show that neither before nor after 1956 was Hungary in any sense socialist. The fact that the councils involved workers seizing control of the means of production should also show that what was wrong with Hungary was not some 'political degeneration' at the top but a system which exploited and oppressed workers both politically and economically. 'The communists nationalised all the factories and similar enterprises, proclaiming the slogan, "The factory is yours—you work for yourself." Exactly the opposite of this was true. They promised us everything, at the same time subjugating us and pulling us down to the greatest misery conceivable,' said one Csepel worker.[31]

But these are only the first questions posed by the workers' councils in 1956. Clearly the councils were tools of destruction through which the old regime was being brought down. But were they, and can they again be, tools of creation through which a new democratic economic and political order can be built?

There is a horrible irony in the fact that many historians today, and not least those in Hungary, are as anxious to dismiss this possibility as was the Kádár regime that destroyed the workers' councils in 1956. Those for whom the only alternative to dictatorship is a Western style bourgeois democracy solve the problem of 1956 by concentrating on the political demands. The re-emergence of some 20 political parties, with the potential to compete for parliamentary power, was bound, they suggest, to lead to a market transition and, sooner or later, a degree of privatisation. Nineteen fifty six is made to anticipate 1989. It was a 'bourgeois revolution', said the Hungarian politician Viktor Orban in 2001. For Peter Kende, one of a number of participants who now doubt their own past, 'by history's inscrutable logic the Hungarian people seem to have achieved in 1989 what they fought for in 1956'.[32] Litván, another participant historian, is less direct, redefining 1956 (in a phrase of István Bibó) as a 'revolution in human dignity'. But all revolutions involve the oppressed asserting their dignity against the oppressor. Moreover dignity comes in different forms— not all of them compatible. If people in 1956 did not believe it could be found in the old system, they equally did not seem to believe it could be found in the restoration of other discredited forms. Istvan Bibó, who attempted to theorise what was happening at the time, called it 'the beginning of one of the most exciting socialist experiments of the century'.[33] 'The intended economic order', writes Litván's group of historians, 'would place decision making in industry, mining and transport in the hands of the producers.' But sooner or later, they also imply, workers would have been forced away from this 'possibly utopian' road. 'The healing of a ruined economy was impossible without a more or less free market'.[34]

But if the workers' councils were incompatible with a Stalinist state capitalism masquerading as 'socialism', how could they have been compatible with more free market capitalism either? It is true that what was called 'workers' participation' existed in some social democracies and in Yugoslavia in the 1950s, but participation is not control. These were top down initiatives in which real influence from below was severely constrained. The importance and challenge of the Hungarian councils lie in their contradiction to these lesser visions of change.[35]

The Hungarian workers' councils grew from the bottom up and were marked by the breadth and depth of participation. They combined national demands with a fundamental social agenda which looked to a new system moulded from the workers' councils, independent free trade unions and competing socialist parties. This idea is less distinctive than some have suggested. It recaptured elements of an earlier socialist tradition (even, we would suggest, a Bolshevik one) that had been squeezed out by the statism of social democracy and the one-party developmental dictatorship of Stalinism. Its base would lie in the claim that 'the factories must become truly collective, and not capitalist property' and the argument, expressed in different forms, that 'the working class itself wants a guarantee that it will be armed so that it can stop any force from negating the basic aim of the revolution and its achievements so far'.[36]

Here at least we must grant the Kadar regime the virtue of consistency. For it the workers' councils were a fantasy in theory and mob rule in practice. They had no creative element; they were simply destructive. The regime was quick to identify every incident and build it up as one of the crimes of 1956. The most notorious, perhaps, was on 30 October when state security police opened fire from inside the Budapest Communist Party headquarters. Protesters returned the fire, killing, among others, Imre Mezö, the local party secretary and Nagy supporter, and then lynched a number of the people in the building, some of whom may not have been involved in the shooting. But the regime's own data puts any popular violence into perspective. There were, it claimed, 215 'victims of counter-revolution' of whom were 169 were military; 14 of these were claimed to have died from summary execution. Forty six deaths were civilians, of whom eight were Communist officials killed or lynched by crowds. 'Believe me, we are not sadists, but we cannot bring ourselves to regret those kind of people,' said one contemporary who was asked.[37] The majority of deaths, even if they were all regime deaths, clearly came in the fighting. All the occasional indiscriminate 'crimes' of the real revolution cost no more lives than a single massacre by the forces of the Hungarian state or the Russian army. Far from the revolution involving widespread mob rule, the Litván group writes, 'there is abundant evidence that the freedom fighters themselves penalised any lawlessness resolutely'.[38]

Most present day accounts want to claim that the councils had limited capacity. But the creative energy and self-discipline of the councils create a problem for them. The historical undermining of the legacy of the workers' councils today does not derive from a grand theory of bourgeois democracy or the majesty of its reality. Where is such a reality today? Rather it derives from an accommodation to current practice. Historical accounts inevitably reflect the time in which they are written. The best can partly rise above this and connect past, present and a range of new futures; the worst bludgeon the present into the past to deny any future other than what is. The political vision that emerged out of the transition in Hungary was a narrow one, and leading Hungarian intellectuals accommodated to it. It does past, present and future a grave disservice.

Street fighting people: round two

'Today at dawn', Imre Nagy broadcast on Sunday 4 November, 'Soviet troops attacked our capital with the obvious intention of overthrowing the legitimate government.' The second Soviet intervention, 'Whirlwind', was more massive and better organised than the first. The Hungarian army was immediately demobilised by Russian troops. The new National Guard had had no time to organise for such a contest. Potential leaders like Maléter were arrested. Kopásci was soon rounded up. Resistance again had to come from below. The Soviet general Zhukov later claimed that his forces had to disarm 35,000 Hungarians. This may be true but they could never have matched a major army. Nevertheless, the stand taken in key areas was heroic in the face of often overwhelming force. Fierce fighting took place in several provincial centres including Pecs in the south. But generally the stiffness of resistance reflected the distribution of sections of the working class. 'The greatest armed resistance to the Soviet forces occurred in the large iron and steel centres of Dunapentele, Ozd and Miskolc, and in the mining regions of Borsod, Tantabánya and Pecs,' writes Lomax. At Dunapentele, the former Sztálinváros, the workers' council faced with the Soviet army declared:

> Dunapentele is the foremost socialist town in Hungary. Its inhabitants are workers, and power is in their hands. The houses have all been built by workers themselves. The workers will defend the town from 'fascist excesses' but also from Soviet troops.[39]

Within Budapest the same pattern emerged. In the centre street fighting was hard at the Kilián Barracks, Corvin Passage and Tüzoltó Street—all these places became legendary. But it was also considerable in Újpest and Kobanya. It was no less fierce on the Cespel Island where workers held out until 10-11 November.

In 1957 the Kádár government was quick to issue its own data to claim that the cost of violence was greater during the first wave of fighting, when the Soviet army withdrew, than in the second wave after its re-entry. Its 'order' was supposedly preferable to the 'disorder' of the revolution. 'Two thirds of the injured were wounded before 3 November and one third after 4 November.' But the figures, based on hospital admissions, can hardly be a guide since arrest was more likely after 4 November. The deaths seem to have been 40 percent in the first round and 60 percent in the second round of fighting. Property destruction was largely a product of the second phase. The regime claimed only 4 percent of housing in Greater Budapest as a whole was damaged but this somewhat foolish statistic could not hide that fact that 23 percent of housing had been damaged in the 9th Ferencváros district and 18 percent in the Jozsefváros district. Fifty percent of the Budapest dead were recorded in these two districts and the 7th.[40] As Peter Fryer wrote:

> I have just come out of Budapest, where for six days I have watched Hungary's new born freedom tragically destroyed by Soviet troops... Vast areas of the city—the working class areas above all—are virtually in ruins. For four days and nights Budapest was under continuous bombardment. I saw a once lovely city battered, bludgeoned, smashed and bled into submission.[41]

The data on the Budapest dead tell an even clearer social story of a predominance of working class youth. Twenty percent of the dead were under 20 years old, and 28 percent aged between 20 and 29. Seventy five percent of the injured were reported to be under 30; 1,330 of the dead were recorded as workers, only 44 as students. Another Kadar source suggested that 'according to the figures supplied by the hospitals, 80 to 90 percent of the wounded were young workers, while students represented no more than 3 to 5 percent'.[42]

Resistance and the struggle for power

With the armed resistance crushed by 10-11 November a month and a half of passive resistance to occupation and counter-revolution began. The Hungarian army had disintegrated, the political leaders had been arrested or had fled, and writers and intellectuals, however prominent, lacked an organisational base of their own. It was the workers' councils which were the basis of opposition and they stood at the head of a general strike. 'We are and shall remain the leaders in Hungary,' said Sándor Racz when he was elected president of the new Central Workers' Council in Budapest. Despite the continued emphasis in some accounts on the role of intellectuals, the Writers Association passed a motion on 12 November which read, 'We throw in our lot with the Hungarian working class, the peasantry and the revolutionary youth, and in the course of further developments we shall work together with their democratically elected organisations'.[43] It is not difficult to see why. If we take industrial production in September as 100 then in October it was 71.1 percent of that level and in November a mere 17.6 percent. Even with the actions of the authorities in December it only rose to a monthly figure of 30.5 percent of the September level. To close down over 80 percent of industrial production effectively for over a month must register as one of the most complete and sustained general strikes in history. And in particular sectors for which data was collected by the statisticians the strike was even more effective.[44]

A journalist writing for the *Observer* in Britain reported the situation in mid-November:

A fantastic aspect of the situation is that although the general strike is in being…the workers are nevertheless taking it upon themselves to keep essential services going, for the purposes which they themselves determine and support. Workers' councils in industrial districts have undertaken the distribution of essential goods and food to the population in order to keep them alive. The coal miners are making daily allocations of just sufficient coal to keep the power stations going and supply the hospitals in Budapest and other large towns. Railwaymen organise trains to go to approved destinations for approved purposes…[45]

The impact of the invasion on the workers' and revolutionary councils was uneven. In some areas they quickly collapsed but those based on factory committees in urban, working class environments proved more resilient and their organisation deepened. So strong was it that the Kádár government was forced to temporarily recognise the workers' councils while trying to gain time to contain and undermine them and pick off their leaders. In some areas arrests began immediately. On 5 November, for example, 12 members of the Borsod workers' councils attempted to negotiate and were arrested and taken out of Hungary.[46] Occasionally, however, such arrests had to be rescinded and negotiations were held with Soviet commanders to this effect.

The biggest developments were in Budapest. On 12 November the Revolutionary Workers' Council of Újpest proposed the creation of a Central Workers' Council for Greater Budapest. In spite of attempts by the authorities to disrupt it, on 14 November the new Central Council met at the Egyesült Izzö plant. The meeting, which was chaotic, elected a provisional committee made up from delegates from the district workers' councils.[47] As in any revolution, individuals were thrown up who quickly proved unequal to the task and were replaced by others who found a strength, courage and vision that perhaps they had not appreciated they had. Two of these were workers from the Beloiannis electrical factory. Sándor Racz was a young tool fitter who was soon elected president of the council. Sándor Bali, another tool fitter, was older and more experienced, having been a past member of the Social Democratic Party and Communist Party but also having conspicuously refused to take advantage of the possibilities of social mobility that the regime offered before 1956.

It was Bali who was the leading influence on the perspectives of the Central Workers' Council. These involved seeing it as the organising centre for the Budapest workers' councils. It became, said Balász Nagy, 'a hive of activity'. New elections were held in the factory committees and workers' councils to ensure the legitimacy of these organisations and hence the Central Council itself. 'The factories are in our hands, the hands of the workers' councils,' said one leaflet from late November. But the key political issue was whether to negotiate with the Kádár regime. The brute face of military power was everywhere. Bali therefore proposed that the Central Council negotiate but refuse any formal recognition of the government. But negotiate to what effect? The Central Council and the councils on which it drew were determined to deepen their role. The big immediate weapon they had was the general strike. But general strikes cannot last indefinitely, especially one so complete. The most conservative voices argued for the strike to be called off to give Kádár time to show his intentions. The most radical argued for it to be maintained to the bitter end, come what may.

In the midst of military occupation, with perhaps 2,000 dead already and many more wounded and under arrest, the difficulty of these choices should not be underestimated. In the event the position that won was to agree to return to work in return for concessions. But what concessions, and could the government be trusted? This produced sharp arguments in some of the Budapest districts and committees. In Csepel, for example, leaders who saw this position as too radical were removed in favour of delegates who thought it too moderate.[48] Racz argued that the workers' councils were in a position of growing strength: 'The government is now beginning to make certain concessions, and it will make still more. We just have to force it to do so. We must wait until work has been resumed every-where, because otherwise the Russians will occupy the industrial centres and replace the workers. The question now is whether we will be the masters or the Soviet command'.[49] Outside of Budapest too there were divisions. Some miners took the view, 'You can work if you want, but we shall provide neither coal nor electricity; we shall flood the mines'.[50] But negotiations went ahead with the Kádár regime for the removal of Soviet troops, the generalisation of workers' councils, and the defence of the right to strike. The return to work was set for 17 November.

But the government's position was well described by a British reporter. Its aim was 'to divert workers' councils into innocuous channels by "legalising" them as organs of economic self-government, somewhat on the Yugoslav model, but denying them the right to put forward political demands or issue a newspaper'. The perspectives were far apart and 'merely led to continued deadlock in Budapest'.[51]

To maintain its position the Central Council could not stand still. The organisation had to be widened. Accordingly on 19 November it accepted a plan to create a new Parliament of Workers' Councils and made an appeal for delegates to meet in Budapest on 21 November. But when delegates arrived at the sports stadium where the meeting was due to be held they found it surrounded by Soviet tanks (some called them 'Kádár taxis'). A smaller meeting was held at the headquarters of the Central Council which, again after debate, accepted its positions. But while the talk was going on, workers, fearing that delegates had been more widely arrested, were coming out on strike again and on 22-23 November Budapest was hit by a general strike which also served to commemorate the outbreak of the revolution a month earlier. The Central Council had no choice but to put itself at the head of this.

The Kádár regime and Soviet forces were far from idle during this time. It is clear now that János Kádár swung to become the figurehead of the Russian invasion quite late on. When he arrived in Budapest on 7 November in a Russian armoured car he had no plan or authority other than that given to him by the Russian army.[52] The secret police had gone, the army had disintegrated, and government was in disarray. His new 'party'—the Hungarian Socialist Workers Party—barely existed (in December it only had 37,000 members, a few percent of the old Communist Party). In the next weeks Kádár talked but refused to yield, supported as he was by the Soviet occupation. Imre Nagy and his supporters were tricked out of the Yugoslav embassy with the complicity of the Yugoslav government on 23 November, arrested and taken out of Hungary. But Kádár also tried to build a new base for himself through the formation of the Hungarian Revolutionary [sic] Home Guard Militia, which was supplemented in early 1957 by a 'Workers' [sic] Guard'. It was the militia, with the Russian army, that would eventually crush the revolution in December. Another strand of Kádár's policy was to send out the signal that there would be no return to the past, whatever repression followed, Attempts were made to buy off working class discontent with backdated pay rises, peasant discontent with concessions on forced deliveries and agricultural process, and the discontent of small craftsmen through tax and property changes. Rákosi and Gerö remained in exile and gestures were made on religious freedom and towards an even more obvious co-option of national symbols. But the regime, like all established orders, had an additional weapon and a very powerful one—time. It could sit it out and try to stretch out negotiations to a point when it felt able to move. By early December Kádár and others seem to have begun to feel that their time was coming.

The Central Workers' Council (CWC) did not want the provocation of a major demonstration on 4 December, a month on from the second Soviet invasion. Fearing the consequences if the authorities used force against a mass demonstration, an evocative procession was organised of some 30,000 women dressed in black. They walked through Budapest until they encountered Soviet troops. The demonstration was deeply symbolic and moving. But in terms for the balance of power between the councils and the government it was too little. The authorities now began to move quickly.

The Kádár regime began to widen arrests and then news came through that on 8 December a massacre had occurred at Salgótarján, with the arrest the leaders of miners' workers' councils and the shooting of 39 demonstrating miners. The Central Council meeting in Budapest called a 48-hour general strike for 11-12 December, 'the like of which has never before been seen in the history of the workers' movement', an official Hungarian paper was forced to report.[53] The government responded by declaring that the CWC and local councils were illegal (but not yet the factory committees) and declaring a state of emergency. Some 200 working class leaders were rounded up and arrested. Racz and Bali were major targets but they were protected for a time by the workers in their factory. They were only induced out by a duplicitous personal offer from Kádár to negotiate. They were then arrested. When other strikes and demonstrations against the arrests were called the response was just as ruthless as it had been in Salgótarján. Workers were shot down in the streets in several places including Miskolc, Eger and Zalaegerszeg.

Workers' opposition was now forced underground and on 5 January 1957 the government announced the death penalty for a refusal to work and strike agitation. Several workers' councils ceremoniously dissolved themselves rather than just fade away under the weight of this repression. The Csepel council said that to continue 'would be to deceive our comrades. We therefore return our mandate to the workers'.[54] When, on 8 January, workers on the Csepel Island demonstrated their support they too were met with Soviet tanks and more were killed. Five days later the Kádár government further widened the death penalty. The regime was able to move on and suspend the Writers Association on 18 January and close the Journalists Club on the 20th. After nearly three months the Hungarian Revolution had finally been crushed.

The pattern of repression

The story of a revolution can also be told through the nature of the victims when it is repressed. The weight of repression has obviously to serve as a warning to the main social forces involved never to attempt the same again. Here too then we find evidence of the absolute centrality of the workers' councils. Arrests began to mount between November 1956 and the end of 1959. Some 100,000 were arrested, 26,000 tried and 22,000 sentenced; 229 formal death sentences were passed but accounts suggest that as many as 350 executions may have occurred. Those of Imre Nagy, Maléter and others were the most prominent. Leading intellectuals were jailed. But the target of repression was much more the working class. The majority of the arrested and sentenced 'were workers 20 to 30 years of age'. Death sentences fell especially on workers accused, rightly or wrongly, of street fighting. Among the arrested 'the group that contributed the greatest number of those sentenced consisted of the members of the workers' councils and revolutionary committees from factories and local institutions'. Death sentences were rarer but long prison sentences the norm, including life (for Bali and Rácz, for example). Despite later amnesties 'quantitatively…this group was hardest hit, by both judicial sentences and by extra-legal measures of repression'. As the Litván history notes, the targeting of this group was hardly an 'accident' but 'a major goal of the repression'.[55]

Fifty years on

Once the threat of the revolution had been overcome Kádár began to build bridges to the Hungarian people. From the early 1960s he became the most successful Eastern bloc leader. But the memory of 1956 still had to be contained through suppression and distortion. The same process is at work today but the politics are different.

When the Soviet bloc collapsed in 1989, 'the transformation in Hungary was perhaps the most tranquil of all'.[56] This was a negotiated transition, negotiated in no small part by those who had made their careers under Kádár and who saw the chance not only to survive but also to prosper in a new Hungary. Manipulating 1956 as a 'national' myth served the interests of these people as well as a new generation of leaders committed to the market and private property. Today Hungary is a member of the European Union. It is an ally of the United States, and the share of multinationals in its manufacturing turnover is over 70 percent—second only to Ireland. Ordinary Hungarians, however, like most ordinary people in the transition regimes, have seen fewer of the benefits of change. This has been especially the case in the industrial areas that were the core of 1956.

In this new situation the radical interpretation of 1956 is unwelcome. So too is a recognition of the hollowness of Western policy in 1956 which was strong on rhetoric but involved standing by to allow Russia to crush the revolution and maintain its sphere of interest and the overall balance of power. 'Alas, the logic of great power policy made accomplices of many otherwise honourable Western politicians', writes the Litván group.[57] This is self-deceit of the worst kind, for 1956 was the year of both Hungary and Suez. It simply writes into history the cynical idea that it is better for a small country to prostrate itself voluntarily before Washington and Brussels than be enslaved by Moscow. Did Hungarian workers want to control their own lives? The self-deceit works again. Of course, but now it must be understood that freedom can never be anything more than the freedom to apply to work for this or that multinational and their freedom to reject you.

But the story of 1956 is bigger than this. Different regimes in France struggled to contain the legacy of its great revolution for 200 years. But it has not always been easy. One of the songs heard on the streets of Budapest in 1956 was in fact the Marseillaise. What Kende now calls 'history's inscrutable logic' is often more inscrutable than those who invoke it suggest. Connecting to the real history of 1956 shows that its legacy is much more open than many would like us to believe.

NOTES

1: M Molnar, *Budapest 1956: A History of the Hungarian Revolution* (Allen & Unwin, 1971), p174.

2: It is ironic that accounts of the post-1956 Kádár regime often paid more attention to the 'counter-revolutionary' role of workers in 1956 than some post-1989 Hungarian accounts. The main translated general history of the post-1989 era, Ignac Romsic's *Hungary in the Twentieth Century* (Corvina, 1999), (which incidentally concludes with a near racist celebration of Hungary's thousand year struggle to resist 'Asian and Eurasian tyranny' in favour of membership of the Christian West) does not mention the workers' councils in its discussion of the first stages of the revolution. It then gives them scant attention in the resistance except when they became victims of repression. 'The spirit of the revolution,' Romsic argues, 'lived on most conspicuously among groups of intellectuals' (p316).

3: Data from M Pécsi and B Sárfalvi, *The Geography of Hungary* (Collets, 1964).

4: There is an element of spurious precision in this data. Although the order of magnitude is correct it is probably an undercount. Some of the losses on the Soviet side may have been hidden. The undercount is probably greater on the revolutionary side. Some urban dead were simply buried by relatives; there was a less accurate count in the countryside and some others died trying to flee the country—G Litván (ed), *The Hungarian Revolution of 1956: Reform, Revolt and Repression 1953-1963* (Longman, 1996), p103. For the Russian data see J Granville, 'In the Line of Fire: the Soviet Crackdown on Hungary, 1956-57', in T Cox (ed), *Hungary 1956: Forty Years On* (Cass, 1996), p82.

5: See M Haynes, 'Accumulation and Working Class Exploitation, Some Origins of 1956 in Hungary', London Socialist Historians Conference on 1956, February 2006 (forthcoming).

6: Quoted in M Kramer, 'The Soviet Union and the 1956 Crises in Hungary and Poland: Reassessments and New Findings', *Journal of Contemporary History*, vol 33, no 2 (1998), p175.

7: J Granville, 'Reactions to the Events of 1956: New Findings from the Budapest and Warsaw Archives', *Journal of Contemporary History*, vol 38, no 2 (2003), pp264-265.

8: Rákosi's comment to Voroshilov quoted in J Granville, 'Reactions...', as above, p268.

9: Quoted in J Granville, 'Reactions...', as above, p277.

10: Quoted in M Kramer, as above, p181.

11: Quoted in M Molnar, as above, p178.

12: Quoted in C Harman, *Bureaucracy and Revolution in Eastern Europe* (Pluto, 1974), p150. Fekete was the imprisoned author of a famous underground pamphlet by 'Hungaricus'.

13: The analysis of Hungary in 1956 as a social revolution forms the centrepiece of Bill Lomax's *The Hungarian Revolution*,

(Allison & Busby, 1976). Since 1989 a mass of material has become available but new Western accounts focus primarily on the international dimensions. Hence Lomax's classic account remains a significant point of reference. Lomax also edited a major documentary collection: B Lomax (ed), *Hungarian Workers' Councils in 1956* (Social Science Monographs, 1990).

14: Quoted in M Kramer, as above, p185.

15: Kopásci later wrote his own account. See S Kopásci, *In the Name of the Working Class: The Inside Story of the Hungarian Revolution* (Fontana, 1987).

16: Quoted in J Granville, 'In the Line...', as above, p101.

17: Quoted in B Lomax, *The Hungarian Revolution*, as above, p111.

18: As above. For a sizeable extract from a first hand account of Maléter's actions see C Harman, as above, pp136-137.

19: G Litván (ed), *The Hungarian Revolution of 1956: Reform, Revolt and Repression, 1953-1963* (Longman, 1996), p68. This is the quasi-official post-1989 history of 1956. Its editor, György Litván, was then a brave history teacher who denounced Rákosi to his face. He was later imprisoned. Now he is one of the most senior historians in Hungary. The 1956 Institute in Hungary has a large website with a mass of materials that I have drawn freely on: www.rev.hu

20: Despite its name this plant was involved in engineering, including military production.

21: Quoted in B Lomax, *The Hungarian Revolution*, as above, p141.

22: B Lomax, *The Hungarian Revolution*, as above, p140.

23: P Fryer, *Hungarian Tragedy* (New Park, 1986), pp44-45.

24: Quoted in B Lomax, *The Hungarian Revolution*, as above.

25: *Hungary* (Corvina Press, 1964), p280.

26: Quoted in B Lomax, *The Hungarian Revolution*, as above, p97.

27: This was the first place Peter Fryer, the *Daily Worker* correspondent, saw. He arrived the day after the massacre and was immediately broken of his Stalinism by what he saw. See P Fryer, as above, pp17-24.

28: S Horváth, 'Everyday life in the first Hungarian socialist city', *International Labor and Working Class History*, no 68 (Fall 2005), pp24-46. Whether Sztálinváros was ever rational is an interesting question but whatever logic it had was further undermined as it was being planned by Stalin's dispute with Tito in Yugoslavia, which denied the iron and steel works expected supplies from that country. Horváth's study of Sztálinváros shows that many of the new workers and especially the skilled ones came from other towns including Budapest. This confirms the pattern evident in the work of Mark Pittaway which stresses the role of skilled workers in 1956. See, for example, M Pittaway, 'The Reproduction of Hierarchy: Skill, Working Class Culture, and the State in Early Socialist Hungary', *Journal of Modern History*, vol 74, no 4 (December 2002).

29: Peter Fryer describes a peasant council at the Bábolna state farm where he spent two days—P Fryer, as above, pp49-54.

30: Calculated from I Romsic, as above, p330.

31: Quoted in B Lomax, *The Hungarian Revolution*, as above, p37.

32: P Kende, 'Afterword', in G Litván (ed), as above, p180. Kende had been an oppositionist journalist in the 1950s.

33: Quoted in B Lomax (ed), *Hungarian Workers Councils*, as above, pxix.

34: G Litván, as above, p126.

35: On the debate on 1956 in Hungary see H Nyyssönen, *The Presence of the Past in Politics: '1956' after 1956 in Hungary* (Sophi, 1999).

36: Quoted in B Nagy, 'Budapest 1956:

The Central Workers' Council'. This is reprinted in B Lomax (ed), *Hungarian Workers' Councils*, as above. It is also more easily available on line in the Marxist internet archive.

37: Quoted in B Lomax, *Eyewitness in Hungary* (Spokesman, 1980), p125.

38: G Litván, as above, p77.

39: See B Lomax (ed), *Hungarian Workers' Councils*, as above, p85.

40: 'Fontosabb adatok az 1956. Október-Decemberi idöszakról', *Statisztikai Szemle*, vol xxxiv, no 11-12 (November-December 1956), p928.

41: P Fryer, as above, p69.

42: G Litván, as above, p103; B Nagy, as above.

43: Quoted in B Lomax, 'The Working Class in the Hungarian Revolution', *Critique*, no 12 (Autumn-Winter 1979-1980), p46.

44: 'Fontosabb adatok az 1956. Október-Decemberi idöszakról', *Statisztikai Szemle*, as above, pp17-918.

45: *Observer*, 25 November 1956, as quoted in A Anderson, *Hungary '56*, available at http://libcom.org/library/hungary-56-andy-anderson

46: G Litván, as above, p135.

47: For the role of the Council see B Nagy's account, as above, and the documents in B Lomax (ed), *Hungarian Workers Councils*, as above, pp91-180.

48: See E Nagy, 'Conflicts Between the CWC of Greater Budapest and the CWC of the Csepel Iron and Steel Workers', in B Lomax (ed), *Hungarian Workers Councils*, as above, pp467-499. Elek Nagy was president of the Csepel Central Workers' Council.

49: This comes from evidence presented in the trial of Rasz and the other CWC leaders after the defeat of the revolution. See B Lomax (ed), *Hungarian Workers'*

Councils, as above, p562.

50: Quoted in B Lomax, *The Hungarian Revolution*, as above, p159.

51: *Observer*, 2 December 1956, quoted in A Anderson, as above.

52: The Russians needed a figurehead. Kádár's shame is that he became it. We now know that he did so after hesitation. See M Kramer, as above, pp200-201.

53: Quoted in P Fryer, *Hungary and the Communist Party* (London, 1957), p27.

54: See Elek Nagy's account in B Lomax (ed), *Hungarian Workers Councils*, as above, pp497-498.

55: See G Litván, as above, pp139-148.

56: As above, pxiii.

57: As above, p155.

Suez and the high tide of Arab nationalism

Anne Alexander

July 26, 1956. A crowd, tens of thousands strong, gathered in Manshiyya Square in Alexandria, to hear a speech by Egypt's president, Gamal Abd-al-Nasser. The atmosphere was tense—only days before Nasser had received a humiliating rebuff from the US Secretary of State, John Foster Dulles, to his request for a loan to build the High Dam on the Nile. Egypt had received arms from the Czech Republic in 1955, and Dulles hoped to achieve two aims: to humble Nasser, whose anti-colonial rhetoric was winning support across the Middle East, and to remind other aspiring Third World leaders that there was no neutral ground in the Cold War.

Nasser joked with the crowd, describing Eugene Black, president of the World Bank, as a peddler of 'mortgage colonialism'. Black reminded him, he said, of Ferdinand de Lesseps, whose company constructed the Suez Canal in the 19th century.[1] As the crowd laughed and cheered, Egyptian commandos were taking control of the Suez Canal Company's headquarters in Port Said. The hissing syllables, 'de Lesseps', were the code word to set the secret operation in motion.[2] Nasser finished his speech with a simple statement:

> Everything which was stolen from us by that imperialist company, that state within a state, when we were dying of hunger, we are going to take back…
> The government has decided on the following law: a presidential decree

nationalising the International Suez Canal Company. In the name of the nation, the president of the republic declares the International Suez Canal Company an Egyptian limited company.[3]

The crowd in Alexandria erupted with delight. Here at last was proof that the era of colonial domination was over: the greatest powers on earth would no longer determine Egypt's fate. In Washington, Nasser's reply to Dulles was received with consternation. The US Secretary of State told Anthony Eden, British Tory prime minister that Nasser must 'disgorge' the canal.[4] Dulles's reaction pales compared to the blind rage which descended on the leaders of the old imperialist powers, Britain and France. In London and Paris politicians competed in insulting Nasser. Hugh Gaitskell, leader of the Labour Party, then in opposition, likened Nasser to Hitler. Anthony Eden made the same analogy, warning that 'we all know this is how fascist governments behave, and we all remember only too well what the cost can be of giving in to fascism'.[5]

In reality, the British and French governments were waiting for an excuse to humble Nasser. French forces were fighting a brutal war to retain control of Algeria in the face of a nationalist uprising which had united thousands of Algerians in the struggle for liberation. Leaders of the Algerian National Liberation Front (FLN) found sanctuary in Cairo, and Nasser provided arms and financial assistance for their struggle. Eden, meanwhile, had developed an intense personal hatred of the Egyptian leader. In March 1956 he told Anthony Nutting, Minister of State at the Foreign Office:

> But what's all this nonsense about isolating Nasser, or 'neutralising' him as you call it? I want him destroyed, can't you understand? I want him removed, and if you and the Foreign Office don't agree, then you'd better come to the cabinet and explain why.[6]

Eden's rage reflected his sense that the Middle East was slipping away from British control. At the end of the Second World War Egypt, Iraq and Jordan were ruled by pro-British monarchs. Hundreds of thousands of British troops were stationed across the region. The Suez Canal, route to the empire in India and beyond, was firmly in British hands. Just over ten years later the Egyptian monarchy had been overthrown by nationalist army officers, led by Nasser, British troops forced to leave the Suez Canal after a long-running campaign of guerrilla attacks and mass demonstrations, while popular pressure had forced King Hussein of Jordan to sack the British commander of the Arab Legion, John Bagot Glubb.[7] Only the Iraqi government remained as subservient to British interests as ever. It was in Iraq that British officials hoped to find a counterweight to the rising tide of nationalism across the Middle East. Nuri al-Said, the Iraqi prime minister, was the architect of the Baghdad Pact, a military alliance signed in 1955 which linked Iraq, Iran, Turkey, Pakistan and Britain with the aim of checking Arab nationalism and undermining Soviet influence in the Middle East. A swift blow at Nasser, Eden believed, would tip the balance back in Britain's favour.

The outcome of the Suez Crisis[8] confounded Eden's hopes. A three-sided plot to seize the Canal and topple Nasser cooked up by the British, French and Israeli governments ended in humiliating failure. In the space of a week in November 1956 the British government faced public panic as petrol rationing was introduced, saw the pound plummet in value, the 'special relationship' with the US crack and the cabinet split while protests spread across the country and around the Middle East. Eden was packed off on sick leave and resigned, defeated and broken, in January 1957.

Meanwhile Nasser emerged from the crisis stronger than ever. His picture was everywhere—carried aloft in the streets from Cairo to Baghdad, on the front cover of *Time* magazine. The events of November 1956 seemed to validate the idea that national liberation was possible and that the state could be a weapon in the hands of anti-imperialists. Beneath the surface, however, Nasser's moment of triumph also demonstrated the limits of his strategy. The crisis exposed the weakness of key areas of the Egyptian state, such as the army and state party. The strength to resist the invasion came rather from below, through a popular mobilisation led by Communist activists who had played a central role in the mass movement against the British occupation during the 1940s. They organised civil defence, smuggled arms to keep guerrilla resistance going in occupied Port Said and mobilised thousands of volunteers for military training. Meanwhile, across the region, the massive protests which shook the governments allied to Britain were not brought to life by Nasser's agents, but had a life of their own as the latest episodes in the same long struggle for liberation.

Egypt in movement

After the Second World War Egypt experienced a period of mass protests against British imperialism and the local pro-British ruling class. The national movements at this stage were broad-based coalitions of different opposition groups, including trade unions, left wing nationalist groups, Communist parties, student organisations and peasant groups. Their challenge to imperialism was also a challenge to the existing political order.

By 1952 the protest movement had sapped the strength of the state, with discontent growing in the army, a guerrilla campaign against British forces in the Canal Zone running out of the government's control. The burning of Cairo on 26 January 1952 was the most obvious outward sign of the old order's malaise.[9] The army officers who overthrew the monarchy took advantage of the crisis, but they were not central to the movement which helped to create it. Nasser, for example, had worked with activists from many different political backgrounds including the Muslim Brotherhood and the Communists in the Democratic Movement for National Liberation. Yet he argued that the officers' group needed to keep its independence.[10] Thus when the Free Officers took power in July 1952, they quickly asserted their autonomy, moving first against the independent trade unions and the left, and then against the Muslim Brotherhood.[11]

Nasser's pamphlet *The Philosophy of the Revolution* justifies the officers' actions by painting a picture of a movement in crisis, bereft of leadership:

> I imagined that our role was to act as the vanguard, that this role would not last more than a few hours before the masses appeared behind us, marching in serried ranks to the great goal...the vanguard performed its task, it stormed the ramparts of tyranny, ousted the tyrant and stood by...it waited and waited. Endless crowds appeared, but how different reality is to the imagination: these multitudes were the scattered stragglers from a defeated army.[12]

In the absence of the movement, Nasser believed, the state itself could serve as a tool to change society.[13] And from using the state in the name of the movement it was only a short distance to seeing the state *as* the movement. The Liberation Rally, the single legal party created in January 1953, was designed to replace the old political parties during the three-year 'transitional period' of military rule.

In parallel with the creation of the Liberation Rally, the Free Officers also systematically undermined the organisations which had formed the core of the mass movement. A strike by textile workers in Kafr-al-Dawwar near Alexandria just weeks after the coup was met with fierce repression—two strikers were hanged. Left wing trade union leaders were arrested and supporters of the government elected to head the unions in their place.[14] In October 1952 student unions were dissolved, followed by all political parties in January 1953. The Muslim Brotherhood was initially spared, but Nasser moved against it after an attempt to assassinate him in October 1954.

Using the state to achieve some of the more long term goals of the national movement proved to be a slower process than demobilising the movement organisations. With the exception of land redistribution, enacted in September 1952, the balance sheet of the Free Officers' early years was weighted more towards repression than reform, although the events of 1956 pushed Nasser in the direction of greater state intervention in the economy following the sequestration of assets belonging to British and French nationals. Yet even before 1956 Nasser had begun to articulate a kind of 'anti-imperialism from above'. At the Bandung Conference of 1955 he argued that Arab countries should not align themselves with either the US or the Soviet Union, but preserve their hard-won independence. In September of the same year he also announced the purchase of Soviet arms from the Czech Republic. These policies were all bound together: Nasser was driven to greater radicalism in foreign policy both by the need for economic and social development and by the actions of the Great Powers. He had already approached the US for arms and been rebuffed before the Czech arms deal was agreed.

Conspiracy foiled

Over the summer of 1956, while diplomatic wrangling over the future of the Canal preoccupied the world's media, British and French officials were searching feverishly for a pretext to launch military action against Nasser.[15] By October the detailed outlines of the plan were beginning to take shape. In a secret meeting at a villa in Sèvres, near Paris, British, French and Israeli officials hatched a plot whereby an Israeli attack on the Sinai Peninsula would trigger a British and French ultimatum calling on both the Israeli and the Egyptian armies to withdraw from the Suez Canal

Zone. Confident that Nasser could not accept such terms—which meant abandoning Sinai and the Canal—British and French commanders planned to bomb Egyptian cities and land troops at Port Said to control the entrance to the Canal. The Israelis were to be well rewarded for their role: the French government was already supplying them with arms and fighter planes and it was at the Sèvres meeting that an agreement was reached to provide Israel with French nuclear technology and uranium fuel for a reactor to be built at Dimona.[16] On 29 October Israeli forces crossed into Sinai. As Egyptian troops rushed to engage the invaders, Britain and France made their demands for a ceasefire. The first British bombs were falling on Cairo by nightfall on 31 October. Six days later British and French troops landed at Port Said at the mouth of the Canal.

As the plot against Egypt unfolded, the problems with a conventional military response became clear. The Israeli assault caught the Egyptian command off guard. Nasser believed that the main thrust of any invasion would hit Alexandria first. The garrison in Sinai had been reduced to 30,000 men, including only 10,000 frontline combat troops. Egyptian commanders faced another problem: although well supplied with Russian arms, much of the new weaponry was not yet operational.[17] Despite these difficulties the Israeli assault was not unstoppable. Egyptian units in Sinai fought tenaciously and Israeli paratroops landing at the Mitla Pass suffered heavy casualties. Once British and French forces joined the attack, however, the dice were loaded against them. Nasser quickly realised that his troops would be trapped in Sinai by the British and French invasion and ordered a full scale retreat. According to the journalist Mohamed Hassanein Heikal, one of Nasser's closest advisers, it was at this moment of crisis that cracks began to appear in the Egyptian army command. Abd-al-Hakim Amer, Commander-in-Chief and one of Nasser's oldest friends, lost his nerve and refused to give the order to withdraw, until overruled by Nasser.[18]

The damage caused by confusion in the military command was reduced by the adoption of a new strategy—arming the people in preparation for a guerrilla campaign to resist the invasion. Once again the official mechanisms for mobilisation, in particular the only legal political organisation, the state-run Liberation Rally, showed their weakness. The Liberation Rally was, as John Waterbury comments, 'an unabashed improvisation on the part of the regime to replace the political parties it had outlawed'.[19] It had succeeded in partially co-opting sections of the trade unions—thus weakening the Communist movement—but its main role had been stage-managing rallies and demonstrations in support of government initiatives.

Popular resistance

Nasser now turned to the Communist movement to give life to the inert bureaucracy of the Liberation Rally. Communist activists played a central role in the Popular Resistance Committees, set up by the government in the immediate aftermath of the invasion. They were also involved with organising military training for workers and university students. In the week after the invasion a million small arms were distributed.[20] The trade union lawyer Yusuf Darwish was a leading member of the underground Communist group, Workers' Vanguard:

> I remember a general meeting in the Lawyers' Union against the aggression in 1956, I was in the back row and someone clapped me on the shoulder and said, 'We want you'. I thought he was a detective so I said, 'What do you want me for?' He said, 'We want you in the Liberation Rally'… So I worked with them and wrote propaganda leaflets.[21]

Layla al-Shal recalls helping to set up the Women's Popular Resistance Committee in Cairo. A second year political science student at Cairo University, she was also an activist in the Democratic Movement for National Liberation, one of the largest Egyptian Communist groups:

> A lot of women intellectuals and students and housewives joined us. We set up women's resistance committees across the capital. We had military-style training; how to defuse a bomb, how to shoot a rifle and so on. At that time the government was working in alliance with the Communists. There was a camp in an area near the Canal, where Communist volunteers went for training.[22]

Fathallah Mahrus, a young factory worker and trade unionist in the Workers' Vanguard, remembers how he and his comrades organised military training for workers in the Ramla industrial area of Alexandria, which included huge textile mills such as Sibahy & Co with its 20,000 workers:

In cooperation with the leadership of the armed forces in Alexandria, we set up a weapons training camp on a piece of waste ground next to the area where the factories were. The workers went out with their shift from work and were trained to use weapons. When they finished, the next shift came in.[23]

Communist activists did not only bring their individual talents as organisers and agitators. They delivered their social and political networks: Communist teachers created resistance committees from their pupils, trade unionists recruited their workmates and students brought their friends from university.

On 5 November British paratroops landed at Port Said at the entrance to the Canal, while French forces seized Port Fuad on the opposite bank. With the regular army in disarray as it retreated before the Israeli advance, the city was poorly defended. Here the strategy of popular resistance would be put to the test. According to Fathallah Mahrus:

There was no army to fight in Port Said, just some individuals and a few soldiers and small units. So the popular resistance against the invasion was led by the people of Port Said—women and children as well—armed with cooking pans, kitchen knives, walking sticks and anything they could find.[24]

Amina Shafiq, a young journalist from Cairo, was smuggled into Port Said to join the resistance. She found a town devastated by bombing, but dogged resistance continuing nonetheless. Her role was to turn reports from foreign news broadcasts of demonstrations against the invasion into leaflets:

I used to write about who was supporting us abroad, who had heard of us abroad, about the demonstrations outside Egypt. We were trying to encourage people, to tell them to be steadfast. People were exhausted and supplies were running out, so we were trying to keep their spirits up.[25]

The ferocity of the resistance in Port Said was a grave setback for British and French plans. British officials had convinced themselves that Nasser was a hated dictator, and that the Egyptian people would welcome his defeat and overthrow. But as Fathallah Mahrus explains:

It wasn't about Nasser, it was about our homeland. The imperialists wanted to reoccupy our country, and the invasion was over the nationalisation of the Suez Canal Company which was an imperialist company. And we forgot about what Nasser did to us, and we forgot our differences with him and the prisons and the camps and the torture because there was a common danger and a single enemy: imperialism which wanted to occupy Egypt. All the Communists said the same.[26]

Despite this, there were tensions within the Popular Resistance Committees, as the authorities attempted to prevent Communist activists from gaining too much independence. Workers who took part in weapons training had to return their arms each night, and some government officials tried to exclude Communists from the resistance committees.[27]

Meanwhile events were moving quickly on the world stage. US President Eisenhower was enraged that Britain and France had acted without consulting the US government. In the UN Security Council a motion calling for an immediate ceasefire won the support of both the US and the Soviet Union, only to be vetoed by Britain and France. Soviet premier Nikolai Bulganin made a statement reserving the right to use force to end the conflict in the Middle East, which was widely interpreted as a threat to use nuclear weapons against Britain and France. With sterling in free-fall, and anti-war demonstrations gathering strength, Eden's cabinet began to crack: Minister of State Anthony Nutting resigned. In order to secure US financial support to prop up the value of the pound, Eden announced a ceasefire on 6 November.

Iraq

The attack against Egypt ignited protests across the Arab world. In Iraq the movement in solidarity with Egypt shook the government to the core, demonstrating the weakness and isolation of the pro-British ruling class. Despatches from the British Embassy in Baghdad betray a rising sense of panic throughout November and December. As the protest movement grew in strength, Nuri al-Said feared he might be dismissed by the regent.[28] Embassy officials worked frantically behind the scenes, trying to persuade 'the people at the top' that there was no collusion between Britain and Israel.[29] A despatch from the ambassador at the end of December 1956 spelt out what was at stake:

In the last seven weeks, we have had to struggle with little help from events to prevent a break of diplomatic relations with Iraq. To avert an abrupt dissolution of the Baghdad Pact, to ward off nationalisation or fatal interference with the Iraq Petroleum Company, to keep Nuri in power, and to try and maintain the confidence and support of those in authority here. We have not yet failed (though we may still do so).[30]

The protests in Iraq were not simply the result of Egyptian propaganda. Nasser seems to have played an important symbolic role: his name appears constantly in slogans; his speeches found a huge audience in homes and street cafes across the country. Yet there is little evidence of direct Egyptian intervention in the movement. This is underlined by the dynamic of the demonstrations, which began in response to the Anglo-French-Israeli attack, but quickly became generalised protests against the Iraqi government as a result of police repression.

Instead the demonstrations reflected the growing strength of a mass movement for national liberation. By 1956 the movement had already experienced two major peaks, in 1948 with the revolt against the Treaty of Portsmouth, known as Al-Wathbah (the Leap) in Arabic, and in 1952 another uprising (the Intifada).[31] Nuri al-Said was one of the movement's chief targets. He oversaw repression at home, while working tirelessly for British interests across the Middle East, notably through the creation of the Baghdad Pact.

Hanna Batatu gives a detailed account of the protests in Najaf in early November 1956.[32] Many demonstrations began in the Huwaish quarter. Alongside the Communists, nationalists were also active. Slogans on the protests included 'Down with the Martial Courts', 'Down with the criminal Nuri al-Said', 'Long live Gamal Abd-al-Nasser', 'For a people's government that would live in harmony with the liberated Arab countries'. The protests peaked on 24 November when 'members of the police [were] beset on every side by angry crowds armed with daggers, pistols, stones and huge canes'. According to the official tally, the casualties were two dead, 27 demonstrators and nine police injured. The following day the ulama, or Muslim scholars refused to perform their religious duties, the police disappeared from the streets and troops called out to suppress the protests fraternised with the crowds.

Events in Basra were recorded in regular despatches from Noel Jackson, the British consul-general in the city, to his superiors in Baghdad. The biggest demonstrations in the city took place on 2 December, in response to events in Najaf. The centre of protests was the Girls' Secondary School in Basra City:

> Crowds of students from other schools gathered outside, amongst whom were alleged Communists, who seem to have lead [sic] the demonstration. The usual anti-government and pro-Egyptian and Syrian slogans were used.... I understand that the Acting Director of Education accompanied by a police officer warned the members of the Girls' School, assembled for the purpose, against further activities of that nature.[33]

The northern city of Mosul was the scene of a far more serious confrontation between protesters and the authorities in early December, ending with an armed siege of the city's police headquarters which was broken by the deployment of troops onto the streets. C J Burgess, British vice-consul in Mosul, sent a detailed description of the protests to Baghdad based on an interview with the city governor and the Mosul garrison commander. His report on 5 December 1956[34] gives details of large demonstrations in the city between 30 November and 3 December. On Friday 30 November, students from Adadia Secondary School attempted to join up with students from Gharbia Intermediate School for a demonstration, but were dispersed by police before meeting up. The following morning, Saturday 1 December:

> Students from these two schools and four others, Sharqia Secondary School, near the Mutasarrifia [governor's residence], and three intermediate schools, Muthanna, Hadba and Umm al-Rabi'ain, commenced disorderly behaviour within the schools. Students harangued passers-by from the roofs with the expected anti-Nuri, anti-Western and pro Nasser slogans.

The schools were surrounded by police 'to prevent them from organising demonstrations in the streets'. Around 3pm crowds gathered at the Bab al-Sinjar: 'The mob was led by nondescript adults waving large sticks and shouting for the most part "Down with Nuri", "down with Britain".' The armed protesters attempted to storm the police station. By about 4pm the police headquarters were surrounded by a crowd of up to 3,000 extending up to 400 yards behind the building. At this point the governor called in the army and the protestors dispersed. An attempt at another demonstration following day was dispersed by the army.

The end of empire?

British power in Iraq lasted only another 18 months: in July 1958 revolution swept away the monarchy, Nuri al-Said and the Baghdad Pact. A few months earlier Egypt and Syria had merged to become the United Arab Republic (UAR) under Nasser's leadership and hopes were high that Iraq would soon join a new Arab super-state. The era when Britain's client kings dominated the Middle East had gone forever. Inside Egypt work was soon to begin on the construction of the High Dam on the Nile at Aswan, which Nasser hoped would power a new era of rapid economic growth. Increasing state intervention in the Egyptian economy was followed by an ambitious programme of social reform. By the early 1960s it seemed that poverty, like imperialism, could also be defeated as Nasser pushed forward policies for the redistribution of wealth through land reform, subsidies on basic commodities, free education and a state-led employment drive.[35]

Yet Nasser's moment of triumph was brief. His strategy of using the state to achieve national liberation and economic development reached the limits of its potential within a few years of 1956. The collapse of the United Arab Republic demonstrated the difficulty of carrying out a 'revolution from above' without the support of the mass movement. In early 1958 leaders of the Baath Party in Syria appealed to Nasser to unite Egypt and Syria in a single state, the United Arab Republic. They hoped that the Egyptian leader would be a figurehead, and that his prestige would allow them to dominate Syria and overcome their rivals in the Communist Party. Nasser, however, marginalised the Baathists, appointing them to positions in Cairo while his closest colleagues were sent to rule in Damascus. He also brought the Syrian trade union movement under state control and banned political parties.[36]

However, it was the attempt to extend Nasser's economic reforms, in particular land reform and the 'Socialist Decrees' nationalising major industries and the banks which triggered the collapse of the United Arab Republic. The Syrian landlords and bourgeoisie were in a better position than their counterparts in Egypt to resist Nasser's attempt to expropriate them. In 1961 an army coup overthrew the UAR government in Damascus and handed power to a coalition of liberal politicians who promptly rescinded Nasser's reforms. The UAR's collapse provoked little protest, however. Repression of the left, demobilisation of the independent trade unions and the marginalisation of the Baath Party left Nasser with few allies in his struggle against Syria's old ruling class.

National liberation versus socialist revolution?

There are many reasons why Nasser's route to national liberation turned out to be a dead end. The resources of a single state, particularly an oil-poor country like Egypt, were never going to be enough to challenge either the old or the new imperialist powers. The strength to resist imperialism lay in the fact that the mass movement in Egypt was part of a region-wide anti-colonial struggle. This was British imperialism's real weakness, as events in 1956 showed: invading Egypt meant risking the loss of Iraq.

Nasser's attempt to break out of the nation-state ended in failure, largely because the United Arab Republic simply replicated the problems of Egypt's 'revolution from above' on a larger scale. By undermining the anti-colonial movement's capacity to act independently of the state, Nasser also weakened the state's capacity to realise the goals of the movement. So the UAR fell apart, and even Egypt's state capitalist transformation was short-lived. Only a decade and a half after the 'Socialist Decrees', Nasser's successor, Anwar Sadat, would embark on a programme of neo-liberal reforms. Even before then the hollowness of the Egyptian army's claim to be the Arab world's vanguard against imperialism had been cruelly exposed in June 1967, with Israeli victory in the Six Day War.

Yet the Communists in Egypt, Iraq and Syria were unable to create an alternative to Nasserism which could build on the mass movements of the 1940s and 1950s. As Yusuf Darwish explained many years later:

> Nasser used the Communists as guard-dogs: one day he'd want them out of prison, the next he'd throw them back inside. At that period he wanted us because we were clever: we could write pamphlets, and stir people up, and bear arms and so on... After the war ended and the invasion came to an end and things quietened down...they began to arrest the Communists.[37]

It is true that they faced tremendous objective difficulties. Under the monarchies in Egypt and Iraq Communist organisations were banned, party activists frequently arrested and tortured. In Iraq the general secretary of the CP and other leading figures were hanged. The Egyptian Communist movement was fragmented and small: at its peak, the largest Communist organisation, the Democratic Movement for National Liberation, only counted around 2,000 members.[38] Even in Iraq the CP's explosive membership growth came after the revolution of 1958, and followed a period when severe repression had depleted the party's strength.[39]

Yet repression alone does not explain why the Communists were unable to rebuild and take advantage of the crisis of the nationalist regimes in the 1960s and 1970s. In fact, at the very point when the limits of 'national' revolution in Egypt, Iraq and Syria were becoming clear, the majority of the Communist movement in these three countries dissolved itself into an alliance with the party of the state.[40] Here the problem lay in understanding the relationship between national liberation and socialist revolution. Leon Trotsky's analysis of the link between the democratic revolution and socialist revolution in Russia could have provided a guide for action, but the majority of Communist organisations in the Middle East followed the Stalinist leadership of the Soviet Union and rejected Trotsky's theory of permanent revolution.[41]

Instead Communists in the Middle East looked to an older concept of Lenin's, in which he argued that Russian socialists could not push the democratic revolution 'beyond the scope of bourgeois social-economic relationships'.[42] Therefore, although Lenin argued that the working class, in alliance with the peasantry, would carry out the tasks of the democratic revolution, this 'democratic dictatorship' would be short-lived, soon to be replaced by a conservative bourgeois state.[43] This formula, or a version of it, was accepted by Communist organisations in Egypt and Iraq.[44] In practice its influence can be seen in attempts by the Communists to prevent the army-led revolutions of 1952 and 1958 breaching their 'bourgeois limits'. So the major Communist organisation in Egypt in 1952 refused to organise solidarity for striking textile workers in Kafr al-Dawwar when two activists were hanged by the Free Officers.[45] In Iraq the Communists bolstered the personal rule of Abd-al-Karim Qassim as the means to strengthen a cross-class alliance in support of the revolution, and attacked Qassim's rival, Abd-al-Salam Arif, for raising the slogan of a 'socialist republic' because he risked 'throwing patriotic social strata into the lap of imperialism'.[46]

Trotsky by contrast, agreed with Lenin that the working class was the only class capable of leading the democratic revolution to success, but argued that once in power, the working class could not simply limit itself to constructing a bourgeois democratic state. Instead he said, 'the democratic revolution grows over immediately into the socialist, and thereby becomes a permanent revolution'.[47] As Tony Cliff demonstrated in *Deflected Permanent Revolution*, however, Trotsky's predictions were not borne out in the wave of national revolutions after the Second World War. In country after country the old pro-colonial regimes were overthrown, but not by the working class or the peasantry. Instead sections of the intelligentsia or factions in the army seized control of the state.[48]

The consequences for the Communist movement were profound. The same forces which the Communists saw as leading the struggle for national liberation now turned against them. In Iraq, for example, Qassim feared the Communists' growing power—by 1959 they were capable of mobilising something like a million people for the May Day demonstration in Baghdad.[49] He arrested hundreds of Communist activists, dissolved organisations close to the party and shut the offices of the General Federation of Trade Unions. Although the repression was not as serious as in Egypt, the damage inflicted by Qassim weakened the party, and it was unable to resist the Baathist seizure of power in 1963. In the bloodbath which followed Qassim was killed, and thousands of Communists were also murdered.

Despite the tragic fate of the Iraqi and Egyptian revolutions of the 1950s, the struggle for national liberation in the Middle East still inspires millions of people who want to see a world free of imperialism, poverty and war. The real heroes of the Suez Crisis were the tens of thousands of ordinary people who took to the streets in Egypt, Iraq and around the Middle East to defy the imperialist powers. The same courage and hope can be seen today in the protests against the US occupation of Iraq and the Israeli attack on Lebanon. It will fall to the new generation of socialists in the Middle East to ensure that this time we break imperialism's hold on the region for good.

NOTES

1: He did not, of course, build the canal, whatever it might say in English and French history books. Tens of thousands of press-ganged Egyptian workers built the canal and paid a high price for it in lives lost.

2: In order to make sure that the code word was not missed by the waiting commandos, Nasser repeated de Lesseps' name 14 times in the space of ten minutes. See Gamal Abd-al-Nasser, Nationalisation Speech, 26 July 1956, translated from audio recording in Arabic on the Nasser Foundation web site, http://nasser.bibalex.org

3: Quotes from Nasser's speech retranslated from Gamal Abd-al-Nasser, Nationalisation Speech, 26 July 1956, as above.

4: FRUS (C), 1988, memorandum of a conversation between prime minister Anthony Eden and secretary of state Dulles, 10 Downing Street, London, 1 August 1956, 12.45 pm, document 42, pp 98-99, quoted in A Gorst and L Johnman, The Suez Crisis (Routledge, 1997), pp66-67. Dulles also warned Eden at this meeting against the unilateral use of force against Nasser.

5: Quoted in A Gorst and L Johnman, as above, p69.

6: A Nutting, No End of a Lesson: The Story of Suez (Constable, 1967), pp34-35.

7: Demonstrations in December 1955 also led to a cabinet revolt which prevented Jordan's accession to the Baghdad Pact. See M Oren, 'A Winter of Discontent: Britain's Crisis in Jordan, December 1955-March 1956', International Journal of Middle East Studies, vol 22, no 2 (May 1990), pp171-184.

8: In Arabic the Suez Crisis is known—rather more accurately—as the Tripartite Aggression against Egypt.

9: Jean and Simonne Lacouture give a vivid description of the events of 'Black Saturday'—Egypt in Transition (Methuen, 1958), pp108-109.

10: Khaled Mohi El Din, Memories of a Revolution: Egypt 1952 (American University in Cairo Press, 1995), p25.

11: See R P Mitchell, The Society of the Muslim Brothers (Oxford University Press, 1969), pp105-106, for a discussion of relations between Nasser and the Muslim Brotherhood and Mohi El Din, as above, for details of his relationship with the communists.

12: Gamal Abd-al-Nasser, Falsafat al-thawrah (Dar al-Sha'ab, no date, 9th edition), p22.

13: This picture of defeat provided a convenient justification for the Free Officers' continued hold on power, but the long hard struggle by Nasser to bring the trade unions, political parties and student unions under state control suggests that the movement was far from dead in July 1952.

14: M Pripstein Posusney, Labor and the State in Egypt: Workers, Unions and Economic Restructuring (Columbia University Press, 1997), p45.

15: For decades after 1956, the exact details of the agreement remained secret. At the time British officials denied that there had been any collusion at all. John Selwyn-Lloyd, British foreign secretary, told the House of Commons that there was 'no prior agreement' between the British and Israeli governments over the invasion of Egypt. It was not until 1996 that historian Avi Shlaim published the Israeli government's copy of the secret memorandum signed at Sèvres 40 years previously. See A Shlaim, 'The Protocol of Sèvres: Anatomy of a War Plot', International Affairs 73, 3 (1997), pp509-530.

16: A Shlaim, as above, p523.

17: K Love, Suez, the Twice-fought War (McGraw-Hill, 1969), p493.

18: M H Heikal, Cutting the Lion's Tail:

Suez through Egyptian Eyes (Corgi, 1988), p197.

19: J Waterbury, *The Egypt of Nasser and Sadat* (Princeton University Press, 1983), p312.

20: Heikal, as above, p194.

21: D Hashmat, 'Yusuf Darwish, muhami ummal', *Awraq Ishtirakiyya* (July/August 2004), pp24-25.

22: Layla al-Shal, telephone interview, Cairo/London, 31 March 2006.

23: Fathallah Mahrus, interview, Cairo, 25 March 2006.

24: As above.

25: A Shafiq, telephone interview, Cairo/London, 31 March 2006.

26: Fathallah Mahrus, interview, as above.

27: Abu-Sayf Yusuf, *Wath'iq wa-mawaqif min tarikh al-yasar al-misri 1941-1957* (Sharikat al-Amal, 2000), p357.

28: Telegram, British Embassy, Baghdad to Foreign Office, 1725 23 Dec 1956 FO371/121647.

29: As above.

30: As above.

31: As in Egypt, the movement in Iraq included a number of different political trends, from the communists to Arab nationalists to liberal democrats. Major organisations included the various clandestine communist factions, principally the Iraqi Communist Party (ICP), Arab nationalists organised in the Independence Party, the National Democratic Party led by Kamil al-Chadirchi who identified with the social democracy of the British Labour Party. In addition to the political parties, trade unions and student unions played an important role in mobilising the movement. See H Batatu, *The Old Social Classes and the Revolutionary Movements of Iraq* (Princeton University Press, 1978); K Chadirchi, *Muthakirrat Kamil al-Chadirchi wa tarikh al-hizb al-watani al-dimuqrati* (Cologne, 2002); M Mahdi Kubba, *Mudhakirati fi samim al-ahdath 1918-1958* (Beirut, 1965).

32: H Batatu, as above, pp749-757. Events in Najaf barely register in Foreign Office correspondence, probably because there was no British presence in the city.

33: FO 371 / 121647 British Consul-General, Basra to Embassy, Baghdad, 14 December 1956.

34: As above.

35 See J Waterbury, as above, pp61-82 and p209.

36: See S Heydemann, *Authoritarianism in Syria: Institutions and Social Conflict 1946-1970* (Cornell University Press, 1999).

37: D Hashmat, as above.

38: J Beinin and Z Lockman, *Workers on the Nile: Nationalism, Communism, Islam and the Egyptian Working Class, 1882—1954* (IB Tauris, 1988), p405.

39: See H Batatu, as above, p897.

40: The majority of the Egyptian Communist movement agreed to dissolve into the state-run Arab Socialist Union in 1965. In Iraq, the Communist Party joined the Ba'athist government in 1972, only to face a ferocious campaign of repression led by Saddam Hussein six years later. In 1972 the Syrian Communist Party also joined forces with the Ba'athists in the National Progressive Front.

41: The full text of Trotsky's work is available online at: www.marxists.org/archive/trotsky/works/1931-tpv/index.htm

42: Quoted in T Cliff, *Deflected Permanent Revolution* (1963), http://www.marxists.org/archive/cliff/works/1963/xx/permrev.htm

43: As Tony Cliff notes, Lenin changed his views after the revolution of February 1917. One crucial reason why the working class would be forced to push the revolution beyond the limits of bourgeois democracy, was (as Lenin realised in 1917) that in countries where the bourgeoisie was weak and cowardly, other, more reactionary forces were waiting in the wings to take power, as Kornilov's attempted seizure of power in September 1917 demonstrated. T Cliff, as above.

44: As an internal document of the Egyptian communist movement put it: 'The people's democracy we want to establish in Egypt is not a form of the dictatorship of the proletariat. We aim to establish a democratic dictatorship of all the classes struggling against imperialism and feudalism'—Archives of the Communist Party of Great Britain, National Museum of Labour History, Manchester, CP/CENT/INT/56/03—Note on Communist Policy for Egypt, nd.

45: The DMNL's paper Al-Malayin for 10 September 1952, days after the hangings, ran a lead article entitled ' The Road of the People and the Army—a National Front Against Imperialism and Traitors'—Communist Party Archives, CP/CENT/INT/56/04—Summary of Articles from Al-Malayin, 10 September 1952. Other Egyptian communist organisations did not follow this position, but as the largest group by far, the DMNL's influence played an important role in disorientating the whole movement.

46: Aziz al-Haj in *Sawt-al-Ahrar*, 23 November 1958, quoted in H Batatu, as above, p834.

47: L Trotsky, *Permanent Revolution*, http://www.marxists.org/archive/trotsky/works/1931-tpv/pr10.htm

48: T Cliff, as above

49: For a longer discussion of the role of the Iraqi Communist Party in the revolution of 1958 see A Alexander, 'Daring for Victory: Iraq in Revolution 1946-1959', *International Socialism* 99 (Summer 2003).

The New Left's renewal of Marxism

Paul Blackledge[1]

The birth of the New Left in 1956 marked an important turning point in post-war British history.[2] For the first time since the Second World War a political space opened within which socialists could hope to make headway building a movement independent of both Labourism and Stalinism. Moreover, in struggling for this space, the activists of the New Left made the first steps towards rearticulating a democratic vision of socialism from below to which we remain indebted today. All contemporary anti-capitalists who insist in the face of the collapse of the Soviet Union that 'another world is possible' owe a debt to the New Left's attempt to unpick the authentic socialist tradition from Stalinism. We are also indebted to their challenge to the narrow horizons of contemporary British society: the post-war economic boom had brought relative prosperity in its train, but it did not overcome alienation, and the New Left recognised this fact and aimed to overcome it.

Economic boom did, however, mean that the New Left emerged in a period when the British working class was less radical than it had been for generations. On the one hand, strong growth improved the bargaining power of workers and underpinned a high level of localised shop floor militancy, while, on the other hand, because these strikes were generally very short-lived, they tended not to foster advances in socialist consciousness within the working class: capitalists could afford year on year increases in pay out of increases in productivity, even if strikes were often necessary to push them in the right direction.[3] The resulting working class apathy and parochialism could hardly be less propitious for the rebirth of Marxism. Yet in 1956 a political crisis exploded which challenged the ideological orthodoxies of both sides in the Cold War. Against the inhumanity of both Stalinism and Western capitalism, the New Left embraced the idea of 'socialist humanism', and while the ambiguities of this idea meant that for some it acted as the medium through which they bade their farewells to Marxism,[4] at its most powerful it pointed beyond the morass of Stalinism towards Marx's humanist critique of capitalism.

Marxism before 1956

Before the rise of Stalinism, Marxism developed in close contact with the workers' movement: there was, as Perry Anderson has written, an 'organic unity of theory and practice'.[5] By contrast, Stalinism emerged as a contradictory attempt to represent the defeat of the workers' movement as its victory. Theory and practice were consequently split asunder, and Marxism in the hands of the Stalinists was reduced to a tool which justified the actions of the Soviet bureaucracy.

The success of the Russian Revolution of October 1917 was predicated on the success of similar revolutions across Europe. In July 1918 Lenin argued that 'we never harboured the illusion that the forces of the proletariat and the revolutionary people of one country, however heroic and however organised and disciplined they might be, could overthrow imperialism. That can be done only by the joint effort of the workers of the world'.[6] Unfortunately, while revolutionary upheavals did erupt outside Russia after 1917, these movements had, by the end of 1923, been defeated. In the wake of these defeats the Soviet Union became politically isolated, and the Soviet bureaucracy, which was already evolving as a distinct social layer during the civil war, became increasingly self-conscious. It was in this context that Stalin, in 1924, invented the concept of 'socialism in one country', through which the bureaucracy, as Trotsky argued, came to equate the victory of socialism with 'their own victory'.[7] The importance of this development is hard to overstate. Stalin was no mere dictator who imposed his vision of the future on an unwilling Russia. He was the embodiment of the bureaucracy's project of building a strong Russia in a world of imperialist states. And within a few years the Stalinists had recognised that a strong Russia could only be built on the backs of the workers and peasants who had made the revolution in 1917. While 1924 therefore marked an important watershed in Soviet politics, Michal Reiman has convincingly argued that the key turning point was the period from 1927-29. For it was at this point, after a period of developing structural crisis throughout the 1920s, that Stalinism took final shape as the Stalinists created a socio-political system that was 'diametrically opposed' to socialism.[8] In contrast to Lenin and Trotsky's strategy of fostering world revolution, from the late 1920s onwards Stalin sought to solve the problem of Russia's historical backwardness through a process of state-led industrialisation.[9]

Nevertheless, despite the counter-revolutionary nature of Stalinism, Stalin continued to deploy the—bastardised—language of Marxism to legitimise the Soviet State by reference to the October Revolution, whilst simultaneously robbing socialist opponents of the regime of the language of historical materialism. In so doing, Stalinism marked a fundamental transformation of Marxism. As Herbert Marcuse wrote, 'during the Revolution, it became apparent to what degree Lenin had succeeded in basing his strategy on the actual class interests and aspirations of the workers and peasants.' However, 'from 1923 on, the decisions of the leadership have been increasingly dissociated from the class interests of the proletariat'.[10] Soviet Marxism served not as a guide to working class action, but as a justification for the actions already taken by the Soviet ruling class.[11]

This approach led to all manner of ridiculous pronouncements. Perhaps the most famous of these was Stalin's attempt to square Marx's argument that socialism would be characterised by the withering away of the state with a justification of the growing repression of the Russian state:

> We stand for the withering away of the state. At the same time, we stand for the strengthening of the dictatorship of the proletariat, which is the mightiest and strongest state power that has ever existed... Is this contradictory? Yes, it is contradictory. But this contradiction is bound up with life, and it fully reflects Marx's dialectics.[12]

Nonsense like this led the historian Edward Thompson to suggest that Stalin had transformed Marx's historical and dialectical materialism into 'hysterical and diabolic' materialism. The great virtue of the dialectic, thus conceived, was that it could be used to justify just about any policy because nobody understood what it meant.

More generally, Stalin articulated a social theory that incoherently combined voluntarism with mechanical determinism. History was conceived as a mechanical story of the liberation of the forces of production from the fetters of increasingly regressive relations of production. Marx's revolutionary theory was subsequently reduced to a general evolutionary schema: 'the productive forces of society change and develop, and then, *depending* on these changes and *in conformity with them*, men's relations of production, their economic relations, change'.[13] Whereas Marx had understood the growing contradiction between forces and relations of production as the context within which struggles for freedom were fought out,[14] Stalin judged progress not by the growth of human freedom, but by the growth of the forces of production. This allowed him to equate the industrialisation of Russia with the liberation of the Russian people. He thus twisted Marx's critique of capital's tendency to accumulate for accumulation's sake into a justification of just that process in Russia.

While this model offered very little by way of a rationale for revolutionary practice, Stalin felt compelled to include an account of agency in his social theory if only to justify his own role in Russia. To his mechanical theory of historical evolution, he therefore added a model of bureaucratic activity. The ideology of 'Leninism',[15] invented by the Stalinists in the mid-1920s, served a useful purpose here. 'Theory', as embodied in the party and in practice in the pronouncements of Stalin, acted as the ghost in the machine guiding Russia to liberation. As Nigel Harris put it, as a social theory Stalinism contradictorily combined 'determinism for the masses, voluntarism for the leadership'.[16]

Of course, it mattered little to Stalin that his theory was analytically useless—the point was to justify the actions of the Soviet state not to explain them. Tragically, however, Stalin's domestic policies had disastrous consequences for the international Communist movement. What had been a grouping of revolutionary organisations in the early 1920s were slowly neutered from the mid-1920s through the imposition of, first, tight bureaucratic control from Moscow, then, an ultra-leftist line in the late 1920s, culminating in the mid-1930s in a renewed form of reformism. Following the lead from Moscow, the British Communist Party (CPGB), despite being home to many of the best militants of their generation, effectively ceased to be a revolutionary organisation long before the 1950s. However, a façade of revolutionary rhetoric continued to be used to cover what was essentially a reformist political practice for around two and a half decades before the publication of the party's new programme, *The British Road to Socialism*, in 1951.[17] Reputedly written by Stalin, the publication of this document marked an important turning point in Communist thinking— for the first time the CP made its shift away from revolutionary to reformist politics explicit. In part, this strategic shift was underpinned by an argument, originating in Moscow, but expressed in Britain by CP general secretary Harry Pollitt, that the transitions to 'Communism' in Eastern Europe after the war had proved the viability of reformism. They had shown that 'it is possible to see how the people will move towards socialism without further revolutions, without the dictatorship of the proletariat'.[18] Concretely, the CPGB argued that the Labour Party, once rid of its right wing leadership, could act as the agency for the socialist transformation of society through parliament.[19] Thus, the CPGB's 'Marxism' justified Stalinist rule in Russia whilst being politically reformist at home.

The most important figure to stand out in opposition to Stalinism in the 1930s was Leon Trotsky. In a series of brilliant books and articles he dissected Stalin's domestic and foreign policies and the disastrous strategies adopted by the Communist International. Unfortunately, because Stalinism was a product of the defeat of the workers' movement in Europe, and because Stalin's policies led to further defeats, then, as Trotsky himself argued, the grip of Stalinism over the left was reinforced by the very vices of Stalinism: defeats left socialists feeling isolated and more likely to look to Moscow as the one hope against Hitler. The flipside of this process was, of course, Trotsky's increasing political isolation. This objectively bad situation for the revolutionary left was made worse when a series of Trotsky's key political conjectures were refuted after the war.[20] Unfortunately, the dominant voices within international Trotskyism met this challenge by retreating into dogma. Trotsky had predicted that the war would culminate in a catastrophic economic crisis which would underpin revolutionary movements of workers who would cast aside Stalinism and social democracy. When the Stalinist and social democratic leaderships of the workers' movement in a number of European countries succeeded in stifling the post-war upsurge in struggle,[21] and when the world economy entered upon a period of intense growth, the leadership of the world Trotskyist movement responded by denying reality and vigorously reasserting what were obviously moribund perspectives.[22] Of course some revolutionaries did not follow this course of action, but they were few in number, scattered in small pockets across the globe, and more or less completely isolated from the workers' movement in the early 1950s.

In this context the Soviet regime held out an obvious appeal to Western socialists. In the 1930s Russia could appear for many as the last hope for socialism, and indeed for civilisation in the face of the growing threat of the militarised fascist regimes. Eric Hobsbawm justifiably writes that many of the best militants of his generation joined the Stalinist movement from this point onwards for precisely this reason.[23] John Saville explains that against the backdrop of the Labour Government's attacks on the unemployed in 1931 and in the wake of Hitler's victory in Germany in 1933 'it is not difficult to understand why young people in the mid-thirties chose the Communist Party rather than the Labour Party'. Moreover, even the debased form of Marxism taught in the Communist Movement created 'a growing sense of excitement at the widening intellectual horizons that Marxism offered'.[24] Similarly, in the 1950s the USSR could appear to many as the one hope against the domination of American imperialism. Nevertheless, it was through a rebellion against Stalinism that the best of those men and women who had been attracted to the Communist movement from the 1930s to the 1950s opened the door to a re-engagement with genuine revolutionary Marxism.

1956

If in the 1950s the Communist Party slavishly followed Moscow's line in the Cold War, the leadership of the Labour Party developed a similar relationship to Washington. In fact, the Labour leadership's right wing stance on foreign policy was just part of a consensus between it and the Tory government—labelled 'Butskellism' by the *Economist* in 1954 to highlight the continuity between the policies of the Labour and Tory chancellors Hugh Gaitskell and RAB Butler. To the extent that there existed an opposition to this consensus, its main focus was the Labour Left. However, this opposition was of a very limited kind. Led by Nye Bevan, when this layer rebelled against the leadership it tended to be over foreign and defence policies rather than on domestic issues. Moreover, once Gaitskell succeeded Attlee as Party leader in 1955, Bevan signalled an end to his opposition to the leadership. Bevan was soon to prove his reliability when, as Shadow Foreign Secretary in 1956, he described Nasser's nationalisation of the Suez canal as theft: 'If the sending of one's police and soldiers into the darkness of night to seize somebody else's property is nationalisation, then Ali Baba used the wrong terminology'.[25] If this act helped weaken the Labour left in the run up to the invasion of Suez, other processes were simultaneously creating the conditions for the emergence of a more radical left.

In 1956 four events occurred which helped create a political space to the left of the two faces of the Cold War. First, in February, the Soviet leader Nikita Khrushchev made the so-called Secret Speech[26] at the Twentieth Congress of the Soviet Communist Party within which he detailed some of the crimes committed by Stalin before his death in 1953. Fundamentally, Khrushchev shared with Stalin the aim of fostering economic growth in the Soviet Union so that it might catch up and overtake its Western competitors.[27] However, Stalin's methods, which, from the bureaucracy's point of view, had proved so successful in the 1930s and 1940s, were becoming increasingly inadequate to the continuing needs for economic growth. Russia had gone through a period of primitive capital accumulation, and now needed to switch from extensive to intensive methods of growth. Khrushchev set about liberalising the Soviet regime with a view to unleashing a new period of development. Nevertheless, because he first had to ensure his position against challenges from those groupings within the bureaucracy that wanted to keep to old ways, this extreme Stalinist became Stalin's most prominent critic.[28]

In authoritarian regimes, even small amounts of liberalisation can result in the crisis of the old way of ruling.[29] This is exactly what happened after Khrushchev's speech, when, first in Poland and then much more dramatically in Hungary divisions within the ruling class opened a space for the growth of a workers' movement from below to challenge the Stalinist regimes in both countries. This was the second key event of 1956. Over the summer and autumn of that year there occurred a rapid polarisation and radicalisation in Poland and Hungary culminating, in October and November, in the emergence of a revolutionary workers' movement in the latter country: for the first time since the 1920s workers' councils emerged as a possible alternative form of rule.[30]

All this might have confirmed the hopes of those on the left who believed that the Soviet Bloc would gradually self-reform into democratic socialist states. This illusion was dashed, however, by the third key event of that year. In November 1956 Soviet troops intervened to crush the

Hungarian Revolution. If this gross act of militarism had occurred in isolation, it might merely have weakened the far left in the West as members and supporters haemorrhaged away in disgust at the actions of this 'socialist' state. However, the Soviet intervention in Hungary was not the only act of imperialism that month. The very same weekend, British and French troops in cooperation with Israel invaded Egypt with a view of seizing the Suez Canal. That this act of gunboat diplomacy ended in fiasco did not prevent many in Britain from recognising the parallels between the imperialisms of the ruling classes on both sides of the Cold War.[31] In fact, Suez resulted in the 'largest single upsurge of political activity…in foreign affairs since the war'.[32] While the initial beneficiary of this movement was the Labour Party, which followed Washington in opposing the war, the Party's moderate anti-war slogan—'law not war'—did not reflect the anger of the anti-war demonstrators.[33] In fact, many Labour critics attacked the government, not on any principled anti-imperialist grounds, but because it 'endangered the American alliance and divided the country'.[34] The short-lived and emphatically moderate nature of the Party's opposition to the war, alongside Bevan's position within the leadership, ensured that those radicalised by their opposition to the invasion did not flock to their local Labour Party ward meeting. Unsurprisingly, Khrushchev's invasion of Hungary ensured that neither did this radicalised layer look to the Communist Party.

As a response to these events, a New Left emerged out of dissident groups within the Communist Party, alongside student radicals, left Labourites and members of the tiny revolutionary left.[35] While the New Left had neither fixed political positions, nor an agreed agenda, it did aim at making socialism a living force in Britain. New Leftists developed this message in a number of journals, including *Universities and Left Review* edited by students in Oxford and *The Reasoner/New Reasoner* edited by the historians and Communist activists Edward Thompson and John Saville in Yorkshire. Published initially as a dissident magazine within the Communist Party, and subsequently as an independent journal of socialist theory and practice after its editors refused the Party leadership's demand to stop publishing, *The Reasoner/New Reasoner* made its name as the foremost British voice of socialist humanism. Whereas Stalin had justified his rule by arguing that history was a mechanical process of economic progress, Thompson's socialist humanism placed real human beings at the centre of both the historical process and the struggle for socialism.

The Reasoner was originally published to discuss the reverberations of Khrushchev's speech within the Communist Party. Khrushchev had in fact made two speeches at the Twentieth Congress. In the first, open speech, he denounced 'the cult of the personality' without mentioning Stalin, while in a second, Secret Speech, he made explicit and detailed criticisms of Stalin.[36] While the exact content of the Secret Speech did not become public knowledge until June, everyone knew that criticism of the cult of the personality was a coded criticism of Stalin. The immediate response within the CPGB to this development was a 'stream of questioning letters' to the Party's paper the *Daily Worker*. While some of these were published, the Party leadership attempted to quash the debate as soon as possible: the paper's editor, J R Campbell declared the ensuing debate closed as early as 12th March.[37] However, the crisis within the Communist Party was far too deep for this act of censorship to succeed. Tellingly, a week after Campbell's declaration that the debate was over, John Saville wrote a letter to the Party's general secretary which was sharply critical of the Party's reluctance to be self-critical about the Stalin period.[38] And once the details of the Secret Speech were published nothing could stop the increasingly loud voices criticising the leadership from within the Party.

In July, Saville and Edward Thompson published the first issue of *The Reasoner*.[39] In the editorial of that issue, they wrote that 'We take our stand as Marxists…although…much that has gone on under the name of "Marxism" or "Marxism-Leninism" is itself in need of re-examination'. More specifically, they claimed that '*The Reasoner* is a journal which is, in the main, written by and addressed to members of the Communist Party'. Beyond this, they hoped that 'this journal will perform a practical service in loosening up the constricted forms within which discussion between Communists has taken place in recent years'.[40] This last point was of the first importance. The events of 1956 had proved, if more proof were needed, that that there was very little democratic content to the CPGB's supposed democratic centralism. The closing down of debate on the consequences of Khrushchev's denunciation of Stalin, while essential from the leadership's point of view, was frankly absurd: nothing was more important to the Party's programme than the nature of the Soviet Union, and members found they were unable to discuss the views on this issue of the supposed leader of the international Communist movement! Predictably, the Communist Party leadership attempted to suppress the debate as it was taken up in *The Reasoner*. Responding to this, Thompson and Saville broke party discipline by publishing a third issue of *The Reasoner* in November 1956, signalling their decision, alongside thousands of others, to leave the CP rather than submit to censorship from the party's centre.

Socialist humanism

Upon leaving the Communist Party, Thompson and Saville relaunched *The Reasoner* as *The New Reasoner*. The first issue of this new journal included Thompson's attempt to unpick Marx's humanism from Stalinism in his article 'Socialist Humanism: An Epistle to the Philistines'. This essay opened with the claim that 'a quarter of the earth's surface is a new society, with a new economic structure, new social relations, and new political institutions'.[41] However, despite the suppression of private property within these regimes, the persistence of oppression convinced Thompson of the falsity of the traditional Marxist view that all forms of oppression were rooted in economic exploitation. Against such 'economistic' models of historical materialism, Thompson sought to re-emphasise human agency at the heart of Marxism, and to reaffirm the importance of ideas as the basis for action. Accordingly, he explained the anti-Stalinist revolt of 1956 as a rebellion of the human spirit against the deadening grip of authoritarianism, while Stalinism itself had arisen out of the weaker elements of the Marxist canon. 'Stalinism did not develop just because certain economic and social conditions existed, but because these conditions provided a fertile climate within which false ideas took root, and these false ideas became in their turn part of the social conditions.' Those false ideas were rooted in the classical Marxist tradition which occasionally tended 'to derive all analysis of political manifestations directly and in an over-simplified manner from economic causations'.[42] This mistake linked Stalinism to Marxism, as, in their cruder moments, Marx and Engels understood revolutions as mechanical consequences of the clash between forces and relations of production, rather than as products of the actions of real men and women.

This weakness was most apparent when Marx and Engels deployed the base/ superstructure metaphor. Thompson insisted that this was a 'bad and dangerous model, since Stalin used it not as an image of men changing in society but as a mechanical model, operating semi-automatically and independently of human agency'.[43] This 'denial of the creative agency of human labour', when combined with working class 'anti-intellectualism' and 'moral nihilism', acted to rob Marxism of its human element and to freeze it into the dogma of Stalinism, which was itself 'embodied in institutional form in the rigid forms of democratic centralism'.[44] Thompson wrote that Stalinism was an ideology whose characteristic procedure was to start analyses from abstract ideas rather than from facts. Moreover, this ideology represented the world-view of a 'revolutionary elite which, within a particular historical context, degenerated into a bureaucracy'. The Stalinist bureaucracy had blocked the struggle for socialism, and consequently the revolt which underpinned the struggle for socialism had become a revolt against Stalinism. Negatively, this was a revolt against ideology and inhumanity. Positively, it involved a 'return to man', in the social sense understood by Marx. It was thus a socialist humanism: human, because it 'places once again real men and women at the centre of socialist theory and aspiration', socialist, because it 'reaffirms the revolutionary perspectives of Communism'.[45] Thompson therefore concluded that while Russia was in some sense a socialist state, its oppressive ideological and political superstructure had roots in Leninism.

The obvious problem with this form of anti-Stalinism was that it began from the Stalinist assumptions that, first, Lenin led to Stalin, and, second, that the East European regimes were in fact socialist states! The crushing of the Hungarian workers' councils by the Soviet military in November should have blown this second assumption sky high. However, while events in Hungary led to the *Reasoner* group, alongside thousands of others, leaving the party,[46] in his parting shot to the CPGB Thompson equivocated on this issue. He continued to believe that while the Stalinist States had degenerated, they remained in an important sense socialist. He thus bemoaned the fact that 'Communists' had 'fire[d] on Communists', and claimed that 'Stalinism is socialist theory and practice which has lost the ingredient of humanity'.[47] That Thompson believed this problem could be traced through Stalin and Lenin to the weaker elements of Marx and Engels' thought meant that his moral critique of Stalinism culminated in a call both for a more flexible interpretation of Marx's theory of history, and a rejection of the Leninist form of political organisation.

Thompson's humanist reading of Marx on the pages of *The New Reasoner* dovetailed with a similar re-evaluation of Marx published on the pages of *Universities and Left Review*. In 1958, Charles Taylor returned from Paris to Oxford with a French edition of Marx's 1844 *Economic and*

Philosophical Manuscripts.[48] The Marx who wrote these pages was very different to the mechanical fatalist known through Stalinism. In the 1844 manuscripts Marx brilliantly prefigured his later theoretical and political trajectory by positing socialism as the struggle of the working class against alienation, through a synthesis of what Lenin later termed the *Three Sources and Three Component Parts of Marxism*: German philosophy, English political economy and French socialism. What made these three elements susceptible to synthesis was the place of human labour, understood as purposeful social activity, at the heart of each. First, the political economists had, despite themselves, acted to reveal *alienated* human labour as the essence of value, while, second, the French socialists expressed the collective rebellion against the division of labour. Finally, Marx reinterpreted Hegel's discussion of the self-movement of spirit in terms of human practice.[49] In sharp contrast to the caricature of Marx presented by Stalin, Marx read the resulting conflict between tendencies towards working class association and the alienation arising out of the division of labour as the contradictory essence of capitalism; and through their humanist break with Stalinism, socialists involved in the New Left suggested a reappraisal of this revolutionary core of Marxism.

While Thompson's political optimism was framed through reference to the revolutionary workers in Hungary, the contributors to *Universities and Left Review* were more influenced by the apathy of the British working class. Stuart Hall, prefiguring much of what he was to write on the pages of *Marxism Today* in the 1980s,[50] argued that there had been a 'major shift in the patterns of social life' in Britain, such that those factors which shaped the formation of socialist class consciousness in the past were no longer dominant. By contrast with 19th century capitalism, changes in the economic structure of society meant that the worker in the 1950s 'knows himself much more as consumer than as producer'. Whereas in the 19th century there had been a workers' way of life as collective producer, this had recently been fragmented into so many competing lifestyles. Hall contended that it was these multifarious ways of life, which meant that while Britain remained a capitalist country, the working class had become entrapped in a 'new and more subtle forms of enslavement'.[51]

Hall's essay brought forth two powerful responses on the pages of the next issue of *Universities and Left Review*. Raphael Samuel argued that Hall had mythologised the conditions of the 19th century working class and so created a straw man against which he compared the situation of modern workers:

'the working class community was formed against pressures markedly similar to those upon which attention is focused today'.[52] If Samuel pointed out that Hall's misunderstanding of the past informed his mistaken analysis of the present, Edward Thompson powerfully argued that Hall's model of the present situation of workers was far too static. Prefiguring criticisms he would later lay at the feet of Raymond Williams, on whose work Hall drew, Thompson insisted that cultures were best understood not as static 'ways of life', but rather as an active 'ways of struggle'.[53]

From theory to practice[54]

Following from his model of life as struggle, Thompson consistently brought active political questions to the fore in his writings for the New Left. However, while he pushed for action, he was against the formation of a New Left organisation: his experience of work within the Communist Party convinced him of the folly of building a new socialist party.

> The New Left does not offer an alternative faction, party or leadership to those now holding the field…once launched on the course of factionalism, it would contribute, not to the re-unification of the socialist movement, but to its further fragmentation; it would contribute further to the alienation of the post-war generation from the movement; and the established bureaucracies cannot be effectively challenged by their own methods… The bureaucracy will hold the machine; but the New Left will hold the passes between it and the younger generation': in fact socialist intellectual work was not best 'accomplished by joining anything'.[55]

This perspective emerged out of the break with Communism made by those around *The Reasoner*. Given the hasty closure of debate on the repercussions of Khrushchev's speech on the pages of the *Daily Worker*, it seemed only natural that one of the key essays published in the first issue of *The Reasoner* addressed the issue of democratic centralism.[56] Penned by Ken Alexander, this essay expressed a peculiar limitation of the New Left's break with Stalinism. Alexander pointed to a contradiction within Communist strategy between Lenin's insistence that democratic centralist parties were necessary to smash the old capitalist state, and Moscow's claim, repeated by Communist Party general secretary Pollitt, that peaceful transitions to socialism had occurred in Eastern Europe and could occur in Britain.

Taking the Stalinists at their word, Alexander concluded that the party's militant reformism no longer implied the need for a Leninist party. Moreover, as Leninist parties had been the source of the Stalinist degeneration of the Russian Revolution, then dropping the democratic centralist structure could only be a good thing.[57]

While, Alexander's argument informed Thompson's rejection of Leninism,[58] the problem of political organisation could not so easily be evaded. Precisely because the New Left was much more than a theoretical tendency, its activity brought it into conflict with the Communist and Labour parties. If this tendency was most apparent when Lawrence Daly set up, with a degree of electoral success, the Fife Socialist League,[59] it was also true of the broader New Left's relationship to the Campaign for Nuclear Disarmament (CND). From 1958 onwards New Left activists threw themselves into activity around the newly formed CND,[60] whose marches saw thousands of dissatisfied youth come into conflict both with the government and the leaderships of the Labour and Communist parties.[61] If in CND the New Left gained a mass audience for their ideas, they also experienced the pull of reformism which was ultimately to break the New Left as a movement. Regretably, Thompson's socialist humanism was ill equipped to deal with this problem.

Thompson outlined the strategic consequences of his thought in his essay 'Revolution'. Leninists, he argued, had seriously misconstrued the nature of the coming revolution, and were consequently incapable of adequately preparing for it. He argued that the past century had been witness to a series of structural reforms that had been granted by capital to labour. These reforms were not the product of capital's philanthropic nature; rather they were a corollary of its instinct for self-preservation: capital retreated, inch by inch, before the pressure for reform that originated at the base of society. The weakness with reformism did not lie in the belief in the possibility of reform; these all too palpably existed, but rather in its misdiagnosis of their cause. Leninism, meanwhile, was incapable of reorienting to the changed situation. In particular, Leninists could not comprehend the implications of the enormous reforms that had been brought about through the war: for it was in the period from 1942 to 1948 that the most significant reforms had been won. These changes allowed Thompson, just like the Communist Party, to look forward to a 'peaceful revolution in Britain'.[62] In fact, Thompson suggested, radical change could be instituted relatively easily:

the Establishment appears to rest upon an equilibrium of forces so delicate that it is forced to respond to determined pressure…if we nationalise…if we tax…if we contract out of NATO… At each point the initiative might provoke repercussions which would necessitate a total transformation of relations of production, forms of power, alliances and trade agreements, and institutions: that is, a socialist revolution.[63]

If such a peaceful 'revolution' was possible, then what of the Labour Party, Britain's traditional vehicle of reformist socialist aspirations? Against Thompson's earlier rejection of the case for socialists joining any organisation, others prominent members of the New Left argued that as the Labour Party was 'still a mass movement of the British working class', and 'a battleground in which opposing trends are free to contend for leadership', socialists should join it.[64] These arguments seemed to be confirmed in 1960 when, in the wake of defeat in the 1959 general election, the Labour Party leadership was defeated by the left at the party's conference on the issues of Clause IV of the Party's constitution and over unilateral nuclear disarmament. Ralph Miliband, a New Left activist and the author of one of the most powerful critiques of Labourism, argued at the time that 'it is not inevitable that the Labour Party should continue towards the political graveyard'. He suggested that socialists might act to transform the party into a socialist organisation, 'before it was too late'.[65] Furthermore, in an argument first published in 1961, he claimed that 'the leadership whose purpose it is to reduce the Party's commitment to socialist politics can no longer rely on the trade unions to help it in achieving its aims'.[66] By 1960 Thompson appeared to have gravitated to a similar position. In fact, he suggested that the transformation of Labour into a socialist party was not only possible, but also that this potential was being realised as he wrote: 'Labour is ceasing to offer an alternative way of governing existing society, and is beginning to look for an alternative society'.[67] He argued that the New Left's role should be to encourage this process, while remaining aware that if his more optimistic perspective for the transformation of the Labour Party were frustrated 'then new organisations will have to be created'.[68] Consequently, in the late 1950s Thompson moved to accept both the viability and desirability of working to transform the Labour Party into an organisation capable of realising the transition to socialism.

The bulk of the New Left enthusiastically joined the fight to transform the Labour Party. Concretely, leading members of the New Left believed that a Labour government be the agency of both a 'positive neu-tralist' foreign policy,[69] and a socialist incomes policy. Raphael Samuel suggested that the New Left's 'most influential contribution to Labour Party thought'[70] was John Hughes and Ken Alexander in *A Socialist Wages Plan*, published under the imprint of both the *Universities and Left Review* and *The New Reasoner*. This pamphlet argued for the creation of 'an alliance of gov-ernment and trade unions' to redistribute incomes by taxation, to maintain stable prices, and to raise real wages and salaries.[71] Defending their arguments against criticism from Mike Kidron,[72] Alexander wrote that a suitably trans-formed Labour Party could wield 'government power…behind an egalitarian incomes policy if sufficient political pressure were built up to insist that it were'.[73] For his part, Thompson interpreted the alarm bells sounding in the national press as an indication that bourgeois society was becoming anxious of the developments within the Labour Party, develop-ments which should therefore excite and energise the New Left.[74]

At its heart this perspective greatly underestimated the power of the right wing of the Labour Party. In fact, once the right mobilised its forces at the 1961 party conference the left was easily defeated. This defeat might not have proved fatal for the New Left had it not believed so fervently up to that point in the possibility of transforming the Labour Party. Regrettably, this is exactly what it had done, and consequently it was dragged into the vortex of the Labour left's defeat.[75] The medium through which the right's victory was secured at the 1961 conference was the trade union bloc vote.[76] This came as a huge surprise to most of the New Left's leadership, who had come to believe that the trade union bureaucracy would no longer play its traditionally conservative role.[77] That it had played this role, and after two years of almost continuous advance for the left in the party, was hugely dis-appointing. Raymond Williams argued, 'the reversal of the vote on nuclear disarmament in 1961 came as an astounding blow. There was no idea of the strengths of the labour machine, or of the political skill with which the right was able to organise for victory within it'.[78]

Like the New Left, CND had gravitated towards a programme that aimed to win the Labour Party for unilateral nuclear disarmament, and because they too hoped for so much from this strategy they were also hugely disappointed by the defeat of the vote on unilateralism at the 1961 Labour Party conference. If this defeat effectively signalled the beginning of the end for both CND and the New Left, the Cuban Missile Crisis of October 1962 sealed their fates. Impotent before this global crisis, the very fact that war was averted 'was a blow to those who had based five years of their political life on the' belief that nuclear annihilation was imminent.[79] In these circumstances, the erstwhile activists of the New Left grasped at any sign, however meagre, of a revival in the fortunes of the left. While Thompson was initially enthusiastic about the revival of direct action against the Bomb, with Gaitskell's early death, and Harold Wilson's election to the leadership of the Labour Party in 1963, the reformist illusions which had previously opened the door to the New Left's unsuccessful strategy of transforming the Labour Party into the agency of socialist transformation, now led them to believe that even in defeat the left had been victorious. Wilson it seemed was going to lead the left to the Promised Land; and from that point onwards 'all hopes were now focused on Labour'.[80] Indeed, Perry Anderson, the new editor of *New Left Review*, wrote that Wilson had stepped into the fray just as the objective circumstances favoured the left as they had never done before. Therefore, he argued, Wilson 'may in the end represent a certain moment in the auto-emancipation of the working class movement in England'.[81]

A revolutionary alternative?

There is an unfortunate tendency on the part of many students of the British New Left to dismiss the role of Trotskyism within it. One reason for this attitude is the academic orientation of these authors, which, as Dorothy Thompson has powerfully argued, acts to emphasise the theoretical and philosophical dimensions of New Left activity at the expense of an analysis of its, primary, *political* nature.[82] By contrast with this standpoint, it is useful to remember that a number of key working class activists, alongside some equally impressive journalists and intellectuals, found their way into the Trotskyist movement after leaving the Communist Party in the wake of 1956.[83] Unfortunately, another reason for academic dismissals of Trotskyism during the New Left period is that the perspectives of the largest Trotskyist organisation, the Club/Socialist Labour League (SLL), were even more unrealistic than were Thompson's hopes for the Labour Party. Nevertheless, in the late 1950s and early 1960s the Club/SLL attempted to offer an alternative perspective for the left, and for a short period after 1956 it showed what might have been achieved had it been able to break from both its sectarianism and its catastrophic political perspectives.

The trump card played by the Trotskyists in 1956 was Trotsky's *The Revolution Betrayed*. First published in 1936, this book was a powerful Marxist demolition of the socialist pretensions of Stalinism, which ended with a call for a political revolution in Russia to overthrow the bureaucracy and remake democratic socialism.[84] For those who had first joined the Communist Party in the belief that it was a revolutionary organisation and then left when they discovered their mistake, the message of *The Revolution Betrayed* was, in Duncan Hallas's words, 'manna from heaven'.[85] Among those who were to gravitate towards Trotskyism at this juncture was Peter Fryer. Fryer was the *Daily Worker's* correspondent in Hungary when Russian tanks suppressed the revolution in November 1956. After two of the three reports he filed for the paper were not used, and the third 'severely cut', he resigned from the *Daily Worker* and was shortly afterwards expelled from the party.[86] Subsequently, Fryer joined Britain's main Trotskyist organisation, known as the Club, and in May 1957, he launched *The Newsletter* as an 'independent socialist weekly'. Over the next two years this publication gained a reputation as an excellent socialist newspaper. Indeed, *The Newsletter*, alongside the Club's more theoretical *Labour Review*, through a combination of socialist agitation, propaganda and intelligent debate, came to act as a serious Trotskyist pole of attraction to those ex-Communists who were breaking with Stalinism. Between 1957 and 1959, the socialists who produced and distributed these two publications managed to pull around them a significant grouping of revolutionaries, such that when they launched the SLL in May 1959 this new organisation represented what was a potentially significant breakthrough for the revolutionary left.

Unfortunately, the potential of the SLL was not to be realised. If the most important role for revolutionaries in 1956-57 was to explain to ex-Communists why Russia was not socialist, the Club was able to do this admirably. However, once this grouping moved from a negative critique of Stalinism to a positive presentation of their own perspectives, the limitations of orthodox Trotskyism became all too apparent.

The Club was the dominant local faction to emerge from the crisis of the international Trotskyist movement in the wake of the falsification of a number of Trotsky's key programmatic predictions during and after the war.[87] Led by Gerry Healy, the only way that it was able to maintain Trotsky's catastrophic political perspectives was by expelling all those who pointed to the simple fact that history had refuted the economic analysis upon which they were based. In the early 1950s this meant expelling those, such as Tony Cliff and Ted Grant, who challenged both these perspectives and Healy's leadership.[88] By 1956, the details of these old struggles seemed ancient history, and the Club, as the largest Trotskyist grouping in the country, was able to draw on Trotsky's undoubted moral authority as a critic of Stalinism to attract to it many of the best activists who had recently left the CPGB. However, the undemocratic structure of the Club/SLL ensured that even after the influx of new recruits in the wake of 1956 anyone who challenged Healy's catastrophic perspectives was impotent to do anything about it. Consequently, while by 1959 the SLL had seemed to offer the promise of the creation of a viable anti-Stalinist British Marxist party,[89] within a year Healy had managed to expel or hound out of the organisation just about anyone independent enough to question his absurd perspectives. Indeed, by the autumn of 1959 he had even managed to take Fryer's place as editor of *The Newsletter*.[90] Healy's undemocratic tactics and unrealistic perspectives therefore made it easy for those like Thompson who rejected the project of building a new socialist party to dismiss Trotskyism as a type of anti-Stalinism in the sense that there once existed anti-Popes: the same but different, and with a much smaller congregation.[91]

Similarly, a number of those who had briefly gravitated towards the SLL in the late 1950s reacted to the absurdities of Healy's posturing by rejecting any attempt to unpick Lenin's ideas from the ideology of Leninism. This essentially was the starting point of the grouping around the magazine *Solidarity*, who, under the influence of the French journal *Socialisme ou Barbarie*, embraced the idea that socialism would emerge, more or less spontaneously, from the struggles of the working class at the point of production. While the positive side of the democratic thrust of this reaction to orthodox Trotskyism cannot be denied, like the SLL, *Solidarity* tended to greatly underestimate the barriers to the growth of socialist ideas within the working class. For instance, in 1961 *Solidarity*'s leading figure, Chris Pallis, argued that workers' struggles opened not the *possibility* but the *certainty* of the growth of socialist consciousness within the working class: 'people in struggle *do* draw conclusions which are fundamentally socialist in content' (emphasis in original).[92] Unfortunately, arguments such as this, by downplaying the difficulties involved in socialist activity, fostered a tendency towards the substitution of radical slogans for the long hard work of extending the influence of socialist ideas within the working class. Indeed, it is probably fair to say that, despite their formal differences, *Solidarity* shared with the SLL a weak model of socialist activity: if Healy one-sidedly stressed socialist leadership at the expense of the spontaneous movement from below, *Solidarity* tended to invert rather than to correct this mistake.

This was unfortunate, for what undermined the SLL, beyond Healy's famously authoritarian personality, was not the fact that through it socialists attempted to build their own organisation, but rather that it adhered to a set of catastrophic political perspectives.[93] Understood thus, the SLL had more in common with both Thompson's dominant form of New Leftism and *Solidarity*'s extreme left alternative than either would have liked to admit. They were all hamstrung by unjustifiably optimistic perspectives: the SLL and *Solidarity* for revolution; Thompson for radical reform of the Labour Party and then the British state. What none of these perspective was able to offer was a compelling answer to the rational core of Hall's dismissal of the revolutionary potential of the British working class.

Out of the impasse

In his contribution to *The New Reasoner* debate on socialist humanism, Alasdair MacIntyre formulated a deeper break with Stalinism than that imagined by Thompson, which simultaneously pointed beyond Thompson's domestic political perspectives without collapsing into the dogmatism of orthodox Trotskyism. In 'Notes from the Moral Wilderness', MacIntyre argued that what Marx suggested when he deployed the base/superstructure metaphor was neither a mechanical nor a causal relationship. Rather, he deployed Hegelian concepts to denote the process whereby society's economic base provides 'a framework within which superstructures arise, a set of relations around which the human relations can entwine themselves, a kernel of human relationships from which all else grows'. Indeed, MacIntyre wrote that in 'creating the basis, you create the superstructure. These are not two activities but one'. Thus, the Stalinist model of historical progress, according to which political developments were understood to follow automatically from economic causes, could not be further from Marx's model. For, in Marx's view, 'the crucial character of the transition to socialism is not that it is a change in the economic base but that it is a revolutionary change in the relation of base to superstructure'.[94] If, through this model, MacIntyre criticised the Stalinist attempt to evacuate Marxism of its revolutionary core, he also pointed to weaknesses with

Thompson's anti-Stalinism. Whereas Thompson accepted that Stalinist Russia was characterised by an oppressive political superstructure atop a socialist economy, MacIntyre argued that the Soviet Union was reactionary from top to toe: he insisted Marx's model of socialism as working class self-emancipation 'marks a decisive opposition to Fabianism and all other doctrines of "socialism from above"'.[95] MacIntyre's rejection of the idea that Russia as a socialist or a workers' state, in turn provided a basis from which one might criticise Thompson's militant reformist hopes for Labour Party. For, if the East European states were not socialist, then the Communist Party's assumptions about the possibility of a Marxist justification for a reformist strategy for socialism which had found their way into the New Left thinking were undermined. This, in turn, led MacIntyre to begin to rethink Lenin's legacy, and to unpick his model of democratic leadership from the ideology of Leninism.[96]

MacIntyre's revolutionary articulation of socialist humanism drew him into the orbit of, first, the SLL, from whence, in 1960, he joined the International Socialism group: the forerunner of the Socialist Workers' Party. According to Thompson, *International Socialism* was 'the most constructive journal with a Trotskyist tendency in this country, most of the editorial board of which are active (and very welcome) members of the Left Club movement'.[97] In a generally unsympathetic survey of the politics of IS, Martin Shaw argued that at this juncture it 'came to represent the polar opposite to the SLL: realistic in economic perspectives, able to explain the failures of labour bureaucrats as well as to condemn them, non-sectarian towards other socialists, the champion of thorough working class democracy in all areas of practice'.[98] This perspective was, as Shaw suggests, informed by the break made with orthodox Trotskyism by IS's main theoretician, Tony Cliff.

Whereas Trotsky had characterised the Soviet Union as a 'degenerate workers' state', and his 'orthodox' followers had generalised this model to account for the essentially similar regimes created in Eastern Europe and China after the war—'deformed workers' states', Cliff insisted that it was nonsense to suggest that a workers' state could be created without a workers' revolution. Moreover, as these states were locked into a process of military competition with the West, and as the producers within these states remained wage labourers, the East European states could best be classified as bureaucratic state capitalist social formations.[99] According to Cliff, beyond its specific effects in Russia, military competition between the East and

West had created a global 'permanent arms economy'[100] which under-pinned the post-war boom, and consequently gave reformism a new lease of life.[101] Nevertheless, Cliff was insistent that a contradiction existed between workers' self-activity at the point of production and the ideology of reformism:

> Every struggle of the working class, however limited it may be, by increasing its self-confidence and education, undermines reformism. 'In every strike one sees the hydra head of the Revolution'. The main task of real, consistent Socialists is to unite and generalise the lessons drawn from the day to day struggles. Thus can it fight reformism.[102]

Thus, as opposed to the SLL, Cliff's model of socialist activity was founded upon a model of the spontaneous movement from below, while, as opposed to *Solidarity*, it recognised the limitations of the movement from below and the important role to be played by socialist activists in the growth of working class class consciousness.[103]

According to Alex Callinicos, Cliff's theory of bureaucratic state capitalism afforded his Marxism a number of advantages over orthodox Trotskyism. First, in characterising the Soviet social formation's capitalism through its military competition with the West, Cliff was able to lay the basis for a powerful theory of the post-war boom. Second, this model of post-war capitalism in turn suggested a modification of the classical Marxist theory of imperialism, which immunised his followers from the worst excesses of 'Third Worldism'; the belief that that Western workers had somehow been bought off, and that central locus of the struggle against capitalism had shifted from the point of production to the national libera-tion movements in the South. Third, Cliff's model of the post-war boom informed his analysis of the changing locus of Western reformism: parlia-mentary parties of the left were becoming increasingly irrelevant as the most visible improvements in workers' standards of living were won not through the ballot box but through their self-activity at the point of pro-duction: 'reformism from below' was undercutting reformism from above.[104] Indeed, this perspective allowed the International Socialism group to explain the apathy noted by Hall without dropping their revolutionary politics. While the arms economy had temporarily stabilised capitalism by underpinning the post-war boom, this boom was beset by contradictions, and therefore apathy would be challenged as these contradictions were played out. This standpoint laid the basis for IS's long-term orientation towards the working class, without entailing that it share either the SLL's or *Solidarity*'s simplistic models revolutionary politics.

Conclusion

When, in 1960, *The New Reasoner* and *Universities and Left Review* merged to form *New Left Review*, Thompson envisaged that the new journal would act as a 'point of juncture' between various radical struggles, highlighting their 'inter-connections'. It was thus aimed at facilitating the growth of a general socialist consciousness out of the multiplicity of anti-capitalist struggles.[105] Unfortunately, as the political upturn associated with the birth of the New Left and CND subsided, this perspective was increasingly undermined. At this juncture it became essential that the New Left explain the objective barriers to socialist activism if they were to hope to regroup their forces and orientate towards the long-haul. Unfortunately, neither Thompson nor any of the other leading members of the New Left were able to offer an adequate explanation for their defeat.

In this context the New Left collapsed, and in 1962 a new editorial team transformed *New Left Review* from an activist magazine into an austere theoretical journal which aimed, in part, to make sense of the decline of the first New Left. Unfortunately, in distancing itself from the weaknesses of the first New Left, this second New Left around Perry Anderson came to embrace a more theoretically coherent version of Hall's political pessimism.[106] If it is not too far fetched to claim that the new *New Left Review* therefore continued the *Universities and Left Review* tradition, in 1964 John Saville and Ralph Miliband launched *The Socialist Register* with a view to rekindling something along the lines of *The New Reasoner* tradition.[107] However, without a clear understanding of the failings of the first New Left, and without something like the New Left movement to nourish it, this journal too lost the activist focus that had so enriched *The New Reasoner*.

The British left had to wait until the period after 1968 when an upturn in political and industrial struggles created a space for a third New Left. Unfortunately, Thompson distanced himself from the radicalism of 1968,[108] and it was left primarily to the International Socialism grouping to begin to realise the hopes of 1956: of building a socialist current independent of both Labourism and Stalinism.[109] In 1970 Saville commented that a new socialist party was needed, and that International Socialism might possibly become such an organisation if it moved from being 'a fairly open sect to something approaching a small party'.[110] While International Socialism was able to make this move by explaining the apathy noted by Hall and going beyond both the SLL's and *Solidarity*'s caricatures of revolutionary politics and *The New Reasoner*'s interpretation of socialist humanism,[111] it is also true that it was indebted to the New Left for creating a political space within which an independent left could begin to gain a hearing.[112]

NOTES

1: Thanks to Kristyn Gorton, Chris Harman, John Molyneux and Mark Thomas for comments on a draft of this essay. For anyone interested in reading more of the New Left's original literature, complete collections of *The New Reasoner* and *Universities and Left Review* can be found online at http://www.amielandmelburn.org.uk/archive_index.htm. The Amiel and Melburn trust is to be congratulated for making the content of these magazines widely available.

2: The emergence of 'New Lefts' was an international phenomenon after 1956. Considerations of space mean that I can only deal with the British variant.

3: T Cliff & D Gluckstein, *The Labour Party: A Marxist History* (London, 1996), p257. This situation would only contradict the textbook parody of Marxism as a form of mechanical materialism. By contrast Engels pointed out that socialist class consciousness does not mechanically rise and fall with the ebb and flow of industrial militancy; the class struggle operates at a number of different levels—the theoretical, political and economic—and each of these levels retains a degree of autonomy from the others. F Engels, 'Supplement to the Preface of 1870 for The Peasant War in Germany' in K Marx & F Engels, *Collected Works* vol 23 (Moscow, 1988), p631.

4: It is a weakness of much of the academic literature on the New Left that this aspect of its politics is stressed almost to the exclusion of any other of its strands. See, for instance, L Chun, *The British New Left* (Edinburgh, 1993), p191; M Kenny, *The First New Left* (London, 1995), pp200-206; G Foote, *The Labour Party's Political Thought* (London, 1997), p296. Interestingly, in their eagerness to portray the New Left as a way out of Marxism, all of these studies downplay Alasdair MacIntyre's important contribution to the New Left debate on socialist humanism. In his most recent discussion of the subject, Foote has gone some way to remedy this gap in his earlier argument, but while he comments on MacIntyre's early Marxism, he does so merely to dismiss it (G Foote, *The Republican Transformation of Modern British Politics* (London, 2006), p45).

5: P Anderson, *Considerations on Western Marxism* (London, 1976), p29.

6: D Hallas, *The Comintern* (London, 1985), p7.

7: L Trotsky, *The Revolution Betrayed* (New York, 1972), p32.

8: M Reiman, *The Birth of Stalinism* (London, 1987), pp119; 122.

9: M Haynes, *Nikolai Bukharin and the Transition from Capitalism to Socialism* (London, 1985), p110.

10: H Marcuse, *Soviet Marxism* (London, 1958), p124

11: As above, pp17; 128; N Harris, *Beliefs in Society* (London, 1968), p152.

12: Stalin quoted in N Harris, as above, p162.

13: J Stalin, *Dialectical and Historical Materialism* (1938) available at http://www.marxists.org/reference/archive/stalin/works/1938/09.htm

14: P Blackledge, *Reflections on the Marxist Theory of History* (Manchester, 2006), ch 2.

15: For my comments on this see P Blackledge, 'What Was Done: Lenin Rediscovered', in *International Socialism* 111 (Summer 2006).

16: N Harris, as above, p156; H Marcuse, as above, p121.

17: CPGB, *The British Road to Socialism* (London, 1952). On the Comintern's break with revolutionary politics see D Hallas, *The Comintern*, pp106; 126; 141.

18: Harry Pollitt quoted in J Callaghan, *The Far Left in British Politics* (Oxford, 1987), p163.

19: J Gollan, *Which Way for Socialists?* (London, 1958).

20: A Callinicos, *Trotskyism* (Buckingham, 1990), pp23-29.

21: I Birchall, *Workers Against the Monolith* (London, 1974), pp37-8; I Birchall, *Bailing out the System* (London, 1986), p35.

22: D Hallas, 'Building the Leadership' *International Socialism* 1: 40, (October/November 1969).

23: E Hobsbawm, *Interesting Times* (London, 2002), p127.

24: J Saville, *Memoirs from the Left* (London, 2003), pp8-9; E Hobsbawm, *Interesting Times*, pp127-151.

25: T Cliff & D Gluckstein, as above, pp261-270. The quotation is taken from p268.

26: N Khrushchev, 'The Secret Speech' at http://www.fordham.edu/halsall/mod/1956khrushchev-secret1.html

27: H Marcuse, *Soviet Marxism*, p140.

28: T Cliff, *Russia: A Marxist Analysis* (London, 1964), pp195-204.

29: A Callinicos, *The Revenge of History* (Cambridge, 1991), pp49-50.

30: G Eley, *Forging Democracy: The History of the Left in Europe, 1850-2000* (Oxford, 2002), p334. On the workers' councils see A Anderson, *Hungary '56* (London, 1964), pp66-72, B Lomax 'The Workers Councils of Greater Budapest' *The Socialist Register 1976*, and C L R James, 'Letter 10th February 1957' in A Grimshaw (ed), *The C L R James Reader* (Oxford, 1992), p265. The best first-hand account of the Hungarian Revolution remains Pete Fryer's *Hungarian Tragedy* (London, 1997). For a more analytical discussion see C Harman, *Class Struggles in Eastern Europe 1945-83* (London, 1988), pp119-186.

31: On Suez see J Newsinger, *The Blood Never Dried: A People's History of the British Empire* (London, 2006), pp164-181

32: N Harris, et al, 'Labour and the Bomb' *International Socialism* 1: 10, (Autumn 1962), p24.

33: J Hinton, *Protests and Visions* (London, 1989), p155.

34: P Worsley, 'Imperial Retreat' in E P Thompson, (ed), *Out of Apathy* (London, 1960), p135.

35: Peter Sedgwick famously described the New Left as a 'milieu'. P Sedgwick, 'The Two New Lefts' in D Widgery (ed), *The Left in Britain: 1956-1968* (London, 1976), p143. This classic analysis of the New Left by one of its most prominent participants was originally published in *International Socialism* 1: 17, (Summer 1964).

36: I Birchall, *Workers Against the Monolith*, p84.

37: W Thompson, *The Good Old Cause* (London, 1992), p 100.

38: J Saville, 'Edward Thompson, the Communist Party, and 1956', *The Socialist*

Register 1994 (London, 1994), p22.

39: The prominent part played in the formation of the New Left by members of the Communist Party Historians' Group has been widely noted. For instance, see B Schwarz, '"The People" in History: The Communist Party Historians' Group, 1946-1956', in R Johnson et al (eds), *Making Histories* (Minneapolis, 1982), p84.

40: J Saville & E P Thompson, 'Editorial' *The Reasoner* 1, (July 1956), pp1-3.

41: E P Thompson, 'Socialist Humanism', *The New Reasoner* 1 (Summer 1957), pp105.

42: As above, p108.

43: As above, p113.

44: As above, pp132, 121.

45: As above, pp109.

46: 'Between February 1956 and February 1958 membership slumped from 33,095 to 24,670'. I Birchall, 'The Terminal Crisis of the British Communist Party', *International Socialism* 2: 30, (Winter 1985), p75.

47: E P Thompson, 'Through the Smoke of Budapest', *The Reasoner* 3, (November 1956), reprinted in D Widgery (ed), *The Left in Britain*, pp72; 69.

48: L Chun, *The British New Left*, p34; M Kenny, *The First New Left*, p58. It is often thought that Taylor was the first to introduce the arguments of Marx's 1844 manuscripts to an English speaking audience. This is a mistake. Alasdair MacIntyre referred to the German Edition *National Ökonomie und Philosophie* in his *Marxism: An Interpretation* (London, 1953), a text which formed the core of his *Marxism and Christianity* (London, 1968).

49: This point is spelt out by Chris Arthur in his *The Dialectics of Labour* (Oxford, 1986).

50: C Sparks, 'Stuart Hall, Cultural Studies and Marxism' in D Morley & K Chen (eds), *Stuart Hall: Critical Dialogues in Cultural Studies* (London, 1996), p78.

51: S Hall, 'A Sense of Classlessness', *Universities and Left Review* 5, (Autumn 1958).

52: R Samuel, 'Class and Classlessness', *Universities and Left Review* 6, (Spring 1959), p44.

53: E P Thompson 'Commitment in Politics', *Universities and Left Review* 6 (Spring 1959), p52; See also E P Thompson, 'The Long Revolution', *New Left Review* 1: 9, (1961), p33. For Hall's response, see his 'The Big Swipe', *Universities and Left Review* 7, (Autumn 1959).

54: This section draws on my article 'Reform, Revolution and the Question of Organisation in the First New Left' *Contemporary Politics* vol 10, no 1 (March 2004).

55: E P Thompson, 'The New Left', *The New Reasoner* 9, pp15-7 (Summer 1959); 'Socialism and the Intellectuals', *Universities and Left Review* 1, p34 (Spring 1957).

56: W Thompson, *The Good Old Cause*, p102.

57: K Alexander, 'Democratic Centralism' *The Reasoner* 1, (July 1956), p9.

58: For the influence of this essay on Thompson, see his 'Socialist Humanism', p136.

59: I have discussed the New Left's relationship to Daly's candidature in 'Reform, Revolution and the Question of Organisation in the First New Left', pp26ff.

60: P Duff, *Left, Left, Left* (London, 1971), p128.

61: Both Labour and Communist parties initially opposed CND's demand for unilateral nuclear disarmament. W Thompson, *The Long Death of British Labourism* (London, 1992), p116, and W Thompson, *The Good Old Cause*, p64.

62: E P Thompson, 'Revolution' in

Thompson (ed), *Out of Apathy*, p302. Perry Anderson rightly pointed out that Thompson's politics at this juncture, and thereafter, had much in common with the perspectives he learnt in the Communist Party. P Anderson, *Arguments within English Marxism* (London, 1980), pp145-146; 191.

63: E P Thompson, 'At the Point of Decay' in Thompson (ed), *Out of Apathy*, pp8-10.

64: R Hilton, 'Socialism and the Intellectuals—Four', *Universities and Left Review* 2 (Summer 1957), p20; M Jones, 'Socialism and the Intellectuals—One', *Universities and Left Review* 2 (Summer 1957), p16.

65: R Miliband, 'The Sickness of Labourism', *New Left Review* 1: 1 (1960), p8; M Newman, *Ralph Miliband and the Politics of the New Left* (London, 2002), p76.

66: R Miliband, *Parliamentary Socialism* (London, 1972), p346.

67: E P Thompson, 'Revolution Again' *New Left Review* 1: 6 (1960), p19.

68: As above, p29.

69: I have discussed the bizarrely utopian positive neutralist strategy in 'Reform, Revolution and the Question of Organisation in the First New Left', p29. See also P Sedgwick, 'NATO, the Bomb and Socialism', *Universities and Left Review* 7 (Autumn 1959).

70: R Samuel, 'Born-Again Socialism' in R Archer, et al (eds), *Out of Apathy* (London, 1989), p49.

71: J Hughes and K Alexander, *A Socialist Wages Plan* (London, 1958), p7.

72: In a debate first published in Socialist Review (the precursor of International Socialism) in 1959, Kidron argued that nowhere did Alexander and Hughes 'so much as suggest that a future Labour government would be any different to its predecessors' (M Kidron, 'The Limits of Reform' in *The New Reasoner* 10,

(Autumn 1959), p81). More substantially, Kidron challenged the terms of Alexander and Hughes' argument. He noted the close ties that existed between the British state and private industry, and insisted that, as capital would prevent the state from overturning the rule of the profit motive, these links negated the reformist perspective. He concluded that Alexander and Hughes' perspective was utopian: they 'attempt to substitute a concept—the state—disembowelled of any reality, abstracted from society, for a social force as the agent of reform' (p86). Answering Alexander's claim that Kidron believed that reforms were impossible under capitalism (J Hughes & K Alexander, 'Reply to Critics' in *The New Reasoner* 10 (Autumn 1959), p103), Kidron replied that as 'reforms are palpably with us' his aim was not to deny their reality, but rather to ask whether they were best won by revolutionary or reformist means (M Kidron, 'A Note on the Limitations of Reforming 'Realism'' in J Higgins (ed), *A Socialist Review* (London, 1965), p106).

73: K Alexander, 'Socialist Wages Plan' in Higgins (ed), *A Socialist Review*, p91; J Hughes & K Alexander, 'Kidron and the Limits of Revolution' in Higgins (ed), as above, p103.

74: Thompson, 'Revolution Again', p19.

75: P Anderson, *Arguments Within English Marxism*, p136.

76: P Anderson, 'The Left in the Fifties', *New Left Review* 1:29 (1965), p16.

77: J Rex, 'The Labour Bureaucracy', *The New Reasoner* 6, (Autumn 1958).

78: R Williams, *Politics and Letters* (London, 1979), p365.

79: R Bulkeley, et al, 'Fighting Against the Bomb in the 1950s and 1960s' *International Socialism* 2: 11 (Spring 1981), p9; J Hinton, *Protests and Visions* (London, 1989), p178.

80: R Fraser, *1968: A Student Generation in Revolt* (London, 1988), p61. Dorothy Thompson, speaking at The British Marxist Historians and the New Social Movements conference at Edge Hill College in June 2002, recounted the story of the night that she, Edward Thompson, Robin Blackburn and Perry Anderson euphorically celebrated Wilson's victory in the 1963 Labour Party leadership election.

81: P Anderson, 'Critique of Wilsonism' *New Left Review* I: 27, 1964, p22.

82: D Thompson, 'On the Trail of the New Left', *New Left Review* I:215 (1996), pp94-5.

83: J Callaghan, *British Trotskyism* (Oxford, 1984), p72. Names included Peter Fryer, Cliff Slaughter, Peter Worsley, Brian Pearce, Ken Coates, Peter Cadogan, Chris Pallis (aka Maurice Brinton), Bob Pennington, and Alasdair MacIntyre. Of particular importance was the building worker and ex-CP industrial organiser and executive member Brian Behan, who Alasdair MacIntyre later described as the 'best man who was a revolutionary socialist in Britain in the last 25 years'.

84: L Trotsky, *The Revolution Betrayed*, p288.

85: D Hallas, 'Building the Leadership', p30.

86: P Fryer, *Hungarian Tragedy*, pp1-3.

87: A Callinicos, *Trotskyism*, pp23-38.

88: S Bornstein and A Richardson, *War and the International* (London, 1986), p231.

89: D Hallas, 'Building the Leadership', p31.

90: D Widgery, 'The Double Exposure: Suez and Hungary' in Widgery (ed), *The Left in Britain*, p63.

91: E P Thompson, 'Socialist Humanism', pp139.

92: M Brinton [C Pallis], 'Revolutionary Organisation' in M Brinton, *For Workers' Power* (London, 2004), p46. This essay was first published in *Solidarity* 1, 6 (May 1961). For the politics of *Socialisme ou Barbarie* see C Castoriadis, *Political and Social Writings* I & II (Minneapolis, 1988).

93: D Hallas, 'Building the Leadership', p31.

94: A MacIntyre, [1958-1959] 'Notes from the Moral Wilderness' in K Knight (ed), *The MacIntyre Reader* (Cambridge, 1998), p39. This essay was originally published in two parts in *New Reasoner* 7 (Winter 1958-9) and *New Reasoner* 8 (Spring 1959). For more on MacIntyre's early Marxism see my 'Freedom, Desire and Revolution: Alasdair MacIntyre's Early Marxist Ethics', *History of Political Thought* vol XXVI, no 4 (2005).

95: E P Thompson, 'Agency and Choice' *The New Reasoner* 5 (Summer 1958), p93; A MacIntyre, 'Marx' in M Cranston (ed), *Western Political Philosophers* (London, 1964), p106.

96: A MacIntyre, 'Freedom and Revolution', *Labour Review* (February/March 1960).

97: E P Thompson, 'Revolution Again', p22.

98: M Shaw, 'The Making of a Party?', *The Socialist Register 1978*, p104. Shaw's essay was written as a critique of Ian Birchall's 'History of the International Socialists' *International Socialism* 1:76 & 1:77, (March/April 1975). Birchall responded to Shaw's criticisms in his 'A Premature Burial: A Reply to Martin Shaw', *The Socialist Register 1979*.

99: T Cliff, 'The Nature of Stalinist Russia' in T Cliff, *Marxist Theory After Trotsky* (London, 2003 [1948]). Cliff's arguments built upon those of N Bukharin as presented in his *Imperialism and World Economy* (London, 2003). On the relationship between Bukharin's and Cliff's theories see P Binns, 'Understanding the New Cold War', *International Socialism* 2: 19 (Spring 1983), pp22-27.

100: T Cliff, 'Perspectives for a Permanent War Economy' in Cliff, *Marxist Theory After Trotsky*. This essay was originally published in *Socialist Review* (May 1957). See also M Kidron, 'Reform or Revolution' *International Socialism* 1:7, (Winter 1961); *Western Capitalism Since the War* (London, 1968); *Capitalism and Theory* (London, 1974). Cliff's essay was but one published in *Socialist Review* in the 1950s developing this argument. See also the essays by Mike Kidron and Seymour Papert (latterly professor of artificial intelligence at MIT) collected in Higgins, (ed), *A Socialist Review*.

101: T Cliff, 'Economic Roots of Reformism' in Cliff, *Marxist Theory After Trotsky*. Originally published in *Socialist Review* (June 1957).

102: As above, p185.

103: See T Cliff, *Rosa Luxemburg* (London, 1959), and his 'Trotsky on Substitution', *International Socialism* 1: 2 (Autumn 1960). Both of these essays are reprinted in T Cliff, *International Struggle and the Marxist Tradition* (London, 2001).

104: A Callinicos, *Trotskyism*, pp79-85.

105: E P Thompson, 'The Point of Production', *New Left Review* I:1, 1960, pp68-70.

106: P Blackledge, *Perry Anderson, Marxism and the New Left* (London, 2004), pp12-18.

107: E Meiksins Wood, 'A Chronology of the New Left and Its Successors, Or: Who's Old-Fashioned Now?', *The Socialist Register 1995*.

108: E P Thompson, *The Poverty of Theory* (London, 1978), pp309ff. Tragically, MacIntyre had broken with revolutionary Marxism by this point and elaborated a similarly elitist critique of the movement that erupted in 1968: A MacIntyre, *Marcuse* (London, 1970), pp61; 89.

109: C Harman, 1968: *The Fire Last Time* (London, 1998), pp257-261.

110: J Saville, 'Prospects for the Seventies' *The Socialist Register 1970*, pp212.

111: For my thoughts on why neither Saville nor Miliband were able to make this shift see, on Miliband, P Blackledge, 'On Moving On from "Moving On": Miliband, Marxism and Politics' in C Barrow, P Burnham & P Wetherly (eds), *Reflections on Ralph Miliband's Contribution to State Theory* (London, 2007); and on Saville, P Blackledge, 'A Life on the Left' *International Socialism* 2:105, (Winter 2005).

112: See R Bulkeley et al 'Fighting Against the Bomb in the 1950s and 1960s', pp25-28.

1956: time line

January New government formed in France by Socialist Party leader Guy Mollet to crush FLN liberation movement in Algeria—Francois Mitterrand is minister of interior.

25 February Russian leader Nikita Khrushchev gives secret speech to 20th Congress of Soviet Communist Party denouncing Stalin's crimes.

13 June Last British troops leave Egypt's canal zone after 64 years.

27 June Police shoot down strikers in Polish city of Poznan.

26 July Egyptian leader Nasser nationalises Suez Canal. British prime minister Anthony Eden compares Nasser to Hitler, Labour leader Hugh Gaitskell makes same comparison.

September US attempt to replace nationalisation by international control of canal rejected by Egypt.

16 October Russian troops threaten Poland on border. Arms distributed in Polish factories.

19 October Khrushchev flies to Warsaw and does deal with new Polish leader Gomulka.

22 and 24 October Joint secret meeting between Britain, France and Israel to plan attack on Egypt.

23 October Demonstration in Budapest in support of Polish reforms fired on by security police. Outbreak of Hungarian Revolution, destruction of statue of Stalin.

24 October Imre Nagy becomes Hungarian prime minister.

29 November Nagy government declares neutrality and end of one-party state.

30 October Israeli troops cross Sinai peninsula towards Suez Canal. Britain and France issue an ultimatum to Egyptian troops to withdraw ten miles from Canal. US president Eisenhower opposes ultimatum.

31 October British and French bomb Egypt and destroy airforce. Labour minister Gaitskell denounces ultimatum as 'act of disastrous folly'.

4 November Labour Party supports nationwide protests against war. Russian troops re-enter Budapest and start crushing resistance.

5 November British troops land in Port Said.

14 November Formation of Greater Budapest Central Workers' Council which coordinates general strike.

15 November Faced with run on pound, Britain forced to begin withdrawing from Egypt.

16 November British prime minister Anthony Eden goes on 'sick leave' to Caribbean.

22 November Russian troops kidnap Nagy.

January 1957 Eden resigns.

June 1958 Imre Nagy, Pal Maleter and others executed.

Memories of a seminal year
Stan Newens

For some years prior to 1956 the British labour movement was in overall decline. The 1945 general election had been the crest of the wave for the development of the left in Britain. The British Labour government, which took office, implemented a very radical programme-nationalisation of the Bank of England, coal, gas, electricity, the railways, civil aviation, long distance road haulage, cable and wireless and steel; the creation of the welfare state, the national health service, massive house building, the establishment of the New Town, etc. Even so, electoral support declined before the government had run its course.

Although Labour did not lose any of the 22 by-elections it fought up to 1947, the local elections of that year showed severe Labour losses. Gallup Public Opinion Polls put Labour and the Conservatives at the same level in mid-1947, but thereafter the Conservatives went ahead, until in November 1949 they were ten points in the lead.

Labour managed to rally at this point, however, and in the February 1950 general election actually secured a clear lead of nearly a million votes. Unfortunately, the overall majority of seats fell to five, owing to the concentration of Labour votes in a limited number of constituencies, while many marginals were overwhelmed by small Conservative majorities.

After 1950 Labour also fell back, but once again in the 1951 general election it pulled back and polled more votes overall than the Tories (13,948,833). This time, however, its seats were reduced to 295 against the

Conservatives' 321, which gave the latter a majority of 26 over Labour. As a result, Winston Churchill again became prime minister.

In the years that followed Labour support declined again and in the 1955 general election the Conservatives were returned with a majority of 67. Thereafter the drift to the right continued, with the Labour vote being seriously cut back.

One of the principal reasons for this was the growth of affluence among working people and the coming of age of a generation who were too young to remember the miseries of the inter-war period. Another reason was the Cold War, reports of repressive acts by Communist governments and the trials and executions of leading Communists in Eastern Europe. This destroyed the appeal of the British Communist Party and rubbed off on all who advocated left wing socialist policies—even those who were critics of infringements of human and democratic rights by Communist regimes.

The election of Hugh Gaitskell as Labour Party leader in 1955 and the dominance of right wing leaders in the trade union movement reflected the shift to the right. Great demonstrations or mass struggles for left wing objectives seemed to be remote from reality—the phenomena of an age that had passed. Those who considered themselves to be in the mainstream of post-war life had little sympathy with strikes and mass demonstrations.

In local, ward or general committee Labour Party meetings, in trade union branches and in other areas of activity, it was only too clear that the left was swimming against the tide. There may have been exceptions, but I can vouch from my own experience in urban Stoke on Trent and suburban and rural West Essex that the level of activity and the numbers of members were constantly falling and the majority of those who remained tended to reject left wing proposals. I attended meetings in the old Holborn Hall and such rallies as there were in Trafalgar Square and handed out leaflets, etc. Attendance was sparse and enthusiasm limited to the few.

There was nonetheless an active left throughout this period, albeit in the minority. On 5 March 1952 an amendment in the House of Commons condemning the rearmament proposals was backed by 57 Labour rebels who—despite their variety—essentially represented the Bevanite movement, which had existed as the Keep Left Group even prior to Aneurin Bevan's resignation in 1951, which gave the group its name. At the Morecambe annual conference of the Labour Party in October 1952 the

Bevanites, ie the Labour left, captured six of the seven constituency party seats on the NEC. In 1953-54 the left, joined by some in the centre and even on the right, fought a long campaign to stop German rearmament. In 1955 Aneurin Bevan opposed British membership of the South East Asian Treaty Organisation (SEATO) and was briefly expelled from the PLP.

Other manifestations of the left occurred within the rank and file. In 1954 the Movement for Colonial Freedom was formed at a conference attended by some 300 delegates. Victory for Socialism, originally formed in 1944 by Fred Messer MP and his son, Eric, was still standing in the 1950s to drum up support for domestic and foreign policy objectives. Other groups also existed, including some that began to campaign against nuclear weapons. The *Tribune* had an influential, if limited, readership and the *New Statesman* projected leftish ideas for a more middle class audience.

The Communist Party, though isolated in political terms, still commanded the allegiance of large numbers of key trade unionists—mainly at shop floor level but also some in the higher echelons of the movement. It also had a loyal and influential following among academics and intellectuals.

The Trotskyist Revolutionary Communist Party had dissolved in 1948 but several small organisations, which it had spawned, were active in the movement. The most significant of these was the group led by Gerry Healy, which produced the *Socialist Outlook* and later the *Newsletter*—sometimes called the Club. The group which became the Revolutionary Socialist League led by Ted Grant in 1957 and the Socialist Review Group formed around Tony Cliff, to which I belonged, were also active. All of these groups were entrist and worked within the Labour Party.

Though the situation at the beginning of 1956 appeared to be relatively stable, with no great upheavals in the wings, it was rapidly transformed by the events of that year. The Suez expedition and Soviet intervention into Hungary created a new situation on the left in Britain and made an impact which lasted for at least a generation.

The Suez crisis first boomed into view when the Americans and the British refused to finance the Aswan High Dam in Egypt in July 1956. The Egyptian president, Colonel Nasser, thereafter nationalised the Suez Canal. Initially Hugh Gaitskell backed the hostile stance adopted by the Conservative prime minister, Sir Anthony Eden. In the House of Commons debate of 2 August 1956 he declared, 'I do not object to the precautionary steps, which the prime minister has announced today.' He did, however, warn the government against any breach of international law.

This reflected considerable unease on the back benches and in the spontaneous protests which were voiced outside the House. Here the Movement for Colonial Freedom and Victory for Socialism formed the Suez Emergency Committee, which began to mobilise opinion against the threat of armed intervention by British forces. In the first week of September the TU Congress passed a resolution unanimously against the use of force without UN backing.

However, on 29 October Israeli forces invaded Egypt on the pretext of destroying Egyptian commando bases in the Sinai desert. At this Britain and France, who we now know were colluding with Israel, called on Egyptian and Israeli forces to withdraw to positions ten miles back from the Suez Canal. This was obviously a pretext for armed intervention, which actually began on 5 November with the dropping of British and French paratroops at Port Said and other points on the Canal.

With the prospect of armed intervention imminent, the Suez Emergency Committee booked Trafalgar Square for an anti-war rally on Sunday 4 November. I was in touch with Peggy Rushton, the MCF general secretary, by phone with the object of helping to mobilise support. On Thursday 1 November, when I phoned, she informed me that the Labour Party had been on the line to take over the booking actually, on behalf of the National Council of Labour, representing the TUC and the co-operative movement as well. I was delighted that she had already agreed and carried on with my plans to rally protesters. In addition, using the Epping CLP dupli-cator, I copied 6,000 leaflets drafted by myself and my *Socialist Review* colleagues, calling on workers to strike against the Suez intervention.

The Trafalgar Square rally turned out to be a seminal event in British Labour history. My 6,000 leaflets, which a crowd of dockers helped us to distribute, disappeared in a flash. All afternoon people were pouring into the square until it was impossible to move. At the height of the proceedings, a great chant went up in the north western corner of the square as a massive column of student demonstrators began to come in and went on endlessly.

'One, two, three, four! We won't fight in Eden's war', they chanted. The whole square and its environs were engulfed in a vast array of protesters who were jammed in tight. The sense of mass solidarity in a just cause held us spellbound and instilled in us all a common will to carry our protest forward.

At the end of the protest speeches, part of the crowd made for Whitehall, perhaps hoping to besiege Downing Street, and bitter clashes with the police followed in which 27 people were arrested. It was clear that the rally had awakened many thousands from their apathy and fired them as well as the pre-committed with an unbending determination to oppose British intervention in Suez.

The impetus did not fade as we returned to our homes and it was contagious—inspiring many who were not present, throughout the country, to oppose Eden's war.

In Trafalgar Square Mike Kidron, a fellow *Socialist Review* supporter, told me (as he had left home much later) that the Russians were apparently going in to crush the uprising in Hungary, which had occurred in the latter part of October. The British Communist Party was already in deep crisis. Ever since Nikita Krushchev, the new Soviet leader, had repudiated Soviet changes made under Stalin against Tito in Yugoslavia, which the CPGB leaders had supported, there had been widespread unease. Since then there had been Krushchev's secret speech to the 20th Congress of the CPSU on 25 February, which the *Observer* had published in full on 10 June. The Hungarian prime minister, Matyas Rakosi, had confessed that the trial of Laszlo Rajk, a Hungarian Communist leader who had been executed, had been rigged. In Poland Gomulka had assumed power in defiance of Soviet wishes after riots in Poznan in June. The Hungarian revolt had been the last straw, particularly when the case of Edith Bone, a British Communist who had been tortured and ill-treated in a Hungarian prison, hit the news. A huge swathe of Communist Party members were in revolt at the unwavering support given by their leaders to Soviet policy under Stalin.

Peter Fryer, the *Daily Worker* correspondent in Hungary, sent in reports which the paper refused to publish. It found another journalist, Charlie Coutts, who was prepared to defend Soviet action. Peter Fryer resigned from the Communist Party, wrote a book *The Hungarian Tragedy* in record time and joined Gerry Healy and his group.

Edward Thompson and John Saville were publishing *The Reasoner*, a duplicated magazine, which they refused to close down. A third of the *Daily Worker's* journalists left. Key trade unionists like John Homer, general secretary of the Fire Brigades Union, Jack Grahl, Leo Keely, Laurence Daly (a leading Scottish miner), Les Cannon of the ETU and many others left the party. The historians Edward Thompson and John Saville quit. Christopher Hill, another historian, who with Peter Cadogan and others produced a minority report on inner party democracy, left afterwards. Besides these and other well known figures, thousands of other members were in revolt.

The *Newsletter* and the Socialist Review Group went into overdrive to try to attract dissident CP-ers into their ranks. With its greater resources and the attraction of its printing press, Gerry Healy and the *Newsletter* group were by far the most successful. When the April 1957 Communist Party Congress took place in Hammersmith Town Hall many of them, including Gerry Healy himself, were outside selling journals and lobbying delegates.

I met Pat Jordan from Nottingham, for example, and took him back to see Tony Cliff. As a result *Socialist Review* made contact with a group of dissidents which included Ken Coates and John Daniels besides Pat. We helped them publish a brochure, 'Why We Left the Communist Party'. Several Socialist Review Group members travelled many miles to meet other dissidents and win them over, as did members of other groups.

Eventually a very considerable number of the rebels joined the Labour Party, though not necessarily immediately after leaving the CPGB. Laurence Daly, for example, would not touch the Scottish Labour Party to begin with, and formed the Fife Socialist League which existed for some time before he decided to become a Labour Party member.

The right wing of the Labour Party was by no means happy about all that was happening. Bernard Dix—then a Socialist Review Group member but later a key official in NUPE—told me of a conversation which he over-heard between Sam Watson, a pillar of the Labour right on the NEC of the Labour Party, and a colleague: 'It's great!' said Sam Watson's colleague. 'The Communist Party is falling totally apart.' 'Not so!' replied Sam, 'It's the worst bloody thing that could happen! We'll have half of that lot trying to get into the Labour Party!'

Sam Watson's forecast was basically correct, as later events proved. The revolt in the Communist Party threw up an army of potential Labour Party recruits who were steadily absorbed. But at the same time the protests against Suez politicised and reinvigorated a host of others. Trade unionists, highly experienced political workers, gifted intellectuals and many new, dedicated young people joined the ranks. The experience of the anti-Suez campaign and the fight against repression in Hungary and elsewhere in

Eastern Europe generated a new breed of political activists who joined the political struggle throughout Britain.

The *New Reasoner*, developed out of the *Reasoner* by John Saville and Edward Thompson, commenced publication in summer 1957 with an editorial board consisting of Ken Alexander, Doris Lessing, Ronald Meek and Randall Swingler. It represented dissident Communists. The *Universities and Left Review* started in spring 1957, edited by Stuart Hall, Gabriel Pearson, Raphael Samuel and Charles Taylor. They merged after a time to form *New Left Review*—an extremely influential journal expressing the views of a wide spectrum of writers representative of the New Left.

Many of the New Left joined reinvigorated old lefts to back the struggle against nuclear weapons, and the Campaign for Nuclear Disarmament was formed rallying huge support for the first Aldermaston march in 1958 and still more in later years.

The new atmosphere engendered in the Labour Party was reflected in the struggle for unilateral disarmament, which surfaced in the 1959 Labour Party conference and only just failed to win, when Aneurin Bevan stood against it and said it was unacceptable to send a potential Labour Party foreign secretary naked into the negotiating chamber.

A new spirit also permeated the trade unions. Frank Cousins came to the helm in the Transport and General Workers Union, but even in the reactionary National Union of General and Municipal Workers a left wing tendency began to emerge.

It is important to recognise that the new spirit was not automatically reflected in the electorate as a whole. In fact, at the same time as anti-war feeling was generated by Suez, a wave of chauvinism and misplaced patriotism was also produced and this made considerable headway among some working class voters. Although Labour moved temporarily ahead in the opinion polls as a result of the Suez debacle, by 1958 the Conservatives had turned the tide back under Harold Macmillan. 'Most of our people', he said, 'have never had it so good.' And many believed him.

By the time of the 1959 general election the Conservatives were five points ahead of Labour, and in the poll they increased their seats by 21 to achieve a majority of 100. Labour's vote actually declined by 12.2 percent to 43.8 percent against the Conservatives' 49.9 percent.

However, within the Labour Party and across the movement as a whole the reinvigorated left was steadily winning ground. After the 1959 general election Hugh Gaitskell attempted to dump Clause IV and repudiate the wide commitment to public ownership. He failed. In 1960 the annual conference passed a resolution in favour of unilateral nuclear disarmament. Although this was reversed in 1961, the leftward tide was still rolling.

In public meetings, particularly in Manchester and Liverpool, Gaitskell's views were strongly contested from the floor by left wingers. In 1962/3 Edward Janosik found in a survey that 54 percent of CLPs favoured a move to the left, compared with 46 percent favouring the status quo or a shift to the right. This was reflected in the selection by CLPs after 1959 of numerous left wing parliamentary candidates.

This was not, however, a matter of chance. The left organised through a reconstructed Victory for Socialism, of which I became the organising secretary and This Way to Peace, set up by Richard Fletcher and Walter Kendal in which I also became involved. We had to counter the operations of the right wing group the Campaign for Democratic Socialism under Dennis Howell, Bill Rogers, backed by the Socialist Union, Socialist Commentary and the Fabian Society. Of course *Tribune* was an immensely important force which organised the biggest fringe meeting at Labour Party conference and kept the left in contact throughout the country.

The 1964 general election was our triumph. Labour regained power—albeit only just—and among those elected was a new intake of left wing Labour MPs who reflected the revival initiated by Suez and Hungary in 1956. John Homer, Norman Buchan and Eric Heffer were in fact former Communist Party members who joined Labour after 1956. Others, including me, had been part of that movement.

1956 was therefore a seminal year in British Labour history and it is appropriate that we should consider its impact and aftermath on its fiftieth anniversary. Of course, the uplift could only last a finite period and it is sad to reflect that we are today more deeply sunk in the mire than we were in the early 1950s before the events of 1956.

But say not, the struggle naught availeth.

We shall rise again.

C L R James: the revolutionary as artist

Christian Høgsbjerg

> I have long believed that a very great revolutionary is a great artist, and that he develops ideas, programmes, etc, as Beethoven develops a movement.
>
> C L R James[1]

Cyril Lionel Robert James (1901-1989) was a towering intellectual of what has come to be known as 'the black Atlantic' and also one of the outstanding anti-Stalinist Marxist theorists of the 20th century. Yet, while the late Trinidadian historian may not need any introduction to many readers of *International Socialism* (especially those who are also devout cricket fans), for almost all of his quite remarkable life James was a rather marginalised and isolated individual, apparently too 'extreme' for even an 'age of extremes'.[2] In 1981 Paul Buhle predicted that this neglect would not last, and that 'if civilisation survives the threat of nuclear annihilation another quarter century, James will be considered one of the few truly creative Marxists from the 1930s to the 1950s, perhaps alone in his masterful synthesis of world history, philosophy, government, mass life and popular culture'.[3]

Twenty five years on, while humanity has (so far) managed to avoid Armageddon, James's insistence that the history of civilisation could be explained through an understanding of the history of class struggle is a view that today could not be a more denigrated theoretical perspective. The dedicated followers of contemporary intellectual fashion casually dismiss those who attempt to defend Marxism's relevance today, gently reminding them that notions of 'totality' somehow inevitably lead to Stalinist 'totalitarianism'. As a result, few of those scholars who do discuss C L R James today bother to pay a great deal of attention to his own insistence that his 'greatest contributions' had been 'to clarify and extend the heritage of Marx and Lenin' and 'to explain and expand the idea of what constitutes the new society'.[4] Instead many scholars celebrate James simply as a 'pioneering icon' of 'post-colonial studies' and 'cultural studies', almost as if all he ever did in life was sit around watching cricket matches and then go home and write brilliantly about the spectacle.[5] In this article I argue that as a new global movement emerges against capitalism and war, in protest at Bush and Blair's bloody 'war on terror' and the growing power of multinational corporations (arguably the real 'totalitarian' institutions of our age), James surely deserves to be remembered differently.

To attempt in a short article like this to do full justice to James's contribution to revolutionary politics, which ranged widely in both space and time, covering three continents over 50 years, would be to do an injustice. Instead I will give a necessarily condensed overview of his life, in particular focusing on his early political thought, before turning to the question of how Marxists today might try to build on the best elements of James's rich and inspiring legacy, a question that may not be an entirely new one to some readers of this journal.[6]

A portrait of the artist as a young man

C L R James was born on 4 January 1901 in Trinidad, a tiny island then languishing as a 'crown colony' in the economic backwaters of the British Empire. His parents, Robert and Ida Elizabeth James, were black and lower middle class, and both their fathers had worked their way up from almost nothing as immigrants from Barbados.[7] On his father's side, James's grandfather made it as a pan boiler on one of Trinidad's huge sugar estates (a post traditionally reserved by the white owners for other whites) and so into the nascent emerging black middle class of Trinidad after the abolition of colonial slavery in the 1830s. His struggle enabled his son Robert James to escape a life of manual labour on the sugar estates to become a respected teacher, and later headmaster. Possessing only 'cultural capital', the James family invested this in the only place they could, preparing their son to sit the entrance examination for the island's elite school, Queen's Royal

College (QRC). C L R James was an uncommonly gifted boy and, aged just nine, became the youngest boy ever to win the necessary exhibition. Given that James's great grandmother had been a slave, and he had 'often heard her speak of what slavery meant', the fact that he was now attending the same school as the sons of white colonial officials was of course a huge source of vindication and pride for his whole family and their friends.[8]

Yet expectations that he would graduate from QRC with a scholarship to go abroad and study for a profession were to be dashed. James clearly could have chosen such a route had he wanted to, but his interest was increasingly distracted by life outside the classroom. Instead of paying full attention to Oxbridge educated teachers of Latin and Greek, James indulged his love for the game of cricket and for reading English literature. He happily absorbed the English 'public school code' of morals and graduated from QRC transformed, as he put it, 'into a member of the British middle class with literary gifts'.[9] The problem was that though officially a British subject, he was black and stuck in a tiny Caribbean colony where mass illiteracy and poverty ensured his dream of writing novels was hardly a lucrative career option, indeed hardly a career option at all. His mother, from whom he had inherited his love of reading, was supportive but his despairing father would repeatedly ask, 'Well, where are you going?' 'That is all very well, but what about money?'[10]

After leaving QRC in 1918 all the contradictions of colonial rule slowly but steadily dawned on James. His public school education had trained him to lead men forward for 'King and Country', but when James tried to do just this by enlisting with the army officer's regiment in 1918, he was blocked on account of being black. Those black members of the British West Indies Regiment who did fight in the First World War revolted in Italy against both the war and the institutional racism of the army, and their anger as they returned to price rises, poverty and overcrowded housing was the spark that threw Trinidadian society into turmoil.[11]

After a general strike led by dock workers rocked Trinidad's capital Port of Spain in late 1919, the British introduced a token element of democracy into the island allowing Trinidadians to vote for a few members of the Legislative Council. In 1925 Captain Arthur Andrew Cipriani, the popular leader of the social democratic Trinidadian Workingmen's Association and a former Port of Spain mayor, was elected.[12] Now, as a mass nationalist movement took off around this charismatic workers' leader, who often declared himself 'the champion of the barefooted man', James took notice:[13] 'My hitherto vague ideas of freedom crystallised around a political commitment: we should be free to govern ourselves'.[14] From his reading of literary figures like Thackeray, Dickens and Hazlitt, James had developed a respect for the 'British' ideals of liberalism and democracy, and now he could see the clear hypocrisy of the British colonial elite, something he raged against in his first book, *The Life of Captain Cipriani: An Account of British Government in the West Indies* (1932):

> Any man who tries to do for his people what Englishmen are so proud that other Englishmen have done for them, immediately becomes in the eyes of the Colonial Englishman a dangerous person, a wild revolutionary, a man with no respect for law and order, a self-seeker activated by the lowest motives, a reptile to be crushed at the first opportunity. What at home is the greatest virtue becomes in the colonies the greatest crime.[15]

In this work James tore into the British government's line of 'self-government when fit for it', amply demonstrating that the people of Trinidad had always been manifestly 'fit' to govern themselves.[16]

When he was not teaching English and history, playing cricket (or covering matches in his capacity as a journalist), James spent time in the 1920s and early 1930s with a group of young black and white intellectuals in Port of Spain. They wrote 'barrack-yard' stories about the lives of the poor in shanty towns by way of implicit critique of colonial society, often publishing them themselves. As James later noted, 'the basic constituent of my political activity and outlook' was already set out in 'the "human" aspect' of *Minty Alley*, the unpublished novel he wrote in 1928 about the working people of one 'barrack-yard' he stayed in that summer.[17]

James's humanist spirit would not be diminished when he left Trinidad for Britain in 1932 in order to try and make it as a writer. After all, colonial Trinidadian society with its clear divisions of race, class and power, which James had been able to view in its totality, from top to bottom, was in a sense only a microcosm of the world system, where white supremacy ruled under the flags of competing European empires.

The artist becomes a revolutionary

It is not altogether surprising, after his voyage into a Europe still scarred irrevocably by the horrors of the First World War, and then engulfed by the

Great Depression and the rise of fascism, that James would be attracted by the ideas of Marxism. What is quite remarkable is that he was not to be attracted by what Isaac Deutscher called the 'vulgar Marxism' of Stalinism, but instead independently orientated towards Trotskyism. In the 1930s Leon Trotsky was a politically isolated exile, the 'prophet outcast' from the land of the October Revolution. Under Stalin, Russia was now in the midst of an industrial revolution and apparently proving the virtues of a 'planned economy' while capitalism slipped into the abyss. James's political evolution in this period therefore arguably deserves additional explanation, and was clearly rather contingent on the circumstances in which he found himself on arriving in Britain in 1932.

It is important to note that when James arrived in Britain as an aspiring novelist he was still quite a long way from the revolutionary Marxist he would become. Indeed, if he could be called a socialist at this stage, his socialism was of the rather elitist Fabian variety. In an article he wrote for the *Port of Spain Gazette* in mid-1932, James declared he was 'not impressed' by 'the English people' he had met so far in London. As he put it, 'it does seem to me that millions of these people are still mentally adolescent. They live on cheap films and cheap newspapers'.[18] The Fabians themselves, around Sidney and Beatrice Webb, were soon to argue for the importation of a 'new civilisation' from Stalinist Russia to overcome the apparent intellectual backwardness of the English working class. However, before James could consider such things he left London for the Lancashire textile town of Nelson to stay with the family of his friend the legendary Trinidadian cricketer Learie Constantine, then playing professionally in the Lancashire League.

James arrived in Nelson in late May 1932 and left in late March 1933, and these were clearly ten months that shook his world. James saw the devastating effects of the collapse of the Lancashire cotton industry, but alongside mass poverty he also saw a community of resistance proudly fighting back. 'Red Nelson', as it was known locally, was a solidly working class town, pervaded by an ethos of anti-militarism and ethical socialism, stemming in part from radical, independent Christian Methodism. When, in August 1932, mill-owners across Lancashire started to tear up existing agreements and bring in scab labour to try and restore profitability in the cotton textile industry, cotton workers and weavers struck back to save their livelihoods. The mass strike, which raged for over a month, was a powerful demonstration of the power and resourcefulness of the working class, something James had not witnessed since the general strike of 1919 in Trinidad.[19]

When he arrived in Nelson, James remembered, 'my Labour and socialist ideas had been got from books and were rather abstract'. He joined the Labour Party in Nelson because he saw it as an organisation that was on paper committed to West Indian self-government. However, Lancashire cotton workers remembered Gandhi's recent visit to Lancashire and how the Labour government of 1929–31 had brutally repressed Indian national-ists. Moreover, that Labour government had collapsed after having abjectly failed to defend the interests of those who had elected it as mass unemploy-ment grew, and insult had been added to injury when in late 1931 many of Labour's leaders jumped ship to form a new 'national' government in coali-tion with the Tories. As James recalled, 'These humorously cynical working men were a revelation and brought me down to earth.' When he told these betrayed former Labour supporters of his hopes in a future Labour govern-ment to deliver colonial liberation, they said, 'You make a mistake. Ramsay MacDonald, [Arthur] Henderson, Phillip Snowden, [Herbert] Morrison, they never gave us anything and we put them there; why do you think they would give you any?'[20]

James wrestled with the answer to such questions while in Nelson, and later described how his previous passion for literature 'was vanishing from my consciousness and politics was substituting itself'.[21] The massive economic crisis also opened up a quite profound ideological crisis. As the British historian Arnold Toynbee noted in 1931, 'Men and women all over the world were seriously contemplating and frankly discussing the possibility that the Western system of society might break down and cease to work'.[22] One popular work at the time was the German author Oswald Spengler's *The Decline of the West*, written in 1917 during the First World War, which predicted the inevitable triumph of irrational brutal dictatorships in the heartlands of 'Western civilisation'. Its prophetic title alone, given the alarming rise of fascism, made it a bestseller and James was deeply impressed but remembers he 'did not accept the decline that Spengler preached'.[23] After all, meeting class conscious workers in 'Red Nelson' had completely and permanently altered his attitude towards 'the English people'. As he wrote in 1932, after hearing stories of past class struggles in Nelson:

I could forgive England all the vulgarity and all the depressing disappoint-ment of London for the magnificent spirit of these north country working people. As long as that is the stuff of which they are made, then indeed Britons never, never shall be slaves.[24]

In Nelson, James also happened upon the first volume of Leon Trotsky's *History of the Russian Revolution* (1931), which had just been published in England and which immediately captured his imagination with its powerful analysis. As he remembered, Trotsky 'was not only giving details of the revolution itself, but he was expounding the Marxist theory of historical materialism', even making 'references to literature as expressing social reality and social change'.[25] Trotsky explained why workers, especially those in Britain, could follow conservative ideas much of the time, yet still retained the possibility of transforming themselves into masters of their own destiny through collective struggle and organisation. James saw that Marxism not only offered a serious explanation of the world crisis but also pointed to where the hope for the future lay.

In 1933 James returned to London and, having secured a prestigious job as a cricket correspondent with the *Manchester Guardian*, continued his campaigning work for West Indian self-government inside the Labour Party. Yet while someone with his talents could have risen up the ranks of the Labour Party with ease had he wished, James was increasingly tiring of having to always invoke his 'Britishness' and 'respectability', as most colonial subjects did, in order to then be able to criticise colonialism and racism. The rise of Hitler onto the world stage proclaiming himself the saviour of the Aryan race meant James now defiantly adopted a more radical, transnational identification with other black people (and their culture). That summer James attended a meeting in London to hear the legendary George Padmore, the leading black figure in the international Communist movement, speak. James remembers that 'I was going to every meeting in those days and the race aspect of the matter was an added attraction'—not least because the Labour Party, for some reason, never seemed to hold any meetings on the colonial question.[26]

James would not regret going to that meeting, not least because 'George Padmore' unexpectedly turned out to be a boyhood friend of his from Trinidad, Malcolm Nurse. The two had not seen each other for about eight years, since Nurse had left for America.[27] After hearing the inspirational Padmore speak about the 'coming African revolution' James had even more questions that needed answering. How could the 'Stalinist'

Communist movement be so bad if such a good friend like Padmore could rise so high in it, so soon after joining it in America in 1927? Surely in the interests of fair play at least, after reading Trotsky's *History*, he should try to understand what the 'other side' was saying as well? As James later put it, he felt 'it was necessary to read the relevant volumes of Stalin. And, of course I had to read Lenin in order to trace back the quarrel... I realised the Stalinists were the greatest liars and corrupters of history there ever were. No one convinced me of this. I convinced myself.' After Lenin, James turned finally to the writings of Karl Marx 'and thereby I reached volume one of *Das Kapital* and *The Eighteenth Brumaire* [*of Louis Bonaparte*]'.[28]

However, the final clue to James's commitment to Trotskyism lies less in his study of the Marxist classics, but with his experience of how disastrous Stalinism was in practice. In late 1933 James spent six months in Paris researching the life of Toussaint L'Ouverture, the leader of the victorious slave revolt in Haiti at the time of the Great French Revolution. In early February 1934 Paris was experiencing massive civil unrest as the French far right hoped to emulate Hitler's success the year before, through exploiting growing middle class discontent with the economic crisis and blaming 'corrupt' financiers and Jews. Yet both the social democratic Socialist Party (SFIO) and the French Communist Party did nothing when a violent fascist protest on the 6 February forced the resignation of the Liberal prime minister and his replacement with a more right wing politician, a massive boost to the fascists. The Communist paper *L'Humanite*, following the Stalinist line that revolution, not counter-revolution, was imminent, carried the headline 'No Panic' and declared that the choice between fascism and the current government was like the choice between 'plague and cholera'.[29] As James noted later, 'the utter imbecility of all Stalinism was never more completely shown than in the actions of the Communist Party of France in this grave crisis'.[30]

Just as James must have been wondering whether it was time to get out of France while he could, the working people of Paris instinctively felt the need for unity against the fascists, something only a minuscule group of Trotskyists were arguing for. On the night of 10 February, James later described how there was 'fierce fighting' and 'men were killed. The proletariat, the stock of 1789 and 10 August 1792, of 1830, of 1848 and 1871, came out in their thousands, whether Socialist or Communist.' On 12 February the main union federation, the CGT, called for a general strike and at the last minute the Communist Party called for a demonstration, albeit separately to the main Socialist Party/CGT one. However, instead of the two demonstrations showing their traditional animosity towards each other, on meeting workers spontaneously and gloriously came together to sing anti-fascist slogans. As James wrote, 'It was in the streets that French parliamentarism was saved. The coup had failed'.[31]

Yet on his return to London in March 1934 Oswald Mosley's British Union of Fascists were now a growing threat, and so when James came across some Trotskyists leafleting a Labour Party meeting he decided to leave the Labour Party and join them. The entire Trotskyist movement in Britain at this point consisted of about 50 people, most of whom, like James, were new to revolutionary politics. James remembers that 'there were some people from Oxford and Cambridge who...brought some criticism to the official Trotskyists and they couldn't answer. So on the same night I joined I had to speak on behalf of Trotskyism'.[32] If James was pleased to finally meet the 'official' Trotskyists, we can only imagine how happy they were to see him.

The artist as revolutionary

Joining the Trotskyist movement in Britain at this time for James meant joining the tiny 'Marxist Group' inside the Independent Labour Party (ILP). The ILP had split away from Labour in 1932 in disgust at its betrayals and in order to try to build a socialist alternative. James's talents as a journalist and writer meant he soon not only became a leading member of British Trotskyism but also quickly came to the notice of the ILP leadership. Within a year James had established his reputation on the British left for his leading role in attempting to organise opposition to Fascist Italy's barbaric war against the people of Abyssinia (now Ethiopia), which began in October 1935.[33] In time-honoured fashion, Mussolini declared his criminal invasion and occupation of a sovereign nation was 'a war of civilisation and liberation', even a war 'of the poor, of the disinherited, of the proletariat!'[34] As chair of the newly formed International African Friends of Abyssinia (IAFA), James cut through what he called 'the mountain of lies and nonsense' which surrounded the war, lies which had confused even sections of the left in Britain, damning the role of not just Fascist Italy in Abyssinia but European imperialism in Africa more generally, in a series of outstanding articles and speeches.[35] In March 1936 James turned his research on the Haitian Revolution into a play, *Toussaint L'Ouverture*, starring the legendary black American singer Paul Robeson, staged in London.

The betrayal of Abyssinia by Stalinist Russia, which sold oil to Fascist Italy during the conflict, was one of the most visible demonstrations of the way in which the Communist International under Stalin had steadily abandoned world revolution in favour of building up 'socialism in one country'. After Hitler came to power, Stalin moved to try and make diplomatic approaches with Britain and France and so the Stalinist bureaucracy now drew a distinction between the 'democratic imperialist' countries of Britain, America and France on the one hand and the 'fascist imperialist' powers of Germany, Italy and Japan on the other. When the Communist International instructed George Padmore to explain to African workers and peasants resisting British and French colonial dictatorships that the British and French governments were now 'democratic' and even 'peace-loving', he refused on principle. After resigning his Comintern post in disgust, Padmore returned to London to join up with James and work in the IAFA.[36]

Amid the tumultuous events of 1936, a year which saw among other things Spain in revolt and the election of a Popular Front government in France, and despite only being in the Trotskyist movement a few years, James now wrote *World Revolution, 1917-1936: The Rise and Fall of the Communist International* (1937). This was one of the first serious and detailed examinations of the terrible international consequences of the rise of the Stalinist bureaucracy in Russia, and as Kent Worcester has noted, 'there were not even academic studies that covered the same ground'.[37] In fact, plenty of Western intellectuals at this time were writing about the Stalinist bureaucracy. However, these were lyrical hymns of praise to a new ruling class, which in 1936 had congratulated itself on achieving 'the final and irrevocable victory of Socialism' in Russia. James was motivated not only by the need to defend the relevance of the rich revolutionary legacy of Bolshevism, but more fundamentally to uphold the truth in the face of Stalinist distortions about what had really happened to the international working class movement since the end of the First World War. As he put it in *World Revolution*, 'for suppression, evasion and hard lying the documents of the Soviet Union and the Third International today form, along with British colonial propaganda and fascist demagogy, a trilogy which future historians will contemplate with wonder'.[38]

James's growing sense that any authoritarian regime or police state, whatever its particular official ideology (whether 'communist', 'fascist' or 'democratic'), shared a fundamental common ethos and logic gave the work a certain prophetic power. It is not surprising that George Orwell, who, like James, had had first hand experience of both British imperial rule (in Burma) and the counter-revolutionary nature of Stalinism (in the Spanish Civil War), was impressed by *World Revolution*, describing it as a 'very able book'.[39] Communist officials who crossed swords with the eloquent Trotskyist from Trinidad were obviously less impressed. In the finest traditions of Stalinism, they attempted to persuade their supporters that James, one of the most prominent black figures in British politics who had made his name opposing Mussolini's war, was actually not only on the same side as 'German and Italian Fascism, British imperialism and Japanese militarism' but even directly engaged in 'fascist activity'.[40] When this line of argument, for some reason, failed to convince, James was made out to be some sort of confused liberal (the '*Manchester Guardian* Trotskyist' with his 'easily detected' forgeries and lies, etc).[41]

James was not, however, to be deterred from his support for Trotsky (who despite being Jewish was now accused by Stalin's regime of being in cohorts with Hitler) and risked beatings by disrupting large meetings organised by the British Communist Party to attempt to justify the Moscow Trials.[42] James by now was also working closely with George Padmore, who in justified disgust with Stalinism had moved towards Pan-Africanism and in 1937 had founded the International African Service Bureau (IASB) to continue his work for the liberation of Africa from colonialism. While this organisation was inevitably overshadowed somewhat by the more respectable League of Coloured Peoples and the presence of Marcus Garvey, the Jamaican born Pan-Africanist and founder of the Back to Africa movement, in London during this period, the bureau's political independence allowed it to punch well above its weight regardless. Nor were James (who edited the IASB paper alongside the Trotskyist paper *Fight*) and Padmore afraid to pull any punches, heckling Garvey in Hyde Park for his conservative reaction to the mass labour revolts sweeping the Caribbean during this period.[43]

In 1938 James published *The Black Jacobins: Toussaint L'Ouverture and the San Domingo Revolution*, his panoramic account of the Haitian Revolution of 1791-1803, 'the only successful slave revolt in history'. As James Walvin has written, in the 1930s 'the scholarship on slavery and abolition had changed little in direction and tone for more than a century, and continued to concentrate on the rise of humanitarianism and its effective campaign in ending the cruelty of the slave system. C L R James effectively turned the tide,' restoring the actions of the slaves themselves as being central to their own liberation.[44] However, few were willing to even entertain such a thought when it first came out. Flora Greirson, writing in the *New Statesman*, dismissed *The Black Jacobins* because of its bias, noting James was 'a Communist and wants us to see the worst'.[45] Leaving aside the question of what might possibly constitute the 'best' bits of the slave experience, in reality had James actually been a Communist with a capital 'C' the work would undoubtedly have received more favourable attention on publication. As Eugene Genovese noted in 1971, *The Black Jacobins* 'deserves to rank as a classic of Marxian historiography but has been largely ignored, perhaps because of the author's Trotskyist politics'.[46] There was no 'perhaps' about it, though Eric Hobsbawm has recalled that 'in spite of the author's known Trotskyism' the work did influence and inspire at least some members of the Communist Party Historians Group in Britain. This group of Marxist intellectuals was to be critical for the development of the tradition of 'history from below' after the Second World War.[47]

Yet the intellectual inspiration of Leon Trotsky was central to 'the making' of *The Black Jacobins* as a masterful work of revolutionary history. Firstly, there was the clear influence of Trotsky's *History of the Russian Revolution*, which James once declared 'the greatest history book ever written…the climax of 2,000 years of European writing and the study of history'. For James, Trotsky was the revolutionary historian par excellence, as:

> in pure style, this materialist, as rigid with fact as Scaliger, is exceeded in no sphere by any one of his ancestors, not by Thucidides in proportion and lucidity, nor by Tacitus in invective, nor by Gibbon in dignity, nor Michelet in passion, nor by Macauley, that great bourgeois, in efficiency. There is a profound lesson here not only in history but in aesthetics.

Secondly, there was Trotsky's theory of permanent revolution which James once insisted that 'in analytical power and imaginative audacity' was 'one of the most astounding products of the modern mind'.[48] In the *History of the Russian Revolution*, Trotsky had demonstrated that the combined and uneven development of capitalism allowed apparently 'backward' countries like Tsarist Russia to come to the fore of world history in the age of socialist revolution. Possibly the most striking of James's achievements in *The Black Jacobins* was the way in which he showed how the theory of permanent revolution also illuminated colonial struggles in the age of bourgeois revolution, with the Haitian Revolution inextricably intertwined throughout the 1790s with the Great French Revolution.

In late 1938 James left Britain for a speaking tour organised by the American Trotskyist movement, but the outbreak of the Second World War among other reasons meant he ended up staying for the next 15 years. James would later, rightly, remember his years in America as 'the most important years of my life'.[49]

In April 1939 James spent a week with Leon Trotsky at Coyoacan in Mexico in order to discuss how Marxists might convincingly answer 'the Negro question', the question posed by the massive systematic racism suffered by black people in America.[50] James's radical attempt to solve this question would later influence a group which Manning Marable has argued represented 'in many respects the most significant expression of black radical thought and activism in the 1960s', the League of Revolutionary Black Workers.[51] This is not the place to detail how, alongside Raya Dunayevskaya and Grace Lee Boggs, James formed the 'Johnson-Forest Tendency' within American Trotskyism in order to attempt to deal with the profound crisis the movement was thrown into after Trotsky's murder in 1940. Their highly original attempt to make a 'leap from the heights of Leninism' through breaking with 'orthodox Trotskyism' and returning to the writings of Hegel, Marx and Lenin in order to face up to the new realities after the Second World War has been concisely and critically analysed by, among others, Alex Callinicos.[52]

It is perhaps enough to note here that their development of a theory of state capitalism to understand the Stalinist regimes enabled the 'Johnson-Forest Tendency,' like the French group 'Socialisme ou Barbarie' around Cornelius Castoriadis and the Socialist Review Group around Tony Cliff in Britain, to preserve an orientation around Marx's central theoretical insight that the emancipation of the working class would be the conquest of the working class itself.[53] While both Stalinists and 'orthodox Trotskyists' held on to the notion that state ownership of the means of production meant the Stalinist regimes were 'socialist', those Marxists who held to a theory of state capitalism were free to champion the struggles of workers under Stalinist tyranny fighting back against 'their' states. All three groups had also successfully broken from the ultimately elitist Stalinist and 'orthodox Trotskyist' theory of the party, which arrogantly declared itself the solution to the 'crisis of revolutionary leadership', and then dismissed as 'backward' the vast majority of the working class for not suddenly rallying to its banner.

Yet, unlike Cliff's Socialist Review Group, the 'Johnson-Forest Tendency' and 'Socialisme ou Barbarie' also steadily abandoned the rich Bolshevik legacy of ideas on revolutionary organisation, to be content with merely celebrating spontaneous struggles of the working class, as if these struggles in themselves could overcome what James called the 'crisis of the self-mobilisation of the proletariat'.[54] In 1937, in *World Revolution*, James had noted that 'the pathetic faith the average worker has in the leaders of the organisations he has created is one of the chief supports of the capitalist system'.[55] The post-war economic boom meant the grip of reformism over the Western working class movement grew stronger than ever, as the system was actually able to deliver meaningful 'reforms'. Yet, inspired by the rise of the CIO union in America, the British shop stewards' movement and the Hungarian Revolution of 1956, James wrote as if reformist ideas and organisations were dead or dying, thus rendering revolutionary parties on the Bolshevik model now also redundant.[56]

Antonio Gramsci once suggested that revolutionary Marxists should be guided by the motto 'Pessimism of the intellect, optimism of the will'.[57] Amid the terrible defeats that overwhelmed the movement during the 1930s and 1940s, a period dominated by Stalinism and fascism which the revolutionary novelist Victor Serge aptly termed 'midnight of the century', many radicals fell into a profound pessimism of both intellect and will. It was in this period that the tradition of 'Western Marxism' based around the Frankfurt School now emerged, and as American capitalism boomed, these thinkers now abandoned any belief that the working class could be the central agent of change in the future.

The 'Western Marxists' examined how ordinary people were effectively transformed from active citizens into passive consumers by the power of the mass media, advertising and popular forms of entertainment like Hollywood movies. James, reacting against this fundamentally elitist outlook by a privileged group of intellectuals, now made a 'literary turn' of sorts back to cultural questions to show the contradictions and complexities of 'mass culture'. 'The modern popular film, the modern newspaper (the *Daily News*, not the *Times*), the comic strip, the evolution of jazz, a popular periodical like *Life*, these mirror from year to year the deep social responses and evolution of the American people in relation to the fate which has overtaken the original concepts of freedom, free individuality, free association, etc,' James insisted.[58] This is not the place to discuss his wide-ranging works in this vein which included *American Civilization* (1949-1950), *Mariners, Renegades and Castaways* (1953)—a study of Herman Melville, the author of *Moby Dick*—and of course, *Beyond a Boundary* (1963). They arguably deserve more critical attention from Marxists than they have tended to receive up to now.[59]

Yet despite James's grasp of Marxism as a living, ever-evolving theory, and the creativity he showed as a 'revolutionary artist' in attempting to develop that theory, his abandonment of classical Leninist strategy and tactics ultimately proved costly politically. In *World Revolution* James had approvingly quoted Lenin when he 'called for "determined war" against the attempt of all those quasi-Communist revolutionists to cloak the liberation movement in the backward countries with a Communist garb'.[60] Yet as the 'colonial revolution' erupted after the Second World War, James refused to wage any such 'determined war'. Indeed, perhaps because he knew so many of them personally, James showed a disastrous misjudgement of many leaders of national liberation movements, helping several to cloak themselves in a communist garb. James would have to then break from those he had once declared revolutionary leaders on a par with Lenin.[61]

James's relevance for the movement today

While Marxists should not therefore deify James, nor should we forget that significant aspects of his political thought have a rather poignant resonance and relevance today. Given the context of Bush and Blair's 'war on terror,' it is important to remember James in particular for his implacable opposition to imperialism. Paul Berman, a former 'libertarian socialist' turned miserable apologist for the American Empire, in *Terror and Liberalism* (2003) has warned that unless the contemporary left drops its 'anti-imperialist fervours' and rediscovers its 'ability to stand up to [Islamo-]fascism', Western civilisation will be destroyed by a rising tide of 'Muslim totalitarian movements'. Carried away with his self-appointed role as a 21st century Rudyard Kipling, urging Americans to 'take up the White Man's burden', Berman invokes C L R James as if he might serve as a kind of role-model for a new, pro-war, 'anti-totalitarian left'.[62] This is worse than just another blunder in a book full of blunders: it is a crime. It is not only that James would doubtless have found 'Islamo-Fascism' a disgusting perversion of language; it is that as a Marxist he always saw the growth of religious movements in countries under colonial occupation as both an expression of real suffering as well as an inspiring form of protest against subjugation.[63]

Moreover, in *The Black Jacobins* James reiterated his opposition to imperialist wars, in which 'the great propertied interests and their agents commit the most ferocious crimes in the name of the whole people, and bluff and browbeat them by lying propaganda'. In 1796 the British government of the day sent an army to the rebellious Caribbean island of what is now Haiti in an attempt to reimpose colonial slavery, in what turned out to be a criminal and disastrous invasion that left thousands of innocent people dead. This was justified in parliament at the time by Henry Dundas, the Tony Blair of his day, as 'not a war for riches or local aggrandisement but a war for security'. James wrote that 'Dundas knew that not a single member of parliament would believe him. But parliament has always agreed to speak in these terms in order to keep the people quiet'.[64]

After one reads *The Black Jacobins*, one can only wonder in amazement when careerist New Labour politicians who support Bush and Blair's 'war for security' suddenly sing the praises of C L R James. When culture secretary Tessa Jowell notes that he is 'one of the best black intellectuals' and 'one of the greatest Caribbean writers', one can only speculate that as a member of Blair's 'war cabinet', Jowell perhaps knows better than most the awful truth behind James's point that 'it is easier to find decency, gratitude, justice, and humanity in a cage of starving tigers than in the councils of imperialism'.[65] When David Lammy, minister for culture, tells us in all sincerity that James is his all-time 'hero' for writing the 'exceptionally influential' *Black Jacobins* and so helping him develop his 'sense of history', it is difficult to know whether to laugh or cry.[66]

Overall, that C L R James since his death in 1989 has generally been remembered not as a revolutionary Marxist but as a 'harmless icon' is not altogether a surprise. After Leon Trotsky's murder in 1940, James himself noted that:

> idiots and bourgeois scoundrels always emphasise Trotsky's personal brilliance whereby they seek to disparage Trotsky's method. The two are inseparable. His natural gifts were trained and developed by Marxism.[67]

The same was fundamentally true of James himself, as I have tried to show in this article, and it is above all as a courageous, creative Marxist and a thinker in the revolutionary democratic tradition of 'socialism from below', to use Hal Draper's phrase, that we should remember him.[68] James indicted both Stalinism and social democracy for their perversion of the 'soul of socialism', their belief that it is something that can be imposed on a grateful majority from above, by an enlightened minority. When John Reid, who himself has made a seamless transition from Stalinism to New Labour, tells us that when the American and British governments rain down smart bombs on innocent Iraqi civilians they are fighting a 'socialist war', we can see where such arrogant elitism tends to end up.[69] Such 'socialists' never seem to have grasped the most elementary, essential truth—a truth which C L R James did so much to powerfully elucidate—that liberation from oppression and exploitation can only come from below, from the mass movements and struggles of the oppressed and exploited themselves.

NOTES

1: C L R James, *Notes on Dialectics: Hegel, Marx, Lenin* (London, 1980), p153. Thanks to Paul Blackledge and Osama Zuman for their comments on this article in draft.

2: The allusions here are to Paul Gilroy's *The Black Atlantic* and Eric Hobsbawm's *Age of Extremes; The Short Twentieth Century, 1914-1991*. Much of James's finest writing on his beloved game of cricket is collected in C L R James and A Grimshaw, *Cricket* (London, 1989), while for more discussion of James and cricket, see David Renton's (forthcoming) biography.

3: P Buhle, 'Marxism in the USA', in P Buhle (ed), *C L R James: His Life and Work* (London, 1986), p81. See also Buhle's pioneering biographical study, P Buhle, *C L R James: The Artist as Revolutionary* (London, 1993).

4: P Buhle (ed), as above, p164.

5: When one reads an analysis of James's classic semi-autobiographical social history of cricket, *Beyond a Boundary* (1963), which notes that 'the homoeroticism of James's cricket pitch lends itself to a non-rugged masculinity that can,

again potentially, be opened up as an inclusive social arena, that does not privilege and perpetuate patriarchy', one wonders if we are not perhaps learning more about that particular academic than we are about C L R James. See B A L St Louis, 'C L R James's Social Theory: A Critique of Race and Modernity', unpublished PhD thesis (University of Southampton, 1999), p28. For a critique of the consequences that tend to come with being declared a 'pioneer of postcolonial studies', see D Macey, *Frantz Fanon: A Life* (London, 2000), p26-28.

6: James himself wrote several book reviews for *International Socialism* in the 1960s, one of which, 'Revolutionary Creativity', is reprinted on the C L R James Archive at http://www.marxists.org.uk/archive/james -clr/works/1964/creative.htm. Ian Birchall recalls that in 1967 C L R James shared a platform with Tony Cliff and others for an International Socialists rally on the fiftieth anniversary of the Russian Revolution. If any readers knew James, or perhaps have information on his relationship to the International Socialist tradition, then please feel free to contact me at cjhogsb jerg@hotmail.com

7: P Henry and P Buhle (eds), *C L R James's Caribbean* (London, 1992), p41.

8: See James's *Beyond a Boundary* (1963) for life growing up in colonial Trinidad. The quote comes from C L R James, 'Slavery Today: A Shocking Exposure', *Tit-Bits*, 5 August 1933.

9: C L R James, *Beyond a Boundary* (London, 1969), p41.

10: P Henry and P Buhle (eds), as above, p56.

11: P Buhle (ed), as above, p55.

12: G Farred (ed), *Rethinking C L R James* (Oxford, 1996), p17.

13: C L R James, *The Black Jacobins: Toussaint L'Ouverture and the San Domingo Revolution* (London, 2001), p315.

14: C L R James, *Beyond a Boundary*, as above, p119.

15: A Grimshaw (ed), *The C L R James Reader* (Oxford, 1992), p53.

16: In this James was following in the footsteps of other Trinidadian nationalists. See S Cudjoe, 'C L R James and the Trinidad and Tobago Intellectual Tradition', *New Left Review* 223, (1997).

17: A Grimshaw, *The C L R James Archive: A Readers' Guide* (New York, 1991), p94. *Minty Alley* was published in 1936.

18: C L R James, *Letters from London* (Oxford, 2003), p122. These letters that James wrote for the *Port of Spain Gazette* from London in 1932 give a fascinating insight into his thinking at this time.

19: For more on 'Red Nelson' see J Liddington, *The Life and Times of a Respectable Rebel: Selina Cooper 1864-1946* (London, 1984).

20: C L R James, *Eightieth Birthday Lectures* (London, 1984), p55, and *Beyond a Boundary*, as above, p122. For the British Labour government's repression of Indian nationalists, see the excellent discus-

sion in J Newsinger, *The Blood Never Dried: A People's History of the British Empire* (London, 2006), p144-147.

21: C L R James, *Beyond a Boundary*, as above, p124.

22: A Bogues, *Caliban's Freedom: The Early Political Thought of C L R James* (London, 1997), p49.

23: C L R James, *American Civilisation* (Oxford, 1993), p297.

24: C L R James, *Letters from London*, as above, p124-125.

25: C L R James, *American Civilisation*, as above, p297.

26: A Grimshaw (ed), as above, p291.

27: C L R James, *At the Rendezvous of Victory: Selected Writings vol 3* (London, 1984), p240.

28: D Widgery, 'C L R James', in D Widgery, *Preserving Disorder: Selected Essays 1968-88* (London, 1989), p123.

29: C Harman, *A People's History of the World* (London, 1999), p494.

30: C L R James, *World Revolution, 1917-1936: The Rise and Fall of the Communist International* (New Jersey, 1994), p379.

31: As above, p381.

32: C L R James, 'Interview with Al Richardson' (1986), *Revolutionary History*, http://www.revolutionary-history.co.uk/supplem/jamesint.htm

33: For how James's study of the Haitian Revolution influenced his thought about Abyssinian resistance to imperialism, see my article, C Høgsbjerg, 'C L R James and Italy's Conquest of Abyssinia', *Socialist History* 28 (2006). This issue of *Socialist History* is devoted to 'The Abyssinian Crisis'.

34: The quote from Mussolini was from a speech he gave at Pontinia, December 18 1935, quoted in the *Times*, 20 December 1935. See G Padmore, *Africa and World Peace* (London, 1972), p153.

35: See, for example, C L R James, 'Abyssinia and the Imperialists', in A Grimshaw (ed), as above.

36: C L R James, 'George Padmore: Black Marxist Revolutionary', in *At the Rendezvous of Victory*, as above, p255.

37: K Worcester, *C L R James: A Political Biography* (New York, 1996), p45.

38: C L R James, *World Revolution*, as above, p16. *World Revolution* was banned by the British colonial authorities in India.

39: P Davison (ed), *The Complete Works of George Orwell*, vol 11 (London, 1998), p87. On George Orwell, see J Newsinger, *Orwell's Politics* (Basingstoke, 1999).

40: See *Revolutionary History*, vol 6, nos 2/3 (1996), p53.

41: S Bornstein and A Richardson, *Against the Stream: A History of the Trotskyist Movement in Britain, 1924-1938* (London, 1986), p216.

42: J Archer, 'C L R James and British Trotskyism, 1932-38', *Revolutionary History*, vol 6, nos 2/3 (1996), p64. For a more personal insight on James and British Trotskyism in the 1930s, see the memoir by Louise Cripps, *C L R James: Memories and Commentaries* (London, 1997).

43: B Schwarz (ed), *West Indian Intellectuals in Britain* (Manchester, 2003), p137.

44: C L R James, *The Black Jacobins*, as above, ppviii, xviii.

45: J D Young, *The World of C L R James: His Unfragmented Vision* (Glasgow, 1999), p64.

46: E Genovese, *In Red and Black: Marxian Explorations in Southern and Afro-American History* (London, 1971), p155. For further discussion of 'classic Marxist historiography' see P Blackledge, *Reflections on the Marxist Theory of History* (Manchester, 2006). Stuart Hall has an illuminating discussion of *The Black Jacobins* in *History Workshop Journal* 46 (1998).

47: E J Hobsbawm, 'The Historians Group of the Communist Party', in M Cornforth (ed), *Rebels and Their Causes* (London, 1978), p23.

48: C L R James, 'Trotsky's Place in History', in S McLemee and P Le Blanc (eds), *C L R James and Revolutionary Marxism: Selected writings of C L R James, 1939-49* (New Jersey, 1994), pp94, 118, 123.

49: C Gair (ed), *Beyond Boundaries: C L R James and Postnational Studies* (London, 2006), p129. For personal insight into James's 'American years', see the autobiography of the late Constance Webb, *Not Without Love: Memoirs* (London, 2003), together with A Grimshaw (ed), *Special Delivery: The letters of C L R James to Constance Webb, 1939-1948* (Oxford, 1990).

50: Their discussion is reprinted in G Breitman (ed), *Leon Trotsky on Black Nationalism and Self-Determination* (New York, 1972), and discussed in A Shawki, 'Black Liberation and Socialism in the United States', *International Socialism* 47, (Summer 1990). See also M Shachtman, *Race and Revolution* (London, 2003), and S McLemee (ed), *C L R James on the 'Negro Question'* (Jackson, 1996).

51: D Georgakas and M Surkin, *Detroit: I Do Mind Dying* (London, 1998), ppxi, 16, 262. Georgakas and Surkin in their history of the League note that 'James's ideas were well known to League activists and *Black Jacobins* was the work which struck the deepest chord.'

52: See A Callinicos, *Trotskyism* (Minneapolis, 1990), which is online at: http://www.marxists.de/trotism/callinicos/index.htm See also my brief discussion in C Høgsbjerg, 'Beyond the Boundary of Leninism? C L R James and 1956', *Revolutionary History* vol 9, no 3 (2006), (forthcoming). Grace Lee Boggs's autobiography, *Living for Change* (Minneapolis, 1998), also sheds much light on the 'Johnson-Forest Tendency'. In America James used the pseudonym 'J R Johnson' while Raya Dunayevskaya was 'Freddie Forest'. In 1955 the tendency, by then called 'Correspondence', split when Dunayevskaya broke away to form her own 'Marxist-Humanist' group, News and Letters.

53: As James put it in 1950, Stalinist Russia represented a 'desperate attempt under the guise of "socialism" and "planned economy" to reorganise the means of production without releasing the proletariat from wage slavery.' See C L R James, R Dunayevskaya, and G Lee, *State Capitalism and World Revolution* (Chicago, 1986), p7.

54: As above, pp58-59.

55: C L R James, *World Revolution*, as above, p171.

56: For a spirited defence of James's theory of the party, see M Glaberman (ed), *Marxism for Our Times: C L R James on Revolutionary Organisation* (Jackson, 1999). Contrary to popular belief, James never dropped his belief that Marxists needed to form some sort of revolutionary organisation, but he seemed perfectly content to replace Lenin's ideas on the party with the rather general formulations of Marx, despite the fact that Marx developed his ideas about revolutionary organisation at a time when reformism had a much weaker hold on the organised working class movement. For a discussion of the difference between Marx and Lenin on this question, see John Molyneux's *Marxism and the Party* (London, 1978).

57: Q Hoare and G Nowell Smith (eds), *Selections from the Prison Notebooks of Antonio Gramsci* (London, 2003), p175.

58: K Worcester, as above, p106.

59: See B Schwarz, 'C L R James's American Civilization', in C Gair (ed), as above. I have drawn attention to the circumstances in which James came to write *Beyond a Boundary* in C Høgsbjerg, 'Facing post-colonial reality? C L R James, the black Atlantic and 1956', in K Flett (ed), *1956* (Cambridge, 2006) (forthcoming).

60: C L R James, *World Revolution*, p234.

61: See James's speech praising Kwame Nkrumah in Accra, Ghana, in 1960. C L R James, *Nkrumah and the Ghana Revolution* (London, 1977), p164.

62: P Berman, *Terror and Liberalism* (London, 2003), pp22, 206-207.

63: See, for example, James's discussion of voodoo in *The Black Jacobins*, or his pioneering study of millenarian movements in colonial Africa in C L R James, *A History of Negro Revolt* (London, 1938), p85. In a lecture James gave in Trinidad in 1960, he told his audience that 'if you want to read about anti-imperialism and anti-colonialism, take the Bible and read the last book, that is the Revelations of St John'. Quoted in A L Nielsen, *C L R James: A Critical Introduction* (Jackson, 1997), p144.

64: C L R James, *The Black Jacobins*, as above, pp109, 300.

65: Jowell's comments were made as an English heritage plaque was unveiled to C L R James in Brixton in October 2004, reported on the BBC website at the time. See also *The Black Jacobins*, as above, p229.

66: D Lammy, 'My History Hero: C L R James', *BBC History*, October 2005.

67: C L R James, 'Trotsky's Place in History', as above, p105. On the fate of revolutionary leaders after their death, see V I Lenin, *The State and Revolution* (London, 1992), p7.

68: See H Draper, *The Two Souls of Socialism* (London, 1996).

69: See Reid's interview in the *New Statesman*, 3 March 2003.

The real Simon Bolivar

Andy Brown

A review of John Lynch, **Simon Bolivar: A Life** *(Yale University Press, 2006), £25*

The Communication and Information Ministry of the Bolivarian Government of Venezuela has recently published a short pamphlet called *Simon Bolivar: Liberator of Nations, Homeland Creator*. It is in English and for free distribution. The foreword is two quotes, one from historian Guillermo Sherwel:

'Those who studied Bolivar feel at the end of their task the same reverence one feels on leaving a sacred place, where the spirit has been under the influence of the supernatural and the sublime.'

The second quote is from the hero of Cuban nationalism, Jose Marti:

'One cannot speak calmly of someone who never lived in peace; of Bolivar one can speak with a mountain as a rostrum, or in the midst of thunder and lightning, or with a bunch of free peoples in one's grip and the tyranny beheaded at one's feet!'

The legacy of Bolivar is key to the rhetoric of Chavez's government in Venezuela, yet in reality little is known of his real life or his political ideas. These were fundamentally important in Spanish America, but translate into the 21st century only with considerable difficulty. John Lynch's new biography, *Simon Bolivar: A Life*, is very significant, being the first major work about him in English in decades. It is an excellent and exhaustive account of his career, especially the military campaigns. It also reveals the political ideas of Bolivar's generation and the eventual failure of his project in his own time.

Spanish America at the turn of the 19th century was a society under pressure and ripe for change. The Spanish Bourbon state had reasserted a heavy-handed control of its colonial possessions in South America. Its political character was absolutist. Its economic function was, in the words of Simon Bolivar, 'to satisfy the insatiable greed of Spain' through the export of primary products from agriculture and mining. This was done mainly through imported black and indigenous labour, which was inefficient in production and low in consumption. There was a Spanish elite in charge, from the mainland and sometimes from the Canaries, with its local royalist collaborators.

There was also dissent among the local elite. A creole (American born) faction had considerable wealth with some European and university learning and commercial links, especially with the British West Indies. There were the beginnings of manufacturing for export and trade and with it increasing autonomy from the centres of Spanish colonial rule. Deprived of political representation, these people found themselves with a growing identity but without power.

Dangerous ideas from abroad were knocking at the door of South America. In North America the colonists had revolted against the taxation without representation of the British and fought their war of independence in 1776. From Europe and North America came the ideas of the Age of Reason. Most important was the French Revolution of 1789 which struck terror into the crowned heads, the religious leaders and the political establishment, and reverberated across the Atlantic. Directly in its wake came the massive slave uprising in St Domingue, where the 'Black Jacobins' ended slavery in the island and inspired black rebellion from New York to Sao Paolo. The simmering cauldron of hundreds of thousands of slaves along with free blacks and mixed race descendants threatened to boil over anywhere.

Simon Bolivar was one of the new generation in Venezuela, which did not accept the absolutism and centralism of Bourbon Spain. Born into the white elite as a seventh generation descendant of Basque migrants, he enjoyed the privilege of wealth and the status of his race. He followed a fairly typical upper class education, including the grand tour to Spain at the age of 15. He returned to Europe in 1803 to visit France and Italy, there to witness the march of republican France and the maelstrom of new ideas. John Lynch says 'it was the French authors of the Age of Reason who unlocked the minds of Americans and infused the thinking of Bolivar'.

Bolivar himself summarised his ideals like this:

'A republican government: that is what Venezuela…should have. Its principles should be the sovereignty of the people, division of powers, civil liberty, prohibition of slavery and the abolition of monarchy and privileges. We need equality to recast, so to speak, into a single whole, the classes of men, political opinions and political custom.'

As Lynch comments, these words not only state his ideas for Venezuela, but describe the model of revolution evolved in the Western hemisphere since 1776. But Bolivar was not an idealist. His ideas were a guide to action and he stressed pragmatism

as well as ideology. As much as ideas, he saw American interest as a motivator for change. The idea of colonial independence was not integral to the ideas of all Enlightenment thinkers. Spanish liberals, for example, often saw the possibility of a liberal government running a more enlightened empire. There was no agreed vision either of equality between peoples or of colonial wars of independence. Some were indeed passionate advocates of colonial liberation. Abbe Reynal and Thomas Paine were outstanding in this. Paine fiercely defended the right to American independence with the blinding logic that 'there is something absurd in supposing a continent to be perpetually ruled by an island' and Reynal prophesied the imminent separation of Spain from its American colonies. These, however, were the exception.

Bolivar's fusion of the ideas of the Enlightenment with a distinctively pro-independence position took him further than many in Europe and indeed in Venezuela. Some there wanted more autonomy from Spain but, fearing the social upheaval which this might bring, drew back from support for independence. His whole-hearted commitment made him a figurehead in the South American independence movement and marked, I think, a genuine advance in the logic of Enlightenment ideas.

It was Spain's collapse as a major European power which opened the door to revolt in South America. Thoroughly eclipsed by a vibrant commercial Britain and an aggressive and confident republican France, it lost the ability to hold its colonies as the new century began. The growing prominence of the US as a market and producer also loosened ties between South America and Europe. The British fleet cut links to Spain and threatened territory. Revolts of autonomy-minded Venezuelans and freedom-minded slaves showed what was to come. In 1810 independent juntas sprang up in various parts of Spanish America, confused and divided among themselves about autonomy, independence or loyalism. Bolivar acted as unofficial ambassador in London and became more and more convinced that only outright independence would safeguard both the interests of his country and of his class. Meanwhile the Spanish reasserted control and the junta in Caracas fell.

Returning to America in 1812 Bolivar operated from New Granada (now Colombia) from which Venezuela was ruled. His *Cartagena Manifesto* declared roundly for independence, but in an interesting precursor of his moves away from mainstream liberal ideas, also for strong central government in order to secure military survival and social peace. With a small army of around 700 he moved down the Magdalena River and began raiding Spanish positions and invaded Venezuela. Entering Caracas in August 1813, he was granted supreme power in January 1814. His favourite occupations, history records, were 'being in the company of his numerous mistresses and lying in his hammock'. His struggle with the Spanish was ruthless and bloody on both sides, including the execution of prisoners. The Venezuelan elite was divided between the republic and the monarchy as to how best to protect its interests. The new republic was threatened not only by the colonial power but also by the possibility of slave revolts and attacks by the llanero warlords of the interior, also mainly black. The republic fell and Bolivar went into exile in British Jamaica in 1815.

Once there Bolivar developed and reconstructed his vision of colonial emancipation. It was an exercise in applied liberalism, featuring natural rights, resistance to oppression, and economic and political opportunity. It also argued for strong central authority, in the belief that:

'Events…have proved that wholly representative institutions are not suited to our character, customs and present knowledge. In Caracas this led us back into slavery.'

In 1816 he moved to Haiti, where he was promised aid in return for a pledge to free the slaves in Venezuela. A thwarted invasion from there was followed by another from Guyana. Bolivar widened his base this time, incorporating the main llanero leaders into the republican army and co-opting the aspirations of many mixed race (pardo) Venezuelans. Offering freedom in return for military service, he also neutralised the threat that slaves could be used against the republican cause. A new assembly was called to combine politics with his military strategy. He demanded an explicitly Venezuelan model of government, with legal equality between races, and a two chamber parliament with a strong and centralised executive. The army grew, including up to 6,000 British and Irish volunteers, and crossed the Andes in one of Bolivar's epic marches. Routing the Spanish at Boyaca he entered Bogota in August 1819 and declared a joint republic of Colombia, Venezuela and the as yet untouched Ecuador. By 1821 the Spanish Empire was crumbling across the continent—in Buenos Aires, Chile and Guayaquil. Bolivar mopped up along the Caribbean coast and re-entered Caracas to establish the joint republic.

Bolivar's republic had in theory a strong central government with provincial governors. It was torn from the very start between centralisers and federalists. Bolivar himself was strongly centralist and also believed in the use of the army as an agent to unify and to impose national identity. A rstricted franchise left power firmly in the hands of the elite. The indian tribute was abolished, but slavery was not. Liberation released a flood of incompatible interests, over land, power, race and slavery. Wealth replaced hereditary status as the key to access to power, with a shift in favour of wealthy agricultural producers and traders (though much trade was dominated by foreigners). The republic defended the interests of the creole elite. Beneath was a volcano of social tension.

In his section on Bolivarian society, John Lynch states the following:

'Bolivar conceived the American Revolution as more than a struggle for political independence. He saw it also as a great social movement, which would improve as well as liberate.'

However, the project of improvement had very severe limits. Bolivar aspired to a society of property owning citizens. Land was given to the soldiers of liberation, but largely in the form of bonds, which were promises of land. There was anyway an inequality between grants made to officers and those to men, but the ordinary soldiers often sold their bonds for cash, resulting in a concentration of granted land in the hands of the officers. Independence produced greater land concentration than before. There was little economic development or investment and a systematic attempt by the rich to avoid taxes. Bolivarian society did not materially benefit the poor. Nor did it break from the dependence on trading raw materials for manufactured goods. Arguably those who benefited most from the post-colonial economy were the British, who dominated trade in the region.

Bolivar was an abolitionist and never a racist. He stressed that it was 'madness that a revolution for liberty should try to maintain slavery'. However, no abolition legislation was passed. There was some

manumission in return for military service, but it was not until 1854 that abolition came to Venezuela.

Bolivar had a paternalistic regard for the indigenous people:

'The poor indians are truly in a state of lamentable depression. I intend to help them all I can. First as a matter of humanity, second because it is their right and finally because doing good costs nothing and is worth much.'

The indian tribute was abolished, but paradoxically this tended to work against indigenous people. Tribute had at least conferred some implied entitlement to communal lands. Now the land was privatised and generally taken over by creoles. For the indigenous there was a cycle of debt, sale and encroachment.

Bolivar was frustrated by the faction fighting among the creole elite in Colombia and still had ambitions for a greater vision, so he headed south in 1822 to incorporate Quito, only nominally part of the republic, and Guayaquil, now under a republican junta. He met considerable resistance but the royalists were defeated at Pichincha by General Sucre, advancing from Guayaquil. Peru was largely royalist and hostile and the Bolivar bandwagon moved down in 1823. Fighting first on the coast and then again crossing the Andes, the multinational republican army of Colombia defeated the Spanish first in Peru at Junin and Ayacucho and eventually in 1825 in Upper Peru, now Bolivia.

Bolivar was now the figurehead of a liberated territory stretching from Potosi to the Orinoco. Sucre had done much of the crucial fighting in the later southern campaigns. His military brilliance was matched by his unswerving loyalty to Bolivar and his insatiable desire, like so many of us, for early retirement. Bolivar was usually acclaimed in office by a local creole elite, which sometimes had not even fought for liberation. Here he devised his political constitutions, with the Bolivian one thought to be the culmination of his political thought.

His commitment to his original liberal ideas was matched by a desire for strong central control. The aide de camp and chronicler Daniel O'Leary records that:

'He sought a system of controlling revolutions, not theories which might foment them; the fatal sprit of ill-conceived democracy which had already produced so many evils in America had to be curbed.'

Bolivar himself echoed this:

'The sovereignty of the people is not unlimited, because it is based on justice and constrained by the concept of perfect utility... How can the representatives of the people think they are authorised constantly to change the social organisation? What then will become the basis of rights, properties, honour and the life of citizens?'

The constitution was a liberal document. It held commitments to legal equality, civil rights, security and property. It had an independent judiciary and an elected legislature. The slaves in Bolivia were declared free. But it also provided for a president for life who could appoint his successor. The vice-president was also selected and acted as prime minister. Thus, as Bolivar put it, 'elections would be avoided, which are the greatest scourge of republics and produce only anarchy'. The British consul claimed it was based on the British model of 'useful liberty but obviating any mischievous excess of popular power'. The faithful Sucre was left running Bolivia in what Lynch describes as 'a model of enlightened absolutism'.

In fact, Bolivia and the rest of the liberated territories suffered the same fate. The economy stagnated. Progressive initiatives were either unaffordable or strangled by the ruling class, who fought among themselves and agreed only in preserving their own self-interest against the volcano beneath. The identities which had galvanised the revolt against the Spanish fractured against each other. Bolivar himself undoubtedly had a vision of continental unity, even attempting a Congress of the Americas in Panama in 1826. This was not shared by most of the creoles. Bolivar returned to Bogota to preside over internecine strife and to hear of revolts in Bolivia, Peru, Ecuador, Venezuela and parts of Colombia itself. By 1830 Venezuela and Ecuador had declared independence. Bolivar, unable to contain a fractious Congress and a homicidal vice-president or resolve the political problems, left for exile and died en route.

Bolivar's most famous quote is from 1830 as he surveyed the wreckage of his dream. As self-assessments go, it is not very positive:

'I have ruled for 20 years and from these I have gained only a few certainties:
    America is ungovernable, for us;
    Those who serve a revolution plough the sea;
    The only thing one can do in America is emigrate;
    This country will fall inevitably into the hands of the unbridled masses and then pass almost imperceptibly into the hands of petty tyrants, of all colours and races;
    Once we have been devoured by every crime and extinguished by utter ferocity, the Europeans will not even regard us as worth conquering;
    If it were possible for any part of the world to revert to primitive chaos, it would be America in its final hour.'

It should be said that this was followed by a final message of stubborn commitment to republican Colombia.

So what about our own assessment of Bolivar? He was the pioneer of the independence movement first and foremost, but also the most important figure in establishing the political ideas of the Enlightenment in the continent. In his attachment to colonial liberation from empire, he pushed the logic of those ideas further than many. In his implementation of them in constitutions and political regimes he was pragmatic before being idealistic, especially in his commitment to (some would say, his obsession with) strong, centralist government. Lynch says he advocated 'not the best system of government, but the one most likely to work'. However, his influence was still behind the establishment of modern notions of governance such as constitutional government, the sovereignty of the people and the rule of law. He was the bearer of the most important ideas of the French and North American revolutions into South America, as well as some advanced views on education, literacy and social improvement. He was a man of his time and a man of his class, the privileged creole elite which defended its economic interests through new, modern political means in the early 19th century. His ignorance of the mass of the people in his political vision makes him part of the mainstream of liberal ideas of the time, not a betrayer of them. We should neither be surprised nor disappointed by the limitations of his project.

Bolivar's legacy is being claimed by all and sundry in Latin America and has been for decades, if not centuries. His body was returned to Venezuela from its grave in Colombia to help a president in trouble in 1842 and transferred in 1867 to a suitably impressive pantheon. His legacy remains a subject for debate, appropriated by many and shaped to fit their political needs.

The Chavez government's biographical pamphlet assesses him thus:

'Rather than a valuable American historic symbol, he is the citizen who changed the course of our history; he is the Caracas man whose glory is immortalised in each of the main squares of Venezuela and other countries. Whether on horseback, in bust or standing, he looks to the North as a rule, without losing sight of victory; living in the memory of the Bolivarian Republic of Venezuela, the Fifth [Chavez's] Republic that dignifies the memory and puts into practice the thought of Simon Bolivar, The Liberator.

'That is why, at this historic moment, the Venezuelan people honour The Liberator, not only by calling themselves Bolivarian, but also by giving continuity to his anti-imperialist struggle for the integration and vindication of the peoples.'

Most of this notion that Bolivar's ideas are a model for modern political processes is at best insubstantial and at times, frankly, bogus. In a process which seeks a new socialism for the 21st century, Bolivar's notions of democracy, sovereignty, even equality, are not models or ideas to be put into practice. Even in his anti-imperialism this is questionable. James Dunkerley has pointed out that Bolivar's hostility to colonial powers is restricted to Spain. His view of Britain's government and empire is much more generous.

There remain, however, two central parts of Bolivar's dream which are still valid and explain the attraction of his mantle. The first is the vision of unity, common interest and solidarity, which is shared by millions of ordinary Latin Americans. The second is the vision of liberation in which the resources, sovereignty and political mastery of the continent lie firmly in the hands of Latin Americans themselves.

What is fascism?
Jim Wolfreys

A review of Michael Mann, **Fascists** *(Cambridge University Press, 2004), £15.99, and Robert Paxton,* **The Anatomy of Fascism** *(Penguin, 2004), £8.99*

Fascism has always been the hardest of political movements to understand. This is largely because of its complex relationship to capitalism. Emerging in an era of capitalist expansion, imperialism and democratisation, fascism articulated anger at political and economic elites but then forged alliances with them once in power. During the inter-war period a number of Marxist theories of fascism were developed which identified the middle class, or petty bourgeoisie, as the key component in its make up. Several decades earlier Marx's own analysis of the petty bourgeoisie had underlined its distinctive outlook,

'In the most advanced societies...the situation of the petty bourgeois predisposes him towards both socialism and capitalism...he is dazzled by the expansion of power of the big bourgeoisie on the one side, yet he shares in the suffering of the people on the other. He is bourgeois and people simultaneously. At heart he prides himself on being neutral, on having found the true balance, albeit without falling into mediocrity. This petty bourgeois is the glorification of antithesis, since antithesis is the basis of his existence. He himself is nothing other than the personification of social contradiction'.[1]

During the crisis years of the inter-war period mainstream parties were no longer capable of providing political solutions for these people. Fascism offered them an authoritarian alternative which shifted social frustrations onto the symbols of national decline and renewal, offering individuals who felt powerless a sense of superiority through militant nationalism and violence, initially against the labour movement, but later against all groups considered a threat to the 'community of destiny'.

'In the atmosphere brought to white heat by war, defeat, reparations, inflation, occupation of the Ruhr, crisis, need, and despair, the petty bourgeoisie rose up against all the old parties that had bamboozled it,' wrote Trotsky in the most urgent and compelling of all analyses of fascism. 'The sharp grievances of small proprietors never out of bankruptcy, of their university sons without posts and clients, of their daughters without dowries and suitors, demanded order and an iron hand'.[2]

What set fascism apart from other forms of conservatism or authoritarianism was its ability to mobilise on the streets. Fascism had to prove itself in practice, not just as an alternative to political opponents, but also to the state. The hierarchical structure of fascist organisations fuelled a desire to dominate while reconciling members to their personal insignificance before a higher power, summed up in Hitler's maxim, 'Responsibility towards above, authority towards below.' Fascist ideology was geared towards building an independent mass movement and relates, as Geoff Eley has underlined, not just to the party's ideas or formal aims, but to 'its style of activism, modes of organisation and forms of public display'.[3]

The autonomous development of fascism as a movement means that theories which claim it ended up as simply a puppet of big business once in power are wide of the mark. 'Fascism', argued the Italian Communist Antonio Gramsci, 'is a movement which the bourgeoisie thought should be a simple "instrument" of reaction in its hands, but once called up and unleashed is worse than the devil, no longer allowing itself to be controlled'.[4] But neither is it true that fascist parties were able to subordinate all aspects of the state and the economy to their will. Both Hitler and Mussolini repressed 'radical' elements within their ranks on taking power. In Germany and Italy the fascist regimes shared common interests with sections of the ruling class.[5]

There is nothing to suggest, however, that the Holocaust was a requirement of German business interests or that it served any economic purpose. No explanation of the Holocaust is possible without an understanding of the Nazis' biological racism. This does not mean counterposing 'ideology' to 'economics', as if only one frame of reference is valid, but attempting to explain why Nazi ideas took such a hold. This, in turn, as Alex Callinicos has argued, means locating these ideas within the wider web of relationships which shaped the evolution of the National Socialist regime.[6]

To identify fascist ideology as a projection onto another plane of fears and anxieties deriving from social turmoil is not to dismiss its role, but to begin to explain why so many took it so seriously. Studies within the Marxist tradition which have situated ideological, programmatic and organisational features of fascist parties in the context of their relationship to broader social, political and economic questions have been able to provide rich and detailed analyses of the phenomenon, and to distinguish it from other forms of reaction in a way that makes it possible to identify contemporary variants of fascism.

Central to such studies has been a nuanced grasp of the relationship between fascist parties and their predominantly middle class base on the one hand, and their allies within ruling circles on the other. But the richness of analyses in the classical Marxist tradition, supplemented by others whose work was influenced by it, became obscured by the line developed by the Communist International, or Comintern, under Stalin's influence, which saw fascism as a tool of the ruling class: 'The open, terroristic dictatorship of the most reactionary, most chauvinistic and most imperialist elements of finance capital'. The arguments of those, like Klara Zetkin and Trotsky, who had insisted on the strength of fascism as an autonomous movement, were cast aside in favour of a crude analysis which saw it as an instrument of big capital. How and why fascism developed as a movement, what the motivations of its supporters were, how the organisations held themselves together, what their ideas consisted of, all these were arbitrary considerations beside the outcome—an extreme form of capitalist rule.

More recently, Marxist or 'social' analyses of fascism have been further overshadowed by studies which identify ideas as the defining element in the make-up of fascist organisations. Adrian Lyttelton, author of a number of important studies of Italian fascism, recently summed up prevailing attitudes in academic circles:

'By way of self-criticism, I would say that my approach to the study of fascist ideology was too much influenced by

Marxist or sociological theories. After the "linguistic turn" we are all more sensitive to the autonomy of political discourse, or we should be'.[7]

One of the features of recent studies has been their obsession with elaborating a concise definition of fascism. As with the Comintern's maxim, these tend to focus on one aspect of the phenomenon at the expense of others. Zeev Sternhell, whose work on the French extreme right has prioritised the history of ideas, sees fascism as a revolutionary movement which is 'neither left nor right'. The British historian Roger Griffin has won an audience for his view that fascism is above all a movement of national rebirth. But this emphasis on ideology above all else has made it harder to understand the link between fascist movements and regimes, and between different national variations of fascism. For the Italian historian Renzo de Felice, for example, Italian fascism and German Nazism were two entirely separate things. Sternhell also concluded that Nazism could not be considered fascist because of its biological determinism, which was not part of the ideology of fascism.

One of the effects of this 'linguistic turn' has been to deprive historians of the tools required to understand contemporary fascism. The scope for comparison between movements of the inter-war period and those emerging today has been limited by the notion that fascist ideas must be treated as a 'pure' ideology. So the response of many French historians, for example, to the emergence of Jean-Marie Le Pen's Front National in the 1980s was to dismiss comparisons with inter-war fascism on the grounds that Le Pen, in contrast to 'totalitarian' regimes, was in favour of individual freedom and economic liberalism.[8] This reflex, of relating the characteristics of actual organisations to a so-called 'fascist minimum' or checklist, generally results in too much credence being given to the stated aims of the parties in question. The largely uncritical reception which greeted Gianfranco Fini's assertion that the Movimento Sociale Italiano (MSI), the only major party of the post-war extreme right to identify openly and consistently with fascism, had by the mid-1990s become a 'post-fascist' organisation as the Alleanza Nazionale, is a case in point. Whether the party's integration into Italy's political establishment has definitively put an end to its potential to mobilise a radicalised mass base is a question which cannot be answered simply by relying on the pronouncements of its leadership, particularly since most fascist parties have by now understood that they will not succeed without distancing themselves from the regimes of the inter-war period.

But how then can we distinguish between fascism and other forms of authoritarian reaction? How do we know what makes a Le Pen or a Fini or a Haider a 'real' fascist or not? Robert Paxton's The Anatomy of Fascism provides the best recent guide to unpicking these questions, and offers the most authoritative and convincing challenge to the prevailing trends of post-war studies of the subject. For this reason alone, it is the most important work on fascism of the past 20 years. Definitions, he argues, are static: 'They succumb all too often to the intellectual's temptation to take programmatic statements as constitutive, and to identify fascism more with what it said than what it did'.[9] According to Paxton it is not the themes taken up by fascism that define the phenomenon, but their function. Since fascism is based on a rejection of universal values, it is more disparate than other political movements, and must be understood not 'as the expression of the same fixed essence', but within specific historical contexts. He rejects the way some historians have offered separate definitions of fascism and Nazism, arguing that this leads to the study of fascism in isolation from other factors. Analyses which reduce fascism to a tool of a particular interest group, meanwhile, ignore the fact that the movement won independent popular backing. Instead Paxton proposes to examine the development of fascism through five stages: the creation of a movement; its rooting in the political system; the seizure of power; the exercise of power; its fate in the long term (radicalisation or entropy).

The development of fascist parties unfolds as a series of processes and choices: 'seeking a following, forming alliances, bidding for power, then exercising it'. And this, he argues, 'is why the conceptual tools that illuminate one stage may not necessarily work equally well for others'.[10] While ideas may be important in the early stages of fascist movements, fascism relies more on 'immediate sensual experience' than on reasoned argument, appealing to followers through mobilising passions (the subordination of the individual to the group, perceived as a victim and threatened by decline; the cult of voluntarism, violence and leadership) rather than dogma. Paxton also stresses the extent to which fascism is influenced by context, forced to shift course according to the possibilities open to it. The strength of the Italian left at the end of the First World War, for example, closed off the use of socialist rhetoric to Mussolini. Fascism was constantly reshaped as it grew into the space available to it. In action, then, fascism 'looks much more like a network of relationships than a fixed essence'.[11] Those who ended up as allies of fascism made choices that were not necessarily their preferred options, proceeding, 'from choice to choice, along a path of narrowing options. At each fork in the road, they choose the anti-socialist solution'.[12]

Sternhell has objected that Paxton is guilty of dismissing the intellectual output of fascist parties and their supporters as 'distractions of little importance'. Since Paxton claims that it is practice, rather than ideology, which counts in analysing fascism, how can we distinguish between fascism and authoritarianism? For Sternhell, it is 'the ideology, the vision of man and society, the aims a movement sets itself, its philosophy of history, that are important'.[13] And since no party has ever acted on all of its stated aims, he argues, Paxton's methodology is invalid unless it can be applied to any political movement.[14]

For his part, Paxton claims that fascism is not like other 'isms' (socialism, conservatism, liberalism), which are based on 'coherent philosophical systems laid out in works of systematic thinkers'.[15] Fascism emerged as a response to the development of mass democracy, seeking out, 'in each national culture those themes that are best capable of mobilising a mass movement of regeneration, unification and purity', and directing it against liberal individualism, constitutionalism and the left.[16] Here the distinction between function and themes becomes clearer. Action, not doctrine or philosophy, is what drove the major fascist movements of the inter-war period. In a new era of mass politics, 'emotions…carefully stage-managed ceremonies, and intensely charged rhetoric' counted for more than 'the truth of any of the propositions advanced in its name'. In place of rational debate, fascism substituted the immediacy of sensual experience, turning politics into aesthetics.[17]

Paxton stresses that fascism is shot through with tensions, between radical and more conservative activists, and, once in power, between the normative or legal state apparatus and what he calls the prerogative, or party, state. The basis for this 'dual' state is laid during the development of fascist organisations with the establishment of parallel structures. These structures, a defining feature of fascism, duplicate the functions of the state and present themselves as more viable alternatives, particularly when confronting the left.

This emphasis on what fascists do, rather than what they say, is also present in Michael Mann's detailed survey of European fascism. He deals bluntly with the fashionable academic preoccupation with fascism's 'mythic core':

'How can a "myth" generate "internal cohesion" or "driving force"?... A myth cannot be an agent driving or integrating anything, since ideas are not free-floating. Without power organisations, ideas cannot actually do anything... Fascism was not just a collection of individuals with certain beliefs. Fascism had a great impact on the world only because of its collective actions and its organisational forms'.[18]

Mann claims that the idealism which affects so many studies of fascism is best countered by examining not just the key values of fascism, but also its organisational forms. But, he goes out of his way to add, this does not imply that the 'traditional' alternative to idealism—a materialist analysis of fascism's relationship to capitalism and class—should be embraced. According to his own definition, fascism 'is the pursuit of a transcendent and cleansing nation-statism through paramilitarism'.[19] Like so many of the concise definitions of fascism proffered by innumerable studies on the subject, formally there is little to dispute in what Mann proposes. Despite his apparent

rejection of 'materialist' analyses, he does situate the development of fascism in the context of the social, political and economic crisis of inter-war capitalism and acknowledges the importance of understanding fascism's social base. He is at pains to stress, however, that 'social' should not be associated with class, despite its importance as a constituency of fascist support. Alongside class, he argues, we need to identify the 'core nation-statist and paramilitary constituencies' of fascism.

A strong subtext to this book, which clearly exercises Mann at least as much as its actual subject, is what he refers to as 'class theory', by which he means explanations of fascism which focus either on its relationship to capitalist elites or on its middle class base. Mann claims that Marxists simply reduce ideas 'to their supposed socio-economic base'.[20] His argument is that most 'class theorists' do not take enough account of fascists' own beliefs, which reject both class theories and materialism of any kind. Leaving aside the question as to whether fascists must believe they are pursuing class interests for that to be the case, 'class theory' appears, in Mann's hands, as something of a straw man. This is unfortunate because his determination to portray class as just one sociological descriptor among many diminishes his own attempt to provide an adequate explanation of what makes fascism tick.

We know that fascists in the inter-war period did not advance by proclaiming only their defence of petty bourgeois self-interest or an identification with historical materialism. It is also clear that part of the attraction of fascism was its appeal to the values embodied in the nation and the personality of the 'leader' who stood 'above classes'. Mann observes that fascism recruited from across the social spectrum, including a significant proportion of people who were 'indirect, not direct, observers of the most pronounced class struggle'.[21] But he over-reaches himself in making claims about the centrality of the 'nation-statist' bourgeoisie in fascist parties. A wealth of sources exist which demonstrate a preponderance of middle class elements in the Nazi Party, but Mann argues that in both Italy and Germany it was the educated 'nation-statist' bourgeoisie that was over-represented.[22] Yet his own evidence shows that the proportion of these elements was in many cases higher in rival right wing parties.

'Transcendental nation-statism' remains too nebulous a concept and plays too abstract a role in his explanation, which does not provide enough detail on how and why these ideas came to exert such an influence. As a consequence—and this is also true of Paxton's book—there is no satisfactory explanatory framework for the conflict between radicals and opportunists at the heart of fascist movements and regimes. Mann refuses to accept that fascism represented one side of the class struggle, 'or indeed any single class at all'.[23] As others have pointed out this does rather beg the question as to what the paramilitaries were engaged in, if not a ruthless class struggle against the organisations of the labour movement.[24] Despite acknowledging that once they neared power fascist movements 'became biased on questions of class struggle' and 'tilted toward the capitalist class', he offers little explanation as to why this should be the case and overall his analysis lacks sufficient feel for the texture of the motivations exercising fascist activists.

Despite the impressive scope and detail of Mann's six separate case studies, his insistence on the fixed nature of its values means that he is unable to conceive of fascism existing in a modern context. Inter-war fascism was, he claims,

'European epochal' rather than generic. His characterisation of modern parties like Le Pen's Front National and Jörg Haider's Freedom Party as 'rightist populist' borrows from precisely those analyses whose idealism he criticises at the start of the book. That these organisations are economically liberal and electoralist, and promote neither class transcendence nor militarism, does not justify the complacency of his conclusion:

'These radical populist parties may be disturbing, but provided that European "system parties" adapt themselves to the changing macro-environment, remaining responsive to citizen demands, European fascism is defeated, dead and buried. After their terrible 20th century, Europeans can at least take comfort from this'.[25]

Of course it may simply be coincidence that in France, Italy, Germany and Austria so many veterans of the Mussolini and Vichy regimes, and of the SS and the inter-war leagues, found themselves alongside self-styled 'nationalist revolutionaries' in organisations like the Freedom Party and the National Front, where identification with inter-war fascism remains an open secret and a cult of militarism is actively, if discreetly, encouraged. But one might have expected someone who, over the course of a 400-page book, had expressed such disdain for those who belong to a 'tradition of not taking fascists seriously', to take the trouble to find out how the members of such parties viewed themselves. Had he done so he would have found, in France for example, a fairly extensive analysis undertaken by far-right activists in the 1960s and 1970s which led to the formation of the Front National. For these 'revolutionary nationalists', changes to the post-war state and society—notably greater economic stability and the development of a white-collar bureaucracy loyal to state institutions—meant that fascists would have to organise along different lines to their predecessors, not least because open identification with their legacy would have negative consequences.

Although Paxton does not seriously engage with the role class plays in shaping the motivations and fortunes of fascist organisations, which limits the amount of light he is able to shed on their dynamic, his analysis is far more fluid and nuanced than Mann's. In particular he keeps pace with post-war developments by situating them within the stages of development outlined earlier. 'Since the old fascist clientele had nowhere else to go', he argues, 'it could be satisfied by subliminal hints followed by ritual public disavowals. For in order to move toward Stage Two [integration into the political system] in the France, Italy or Austria of the 1990s, one must be firmly recentred on the moderate Right'.[26]

The Anatomy of Fascism provides a lucid and accessible antidote to prevailing trends in the study of fascism. Its sensitivity to settings and to the way fascist parties adapt to changing contexts will help those who want to make sense of the contemporary extreme right without the hindrance of narrow, inflexible definitions which portray fascism as a danger that has passed:

'Armed by historical knowledge, we may be able to distinguish today's ugly but isolated imitations, with their shaved heads and swastika tattoos, from authentic functional equivalents in the form of a mature fascist-conservative alliance. Forewarned, we may be able to detect the real thing when it comes along'.[27]

NOTES
1: K Marx, Letter to Annekov, cited in D Beetham, *Marxists in Face of Fascism* (Manchester, 1983), pp242-243.

2: L Trotsky, *The Struggle Against Fascism in Germany* (New York, 1971), p400.
3: G Eley, *From Unification to Nazism: Reinterpreting the German Past* (Boston, 1986), p270.
4: A Gramsci, cited in D Beetham, as above, p9.
5: A Sohn-Rethel compares the relationship between the Nazi regime and the German ruling class to that found between capitalist moguls and management in large scale private companies: *The Economy and Class Structure of German Fascism* (London, 1987).
6: A Callinicos, 'Plumbing the Depths: Marxism and the Holocaust', *The Yale Journal of Criticism*, 14/2 (2001).
7: *New York Review of Books*, 12 May 2005.
8: See, for example, P Milza, *Fascismes Français* (Paris, 1987).
9: R Paxton, *The Anatomy of Fascism* (London, 2004), p14.
10: As above, p23.
11: As above, p207.
12: As above, p118.
13: Z Sternhell, 'The Anatomy of Fascism', *New York Review of Books*, 12 May 2005.
14: Z Sternhell, 'Morphology of Fascism in France', in the interesting collection of essays edited by B Jenkins, *France in the Era of Fascism* (Oxford, 2005), p54.
15: R Paxton, as above, p16.
16: As above, p40.
17: As above, pp16-17.
18: M Mann, *Fascists* (Cambridge, 2004), pp12-13.
19: As above, p13.
20: As above, p17.
21: As above, p172.
22: For a clear and measured analysis of the social base of the Nazi party see D Gluckstein, *The Nazis, Capitalism and the Working Class* (London, 1999).
23: M Mann, as above, pp359-360.
24: D Riley, 'Enigmas of Fascism', *New Left Review*, November/December 2004, p141.
25: M Mann, as above, p370.
26: R Paxton, as above, p185.
27: As above, p205.

bookmarks
the socialist bookshop

The Blood Never Dried: A People's History of the British Empire

by John Newsinger   *£11.99*

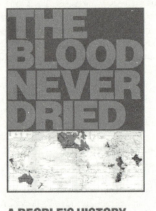

George's Bush's 'war on terror' has inspired a forest of books about US imperialism. But what of Britain's role in the world?

The Blood never Dried challenges the chorus of claims that the British Empire was a kinder, gentler force in the world.

At the heart of the Empire was the coercion of conquered peoples and their heroic struggles for freedom. But too little of this known.

John Newsinger has set out to uncover this neglected history of repression and revolt, from slaves in Jamaica to the brutal war for independence in Kenya.

He also looks at why the declining British Empire has looked to an alliance with US imperialism.

To the boast that 'the sun never set on the British Empire', the Chartist Ernest Jones, replied 'and the blood never dried'.

Deciphering the past

Megan Trudell

*A review of Paul Blackledge, **Reflections on the Marxist Theory of History** (Manchester University Press, 2006), £14.99, and Matt Perry, **Marxism and History** (Palgrave, 2002), £13.99*

Why does history matter? Two interconnected reasons present themselves for the serious study of history. The first is that the past is not simply a series of factual events, but is disputed. For ruling classes everywhere, their rule is the natural pinnacle of humanity's achievements. To portray the past as a seamless march of progress towards this point, and to write out or downgrade class conflict and revolutions, is part of legitimising that rule. Think of the revisionism of Niall Ferguson writing the history of the British Empire as one of a benevolent force, or of Simon Schama and Orlando Figes writing on the French and Russian revolutions respectively in terms which stress the aspects of terror and ignore those of popular democracy—as George Orwell wrote in 1984, cited by Matt Perry, 'Who controls the past controls the future: who controls the present controls the past' (cited in Perry, p22).

But, as importantly, activists today engaged with confronting wars and fighting for an alternative world need to know what forces and processes have shaped the present in order to make sense of what happens around us and draw the correct conclusions to decide on the most effective action. To view the current wars in Iraq, Afghanistan and Lebanon, for example, without an understanding of the development of imperialism, the impact of the Cold War, the foundation of the state of Israel, the historical role of Arab leaders, the economic pressures on the US ruling class and so on, can lead to a range of responses and courses of action that lead away from collective resistance to the system that breeds wars.

If we simply look at a situation at any given moment as a snapshot, the general trends or underlying processes are hidden from us, making political misunderstandings and mistakes more likely. In other words, history matters both in fighting against a suppression of a human past that has developed through struggle and conflict, and in guiding present day activists' engagement with current struggles.

Historical materialism—Marx's theory of history—looks at societies as totalities where change happens because of internal contradictions within those societies. Historical 'truth' is in the process of change, not in any individual part or event, or even in the end result. The 'outcome' of events is not determined in advance, as the distortions of Marxism would have it. The ways in which contradictions in society are resolved open up new possibilities—only constrained by the material capabilities of society at a given historical stage. If real material circumstances change, so must the strategies that people use for further change, and the ideas they hold about the world.

For historians today, who are usually not engaged in present struggles but solely in examination of the past, the hostility to Marxism and a rejection of any such 'total' theory of history all too often result in an inability (or unwillingness) to grasp this historical process. Instead a kind of kaleidoscope approach to history—where all aspects of the past, whether political, social, economic, ideological, the voices of all participants, assume an equal weight and are thrown together in confused patterns—is employed, which does more to obscure than it does to shed light on the central dynamics of past movements. This, at least, is the current fashion exerting a pull on many historians.

Given this, the refreshing and very welcome argument from these two books written from the standpoint of Marxist historical materialism is that understanding and implementing the Marxist theory of history represents the best chance for the reinvigoration of history writing today, as well as being indispensable for informing present struggles.

Although covering much of the same ground, the two books are aimed at somewhat different audiences. Matt Perry's is part of an introductory series from Palgrave on Theory and History and as such is the more accessible of the two for readers new to the subject. He outlines the key concepts as developed by Marx and Engels in admirably clear language, reasserting the dynamic content against the subsequent distortions by Stalinism, before turning to a fascinating examination of their historical writings. Subsequent chapters deal with the contributions of Trotsky, Gramsci and Lukács in history writing and the theoretical development of Marxism; the Communist Party Historians Group and the emergence of 'history from below'—the work of Christopher Hill on the English Revolution, and E P Thompson, notably in his *The Making of the English Working Class*.

Perry discusses the debates between Thompson's 'history from below' approach and the structuralist Marxists who emphasised the structures in society that acted as constraints on human action and downplayed the influence of human agency on history. Understandably Thompson et al reacted against the Stalinist impulses they read in the structuralists' accounts. Perry concludes that their associated rejection of categories like those of base and superstructure weakened historical materialism.

Finally, an explanation of postmodernism's development critiques its internal incoherence and its impact on history writing. There is also a very useful glossary at the back, something that more academic introductions would benefit from.

Paul's book deals with many of the same questions, although it is organised slightly differently and the discussion is conducted in more complex language which assumes some prior understanding of concepts and historical developments. For those readers seeking a more in-depth (and more recent) discussion of Marxism's contribution and continuing relevance in historical studies, *Reflections* is a significant resource. It is a cogent defence of the contribution of Marxist historians to the discipline, from Marx to the present via Trotsky's *History of the Russian Revolution*, Geoffrey de St Croix's *Class Struggles in the Ancient World*, and the British Marxist historians Hill, Hobsbawm and Thompson. In the face of current academic hostility to theoretical interpretations of historical events it is a powerful argument for historical materialism as a critical tool to interpret the past.

Paul devotes more detailed space to key debates within the Marxist tradition—on the transition between modes of production in society, for example the way in which society moved from feudalism to capitalism (including the contributions of Robert Brenner, who debated with Chris Harman in *International Socialism* 111), the associated controversy over English historical development and bourgeois revolutions, and the structure and agency debate. He looks in more detail at the various contributions of Marxist writers, both in history writing and in theories of historical development, including contemporary writers.

Both books contextualise the political background to intellectual arguments, helping to explain the debates within British Marxism in the light of the new social movements from the late 1960s and the increasing influence of the right in the late 1970s and 1980s. In both also the interaction of these and other external pressures with intellectual developments within Marxism and those breaking from it—like the work of Michel Foucault—is dealt with in a more sophisticated and nuanced fashion than I can do justice to here.

There is an understandable emphasis in both books on developments in British Marxism. Nonetheless there is also much useful and suggestive material for those working on the history of other countries, where often the influences of Stalinism and posmodernism are even more pronounced.

These books stress the interconnectedness between past and present, expressing the conviction that history is not a separate world but a process we are part of. How people make history, the constraints they live within, and how human agency and societal structures interrelate and pressurise one another are crucial processes for activists, and historians, to study and learn from.

The influence of Stalinism, and its distortion of historical materialism into a determinist mockery with the contradictions and contingencies written out, weighed heavily on history writing. The work of those British historians who remained in the Communist Party after 1956—like Hobsbawm, outstanding though so much of his work is—suffered the closer it came in historical time to the Russian Revolution and its aftermath, while that of many who rejected Stalinism reflected an inadequate explanation for its development and often led to a rejection of Marxism itself as a theoretical tool.

That weight, as both writers point out, has lifted. The result has often been disorientation and accommodation, the attractions of posmodernism and new 'cultural history', but the collapse of Stalinism in combination with the rise of the global anti-capitalist movement and its theoretical challenges also opens the possibility for new history writing informed by Marxism from historians and students engaged in the struggles against neo-liberalism and war.

These excellent books offer intellectual support and much valuable theoretical suggestion to those attempting to write Marxist history today as well as illustrating the key concepts, rich tradition and current debates of Marxist history writing for newer readers.

Beyond the Pankhursts
Judy Cox

*A review of Jill Liddington, **Rebel Girls: Their Fight for the Vote** (Virago Press, 2006), £14.99*

The front cover of this book shows a picture of a furious 16 year old Dora Thewlis being arrested by two huge policemen after an attempt to storm parliament in 1907. It is strongly reminiscent of the pictures of young women school students being arrested while protesting in Parliament Square on the day the Iraq war was launched in 2003. This spirit of youthful protest runs throughout this fascinating story of previously unsung women activists.

Most histories of the women's suffrage movement have concentrated on the hugely influential and charismatic Pankhurst family. In so doing, they have also focused on suffrage activity in the capital, a perspective which was pioneered by Sylvia Pankhurst herself in her 1931 book *A History of the Suffrage Movement*. Jill Liddington has challenged this view by bringing to light the enormous number of working women who made the women's suffrage movement one of the most geographically penetrating and socially diverse political movements in history.

In 1978 Jill Liddington and Jill Norris published *One Hand Tied Behind Us: The Rise of the Women's Suffrage Movement*, which rapidly became a classic of women's history. Rather than focusing on the glamorous and daring suffragettes, the authors researched the activity of the working class women suffragists of the Lancashire coalfields. These were women like Selina Cooper, who drew their confidence and experience from their work as trade union activists and labour organisers. Unlike Emmeline and Christabel Pankhurst and their Women's Social and Political Union, they refused to break from the labour movement. They were alienated by the window smashing and firebombing of their London sisters and instead they developed the tactics of the mass movement, travelling from town to town collecting signatures on monster petitions, organising caravanning tours that took the suffrage message across the region.

In *Rebel Girls* Liddington adds a new dimension to the story of the women's suffrage campaign. Using new research techniques, Liddington has unearthed the amazing stories of mainly young women from the Yorkshire area, who showed tremendous courage and verve in defying the conventions of their communities and hurling themselves at the Liberal government which denied them the vote.

These were the women who, like Mary Gawthorpe, gave up their jobs in the mills to be full time suffrage organisers. They built meetings, harassed Liberal politicians, sold newspapers, and organised demonstrations and election campaigns. They volunteered to be arrested on protests in London, braving harsh treatment as well as ridicule and abuse. Some, like Isabella Ford, spent months during 1908 and 1909 enduring hard conditions visiting the most isolated villages in Yorkshire in caravans from which they distributed leaflets and held meetings.

Old photographs show suffrage meetings in the fishing port of Whitby and the tiny village of Goatland. Newly discovered minutes of a local suffrage organisation in Huddersfield for 1907 provide an intimate portrait of the initiatives, frustrations and triumphs of working class women suffragists during a dramatic era of political activism. Other chapters in the book focus more on the local roots which fed into the national militancy and a genuine mass movement that engaged hundreds and thousands of working class women.

This book tells some thrilling stories. It explores the relationships between class and women's struggles, between individual heroism and the patient building of mass movements, between propaganda and agitation. It is brilliant in its own terms and full of relevance for the campaigns of today.

Trotsky slandered
John Molyneux

A review of Geoffrey Swain, **Trotsky** *(Pearson Longman, 2006), £14.99*

'Readers of this biography', writes Geoffrey Swain, Professor in Russian and

East European Studies at Glasgow University, 'will not find their way to Trotskyism.' Well, some might despite the author's best intentions, but this cannot be regarded as an overstatement.

There are now many books on the life and politics of Leon Trotsky[1] and this is one of the worst. It casually, but outrageously and repeatedly, slanders Trotsky. Perhaps such slander should be ignored, but I, for one, am fed up with the casual 'academic' slandering of great revolutionaries. Such books do real damage. They find their way onto university booklists, especially the booklists for the author's courses, and exercise an influence on some students. They say, with the full weight of academic authority behind them, 'Don't even begin to look to Trotsky (or Marx or Lenin—Lenin is a favourite for this kind of treatment) for an intellectual alternative to the present system,' and, inevitably, many of the students lack the resources to reply or even to discern the fraud that is being perpetrated. I, therefore, intend to respond—without academic diplomacy.

Swain does not hang about. On page 3 of his introduction he offers the following assessment of Trotsky's intellectual capacity and theoretical contribution:

'Trotsky scholars might be surprised to find in this biography that there are no references to Baruch Knei-Paz's great study *The Social and Political Thought of Leon Trotsky*…[his] approach makes Trotsky a far greater thinker than he was in reality. Trotsky wrote an enormous amount and, as a journalist, was always happy to write on subjects about which he knew very little. Trotsky could write beautifully, but he was no philosopher. Knei-Paz does a better job than Trotsky himself in synthesising his ideas. Trotsky was a jobbing journalist and revolutionary activist

and his writings cannot be divorced from their context. Trotsky's first revolutionary comrade, Grigorii Ziv, doubted that Trotsky had the patience to fully engage with Marxism as an intellectual tool. A similar verdict came from Lunarcharskii …[who] concluded… "He is as bold as can be in opposing liberalism and semi-socialism, but he is no innovator".'

Leaving aside the merits of Knei-Paz,[2] this is, by any standards, a monstrous, in legal terms 'perverse', judgment. I am well aware that journalism can be an honourable profession—one thinks of John Reed, Paul Foot, John Pilger, Eamonn McCann, Robert Fisk (all of them more than journalists)—but to describe the author of *The History of the Russian Revolution* as just a 'jobbing journalist' is laughable. No, it is slander of the first order.

For those who have read *The History* further comment is superfluous; for those who have not it is in three volumes, runs to more than 1,200 pages, and combines in one majestic whole a broad theoretical analysis of the revolution's place in history and an exposition of its internal dynamic as it unfolded day by day in the deeds and thoughts of the different classes and parties and their leading, and not so leading, spokespersons. It is widely considered to be the greatest historical work of the 20th century. Nor does *The History* stand alone: Trotsky's other major theoretical works include *Results and Prospects* (which sets out the theory of permanent revolution), *The Third International After Lenin*, *The Struggle Against Fascism in Germany* (which to date remains the foremost Marxist analysis of Nazism and how to fight it), *The Revolution Betrayed* and *Literature and Revolution*. Swain 'deals' with this large body of inconvenient evidence by simply ignoring it. Not a single one of the works I have cited, nor the theoretical analyses they contain, are either summarised or discussed anywhere in Swain's book.

Instead Swain offers as corroboration a quotation from the esteemed Ziv (whose own contribution to Marxist theory stands at zero), who only knew Trotsky as a youth and whose last, fleeting, contact with him appears to have been in New York in early 1917, by which time Ziv had become a supporter of the First World War. This is backed by a quote from Lunarcharskii, which dates from 1923 (before most of Trotsky's main theoretical works were written), which is unrepresentative of Lunarcharskii's overall assessment of Trotsky and which is anyway palpably false: Trotsky's theory of permanent revolution is clearly one of the most important innovations in Marxist theory since Marx, likewise his analysis of fascism. This is a bit like saying Shakespeare was a good comic dramatist but couldn't handle tragedy and then writing a book about him which doesn't mention Hamlet, King Lear and Macbeth.

Even worse, because it denies one of the central principles of Trotsky's entire life, is the following assertion, also in the introduction but repeated in the conclusion:

'There is little [in this book] about world revolution. Trotsky believed in world revolution, but no more and no less than every other Bolshevik, and like all other Bolsheviks this belief was largely rhetorical... It was only in exile in 1933 that internationalism actually became central to Trotsky's purpose'(pp2-3).

Here only the first sentence is true. The rest is arrogant garbage. Reading the comment on the Bolsheviks I could not avoid thinking of Professor Swain secure in his Chair at Glasgow University and wondering whether this man had ever in his life held a principle for which he was required to make a serious sacrifice. The Bolsheviks were men and women who risked their liberty and their lives for their ideas, who suffered, not by way of exception, but virtually as a rule imprisonment, Siberia and exile, and who, almost alone among Europe's socialist parties, took an internationalist position in August 1914. And he has the gall to say they were not serious about their beliefs.

As for Trotsky, the evidence for the centrality of internationalism to his theory and practice long before 1933 is so abundant that to present even the main body of it would fill this whole journal. In 1904 Trotsky opposed the Russo- Japanese War on an internationalist basis.[3] The theory of permanent revolution developed in 1905-06 is internationalist in its premise—Russia's combined and uneven development is a product of its relationship to international capitalism; and in its conclusion—that a victorious socialist revolution in Russia would be able to sustain itself only if the revolution spread to Europe.[4] In his years of exile prior to 1917 Trotsky was actively engaged with the revolutionary movement in a number of countries, including Austria, the Balkans, France and the US. In 1914 he, with the Bolsheviks and Luxemburg and Liebknecht, was one of the few to remain loyal to internationalism and played a leading role in the famous anti-war Zimmerwald Conference in 1915. After October he was appointed Commissar for Foreign Affairs, in part because of his internationalism, and at Brest-Litovsk he, at first, refused (mistakenly) to sign a peace with the Germans on internationalist grounds. From 1919 to 1922 he played an active and leading part in the Communist International.[5]

Swain knows all this and mentions much of it but only as isolated individual 'facts' and he does not allow these facts to affect his argument. He even claims that Trotsky really supported Stalin's doctrine of socialism in one country. He bases this claim on Trotsky's silence on the question in 1925-26 (which was for tactical reasons and did not at all signify agreement) and a couple of quotes taken out of context from Trotsky's discussions of economic construction.[6] He completely ignores a) that Trotsky had opposed socialism in one country in advance in *Results and Prospects*, and b) Trotsky's major theoretical critiques of socialism in one country in *The Third International After Lenin* (which runs to 72 pages and predicts with striking accuracy the effect the doctrine will have on the international communist movement), *Permanent Revolution* and Appendix II of *The History of the Russian Revolution*—all of which were written before 1933.

Faced with the undeniable importance of international questions (principally Germany 1923, Britain 1926 and China 1925-27) for Trotsky in these years, Swain has a neat solution:

'His critique of the failed German Revolution in 1923 was simply camouflage for an attack on his then domestic opponents Zinoviev and Kamenev. It was the same with his writings on the British General Strike, although here his opponents were Bukharin and Stalin. As to his enthusiasm for China in 1927, that too was essentially domestic in focus, for Chiang Kai-shek's destruction of the Chinese Communist Party was simply a metaphor for Thermidor, for what would happen in Russia if the kulaks ever found a general' (p3).

Swain is trading, for this cheap slur, on his audience not having read the texts in question, for it is hard to imagine how anyone who had read them, with their combination of passionate polemic and

theoretical acuity (I wish I had space to quote them) could accept his cynical interpretation. Nevertheless it is obviously a line of argument with a future. How about, 'The anti Vietnam War protesters didn't care about Vietnam, they just had a grudge against LBJ over the draft'? Or, 'The SWP only opposed the wars on Afghanistan, Iraq and Lebanon because of what Blair was doing on privatisation and the Labour Party'? Nearer the mark might be, 'Swain has no real interest in Trotsky, he has only written this book for the money and another entry on his publication list.'

Sadly, refuting slanders takes much longer than issuing them and it is therefore impossible in the space of a review to pursue any but the grossest of Swain's falsehoods and misrepresentations. One that has to be noted, however, is his insistent repetition of the old Stalinist charge that Trotsky 'underestimated the peasantry'. Swain tells us that 'Trotsky's attitude to the peasantry was his Achilles' heel' (p216). In fact Trotsky *never* denied, in theory or in practice, that the peasants would play a crucial role in the Russian Revolution. What he argued was that the peasantry was unable to play an *independent* role, ie independent of the leadership of one of the main urban classes, the bourgeoisie or the proletariat. In this Trotsky based himself on Marx's famous analysis of the peasantry in *The Eighteenth Brumaire of Louis Bonaparte* and the whole history of peasant revolt in Russia and internationally.[7] Moreover he was vindicated by the actual course of the Russian Revolution.

What the Stalinists did in accusing Trotsky of 'underestimating the peasantry' was run together, in a single demagogic phrase, Trotsky's attitude to the peasantry *before* and *after* the October Revolution. Prior to the revolution the 'underestimation' consisted of rejecting Lenin's view that the existence of a large peasant majority in Russia excluded the establishment of workers' power (in this Trotsky was proved right). After the revolution it consisted of overestimating the obstacle the peasants constituted to the construction of socialism and exaggerating the threat of kulak (rich peasant) inspired counter-revolution. If Trotsky did exaggerate the kulak threat it was not because he was wrong about the peasants but because he underestimated the threat posed by the Stalinist bureaucracy. Swain sheds no light on this question, but simply echoes the Stalinist line.

Swain's book also contains an absolutely astonishing omission. There is *no* mention of, not a *single* sentence on, Trotsky's campaign in 1930-33, from exile in Prinkipo, to alert the German Communist Party to the danger posed by Hitler, to criticise the strategy imposed by Stalin, and to urge the formation of a united front against the Nazis. Given the brilliance of Trotsky's writings on the subject and the extreme importance of the events, this omission amounts virtually to historical censorship. How can it possibly be justified? Not, I assume, by ignorance, or by considerations of space—Swain manages to devote a couple of pages to Trotsky's affair with Frida Kahlo (the priorities of the *News of the World* at work here, I suspect), and whole sections to the relatively minor episodes such as the Vienna Pravda of 1908-10 and the Vienna Conference of 1912.[8] Presumably Swain did not think he could get away with claiming that for Trotsky Hitler was just a 'metaphor'.

The book also says next to nothing about such minor matters as the Spanish Civil War, the Moscow Trials, the international slander and persecution of Trotsky as a fascist agent, Stalin's purges and gulag, or the little question of whether socialism was actually built in the USSR. Trotsky's spats with Victor Serge and Ante Ciliga are, however, featured, while the struggle for the Fourth International is, of course, dismissed as a trivial irrelevance.

All these slanders, distortions and omissions do serve a purpose, however. Swain's avowed focus is on the period when Trotsky was in power or near to power, the decade of 1917-27 and the years of Trotsky's direct struggle with Stalin.[9] What they enable Swain to do is to treat that struggle in largely personal terms, as a battle for power between rival individuals, devoid of real principles and in isolation from wider social forces (I imagine he thinks of it as something like the rivalry between Blair and Brown). He attributes Trotsky's defeat partly to 'personality failings', characteristic of Trotsky from his youth, partly to a 'disagreement about how the party should operate', with Lenin as much as with Stalin, and partly to his 'ideological obsession with the kulak danger' (p4). I doubt Swain realises it but this is all taken more or less directly from Stalin. It is not only factually false but also a miserably inadequate methodology—a species of the long discredited 'great man' theory of history.

'History', wrote Marx, 'is the history of class struggle.' This applies as much to Russia in the 1920s as it does to everywhere else. Trotsky lost to Stalin because at the time in question the social force he represented—the working class—was weaker than the social force Stalin represented, the rising bureaucracy. There were two ways in which Trotsky could have won: through the victory of the international revolution or, possibly, through abandoning the working class to engage in an unprincipled personal power struggle—in that case he would have ceased to be Trotsky. That the first option did not materialise is Trotsky's and humanity's tragedy; that he rejected the second, despite extraordinary difficulties and pressures, is his greatness. Swain's inability or unwillingness to comprehend any of this leaves him with the distinction of having produced what is probably the most mendacious account of Trotsky since the days of high Stalinism.

NOTES

1: These include Isaac Deutscher's magnificent trilogy, *The Prophet Armed*, *The Prophet Unarmed* and *The Prophet Outcast*; Tony Cliff's *Trotsky* (4 vols); Pierre Broue, *Trotsky*; Victor Serge and Natalya Sedova, *The Life and Death of Leon Trotsky*; Ernest Mandel's *Trotsky—a Study in the Unity of his Thought* and *Trotsky as Alternative*; Baruch Knei-Paz, *The Social and Political Thought of Leon Trotsky*; Ian Thatcher, *Trotsky*; Dimitry Volkogonov, *Trotsky: the Eternal Revolutionary*; John Molyneux, *Leon Trotsky's Theory of Revolution*; Duncan Hallas, *Trotsky's Marxism*. Of these Deutscher's is the finest literary-historical achievement, Cliff's the best and most detailed politically, and Hallas's the best introduction. Unsurprisingly Cliff, Mandel, Hallas and Molyneux receive no mention in either Swain's book or his bibliography—presumably lest the readers might find their way to Trotskyism!

2: Long ago I wrote a highly critical review of Knei-Paz's book for the *Critique* journal. Unfortunately I cannot find a reference for it, but it was reprinted in H Ticktin and M Cox (eds), *The Ideas of Leon Trotsky* (London, 1995).

3: Bizarrely for his own argument, Swain actually records this fact (p18) but presumably fails to notice the contradiction.

4: Again Swain quotes Trotsky to this effect (p29).

5: Trotsky's articles and speeches fill two volumes—see Leon Trotsky, *The First Five Years of the Communist International*, vols 1 and 2 (New York, 1972).

6: Trotsky's silence in 1925-26 was one of a number of hesitations and tactical compromises he made in order to avoid an irrevocable split. In my view these were mistakes and derived ultimately from Trotsky's failure, because of his lack of a theory of state capitalism, to see that the Stalinist bureaucracy could become a new ruling class. These matters are discussed in some detail in J Molyneux, *Leon Trotsky's Theory of Revolution*, and T Cliff, *Trotsky: Resisting the Stalinist Degeneration* (vol 3). What Swain does is exploit these hesitations to misrepresent Trotsky's fundamental views.

7: There is a basic Marxist principle at stake here. Until very recently the overwhelming majority of the world's exploited and oppressed were peasants, not workers. If it were not for this political weakness, produced by their objective economic and social circumstances, they and not the proletariat would be the main revolutionary class, as was argued by the Narodniks in Russia and by various third worldists in the 1960s.

8: What these events do show is Trotsky at odds with Lenin, and Swain follows the Stalinist practice of highlighting every disagreement with Lenin, no matter how minor or superseded by history.

9: Swain claims that 'the decision to concentrate on the years in power enabled me to do justice for the first time to Trotsky and Russia's Civil War'(p2). Our ideas of justice obviously differ, but, once again, this is not even factually true. Tony Cliff, unmentioned by Swain, dealt with the Civil War and Trotsky's role in it, at greater length and in greater detail (and with much greater political understanding) in *Trotsky: the Sword of the Revolution* (vol 2).

Delving behind the screen
Chris Nineham

A review of Mike Wayne (ed), **Understanding Film: Marxist Perspectives** *(Pluto, 2005), £16.99*

At various times over the last century Marxists have been central in debates about culture in academia and beyond. Marxist perspectives were key to discussions about realism and modernism in the 1920s and 1930s and to controversy about high and low culture and the role of ideology in the 1960s and 1970s. With some honourable exceptions Marxist input petered out in the 1980s. This book is just one indication of a revival in the Marxist study of culture. In itself it is an attempt to reassess and reapply some of the best work of the past.

Some of the the essays recap Marxist debates and in the proccess show how many different 'Marxist' positions on culture there are. Esther Leslie describes the three-cornered 1930s controversy between German Marxists Bertolt Brecht, Walter Benjamin and Theodor Adorno about the impact of mass production and modernism. Brecht's philosophy was to embrace and use 'the bad new things'. Adorno was more pessimistic, championing the avant garde only because he felt mass produced culture was contributing to a 'repressive collectivism'. Walter Benjamin argued that in certain circumstances new technology could demystify and had a shock value that could jolt people out of complacency.

Deborah Phillips describes how Althusser's brand of Marxism came to dominate in the 1970s and 1980s. She marvels at the venom and obscurity of some of the debates he generated but shows how the real impact of Althusser was to open the way to various forms of poststructuralism and identity politics: 'Foucault, Derrida and Baudrillard are now more likely to be invoked as theorists than Althusser, but all forged their work in the context of his intervention into Marxist theory.'

Mike Wayne develops the critique of Althusser. Althusser's trick of deconstucting the ideology 'written in to' texts was a useful innovation. But in the end he took cultural critique down the road to relativism and obscurity. Though he hung on in theory to the notion of scientific truth, he came to see ideology as all pervasive in practice. He followed Lacan in declaring that ideology was

written in to language itself. From here there is no escape.

Apart from containing a paradox (from what vantage point can you identify the role of ideology if it dominates all human practice?), this is clearly a position that leads away from struggle or even hope for the future. It also leads away from a real Marxist understanding. As Mike Wayne points out, Marxism should remind us 'how important socioeconomic relations are and any authentic Marxism understands the complexities of the cultural arena within those relations'.

There are essays in this spirit on corporate ownership in Hollywood, an examination of the conflict between two core functions of capitalist film and culture; 'sales' and 'uplift', and an interesting comparison between the cinema of the Russian and Cuban revolutions.

There is also an entertaining look at the (absence of the) working class in the films of Alfred Hitchcock and a fascinating study of one film by Ousmane Sembene which examines the complex way dominant ideas are disseminated.

Mike Wayne's introduction is one of the highlights of the book. Wayne summarises many of the key Marxist debates but takes positions. He argues against the pessimism of even soft versions of postmodernism and challenges the once fashionable post-structuralists who argued that texts write themselves, that cultural products are shaped unconsciously by institutions, history, subconscious desires and so on. As he says, 'While the dominant version of authorship had rightly been taken to task, we cannot do without some sense of agency, collective and individual... There is no reason to suppose that authors of cultural texts are any less able to consciously shape meaning than academics.'

In his discussion of Italian revolutionary Antonio Gramsci, Wayne places the role of ideas in the context of economic developments and class struggle, something most self-declared Gramscians failed to do in the 1980s: 'The forging of hegemony is the process by which the dominated or subaltern groups are brought into the social economic and cultural order... As the competitive struggle to accumulate profits intensifies capital must establish a new neo-liberal order in which capital compromises rather less and labour concedes rather more. The struggle for moral and intellectual leadership is today fought out in such topics as war, the environment, sexuality, public services, poverty, wealth and trade.'

Just two connected observations: first, none of the contributors draws out what seems to me an important conclusion from the quote above. Some of the essays point to growing cultural opposition in the margins, on the internet or through culture jamming, for example, but none consider the impact that neo-liberalism and war have had on the cultural mainstream. Though big corporate control of the studios is tighter than ever, there is a widening strand of dissent even in Hollywood.

One unexamined paradox is that though the cultural world is ideologically important for the ruling class, it is a social sphere which must at least appear to allow dissent and freedom of expression. It needs to do this to legitimise a society that denies them in practice to the rest of us. In normal times this works okay for the establishment. The free market can be invoked to justify the predominance of pap, and the alienation of audience and cultural producers alike is a barrier to engagement in social isues. At times of growing social stress, however, polarisation in society can carry over into the realm of culture. It is at times like these that corporations like Disney find themselves involved in Michael Moore films, or pin-ups such as George Clooney rail against permanent war.

Hidden communities
John Newsinger

A review of Alvin O Thompson, **Flight To Freedom: African Runaways and Maroons in the Americas** *(University of the West Indies Press, 2006), £27.95*

Black resistance to slavery in the Americas was continuous. It began even before the enslaved were loaded on board ship, continued during the horrific voyage to the Caribbean, South America or the United States, and was a permanent feature of plantation life. This resistance manifested itself in a petty day to day opposition to the slave regime, but on occasions broke out into full-scale rebellion. While the great Haitian Revolution (1791-1804) is history's only instance of a successful slave revolt, there can be no serious doubt that the Jamaican revolt of 1831, even though it was brutally suppressed, signed the death warrant of slavery in the British Caribbean. In this important book Alvin Thompson chronicles a form of resistance that lay between petty day to day opposition and full-scale rebellion: the resistance of the runaway and the establishment of hidden Maroon communities.

Thompson establishes the importance of 'running away' as a phenomenon central to slave societies. He estimates that hundreds of thousands of slaves ran away throughout the Americas, some for only a short time as an act of petty resistance, but for others it was a 'flight to freedom'. In Haiti between 1764 and 1793 some 48,000 slaves escaped their enslavers, and while these figures are inflated by those who ran away more than once, most were never recaptured. The youngest runaways were children aged ten, while the oldest he has found a record of was 'a 90 year old unnamed Fulani man in Haiti'. Most were under 35 years of age, and they included both men and women.

Once they had made good their escape, the runaways established or joined hidden Maroon communities that existed everywhere where slavery operated. Thompson argues for the existence of thousands of these communities throughout the history of slavery in the Americas. The first were established in Mexico, the Dominican Republic and Brazil in the early decades of the 16th century. As early as 1503 the Spanish authorities were complaining of Maroon activity in the Dominican Republic.

As soon as black slaves arrived, they began escaping and trying to establish communities of free men and women. Sometimes these communities remained hidden and sometimes they waged war against the slave regimes. Generally the Maroon communities were small, but some became substantial settlements with fortified towns, farming hundreds of acres.

The largest was the Republic of Palmares, a federation of Maroon communities established in Brazil in the 17th century. At its height, Palmares had a population of 15,000 to 30,000 people and its capital city, Cerca do Macao, was a fortified stronghold with over 2,000 houses. One historian has written of 'the new socialist form of life and work which the settlement of Negroes in Palmares assumed'. When Palmares was finally destroyed by a Portuguese military expedition in 1695 most of its inhabitants

made good their escape, establishing new hidden communities that continued to alarm the slave-owners into the 19th century.

The danger that the runaway posed to the slave regimes was demonstrated by the ferocity of the punishment for the offence. In Mexico in 1590 30 lashes were prescribed for even one night's absence. The punishment for a second offence was 200 lashes and the amputation of both ears, for a third 200 lashes and the amputation of a limb, and for a fourth offence death. The French Code Noir of 1685 prescribed death for the third offence. In Peru absence for more than six days was punished by castration. As Thompson points out, castration was not unique to Peru, but was used as a punishment in many other slave societies—Brazil, Mexico, the British Caribbean and the US. In Barbados in 1692 the authorities paid a certain Alice Mills ten guineas for castrating 42 slaves implicated in a revolutionary conspiracy. In 1697 three runaways were castrated in South Carolina and in 1722 that colony's legislature prescribed castration for a fourth offence. As late as 1831 a Louisiana jailor advertised that he had in custody a runaway who was recently castrated and not quite healed.

Castration was by no means the worst punishment in a slave regime's armoury. Captured Maroons were often tortured to death in the most brutal fashion. In 1795 the Maroon leader, Amsterdam, in the Dutch colony of Demerara was forced to watch his followers executed and then to walk over their bodies to his own place of execution. He was horrifically tortured and then burned alive. As Thompson recounts, many Maroons committed suicide rather than fall into the hands of their oppressors. When Palmares fell in 1695, some 200 of the inhabitants, who could not make good their escape, killed themselves rather than return to slavery.

Many Maroon communities waged war against the slave regimes. Most famously, the Jamaican Maroons fought the British for 70 years before their freedom was recognised in the treaties of 1739. In Suriname the Dutch similarly fought the Maroons for years but eventually in the 1760s concluded treaties that recognised their freedom. One community, the Aluku Maroons, were excluded from the treaties. Under their leader, Boni, they became a major threat to the Dutch that was only eliminated after two brutal wars. The second war of 1789-93 saw Boni himself killed and his followers escaping into French Guiana. One of the participants in this war was the British mercenary John Gabriel Stedman, whose *Narrative* was illustrated, in part, by William Blake.

In many ways the most remarkable of the Maroon wars was that fought out in Florida where black runaways allied themselves with the Seminole Indians, becoming perhaps a third of the tribe. The Second Seminole War (1835-42) was at least in part an American attempt to eliminate this sanctuary for runaway slaves and to re-enslave those who had already made the flight to freedom. Escaped slaves played a major role in the armed struggle against the US, which cost the lives of some 1,500 American soldiers and militia, and was the most hard-fought of the so-called 'Indian Wars'. The Seminole Maroons remained free.

One last point is worth making here. A number of the Maroon communities that concluded treaties with the slave regimes actually became part of the security apparatus that helped sustain them. In Jamaica in 1739 the Maroons agreed to return future runaways and went on to serve as slave catchers for the British, hunting down runaways for a bounty. They played an important role in suppressing slave revolt, most notably the great slave revolt of 1760, 'Tacky's revolt'. Similarly in Suriname, the Ndjuka Maroons, allied with the Dutch, were decisive in the defeat of Boni's Aluku Maroons. Without any doubt this coming to terms with the slave regimes was an important feature of Maroon history, but it must not be seen as an inevitable development. Most Maroon communities never entered into such pacts and, as Thompson insists, one has to remember the part that the Haitian Maroons played in unleashing the great Haitian Revolution.

Thompson's admirable volume is a welcome addition to the select library of recommended books on the resistance to black slavery in the Americas, alongside C L R James's *The Black Jacobins*, Robin Blackburn's *The Overthrow of Colonial Slavery*, Michael Craton's *Testing the Chains*, Richard Hart's *Slaves Who Abolished Slavery* and Emilia Viotta da Costa's *Crowns of Glory, Tears of Blood*. It deserves the widest possible readership.

Carnival, march, riot
Neil Davidson

A review of Dave Renton, When We Touched the Sky: the Anti-Nazi League, 1977-1981 (New Clarion Press, 2006), £13.95

Over three years one organisation distributed 9 million leaflets, sold 750,000 badges, had 250 branches with 50,000 members, held a conference attracting 800 delegates and received affiliations from—

among other bodies—50 constituency Labour parties, 30 AUEW branches, 25 trades councils and 13 shop steward committees. These are some of the materials produced, activities undertaken and supporters enlisted, not by the Stop the War Coalition since 2002, but by the Anti Nazi League (ANL) between 1977 and 1980.[1]

The goal of the ANL was to stop and reverse the growth of the fascist National Front (NF), and it may be worth reminding ourselves of the extent of the Nazi threat during the latter half of the 1970s, since today this is often downplayed. One estimate, by the journal *Searchlight*, has 64,000 people passing through the ranks of the NF between 1967 and 1979, with its highest membership level in any one year reaching 17,500 in 1976-77. In the general election of October 1974 the NF stood 90 candidates who received 113,844 votes. Three years later, in the local and Greater London Council elections, NF candidates received an average of 5.7 percent of the vote, pushing the Liberals into fourth place in a quarter of the seats.

For many black and Asian people the threat was immediate and direct, in the shape of violent and sometimes fatal racist attacks, such as those which took the lives of Gurdip Singh Chaggar and Altab Ali. Yet by the time the ANL was effectively disbanded towards the end of 1981, the NF was unable to demonstrate without challenge, had seen all its candidates in the 1979 general election lose their deposits and had suffered disabling internal leadership battles provoked by their failure. By the end of 1984 the NF had lost nine tenths of its membership.[2]

The marginalisation of the NF was, by any standards, a remarkable success for a movement initiated by the revolutionary

left, particularly in a period otherwise marked by the beginning of a generalised retreat by the labour movement. It was the formative political experience of an entire cohort of activists, many of whom ended up far from revolutionary politics. 'Leon Trotsky has not made a big impact on my life, except for the circles and the arrows', wrote *Guardian* journalist Jackie Ashley recently:

'Everyone on the left in my generation probably remembers them: the symbols of the Anti Nazi League. It may have been kicked off by the Socialist Workers Party, but thousands of Labour activists, trade unionists and students carried the circles and arrows, back in the 1970s as we marched against the National Front'.[3]

It is not an achievement which has hitherto been studied in any detail. Until now the major book dealing with this period had been David Widgery's *Beating Time*, a work of literary and visual fusion which displays all the characteristic panache of its author, but—mainly because of his role as a leading participant—lacks the necessary historical distance from the material.[4] More to the point, it is focused mainly on the role of Rock Against Racism (RAR), rather than the ANL.

RAR was launched in September 1976, over a year before the ANL, and was a more specifically cultural intervention with a wider remit, indicated by the opposition to racism rather than fascism in its name—although the two organisations did of course work closely together.[5] As Dave Renton points out in the preface, *When We Touched the Sky* is therefore 'the first book-length study of the Anti Nazi League' as such.[6]

Renton begins with two brief chapters setting out the crisis-ridden situation of

Britain by the mid-1970s and the history of racism down to that time. The book then moves, more or less chronologically, from 1976 and the formation of RAR in response to racist comments by Eric Clapton—a process which fortuitously coincided with the emergence of punk (Renton has some interesting comments about the relationship of specific forms of music to RAR); 1977 and the great counter-demonstration against the NF in Lewisham which led directly to the formation of the ANL; 1978 and the carnivals in Victoria Park and Manchester (subject of a particularly exhilarating chapter); 1979 and the Southall demonstration in which the police murdered Blair Peach; then through to 1980-81 and the collapse of the NF.

It is clear from this account that the ANL strategy had three main components: mobilisation of the largest numbers of people possible solely on the basis of their opposition to the NF; physical confrontation to stop the NF from marching or assembling; and political identification of the NF as fascists whose ideology was the same as those responsible for the Holocaust. These elements were dependent on their mass character for success. There is a difference between the defensive force of tens of thousands of people, many of whom belong to the threatened community, blocking the path of the NF and their police protectors, and the violence of small gangs of young anti-fascist men fighting with other small gangs of young fascist men: the first is a political act, the second is not and, indeed, it obliterates political difference. These elements were also interlinked. The carnivals were important cultural events, but would have merely left the audiences as consumers affirming their collective anti-fascism if they had not also been involved in the great demonstrations.

Renton is a prolific author, perhaps too prolific. At least some of his previous books—which include three studies of fascism and anti-fascism[7]—give the impression of being over-hastily compiled from research, with all the attendant problems of avoidable errors and incautious judgements, many of which might have been avoided by a longer gestation period. None of this is true of *When We Touched the Sky*, perhaps because (on his own account) it took seven years to complete and therefore involved a greater deal of consideration. At any rate, Renton's strengths are on display here. In addition to archival research, he employs the techniques of oral history and has interviewed the organisers of the ANL and a wide range of other activists, including members of other anti-racist groups. As has been his practice for previous books, Renton refuses to interview fascists, but he has used their publications as a source. And, disgusting though the experience of reading the likes of *Bulldog* and *Spearhead* no doubt was, it has been useful in confirming that the NF did indeed see the ANL as a threat to their activities.

The point is important, since it is sometimes claimed that the Nazi vote did not collapse because of ANL activity but because NF voters switched to supporting the Tories in the general election of 1979. If this is true then the future of anti-fascist activity is bleak, because apparently the only way to demobilise the fascist right is for conventional right wing politicians to take their place. Renton rightly rejects this position on two grounds. One is that it rests on the highly implausible assumption that all the ANL activity had precisely no effect, in either demoralising the NF activists who were for years unable to appear publicly unopposed, or in separating out hardcore supporters from the soft racists through emphasising the fascist nature of the former. The second is that we have the counter-examples from those countries where opposition to the fascist right did not take a similar form to that of the ANL. France, where Le Pen and the Front National were able to establish themselves, at least until 1995, without serious political opposition, is the key example in this respect.[8] (Indeed, partly as a result of the failure of the French left, voters ended up in the final round of the presidential elections of 2002 precisely with a choice between the conservative Chirac and the fascist Le Pen.)

When We Touched the Sky is therefore an invaluable guide to one of the most important movements in recent British left wing history, perhaps the most important prior to the Stop the War Coalition. My criticisms mainly concern areas which Renton has omitted from consideration.

'Social movement history', of which this is a fine example, does seem to have inherited from labour movement history a certain narrowness of focus, particularly in relation to wider issues of the state and economy. The introductory chapters apart, the protagonists here are the ANL/RAR, the NF and the people they were trying to mobilise or influence. The state enters in the form of the police, usually defending the NF, sometimes remaining neutral, very occasionally siding with anti-fascists. From the sidelines we hear the babble of a press typically more concerned with denouncing anti-fascist responses than the fascist activities which provoked them. But the broader social context in which all this took place—the economic crisis and the origins of neo-liberalism, the rightward turn in British society as a whole, the downturn in industrial struggle (the very existence of which was contested within the SWP at the time)—is mentioned, but never

integrated into Renton's account. As a result the conflicts he describes often appear self-contained. The most obvious question which the book implicitly raises—how it was possible for a political victory on this scale to be achieved at a time when the industrial class struggle was stalling or going down to defeat—remains unanswered. In the absence of a revival of generalised trade union militancy it is one which remains relevant to us today.

In other respects, however, the book does provide material of major importance to contemporary debates. I have already referred to the Stop the War Coalition, which is linked to the ANL, not just by the presence of the SWP, but by the common approach both took to building alliances with people who were not revolutionaries.

The models of the united front and the popular front are not useful here if we expect them to take the form that they did between the First and Second World Wars of the last century. The strategy of the united front, as it was codified at the Second Congress of the Communist International in 1920, involves revolutionary working class organisations offering to work alongside reformist working class organisations in pursuit of specific goals. It is not about reaching agreement on an entire political programme, otherwise there would be no need for two organisations in the first place. Nor does it aim for the immediate overthrow of capitalism: it is a genuine attempt to achieve the specific goals as stated (although revolutionaries obviously try to demonstrate to reformist workers the superiority of their ideas and strategy through the experience of joint work). On the other hand, the popular front, first launched in France in 1935 but a key component of Stalinist politics ever since, involves alliances between revolutionaries and bourgeois political parties solely for electoral purposes.

Several critics have seen the ANL as having most affinity with the popular front. One of the most serious of these, the black cultural theorist Paul Gilroy, wrote:

'Rock Against Racism had allowed space for youth to rant against the perceived iniquities of "Labour Party Capitalist Britain". The popular front tactics introduced by the ANL closed it down. Being "anti-Nazi" located the political problem posed by the growth of racism exclusively in the activities of a small and eccentric, though violent, band of neo-fascists'.[9]

These remarks involve a fundamental misunderstanding of what both 'united' and 'popular' strategies involve. Fairly obviously, the ANL was not an electoral alliance between revolutionaries and bourgeois political parties, but was it then a united front? In fact, united fronts in the 'classic' Comintern or Trotskyist sense are actually very rare in working class history, although the essential principle is used every day by Respect or Solidarity activists who convince Labour Party members to jointly take a petition or a collection round their workplace. And it is the principle which is important. Renton quotes one ANL activist:

'The Anti Nazi League wasn't a united front, but it was a united front type organisation. It wasn't a pact between mass organisations, but there was an alliance between reformists and revolutionaries, unity around specific organisation demands which left the organisations free.'

The SWP was not in a position to offer 'unity' in action with the Labour Party—an organisation which then had a membership around 100 times larger—but it could approach individual members and constituencies in the spirit of the united front in order to conduct joint activity. As Renton writes, with commendable restraint, 'Perhaps one lesson of the Anti Nazi League is that unity can be too narrowly conceived'.[10]

Gilroy's main point lies elsewhere though. It is that the ANL, unlike RAR, wrongly focused on fascism at the expense of the far greater racist threat posed by the British state and what we, post Lawrence inquiry, would now call institutional racism: this was what gave the NF the ideological basis for their appeals to the white population. Essentially this means that, unless you are prepared to challenge every aspect of a threat, it is wrong to challenge any aspect of it, even if the aspect in question poses the most immediate threat.

Similar arguments to those of Gilroy were made at the time by groups on the sectarian left, for whom the very idea of the united front itself was counter-revolutionary. According to one typical example of the genre:

'The standpoint of the ANL is that of the Labour racists. They are loyal to British imperialism, loyal to the British state, support immigration control and all the actions of the racist Labour government. Thus the ANL has not been for one moment concerned to defend black people. Its sole and single purpose is to prevent the growth of the influence of the National Front...the ANL attempts to mobilise working class patriotism (to British imperialism) against the National Front's threat to British bourgeois democracy'.[11]

The usual 'proof' offered by critics of this sort is that the ANL leadership refused to support calls for the abolition of all immigration controls. In fact the ANL *did* adopt a policy of opposition to all immigration controls at its first conference in 1978 (and the SWP carried placards saying 'Stop the Nazis; No Immigration Controls' at the Victoria Park carnival); what it did not do was make this position either a condition for membership or the basis of its activity.

Why not? As Renton asks, 'What was the point of the League, to represent internally all the considered positions of the left or to challenge fascism?... The League was not a political party'.[12] If people already agree with opposition to all immigration controls, they would be revolutionary socialists and there would be no need for alliances; if not, then making their participation in an organisation dependent on their adopting this position is unlikely to result in a mass of recruits. It is important to challenge views of people who support immigration controls, but you are far more likely to convince someone of the need to oppose them while working together against the Nazis than as a result of demanding that they adopt all of your politics before you condescend to speak to them.

Anyone who has been active in both the anti-Nazi movement of the 1970s and the anti-war movement of the 2000s will experience a sense of deja vu in relation to these arguments. Instead of criticism for allying with a supposedly entirely racist and imperialist Labour Party, the left has been criticised for allying with a supposedly entirely homophobic, sexist Muslim Association of Britain.[13] In both cases whole groups of people are written off in advance as incapable of engaging in dialogue or ever changing their views.

Towards the end of the book Renton quotes the speech by Darcus Howe at a memorial meeting for David Widgery:

'Howe said that he had fathered five children in Britain. The first four had grown up angry, fighting forever against the racism all around them. The fifth child, he said, had grown up "black and at ease". Darcus attributed her "space" to the Anti Nazi League in general and to Dave Widgery in particular'.[14]

Not for the first time, Howe is exaggerating, but there is something in this nevertheless. Perhaps the longer term achievement of the ANL was to help forge a black and white unity deeper than that required by the immediate needs of anti-fascist mobilisation. As Renton suggests, perhaps it 'had been a necessary precondition for the recent alliance between Muslims and non-Muslims in the movement against the Iraq war... In that sense, the 1970s provide a stock of experiences on which present-day activists can draw'.[15]

NOTES

1: D Renton, *When We Touched the Sky: the Anti-Nazi League, 1977-1981* (Cheltenham, 2006), p175.
2: As above, pp23, 174.
3: Quoted in D Renton, as above, pviii.
4: See D Widgery, *Beating Time: Riot 'n' Race 'n' Rock 'n' Roll*, designed by R Gregory and A Dark (London, 1986). To be fair, the book was not intended to be a scholarly or objective account. See D Widgery, 'Beating Time—a Response to Ian Birchall', *International Socialism* 35 (Summer 1987).
5: It is possible to exaggerate the distinction between the two organisations. If my own experience in Aberdeen is anything like typical, then in many parts of the country the same

people probably ran them both, as two aspects of essentially the same operation.

6: D Renton, as above, p3. Renton admires Widgery's work, without necessarily accepting all his conclusions. See D Renton, as above, pp47-50, 181-182, and D Renton, 'David Widgery', in *Dissident Marxism* (London and New York, 2004), pp217-227.

7: D Renton, *Fascism: Theory and Practice* (London, 1999); *Fascism, Anti-Fascism and Britain in the 1940s* (London, 2000); and *'This Rough Game': Fascism and Anti-Fascism in European History* (London, 2001).

8: D Renton, *When We Touched the Sky*, as above, pp175-180.

9: P Gilroy, *There Ain't No Black in the Union Jack: the Cultural Politics of Race and Nation* (London and New York, 2002), p174.

10: D Renton, *When We Touched the Sky*, as above, pp105, 106. And see pp102-106 more generally.

11: M Williams, S Palmer and G Clapton, 'Racism, Imperialism and the Working Class', *Revolutionary Communist* 9, June 1979, pp41, 42.

12: D Renton, *When We Touched the Sky*, as above, pp104, 118. Gilroy's other main argument is that the ANL retreated into a patriotic Britishness based on memories of the Second World War to oppose the NF. In fact, the main ANL slogan was 'Never again!' Contrary to what Gilroy appears to believe, this was a reference to the Holocaust, not the Battle of Britain. See the discussion by Renton in *When We Touched the Sky*, as above, pp126-127.

13: For the Stop the War Coalition as a form of united front, see A Murray and L German, *Stop the War: the Story of Britain's Biggest Mass Movement* (London, 2005), pp3-5, 47-63.

14: D Renton, *When We Touched the Sky*, as above, p180.

15: As above, p183.

Imagining other worlds

Michael Löwy

A review of Matthew Beaumont, **Utopia Ltd: Ideologies of Social Dreaming in England 1870-1900** *(Brill, 2005),* €58

This book is a remarkable contribution to a materialist history of utopias in the form of a study of English utopian novels of the late 19th century. Inspired by Marx, William Morris, Ernst Bloch[a] and Walter Benjamin,[b] it stands apart from most works on this subject area by its Marxist culture and philosophical depth.

In a historical context defined by the Paris Commune, the Great Depression of 1873-1896, and the first social struggles of English workers, a large number of utopian novels were published in England. In their most radical manifestations they offered the possibility of a utopian/critical perspective on contemporary society from the standpoint of a fictitious future. In their more conventional forms, they remained prisoners of the (bourgeois) present, unable, to use Benjamin's phrase, to 'shatter the continuum of history'.

William Morris, in his famous utopian novel *News from Nowhere* (1891), inspired by the English Romantic anti-capitalist tradition, is an example of the more radical type; his rival, the American Edward

a: Ernst Bloch (1885-1977), German philosopher who moved towards Marxism in the late 1920s, went into exile under the Nazis and then lived in East Germany until disagreements with the authorities led him to move to West Germany in 1961.

b: Walter Benjamin (1892-1940), German Marxist theorist of literature and art, committed suicide just as he was about to be handed over to Gestapo in 1940.

Bellamy, with *Looking Backward* (1888), is the most influential representative of the other type, that is, of state socialist utopias 'from above', which in no way call into question modern (capitalist) civilisation.

From a position close to Fabianism, Bellamy puts forward a reformist, evolutionist, modernist, philanthropic, profoundly 'petty bourgeois' utopia, a sort of 'third way' between laissez-faire capitalism and socialist revolution. In his utopian novel the future is presented in the form of what he calls 'nationalism'—the word 'socialism', too compromised by its associations with the red flag and the smell of petroleum from the fires of the Commune, is avoided. It is a system thanks to which the nation becomes 'one great business corporation...the one capitalist in the place of all other capitalists', while the workers are mobilised into an 'industrial army' under military discipline.

This future is the natural and inevitable result of the concentration of capital, so society simply needs to 'recognise and cooperate' with 'industrial evolution'. As a critic of liberal capitalism, Bellamy is a supporter of 'prophylactic' reform. 'Let no mistake be made here, we are not revolutionarists but counter-revolutionarists', he explained in a lecture of 1890 in response to middle class anxieties.

The huge success of *Looking Backward* in the US and, to a lesser extent, in England convinced William Morris that the utopian novel was a site of cultural struggle within the socialist movement. His response, *News from Nowhere*, was that of a revolutionary utopia, that is, a future resulting from the active struggle of the exploited, and which represented a radical alternative to capitalist civilisation. His *concrete utopianism*—in the sense which

Ernst Bloch gives this term—is not contemplative, but fulfils a dialectical function—to introduce reality into utopia and utopia into reality.

Apart from these two key figures, the author analyses in detail two other forms of futuristic fiction: feminist utopias and anti-communist 'cacotopias'.

The utopian feminist novels of the late 19th century are the product of a complex convergence between two streams of thought: the 'warm stream' (another of Ernst Bloch's terms) of the Owenite socialist-feminist utopia of the first half of the century, and the 'cold stream' of the pragmatic feminist reformism of the late 19th century. What they have in common is the hope of 'constructing a New World inside the shell of the Old', in the words of the feminist historian Barbara Taylor.

These utopian novels are, in part, a response to misogynist dystopias such as J M Allan's novel *Woman Suffrage Wrong* (1890), which brandishes the threat of an 'Amazonian army...ready and willing to copy the excesses of Parisian women at Versailles on 6 October 1789'. We find 'Amazonian armies', but with an emancipatory dimension, in Florence Dixie's utopian novel *Gloriana, or the Revolution of 1900* (1890), in the form of a Woman's Volunteer Corps composed of militant suffragists capable of defeating 'the demon armies of Monopoly and Selfishness'. The whole new society is inspired by the myth of the Amazons in Elizabeth Corbett's novel *New Amazonia* (1899): she shows us Ireland in 2472 ruled entirely by women.

According to Beaumont, the epistemology[c] of these utopias is that of an heuristic exercise, ie a counter-factual

---

c: Epistemology—theory of knowledge

thought experiment, an imaginative leap into the future beyond empirical data, an attempt to import the redemptive perspective of the future into the present.

A quite different phenomenon is presented by the anti-communist dystopias or cacotopias—from the Greek kakos meaning 'bad'—inspired by the terrifying spectre for the ruling classes of the Paris Commune of 1871. The task for these fictions of social catastrophe, which describe revolution as a sexual and political apocalypse, is to stave off the danger of an 'English Commune', a spectre nourished by the emergence of the socialist movement and by the class struggle in England in the last third of the 19th century. The prototype of this sort of futuristic fiction is *The Commune in London: A Chapter of Anticipated History* (1871) by S B Hemyng, who describes, with a wealth of detail, the ravages and crimes committed in the good city of London by a bloodthirsty working class mob led by demonic female insurgents and secretly controlled by agents of the International. In *The Decline and Fall of the British Empire* (1890) by Henry Watson, a dirty, unwashed crowd sets fire to Buckingham Palace, to Kensington Palace, and, worst of all, to the gentlemen's clubs of London. The role of the women 'incendiaries' recurs in almost all these cacotopias: in the hands of these women, writes an anonymous commentator, 'the torch of Enlightenment had become the brand that set Paris alight'.

Paradoxically, observes Beaumont, these cacotopias are conceived as false prophecies, starting from the optimistic hypothesis that their readers will be able to prevent the disaster; but they are also anxious and uncertain of their effectiveness. There is also a 'utopian' aspect to these dystopias: in comparison with the hell that threatens us, present day capitalism appears as an ideal society.

In the final chapter of the book the author returns to William Morris's utopia, which enables us, thanks to the perspective of the future, to see the 'view from the rooftop' embracing present day society in all its contradictions. As Ernst Bloch wrote, 'We need the most powerful telescope, that of polished utopian consciousness, in order to penetrate precisely the nearest nearness.'

In the utopian future described in *News from Nowhere*, work ceases to be a curse and becomes 'the pleasurable exercise of our faculties', the product of which is freely distributed by the workers to the consumers. Use value and the beauty of objects replace the commodity and its price. In a famous scene of the novel, the visitor from the past accepts the gift of an object of beauty (a pipe), richly decorated with gold and gems. This happy future, where the pleasure principle and the reality principle seem to have become reconciled, has not fallen from the sky but has been the result of a bitter revolutionary struggle described by Morris in the chapter 'How the Change Came'.

News from Nowhere is an exercise in critical historiography. It understands the last years of the 19th century from the perspective of a possible future history, of a communist alternative. The aim of this dream of the future is, for its author, to act on the present, that is to say on the 'Now', which is the 'strait gate' by which the Messiah—ie the Revolution—might enter history (Walter Benjamin). William Morris is thus virtually alone in the late 19th century in his aspiration to 'transform utopian writing into a necessarily partial and provisional moment of revolutionary practice' (Miguel Abensour).

My only criticism of the enthralling analysis put forward by Matthew Beaumont is that he too rapidly passes over the structure of William Morris's romantic anti-capitalist sensibility, briefly referred to (p43), but subsequently abandoned. To me, this seems decisive in the understanding of his work, inasmuch as it introduces an essential dimension of his utopian novel: the relation to the past. Like all the Romantics, Morris refers to the pre-capitalist past to criticise modern bourgeois civilisation. However, unlike the conservative Romantics, such as his friend John Ruskin, he does not advocate a return backwards, but rather a detour via the past on the way to the utopian future. This romantic/revolutionary dialectic between the past and the future—against the wretched capitalist present—is visible in numerous aspects of the novel, as in the scene of the gift, the ornamentation of which suggests artisanal and/or artistic labour, or in the scene which describes London transformed into a sort of pastoral city surrounded by greenery. This romantic moment does not in any way detract from the visionary strength of *News from Nowhere*, quite the contrary!

In any case, Beaumont's work is of a high intellectual and political quality, and will undoubtedly become a reference work for all those interested in the fortunes of the *Principle of Hope*[d] dear to Ernst Bloch.

---

d: *Principle of Hope*—Ernst Bloch's best known work, a critical history of the utopian vision.

Between ritual and revolt
Chris Harman

A review of Ali Rahnema (ed), **Pioneers of the Islamic Revival** *(Zed books, 2006), £18.95*

The great threat to civilisation is, according to George W Bush, 'Islamofascism'. Many liberals who do not agree with Bush on much else and even some groups who claim to be part of the revolutionary left share this analysis. They lump all strands of political Islam (or 'Islamism') together, designate them as 'fundamentalism' and treat them as an evil at least as great as that of the IMF, the World Bank, the Pentagon, the WTO, structural adjustment and NATO combined. In doing so they show their complete ignorance of the history of political Islam and of the myriad of different organisations and beliefs that fall under that title today.

For this reason alone, the new edition of this book is welcome. Its essays dissect the contrasting approaches of eight of the most significant figures to develop political Islam.

The pioneer is usually seen as Sayyid Jamal al-Din al-Afghani (Afghani for short), born in Iran in 1838-39 and then living variously in Turkey, Afghanistan, Egypt, India, the Arabian peninsula and briefly, London and Paris. He came to adulthood at a traumatic moment for the more intellectually concerned members of the middle class in the vast region that stretched from the Atlantic to the Bay of Bengal. Its rival states had, not long before, shared some elements of a single civilisation, in which a layer of religious scholars (the 'ulama'), trained in classical Arabic and referring to the same classical texts, administered the traditional civil law (the 'sharia') as well as preaching in the mosques. But that civilisation was now being destroyed from outside.

Britain, which had begun its encroachment into Muslim-ruled India in 1757, completed its takeover of the subcontinent with the annexation of the kingdom of Oudh (sometimes spelt Awadh) in 1856 and the bloody crushing of the rising (the 'mutiny') of 1857. France had begun grabbing Algeria in 1830 and was soon casting its eyes on Morocco and Tunisia. Tsarist Russia was continuing a century long southward march to grab the Caucasus and historic centres of Islamic culture like Samarkand and Bukhara. In 1882 Britain seized control of Egypt so as to enforce payments of the ruler's debts. It would not be that long before the whole vast region was under foreign rule. The result was not only poverty for the lower classes; there was also a deepening sense of humiliation for the middle classes, including the clerics, as the Europeans who lorded it over them treated them as ignorant inferiors. Out of this emerged two often intertwined strands of ideological opposition—nationalism on the one hand, political Islam on the other.

Afghani and those influenced by him like the Egyptian Muhammad Abduh could see that to develop resistance the Muslim lands had to learn from the technical and scientific advances of the West. Islam, they argued, is not superstitious like Christianity, with its belief in miracles and its myriad saints who are supposed to be able to intervene magically on behalf of their worshippers. But they refused to accept that capitalist values, with their commodification of all human relations, were intrinsically superior to the Islamic ones.

One of their central concerns was to work out why the Islamic lands had succumbed to the West. Their conclusion was that the Islamic societies had become weak during centuries of despotic rule. The only way to reinvigorate them was to go back to the values of the 'pure' Islam of the time of the prophet Mohammed and his immediate successors (the 'four righteously guided Caliphs'). In this way, it would be possible to construct a society which avoided the all too obvious horrors of the capitalist West but which was able to incorporate its scientific insights.

It is this project which, in one way or another, different versions of political Islam have been trying to implement ever since.

But it is a project which is necessarily subject to very different interpretations.

There was, for instance, the question of what the original Islam was. All agreed it was based on the Quran and the hadiths (the sayings) and sunna (reported actions) of the prophet. But there was already a great debate at the time of the formulation of Sunni Islamic orthodoxy 1,200 years ago about how these were to be interpreted. Some scholars are argued that the Quran was the word of god and had to be taken literally even when it did not seem to make sense: if it seemed confusing to humans that was because we could not possibly decipher the mind of god. Others argued, by contrast, that god, as all-perfect, could not possibly be irrational and that therefore, where the words of the Quran, read literally, contradicted reason they had to be read allegorically in a rational sense.

There was the question of what was most important—keeping strictly to religious rituals or abiding by the values embodied in the religious teaching, above all the value of resisting oppression.

Then, there was the question of how to apply the original doctrine today. Thinkers like Afghani and Abduh argued that modern society was so different to that of the prophet, early 7th century Arabia, that a new interpretation ('ijtihad') of the written doctrine was necessary—a break with the practice of Sunni Islam (although not Shia) since the 11th century when 'the gates of *ijtihad* were closed'. Others regarded this as a heretical break with pure Islam.

Finally, there was the question of whether Muslims joined with others fighting against oppression from Western imperialism, or whether they saw them as an enemy who would pollute the minds of other Muslims.

These issues have divided different proponents of political Islam ever since. They mean there are different directions in which political Islam can go. At one extreme are puritan doctrines, based upon literalist interpretation of the texts and a stress on the perfection of rituals. 'Degeneration' in Islamic societies is seen as a result not of the existence of oppression or exploitative classes, but of moving away from what are seen as religiously sanctified practices (women not wearing the veil, drinking alcohol, looking at pictures that are deemed to be 'graven images'). This prioritises attempting to 'purify' the behaviour of people while maintaining a conservative attitude to oppressive social structures. It also necessarily leads to narrowing down the forces prepared to struggle for change, since not only does it rule out joint struggle alongside groups of the exploited and oppressed who are not Muslims, but it also means attacking those who practise different versions of Islam. So Zarkawi, who proclaimed himself leader of Al Qaida in Iraq, issued a call for war against 'Shia idolaters' and 'apostates'—a position then criticised by Bin Laden's lieutenant Zawahiri as detrimental to 'Muslim unity' in the struggle against the West.

At the other extreme are interpretations like that developed by the Iranian Islamist Ali Shariati, who put the stress on political

and social activity directed against oppression and the state, so inspiring sections of the left in the revolution which took place in 1979 (two years after he died).

Most of the thinkers dealt with in this book took an ambiguous position, seeing a role for reason, *ijtihad* and political and social struggle, but repeatedly reverting to literalism or a stress on ritual purity. In different ways this was true of Maudidi and the Jamaat-i-Islam in the Indian subcontinent, of Khomeini in Iran, and of Banna, the founder of the Muslim Brotherhood in Egypt. This was because each developed a project for political change which left intact the central features of the existing social structure—symbolised by their insistence that support for private property was a central tenet of Islam (as if the private property of the modern billionaire is the same as the private property of the 7th century nomad). This was facilitated by shying away from a challenge to the structures that created oppression and putting the emphasis on personal behaviour.

Such a programme could mobilise sections of the classic petty bourgeoisie and the new middle class, and draw many of the urban poor behind them, while at the same time leaving room for deals with sections of the bourgeoisie proper or the state. Such deals could be accompanied by attacks on religious minorities (Muslim as well as non-Muslim), on those alleged to have infringed sexual norms (non veil wearing women, gays, 'adulterers' and so on) or on the left. In such cases those whose starting point was a reaction against the imperialist destruction of the old Islamic societies ended up allying themselves with sections of the ruling classes from those societies—and through them on all too many occasions with imperialist actions against nationalist and left wing movements. So it was that in the third quarter of the 20th century political Islam was often characterised by its willingness to physically attack the left—and it still is today in some important cases.

It is this record which supposedly left wing talk of 'Islamofascism' rests on. But such talk misses out a central point. The behaviour of imperialism continually causes many of those with Islamist ideas to react against the compromises with the old ruling classes and imperialism that they themselves once accepted. Witness the way in which those who worked with the CIA in Afghanistan have turned against imperialism because of the behaviour of the US in Iraq and the continuing oppression of Palestine. That is why some of those from Islamic movement like the Muslim Brotherhood who were fighting the left 40 years ago are now prepared to march act alongside it against what they can see is a common enemy.

This does not mean that all Islamist organisations automatically act in a progressive fashion. Far from it. Some remain wholeheartedly on the side of reaction (although this does not make them necessarily 'fascist', any more than conservative Catholic theology makes Christian Democrat parties fascist). Others can claim to act against imperialism, but then do things that disrupt the anti-imperialist movement (as with the behaviour of Zarkawi in Iraq). Their characteristic methods of struggle are still those which turn away from direct class conflict -which is why they oscillate between individual heroic 'martyrdom actions' (often with no concern for civilian casualties) on the one hand and attempts to permeate existing capitalist states from within. And their attempts to bridge the class gap between Islamic capitalists and Islamic workers and peasants mean that some of them may well work against the left (including the Islamic left) on behalf of the Islamic bourgeoisie at some point in the future, just as Khomeini did in order to consolidate his power after the Iranian Revolution.

But this does not make them all a single, homogeneous Islamo-fascist force. It means, rather, that their followers can be pulled in different directions, and the degree to which this happens depends in part on the reaction of the left. Where the left is uncompromising in its anti-imperialist struggle and attempts to draw in the masses influenced to greater or lesser degrees by Islamic religious ideas, it has the chance of isolating those Islamists who would do deals with state and the bourgeoisie to smash the left. Where the left itself unites with the state and imperialism in order to attack supposed 'Islamofascism', it makes it easier for the most reactionary interpretations of political Islam to have an impact.

In the essay in this book on the Egyptian Islamist Qutb (executed by Nasser in 1966), Charles Tripp draws out the 'communitarian' character of his thought.

'In common with many communitarian thinkers,' Tripp writes, 'Qutb was dissatisfied with the utilitarian philosophy of hedonistic egoism. Although it had apparently contributed to the material success on which the power of the west was founded, he believed not only that it led to deplorable moral conduct, but also that the conception of society that underpinned it was, in the final analysis, a soulless, rootless and empty one... He was therefore searching for something that would meaningfully fill the void, a lost harmony and an implicit faith.'

There is a problem with this approach which is not something peculiarly Islamic. It is common to all forms of communitarianism today, just as it was to romantic reactions against the destructive effects of capitalism in the first half of the 19th century. It is that there are diametrically opposed ways of seeking to counter with 'community' the atomism, the disorientation and the rat-race mentality built into present day society.

One is to try to restore an imaginary communal past by attacking some of the superficial features of a society whose productive base has been transformed by capitalism. This was characteristic of what Marx and Engels called 'feudal socialism' and 'petty bourgeois socialism' in the *Communist Manifesto* and it is characteristic of a big section of political Islam today. Faced with the complete destruction of the old society by more than a century of capitalist development, this trend tries to reimpose certain old social practices while leaving intact the various processes of capitalist exploitation and accumulation that have undermined them.

The second is to retreat from existing society, so as to try to establish harmonious, communal enclaves of the pure outside of it. This was the path of the utopian socialists in the 19th century, of the counter-culture communes of the late 1960s and early 1970s, and it is the path of some of the non-violent Islamist sects today.

But a third is to move forward to revolutionary reorganisation of society, so that the 'the free development of each is the condition for the free development of all'. There are trends within political Islam which are capable of moving in this direction, The task of the left is not to spurn them out of hand as 'reactionary', still less as fascist, because they do not like capitalist 'modernisation'. There have to be strategies and tactics that try to draw them into common struggle against imperialism and capitalism, so leading them to break with those who share their religious language but draw completely opposite conclusions from it. Every time sections of the left repeat the neocons mantra about 'Islamofascism' they make this task more difficult.

Pick of the quarter

New Left Review continues to amaze those of us who got put off it by the academic obscurantism of many of its articles in the mid-1990s. The July-August issue contained at least three articles well worth anyone reading. R Taggart Murphy's article 'East Asia's Dollars' provides an interesting and provocative analysis of the contradictions facing Japan's capitalism in its relations with the US and China (http://www.newleftreview.net/?page=article&view=2625).

Immanuel Wallerstein's 'The Curve Of American Power' provides an analysis of the problems facing American imperialism, which comes to similar conclusions to those we have presented in this journal, despite some methodolgical dfferences. He insists, 'The net result of the entire Bush foreign policy has been to accelerate the decline of US hegemony rather than reverse it. The world has entered into a relatively unstructured multilateral division of geopolitical power, with a number of regional centres of varying strengths manoeuvring for advantage—the US, the UK, Western Europe, Russia, China, Japan, India, Iran, Brazil at the very least.'

A short piece by Gadi Algazi, 'Offshore Zionism', shows how multinational capital is managing to use the Zionist structures of the Israeli state to its own profitable advantage (www.newleftreview.net/?page=article&view=2624).

And anyone who wants to know about the background to the military coup in Thailand should read the piece by Kasian Tejpira in the May-June issue.

But not everything has changed in **NLR**. I found the first article in the July-August issue, 'States of failure' by Malcolm Bull, virtually incomprehensible. If theory is to guide practice, it needs to be expressed in language the practitioners can understand.

Comprehensibility is one merit of nearly all the articles that appear in **Monthly Review**. And the last two issues are no exception. The July-August special issue on class in the US contains two pieces of speical interest. 'Some Economics of Class' by Michael Perelman (http://www.monthlyreview.org/0706perelman.htm) provides careful analyses of statistical information to show the degree to which exploitation has risen over the last three decades. 'Probably 80 percent of the population was worse off in 2002 than in 1970', despite a doubling of per capita national output in the interim. In other words, nearly all of the enormous increase in output in these years has gone to the ruling class.

'Six Points on Class' by Michael Zweig (http://www.monthlyreview.org/0706zweig.htm) includes a breakdown of the US population in class terms which sees the central divide as between 'the corporate elite (or capitalist class), who make up only 2 percent' of the US labour force, and 'the working class' who make up 62 percent. 'In between these classes is the middle class (36 percent)'—a figure which I would regard as too high since it includes groups like 'public school teachers'. Zweig shows how mistaken it is to talk of the poor as being an 'underclass'. 'Poverty is something that, in fact, happens to the working class', he insists. 'Most poor people in the US are in families where the adults experience periodic spells of unemployment or work only part-time or on low wages. Two wage earners, one year-round full-time and one year-round half-time, each earning minimum wage, does not make enough to bring a family of three out of poverty. The "underclass"—people entirely marginalised from the legal economy—is only a small fraction of the poor.'

He also cuts through some of the confusion over race and class which enables politicians to give the impression that it is only blacks and minorities who are excluded from the American Dream. 'In the US two thirds of all poor people are white and three quarters of all black people are not poor. Racism accounts for the fact that poverty is experienced disproportionately among blacks and Hispanics (and among women because of sexism). But we should not allow their comparatively heavy burden to blind us to the full realities of poverty in America.'

In September's issue of **MR** Michael Watts' 'Empire of Oil: Capitalist Dispossession and the Scramble for Africa' (http://www.monthlyreview.org/0906watts.htm) is about how neo-liberal policies have led to a fall in per capita income across Africa and, at the same time, to bitter and often barbaric armed conflicts in the enclaves where there are valuable raw materials, especially oil.

Readers who have liked two of the articles in this ISJ might like to read other recent articles by their authors. Christian Hogsbjerg's 'C L R James and Italy's Conquest of Abyssinia' appears in **Socialist History** no 26, while Paul Blackledge's 'Karl Kautsky and Marxist Historiography', in **Science and Society**, July 2006, argues that Kautsky's political degeneration at the time of the First World War has often led to an unnecessary dismissal of his historical writings.

Our last issue contained two pieces on the successful student and youth revolt against the French government's CPE attempt to extent precarious working. The July issue of **Critique Communiste** contains five articles which will enable those who can read French to learn much more about an immensely important struggle.

CH

Feedback: Cuban myths

Samuel Farber

I am grateful for Chris Harman's positive review of my book *The Origins of the Cuban Revolution Reconsidered* (*Internatioanl Socialism* 111). Nevertheless, I would like to address an issue that Chris mentioned almost in passing but which I feel requires clarification.

I don't recall engaging in a polemic with Tony Cliff, or any other leader or member of the Socialist Review/International Socialism group, on the issue of whether 'Castro was an enemy in the same league as US imperialism'. My opposition to both, then and now, has nothing to do with whether they are in the same league or not.

I do recall a tactical/political disagreement with Cliff that lasted literally a few hours. When the missile crisis of October 1962 broke out I went over to Cliff's (and, of course, Chanie Rosenberg's) house near the Arsenal tube station to discuss the situation. Initially Cliff supported the slogan put forward by the orthodox Trotskyists demanding 'US missiles out of Cuba'. I, on the other hand, agreed with the slogan put forward by the anti-nuclear, direct action Committee of 100 for 'all missiles out of Cuba'. As a number of comrades active in the Young Socialist newspaper *Young Guard* began to drop by the house, it became evident that they agreed with the Committee of 100's slogan and not with Cliff's. By the end of the day, Cliff dropped the matter and the group ended up supporting the slogan 'All missiles out of Cuba'.

On a different subject, I want to note that my recent book is also available in paperback at £13.95, a much lower price than the hardcover edition noted in the review.

Finally, I wholeheartedly endorse the sentiments expressed by Chris in his concluding remarks that 'support for Cuba against US imperialism, its threats and its embargo must not turn into support for a Cuban model that offers nothing to the new revolutionary movements'.

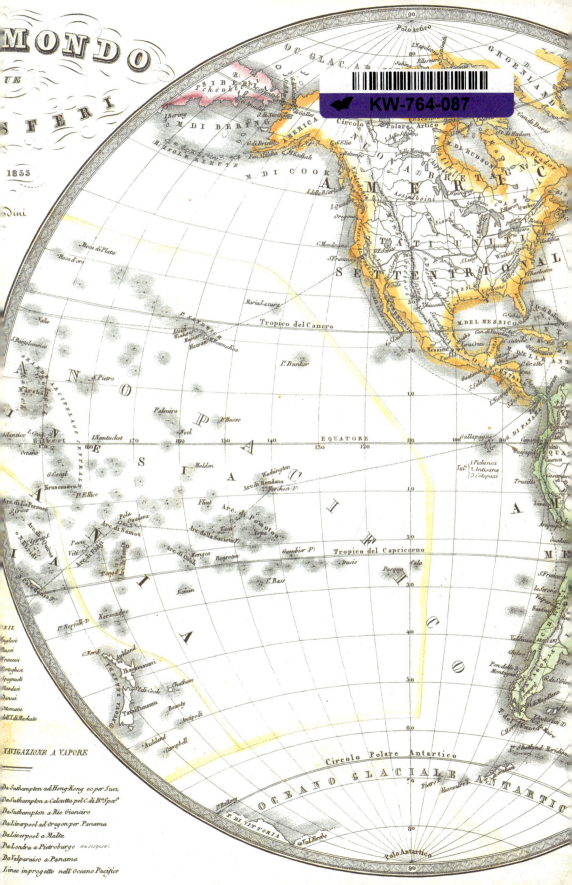

Ingrandimenti

I MARI DEL SUD
di Folco Quilici

Fotografie dell'autore

ARNOLDO MONDADORI EDITORE

Dello stesso autore

Nella collezione Ingrandimenti
L'avventura e la scoperta
L'India di Folco Quilici

Nella collezione Omnibus
Cacciatori di navi

Nella collezione Illustrati
Coste e mari d'Italia

Nella collezione I grandi libri
Il grande libro dell'Europa

Folco Quilici ringrazia Luca Tamagnini per le foto di copertina e per quelle del branco di squali scattate al largo di Rangiroa.

Ed è grato al professor Romeo Lucchese per la sua collaborazione alla revisione dei testi.

Inoltre, anche a nome dei collaboratori che lo hanno seguito in tanti viaggi nei Mari del Sud, ringrazia:
– la LUFTHANSA per l'assistenza ai voli attorno al mondo, sino ai margini orientali e occidentali dei Mari del Sud;
– la KODAK per l'assistenza al lavoro fotografico e cinematografico;
– la MARES per l'assistenza – con le sue attrezzature – alle immersioni;
– la FOWA e la NITAL per l'assistenza all'impegno di documentazione fotografica, con attrezzature Hasselblad, Contax e Nikonos.

ISBN 880435268-X

I MARI DEL SUD
di Folco Quilici

Il perché di una dedica

Nei quasi quarant'anni che intercorrono tra il mio primo viaggio nei Mari del Sud e il più recente, ho narrato di esperienze, avventure e ricerche in quel mondo di isole e atolli in più occasioni; una di esse fu quando, nel 1971, assieme al film Oceano *firmai un libro dallo stesso titolo; e lo dedicai a mia madre.*

Con lo stesso affetto e le stesse motivazioni intendo ora dedicarle questo.

Aggiungendo il perché di quella dedica. Che non era solo un debito di sentimento ma, senza dirlo esplicitamente, suggellava una particolare alleanza, una comunità d'intenti; o meglio, come oggi spesso si dice, di quella unità nella diversità che collegava per vie istintive e in certo senso inspiegabili il mio lavoro al suo.

La dedica di Oceano *voleva evocare un episodio di questa sintonia, quando io, per molti mesi, avevo navigato tra gli atolli delle Tuamotu, e mia madre nello stesso periodo aveva deciso di tornare a dipingere quel paesaggio delle «Valli del Po» che era stato il suo tema poetico in età giovanile. Al mio ritorno in Italia, le avevo mostrato film e foto raccolti in Oceania; e lei mi aveva fatto vedere i suoi quadri e disegni realizzati nelle «Valli». Ci accorgemmo quel giorno – con emozione, anche se lì per lì ci scherzammo sopra – che ai due poli opposti del pianeta avevamo percepito, fatte nostre – e riproposto in immagini – atmosfere di luci e colori che sembravano riflettere un'identica visione del mondo.*

In quel caso: gli spazi dei miei atolli e quello delle sue «Valli». Nulla di più diverso e lontano, e tuttavia nulla di più simile nelle nostre interpretazioni; identiche linee orizzontali tracciate da basse, piatte terre disposte a chiusura di lagune dalle acque immobili, specchio perfetto del cielo, delle nubi e delle loro luci perennemente cangianti. Per entrambi si era trattato di raccontare in immagini paesaggi che avevano in comune l'esser chiusi, limitati, finiti; dilatati, però, all'infinito nella moltiplicazione dei riflessi al loro interno. Sorta di magia che aveva permesso, a lei e a me, di entrare in una quarta dimensione reale e irreale allo stesso tempo; e di ritornarne, seguendo vie diverse ma con esperienza identica di forme, colori. In un'unica, eguale emozione.

Ritorni in Polinesia
(molti e sempre stupefacenti)

Tutto è cambiato, l'aveva detto Cook a Tahiti, al suo secondo viaggio – La
tivù nelle capanne – Il lamento di Gauguin – I polinesiani e la loro ecologia
istintiva – La rivincita della natura nelle «isole minori» – La matriarca
dell'isola di Pasqua.

Ritorno in Polinesia: dopo vent'anni dal mio ultimo itinerario nelle isole, dopo trentacinque dal primo. Sento fisicamente l'inizio di questo viaggio nel passato, quando la poltroncina del DC10 che mi trasporta a novemila metri di quota sul Pacifico cambia natura e diventa una asimoviana macchina del tempo. Accade nell'istante preciso in cui l'aereo inizia la sua discesa, con l'impercettibile mutazione d'assetto.

Dopo 6250 chilometri di volo dalla costa americana, l'aereo s'appresta ad attraversare le nubi. Sullo schermo ove abbiamo visto scorrere immagini di Woody Allen sino a un'ora prima, si accende una mappa luminosa elettronica; al suo centro appare una macchia scura sulla quale si sovraimprime la scritta *Tahiti*. Verso quelle lettere luminose punta la sagoma dell'aereo sul quale siamo imbarcati; e intanto sulla mappa stessa appaiono informazioni che il computer di bordo elabora a getto continuo. Stiamo scendendo di trecento metri al minuto; la distanza con la pista di Faa è di quaranta miglia, poi trentanove, poi trentotto e via così, mentre il segno sulla mappa si ingrandisce, e altre cifre ci informano di quanto non possiamo renderci conto dato che l'atterraggio avviene a notte fonda: il tempo a terra è molto nuvoloso, su Papeete piove, la temperatura è di 22 gradi, il vento è di dieci miglia da nord-est.

Non diversamente dalle indicazioni del libro di bordo di uno dei primi velieri giunti a questo ancoraggio al centro del Pacifico meridionale, le note sommano e precisano dati che riassumono le coordinate dell'approdo. Ora dal cielo, ieri dal mare, la stessa sensazione di giungere a una meta estremamente lontana, a un punto remoto nell'immensa vastità dell'oceano. Certo un DC10 non è uno *schooner*, i suoi quattro Pratt & Witney producono molta più energia di quaranta vele, otto ore di volo sono molto più rapide di otto settimane di traversata oceanica. Eppure, anche se ora si sentono *vicine* Tahiti e la Polinesia intera, la sensazione d'aver superato uno spazio marino vastissimo è la stessa; ne sono sicuro.

La lunga pista in cemento si distende all'interno della laguna corallina di Tahiti proprio là dov'era il villaggio di Faa da cui ha preso il nome, ed è stata costruita sullo stesso asse est-ovest dove ammarava l'idrovolante della *Teal-Tasman and Australian Airline*, il primo collegamento aereo con Tahiti, agli inizi degli anni Cinquanta. Un volo ogni quattordici giorni, con un panciuto *Sunderland* quadrimotore militare adattato a versione civile. Il volo durava allora tre giorni dall'Australia al cuore della Polinesia; l'idrovolante si fermava ogni sera perché non abilitato al volo notturno, faceva scalo ogni tramonto a un'isola diversa: alle Figi, a Samoa – con possibilità di visita alla tomba di Robert Louis Stevenson – e poi agli atolli Cook. L'arrivo e l'ammaraggio nella laguna di Tahiti avveniva al tramonto del sole della terza tappa, in un tripudio di luce, in cielo, e di feste, a terra.

Infatti dal momento del primo ammaraggio la solitudine dell'isola – se mai è esistita un'epoca in cui quest'isola e quelle tutt'attorno furono veramente «lontane» dal resto del mondo (presupposto che io ritengo errato perché, dal momento della loro scoperta in poi, gli arcipelaghi polinesiani sono stati meta ininterrotta di pellegrinaggi marini d'esploratori, missionari, mercanti, militari, poeti, istitutori, pittori e infine turisti) – era finita.

Era finita un'epoca, la Polinesia non era più fisicamente lontana; era – si fa per dire – a portata di mano e iniziava, con l'ammaraggio di quel primo idrovolante, un altro capitolo della sua storia, quello legato alla sua trasformazione in «paradiso turistico».

Quando Capitan Cook, primo europeo a gettar l'àncora in una baia di Tahiti, tornò allo stesso approdo nel 1769, ovvero solo due anni dopo la sua prima visita, annotò nel suo *Diario* – destinato a diventare famoso – di aver trovato Tahiti «profondamente cambiata». Dal momento in cui la sua penna d'oca scrisse queste parole, la sua osservazione è diventata il *leit-motiv* di tutti i viaggiatori tornati a quest'isola dopo un primo sbarco. Famosi e sconosciuti, banali cronisti e illustri scrittori, semplici visitatori, funzionari di dogane, avventurieri squattrinati o ricchi turisti del jet-set internazionale, insomma tutti coloro che approdano «per una seconda volta in Polinesia» s'affannano a ripetere, da duecento anni, che «le isole» sono cambiate, non sono più le stesse; e aggiungono che ancor di più si sono trasformati – in peggio, naturalmente – i polinesiani.

Per la verità, si potrebbe addirittura dire, oggi, che sono scomparsi, perché nei due secoli trascorsi da quando «furono scoperti» – quale disgrazia, per loro! – nei Mari del Sud sono giunti con successive e alternate «invasioni» inglesi e francesi; e poi, in ordine sparso, cinesi, indiani, giapponesi, e tanti, tanti altri americani ed europei. Non pochi persino gli sbarchi di italiani, dato che oggi, a Tahiti, di nostri «oriundi» se ne contano circa ottocento.

Tutti questi *poopà* (così siamo chiamati, noi bianchi, da «loro») si sono confusi, mescolati, accoppiati con i polinesiani mutandone usi e costumi, ben diversi dagli originali: dalla cucina alle abitudini sessuali, dalla maniera di abitare a quella di pescare.

Confesso d'essermi anch'io confuso più volte nell'eterogenea compagnia «dei nostalgici». Anch'io, a ogni ritorno nell'Oceania del Sud, ho ripetuto la stessa monotona osservazione. Lamento che non è poi nemmeno riservato alla sola Polinesia: in fondo non facciamo altro che ribadirlo, soprattutto noi della generazione a cavallo di questo secolo, applicandolo – con spenta afflizione – a genti e paesi, usi e costumi del mondo intero. A cominciare da quelli di casa nostra.

«Tahiti è cambiata» affermò Cook due anni dopo averla scoperta: sono arrivati i missionari, hanno dato fuoco ai sacri *tiki* di legno, hanno tagliato i capelli alle ragazze, non c'è più libero amore; abbiamo portato il peccato o quanto meno l'idea del peccato, il senso di colpa per ogni atto anche più innocente, basta sia *diverso* da quanto codificano le nostre leggi, le nostre abitudini, la nostra morale.

«La natura dei nativi delle isole è cambiata molto, o poco? è riconoscibile o irriconoscibile?» «Quant'è diversa la Polinesia degli anni Novanta, rispetto a quella che tu hai visto?» Sono queste le domande che mi rivolgono – con petulante ma giustificata insistenza – i miei compagni di viaggio mentre d'isola in isola visitiamo l'arcipelago delle Tuamotu. Sono al «primo approdo», qui; e i loro interrogativi sono comprensibili. Si sentono quasi turlupinati: le isole che s'aspettavano – «un incanto» – sono ben diverse.

Il loro paesaggio è punteggiato di alberghi e nuove costruzioni. A Papeete il traffico si è fatto caotico (alla mattina e alla sera per entrare o uscire dalla piccola capitale occorre un'ora di sofferta fila, incolonnati in automobile come in qualsiasi altro centro europeo, americano, giapponese).

Sì, Papeete, Tahiti e le isole vicine sono ogni giorno diverse, sempre più diverse dal loro modello ideale. Ma fino a che punto siamo autorizzati a piangere su queste trasformazioni? In realtà, in quarant'anni di viaggio ho visto mutare in tante parti del mondo di più e in peggio isole, coste, paesi, porti, spiagge. Talune isole e tanti litorali di casa nostra sono spesso irriconoscibili da una stagione all'altra.

Dopo James Cook, un altro personaggio famoso lamentava questi mutamenti con accenti rabbiosi: Paul Gauguin. Nelle lettere agli amici, e al suo mercante d'arte e nel diario *Noa-noa*, così come in quel giornaletto «Les Guêpes» (Le Vespe) a sue spese pubblicato a Papeete, predicava contro le innovazioni colpevoli di «tagliar alla base», in Oceania, le radici della nobile cultura locale.

E per chi gode nel leggere parole di nostalgia ed evocazioni e rimpianti, consiglio vivamente uno dei più bei libri mai scritti sulla Polinesia, *Les immémoriaux*, romanzo di Victor Segalen.

Ma se alla nostalgia si vuol aggiungere una riflessione più ragionata, meno sentimentale, ci si può render conto di alcune «verità» che sopravvivono, malgrado tutto, in Polinesia. Certo, nelle isole le trasformazioni hanno assunto un ritmo frenetico da quando a Tahiti, a Bora-Bora, a Rangiroa sono state attrezzate piste ove atterrano jet capaci di scaricare trecento passeggeri per volta, pronti a una fulminea vacanza in un «mare del Sud» esemplificato da cartoline e dépliants. *Inclusive tour* dall'immancabile conclusione con cena alla luce delle torce e équipe tahitiana impegnata nel classico *tamurè*; il ballo «sfrenato-come-un-atto-d'amore», che si conclude con l'invito dei danzatori polinesiani a turisti maschi e femmine perché – ballando insieme – anch'essi assaporino la gioia di questa danza così sexy da essere proibita come «diabolica» dai primi missionari.

La riflessione controcorrente che poco sopra suggerivo potrebbe prender spunto proprio dalla danza serale offerta – alla luce delle torce – ai *poopà* in cerca d'emozioni. Può sembrare – e lo è! – frutto di un'attenta organizzazione turistica; eppure, anche se nel corpo di ballo non tutte le ragazze sono polinesiane (ben abbronzate, si confondono tra loro parigine, milanesi, californiane, che si pagano così una lunga vacanza nelle isole), questo «ballo d'accoglienza e d'addio» non è *un falso*, in quanto dal diario di Cook – che continuo a citare come punto preciso di riferimento tra *ieri* e *oggi* – sappiamo che proprio con simile danza collettiva i tahitiani *veri* di allora accolsero l'equipaggio della prima nave europea; e sappiamo che uomini e donne invitarono i pallidi marinai e ufficiali inglesi a unirsi a loro. Perché la danza era – ed è ancora – il linguaggio, il *modo di comunicare* preferito dai polinesiani; tra loro, e tra loro e gli *altri*.

Le isole sono cambiate, dunque? Né più né meno di quanto tutto il mondo cambia, giorno dopo giorno.

In meglio o in peggio? Per Gauguin e i suoi epigoni romantici, nostalgici del «paradiso naturale delle isole» (ma è poi mai esistito?), le isole e la gente che le abita sono certamente cambiate. E in peggio.

Ma si tratta di un giudizio superficiale. Occorrerebbe distinguere tra certe apparenze – irritanti, è vero – e talune realtà che lasciano interdetti. Per esempio, mi sono accorto che il *modo spontaneo* dei polinesiani – e dei loro figli meticciati con tutti noi – di intessere un preciso rapporto con la natura non solo non è cambiato, ma costringe anche i *poopà* ad adeguarsi a norme mai scritte ma ben precise. Ben severe nel regolare certi rapporti con l'ambiente circostante, come il considerare peccato grave qualunque atto capace di inquinare le acque interne delle splendide lagune; o di tagliare un albero di cocco senza provvedere a piantarne subito altri tre.

Potrei continuare con altri esempi. Ma mi pare che questo basti a capire come sia necessario andar cauti, prima di piangere «sui cambiamenti» delle isole. È necessario stare attenti quando se ne parla, e ci si esibisce in facili e strazianti lamenti. Taluni sono proprio inutili, soprattutto se siamo noi *poopà* a levarli al cielo, dimenticando – ancora una volta – di guardarci allo specchio.

È una riflessione che già avevo espresso a voce alta, al mio arrivo nel '70, in Polinesia. Alla sera stessa del mio sbarco a Papeete ero andato a far visita a un polinesiano che molto mi aveva aiutato nel realizzare le scene di mare più difficili per il mio film *Tikoyo* del 1960, ed ero entrato nella capanna sua e di sua moglie Vahirià.

Una capanna che non era più una capanna. Il suo interno – di cui s'intravedeva un arredamento standard con mobili di plastica – era rischiarato da una tenue luce azzurrognola. Nella capanna di *niau* – esternamente ancora eguale a quelle che videro i primi esploratori, nello stesso luogo, alla fine del Settecento – in un villaggio chiamato Arué troneggiava un televisore a colori. In un notiziario in lingua francese, un telecronista parlava dei problemi di parcheggio nella Città del Vaticano e un altro, subito dopo, annunciava i risultati di un torneo di pelota basca in non so quale città iberica. La famigliola dei padroni di casa e un'altra decina di vicini, tutti polinesiani vestiti con pareo e camiciola, ascoltavano in silenzio; del tutto privi d'interesse verso quelle notizie, ma certamente ipnotizzati dal quadro fluorescente del video.

La televisione a Tahiti era allora un dono di un lontano ministero parigino «della cooperazione», nel quadro degli aiuti ai paesi in via di sviluppo ancora sotto amministrazione europea. La stessa amministrazione, mentre elargiva ai polinesiani i piaceri della tivù, decideva di eliminare lo studio della loro lingua nelle scuole di tutte le isole e di vietarne l'uso negli atti ufficiali. I due divieti, sommati, hanno minacciato di eliminare tradizioni orali, poesie, costumi, ricordi storici preziosi; e di contribuire con l'aiuto dei mutamenti sociali ed economici che investono le isole del Pacifico (il più disastroso «ciclone» della storia di questo oceano) a far dimenticare le proprie origini a un intero popolo. Negli arcipelaghi centrali del Pacifico, nel cuore cioè della Polinesia, s'è corso il rischio di una catastrofe culturale; che per fortuna s'è avverata solo in parte, perché la temeraria decisione del ministro parigino fu revocata pochi anni dopo la sua promulgazione; e se la tivù continua a far danni (là come ovunque, peraltro) perlomeno li causa parlando in lingua polinesiana.

Tahiti e la Polinesia orientale sono così salve dal «contagio linguistico» europeo che invece ha travolto isole come le Samoa, le Hawaii e le Figi – potrei citarne anche altre – dove da tempo si parla solo inglese.

Negli anni Settanta su tutti i limiti delle terre emerse dell'Oceania, nelle lagune coralline e lungo le coste vulcaniche, anche la natura sembrava voler iniziare mutazioni simili a quelle che cambiano il mondo degli uomini. Era stata una stella di mare a dare il primo segno d'allarme.

La cosiddetta *acantasther*, una delle mille e mille forme di vita che popolano le acque tropicali, e si nutre di corallo, aveva dato segni di squilibrio biologico. Forse per le radiazioni atomiche, forse per altre contaminazioni, fatto è che, dall'Australia agli atolli della Micronesia, l'*acantasther* si era moltiplicata vertiginosamente e divorava e sgretolava ogni giorno vasti tratti di barriere madreporiche cresciute in milioni di anni intorno alle terre emerse, proteggendole dalle furie dell'oceano, permettendovi la vita.

Nell'immensità dell'oceano, nel lento ciclo degli eventi naturali, nel respiro vastissimo dei fatti biologici, quello dell'*acantasther* fu un episodio particolare di proporzioni quasi insignificanti. Eppure è sintomo – e simbolo – di questo mondo che alle trasformazioni e alle mutazioni reagisce spesso con fenomeni incomprensibili. Inspiegabili.

Tornando in Polinesia nel '91, e osservandola quindi con il distacco di tanti anni, troverò molte conferme al mio pessimismo degli anni Settanta, ma anche molte sorprese. Alcune delle quali mi permetteranno di annotare *oggi* mutazioni positive. Coincidenze di eventi negativi hanno permesso – ecco un esempio – lo sviluppo di una serie di concause per le quali l'antropizzazione delle isole minori, e la conseguente mortificazione della natura, non solo s'è arrestata, ma in certi casi è addirittura stata cancellata (e vedremo più avanti il perché). Quel pericolo incombeva, a mio avviso, in molte isole tra il 1955 e il 1970. Quando, a più riprese, avevo percorso più di trentamila miglia da est a ovest, dalla costa americana a quella australiana toccando le Galapagos deserte, le Hawaii sovrappopolate, la Micronesia, la sacra Isola di Pasqua e le paludose Trobriand, la turistica Tahiti e le lontane Tuamotu contaminate da centinaia di funghi atomici «sperimentali»; e la Nuova Guinea, le Sottovento, le Samoa, le Salomone, le Nuove Ebridi, la Nuova Caledonia.

A Huahine, nelle isole Sottovento, c'è una scogliera, di traverso tra l'oceano e la laguna, dove in un giorno del 1970, mi era sembrato possibile godere due sensazioni molto contrastanti: da un lato il sentirmi di fronte alla natura come nel momento della creazione e trovarmi tra gente che aveva saputo istintivamente elaborare un rapporto quasi perfetto tra se stessa e l'ambiente; al contrario sentivo però che quell'equilibrio era sul punto di spezzarsi e per sempre. Per questo mi sentivo felice e infelice allo stesso tempo. Su quella scogliera tra oceano e laguna, assordato da centinaia di uccelli marini, vedevo muoversi sotto il pelo dell'acqua la vita sottomarina come in un acquario di cristallo: in quella opalescenza guizzavano pesci di ogni forma e colore, testuggini portate dalla corrente, l'ombra nera delle mantas, e – dappertutto – coralli e madrepore.

A specchiarsi in quel cristallo era un villaggio (alcune capanne e rare case) inserito con grazia naturale nel quadro d'insieme. E tra quelle case, e sul mare e nella laguna, la comunità dei pescatori viveva un'esistenza sotto molti aspetti straordinariamente serena, traendo dall'ambiente circostante il massimo beneficio senza violarne regole maturate di generazione in generazione.

Vigevano là due sistemi diversi per ricavare dalle acque il cibo necessario alla sopravvivenza e al commercio: reti o nasse di canne in laguna; e pesca alla traina, all'amo e all'arpione subacqueo in mare aperto o nella *pass* (il canale tra acque interne ed esterne di ogni atollo, quasi un'anticamera dell'oceano). Non attribuivo altro significato se non quello pratico a questa differenza di sistemi; invece essi rispecchiavano non solo un sistema di vita, ma un complesso intreccio di rapporti con l'ambiente.

«C'è una ragione» mi dice il mio più vecchio amico delle Sottovento, Garnier, pescatore polinesiano che spesso ricorderò in queste pagine, «se attorno alle scogliere, dove fino a ieri la vita sottomarina era così ricca, le acque sembrano ora morte è perché sono state violate regole precise che insegnavano come l'uomo doveva rispettare le lagune; lagune che erano la nostra vita, tu lo sai. L'uomo delle nostre isole viveva di quella ricchezza. E i nostri vecchi avevano capito che, per restare sempre uguali, quelle acque *non dovevano sentire* la presenza dell'uomo.»

Era una lezione di ecologia istintiva quella che ascoltavo; norme certo mai studiate dai polinesiani, eppure parte essenziale della loro conoscenza sperimentale.

I polinesiani sapevano bene che, per turbare l'equilibrio naturale delle loro lagune, bastava *contaminare* appena quelle acque con rifiuti del villaggio o addirittura con molto meno: per esempio, il sangue di un pesce pescato all'amo o all'arpione. Quelle poche gocce di sangue sarebbero a poco a poco marcite nell'acqua (che nello specchio liquido chiuso dell'atollo è quasi stagnante), provocando la fuga in oceano aperto dei pesci di specie più delicata; e quella prima rottura d'equilibrio avrebbe causato altre fughe a catena. Per questo nelle acque «interne» i pesci dovevano essere catturati vivi senza il minimo spargimento di sangue; e potevano essere uccisi, poi, solo lontano dall'acqua. C'erano pene severe per chi trasgrediva queste regole, garanzia di un equilibrio tanto delicato da misurarsi nel rapporto tra poche gocce di sangue e l'enorme massa d'acqua di una laguna.

Proprio in quell'anno, e proprio in quelle stesse isole vidi però com'era facile turbare o addirittura cancellare quell'equilibrio. Era bastata l'apparizione, in quel mare, di flottiglie di pescatori giapponesi, e il loro lavoro frenetico, indiscriminato. Successivamente la situazione era peggiorata con l'arrivo di sempre più numerose comitive di turisti, la costruzione d'alberghi e piccoli aeroporti creati per lo «sviluppo delle isole». Nuove costruzioni che hanno trovato, tutte, il loro punto di scarico proprio nelle lagune.

«È stata questione di poco tempo» mi ha detto il capo villaggio di Rangiroa, e le sue parole mi sono state ripetute da tanti altri abitanti delle isole, «e molto è cambiato attorno a noi. È difficile continuare a essere pescatori se non c'è pesce nella laguna, e resta da catturare solo quello dell'oceano, rischioso e difficile. Meglio lavorare all'aeroporto, o in albergo; oppure andare a Tahiti dove viene richiesta ogni giorno più manodopera, e a chiunque di noi viene offerto tanto denaro per un mese quanto un polinesiano delle isole non ne ha visto durante tutta la sua vita.»

Dall'esodo verso le città nelle «isole grandi» e l'abbandono di quelle piccole derivano quelle conseguenze relative all'antropizzazione, delle quali parlavo poco addietro; e sono esattamente l'opposto di quelle sino a ora esposte: infatti dove l'uomo abbandona il suo mondo, l'ambiente naturale (altrove umiliato e annientato) si prende la sua grande rivincita. Ma se questo rassicura sulla sopravvivenza di tante specie animali, tuttavia anche qui ci troviamo di fronte a una sconfitta, quella di una cultura unica al mondo, le cui basi poggiavano tutte sul rapporto uomo-natura, che specialmente nelle «isole minori» era particolarmente sviluppato, perché era l'unico «sistema di rapporti» che permetteva la sopravvivenza di minuscole comunità isolate in atolli fuori da ogni rotta, e quindi preclusi a periodici regolari contatti con i centri maggiori.

Quando si dice «cultura» parlando dei polinesiani, si intende la parola nel suo significato letterale. Ogni popolo ha sviluppato un suo sistema di vita creando, di volta in volta, civiltà grandi e memorabili in campi sempre diversi a seconda di differenti componenti storiche. Per i polinesiani la cultura ha significato soprattutto *ricerca di un rapporto, di un equilibrio con l'ambiente circostante*; altri popoli hanno elaborato sistemi filosofici o religiosi, edificato opere grandiose, creato imperi secolari; i polinesiani hanno perseguito invece solo questo scopo, da noi occidentali ritenuto «minore» fino al momento in cui ci siamo resi conto, improvvisamente, dell'importanza dell'ecologia, e s'è cominciato a capire che l'uomo morrà se non riuscirà a salvare l'ambiente naturale in cui vive. Una cultura che ha trovato questo equilibrio, ed è stata capace di porlo come base stessa della sua esistenza, merita dunque una ben profonda considerazione nella storia dell'uomo e delle civilizzazioni. Ed è per questo che, là dove i polinesiani abbandonano le loro isole, ci sentiamo di fronte a una comune sconfitta. A consolarci resta il fatto che nei luoghi da cui l'uomo fugge subentra una natura trionfante: lo abbiamo visto, nel nostro ultimo viaggio, in tante piccole isole di varie zone del Pacifico; con maggior evidenza nelle Wallis, nelle Loyalty e nei microscopici *motù* corallini delle Tuamotu; e in particolare quelli «periferici» verso le Gambier. Qui, soprattutto, il fenomeno si mostra in immagini stupefacenti.

Sbarcati in uno di questi *motù*, l'abbiamo trovato popolato da decine di migliaia di esemplari di una famiglia di uccelli marini che erano ritenuti in via d'estinzione, le *kaveka*, le rondini di mare. Ormai l'isola è loro, l'ultimo uomo è partito da qui oltre dieci anni addietro; noi siamo i primi a tornare, camminiamo su una spiaggia palpitante, tappeto di piccoli appena nati o di femmine ancora intente a covare. Parlare fra noi non è facile, tanto le *kaveka* stridono al nostro apparire.

«A mezzogiorno mangeremo frittata d'uova di *kaveka*» ci grida per farsi sentire la nostra guida polinesiana; e ci spiega come distinguere le uova fresche da quelle vecchie: bisogna calpestare tutte le uova che capitano sotto i piedi lungo un tratto di spiaggia e ritornare poi all'ora del pasto; le uova che troveremo sopra quelle da noi schiacciate saranno evidentemente appena deposte, ottime da mangiare. Un sistema analogo mi fu illustrato da Bernard Motissier, il navigatore solitario francese, che incontrai a Tahiti reduce dal suo doppio giro del mondo a vela. Gli raccontai l'episodio del nostro sbarco all'isola delle rondini e di come la nostra guida ci aveva insegnato a sfamarci con uova appena deposte. «Anche in altri arcipelaghi» mi disse «le isole piccole sono sempre meno abitate dall'uomo; e anche lì tornano a migliaia, decine di migliaia, gli uccelli che sembravano destinati a scomparire. Quando approdo su quelle piccole terre, mi comporto così: getto in mare le uova d'un tratto di spiaggia, che delimito poi con quattro frasche. Mi metto a dormire sotto un albero e mi sveglio dopo un paio di ore, e, se nel tratto da me recintato ci sono uova, posso essere certo della loro freschezza.»

Solo venticinque anni fa, nel '66, sembrava che l'uomo avrebbe cancellato nel giro di una generazione ogni traccia di vita animale da queste isole. Si parlava di turismo, di industrie del pesce, della *coprah*, del petrolio. È successo tutto quanto era previsto – e forse anche peggio – ma solo nelle isole e negli atolli più grandi; nelle «piccole terre» ogni pronostico è stato sovvertito, appena l'uomo che le abitava non ha saputo resistere al richiamo delle città; come i nostri contadini, come i montanari, come i nomadi del deserto. Lo stesso fenomeno si ripete a tutte le latitudini.

È cominciato in Micronesia, con gli isolani di Bikini, l'atollo degli esperimenti atomici americani: vent'anni d'esilio, poi li riportarono alla terra nativa, ormai decontaminata. Ma dopo pochi mesi, i giovani sono tornati nelle *bidonvilles* alla periferia della città ove erano stati un tempo trasportati di forza. Preferivano le baracche – margini miserabili della vita urbana – alle capanne dei villaggi felici sull'oceano.

Poi fu la volta dell'atollo di Mururoa; altri esperimenti atomici (francesi, questi) e altro esodo forzato degli abitanti di molti villaggi, i quali non volevano lasciare, quasi ovunque, le case e le rive degli avi. Ma appena a Papeete, nella Tahiti ormai «grande città», hanno cambiato idea e hanno fatto intendere di preferire la carne in scatola al cibo strappato alle onde del Pacifico.

Le due notizie (attraverso la fitta rete degli scambi, delle golette, dei parenti, degli amici) hanno compiuto rapidamente il giro dell'oceano, isola dopo isola. E così oggi i villaggi di troppi arcipelaghi hanno cominciato a spopolarsi. Un esodo che si è completato quando per due volte, negli anni Ottanta, la violenza di un ciclone tropicale, quale non se ne ricordava di simile da quasi un secolo, ha sconvolto gli atolli orientali, seminando distruzione e morte. Anche, e soprattutto, per questo oggi i villaggi di quello che fu la coraggiosa e orgogliosa gente *puamutu*, offrono il desolato spettacolo di case e capanne in rovina.

Tutt'attorno la natura si prende, come ho già detto, la sua rivincita; nelle acque basse, lungo le coste e negli specchi interni delle isole abbandonate, la vita subacquea è sempre più ricca e il mare si ripopola.

Ho visto una sera le acque della laguna di Maupiti scendere sotto il livello medio della marea, per qualche misterioso gioco di correnti o di luna. Restarono allo scoperto tutti i coralli del basso-fondo e parve che l'orizzonte davanti a noi palpitasse affannato: migliaia, milioni di pesci erano rimasti quasi all'asciutto e guizzavano, balzavano, s'ammucchiavano.

Venne dall'alto una nuvola nera: erano *sule*, predatrici del cielo; piombarono su quel cibo facile, un tuffo dopo l'altro, senza arrestarsi mai finché fu notte.

A quell'ora a Papeete, a soli trecento chilometri in linea d'aria, la stessa notte era tagliata dalle luci delle automobili bloccate negli ingorghi del traffico cittadino, ormai di dimensioni europee.

Quando giunsi per la prima volta a Papeete nel 1955 le automobili erano meno di cento. E nel '64, tornato per un secondo viaggio, mi parve incredibile che fossero quasi mille. «Questa cittadina non può contenerne tante» si diceva. A dimostrare il contrario, già nel '70, a Papeete erano immatricolate ventiduemila vetture, a parte le moto e i camion.

Nel gennaio del '91 il tutto è più che triplicato, si sono dovuti creare parcheggi multipiani e superstrade a quattro corsie attorno alla cittadina.

Eguale boom nell'edilizia, tale da mutare alla base il rapporto tra uomo e uomo. A Papeete, benché il nucleo urbano fosse già molto sviluppato, negli anni Cinquanta e negli anni Sessanta non esisteva una vera e propria «barriera sociale». Come in tutta la

Polinesia, non esisteva in quella cittadina una nozione di società urbana come noi la conosciamo, e cioè divisa da classi «discriminate» in quartieri dei ricchi e in quelli dei poveri. I ricchi e i poveri, ovviamente, esistevano, anzi c'erano pochi individui ricchissimi (la stessa natura estremamente povera «coloniale» dell'isola favoriva l'accumulazione di spropositate ricchezze nelle mani di un'élite) e una maggioranza di poveri. Ma la «non esistenza» di una vera e propria città con le sue barriere aveva fatto in modo che le differenze economiche non avessero mutato l'antica facilità di rapporti umani. In base ai quali, per esempio, Monsieur Martin, il miliardario padrone della locale industria della birra e delle bevande in bottiglia, poteva tranquillamente invitare a cena allo Sporting Club la cameriera addetta alla pulizia dei pavimenti nella sua villa, o il governatore poteva ballare allegramente all'Hôtel Tropiques con la cuoca del «palazzo» senza stupire o scandalizzare nessuno. Questa assenza di confini era il riflesso di una urbanistica che non conosceva, appunto, l'esistenza di quartieri ricchi e quartieri poveri; le grandi ville coloniali liberty, le abitazioni modeste e le capanne s'alternavano casualmente, e nessuna rete, muro, cancello divideva un'abitazione dall'altra.

Tutto è cambiato, oggi. Da tutte le piccole isole giunge alla «capitale» gente che vuol vivere l'avventura cittadina. Uomini e donne s'affollano in questa città dove lo sviluppo turistico crea una continua domanda di lavoro. Crescendo di misura, la città polinesiana non è solo mutata di forma e di stile (dalle case di legno di cocco intarsiate al cemento armato e acciaio) ma è cambiata nel suo spirito. Le barriere di classe fino a ieri inesistenti ora dividono i polinesiani inurbati in rigidi strati sociali. La città è lo specchio dell'uomo: e questa città che non aveva quartieri, ora li ha, creati dai gruppi che giungono dalle piccole isole; nuovi venuti che hanno meno mezzi dei cittadini si vestono differentemente, parlano dialetti incomprensibili. Solo per essere già da tempo inurbati, i polinesiani di Papeete chiamano i cugini venuti dalle isole Marchesi o dalle Gambier *sauvages*. E li confinano in periferie provvisorie e miserabili.

Quello che accade a Papeete in Tahiti si ripete a Noumea in Nuova Caledonia, a Suva nelle Figi, ad Apia nelle Samoa – e cito solo le maggiori «isole di cemento» che ho visto, ma certo altri esempi potrebbero essere aggiunti.

Le «catastrofi culturali e sociali», nelle isole polinesiane, non datano però solo da oggi.

All'«isola sacra» della cultura oceanica, l'Isola di Pasqua, giunsero, nei secoli dello splendore polinesiano, coraggiose spedizioni che percorsero migliaia di miglia attraverso i Mari del Sud e popolarono la piccola isola creandovi un centro di civiltà unico nella storia dell'uomo. Poi, da quando Roggeveen la scoprì, oltre due secoli e mezzo fa, questa terra a duemilacinquecento chilometri dal Cile e ad altrettanti da Tahiti fu meta di continui saccheggi, rapine e violenze, e così fu distrutta quella comunità dalla quale erano nati sacerdoti che avevano popolato il cielo e la terra della Polinesia di divinità dai simboli impenetrabili; e dalla quale erano nati gli scultori di quelle statue giganti (i *moai*), simboli dell'arte oceanica e misura della sua universalità e del suo mistero.

Viaggiatori, scienziati, archeologi ed etnologi giungendo, dall'inizio del secolo a oggi, a questo approdo del Pacifico, si sono posti sempre un'unica domanda, non accorgendosi che altri e più angosciosi interrogativi gravavano sul futuro della piccola isola con un'ipoteca la cui scadenza è andata avvicinandosi di anno in anno.

E così, anziché chiedersi come riuscire a salvare gli ultimi resti di quella civiltà e della gente che la creò, studiosi, archeologi, viaggiatori hanno concentrato la loro attenzione su un problema certamente secondario al primo: queste sculture scolpite nella roccia dei vulcani spenti dell'isola ed erette lungo le sue coste, sulla sommità dei colli, nel fondo delle valli, oltre a testimoniare una tanto matura e perfetta abilità artistica, quale sconosciuta pagina della storia locale documentano? In altre parole: *perché* gli abitanti dell'Isola di Pasqua per oltre sei secoli lavorarono a erigere centinaia di enormi monumenti di pietra, così difficili da tagliare e da trasportare? Una domanda rimasta senza risposta. Si è sostenuto che Pasqua fosse l'estremo resto di un continente inghiottito dal mare, o di una civiltà megalitica partita dall'Asia e giunta sino al Sud America passando per questo lembo di terra d'un soffio emergente dall'oceano; altri ancora hanno suggerito che essa fu «l'isola cimitero» di un arcipelago oggi scomparso, il luogo ove venivano sepolti i re e i capi di un grande popolo estinto.

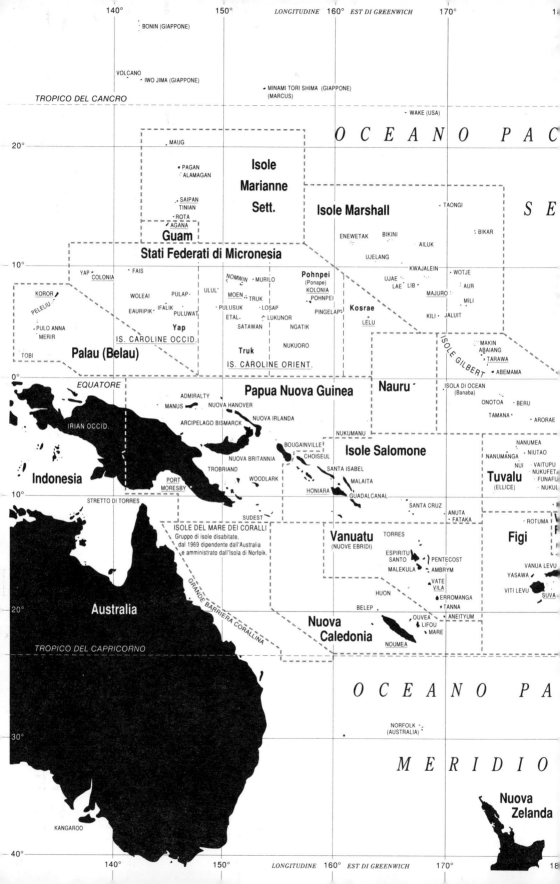

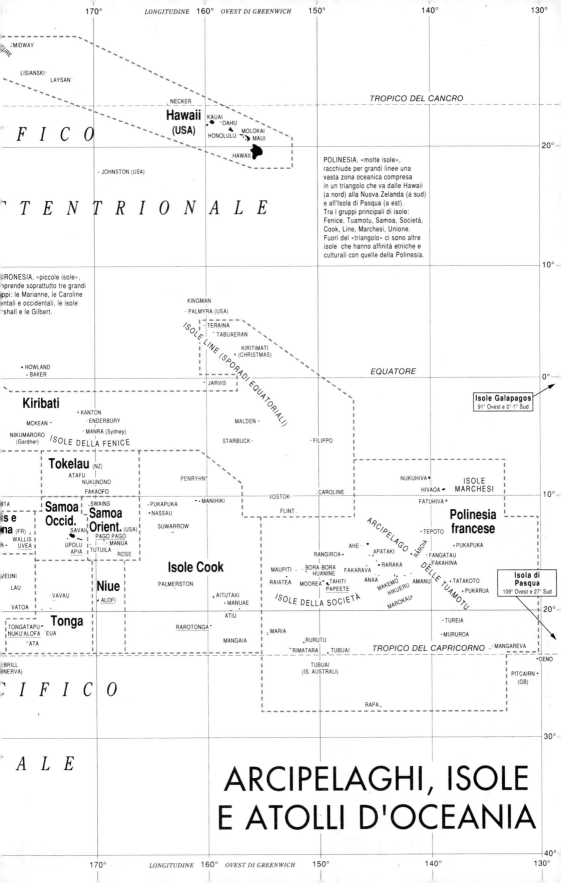

ARCIPELAGHI, ISOLE E ATOLLI D'OCEANIA

Interpretazioni diverse, ma da sembrar dettate da una sorta di fede in una «età dell'oro» popolata da una umanità tutta grandezza e mistero. L'archeologia e l'etnologia degli anni più recenti hanno però, se non altro, cancellato queste fantasie chiarendo un dato di partenza inconfutabile: Pasqua fu popolata, all'incirca un millennio fa, da trasmigratori polinesiani che vi giunsero dopo aver conquistato tutto il Pacifico meridionale, isola dopo isola. Essa rimane la punta estrema raggiunta dalle loro fragili imbarcazioni, il luogo da cui non poterono mai più ripartire perché sull'isola non cresce, né crebbe mai, un solo albero di dimensioni tali da permettere la costruzione di uno scafo capace d'affrontare l'oceano per un così lungo viaggio di ritorno. E furono loro, i polinesiani di Pasqua, a creare autonomamente un'arte assolutamente originale.

Appena sbarcati a Pasqua, sentendoci come a disagio davanti a quei giganti di pietra dallo sguardo fisso nel vuoto, abbiamo sentito innanzitutto l'angoscia di vedere le grandi statue cadere a pezzi; molte sono già a terra calpestate quotidianamente da migliaia di montoni che l'amministrazione cilena alleva nell'isola per creare «un'economia locale». La pietra scolpita ha resistito per secoli alle intemperie, al sole torrido come al vento gelido del Sud; ai terremoti e alle guerre feroci tra gruppi rivali; oggi, come presa da una repentina, profonda stanchezza, cede, giorno dopo giorno.

Nell'isola i polinesiani sono sempre di meno; aumentano *gauchos* e *peones* cileni che con un'operazione certamente non casuale vengono qui inviati per «ripopolare» l'isola.

A questi «coloni» imposti, si aggiungono altre presenze estranee. Un esempio fra tanti è quello della famiglia che ci ha ospitato durante la nostra permanenza nell'isola, di origine, come prova il suo nome, italiana: Cardinale. La padrona di casa, la *señora* Rosa, è nipote di un marinaio siciliano scampato a un naufragio e rimasto poi per sempre a Pasqua. Il sindaco, «el señor Alcade» (occorre ricordare che Pasqua è un'altra isola del Pacifico ove la lingua originale è stata sostituita da quella degli invasori coloniali: lo spagnolo), oltre a guidarci nei luoghi ove dovevamo filmare le grandi statue, ci ha presentato durante i nostri quotidiani spostamenti, durati tutto il periodo del nostro lavoro nell'isola, le famiglie più eterogenee dell'inventario multinazionale locale. Abbiamo così conosciuto gli anglo-maori, gli svevo-iberici, i franco-australiani: per ricordarci di essere nella sacra isola dei grandi trasmigratori oceanici, cercavamo di passare ogni sera dai Pakarati, l'unica famiglia le cui origini polinesiane sono saldamente radicate nelle più remote vicende isolane. Una famiglia chiassosa, allegra, numerosa: certo molto simile a quelle incontrate dai primi viaggiatori.

Un'unica famiglia a serbare il carattere, e qualche ricordo, di quella società indigena profondamente evoluta già da oltre mezzo millennio, da quando la prima vela europea apparve all'orizzonte e cercò approdo su quelle coste allora sconosciute ai marinai che s'avventuravano sul Pacifico. Bisogna ripartire da quel giorno per comprendere quanto avviene oggi in quest'angolo perduto dell'Oceano Pacifico ove la violenza dell'uomo sull'uomo ha conosciuto la stessa selvaggia drammaticità di cui furono vittime altri popoli, in altre terre, e, anche di recente, tra noi.

Quella domenica del 1722 (giorno di Pasqua, da cui il nome dato all'isola) la prima nave europea apparsa in quei mari era certo sembrata agli occhi degli isolani immensa, rispetto alle loro fragili canoe. Tuttavia non ne avevano avuto paura. Gli uomini e le donne saliti a bordo si comportarono con infantile curiosità ma, a modo loro, dignitosamente: non erano «selvaggi» terrorizzati dalla presenza di esseri sovrannaturali, ma uomini, marinai, sorpresi e incuriositi da nuovi problemi tecnici; misurarono in lungo e in largo l'imbarcazione e le sue vele, le cime, il timone. Quando suonò la tromba di bordo, gli isolani risposero con i loro strumenti danzando in onore degli ospiti a significare quanto anch'essi conoscessero e amassero la musica.

Nel pomeriggio dello stesso giorno i marinai olandesi scesero a terra e ricambiarono l'accoglienza e i doni ricevuti con una nutrita scarica di fucileria, che fece qualche decina di morti e di feriti gravi: avevano voluto subito dar la misura del superiore grado di civiltà degli europei. A confermarlo, giunsero poi all'isola nei successivi sessant'anni spagnoli, inglesi, francesi; agli inizi dell'Ottocento gli americani, i russi e ancora gli inglesi e infine i peruviani.

A tutti loro si deve quella serie di «mostruosi crimini commessi dai bianchi su una popolazione inerme» (come li ha definiti Alfred Métraux, il maggiore studioso di Pasqua) che non hanno praticamente altra definizione se non quella di genocidio.

Nel 1808, la nave americana *Nancy* compì la prima deportazione di uomini e donne con l'intenzione di adibirli come schiavi alla caccia alle foche nell'isola di Masaguera. Furono incatenati e rinchiusi sottocoperta, e solo dopo tre giorni di viaggio venne deciso di portarli sul ponte. Furono tolte loro le catene, agli uomini per farli lavorare alle pompe, alle donne per «intrattenere» gli ufficiali di bordo. Ma accadde qualcosa di incredibile: i prigionieri, appena liberi, si gettarono in mare e si misero a nuotare con disperazione, sperando forse di riuscire a tornare alla propria terra, nemmeno più in vista. Il comandante americano, pensando che la paura dell'oceano avrebbe fatto ritornare i fuggiaschi, fece fermare la nave e osservò da lontano la discussione sorta tra i fuggitivi sulla direzione da prendere: non essendo riusciti a mettersi d'accordo, alcuni si allontanarono verso sud altri verso nord. Furono allora mosse in acqua alcune imbarcazioni ma i fuggitivi rifiutarono di salirvi, lasciandosi inghiottire dal mare.

Dopo la *Nancy*, a più riprese altre navi tornarono a rifornirsi di schiavi a Pasqua. Razziatori di varie bandiere compirono incursioni ai danni di quel piccolo popolo, e il 12 dicembre 1862 una vera e propria piccola flotta arrivò all'isola: erano peruviani e loro mercenari. Sbarcarono e rastrellarono l'interno, le valli, le colline, le pendici dei vulcani. Pochi polinesiani riuscirono a scampare: gli altri, portati in Perù, vi morirono in breve di malattie, di disperazione, di maltrattamenti. Tra loro c'erano quasi tutti gli anziani, coloro «che sapevano» gli *huarè-po*, depositari della tradizione orale maturatasi nei secoli, e il re dell'isola, Kamakoi. Solo quindici isolani vennero liberati, quando il mondo seppe della razzia; tornarono all'isola ma portarono il vaiolo che si diffuse rapidamente trasformandola in un grande cimitero. All'epidemia si aggiunse la fame (nessuno pescava, nessuno più lavorava la terra). E così l'isola conobbe le lotte interne per il possesso dei pochi beni rimasti. La popolazione si ridusse a 600 abitanti e scomparvero gli ultimi sacerdoti depositari dei segreti del passato.

Quando i bianchi si insediarono nell'isola vi trovarono soltanto i resti di una civiltà agonizzante, distrutta fisicamente e moralmente, incapace di creare opere come quelle di cui l'isola era disseminata: statue, petroglifi e bassorilievi; nacque così l'interrogativo sulla provenienza di tanti tesori d'arte.

Da allora a oggi poco è cambiato. E quel poco, naturalmente, in peggio. Non solo aumenta di anno in anno la popolazione dei «coloni» cileni, ma è vicino il momento, anche qui, del boom del cemento armato e del turismo; e presto sarà difficile incontrare un uomo o una donna di diretta discendenza polinesiana.

Quando visitai Pasqua negli anni Settanta, la linea aerea regolare, dall'America e dall'Australia, era ormai una realtà settimanale; e si ponevano le fondamenta di un grande albergo in riva al mare. Una nuova ondata di invasori stava per metter piede sull'isola: ondata certo pacifica e tale da portare un sensibile beneficio economico agli abitanti di laggiù, vissuti sino a oggi in condizioni di miseria assoluta, ma che *ha* contribuito a metter la parola fine anche per l'ultima autenticità dell'isola. Nel piccolo villaggio di Hanga Roa, dopo che di stagione in stagione i turisti aumentano, e ora sono *l'unica realtà economica* dell'isola, i giovani si son messi tutti d'impegno a tagliare e produrre in serie statuette di pietra a imitazione dei sacri *moai*, per venderle all'aeroporto e nei due alberghi costruiti dai cileni.

Nella «sala partenze» di quell'aeroporto, quando abbracciai la donna che più d'ogni altra isolana mi aveva aiutato a conoscere la sua piccola terra – la vecchia Palarati, ultima matriarca polinesiana dell'isola – mi disse: «Quando tornerai, io non ci sarò più. Ma non ci sarà più nemmeno l'Isola di Pasqua».

Eguale problema a oltre novemila chilometri di distanza, all'altro estremo del Pacifico, dove ho disegnato molti dei miei itinerari nell'oceano di Balboa. Nel mondo papua degli arcipelaghi occidentali è fiorita – negli statici millenni delle culture primitive – un'altra dimensione umana: un'eredità di equilibri con la natura in un certo senso più «barbara» di quella polinesiana, ma certo non meno importante nella storia dell'uomo. Infatti le forme

d'arte – in particolare quella statuaria rituale – fiorita nell'«Oceania nera» sono ormai parte del patrimonio figurativo dell'umanità; e arricchiscono non solo i musei d'antropologia del mondo
intero, ma le gallerie d'arte (per non parlare dei prezzi astrono-
mici che alcuni «pezzi» hanno raggiunto nel mercato antiquario e
collezionistico di New York, Los Angeles e Londra).

Anche qui l'acculturazione già da tempo corrode usi, costumi e
ricordi. Oggi è fenomeno sempre più rapido e totale: ne sono
testimone diretto, e anche qui posso dire di avere visto dal 1965 al
1989 un altro mondo primitivo nel momento in cui sta per scomparire. Nei miei itinerari più recenti sotto le ali di piccoli aerei
diretti verso l'interno, ho visto passare la geografia difficile delle
grandi isole, le Salomone, la Nuova Guinea, la Nuova Britannia:
vulcani e montagne a picco, vallate strette e tortuose, fiumi a
spirale nella foresta ove il verde impazzisce in infinite gamme (le
zone paludose, in toni chiarissimi, e le zone nel tono cupo che ha il
verde là dove la vegetazione è così fitta da impedire qualsiasi
forma di vita animale). Voli ai quali sono seguiti itinerari in auto
e, per giorni e giorni, a piedi e in canoa; sino all'arrivo ai superstiti
villaggi ove è riuscita a sopravvivere una vita tribale primordiale e
antica quanto l'uomo.

Alle *high-lands* dell'Asaro Valley in Nuova Guinea, nel 1970, ero
arrivato a piedi. E oltre Kambaramba, ho trovato in canoa a
motore i dedali forse mai battuti del bacino del Sepik, una zona di
canali, fiumi, acquitrini e laghi più vasta della valle Padana. Cito
questi luoghi perché rappresentavano (nel maggio 1970, quando li
abbiamo raggiunti e oltrepassati) una sorta di confine ideale tra le
terre realmente sotto controllo dell'Amministrazione australiana
(il TPNG) e quelle ancora immobili sotto il sole del Neolitico.
Oltre quel confine ogni villaggio, ogni gruppo umano era ricco di
un patrimonio di tradizioni; assieme agli arcipelaghi papua più
lontani e al gruppo delle Trobriand, questa zona è stata sino a
oggi uno dei campi di ricerca più ricchi e stimolanti per gli etnologi del mondo occidentale (da Malinowski negli anni Venti ai
giovani studiosi delle ultime generazioni).

Spinto dall'incredibile interesse di quanto ero riuscito a vedere
nei primi itinerari, sono poi tornato sui miei passi con viaggi
successivi. Certo, era passato qualche anno; ma cos'è una simile

frazione di tempo, in rapporto all'età di una cultura, di una società, e al lentissimo suo mutare, là ove le condizioni naturali hanno per millenni garantito condizioni di stabilità? Invece ho potuto misurare in un arco di tempo tanto preciso e breve (come in un esperimento di laboratorio) la velocità con la quale in Oceania una cultura autoctona oggi scompare, annullandosi.

Per oltre un secolo gli studiosi hanno ritenuto che il fenomeno dell'acculturazione in paesi molto isolati come la Nuova Guinea si svolgesse lungo un lento arco generazionale: nel tempo in cui i giovani si sostituivano agli anziani, il passaggio dalla cultura «primitiva» a quella «industrializzata» era cosa fatta. Poi si è visto quanto elementi imprevisti – e nel Pacifico soprattutto la seconda guerra mondiale – abbiano accelerato il progressivo dissolversi di tradizioni uguali a se stesse dall'alba dell'umanità a oggi; nell'ultimo decennio, infine, la metamorfosi del mondo papua ha assunto un ritmo vertiginoso: ormai non è più il caso di parlare di generazioni né di «agenti» straordinari. Le ultime aree dove le culture papua sopravvivono sono state cancellate nel giro di pochi mesi; a distanza di un solo anno i villaggi e le comunità dell'Alto Asaro e sul Sepik (mi erano sembrate irraggiungibili!) sono già meta di intraprendenti comitive di turisti, e di quel nuovo viaggiatore del mondo tribale, il «raccoglitore di maschere», operatore di quel commercio dell'arte «primitiva» il cui mercato si va sviluppando sempre più, in America come in Europa.

Ed è proprio la maschera il simbolo inequivocabile della fine di questo ambiente umano, nell'istante in cui essa decade da oggetto sacro a oggetto di scambio; un anno fa nell'Alto Asaro ne vidi alcune bellissime; e fui sorpreso nel rendermi conto che nessuno (nemmeno per cifre astronomiche in relazione all'ambiente) accettasse di vendermele; davanti a tanta fermezza mi rimproverai d'aver tentato di «corrompere» un mondo tanto autentico e sincero da non violare la sfera del magico e del rituale cedendo alle lusinghe del denaro.

Doveva essere un rimorso di breve durata. Tornando sugli stessi luoghi, le maschere (a decine e già false, prodotte in serie) mi sono state offerte con smaglianti sorrisi. Fu la prima sorpresa ma non l'unica. Né la più indicativa. Fra tutte la più esemplare resta per me quella del «funeralino».

Anche in questo caso si tratta di un'esperienza in due tempi (a breve distanza l'uno dall'altro) in un villaggio non lontano dalla Roka Valley, nel centro della Nuova Guinea. Quando vi giungemmo per la prima volta, nel maggio del '70, era morto un bambino. Gli uomini s'erano coperti di fango giallo, le donne di terra rossa; un canto flebile si era levato dalle capanne e s'alternava a sommesse grida di dolore, in un ritmo rituale ma non per questo meno umano. Fummo allora testimoni di una cerimonia cui poche volte, nell'arco di tanti anni di viaggio nel mondo primitivo, m'era stato dato d'assistere. Gli uomini e le donne con lo sciamano del villaggio stavano accanto al corpicino inerte: alcuni si erano infilati alle dita corte canne di bambù che battevano ritmicamente, altri ne muovevano di più lunghe e sottili. D'un tratto queste vennero agitate con velocità sempre maggiore sul corpo del bambino come in un ronzio d'alveare, producendo un soffio d'aria che sfiorava gli astanti e anche noi. Tentava, lo sciamano, di vincere la morte e far tornare la vita; e la vita era quel muoversi veloce di canne davanti agli occhi chiusi del corpicino senza vita, quel ronzio quasi animale, quel soffio leggero che doveva suggerire il respiro a quella bocca inerte.

Tutti sapevano, ne sono certo, dell'inutilità finale di quello sforzo tentato al limite tra il mondo naturale e quello sovrannaturale; ma tutti erano coinvolti nel dovere di credere e di sperare.

Dopo circa sei mesi siamo tornati in quel villaggio, sperando di cogliere documenti filmati altrettanto autentici. Appena giunti alle prime capanne, già ci attende una sorpresa. Malgrado le zanzare, il pericolo di dissenteria, i disagi di una lunga marcia in alta montagna, qualcuno ci ha preceduto: al centro del villaggio c'è un gruppo di turisti intenti a fotografare, e notiamo che la popolazione osserva quella comitiva di estranei come se non fosse la prima a essere giunta fin là. Delusi, pensiamo di riprendere subito il cammino verso un altro centro abitato, ancor più nell'interno, quando una nenia si alza alle nostre spalle e non tardiamo a riconoscerla. È quel canto funebre udito nello stesso luogo al tempo della nostra prima visita; al canto segue l'apparizione del corteo di morte, gli uomini nei loro colori, le donne, lo sciamano. C'è anche il bambino morto. Ma come lui, tutti stanno recitando; la cerimonia è diventata spettacolo, la verità folclore.

Il gruppo di estranei in camicie a fiori fotografa quello che la guida chiama «show», poi il capo villaggio chiede un compenso in forma precisa: tante persone, tanti dollari. A far da contabile è lo sciamano nella insolita funzione di cassiere.

Per lui e per la sua gente il tempo dell'eternità è lontano, svanito per sempre. Rimane un presente squallido, sordo ormai a ogni voce del passato.

La voce del passato: un richiamo inutile se inteso solo in senso retorico; ma chiave precisa di ricerca per capire un paese, un mondo.

Un viaggio in Oceania, oggi, ove le tracce del passato sono ormai scomparse, o stanno scomparendo o mutandosi, può solo significare un meccanico trasferimento da un'era geografica a un'altra, senza alcun contatto reale e profondo con complesse e tanto diverse culture.

Così, per ancorare il nostro viaggio attraverso questo continente a quel passato senza il quale sarebbe impossibile comprenderlo, il racconto di queste pagine avanzerà su due piani sempre diversi: a livello della cronaca, della testimonianza di quanto da me vissuto; e nella proiezione di una realtà oggi non più esistente, riscoperta nei testi tratti da fonti locali, e nelle pagine di protagonisti di viaggi, esplorazioni e studi su quello che fu un tempo il mondo delle isole nel Pacifico.

Sulle rotte dei primi oceaniani, i «vichinghi d'Oriente»

La preistoria delle isole – Il mistero delle migrazioni oceaniche – Da dove provengono questi isolani? dall'Asia o dall'America? – L'enigma del «Continente di Mu» – Le epopee delle zattere *Tahiti Nui* e *Kon-Tiki* – Il più grande pescatore del mito: Maui – L'enigma dell'aragosta gigante – Teriakai e gli squali – Il cielo ove non brilla la stella polare.

L'acqua, il fuoco, la terra: dei tre elementi che in tante cosmogonie dei popoli primitivi sono presenti, solo i primi due nel Pacifico
meridionale hanno vera importanza. La terra, quando c'è, è solo
una manciata di isole, punti più di partenza che non d'approdo
perché raggiunte e popolate solo per riguadagnare ancora l'immensa distesa dell'oceano: «la nostra terra è il mare».

Da dove vengono questi abitatori dell'acqua, il popolo dei polinesiani, la cultura «più marina» di tutto il Pacifico? Dall'India,
forse, spingendosi verso oriente, o da un mitico continente che
avrebbe avuto sede nel Pacifico settentrionale prima di essere
inghiottito da una spaventosa catastrofe, oppure dalla Cina, o da
un ceppo vichingo?

Le ipotesi scientifiche e le fantasie meno attendibili si accavallano, ma il mistero rimane fitto, anche per l'incontro con un
complesso di miti religiosi altrettanto ermetici. Questi miti fanno
della patria di ciascuna popolazione dell'Oceania il centro dell'u-
niverso, perché di ogni arcipelago si può dire che la genesi fu
opera di dèi e di semidei autoctoni; ogni arcipelago costituì una
sua cosmogonia, perché ognuno di essi divenne un mondo a sé –
caso estremo l'Isola di Pasqua, che è addirittura un microuni-
verso.

I miti sulla genesi del cosmo parlano tutti di una tenebra, di
un vuoto, di un caos originari, ma pure di un diverso autoctono
demiurgo, creatore di tutte le cose; tutti simboli sotto i quali le
caste dei capi e dei sacerdoti celarono i princìpi che presiedono

alla conservazione della vita e al ripetersi del ciclo delle stagioni, per una popolazione di contadini e di marinai.

Ogni arcipelago ha genealogie di capi, che prendono radice in quella degli elementi e dei fenomeni naturali, con l'unico fine di asserire la continuità del sangue divino della propria dinastia; e talvolta queste genealogie furono d'aiuto a chi volle computare le generazioni per tentare ricostruzioni di vicende perdute nel tempo.

Società agricola di marinai, quella dei polinesiani; meno marinara quella dei micronesiani; e ancora meno quella della Melanesia; tre diversi ceppi culturali del Pacifico meridionale dei quali solo la prima risentì la potente necessità di navigare, di tentare la scoperta di nuove isole, quando lo richiesero l'eccessivo popolamento delle terre coltivate, o la sconfitta militare, o l'ambizione dei capi, o lo spirito di avventura. Ciò diede inizio a quell'epopea delle trasmigrazioni transpacifiche del nostro millennio che restano fra le imprese più gloriose della storia dell'uomo, azzardate avventure degne di eroi, che condussero alla scoperta e alla colonizzazione di isole vaste e verdeggianti e di atolli sperduti e poverissimi. Grandi e piccole, le isole – a una a una – furono nuove patrie, i capi ricrearono, come lo permetteva l'ambiente naturale, le condizioni di vita economica, sociale e religiosa della patria abbandonata.

Non sappiamo a quale isola o arcipelago della loro protostoria i polinesiani si riferissero citando una mitica Hawaiki come prima terra uscita dal caos, durante la genesi, patria primordiale, regione indecifrabile, da loro abbandonata allorché penetrarono nel Pacifico, nome che essi rinnovarono nell'isola di Raiatea, il loro centro culturale e religioso nel cuore del cosiddetto «triangolo polinesiano».

L'Oceania, mondo insulare che la geografia divide convenzionalmente in Melanesia, Micronesia e Polinesia, è variatissima nelle dimensioni e nella natura delle sue isole, alcune di vastità continentale (come l'Australia, da noi volutamente esclusa, o come la seconda isola del mondo, la Nuova Guinea), ma nella generalità è costituita da miriadi di isolette, raggruppate in infiniti arcipelaghi. Differente è pure la natura di tali isole, distinte in alte e basse, vulcaniche e coralline. Si può dire soltanto che la loro grandezza va decrescendo a mano a mano che ci si allontana dall'Asia sud-orientale e dall'Indonesia, verso oriente, come vi decresce pure il numero delle specie vegetali presenti. Inoltrandosi nel Pacifico, lo sterminato numero di arcipelaghi ci si rivela in altrettante manifestazioni del vulcanismo sottomarino, meglio visibile lungo le coste asiatiche e americane, per cui il Pacifico può dirsi come chiuso da una cintura di fuoco.

La credenza di una miracolosa fertilità e di una esuberanza tropicale delle terre dell'Oceania è un luogo comune. È vero che i terreni vulcanici possono essere ricchi di sali per le coltivazioni, ma le piogge non sempre le assecondano. «L'ultimo paradiso» non esiste? (Ancora una volta ripeto un identico interrogativo...)

Terra di contrasti [come ha scritto Guaiart] fra la presenza idilliaca di certe isole e la precarietà della vita che l'uomo vi conduce, per esempio: si pensi agli atolli micronesiani, sui quali la minaccia della fame è continua in mezzo a uno scenario paradisiaco.[1]

L'habitat offerto all'uomo dalla natura è variatissimo. A differenza delle grandi isole papua, ove sono presenti estesi altipiani, climi temperati e buone precipitazioni, nella maggior parte delle isole del Pacifico meridionale la terra coltivabile non abbonda, e l'uomo ha dovuto anche conquistarsela, adattando a un terreno salmastro certe piante per il suo sostentamento, scavando fino a raggiungere la falda inumidita delle infiltrazioni marine, o addirittura portando la terra là dove la terra non c'è, negli atolli di solo corallo.

In questa varietà di ambienti, l'uomo ha ideato vari espedienti per procurarsi il cibo o per ripararsi dalle intemperie. Per proteggersi dal freddo delle isole sulle frange estreme a nord e a sud, o dal caldo equatoriale di altre, e dalle furie distruttive dei cicloni si sono create abitazioni di tipo diverso: i polinesiani delle isole australi, ad esempio, a differenza dei loro cugini della Polinesia centrale che vivono in leggere capanne, hanno dovuto costruirsi case parzialmente interrate, con pareti e coperture di tale spessore da conservare il calore.

[1] J. Guaiart, *Oceania*, trad. it. G. Veronesi, Feltrinelli, Milano 1963.

In vari arcipelaghi le case degli uomini (le grandi capanne per le riunioni) erano, e sono, abbellite da artistici intagli nei pali di sostegno o dalle decorazioni dei fronti. Comuni a tutti gli arcipelaghi polinesiani erano, e non sono più, i monumenti funerari dei grandi capi, i santuari, le sculture e le costruzioni monolitiche di un genere peculiare, anche se si sono ravvisati influssi da o verso ambo le coste continentali del Pacifico.

Autentico laboratorio umano, dove la tradizione, di una stupefacente molteplicità di forme, ha dato origine a una grande varietà di strutture sociali tra loro assai differenti... l'Oceania può attirare la curiosità e la passione [...].[1]

Molto è stato indagato e pubblicato sulla preistoria dell'Oceania, e se ne sono pure tentati quadri d'insieme, prematuri, servendosi di materiali archeologici e delle tradizioni, analizzando genealogie, miti e canti, comparando complessi culturali e caratteri antropologici, per determinare come sia avvenuto il popolamento dei vari arcipelaghi, quali le etnie che vi parteciparono, e la loro provenienza, quali le rotte e gli scali per raggiungere quelle sedi nelle quali le varie popolazioni furono scoperte per la prima volta dagli europei negli ultimi quattro secoli, quali gli scambi culturali e i legami di parentela.

Una sola cosa è certa: l'arrivo dei polinesiani nel Pacifico meridionale – problema fra i più intricati e dibattuti sull'Oceania – non è evento remoto, se fino a qualche secolo fa era viva tra essi la tradizione di una loro provenienza da terre a occidente, quella remota patria Hawaiki che abbiamo citato, situata nella direzione del sole morente, «dove ritornano le anime dei morti».

La nostra scienza è insufficiente su molti punti. Si riconoscono oggi certe linee generali che richiedono di venir precisate, ma nessuna asserzione definitiva può essere affermata senza ciarlataneria.

Quali sono, infatti, le nostre fonti di informazione? I risultati degli scavi archeologici compiuti ora e, in particolare, un certo numero di date ottenute col metodo del carbonio 14. E poi, gli studi comparativi che hanno per oggetto la cultura materiale, la sociologia e i miti.

Ci si è basati per molto tempo, a questo proposito, su relazioni supposte, da causa a effetto, secondo le quali la presenza simultanea in due punti di

---

[1] J. Guaiart, *op. cit.*

certi oggetti o di certe tecniche dimostrerebbe precedenti migrazioni di popoli.[1]

La realtà non è così semplice e questo anche a causa dell'estrema mobilità dei popoli marinari di cui si tratta. L'abilità navigatoria dei tre principali gruppi di popoli dell'Oceania ha reso possibili viaggi su grandi distanze e su ogni rotta, favorendo i contatti tra i gruppi stessi.

Al formicolare e al disperdersi dei tipi fisici si aggiunge così una grande varietà di culture materiali e sociali meticce, nessuna delle quali è esattamente riducibile alla sua vicina.[2]

I materiali archeologici non sono, purtroppo, né molteplici né in evidente successione cronologica.

I principali oggetti sono stati vasellame in ceramica, ritrovati sia in Polinesia che in Melanesia; collane e ami di madreperla e di conchiglie; oggetti in osso o di tartaruga; resti di alimenti (ossi e conchiglie); e resti di focolari.

L'esame stesso di questi oggetti induce a tentare di identificare delle «serie» di apparenza cronologica, per esempio nella forma delle lame delle accette, degli ami e nella decorazione delle ceramiche. In generale si resta però sempre nel campo delle ipotesi, perché l'Oceania non ha dato quasi mai, almeno fino a oggi, delle serie di strati di scavo ricchi, separati fra loro da zone sterili.[3]

Gli interrogativi che si pongono soprattutto antropologi ed etnologi, relativamente al popolamento del Pacifico centrale, vertono sull'origine di una gente con cultura neolitica, di contadini e marinai, che si stanziò in migliaia di isole, su una vastissima regione oceanica. La tesi generale di una sua origine composita trova consenziente la maggior parte degli studiosi, e così quella di una provenienza dall'Asia, dov'essa si formò, come tale, in una regione marittima del Pacifico occidentale. Dopo di ciò questa gente navigò verso oriente, infiltrandosi nel Pacifico centrale, sebbene non in vere e proprie ondate migratorie, ma a gruppi. Per giungere nel cuore del Pacifico, ci si domanda, seguì una rotta settentrionale, lungo la catena di isole della Micronesia, oppure

---

[1] J. Guaiart, *op. cit.*
[2] *Ibidem.*
[3] *Ibidem.*

seguì una rotta meridionale, lungo la catena insulare della Melanesia? È stata avanzata e sostenuta anche una terza teoria, molto meno credibile, di una provenienza dall'America meridionale – di moda al tempo dell'avventura del *Kon-Tiki* – basata appena su certe affinità di elementi culturali, non certo negabili, ma la cui spiegazione è piuttosto in una serie di contatti che su una ipotesi di origine.

Il primo studioso che ha messo un po' d'ordine in queste idee, basandosi soprattutto sulle leggende e le genealogie dei polinesiani, fu il neozelandese Percy Smith, che degli studi sui polinesiani fece lo scopo della sua vita; nel 1891 fondò la Polynesian Society, e ne diresse l'autorevolissimo «Journal», finché morì, a ottantadue anni, nel 1922. L'anno prima, quasi a suo testamento dottrinario, egli aveva fissato queste conclusioni, su cui allora era d'accordo la maggioranza dei polinesiologi, pubblicandole in un articolo sulla propria rivista, sotto il titolo *I polinesiani in Indonesia*. Da allora molta acqua è fluita sopra quelle sue conclusioni, ma esse meritano di essere ricordate, in paragrafi, come egli le formulò:

1. I polinesiani sono «caucasici», anche se mescolati con altre genti, e sono un ramo dei popoli protoariani dell'India.
2. Furono cacciati dall'India da una gente slanciata, nera, crespa e pelosa.
3. Lasciarono l'India al principio del IV secolo avanti Cristo.
4. Emigrarono verso est, verso l'Indonesia, occuparono Sumatra (forse la Tauhiti-Roa della tradizione più antica polinesiana?), Giava (forse Hawaiki?), Borneo (forse Taihiti-nui?), Ceram (forse Horangi?).
5. Lasciando l'Indonesia, gli emigranti presero diverse direzioni: una parte arrivò alle Hawaii (direttamente); l'altra, attraverso la costa nord della Nuova Guinea, le Salomone e le Nuove Ebridi, si stabilì nel gruppo Lau delle Figi, alle Samoa e alle Tonga. La prima emigrazione lasciò l'Indonesia verso l'anno 65 della nostra èra, e la si trova nel gruppo delle Lau verso l'anno 450; ma è possibile che vi sia arrivata molto prima.

6. Da Samoa e dalle isole vicine essi si allargarono verso la Polinesia orientale tra il 700 e il 900 circa.

7. La Nuova Zelanda fu scoperta dal navigatore Kupe nel 925, e abitata, poco dopo, da melanesiani-polinesiani; ma nel 1150 circa vi arrivarono i polinesiani partiti dal Pacifico orientale; e infine ci arrivò la cosiddetta «Grande Flotta» polinesiana della trasmigrazione partita da Tahiti, nell'anno 1350.

I «misteri del Pacifico», come li ha chiamati Eric de Bisschop, hanno fatto pullulare l'Oceania di «scoperte» preistoriche, sempre sensazionali, anche se quasi sempre fantastiche. Una fu quella di J. M. Macmillan, che contestò la tesi di Percy Smith.

Egli sostenne, nella sua opera *The riddle of the Pacific*, un arrivo di polinesiani nel Pacifico che non manca di suggestione: [...] un potente impero, oggi sommerso, un centro originale di civiltà sarebbe esistito nel Pacifico, del quale la cultura polinesiana sarebbe l'ultima traccia.[1]

Naturalmente, la «spiegazione», in quegli anni, trovò nel pubblico dei lettori di giornali un successo imprevisto e diventò la leggenda di un mitico «Continente di Mu», che sarebbe esistito, nel Pacifico, migliaia di anni fa, come un'altra Atlantide di Platone, là dov'è il Sahara. Questo fantascientifico impero avrebbe avuto il suo apogeo 70.000 anni prima di Cristo e sarebbe stato inghiottito dalle onde, 12.000 o 12.500 anni prima della nostra èra.

Vittorio Lanternari[2] ha evocato un accenno (nelle tradizioni polinesiane) a certe «terre fredde» e a un paese remoto, dove «gli uomini camminavano nell'acqua», che forse può aiutarci a risolvere il mistero.

Un nativo dell'Isola di Pasqua aveva creduto di leggere in una «tavoletta parlante» della sua terra questa frase curiosa: «In quella terra semplice e bella... gli dèi del cielo trascorrono il loro tempo nell'acqua durante la stagione fredda... l'uccello nero-

---

[1] In E. de Bisschop, *Vers Nousantara*, 1957.
[2] In *La grande festa*, Il Saggiatore, Milano 1959.

bianco vorrebbe raggiungere il cielo, ma glielo vieta la crudezza del freddo». È una fugace visione di un paese dove vissero quegli antenati che i polinesiani avevano poi deificato? Lanternari scrive a proposito:

di ravvisare [in questo] una variazione del tema mitico di *Ra* che discende «sotto l'oceano» quando sopravviene l'inverno. Comunque si allude a una regione dal clima invernale, particolarmente rigido [...]. Un mito di Rarotonga racconta che nel paese degli antenati gli alberi verdeggiavano soltanto per metà dell'anno, e gli uomini camminavano nell'acqua. È il quadro sommario di un paese a inverno freddo, con vegetazione a foglie decidue e con terreni presumibilmente inondati. Certamente gli erti isolotti vulcanici nei quali vivono i polinesiani oggi non hanno nulla a che fare con il mitico remoto paese degli antenati. [...]
Atia-te-varinga-nui è il nome mitico della patria originaria [...] e corrisponde per molti aspetti a quella che a loro volta le tradizioni polinesiane designano come patria degli antenati.
Partiti da Atia-te-varinga-nui, gli antichi fondatori della stirpe sarebbero pervenuti, dopo varie peregrinazioni, al paese di Hawaiki, ove avrebbero trovato l'albero del pane. Secondo la tradizione essi cominciarono allora a coltivarlo.

Questi nomi e queste ipotesi ci riportano alla già citata teoria di Percy Smith che avanzò per primo l'idea che *Atia-te-varinga-nui* significherebbe «Aria-coperta-di-riso»; il che farebbe pensare che nella loro patria di origine i protopolinesiani sarebbero stati *risicoltori* e si sarebbero trasformati successivamente in *arboricoltori* (albero del pane) al loro arrivo in Polinesia, nelle isole centrali (Samoa, Tonga, Tahiti) corrispondenti forse alla mitica Hawaiki di cui parlano le tradizioni. Di qui si sarebbero irradiati alla periferia (Hawaii, Marchesi, Pasqua e Nuova Zelanda). L'opinione è stata modificata da Sir Peter Buck, che propende a fissare un itinerario settentrionale moventesi dall'India alla Micronesia, di qui alla Polinesia centrale, quindi orientale. Altri hanno suggerito un'origine dall'Assam, mentre l'opinione fondamentale di un altro studioso, l'inglese Handy, è che in Polinesia sopravvivano sostanziali elementi di provenienza cinese.
Anche il Guaiart propende per una regione d'origine dei protopolinesiani in una parte della Cina sud-orientale. Egli suggerisce che i melanesiani possano essersi formati da un miscuglio di tre diversi gruppi umani: di tipo *ainoide* (europoide), lontani parenti

degli *ainu* del Giappone; di tipo *veddoide*, per la somiglianza con i *vedda* dell'India; e di tipo negroide oceanico.

Il miscuglio di questi tre elementi [egli scrive] doveva già provocare una situazione assai complessa; i vari gruppi che ne risultarono hanno potuto disseminarsi vivendo di caccia e di pesca in quasi tutta la Melanesia, compresa la Nuova Caledonia. Questo processo si sarebbe svolto in un numero rispettabile di secoli.

A un certo momento, secondo Guaiart, sopraggiunse l'infiltrazione polinesiana:

Le tecniche agricole sarebbero state introdotte dai nuovi arrivati, venuti non in migrazioni massicce ma per lenta infiltrazione lungo la costa, da un arcipelago all'altro. Con i loro mezzi di trasporto marittimo, le piroghe a bilanciere, potevano permettersi i più audaci viaggi, a ventaglio, partendo dalla Nuova Guinea, e percorrere quindi itinerari diretti, che si aggiungevano a quelli classici lungo le coste dell'arco melanesiano. Così essi avrebbero potuto colonizzare la Micronesia, poi, grazie anche alla pressione demografica, sarebbero ridiscesi sulla frangia nord delle isole Bismarck, e, sempre più mescolandosi con i loro predecessori, avrebbero occupato una parte delle isole Salomone, delle Nuove Ebridi e della Nuova Caledonia, le isole Loyalty e le Figi.
[...] Ciò che doveva essere l'etnia polinesiana si è costituita da qualche parte in questo complesso, prima di spingersi al di là di Samoa.

Con questa asserzione, l'etnografia più recente prende posizione contro certe ipotesi «solo affascinanti» come quella del *Kon-Tiki*:

Lo scrittore norvegese Thor Heyerdahl ha voluto spiegare il popolamento della Polinesia con una migrazione sudamericana, che sarebbe [...] una delle vie di navigazione dal nord. [...] Non c'è interesse a discutere sui particolari del modo di argomentare di questo navigatore sportivo e coraggioso; egli si vale del metodo comparativo così come lo si praticava mezzo secolo fa. [...] Oggi i paragoni si fanno non fra elementi isolati, ma fra complessi e strutture; e questo è possibile solamente, allo stato attuale delle nostre cognizioni, paragonando popoli limitrofi o vicini.
Ciò non toglie che il problema delle relazioni fra l'Oceania e l'America sia posto. Nulla impedisce di pensare che quegli straordinari strumenti di navigazione che sono le piroghe doppie polinesiane abbiano potuto raggiungere certi punti dell'America del Sud, del Centro e del Nord; in quel caso, invece che nordici, i famosi «indiani bianchi» del Darien potrebbero essere polinesiani. E perché no?[1]

[1] J. Guaiart, *op. cit.*

The Rangi Hiroa è il nome polinesiano di un autore che abbiamo già citato, Sir Peter Buck, neozelandese, uno dei più autorevoli studiosi della Polinesia; è il nome polinesiano che egli ricevette dai parenti di parte materna, e che non ha voluto dimenticare.

In un suo libro,[1] che potrebbe dirsi l'Odissea dei polinesiani, egli ci ha dato, insieme all'espressione del suo amore per i progenitori, un prezioso contributo per la conoscenza dei «vichinghi d'Oriente».

Che razza di uomini erano essi [si chiede Peter Buck] se riuscirono a superare le imprese dei fenici nel Mediterraneo e dei vichinghi nell'Atlantico, e meritano perciò di essere chiamati i più grandi navigatori della storia?

Egli cerca di fissare i termini del mistero che avvolge le origini dei polinesiani:

Possiamo dire che in età remote i progenitori dei polinesiani probabilmente vissero in qualche regione dell'India e si spinsero poi verso oriente; ma i miti e le leggende trasmessi per via orale non giungono così addietro nel tempo. Quei viaggiatori dovettero far tappa in Indonesia, com'è dimostrato dal fatto che la lingua polinesiana mostra affinità con i dialetti indonesiani. Durante la dimora in Indonesia, il salmastro penetrò nelle loro vene, e da uomini di terraferma li trasformò in lupi di mare; e quando le pressioni delle popolazioni mongoloidi provenienti dall'entroterra diventarono insopportabili, i progenitori dei polinesiani volsero lo sguardo verso l'orizzonte orientale e si imbarcarono per una delle più grandi avventure marinare di tutti i tempi.

Quando poté avvenire questa supposta emigrazione dall'India, oggi contraddetta da altri?

Le genealogie dell'isola di Rarotonga risalgono per novantadue generazioni fino al progenitore Tu-te-rangi-marama, che dimorò in una terra identificata da Percy Smith con l'India. Stabilendo arbitrariamente per ogni generazione una media di venticinque anni, arriviamo al 450 a.C. La distanza nel tempo è di 2300 anni, la distanza nello spazio [deducendola dai luoghi citati nelle genealogie] equivale a circa quella che separa l'India da Rarotonga, nelle isole Cook.[2]

---

[1] P. Buck, *I vichinghi d'Oriente*, trad. it. E. Spagnoli Vaccari, Feltrinelli, Milano 1961.
[2] P. Buck, *op. cit.*

Il barone Eric de Bisschop, che visse i suoi ultimi venticinque anni per i «misteri del Pacifico», rischiando molte volte la vita, morì nel 1958, quasi settantenne, sulla zattera *Tahiti Nui II*, che stava per inabissarsi, al ritorno dal Perù, dopo aver attraversato l'oceano, quasi in vista dell'arcipelago polinesiano di Rarotonga. Entusiasmatosi per lo studio della navigazione e dell'antropologia dei polinesiani, aveva cominciato a studiare il problema delle emigrazioni marine sin dal 1932, navigando egli stesso, e costruendosi e rabberciandosi, dopo ogni naufragio, le sue quattro o cinque bizzarre imbarcazioni, giunche, catamarani, zattere. Ne sentì tante di critiche e di consigli, in ogni suo cantiere improvvisato, che teneva sempre in vista un bel cartello: «Sappiamo di essere considerati pazzi. Siete pregati di non tentare di dimostrarcelo». Si era proposto di studiare le allora poco note correnti equatoriali del Pacifico, per ricostruire il quadro delle conoscenze marine in cui agirono realmente i navigatori della Polinesia. Le sue imprese, benché meno propagandate, non furono affatto inferiori a quelle di Heyerdahl con il *Kon-Tiki*. E ancora nell'ultimo dei suoi libri,[1] riaffermò la sua vecchia convinzione sull'origine asiatico-caucasica dei protopolinesiani, oltre alla tesi di antiche navigazioni di polinesiani fino in America.

De Bisschop ha ricordato che le popolazioni della Polinesia attendevano un ritorno dal mare «degli dèi dalla pelle bianca», da cui essi erano discesi. Tra tali dèi arcaici (che vivevano sempre sul mare e avevano i capelli biondi o rossi e la pelle bianca), tre erano quelli principali: Tu, dio della guerra, Rongo, dio delle messi, e Tane, dio della virilità. Un giorno essi furono spodestati da Tangaroa (o Ta'aroa), che tenne «il ruolo di creatore del mondo», senza per questo perdere il suo attributo universale di «Padrone dell'Oceano». Da questa famiglia di dèi tradizionali, de Bisschop volle mettere bene in luce un dato essenziale, desumibile dalle stesse tradizioni:

A una data epoca, ancora da stabilire, un gruppo di individui, aventi un'apparenza caucasica, il cui capo fu chiamato Tangaroa, apparve nella Polinesia centrale. Vennero allora introdotti elementi nuovi di cultura, le cui caratteristiche più sorprendenti furono soprattutto marittime.

[1] *Vers Nousantara*, cit.

Queste caratteristiche sono da lui definite stupefacenti perché «non si riscontrano nella storia tradizionale di nessun'altra nazione, popolo o tribù del mondo», e fanno dei polinesiani esseri dalla natura quasi anfibia: non occorre leggere tutti i racconti leggendari e le tradizioni polinesiane, per notare che gli eroi agiscono in un ambiente geografico tutto speciale. Non si tratta mai di lotte epiche con animali leggendari di terra, ma di terribili e mortali scontri, in mare, con pescecani, testuggini giganti, anguille feroci e la «grande tridacna» che inghiottiva navi e interi equipaggi.

Dopo un esame di vari elementi tecnici con i quali de Bisschop conferma la «*natura così marcatamente anfibia*» dei polinesiani, egli proprio da questa natura trae spunto per negare un'origine indoeuropea dei polinesiani, e per una buona ragione:

A qualsiasi conclusione gli studiosi giungeranno, un dato è comunque certo: che è impossibile, con il solo pretesto di una apparenza caucasica, immaginare un rapporto tra polinesiani e una qualsiasi famiglia di origine indoeuropea; non ci fu mai gente più estranea, direi più ostile, alle cose di mare, della popolazione di quella origine.

Quell'orrore che essi provarono per i «flutti maledetti» si rifletteva anche nelle loro concezioni religiose, per cui si credeva che il colpevole di aver viaggiato per mare si fosse macchiato di una colpa, la cui contaminazione indelebile non poteva essere cancellata che dalla morte.

De Bisschop chiuse i suoi vagabondaggi più che ventennali nei Mari del Sud al termine del suo riuscito tentativo di controdimostrare la tesi di Heyerdahl, che cioè furono i polinesiani a raggiungere il Sud America, non viceversa, avendo egli dalla sua parte studiosi come Erland Nordenskiöld, Frederici, Dixon, Rivet, Buck, Hornell, Emory e altri.

Per questo scopo compì un viaggio doppio di quello del *Kon-Tiki*, su una zattera di bambù, all'andata, da Tahiti alle coste del Cile, lungo il 35° parallelo sud, profittando della corrente oceanica verso levante. Intendeva poi farsi portare a nord dalla corrente di Humboldt, e quindi allontanarsi dalle coste del Perù, per il viaggio di ritorno, profittando della corrente sub-equatoriale, già utilizzata da Heyerdahl, corrente che egli aveva tentato di studiare già nel 1933 con la sua giunca *Fou Po*. Furono tredici mesi di navigazione, con due naufragi. I bambù della zattera dell'andata assorbirono tant'acqua da non galleggiare più, e l'imbarcazione fu abbandonata a 600 miglia da Valparaiso; così avvenne pure per i tronchi di balsa della zattera del ritorno, anche se con essa la spedizione raggiunse la Polinesia, addentrandosi negli arcipelaghi molto più a nord di Tahiti.

Malgrado le drammatiche disavventure, con quella doppia traversata del Pacifico, de Bisschop aveva cercato di dimostrare non soltanto quale aveva potuto essere il genere d'imbarcazione dei polinesiani nelle traversate transpacifiche (zattera, del resto, perfezionata su ambo le coste dell'oceano stesso), ma anche la rotta percorsa dai polinesiani col favore di ben conosciute correnti oceaniche.

De Bisschop, dopo quel ventennio di esperienze oceaniche, era giunto alla conclusione che i «*lupi di mare polinesiani effettuarono ripetutamente la traversata fino al Sud America, e il relativo ritorno, in tempi preistorici, e di conseguenza influenzarono e rimasero a loro volta influenzati da varie tribù indiane*».

Questa è una sintesi di quanto opinano gli studiosi. Ma cosa ne pensano i diretti interessati? A risponderci, sia pur in forma velata, talvolta oscura, ma sempre stimolante, sono i loro miti e le loro leggende.

Le cosmogonie dell'Oceania sono numerose come la proliferazione dei suoi arcipelaghi. Ciascuna attribuisce a un demiurgo locale la creazione dell'universo, traendo egli ogni cosa e la vita stessa dal vuoto, dal buio, o separandole a gran fatica di mezzo al caos.

Senza voler tentare una comparazione fra miti e tradizioni culturali così diversi come quelli dei polinesiani, dei melanesiani e dei micronesiani, accenneremo ad alcuni di essi, fra i più significativi. Li abbiamo scelti tra le cosmogonie dei papua nella Nuova Guinea, e delle isole Trobriand in Melanesia; e tra quelle delle isole Gilbert in Micronesia, delle isole della Società (rappresentate da Tahiti) e tra altre ancora ai vertici del «triangolo polinesiano» (Hawaii, Nuova Zelanda e Isola di Pasqua).

Queste cosmogonie, narrate in cerimonie rituali dinanzi al popolo riunito, erano sempre una specie di glorificazione di genealogie dei capi, eroi deificati che i polinesiani chiamano «i pescatori di isole», i grandi navigatori ed esploratori del passato. Anche certi elementi e fenomeni naturali, e talune piante e animali ebbero una loro genealogia e un loro particolare creatore, quando il demiurgo supremo si era dimenticato (o aveva disdegnato) di farlo, ritenendo quell'essere indegno della sua divina fatica (come fu per il pescecane o per la mosca).

«Naareau l'Anziano fu il Primo di Tutti», così incomincia il racconto di ogni buon *huarè-po* alle isole Gilbert.

Non un uomo, non un animale, non un pesce, non una cosa esisteva prima di lui. Egli non dormiva perché non c'era sonno, non mangiava poiché non c'era fame. Si trovava nel vuoto. Non v'era che Naareau nel vuoto. A lungo sedette, e non vi fu che lui.

Poi, Naareau disse dentro di sé: «Creerò una donna». E, miracolo, una donna sorse dal vuoto: Nei Teakea. Egli disse ancora: «Creerò un uomo». E, miracolo, un uomo nacque dal suo pensiero: Na Atibu, la Roccia. E Na Atibu giacque con Nei Teakea. Ed ecco!, ebbero un figlio... vale a dire Naareau il Giovane.

E Naareau l'Anziano disse a Naareau il Giovane: «Tutta la conoscenza è racchiusa in te. Creerò per te una cosa sulla quale tu possa agire».

Egli, quindi, creò le Tenebre e il Caos, dopo di che se ne andò via, abbandonando Naareau il Giovane, figlio dell'uomo e della donna, a cavarsela da solo. E il suo giovane alunno non fu inferiore all'incarico, almeno per intelligenza, se non per potenza, ben munito com'era di una buona dose di incantesimi, per ogni evenienza.

Il Cielo, la Terra e il Mare allora erano una cosa sola, e bisognava separarli, cominciando a sollevare il cielo, che pesava inerte sulla terra. Come fare? Naareau cercò in tutti i modi di cacciare le dita fra il cielo e la terra, per trovare un appiglio. Ci riuscì con un incantesimo, uno spiraglio si aprì: vide, sotto, una voragine buia, e udì un coro di sospiri e di esseri che russavano. Per fortuna uscì dal basso la prima creatura, il Pipistrello; e Naareau lo mandò giù, in esplorazione: «Tu riesci a vederci nel buio. Precedimi, e scopri quello che potrai scoprire».

Il Pipistrello ubbidì a Naareau, e dalle profondità della voragine gli venne ripetendo i nomi degli esseri che andava incontrando addormentati.

Quando gli furono citati tutti, Naareau capì che da laggiù non poteva sperare aiuto, per alzare il cielo al di sopra della terra: quella era l'Accolta degli Sciocchi e dei Sordomuti, una «razza di schiavi». Si calò egli stesso nella voragine, dette la sveglia sonoramente a tutti, e quelli finalmente si mossero; e quando si misero seduti, il cielo si sollevò un po'. Li incitò a sollevare di più, dette loro anche un palo, perché si aiutassero, ma più di quello non potevano fare: «Non è più possibile» dissero «perché il cielo ha le radici nella terra».

Naareau allora levò alta la voce: «Dov'è l'Anguilla?». [...]

L'Anguilla marina dormiva con la moglie, l'Anguilla dalla Coda-Corta. [...] fu catturata, e costretta a collaborare, sollevando il cielo col capo e abbassando la terra con la coda. Il cielo e la terra gemevano, non volevano essere separati. [...]

Infine, le radici del cielo vennero strappate dalla terra: il Caos era stato suddiviso.

Naareau si accorse di qualche difetto della sua opera: pure il mare si era separato dal resto, e l'Accolta degli Sciocchi e dei Sordomuti vi nuotava senza meta; inoltre, il cielo, salito così in alto, non racchiudeva più la terra che era rimasta senza confini. E creò i punti cardinali, abbassando i corrispondenti lembi del cielo fino a terra, balzando da un estremo all'altro della terra, e dando nomi propri ai vari cardini dell'orizzonte, finché il cielo, abbassandone i lembi, ebbe assunto la forma di una semisfera. A quel punto, Naareau s'avvide dell'Accolta degli Sciocchi e dei Sordomuti che continuavano a sbracciarsi nel mare, e decise: «Vi sarà la prima terra nel mare», e gridò loro: «Tuffatevi, tuffatevi! Agguantate con le mani. Issate il fondo roccioso. Issate!». E infatti quelli, tuffatisi, sollevarono la prima terra dal fondo del mare e il suo nome fu Aba-la-Grande. Nel suo mezzo c'era una montagna che fumava, un vulcano, nato dalle Tenebre. [...]

Tutte le terre furono create da Naareau il Giovane. Così, infine, tutte le cose vennero da lui completate secondo il suo pensiero. Ed egli disse dentro di sé: «Basta. È finito. Me ne vado per non più tornare». E se ne andò e non tornò più.[1]

Questa è la genesi che si narra alle Gilbert; a ponente di questo arcipelago, nella Melanesia, ecco come la narrano i papua delle Trobriand, secondo la versione raccolta in queste isole da Buehler, Borrow e Monthford:

Il cielo, nell'epoca pre-umana, stava sotto e la terra stava sopra. Nel corso di un violentissimo temporale, le «divinità» rivoltarono il mondo, conferendogli la sua configurazione attuale. I primi uomini nacquero dal sangue di una colomba [principio femminile], per l'azione di un vecchio [principio maschile], con l'aiuto del fuoco e di canne di bambù. Il cielo, il sole, la luce e il fuoco furono associati con la figura del padre, alla quale sono strettamente collegati gli animali selvatici. Tutto ciò sta a indicare una cultura di cacciatori e debbiatori, oggi praticamente scomparsa. [...]

Le potenze celesti rappresentano il principio maschile. Sono collegate a

---

[1] In A. Grimble, *Le isole delle anime*, trad. it. B. Oddera, Bompiani, Milano 1954.

esse i fulmini, i tuoni, la luce, il fuoco, il sole e la luna. L'acqua, il mare, la superficie della terra devono la loro nascita al principio terrestre, femminile.[1]

Gli stessi autori hanno rilevato altri miti della creazione nelle isole di Huon, in Nuova Caledonia, presso popolazioni di una cultura agricola e marittima, collegata alla corrente meridionale dell'immigrazione austronesiana; agricoltura e pesca erano egualmente vitali per l'economia della società nativa.

Bronislaw Malinowski, l'etnologo inglese di origine polacca, che, per i suoi studi, soggiornò alcuni anni nelle isole del Pacifico occidentale ci ha lasciato un'opera che fa testo,[2] nella quale ricorrono spesso accenni a miti sulla creazione, ancora vivi nella tradizione orale papua.

Gli esseri umani sono emersi di sotterra attraverso buchi praticati nel terreno. Ogni sottoclan ha il proprio posto di nascita, e gli avvenimenti che si verificano in tale decisiva occasione determinano talvolta i privilegi e le particolari incapacità del sottoclan. [...] Il primo gruppo ancestrale, la cui apparizione è menzionata nel mito, consiste sempre in una donna, accompagnata dal fratello, talvolta dall'animale totemico, mai dal marito. In alcuni miti è descritto esplicitamente il modo di propagarsi della prima antenata. Essa dà inizio alla linea dei propri discendenti esponendosi imprudentemente alla pioggia; o mentre sta distesa in una grotta viene forata dallo sgocciolamento delle stalattiti; o, facendo il bagno, è morsa da un pesce: viene «aperta» in uno di questi modi e lo spirito di una creatura entra nel suo grembo e la feconda. Così, invece della forza creatrice del padre, i miti rivelano la spontanea potenza creatrice della madre ancestrale.[3]

Veniamo ora alla Polinesia, e cominciamo dal suo ombelico, l'isola di Tahiti.

Verso il V secolo della nostra èra, un'avanguardia degli emigranti polinesiani, veleggiante verso oriente, s'imbatté nelle isole della Società; e là, poi, col passare del tempo, si stabilirono le famiglie di quei primi e dei successivi colonizzatori.

Con il passare delle generazioni, Tahiti, come la maggiore isola, la più vasta e la più fertile del gruppo delle Sottovento, finì

---

[1] In Buehler, Borrow, Monthford, *Oceania e Australia*, trad. it. Q. e E. Maffi, Il Saggiatore, Milano 1961.
[2] B. Malinowski, *Sex and repression in savage society* (1927), trad. it. T. Tentori, *Sesso e repressione sessuale tra i selvaggi*, Boringhieri, Torino 1969.
[3] B. Malinowski, *op. cit.*

per ospitare il grosso dei coltivatori, mentre un'altra isola, alla quale era stato dato il nome augurale di Havaii (in ricordo della mitica patria abbandonata nell'Occidente, cui essa somigliava), divenne sede dei capi e dei sacerdoti. Questi ultimi organizzarono la nuova comunità, la quale secoli dopo, essendosi moltiplicata, cominciò a sciamare in tutti gli altri arcipelaghi della Polinesia. In quell'isola di Havaii, l'attuale Raiatea, nel centro sacro di Opoa, presero forma precisa le leggi, i miti, le genealogie, le cerimonie rituali, già note, embrionalmente, a Tahiti. Peter Buck ne ha raccolti diversi:

I sacerdoti e dotti di Opoa misero insieme frammenti di memorie e briciole di miti per comporre una genesi della loro nuova patria e delle terre che le sorgevano intorno nell'oceano.

Deificarono i capi delle prime spedizioni (che li avevano guidati fin là), i quali con l'andar del tempo divennero gli dèi più importanti dell'Olimpo tahitiano: Ta'aroa, Tu, Tane, Ro'o e altri. Come dèi, fu loro attribuito una parte nella creazione della volta del cielo, della terra e degli esseri venuti a popolare la terra e le acque. L'uomo fu fatto discendere dagli dèi (il che era pura verità, perché gli dèi, prima di essere deificati, erano stati uomini, progenitori di quelli ora viventi); e in aggiunta a dèi e semidei, il Pantheon tahitiano fu arricchito con la personificazione di certi fenomeni naturali e di concetti connessi con l'evoluzione: *Atea* (lo Spazio), *Papa* (Fondamento-terrestre), *Te Tumu* (Fonte, Causa) e *Fa' ahotu* (Cominciare-a-formarsi).[1]

Lo stesso problema del distaccare il cielo dalla terra, presentatosi al demiurgo delle Gilbert, si presentò al creatore dell'arcipelago tahitiano.

Ta'aroa, il Creatore, nacque da se stesso, non avendo né padre né madre. [...] Sedette in un guscio chiamato Rumia, fatto a forma d'uovo, per secoli innumerevoli in uno spazio infinito, dove non esistevano né terra né cielo né mare, né luna né stelle. Questo fu il periodo dell'oscurità continua, infinita (*Po-tinitini*), profonda e impenetrabile (*Po-ta'ota'o*). Infine Ta'aroa spezzò il guscio, vi si mise in piedi e chiamò in tutte le direzioni, ma dal vuoto non gli rispose alcun suono. Allora si ritirò dentro a Rumia, ma in un guscio più interno, chiamato *Tumu-iti* (Strato inferiore), dove giacque torpido e sonnacchioso per un altro periodo non si sa quanto a lungo. Alla fine decise d'agire. Emerse dal suo rifugio, e del guscio interno di Rumia fece le fondamenta delle rocce e del suolo terrestre, del guscio esterno fece la volta del cielo. [...]

[1] Peter Buck, *op. cit.*

Ta'aroa creò le rocce, la sabbia, la terra, e si fece aiutare anche da Tu, il grande artefice, insieme al quale formò le mille e mille radici. Quindi spinse il cielo un po' più in alto.

La volta formata con Rumia fu alzata su pilastri e così lo spazio sottostante si slargò: ebbe il nome di Atea e fu pervaso di uno spirito personificato con quello stesso nome. Terra e spazio furono allargati, e il mondo sotterraneo separato da essi. Crebbero alberi da foresta e da frutto e piante commestibili, ed esseri viventi cominciarono ad apparire sulla terra e nel mare.

Restava il grosso impegno di sollevare ancor più in alto la volta del cielo.

Molti artigiani furono messi all'opera per alzare il cielo e far sì che la luce entrasse nel mondo, ma tutti si ritirarono con i loro utensili, quando furono davanti alla terribile e augusta faccia di Atea, il dio dello Spazio, sotto la cupola di Rumia. Ru, nonno del grande Maui, fece il primo tentativo di innalzare il cielo: volle sollevarlo al di sopra delle cime delle montagne, dove si appoggiò sulle foglie dell'*arrow-root*, che in conseguenza divennero piatte; ma lo sforzo lo fece diventare gobbo, ed egli rinunciò all'impresa. Tentò poi Tino-rua, Signore dell'Oceano, ma neanche lui riuscì. Maui, sotto il nome di Maui-ti'iti'i, studiò il problema e si convinse che l'unico modo per risolverlo consisteva nel togliere i pilastri su cui Rumia poggiava, distaccare i tentacoli del Grande Octopus che tratteneva il cielo, e allentare la stretta con cui Atea teneva la terra.

Non ci riuscì nemmeno lui, e dovette ricorrere all'aiuto di Tane, dio degli artigiani, il quale sapeva far miracoli con i suoi attrezzi:

Con strumenti taglienti e perforanti fatti con gusci di molluschi e usando come leve grandi tronchi d'albero, distaccò Atea dalla terra e lo spinse verso l'alto. Così la luce entrò nel mondo, e terminò la lunga notte di Rumia.

Fu rimesso in ordine il firmamento, spostato dal sollevarsi di Atea, e il sole, la luna e le stelle furono rimesse al loro giusto posto.

L'uomo imparò ad adattarsi a un ambiente naturale che gli offriva cibo sia nel mare sia sulla terra.

La prima terra creata era stata chiamata Havaii, e i bardi tahitiani sembrano sicuri che questa Havaii fosse l'isola nota come Raiatea. L'oceano a occidente di Havaii fu chiamato il Mare-dall'odore-rancido, e l'oceano orientale fu chiamato il Mare-della-Luna.

La prima terra creata era stata chiamata Havaii, ed ecco come gli antichi poeti descrivono la nascita di nuove terre, generate dalla stessa Havaii, nel fragore tambureggiante della tempesta, o nel furore delle orrende esplosioni vulcaniche sottomarine:

> Che altre terre nascano da Havaii,
> Da Havaii, luogo natale delle terre.
> Il ridesto spirito dell'alba cavalca
> Sulla nube lieta di là da tutti i confini.
> Continua a crear nuove terre!
> Dove batte il tamburo?
> Batte laggiù, nel mare occidentale
> Là dove il mare ribollendo getta in alto Vavau;
> Vavau, primogenita della famiglia,
> Con flutto che rovescia da due parti.

«Kumulipo è il nome di un canto di creazione delle Havaii composto in onore di un antenato del Re Kalakaua» riferisce ancora Peter Buck. Il poeta che lo compose fece un'opera prodigiosa, radunando ben duemila nomi propri, e affidandola alla memoria umana. Il fatto che esso sia stato tramandato oralmente per più di cent'anni, prima che l'introduzione di un alfabeto permettesse di trascriverlo, fornisce un indizio della straordinaria memoria dei polinesiani.

Il canto Kumulipo narra che durante il periodo di impenetrabile oscurità nacquero, successivamente, molluschi, alghe, erbe, piante, pesci, insetti, uccelli, topi, cani e pipistrelli. Nell'ottava èra le Innumerevoli-Notti si persero nelle Notti-allontanantisi-su-remote-onde, e il Giorno succedette alla Notte. In questo periodo nacquero l'uomo Ki'i (Tiki in maori), la donna La'ila'i e gli dèi Kane (Tane) e Kanaloa (Ta'aroa o Tangaroa). È menzionata anche la Piovra-Gigante che compare nei miti delle altre isole.

Nella nona e decima èra, la scena è occupata principalmente da Ki'i e La'ila'i che aumentarono la popolazione del mondo, e dai quali derivò il sacro diritto di primogenitura dell'uomo.

Terminato questo lavoro il poeta canta:

> I cieli furono sospesi
> la terra è sospesa
> nello spazio stellato.

Giunti finalmente ai progenitori umani, il canto termina con Lonoikamakahiki, il grande capo in cui onore esso è stato composto.

Il ciclo dei pescatori di isole è la deificazione dei grandi navigatori polinesiani, scopritori di isole lontane. Secondo i miti, essi non scoprirono terre, ma le trassero dalle profondità dell'inconoscibile oceanico alla luce del sole.

Gli uomini avventurosi che guidarono le loro navi nel cuore dell'ignoto Pacifico erano abili pescatori, oltre che bravi marinai. Pescavano pesci e isole. Grazie all'aggiunta di un potere magico ai loro utensili da pesca, pescatori semimitici poterono trarre isole dal fondo del mare. Il più grande pescatore di tutta la Polinesia fu Maui, un antico scopritore di terre che divenne un eroe da leggenda: è infatti il protagonista di un ciclo di imprese leggendarie che generazioni di nonni hanno raccontato ai loro nipotini muti di ammirazione. [...] Maui compì molte imprese straordinarie, ma in tutto il corso della sua carriera fu un empio e un mariolo.[1]

Ecco, per esempio, con quale atto crudele creò il cane: ingelosito della fortuna del cognato nella pesca, quando sbarcarono, lo schiacciò sotto la piroga, e gli tirò il naso, le orecchie e la spina dorsale, facendone appunto il primo cane, Irawaru per i maori, Ri per gli abitanti delle Tuamotu. In compenso,

rubò il fuoco a Mahuike, nel mondo degli Inferi, e insegnò all'uomo come farlo sprizzare per attrito dal legno in cui era racchiuso. Grazie al fuoco, l'uomo poté cuocere il cibo che sin allora aveva mangiato crudo.

Un'altra volta si recò alle porte orientali del giorno e con un nodo scorsoio fatto di capelli umani imprigionò Ra, il Sole, nel momento in cui usciva dal pozzo della notte, per cominciare il suo troppo rapido viaggio diurno. Bastone alla mano, Maui impose le sue condizioni, e Ra acconsentì a percorrere lentamente la volta del cielo, concedendo così all'umanità più ore di luce in cui procurarsi e coltivare il cibo.[2]

Per giungere a tanto, Maui dovette lottare; sostenne una battaglia, durante la quale, battendo forte i piedi a terra, egli spaccò l'isola in due: l'atollo di Rakahanga e quello di Manihiki.

Ecco [è sempre Buck che scrive] come si parla della pesca delle isole nel canto dei naviganti che invitavano Lono-Kaeho di Tahiti a seguirli nella loro isola di Hawaii:

> Vieni con noi ad abitare in Hawaii-dal-dorso-verde,
> La terra che si formò nell'oceano,
> Che fu tratta su dal mare,
> Dalle profondità delle cave dell'oceano,
> Che fu presa all'amo da un pescatore,

[1] P. Buck, *op. cit.*
[2] *Ibidem.*

Il grande pescatore di Kapaahu,
Il grande pescatore Kapu-he'e-ua-nui.

I miti dell'Oceania si rifanno sempre alle genealogie proprie delle cose create. A questo proposito, Métraux scrisse:

Le società polinesiane erano profondamente imbevute di spirito aristocratico: il rango dipendeva da una supposta «purezza del sangue» e dal numero di antenati conosciuti. [...] Il valore attribuito alle genealogie ha contaminato la religione e la letteratura. Le stesse divinità furono provviste di una genealogia e presentate come il frutto di una lunga successione di unioni fra esseri immaginari. Questa mania si estese alla natura e fu così che anche ai minerali, alle piante e agli animali furono attribuiti dei genitori. [...]

Il Dio dal-volto-terribile, accoppiandosi con Rotondità, generò le piccole baie chiamate «poporo».

Il *ti* (*Dracena terminalis*), accoppiandosi con Tatuaggio, generò la pianta *ti*.

Altezza, accoppiandosi con Altitudine, generò le erbe alte del paese.

Taglio, accoppiandosi con Ascia, produsse l'Ossidiana.

Rampicante, accoppiandosi con l'Anguilla-irascibile, generò l'albero di cocco.

Boschetto, accoppiandosi con Tronco, generò il marikuru (*Sapidus saponaria*).

La Mosca-pungente, accoppiandosi con Nugolo-di-mosche, generò la mosca.

Ramo, accoppiandosi con Forcella-d'albero, generò lo scarabeo-che-vive-nel-bosco.

Donna-lucertola, accoppiandosi con Zolla-di-terra, generò la canna-da-zucchero.

Assassinio, accoppiandosi con Filo-dalla-lunga-coda (striscia), generò il pescecane.

Piccola-cosa, accoppiandosi con Cosa-impercettibile, generò il pulviscolo dell'aria.

Tiki-il-signore, accoppiandosi con Donna-di-sabbia, generò Hauhara.

Tiki-il-signore, accoppiandosi a una pietra, generò la carne-rossa.

Concludendo la mia rassegna antologica sul tema delle origini delle civiltà polinesiane del Pacifico meridionale, inevitabilmente debbo citare testi e note relativi all'Isola di Pasqua, quel piccolo universo della cultura oceanica del quale ho già detto nel capitolo precedente. E dove torno, ora, perché in quella «piccola terra» ai margini del mondo l'angoscia degli interrogativi sin qui posti dalla scienza e dal mito trova eco in una quantità considerevole di libri, di saggi, di romanzi, frutto di ricerche, di studi o della fantasia. È quasi incredibile l'attrazione esercitata, dal momento della sua scoperta a oggi, da quel misterioso relitto vulcanico, sperduto tra l'Oceania e le coste del Cile, e simboleggiato dalle sue statue gigantesche ed enigmatiche. L'isola merita un'attenzione particolare a sé in questa antologia; non solo per la sua fama e la sua forza evocatrice; ma soprattutto perché resta come un preciso modello-tipo di tanti altri centri dell'Oceania, dove la cultura polinesiana ebbe un suo sviluppo. Nessuno degli scritti pubblicati finora ci è parso più chiaro ed efficace, per illustrare l'isola dei Lunghi-Orecchi, del libro che Alfred Métraux ha destinato al grande pubblico,[1] dopo la monografia, molto più dotta e voluminosa, per gli archeologi e gli etnografi, edita nel 1940 dal P. Bishop Museum di Honolulu, e dopo l'opera della studiosa americana Routledge (*The Mistery of Easter Island*, Londra 1919), cui va il merito di aver per prima affrontato scientificamente il grande enigma di Pasqua. Nell'intento di far conoscere il piccolo universo pasquense, abbiamo qui riunito una scelta dei brani più esemplari di Métraux.

L'Isola di Pasqua [scrive Alfred Métraux nelle prime pagine della sua opera] ci è apparsa in un giorno piovoso dell'inverno australe, sul finire del luglio 1934. Rivedo ancora sfumate nella nebbia le alte scogliere della penisola di Poike, la massa tondeggiante dei vulcani e quella scogliera nerastra, contorta, irta di creste e di picchi rocciosi contro cui si infrangono le onde. [...] Questa prima giornata all'Isola di Pasqua resterà per sempre impressa nella nostra memoria. Il vento, che soffiava a raffiche, spingeva verso terra enormi ondate e la navigazione, vicino agli scogli, si faceva sempre più pericolosa.

C'era il problema di dove e come sbarcare la missione franco-belga di cui Métraux faceva parte. Dalle parti di Hanga Roa, dov'era il porto, il mare era grosso, e il comandante si ancorò al largo; i pasquensi avrebbero mandato le loro barche a remi sottobordo con quel mare?

Radunatisi in massa sulla spiaggia, non sembravano sulle prime disposti a venirci incontro. [...] Sulla spiaggia, vicino alla «casa delle barche», i capi tenevano consiglio e noi seguivamo le peripezie di questa assemblea

[1] *Meravigliosa Isola di Pasqua*, trad. it. A. Hausman, SugarCo, Milano 1967.

ISOLA DI PASQUA

Ru Motu

Motu Kau

Rua Honu

TEREVAKA

Puapau

Te Taki

Te Nui

Ana-o-Keke

CRATERE DEL
PUACA TIKI

CRATERE DEL
RANO RARAKU

Te Epa

(dove venivano scolpiti
i grandi *maoi*)

Hanga Roa

Moeroa

Motu Mariu

Mataveri

(luogo sacro
al culto del
dio-uccello)

CRATERE DEL
RANO KAU

Motu Toa Toa

Orongo

OCEANO PACIFICO

Motu Iti

Motu Nui

28°

km 0 1 2 3 4 5 6 7

109°

108°

improvvisata, impazienti e allarmati dal suo prolungarsi. Se gli indigeni rinunciavano ad abbordare la nostra nave, saremmo stati spiacevolmente costretti a ritornare verso il nord dell'isola, al riparo del vento ma lontani da ogni luogo abitato. Fu con molto sollievo che vedemmo venire verso di noi prima una, poi due, poi tre barche indigene.

Métraux giungeva a Pasqua pensando di risolvere i principali enigmi «attraverso l'uomo»: avvicinando e interrogando i superstiti abitanti dell'isola; il suo collega Charles Watelin, incaricato delle ricerche archeologiche, sperava, invece, di «scoprire la verità» portando alla luce vestigia di città sepolte, paragonabili a quelle protostoriche del Medio Oriente. I fatti avrebbero poi dato ragione a Métraux e al suo sistema di ricerca.

L'Isola di Pasqua non ha ricevuto mai nome dai suoi abitanti. Perduta nell'oceano per almeno mille miglia intorno, l'isola era per essi semplicemente la Terra, come l'Isola Grande per i malgasci. Come in tutte le isole sperdute dell'Oceania, la popolazione che la colonizzò, sbarcandovi nei primi secoli del nostro millennio, recava i semi di una precedente cultura, e quei semi sviluppò poi a suo modo, in dipendenza dell'ambiente pasquense. L'isola non ebbe, nel suo apogeo, più di 7-8000 abitanti; tuttavia, in quella sua solitudine, priva di battelli oceanici, in un confine preciso e ristretto, ebbe organizzazione politica, sociale, religiosa, economica; ebbe capi, sacerdoti, guerrieri e schiavi, divisioni in clan e in classi, e una volontà di potenza nei suoi capi, i quali riuscirono a fare scolpire ed erigere in loro memoria, sui propri mausolei, le statue gigantesche, i *moai*.

In quell'isoletta, quella spora giunta fin là della cultura polinesiana non inaridì, ma si sviluppò con caratteri propri.

La cultura di quest'isola [scrive Métraux], la più solitaria della Polinesia, risente molto, dal punto di vista tecnico, delle particolari condizioni ambientali. Risente ad esempio, dal punto di vista economico, della mancanza di palma di cocco e di certi tuberi; dal punto di vista tecnico, della mancanza del legname.

Questa penuria d'alberi non poté essere sanata dal legname di deriva che, di rado, le correnti portavano ad arenarsi sulle sue spiagge (forse «inviato ai figli», come i genitori promettevano loro di fare, in punto di morte). La prima «industria» che soffrì di questa mancanza fu la navigazione, per cui l'imbarcazione polinesiana si ridusse a miseri zatterini di giunchi. Non poté neppure svilupparsi la scultura lignea, e i suoi artisti dovettero rivolgersi alla scultura del tufo e del basalto. Le piante coltivate, stante la scarsa piovosità, tesorizzarono l'umidità, conservata grazie ai sassi di cui era ingombro il terreno e che per questo motivo non furono rimossi.

A quest'isola i polinesiani sono certi d'esser giunti per un sogno premonitore avuto dal re Hotu-matua; l'episodio è parte di una leggenda raccolta da Peter Buck il quale riporta il testo orale ove si precisa che Hotu-matua viveva nella terra di Marae-renga, e aveva sognato un'isola con una spiaggia meravigliosa, oltre l'orizzonte orientale.

Ordinò dunque a un certo numero dei suoi uomini di mettersi in mare, con una canoa chiamata Oraora-miro, in cerca della spiaggia dell'isola sognata; e li seguì da presso con la sua grande canoa doppia, lunga trenta metri e profonda due. In un'altra canoa seguiva Tu-koihù, il capo dei carpentieri del re. Dopo molti giorni di viaggio, le due imbarcazioni avvistarono un'isola, in cui Hotu-matua riconobbe quella da lui sognata. Avvicinandosi all'estremità occidentale dell'isola le due canoe si separarono; quella del re andò a esplorare la costa meridionale, quella di Tu-koihù la settentrionale. La canoa del re procedeva rapida, gli uomini si erano messi alle pagaie per aumentare la velocità; ma il re doppiò la punta orientale dell'isola senza aver visto la spiaggia che cercava.

Chi la scoprì fu, invece, il suo capo dei carpentieri; per cui, Hotu-matua, quando se ne accorse, con un sovrano atto di prepotenza, lanciò la sua magica invocazione «fermate le pagaie», e la canoa di Tu-koihù, per quanto le sue pagaie agitassero l'acqua, rimase inchiodata dov'era; cosicché il sovrano poté prendere possesso della spiaggia dei suoi sogni.

Resta da chiedersi se il mitico sovrano fosse poi eternato in uno dei grandi *moai* di pietra in gran parte eretti per onorare i grandi re e i grandi trasmigratori.

Quei *moai* che Métraux studiò a lungo, a uno a uno, ricordando il giorno in cui Roggeveen, il primo europeo che li vide, scrisse sul giornale di bordo: «Queste figure di pietra ci riempirono di meraviglia, perché non riuscivamo a renderci conto come uomini sprovvisti di grosse leve e di funi fossero riusciti a sollevarle».

Il nostro primo contatto con le grandi statue [scrive Métraux] ci lasciò un po' delusi. Poco dopo lo sbarco e sotto una fitta pioggia, andammo a vedere i resti di quelle che sul medesimo tratto di spiaggia si erano offerte alla vista di Cook e di La Pérouse. [...] Ma sarebbe ingiusto non riconoscere l'imponenza di quelle sculture soltanto perché non sono più al loro posto, sulle piattaforme dei mausolei, e solo perché hanno subito l'oltraggio del tempo e degli uomini. Ci rendemmo conto della loro maestosità quando, facendo il giro dell'isola, arrivammo all'*ahu* di Tonga-riki: il santuario era infatti una volta sormontato da quindici statue; anch'esse, come le altre, giacciono al suolo a eccezione della parte inferiore di una sola statua, che si erge ancora sul suo piedistallo di basalto. [...] Più che le loro dimensioni, è il disordine in cui si presentano, che opprime. Se fossero disposte con una certa regolarità si potrebbe meglio cogliere la volontà e il pensiero dei loro costruttori; così invece si rimane in preda al turbamento generato dalla confusione quasi umana e dal carattere tumultuoso di questa assemblea di colossi dall'enorme naso e dalla nuca completamente piatta.

Le statue sono tutte scolpite secondo un unico modello, ma il modo disordinato con cui sono disposte conferisce a ognuna di esse una precisa individualità.

Dietro allo sciame di statue erette sul pendio erboso del vulcano c'è la schiera di quelle ancora in costruzione. Il cantiere ha un bell'essere abbandonato e silenzioso, gli operai morti da lungo tempo, queste statue abbozzate, scolpite a metà, pronte a essere fatte scivolare verso la pianura, creano un'atmosfera di vita, che manca invece in mezzo alle statue già terminate. Qui tutto suggerisce l'idea del lavoro e dello sforzo. [...]

Si cammina attraverso la cava come se fosse giorno di riposo: gli operai sono andati al villaggio, ma domani ritorneranno, e i fianchi della montagna risuoneranno nuovamente dei colpi di piccone; si sentiranno le risate, le discussioni e i canti ritmati degli uomini al lavoro. Perché non dovrebbero tornare anche gli scultori, loro che hanno lasciato gli attrezzi ai piedi delle opere: basta chinarsi per poterli raccogliere. [...]

In una cripta pazientemente scavata col piccone dorme un colosso di quindici metri steso su un letto di pietra. Un mese ancora, e sarebbe stato pronto per lasciare il suo incunabolo e scendere in pianura. Adesso rimarrà per secoli nella sua nicchia circondato dalle felci come un morto abbandonato. [...]

Alcune statue sono quasi finite: sarebbe bastato qualche colpo di piccone perché la lunga e fine lamina, che unisce il corpo alla matrice, fosse spezzata e la statua pronta a scivolare sull'erba densa e fitta. [...] Uno di essi è lungo diciotto metri e occupa la cresta di un'intera montagna.[1]

Quale sarà stata la causa del gigantismo di queste statue? Métraux l'attribuisce a una tendenza a stupire mediante il colossale.

Come nelle antiche civiltà dell'Asia, si ha l'impressione di una identica e orgogliosa volontà di unire la preoccupazione estetica al senso di meraviglia, la forma alla massa della materia dominata. La vertigine del colossale su di un universo minuscolo presso uomini con risorse limitatissime: ecco il miracolo estetico dell'Isola di Pasqua. [...]

Le statue che sormontavano i grandi mausolei sono trecento, cifra approssimativa in quanto molte sono state completamente distrutte dagli indigeni durante questi ultimi anni. Altre sono rimaste sepolte sotto le rovine dei loro *ahu*. [...] Le dimensioni variano dai 3,50 ai 5,50 metri. Quelle della costa sud sono in genere più alte e più voluminose di quelle della costa ovest. La più alta, chiamata Paro, oggi giace sull'*ahu* Te Pitote-kura: misura 10 metri di altezza, ha una circonferenza di 7,80 metri e pesa più di 20 tonnellate. Era sormontata da un cilindro alto 1,80 metri e largo 2,40. [...]

L'interpretazione che sorge più immediata nella mente, quando si cerchi di penetrare il significato delle grandi statue, è di considerarle delle raffigurazioni di divinità adorate dagli antichi pasquensi. [...] Gli indigeni moderni, interrogati... si limitarono a rispondere che servivano da ornamento ai «mausolei». Ed è questa anche la spiegazione che i pasquensi, cresciuti fra le antiche tradizioni, avevano dato ai primi missionari.

Il motivo per cui si smise, a Pasqua, di scavare e innalzare statue, è legato alla leggenda che i polinesiani chiamano «della grande aragosta»; ce la racconta Métraux prendendo spunto dal fatto che una visita alla cava ove le statue erano scolpite suggerisce a prima vista una brusca interruzione dei lavori.

Circa cento statue rimaste incompiute e altre sono state abbandonate nel momento in cui stavano per uscire dal cantiere. L'improvviso arresto di una febbrile attività fa pensare a un cataclisma o a una tragedia che abbia completamente sconvolto la vita dell'isola. Gli indigeni hanno ancora coscienza di un evento che per la sua gravità deve aver paralizzato l'attività degli scultori.

Gli scultori solevano nutrirsi di pesci pescati apposta per loro. Un giorno i loro pescatori scoprirono una enorme aragosta, in una grotta sottomarina,

[1] A. Métraux, *op. cit.*

63

così mostruosa che né tre né altri tre giovani riuscirono a catturarla; anzi: ci perdettero la vita. Infine tre altri giovani riuscirono a portarla a riva; la portarono agli scultori, e questi la affidarono a una vecchia maga, là vicino, la quale acconsentì di cucinarla, a patto che gliene lasciassero poi una buona porzione. Mentre il crostaceo cuoceva lentamente nel forno sottoterra, la maga andò a visitare un fratello. Quando ritornò, gli uomini, dimenticando la promessa, avevano mangiato tutta l'aragosta, distribuendone ad altri gli avanzi. Intanto stavano lavorando a una statua, che si chiamava Tokanga: mancava soltanto di tagliare la lama di tufo che la univa alla roccia, per portarla sull'*ahu* Matarai a Vinapu. La maga, al vedere la carcassa dell'aragosta spolpata e nel sentire che non ne era rimasto più nulla, si infuriò e recitò un incantesimo: «*Statue che siete in piedi, cadete! E voi mai più mi ruberete il cibo: immobilizzatevi per sempre!*». Così le statue crollarono e fu la loro fine per sempre, perché anche gli scultori divennero di sasso.

La cava, colpita dal tabù, è come rimasta sotto l'incantesimo della maga [annota Métraux. E aggiunge la sua opinione sull'unica reale spiegazione del fenomeno:] Se, come abbiamo modo di supporre, la fabbricazione delle statue era compito di una corporazione di scultori, sarà bastata una guerra o qualche epidemia, portata da una nave europea, per spiegare l'abbandono dei cantieri.

Una quantità di dilettanti e di studiosi si è torturata il cervello cercando di capire che cosa fossero certe tavolette fittamente incise di ideogrammi e simboli, unicamente conosciute nell'Isola di Pasqua. Buck ce le descrive come «pezzi di legno piatti, oblunghi, con angoli arrotondati; sono solcati da scanalature poco profonde, parallele, tracciate con cura, e circondate da un margine netto», ogni scanalatura ricoperta di fitti e ordinati segni.

Il mistero di queste tavolette «parlanti» è forse ancora più oscuro di quello delle statue, perché tutti si sono intestarditi nel voler vedere in esse un tipo di scrittura, e si è tentato in tutti i modi di decifrarla. Il guaio è che i pasquensi, coscienti o non, hanno ingarbugliato il gioco, quali interpreti: mettendo una di tali preziose reliquie nelle mani di uno di loro, l'uomo si metteva subito a cantare o a recitare, come mosso da un potente impulso, e come «leggendo» la tavoletta. Sono state raccolte, così, varie «traduzioni»; ma è giunta, col tempo, la delusione: i testi dettati da uno stesso «lettore», a distanza di tempo, erano di senso del tutto diverso per la stessa tavoletta.

Ci fu, tra gli altri decifratori, un dilettante linguista francese, Guillaume de Hevesy, che credette addirittura di avere scoperto un'affinità tra i segni delle tavolette e quelli sui sigilli della civiltà di Mohenjo-Daro, nella valle dell'Indo. Si sarebbe dovuto dedurre un rapporto della civiltà dell'Isola di Pasqua con quella fiorita in Asia intorno al 2000 a.C., a 13.000 miglia di distanza. Ma lo «scopritore» fu smentito presto dagli specialisti.

È stato anche esaminato il legno delle tavolette, per determinarne età e provenienza, ma se ne è concluso che l'origine non pasquense del legno era nell'ordine delle cose, mancando tale materia nell'isola. Ciò non vuol dire, tuttavia, che la provenienza del legname in questione sia remota nel tempo e nello spazio. «*In tutti i tempi, i pasquensi hanno importunato i visitatori per ottenere del legno*» scrive Métraux. «*La più grande tavoletta che oggi si possiede, chiamata "Remo", è fatta con la paletta di un remo europeo di pioppo. Non è dunque anteriore al secolo XVIII.*» Le ragioni addotte da Métraux e da altri studiosi, per negare la natura di documento scritto alle tavolette, riempirebbero molte pagine. Concludiamo perciò con una ipotesi «provvisoria» dell'etnografo francese:

I *rongorongo* o cantastorie dell'Isola di Pasqua usavano bastoni per sottolineare gli effetti della loro recitazione. Sui bastoni erano incisi i simboli sacri. In origine i simboli, come tutti i segni sui bastoni degli oratori polinesiani, hanno avuto forse una funzione di promemoria. Più tardi l'elemento decorativo o mistico dei simboli ha preso il sopravvento su quello pittografico, e sorse la tendenza quindi di moltiplicarli a caso.

Le tavolette potrebbero avere avuto, dunque, tutt'al più, la funzione di promemoria, come fanno altri polinesiani, con l'impiego di nodi diversi, per ricordarsi della successione di una genealogia o di una serie di miti.

Ho visto e fotografato alcune rocce dell'isola dove sono incise strane figure dal corpo umano e dalla testa di uccello: sembra che abbraccino un grande uovo; sono il simbolo di un culto che si celebrava ogni anno, al ritorno degli uccelli che annunciano la bella stagione. Il culto s'accentrava su una gara, a sfondo religioso, fra chi riusciva a catturare il primo uovo deposto sulle rupi di un isolotto a poca distanza dalla costa, il Motu Nui, dove le rondini marine andavano a nidificare. Buck e Métraux ci hanno dato una vivida descrizione di questo genere di gara, che al tempo in cui i due scrittori visitarono l'isola era ancora ricordata dai vecchi pasquensi. Era una gara che impegnava il prestigio dei nobili isolani nel momento in cui le rondini di mare (o *manu tara*) venivano in gran numero (luglio e agosto) a covare le loro uova sulle rocce, al largo della punta sud-occidentale dell'isola, dominata dal cratere del Rano Kau. Da un'iniziale raccolta di uova di rondine, per cibarsene, nacque col tempo la gara fra chi riusciva a scoprire il primo nido; gara alla quale i guerrieri (*mata-toa*) della tribù più forte facevano partecipare i loro servi. Questi dovevano raggiungere a nuoto lo scoglio di Motu Nui recando le provviste per tutto il tempo dell'attesa, e là restavano, isolati, esposti alle intemperie, e, se l'attesa dei volatili si prolungava, esposti anche alla fame. Col tempo furono elaborate regole e riti su quell'avvenimento che divenne il più importante fatto sociale dell'anno nell'isola. Il servo vincitore montava su un promontorio roccioso e di là gridava al suo padrone: «Raditi la testa. L'uovo è tuo!». Una sentinella di vedetta in una grotta al disotto di Orongo (l'*Haka-rongomanu*, o Ascoltatore-di-uccelli) correva allora a recare l'annunzio ai padroni che passavano quei giorni e quelle notti a banchettare e cantare, mentre il servo, se gli erano finite le provviste, si accontentava delle bucce di banana accortamente conservate. Il servo vincitore si assicurava con una benda il prezioso uovo sulla fronte, e quindi sfidava l'impeto dei frangenti, per raggiungere a nuoto la turba festante che l'attendeva. Avuto l'uovo il padrone assumeva, per tutto l'anno, il titolo di *Tangata-manu*, o Uomo Uccello. Veniva scortato con grande onore da tutto il popolo sino a Mataveri.

Non si sa con precisione quali funzioni avesse e quali privilegi gli venissero riconosciuti, ma è certo che era tenuto in grande onore e nutrito a spese pubbliche, fino alla gara dell'anno successivo.[1]

«Il più grande enigma della storia dell'uomo», come molti hanno chiamato il mistero dell'Isola di Pasqua, trova una sua semplice, laconica ma autorevole spiegazione nella conclusione del libro di Métraux:

I pasquensi hanno forse preso parte a ondate migratorie dirette verso est

[1] P. Buck, *op. cit.*

che hanno investito le Marchesi, le Gambier e le Tuamotu. Dopo essere rimaste per qualche generazione nelle Marchesi, una o due tribù partirono alla scoperta di nuove isole. Il caso le condusse nell'Isola di Pasqua, dove si stabilirono. Per mancanza di legno quei polinesiani non tornarono mai indietro, l'arte della navigazione aveva infatti subito un forte regresso. (Fu proprio la sua rarità a rendere prezioso il legno, spiegando così parzialmente l'importanza che assunse la scultura lignea. I suoi prodotti dovevano avere per i pasquensi lo stesso valore attribuito alla giada o all'avorio di balena nella Nuova Zelanda e nelle Marchesi.)

È ormai registrato dalla storia che, alla fine del loro lungo arco migratorio, i polinesiani ridivennero un popolo di terraferma, dopo esser stati un popolo di marinai. Le popolazioni che misero piede nelle Hawaii, nella Nuova Zelanda e lungo la cintura degli avamposti orientali, vi si installarono, abbandonando il mare per l'agricoltura, al contrario di quanto avevano fatto i loro antenati quando, provenendo dall'Asia, avevano sfidato l'oceano per la prima volta. L'arco evolutivo della cultura polinesiana ha dunque due termini nelle grandi trasmigrazioni delle quali vorrei evocare le probabili cause e le ben conosciute tecniche; patrimonio culturale di un intero popolo che navigò nella direzione del sole nascente fino a quando non ebbe popolato ogni isola, anche la più remota del Pacifico meridionale. Virtù e conoscenze solidissime resero possibili queste epopee: il virile senso marinaro, la perfezione della canoa oceanica, l'arte nautica pressoché infallibile, l'abilità marinaresca e non ultime la fiducia nel proprio animo e nei propri mezzi e una non retorica resistenza.

Peter Buck[1] ricorda la devozione affettuosa dei polinesiani per la loro remota terra di origine:

Hawaiki è il simbolo della patria lontana di dove vennero gli antenati dei primi navigatori addentratisi fin nel cuore del Pacifico. Le popolazioni che vivono lungo la base occidentale del «triangolo» polinesiano, nelle Samoa e nelle Tonga, chiamano Pulotu il paese in cui l'anima ritorna «lungo lo scivoloso, il viscido sentiero della morte», mentre la maggior parte di coloro che penetrarono più addentro nel «triangolo» coltivano amorosamente il ricordo di una patria nella lontana Hawaiki. Di là i progenitori fecero vela nella direzione del sole nascente, e là tornarono le anime dei loro morti lungo la grande strada d'oro gettata sulle acque dell'oceano dai morenti

---

[1] P. Buck, *op. cit.*

raggi del sole al tramonto. Così è giusto: il sole nascente per la gioventù, per l'avventura, il sole morente per la vecchiaia e il riposo.

Dove le anime dei nostri progenitori siano arrivate non possiamo sapere, perché, come dice il poeta maori, essi «hanno percorso il sentiero che attira le moltitudini, il sentiero che chiama le miriadi, il sentiero che non manda indietro i messaggi».

Noi sappiamo, però, dove sono arrivati i loro nipoti, e sappiamo che in epoche successive, cresciuta a dismisura la famiglia polinesiana delle prime isole colonizzate, essi ebbero bisogno di nuove terre al di là dell'orizzonte marino.

Secondo il racconto fatto a Henry Teuirà, che lo riportò nel suo volume *Tahiti aux temps anciens*,[1] il tahitiano Papearu ricordava ancora nel 1854 gli itinerari, in parte mitici e in parte reali, del cosiddetto «circuito tahitiano di navigazione», ossia i peripli attribuiti ai navigatori che mossero da Tahiti, in tutte le direzioni.

Dopo che Rua e Hina ebbero scoperto le terre [narrò Papearu] Maui con la sua flotta navigò ancora una volta nell'oceano per il suo re Ama, con la piroga Tai Atea, che vuol dire Bilanciere del lontano oceano. Quando arrivava in qualche regione, con l'aiuto dei suoi uomini costruiva *marae* e li consegnava ai sommi sacerdoti.

Non c'è alcun dubbio che, come scrive Métraux,

le migrazioni dei polinesiani costituiscono uno dei capitoli più singolari della storia umana; migrazioni talmente singolari che se ne è negata la possibilità [...] per spiegare la vasta dispersione di questo popolo, si sono perfino inventate terre immaginarie in mezzo al Pacifico. Queste fantasie non possono tuttavia togliere ai polinesiani la gloria di aver scoperto sulle loro piroghe doppie tutte le isole, alte e basse, disperse in quell'immenso spazio triangolare che va dalla Nuova Zelanda alle Hawaii e dalle Hawaii all'Isola di Pasqua.

Fenomeno navigatorio e migratorio che ebbe come teatro la deserta e sconfinata regione marina del Pacifico centrale compresa fra i paralleli 38° nord e 48° sud e i meridiani 168° est e 110° ovest, vale a dire una regione di mare vasta quattro volte l'Europa, le cui terre emerse, se si eccettua la Nuova Zelanda, hanno sì e no la superficie del Piemonte e della Lombardia messe

[1] Il volume fu iniziato nel 1823 da J.M. Orsmond ed è stato concluso nel 1951 da Teuirà; lo ha pubblicato nel 1951 la Société des Océanistes.

insieme. L'isola maggiore, Hawaii, è un po' più grande della Corsica, e le migliaia di altre sono, in media, quanto l'Elba e le Eolie.

In questa zona d'oceano (Hawaii a nord, Pasqua a est, Nuova Zelanda a ovest) detta il «triangolo polinesiano» il fenomeno migratorio si mosse in tre periodi distinti:

1. quello del popolamento di certe isole nei due ultimi millenni dell'evo antico, da parte di gruppi sporadici, probabilmente «negriti», che i successivi occupanti trattarono come esseri inferiori, con il nome di *menehune*;

2. quello degli arrivi nel Pacifico centrale di genti note oggi come «polinesiani», arrivi che durarono all'incirca dal principio della nostra èra sino al V secolo. Il gruppo principale o più avanzato popolò le isole della Società, nel cuore del «triangolo», mentre altri, distaccatisi prima, si diressero verso sud-est, nella Polinesia occidentale, alle Samoa e alle Tonga, arcipelaghi che sono al centro geografico dell'Oceania;

3. infine l'epoca d'oro delle trasmigrazioni propriamente polinesiane, fra il X e il XV secolo, che si irradiarono come tentacoli di un polpo in tutte le direzioni, presumibilmente dal centro del «triangolo», vale a dire da Tahiti, alle Marchesi, alle Hawaii, alle isole Australi, alla Nuova Zelanda, all'Isola di Pasqua.

È ai grandi movimenti umani *dopo l'anno Mille* che ci si riferisce, nel parlare delle «grandi trasmigrazioni» polinesiane. Esse hanno destato sempre il più curioso interesse, sia per l'alone romanzesco di avventura o di epopea di un intero popolo, sia perché ci sono meglio note di quelle che le precedettero, e infine perché fu con queste nuove colonie, scaturite dalle ultime migrazioni, che i primi esploratori europei dell'Oceania vennero a contatto, colmi di meraviglia.

Per esclusione di altri popoli dell'Oceania – come i melanesiani e i micronesiani, che rimasero paghi dei loro primi insediamenti – l'epopea migratoria oceaniana è dunque *quella dei polinesiani* e più precisamente quella di questo millennio. Epopea poi ricostruita a fatica, raccogliendo e analizzando tradizioni, miti, leggende, canti, quando la cultura polinesiana era ormai in gran parte dispersa o distrutta. Quali furono le cause dello sciamare polinesiano nel Pacifico, sino ai confini del loro mondo insulare, ce lo dirà Peter Buck. Intanto il de Bisschop schematizzava così il genere dei grandi viaggi marini compiuti dai polinesiani:

1. viaggi di esplorazione e di scoperta;
2. viaggi di colonizzazione, per migrazione volontaria;
3. viaggi di colonizzazione e di popolamento, per migrazione forzata. La suddivisione ha i suoi motivi che qui citiamo nelle parole testuali del suo autore:

Viaggi di esplorazione e di scoperta: furono intrapresi dai migliori individui della popolazione e sotto la loro guida. La canoa doppia fu molto probabilmente il tipo di imbarcazione maggiormente impiegato; le sue qualità in mare e la sua grande capacità di carico permettevano l'imbarco di un equipaggio numeroso e delle provviste necessarie. [...]
Viaggi di colonizzazione e di popolamento: faccio una distinzione molto importante tra migrazione volontaria o organizzata, e migrazione forzata. Il solo esempio veramente storico del primo caso ci è dato dalla cosiddetta «grande flotta polinesiana», che dal Pacifico centrale arrivò verso l'anno 1350 in Nuova Zelanda. [...] Conosciamo i nomi delle imbarcazioni come quello dei sacerdoti e dei capi che le comandavano. Conosciamo anche il tipo delle barche utilizzate, in maggioranza canoe doppie, dette *pahi* [e il de Bisschop ne aveva usata una di sua costruzione, con la quale navigò dal Pacifico al Mediterraneo].
Viaggi di migrazione forzata: vennero intrapresi da una parte della popolazione, che per una qualsiasi ragione fu costretta ad abbondare la propria isola e a prendere il mare.[1]

La facilità dell'esistenza in Oceania è un allettamento letterario, e solo per l'europeo moderno, ha detto Jean Guaiart. È superfluo ripetere, sulle bellezze del mondo oceaniano, quanto si può leggere su ogni pieghevole turistico. Ma è il rovescio della medaglia che conta per chi deve vivere in quelle isole. E Guaiart annota alcune avversità dell'ambiente naturale e della società polinesiana, e che furono certo causa di molte delle grandi emigrazioni. Per esempio, la sete:

Le precipitazioni atmosferiche, anche abbondanti, non bastano a garantire una provvista permanente. [...] Le isole coralline, per esempio, non dispongono affatto di acqua in superficie; al livello del mare, invece, esiste una polla d'acqua dolce, sospesa sull'acqua del mare, che la sostiene attraverso il basamento corallino forato come una schiumarola; è acqua pota-

[1] E. de Bisschop, *op. cit.*

bile, e il suo livello, che sale e scende a secondo della marea, può essere raggiunto grazie alla tecnica moderna; talvolta quest'acqua affiora in fondo alle grotte. [È proprio quello che avviene in tutte le isole coralline del mondo.] Si dà il caso anche di notevoli porzioni di isole costituite da formazioni calcaree, non sempre coralline, sopraelevate a diverse centinaia di metri d'altezza, e nelle quali i corsi d'acqua sono sotterranei per gran parte del loro percorso. Altrove, da un fiume all'altro [...] le distanze sono grandi, e i villaggi situati in quella zona possono mancare totalmente d'acqua per gran parte dell'anno.

Un'altra rilevante avversità è rappresentata dalla fame, dovuta alla mancanza di sufficienti terreni abbastanza fertili, o peggio inariditi dalla siccità o marciti dal pantano sterile degli acquitrini.

È poco noto pure che nella Nuova Guinea centinaia di chilometri sono preda della mangrovia e che, di conseguenza, la popolazione vi sussiste in virtù della propria non comune ingegnosità.

La popolazione combatte, con lavori di riempimento, questa specie di taiga marittima e tropicale, per creare minuscoli lembi di terreno coltivabile.

La sete [prosegue Guaiart] è un dato di fatto permanente in molte regioni [e la sete vuol dire fame]. Fino a pochi anni fa [...] i raccolti [venivano] bruciati prima di essere maturi, le sementi non attecchivano. Sola risorsa era allora la pesca e la raccolta di piante e di radici selvatiche commestibili.

E non c'è carestia peggiore – notano gli oceanisti – di quella in una piccola isola da dove non si può fuggire. Un tempo questo significava la morte; oggi si giungono a fare distribuzioni di cibo, da parte delle amministrazioni da cui dipendono. Ma se la carestia perdura, o se un ciclone distrugge le coltivazioni, non resta che «emigrare, emigrare ancora, almeno gli uomini, per qualche mese, [...] vendendo la manodopera per guadagnare di che mantenere la famiglia fino al raccolto successivo».[1]

Anche la guerra, tutt'altro che rara e incruenta, come testimonieranno anche i primi esploratori europei, fu sovente motivo di trasmigrazioni collettive. In seguito a una sconfitta, popolazioni o

[1] J. Guaiart, *op. cit.*

capi col loro seguito dovevano cercare scampo su altre isole. In occasioni diverse, sempre per motivi «di guerra», si può parlare di *trasmigrazioni involontarie*: all'epoca dell'impero delle isole di Tonga, per esempio, venivano inviate flotte numerose e ben armate di piroghe, per il loro ciclo di esazioni annuali dei tributi (beninteso in natura, riempendone piroghe e piroghe), flotte che si spingevano, di arcipelago in arcipelago, anche alle più appartate isolette. Non sempre queste imprese finivano com'era nei piani.

Nel corso di simili spedizioni [scrive ancora Guaiart] molte piroghe andarono perdute o sono finite alla deriva fino a scomparire del tutto o a ritrovarsi in Melanesia o in Micronesia, essendo talvolta capriccioso l'incontro della corrente marina e dell'aliseo. Sbarcando, i naufraghi erano massacrati oppure assimilati dalla popolazione indigena.[1]

Se erano assimilati, contribuivano, pur senza volerlo, al popolamento di nuove terre. Un'operazione involontaria che assomiglia alla scoperta e colonizzazione di isole da parte di naufraghi, fatto non nuovo, e comune ad altri mari.

Uno studioso neozelandese, Andrew Sharp, si occupa da molti anni della navigazione degli antichi polinesiani, e ha tentato di rinverdire una vecchia teoria. Egli ha cercato di enumerare i viaggi accidentali di piroghe andate alla deriva, per cause di forza maggiore, e casualmente approdate a isole sconosciute. Si è servito del metodo statistico, e dal suo censimento, scrive Guaiart,

risulta in modo chiaro che, in due secoli, tutti gli arcipelaghi polinesiani hanno accolto piroghe con equipaggi, andate alla deriva fuori dal loro itinerario, e che simili derive hanno avuto luogo in tutte le direzioni... Se si pensa che questo fenomeno può essere durato due millenni, ci si può spiegare come si sia, a poco a poco, popolato l'insieme della Polinesia, tenendo come punto di partenza le isole centrali (Tonga e Samoa).

Questa teoria di Sharp (che non è nemmeno nuova) fu contraddetta già nel secolo scorso; se è certo plausibile come concausa non può invece essere accettata nella sua visione «assoluta», che riduce l'intero fenomeno trasmigratorio a pura e semplice casualità. Su questo punto si sono creati fieri contrasti fra gli studiosi.

Oggi, pur non disconoscendo che *in parte* Sharp ha visto giusto,

[1] J. Guaiart, *op. cit.*

si concorda nel ritenere *volontaria* la grande epopea migratoria polinesiana. Si conosce con certezza l'organizzazione politica e sociale di questa cultura, oltre che i complessi ordinamenti religiosi, e sappiamo bene che «parallelamente allo sviluppo e al progresso della teologia e all'organizzazione sociale, progredirono le arti e le attività artigianali».[1] Questo sviluppo significò anche incremento demografico, necessità di rifornimenti di certe materie, necessità di scambi, e nuovi contatti, maggiori conoscenze geografiche, bisogno di rinnovo: il bisogno di cercare nuovi orizzonti.

Le trasmigrazioni collettive, nella molteplicità dei loro moventi, si giovarono di una conoscenza preventivamente acquisita dalle nuove terre da colonizzare, per sommaria che fosse. In altre parole, non si partì alla ventura, né un'emigrazione marina può immaginarsi come quelle di un'orda del paleolitico. Chi dette una meta a ogni primo gruppo di piroghe fu quasi sempre un antenato che aveva saputo trovare, dopo la scoperta di qualche atollo deserto, la via del ritorno, e aveva lasciato una traccia del suo viaggio, talvolta nella forma artistica di una poesia o di un mito.

Le fasi emigratorie ebbero così un antecedente esplorativo, anche se non furono mandati apposta in avanscoperta i Colombo o i Magellano dei Mari del Sud; ebbero cioè come base le scoperte volontarie o accidentali, delle quali non si fece subito uso, che però andarono ad arricchire la tradizione conservata dai capi e dai sacerdoti, come in un archivio, con la precisa rotta per ritrovare le terre nuove, e delle quali, magari, non si parlò più per generazioni. È risaputo che i polinesiani dopo gli dèi (che erano stati i piloti ad avere condotto nel cuore del Pacifico i primi coloni) veneravano una schiera di eroi esploratori, come Rata (che aveva vinto innumerevoli prove in «oceani multicolori», e aveva ucciso la Tridacna Gigante, divoratrice di intere navi ed equipaggi); come Kupé (che aveva scoperto, fra l'VIII e il X secolo, la Nuova Zelanda), come Hiro (il mitico, geniale padre delle architetture navali oceaniche).

[1] J. Guaiart, *op. cit.*

I viaggiatori succeduti a Rata [narra Peter Buck] esplorarono nuove terre e tornando a casa narrarono le loro avventure, ma furono anche in grado di indicare le rotte da seguire per raggiungere altre isole... Fra i viaggiatori del periodo più tardo furono Hono'ura e Hiro... Oltre a splendide avventure sul mare si attribuisce a Hiro il merito di essere stato il primo a costruirsi una nave con tavole di legno, in luogo di scavare, al solito, un tronco d'albero.

Le scoperte, in ogni caso, non andarono perdute, anche se dovettero attendere il momento decisivo, per essere valorizzate. E quando i tempi furono maturi,

si produsse un movimento migratorio diretto a occupare stabilmente le nuove terre. La migrazione fu determinata probabilmente da conflitti dovuti all'accrescersi della popolazione, cui si accompagna sempre, inevitabilmente, la lotta per il potere. Spedizioni organizzate furono dirette dai membri più giovani delle famiglie potenti, che non vedevano nessuna possibilità di farsi strada se rimanevano a casa loro, ma grazie al prestigio della famiglia erano in grado di farsi costruire imbarcazioni e di armarle con equipaggi di gente avventurosa. Li accompagnavano sacerdoti, che non solo erano esperti dei segreti della navigazione, ma possedevano una profonda conoscenza del patrimonio leggendario e tradizionale del popolo.[1]

Nell'arcipelago delle isole della Società, le isole maggiori di Bora-Bora, Tahà, Huahine e soprattutto Raiatea (la nuova Havaii dei primi coloni) furono le isole venerabili dove la cultura polinesiana si caratterizzò e dove fu fatta la storia della Polinesia. L'isola di Havaii, genitrice di altre isole, il cui popolo fu padre di successive nuove colonie, «diventò il centro intorno a cui ruotava l'universo polinesiano». I sacerdoti della sua nobile città di Opoa ordirono la tela della mitologia polinesiana, nella quale i figli degli dèi ebbero compiti distinti: Tane, dio delle foreste e patrono degli artigiani e dei carpentieri navali, Tangaroa, dio del mare e della pesca, Ra'a, dio della meteorologia. Col passare del tempo i sacerdoti fecero un'innovazione rivoluzionaria: pensionarono Tangaroa, veneratissimo fra gli dèi, e prescrissero, in sua vece, il culto per suo figlio 'Oro, facendone la suprema divinità del grande santuario di Taputapu-atea. Cook vide ancora in piedi, nel XVIII secolo, questo *marae* al dio 'Oro. Col tempo, il santuario

[1] P. Buck, *op. cit.*

74

era «cresciuto in grandezza e importanza, fino a diventare il santuario interinsulare», che richiamava pellegrini da tutto l'arcipelago a quella specie di città santa. Presso la sua spiaggia «c'era un altro *marae*, dove le vittime destinate al sacrificio aspettavano il loro turno nelle cerimonie celebrate in Taputapu-atea», e a uno di tali sacrifici assistette l'esploratore inglese.[1]

La popolazione di Tahiti [prosegue Buck] si rifiutò di accettare il nuovo culto, rimase fedele al suo dio Tane, e fra questo e 'Oro scoppiò una guerra all'ultimo sangue. Alla fine però 'Oro la ebbe vinta, e divenne il dio principale di tutte le isole della Società. Un nuovo tempio, chiamato Taputapu-atea come quello di Opoa, fu costruito in Tahiti e divenne il centro del nuovo culto.
Alcuni tra i fedeli di Tane, che si rifiutarono di accettare 'Oro, lasciarono Tahiti e andarono a stabilirsi sulle isole più marginali del gruppo delle Cook. Così anche nel Pacifico come nell'Atlantico [con i pellegrini del *Mayflower*] l'intolleranza religiosa ebbe la sua parte nel determinare il popolamento di nuove terre.

Il popolamento della Polinesia è apparso sempre come un fenomeno straordinario, quasi inspiegabile, data la vastità oceanica su cui avvenne tale movimento umano. Queste lunghe trasmigrazioni comportavano, infatti, uno dei più ardui problemi tecnici, quello della navigazione oceanica da parte di popolazioni che, secondo un punto di vista «tecnologico», potremmo considerare ancora all'età della pietra. Di conseguenza, come per tutte le storie di antiche navigazioni, da quelle della regina Hashepsut, a quelle dei fenici oltre Gibilterra, dei vichinghi e dell'epoca colombiana, anche quelle dei polinesiani sono state materia di tesi contrastanti e di polemiche, nell'intento di trovare una spiegazione accettabile.

Nel «Journal of the Polynesian Society», in un ampio studio sull'argomento dovuto a un gruppo di studiosi australiani e neozelandesi, sono state approfondite, sotto la direzione dell'oceanista Jack Golson, le questioni relative all'antica navigazione dei polinesiani. Lo studio, apparso nel 1962, non ha presentato conclusioni, ma ha consegnato i risultati delle varie ricerche vertenti sulle conoscenze geografiche e meteorologiche dei polinesiani, il

[1] Vedi pp. 275-276.

tipo delle loro imbarcazioni, il popolamento degli arcipelaghi, la nautica e la navigazione primitiva.

Nel complesso, i risultati raggiunti hanno permesso di raccogliere e confrontare le testimonianze che possediamo sulle canoe, sulla nautica e il genere di viaggi di quel tempo e in questo oceano: attraverso un'analisi di dati specifici e specialistici raccolti, si è capito quali furono per i polinesiani i problemi dell'architettura navale, quelli dell'arte nautica; e come essi poterono raggiungere la loro leggendaria abilità marinaresca, e la capacità di resistenza e di sopravvivenza alla fame e alla sete con la quale riuscirono ad affrontare l'ignoto.

Un episodio narrato da un inglese[1] che visse oltre vent'anni alle Gilbert, nell'Oceania centrale, va al di là della sua stupefacente cronaca; è un fatto indicativo, *visto oggi*, delle possibilità di sopravvivere di un polinesiano in oceano. È una «avventura-tipo», che ci offre la chiave per comprendere la tempra degli uomini che furono i protagonisti della grande epopea delle trasmigrazioni. Epopea della quale mai si potrà comprendere l'esatta misura se non si aggiunga, a quanto la scienza va scoprendo giorno per giorno, anche la cognizione del grado di «acquaticità» degli isolani del Pacifico.

Per capirlo, in una storia su centomila, ascoltiamo quella di Teriakai:

L'impresa di Teriakai, un altro uomo di Taraua, divenne storica. Teriakai era a quel tempo ospite di Sua Maestà,[2] essendosi cacciato nei guai per un'interpretazione alquanto libera delle leggi sul matrimonio. Si trattava di un ospite straordinariamente bene accetto; la sua costituzione robusta e massiccia rendeva, dal punto di vista del lavoro, quanto quella di un gigante, e lo spumeggiare del suo irreprimibile buonumore faceva ridere da mattina a sera sia i guardiani delle carceri sia i compagni di prigionia. [...]

E, ogni volta che v'era qualcosa di speciale da fare, sceglievano sempre Teriakai per affidargli l'incarico. Fu quindi del tutto naturale che, quando il comandante e il primo macchinista del piroscafo *Tokelau* – entrato nella laguna di Tarawa per le pulizie dello scafo – vollero spingersi al largo in

---

[1] A. Grimble, *op. cit.*
[2] Nelle prigioni del Protettorato.

barca a vela, con un tempo che minacciava di mettersi al brutto, Teriakai li accompagnasse per vegliare su di loro.

Accade che la barchetta fa naufragio e i tre uomini siano in pericolo di vita. Teriakai non si perde d'animo, benché

[...] due pericoli soprattutto li minacciavano; ovunque attorno a loro v'erano gli squali-tigre, e inoltre essi si trovavano abbastanza vicini alle scogliere per poter essere risucchiati al largo quando la marea avesse cominciato a calare. Teriakai si preoccupò innanzitutto degli squali. Cominciò col tagliare la vela più grande che galleggiava sull'acqua al completo di stanga e bozzello (gli ospiti di Sua Maestà non avrebbero dovuto possedere coltelli, ma lui ne aveva uno, che Dio benedica la sua infrazione al regolamento). La vela, sorretta alle estremità dall'alberatura, formò sott'acqua un bel sacco, nel quale egli fece entrare il comandante e il macchinista. «State qui dentro» disse, ormeggiando con una drizza l'improvvisato rifugio alla barca capovolta, «e i *tababa* non riusciranno a fiutarvi.» Poi si occupò dell'àncora; la catena era stata per fortuna assicurata a uno dei banchi, ma gli occorse un'ora di tuffi e di tentativi per sbrogliarla, in modo che l'àncora potesse toccar fondo. «Adesso andrò a chiedere aiuto» disse, quando ebbe terminato. «Se riesco a eludere quei *tababa*, forse ci rivedremo ancora.»

Nuotò diritto verso la cerchia degli squali – il comandante e il macchinista lo seguivano con lo sguardo – e i demoni lo lasciarono passare. Gli chiesi in seguito se sapesse spiegarsene la ragione. Mi rispose: «Se in acqua stai fermo, i *tababa* ti attaccano. Se ti allontani a nuoto, spaventato, fiutano che hai paura e ti danno la caccia. Ma se nuoti senza timore verso di loro, si spaventano e ti lasciano in pace». Così, egli scelse il suo squalo, nuotò a tutta velocità verso di esso e, oplà!, l'accerchiamento si ruppe davanti a lui. In tutto ciò non vi era assolutamente che un incredibile coraggio.

Teriakai percorse a nuoto circa sei chilometri e mezzo prima che accadesse qualche altra cosa. [Raccontò poi di essere stato assalito da un *tababa*.]

La rapida notte equatoriale scese su di lui nella successiva mezz'ora. La luna non s'era ancora alzata, ripetute raffiche da nord facevano infuriare le acque. [...] Ma riuscì a passare senza venir meno, a nuotare per un altro chilometro e mezzo fino a riva, a percorrerne ancora tre e a raggiungere la casa di un commerciante bianco, ove svenne sulla veranda. Il commerciante lo fece rinvenire con un bicchiere di rum, ma si rifiutò di andare al salvataggio dei naufraghi con la sua barca in una notte come quella.

La risposta di Teriakai fu più eloquente di ogni parola. Egli afferrò la bottiglia del rum (proibito dalla legge agli indigeni) dalle mani del bianco e fuggì con essa nella notte. Aveva altri otto chilometri da superare per giungere alla casa di un altro commerciante. [...]

Jimmy Anton, figlio di padre austriaco e di madre delle Gilbert, non era

uomo da rifiutarsi di porre a rischio la propria vita e l'integrità della sua
barca. Chiamò la moglie indigena e, tutti e tre insieme, misero subito in
mare l'imbarcazione. [...]

Rinvennero la barca capovolta poco prima dell'alba; il comandante del
piroscafo e il macchinista erano rimasti in acqua dodici ore, ma si trovavano ancora in salvo dentro al sacco di canapa. Teriakai fu premiato con la
medaglia di bronzo della Royal Humane Society.

Attenti osservatori della natura, come tutti i primitivi, i polinesiani avevano un loro patrimonio di conoscenze meteorologiche e
oceanografiche, indispensabili al navigare. «*In questo campo, non solo
un'élite, ma molti tahitiani dimostrano conoscenze fuori del comune che
denotano un vero "senso marinaresco", tanto in quello che concerne il mare,
forza e direzione delle onde, dell'onda lunga e delle correnti... quanto dell'atmosfera: venti, differenze stagionali dei venti, nuvole, predizione del tempo*»
scrive P. Jourdain.[1] Nella cosmogonia tahitiana i venti erano i
potenti rappresentanti degli dèi e prevenivano gli uomini su
alcuni pericoli mormorando cose misteriose.

Per i navigatori polinesiani che effettuavano a vela i grandi
peripli – la pagaia veniva usata solo nei periodi di calma e nelle
manovre d'arrivo e di partenza – la conoscenza della direzione del
vento era essenziale. Essa veniva indicata in rapporto all'est e la
rosa dei venti tahitiana ne enumera i nomi secondo la loro provenienza, e qualche volta la loro forza. Secondo i vari autori, l'orizzonte era suddiviso in dodici, sedici e qualche volta anche in
trentadue parti, che consentivano al pilota di mantenere la rotta.
Anche i venti erano suddivisi e classificati. I più famosi erano il
vento di nord-est, il *Toereau*; il vento dell'est, *Maoae*; il vento del
sud-ovest, *Uru*, che, se è forte, diventa *Urupa*. Infine il più temuto,
quello del sud, il *Maramù*.

Vi erano poi gli strumenti per navigare. È certo che i polinesiani ne conoscevano molti, ma di uno solo la tradizione ci rinvia il
nome e la sua capacità di «dire» ai polinesiani la loro posizione in
mare basandosi sugli astri: è la famosa, ma molto dubbia, «zucca
sacra». Così ne parla de Bisschop:

Era proprio una zucca la cui punta era stata tagliata e vuotata; sotto il
bordo circolare così formato, era stata praticata una serie di buchi, a una

---

[1] P. Jourdain, *Pirogues anciennes de Tahiti*, Société des Océanistes, Parigi 1970.

certa e accuratamente calcolata distanza. La zucca veniva riempita d'acqua, il cui liquido raggiungeva questa serie di buchi. [...] Come se ne servivano? Semplice: facevano vela verso nord. Dopo aver passato l'equatore, scorgevano la Stella Polare, che ogni giorno saliva sempre più sull'orizzonte. Sapevano che essa doveva raggiungere una certa altezza, conosciuta dai grandi preti, perché fossero giunti esattamente al traverso delle Hawaii: veleggiando allora col vento in poppa, non potevano mancare l'arcipelago. [...]

La «zucca sacra» indicava, a quel punto, un «angolo magico»: se era tenuta perfettamente orizzontale (e si sapeva che era orizzontale quando l'acqua raggiungeva la serie dei suoi buchi disposti in circolo), serviva per traguardare la Stella Polare attraverso uno dei tanti buchi, in tangente col bordo superiore quando veniva raggiunta la latitudine delle Hawaii.

Eric de Bisschop, con la sua esperienza più che ventennale di navigazioni nel Pacifico con piccole imbarcazioni, ha fatto questa distinzione fra navigatori e marinai, a proposito dei polinesiani:

Io chiamo «navigatore» colui che si serve di un battello per spostarsi sull'acqua, con una destinazione prestabilita che sa di poter raggiungere. Gli manca una qualità essenziale e caratteristica del «marinaio», il quale si serve di una imbarcazione per correre verso il largo, attirato dal mistero degli orizzonti e da quello che ci può essere al di là. [...] Per nominare due popoli che hanno queste caratteristiche estreme, non posso che scegliere l'egizio e il polinesiano. Il primo fu, probabilmente, fra i più antichi a conoscere la vela; ma non fece altro uso che il navigare sul Nilo, e forse per qualche viaggio costiero molto limitato. [...] Il polinesiano, invece, fu il perfetto «marinaio», il popolo «curioso» del mare aperto, capace di lanciare le sue imbarcazioni alla conquista degli oceani. [...] I melanesiani, anch'essi insulari, anche se le loro imbarcazioni, meraviglie di costruzione, che ci stupiscono per l'arte della loro decorazione, non sono e non furono mai costruite se non per brevi navigazioni costiere.

«Il polinesiano è l'unico popolo della terra che abbia mai concepito un tipo di canoa adatto ai viaggi oceanici» aveva scritto de Bisschop; il quale quando volle provare egli stesso la canoa doppia polinesiana, perfetto tipo di scafo oceanico che essi avevano inventato, dovette costruirsela da sé, la *kamiloa*, della quale ridisegnò con molta fantasia i piani di costruzione, perché di canoe doppie non ne restava più nemmeno una per modello. Con quella sua *kamiloa* egli poi andò dalle Hawaii a Cannes, nel Mediterraneo, passando per il Capo. Anche Peter Buck ci parla della sua delusione nell'annosa ricerca di una vecchia piroga polinesiana di arcipelago in arcipelago:

> In un'isola delle Tuamotu domandai: «E non c'è nessun vecchio scafo o parte di canoa ch'io possa esaminare?».
>
> «No,» rispose Pa «le vecchie canoe, dopo che entrarono in uso le barche a vela, furono ridotte in pezzi per farne pali per le nuove case. Ecco, i pali di questa casa sono fatti con una vecchia canoa. [...] Sono secoli che i polinesiani non compiono più lunghe traversate, ma possiamo avere un'idea approssimativa della grandezza delle loro navi di un tempo dai primi esploratori europei. Varie notizie indicano in generale una lunghezza variante da diciotto a ventiquattro metri; ma qualcuno vide imbarcazioni di trenta metri e più.»

Le ultime vere grandi canoe le aveva infatti studiate Cook: canoe doppie d'altomare o da guerra; una, di una quarantina di metri, poteva portare 144 vogatori e 39 guerrieri.

> Due scafi lunghi da ventuno a ventiquattro metri, con un ponte fra mezzo [ci precisa Buck], potevano ospitare parecchia gente; e infatti le canoe da guerra di Tahiti, partendo per qualche incursione, portavano fino a un centinaio di guerrieri. Nei viaggi di ricerca di nuove terre in cui stabilirsi – nei viaggi nei quali, oltre alle donne e ai bambini, si portavano provviste, piante, semi, tuberi, maiali, cani, pollame – le grandi canoe doppie potevano ospitare senza fatica sessanta o più passeggeri.

Questa canoa doppia, tipica dei polinesiani, nacque dalla necessità di affrontare lunghi viaggi, o per il trasporto di truppe. Per disporre di una imbarcazione più capiente, l'unica soluzione possibile fu di sostituire il bilanciere con una seconda canoa: così nacque «il doppio scafo», imbarcazione con la quale i polinesiani conquistarono il Pacifico.

Sulle prestazioni di questo genere di scafi oceanici non ci sono dubbi, se dobbiamo credere a Cook e agli altri esploratori contemporanei: erano canoe che potevano affrontare normalmente viaggi anche di quindici giorni senza scalo, quando non di più, il che ci indica le distanze che esse potevano compiere senza mai toccare terra. Ma si sa che i polinesiani utilizzarono anche zattere: le incisioni che illustrano le relazioni dei primi viaggiatori ce ne mostrano di diversi tipi: ed è noto che esse furono e sono ancora usate lungo le coste peruviane come quelle della Cina meridionale (beninteso manovrate e guidate mediante opportune derive e con vele e capanne per riparo del carico e dell'equipaggio, su rotte ben prestabilite). Le esperienze transpacifiche di vari europei, negli anni tra il '48 e il '58 hanno confermato l'efficienza oceanica di tali mezzi, in apparenza così rudimentali. Non ci resta che vedere come queste imbarcazioni furono capaci di raggiungere, secondo la tradizione e gli studi, i grandi arcipelaghi ai vertici del triangolo polinesiano, le Hawaii e la Nuova Zelanda.

Per uno dei tanti moventi che abbiamo prima citato, ma pure per quell'imperativo «*che trae origine dalla instabilità congenita del polinesiano, dal suo vecchio istinto migratore che altre volte lo ha spinto, da un'isola all'altra, alla colonizzazione del Pacifico*», come scrisse Jean-Marie Loursin,[1] le colonie originarie delle isole della Società proliferarono nuove e altre colonie via via in arcipelaghi sempre più remoti. Le Hawaii, come conferma l'archeologia, già toccate verso il 350 da gruppi di polinesiani, furono popolate a partire dal 750.

Circa la scoperta delle Hawaii, Bruce Cartwright suggerisce che i polinesiani, acuti osservatori dei fenomeni naturali, abbiano potuto scoprirne l'esistenza seguendo il volo del piviere dorato, uccello di terra che in inverno emigra dall'Alaska verso sud per tornarvi in estate.

È un vanto per i maori poter citare una discendenza dai coloni polinesiani arrivati in Nuova Zelanda, nel XVI secolo, con le prime canoe doppie, delle quali sono ancora ricordati e venerati i nomi, quelli degli occupanti e persino quello della pagaia timoniera.

> Guarda *Tainui, Te Arawa, Mataatua, Kurahaupo e Tokomaru,*
> Tutte galleggiano sulla vasta distesa dell'oceano.
> Il tronco d'albero fu scavato in Hawaiki,
> E così prese forma *Takitumu.*
> Una notte fu spesa a Rangipo
> E *Atea* prese il mare all'alba.
> Queste son le canoe di Uenuku
> La cui fama giunge al cielo.

[1] *Tahiti*, Mondadori, Milano 1961.

A proposito di questi primissimi viaggi della Grande Emigrazione da Tahiti verso la Nuova Zelanda, narra la tradizione orale polinesiana che:

La canoa *Tainui* sotto il comando di Hoturoa si era preparata a partire da Hawaiki nella notte chiamata Orongo (la ventisettesima) del mese lunare di ottobre-novembre; i vecchi consigliarono a Hoturoa di rimandare la partenza finché non fossero passate le tempestose Tamatea (le notti dalla sesta alla nona) del mese successivo, ma Hoturoa rispose: «Voglio partire ora e incontrare le Tamatea in mare aperto». E superando tempeste e pericoli giunse sano e salvo a Capo Runaway.

È diffuso tra gli studiosi delle trasmigrazioni il convincimento che i polinesiani si sarebbero spinti sino ai mari subantartici. Di fatto, nella mitologia di Rarotonga, tra i racconti delle imprese di lontani antenati, si narra di un viaggio nell'estremo Sud di un capo piroga chiamato Ui-te-rangiora.

Vissuto nella prima parte del XVIII secolo, con la sua nave *Te-ivi-o-Atea* egli fece vela verso il lontano Sud, dove vide gli scogli che si levano dal mare chiamato Tai-rua-koko, i lunghi capelli fluttuanti sulla superficie delle acque, il mare coperto di schiuma simile ad *arrowroot*, l'animale che si tuffava nelle profondità del mare, un luogo oscuro dove non si vedeva il sole, con alti scogli bianchi, spogli di ogni vegetazione. Tutte queste meraviglie sono state interpretate rispettivamente con il mare a sud di Rapa, alghe brune, il mare gelato, leoni marini, la notte antartica, gli iceberg: dati che ci offrono la prova del limite estremo verso l'Antartide raggiunto dalle piroghe da pesca polinesiane.

Sostenitore, con Buck, di questa «possibile verità» è Paul-Émile Victor, esploratore ed etnologo del Collège de France.

Queste cronache stupefacenti non sono che una parte di tanti capitoli di tante imprese verso orizzonti diversi; ognuna con il suo episodio particolare, sempre in bilico tra la realtà e la fantasia, tra la storia e il simbolo. Basti citare, per questo, l'episodio che segue.

La scoperta della Nuova Zelanda è generalmente attribuita a Kupé, intorno alla metà del X secolo. Narra la leggenda che, adiratissimo contro i polpi che gli divoravano l'esca mentre stava pescando, egli giurò di uccidere il loro capo, Wheke-a-Muturangi. E infatti lo perseguitò per tutto il mare finché riuscì ad arpionarlo. Ma non a ucciderlo, sicché quel mostro, con la sua grande forza, lo trascinò lontano, verso sud, dove Kupé vide una terra dalle alte colline coperte di nebbia... Quel mitico, infuriato inseguimento del capo dei polpi sarebbe dunque all'origine della scoperta della Nuova Zelanda...

Per confermare la tradizione che vuole il tahitiano Kupé scopritore della Nuova Zelanda, fra l'VIII e il X secolo, in un viaggio di 2100 miglia, occorreva dimostrare che una *pahi*, o piroga a bilanciere, potesse percorrere in media sei nodi l'ora, in un lungo viaggio senza scalo; questa dimostrazione è stata fornita dal viaggio, nel 1965, di David Lewis da Tahiti alla Nuova Zelanda, via Raiatea e Rarotonga; Lewis, a bordo di un catamarano a vela, è riuscito a compiere questo viaggio, utilizzando solo le tecniche dei tahitiani di un tempo, mantenendo la rotta secondo il levare e il tramontare del sole e delle stelle, osservando le stelle zenitali per un approdo di latitudine, e i segni che annunciavano la terra (uccelli, rottami galleggianti, nuvole, moto delle onde). L'approdo in Nuova Zelanda è facilitato dalla distesa di quelle terre, che hanno un'estensione di oltre 700 miglia, secondo l'asse nord-sud, ma ciò non sminuisce il valore dell'impresa e l'efficienza del metodo impiegato.

Un fatto di vitale interesse nella colonizzazione pre-europea della Polinesia fu l'introduzione delle piante e degli animali utili all'uomo. L'ambiente naturale delle isole non offriva molte risorse, se si eccettuano gli uccelli e i pesci. Pertanto le piante di cocco, di banano, canna da zucchero, taro, igname, gelso da carta e di una specie di zucca, la *Legenaria vulgaris*, di cui si fanno recipienti, e la patata dolce furono portate dall'uomo; così pure il maiale, il pollo, il cane, il topo grigio. Non si conosce ancora con sicurezza la via che piante e animali seguirono, insieme all'uomo. «La storia del passaggio delle piante verso la Polinesia» è stato scritto[1] «è avvolta di mistero, non meno di quella dei viaggi dei primi esploratori polinesiani.»

Altro mistero è quello relativo alla patria dei navigatori che

[1] R. Schaeffer, *Oceania, mito e verità*, Edizioni Nautiche di Studio, 1969.

portarono dall'America del Sud in Polinesia la patata dolce, la cui provenienza americana in epoca precolombiana è sicura. Su questo fatto sono fiorite le favole di un preteso popolamento americano della Polinesia, negato, oggi, dall'antropologia; ciò non elimina comunque la curiosità di scoprire come la patata dolce finì in Polinesia, mentre la zucca da recipienti arrivò nell'America del Sud.

Buck scrive in proposito: «Nel dialetto *kechua* del Perù settentrionale, la patata dolce si chiama *kumar*, e il nome polinesiano è *kumara*. Non sappiamo con precisione quando, ma prima del XIII secolo, uno sconosciuto viaggiatore polinesiano fece vela verso est alla ricerca di una nuova terra».

Per diverse considerazioni Buck ritiene che questa ignota spedizione poté partire dalle isole Marchesi.

La distanza dalle Marchesi alla costa peruviana settentrionale è di pochissimo superiore alle 4000 miglia. Dixon pensa che una canoa polinesiana non fosse in grado di percorrere senza sosta più di 2500 miglia, ma questa stima è basata sui viaggi compiuti nell'ambito polinesiano. In realtà, con vento favorevole, possiamo calcolare che una canoa percorresse sette miglia l'ora, e con questa media per andare dalle Marchesi all'America avrebbe impiegato tre settimane o poco più, una prova non troppo dura per uomini vigorosi. Fu tuttavia un viaggio eccezionale.

Al termine del quale Buck suppone che i polinesiani appena sbarcati:

Si trovarono in mezzo a gente strana, troppo diversa da loro, e temendo un conflitto in cui, data l'enorme inferiorità numerica, avrebbero avuto la peggio, decisero di tornarsene a casa loro, in Polinesia. [...] Da qualunque isola sia partita la spedizione, è certo che tornando arrivò alle Marchesi: là crebbe una nuova pianta, e di là fu portata successivamente a Mangareva e all'Isola di Pasqua, a oriente, e alle isole della Società a occidente nel centro della Polinesia.

I nostri navigatori avevano lasciato in cambio ai loro ospiti americani la zucca.

«A Mangareva è tuttora in uso il metodo della sepoltura in mare, proprio dei naviganti d'alto mare» ricorda Peter Buck. È la «restituzione» di se stessi all'elemento primordiale compiuta da «esseri anfibi» come sono i polinesiani. In questa «tomba nel mare» giacciono coloro che diressero le loro imbarcazioni a un'isola amica, seguendo la buona stella, ma non furono fortunati perché finirono «in mari vuoti». Di loro ha detto Peter Buck:

> Essi dormono ora sotto la superficie delle distese deserte. Se un giorno il mare restituisse i suoi morti, che processione di polinesiani sorgerebbe dalle profondità dell'oceano, al suono del *pu* che li chiama all'ultima adunata... Il loro numero renderebbe testimonianza del coraggio di coloro che cercarono una terra dove non c'era. Eroi di imprese non conosciute dagli uomini, ma solo dal mare.

I morti e i vivi, le imprese conosciute e quelle che non lo saranno mai; le sconfitte sull'oceano, le vittorie: nel grande affresco primitivo della trasmigrazione la ricerca scientifica è giunta più volte al limite di una realtà che poteva sembrare frutto di una fantasia poetica, di un'invenzione magica. Ma è anche accaduto l'inverso: una somma di vicende tutte umane in quella loro misura che è eroica ma al contempo umile e dimessa così come possono essere le imprese di pescatori di cui non sapremo mai il nome, non poteva mancare d'ispirare la narrativa e non solo quella locale. In certa misura, infatti, un racconto «romanzato» può riuscire a evocare una grande vicenda storica con una forza che una somma di documenti e di analisi può non riuscire ad avere, almeno sul lettore non specializzato.

Per questo motivo alla fine di una raccolta antologica dedicata alle trasmigrazioni, ci è sembrato non fosse fuor di luogo concludere il nostro testo citando un'opera che riassume in un grande romanzo le più diverse ipotesi, gli studi e le ultime concrete testimonianze sulle trasmigrazioni nel Pacifico. L'americano James A. Michener[1] ha immaginato l'avventura più mitica di quell'epopea: il viaggio di una grande canoa oceanica polinesiana da Bora-Bora alle Hawaii per oltre tremila miglia. Il romanzo come storia!

Il racconto si apre, appunto, in chiave «storica». A Parigi, un mattino, i figli di Carlo Magno litigano per decidere chi ha da governare l'impero paterno; nel frattempo una veloce e nuova canoa a bilanciere, mossa da robusti vogatori, munita di vela triangolare, e con un capannuccio per ospitarvi gli dèi e le provvi-

---

[1] *Hawaii*, trad. it. M. Gallone, Rizzoli, Milano 1960.

ste, dopo aver solcato leggera l'oceano, in una sua prima prova in mare aperto, rientra al solitario ingresso della laguna di Bora-Bora, sulle cui rive l'intera popolazione di quell'isola ne segue l'avanzare. A bordo c'è un re, Tamatoa, che da tempo anela di lasciar la sua patria natale per raggiungere una grande isola ignota sperduta nel Nord, di cui parla una fioca e fumosa tradizione.

Da quest'episodio in poi, tralasciando gli sviluppi di una vicenda che si snoda drammaticamente nel disegno di tanti e diversi personaggi, vorrei qui ricordare solo i brani significativi per evocare il grande viaggio che fa da sfondo alla prima parte del romanzo di Michener; un collage di eventi e di stati d'animo, che hanno inizio dal momento in cui a Bora-Bora il re ha deciso definitivamente di trasmigrare.

Il sogno che decise definitivamente del viaggio fu quello del vecchio Tupuna. Questi vide apparire un arcobaleno proprio sulla rotta della canoa: non avrebbe potuto esservi presagio più funesto. Tuttavia quasi subito Tane e Ra'aroa sollevarono l'arcobaleno e lo posero a poppa dell'imbarcazione, dove rimase a illuminare le acque. Questa seconda parte del sogno rendeva il presagio così augurale (il male si tramutava in bene per intervento divino) che il vecchio non si destò neppure per riflettervi. Il mattino disse al re con l'animo colmo di gioia: «Stanotte ho fatto un sogno meraviglioso. Non ricordo più come fosse, ma stasera salperemo senz'altro». [...]
Così la duplice canoa, carica sino a scricchiolare di uomini, di dèi, di maiali, di speranze, di timori, salpò verso l'ignoto.

Il racconto del viaggio è subito drammatico, perché appena lasciata Bora-Bora la grande canoa deve affrontare una furiosa tempesta: creste irose del mare, un fischiare impazzito del vento, violentissime ondate che sembrano spaccare le due parti dell'imbarcazione (nella capanna di paglia invasa dall'acqua le donne pensavano «questa è la fine»). Ma è uno scontro dal quale gli uomini escono vittoriosi, sì che, calmatasi la furia degli elementi, la robusta canoa ritrova l'equilibrio e prende a filare sicura lungo la grande strada d'acqua che la porta verso l'ignoto.

Uno squarcio del cielo rivelò per un istante le luminose stelle del firmamento, si comprese quanto fosse stato saggio Tupuna a suggerire di partire la sera del primo giorno del nuovo mese allorché, poco dopo, davanti agli sguardi incantati dei navigatori spuntarono scintillanti nel cielo orientale, non offuscati dal chiarore lunare, i «Sette Piccoli Occhi». Era la loro prima apparizione dell'anno, il loro rassicurante ritorno a garantire che l'universo sarebbe continuato a esistere per almeno altri dodici mesi. Con quanta inesprimibile gioia i viaggiatori li salutarono.

«I "Piccoli Occhi" sono tuttora con noi!» urlò Tupuna, e il re alzò il capo in preghiera a ringraziare i custodi del firmamento, la costellazione intorno alla quale l'universo era stato costruito. Quindi gli astronomi si riunirono per interpretare i segni. [...] Tupuna, per tutta risposta, intonò il solo canto che avesse mai mandato a memoria per la navigazione al Nord, il quale diceva in sostanza: «Mantenete la canoa nella scia della tempesta sino a che i venti non saranno totalmente cessati. Virate quindi nel mare morto, dove le ossa marciscono per il calore, e non spira alito di vento. Vogate seguendo la nuova stella, e non appena i venti si leveranno da oriente, sfruttateli per portarvi a ovest, dove sotto i "Sette Piccoli Occhi" scorgerete una terra».

Il re, che non era del tutto digiuno d'astronomia, puntando l'indice verso nord domandò: «Dunque le terre che cerchiamo sono laggiù?».

«Sì» rispose Tupuna.

«Però noi andiamo da questa parte?» seguitò il re indicando l'est, nella cui direzione li stavano sospingendo le ultime raffiche di vento della tempesta.

«Sì.»

Pareva talmente assurdo dirigersi verso una terra fuggendone, che Tamatoa esclamò: «Siete sicuri che questa sia la via giusta?».

«No, non possiamo esserne sicuri» confessò il vecchio.

«Allora perché...»

«Perché quel poco che sappiamo ci suggerisce di agire così...»

«Sicché noi navighiamo lasciandoci guidare dal canto d'un poeta?» domandò Tamatoa.

«Sì» rispose il Sacerdote. [...]

A mano a mano che la canoa avanzava, i compiti quotidiani di ciascuno assunsero un ritmo più regolare. All'alba i sei schiavi smettevano di aggottare e ripulivano la canoa, mentre gli agricoltori si preoccupavano di rifocillare porci e cani, abbeverandoli e nutrendoli di pesce fresco pescato nelle prime ore del mattino, oltreché di patate dolci schiacciate. Ai polli venivano distribuiti noce di cocco secca e un pesciolino a testa.

Chi stava peggio a bordo erano le donne. Logicamente, le razioni più grosse spettavano agli uomini, cui toccava la dura fatica del vogare. Venivano poi i maiali e i cani, che dovevano essere mantenuti in vita per popolare la nuova terra, cosicché alle donne restava ben poco. Per questo, non appena se ne presentava l'occasione, venivano calate le lenze. I primi pesci pescati andavano al re e a Teroro, poi a Tupuna e alla sua vecchia sposa, quindi ai vogatori, e via via porci, cani, polli e topi. Le donne si dividevano soltanto i pesci che avanzavano. [...]

Quando anche le frequenti piogge cessarono del tutto, re Tamatoa fu costretto a ridurre ulteriormente le razioni d'acqua, finché l'equipaggio non ricevette più che due sole manciate di cibo solido e due piccolissime razioni d'acqua, tanto che i giorni in cui non si pescava nulla tutti si trascinavano in preda alla fame.

Ma la sete, prosegue il racconto, non era l'unica angoscia di chi guidava la trasmigrazione. Il re e Teroro avevano fatto una scoperta, la stessa scoperta tormentosa e assillante prima di loro sperimentata da tanti altri navigatori polinesiani che dal Sud avevano puntato al Nord e che ora gli astronomi di bordo confermavano: il viaggio in canoa stava per abbandonare, e per sempre, molte delle antiche stelle familiari. Con dolore, addirittura talvolta con lacrime, ognuno seguiva per l'ultima volta con lo sguardo una determinata stella, forse particolarmente amata in gioventù, e la vedeva tramontare per sempre.

Sebbene questo fenomeno causasse rimpianto, non destava tuttavia preoccupazione. [...] Alla partenza sapevano già che avrebbero perduto per via qualche stella familiare, ma ne avrebbero incontrate di nuove. Con gioia gli scopritori, dunque, contemplavano di volta in volta le stelle, sino a quel momento mai vedute, del Settentrione. Tuttavia, nonostante la loro saggezza, non erano preparati a vedere quel che videro l'undicesima notte.

È questo il punto cruciale del racconto che Michener ha tratto dalla vicenda dei trasmigratori che dal Pacifico meridionale puntarono verso il Nord; il momento dell'emozione profonda di tutti coloro che, durante la grande epopea, tentarono una nuova strada, fuori dalle rotte protette da «stelle amiche» e conosciute.

«Guarda com'è in linea retta rispetto alle due stelle di "Uccello-dal-collo-lungo"» esclamò Tupuna, alludendo alla costellazione del Gran Carro. A tutta prima Teroro non fu in grado di individuarla, tanto tremolava, ma alla fine la scorse; era una stella luminosa, limpida, fredda, risalente con nitidezza in un ampio tratto vuoto del cielo. Parlando da navigatore osservò: «Dovrebbe essere un'ottima stella di orientamento...».
[...] I due uomini non perdetero di vista il nuovo astro, ma al sorgere dell'alba l'uno temette di confidare all'altro ciò che aveva visto; rendendosi conto di trovarsi di fronte a un prodigio di portata eccezionale. [...]
La terribile ipotesi non lasciava adito al dubbio, furono costretti a dar voce all'arcano timore che li divorava.
Il primo a parlare fu Tupuna: «La nuova stella non si muove».
«È fissa» assentì Teroro.

I due uomini erano sgomenti, davanti a quelle parole. Nulla, infatti, è «fisso» nel cielo i cui astri ruotano intorno alla Croce del Sud, ove le costellazioni si levano da una «fossa» per subito calare in un'altra; e altre non scompaiono mai al di sotto delle onde: tutte, nondimeno, si spostano perennemente attraverso i cieli. Quella stella nuova, invece, non si muoveva; e causava nei polinesiani che non la conoscevano paura, prima, e sorpresa, poi. Infine gioia, quando comprendevano che era in grado d'indicare con sempre perfetta esattezza la via da seguire in un oceano completamente deserto. E così fu per la piroga di Teroro e del suo re partiti da Bora-Bora. Dopo la sorprendente scoperta percorsero ancora duemila miglia (spinti dai venti di levante e coprendo circa duecentocinquanta miglia giornaliere) come ipnotizzati da quella luce sempre ferma pressappoco alla medesima altezza sull'orizzonte, alla loro destra. E intanto, avanzando sempre più verso le isole alle quali i trasmigratori puntavano senza conoscerne né l'esatta ubicazione né la natura (e nemmeno, in fondo, la reale possibile esistenza), queste cominciarono a «svelarsi» con segni che solo l'occhio più che esperto dei vecchi poteva interpretare.

Nel ventinovesimo giorno di navigazione avvistarono uccelli neri, dal corpo allungato e dalla coda elegantemente biforcuta; erano certo partiti in caccia dalla loro isola natale, punto imprecisato al di là dell'orizzonte. Quando sorvolarono la canoa

Teroro notò con comprensivo compiacimento che la loro direzione, alla rovescia, era la sua. [...] Dalla presenza dei volatili si poteva dedurre che la terra doveva distare al massimo una sessantina di miglia. Questa supposizione fu confermata allorché Teura e Tupuna riconobbero nelle onde del mare un disegno caratteristico, indicante come poco lontano la profonda deriva occidentale dell'oceano urtasse contro una scogliera, dalla quale rimbalzavano onde di ritorno che tagliavano di traverso il movimento normale del mare.

Prima di concludere la sua narrazione, lo scrittore americano vuole comparare l'avventura della canoa di Bora-Bora ad analoghe imprese della stessa èra storica, attorno all'anno Mille, in altri continenti; solo da questo paragone le imprese dei polinesiani possono essere pienamente valutate, oggi, da un lettore europeo; e così Michener scrive:

Mentre i nostri viaggiatori si stanno avvicinando al termine di una traversata di circa duemilacinquecento miglia, è giusto raffrontare la loro impresa con quelle di altri navigatori dell'epoca in altre parti del globo.

Nel Mediterraneo i discendenti degli orgogliosi fenici, che anche nei loro momenti maggiori di gloria s'erano di rado avventurati fuor di vista della terra, navigavano ora costeggiando lidi ben noti e di tanto in tanto, impresa ritenuta arrischiatissima, osavano addirittura attraversare il loro piccolo mare chiuso, percorrendo al massimo duecento miglia. In Portogallo, s'incominciavano a raccogliere importanti notizie sull'oceano, ma gli uomini non erano ancora pronti a tentare il grande balzo, e sarebbero trascorsi seicento anni prima che fossero scoperte le vicine isole di Madera e delle Azzorre. Alcune navi si erano spinte non oltre le spiagge africane, poiché si sapeva che attraversare l'Equatore, perdendo in tal modo di vista la Stella Polare, equivaleva o a morire bolliti o a rotolare giù dall'estremo limite del mondo. Sul lato opposto del globo le giunche cinesi avevano compiuto il periplo dell'Asia, e nei Mari del Sud s'erano solo spostate da un'isola all'altra senza mai perdere di vista la terraferma, impresa addirittura eroica. I mercanti dell'Arabia e dell'India avevano affrontato viaggi di una certa importanza, senza però allontanarsi di molto dalle coste conosciute. Soltanto nel Nord dell'Europa i vichinghi avevano rischiato avventure che si possono paragonare a quella degli uomini di Bora-Bora; tuttavia in quel tempo neppure essi avevano iniziato i loro lunghi viaggi, pur potendo disporre di metalli, di navi di grande stazza, di vele di stoffa, di libri, di mappe approssimative ma pur sempre valide.

Toccava agli uomini del Pacifico affrontare un oceano da pari a pari e conquistarlo. Benché privi di metallo e di carte, orientandosi solo con l'aiuto delle stelle e provvisti di qualche pugno di *taro* secco e d'una fede incrollabile nei propri dèi, questi uomini compirono prodigi. Dovevano passare ben sette secoli prima che un navigatore italiano chiamato Colombo, battendo bandiera spagnola e sfruttando l'esperienza e i mezzi apprestati da una comunità civile, osasse avventurarsi su tre solide e comode navi in un viaggio assai meno lungo e infinitamente meno rischioso. [...]

Tamatoa sbarcò per primo, e non appena fu a riva s'inginocchiò, prese un pugno di terra e, portandoselo alle labbra, lo baciò ripetutamente, intonando quindi con voce solenne: «Questa è la terra. Questa è la casa dell'uomo. Questa è terra buona su cui stabilirsi, una terra buona sulla quale procreare figli. Qui porteremo i nostri antenati. Qui porteremo i nostri dèi».

Queste pagine, le riflessioni che suscitano, l'emozione che creano, il senso d'angoscia che insinuano in chi dalla loro lettura ha misura di quale patrimonio l'umanità sarà priva nel perdere l'apporto culturale dei polinesiani, possono aiutarci a comprendere la drammaticità di quanto scrive l'antropologo polinesiano Te Rangi Hiroa, osservando i mutamenti della sua gente e la fine del suo mondo; poco prima di morire: «La vecchia rete è piena di buchi,» annotò nella sua opera *I vichinghi d'Oriente* «le sue maglie sono marce e l'abbiamo messa da parte... con quale rete nuova andremo a pescare?».

Capitolo terzo

Cronache di una mia lunga odissea oceaniana

Tanai e la sua storia d'amore – La manta che lo riconduce al suo atollo –
Come si costruisce una canoa *pahi* – I cantastorie di Papeete – I maiali come
bussola – La nuvola verde di Anaa – Alla deriva verso il Mar Antartico –
La grande pesca al *mahimahi* e al *paratà* – I profughi dell'atomica di Mururoa.

È stato alle isole Tuamotu, nel 1961. Mi accadde allora di conoscere la vicenda di un uomo chiamato Tanai e del suo lungo viaggio attraverso il Pacifico in piroga a vela.

Una immaginaria avventura nata molto probabilmente, come spesso accade nei racconti tramandati a voce, da altre e diverse realmente vissute; vicende di navigatori polinesiani così come se ne ascoltano in differenti isole e arcipelaghi da cantastorie e da vecchi *huarè-po*; somma di storie vere che hanno finito con l'identificarsi nella figura di Tanai, pescatore leggendario. Al largo di Rangiroa in una barca a motore, alle due del mattino, me ne parla un vecchio polinesiano.

Su quella barca, immobile sull'oceano appena mosso da onde lunghe come il respiro lento e profondo di un animale addormentato, c'è solo, con me, quel pescatore. Si chiama Tetoèa, il vecchio.

Siamo usciti dalla *pass* dell'atollo poche ore prima, all'imbrunire, prendendo il largo in direzione della punta meridionale dell'isola. Abbiamo un pieno del serbatoio, oltre la riserva di due taniche di venticinque litri di miscela, strappate a Kamin (detto Elastique, per la sua bocca senza denti), commerciante cinese che ha la casa e l'emporio, unico dell'isola, proprio in riva alla laguna.

Ogni pochi minuti c'è un salto di pesci volanti: «*Mamarà!*» grida il vecchio, ridendo; e a gesti mi aiuta a capire che nel silenzio della notte il rombo del nostro motore si propaga, a sferzate, sott'acqua impaurendo i pesci e spingendoli a fuggire; quelli volanti, un salto dopo l'altro, scompaiono in onde lontane, a noi invisibili nel buio della notte. Solo uno sbaglia la traiettoria dei suoi balzi, e ripiegando le pinne tese per infilarsi in acqua, dopo un volo in preda al terrore, finisce in barca; la nostra corsa si è incrociata con il suo guizzo e in quell'istante l'ho visto volare, lampo argenteo nella luce della lampada.

Da quando s'è fatta notte abbiamo navigato ancora per tre ore, allontanandoci sempre più dall'atollo.

Il fatto è abbastanza inconsueto; nel Pacifico con una piccola barca a motore non ci si spinge al largo, oltre la *pass*; le piccole barche difficilmente lasciano le acque interne delle lagune; queste infatti, anche se vaste, anche se infuriate, sono uno spazio sicuro, chiuso da ogni lato dall'anello emergente dell'isola e dei coralli; nell'oceano aperto, invece, è difficile immaginare una motobarca in difficoltà che riesca a riparare in caso di maltempo o di una semplice avaria; le isole sono sempre lontane le une dalle altre, e una imbarcazione piccola, pur ammettendo che non faccia naufragio, scompare in poche ore alla deriva, chissà verso dove, e con pochissime probabilità di averne più notizie.

Eppure quella sera l'unica motobarca di Rangiroa, quella appunto di Tetoèa, aveva lasciato il pontile e la laguna puntando verso il largo non appena la radio aveva annunciato il passaggio di una goletta, la *Mahina-tamurè*, in rotta nelle Tuamotu orientali da Anaa verso Vana Vana; bastava un calcolo semplice per capire che quella goletta avrebbe costeggiato l'atollo sul quale ci trovavamo e dove nessuna nave, grande o piccola, faceva scalo da più di due mesi e dove occorreva di tutto: farina, medicine, carne in scatola, olio, zucchero. Da dicembre non si mangiava più pane, e si era al dieci di gennaio. Mancava la benzina per i motori delle barche e nessuno voleva andare più a pesca per paura di finire le riserve; per questo motivo, avevamo dovuto aspramente contendere a Elastique quei due galloni di miscela necessaria a prendere il largo.

Con la sua autorità di *tavanà*, capo villaggio, Tetoèa pensava, una volta incrociata la goletta, di convincere il comandante a puntare verso l'atollo. Da parte mia, mi ero unito a quella spedizione in alto mare, perché – si fosse o no fermata quella goletta e avesse o no dirottato – avrei potuto affidare a qualcuno di bordo lettere con nostre notizie da spedire agli amici del gruppo, al lavoro in altre isole dell'arcipelago e dai quali eravamo da tanto tempo isolati.[1] La radio del villaggio, dove noi vivevamo ormai da tante settimane, era da tempo in panne: poteva solo ricevere, non trasmettere.

All'una di notte siamo così in alto mare; abbiamo spento il motore; sottovento all'atollo, dove ci troviamo, possiamo ritenere di trovarci nel miglior punto, secondo Tetoèa, per attendere il passaggio della *Mahina-tamurè*.

Nel silenzio Tetoèa comincia a parlare; un discorso fitto, metà in francese, metà in polinesiano, alternato a lunghe pause, per cercare di sentire il battito del motore della goletta, al largo; è la storia di Tanai che mi narra, dal momento in cui essa ebbe inizio, quando un'altra goletta non si fermò, anni prima, a quello stesso atollo. Tetoèa m'aveva indicato una linea nera all'orizzonte, l'estrema punta meridionale di Rangiroa appena visibile nel controluce della luna finalmente apparsa tra cielo e onde.

«In quel punto dell'isola c'è un villaggio, anzi c'era perché ora è abbandonato, deserto... In quel villaggio viveva un ragazzo. A lui serviva qualche sacco di terra...»

«E la goletta?» avevo chiesto cercando di capire l'inizio di quel racconto.

«La goletta?... La goletta doveva portare i sacchi di terra all'atollo; quel ragazzo, Tanai, la attendeva da tempo. Voleva costruirsi una capanna e voleva piantarsi accanto l'albero del pane. Vicino a una nuova capanna, qui alle Tuamotu, si cerca sempre di piantare l'*urù*, l'albero del pane...; e per piantare l'albero del pane serve la terra...»

«L'*urù* è il simbolo della fecondità. Le sue radici debbono entrare nella terra accanto alla nuova casa lo stesso giorno nel

---

[1] Eravamo nel Pacifico per una ricostruzione cinematografica e televisiva dei *Viaggi del Capitano Cook*.

quale la casa è terminata» avevo letto prima di sbarcare alle Tuamotu; l'avevo poi osservato direttamente negli atolli. In quel mondo ormai senza particolari obblighi rituali, il trapianto di un alberello del pane è un atto quasi sacro, tradizione alla quale anche oggi non so quanti abbiano il coraggio di passar sopra. E oltre a questo, il frutto dell'*urù* ha sempre, malgrado il cibo in scatola o quello congelato, una fondamentale importanza nell'alimentazione della gente degli atolli. Si mangia con il pesce, con la carne di maiale e di pollo o con quella in conserva; si mescola, come una insalata, al pesce crudo condito con il latte di cocco: è l'unico farinaceo di tutta l'alimentazione degli atolli. Ma l'albero dell'*urù*, a differenza dei cocchi, dei pandani e di altri cespugli capaci di germogliare e crescere sul terreno corallino, chiede vera terra per attecchire e dar frutti. Vera, grassa terra: quella che, negli atolli, non c'è. Gli atolli sono formati, infatti, dall'accumularsi millenario di incrostazioni biancastre, dure come pietre, levigate dal vento e dall'acqua: corallo morto.

Quindi, chi vive in un atollo e voglia piantare l'albero del pane accanto alla propria capanna deve acquistare due, tre anche più sacchi di terra dalle golette che li trasportano agli atolli dalle Isole Alte; terra da versare, in una buca tra i coralli, accanto alla casa ove la giovane talea dell'*urù* dovrà essere piantata. Nel gesto, nel costume, nell'abitudine di questa operazione, nella rarità di quella manciata di terra e nella sua capacità di far crescere ricco e lussureggiante un albero così prezioso è da ricercare il significato rituale del trapianto di un albero del pane nell'arcipelago delle Tuamotu.

Mentre rifletto su tutto questo, Tetoèa tace. A poppa della barca, in piedi, cerca nel buio della notte le luci di posizione della *Mahina-tamurè*, e tenta ancora una volta di sentirne il battito del motore. Ma l'oceano resta buio e silenzioso.

«Non viene» mi dice «ma noi l'attendiamo... Anche Tanai, in attesa dei sacchi di terra, come noi stasera, scrutava il mare per scorgere la goletta desiderata, tanto importante per lui e per tutta la gente del suo villaggio, da tempo ormai priva, come noi, di rifornimenti, viveri freschi...

«La goletta, un giorno, finalmente, apparve: ma non si fermò all'atollo, non fece scalo, non gettò l'àncora al pontile del villaggio. Apparve alla punta Matibenà, ma anziché prendere la rotta della *pass* per gettare l'àncora nell'acqua della laguna, prese una rotta bordeggiante e sfiorò lentamente costa e barriera di corallo...»

Secondo il racconto di Tetoèa, quando fu chiaro che quella goletta non si sarebbe fermata, la popolazione dell'atollo si precipitò sulla riva dell'oceano, agitando segnali. Tutti avevano bisogno di quella nave, per offrire raccolti di *coprah* in cambio di viveri, di medicine e di indumenti.

«Per questo, uomini e donne corrono lungo la costa, gridano.» Tetoèa vive intensamente il suo racconto. «Sperano di poter fermare la corsa della goletta: un tentativo inutile. La piccola nave ha un carico destinato altrove e scompare oltre la linea dell'orizzonte... Fu allora che Tanai, che voleva acquistare i sacchi di terra per piantare l'*urù*, costruirsi una casa e sposarsi con Tihatiaà, una ragazza del villaggio, ebbe un'idea impossibile.» Tetoèa dice in polinesiano *pohinò*, a significare tutto quanto è illogico, folle. «E sai qual era l'idea impossibile? Era quella di andar da solo a cercar la terra nelle Isole Alte, e di andarci con una *pahi*, una piroga, che lui stesso avrebbe costruito. Tanai era un giovane deciso e non cambiò idea. In meno di un mese, con l'aiuto dei fratelli, costruì una lunga imbarcazione a bilanciere come quelle dei tempi antichi: e anche l'albero per la vela e il grande governale erano tagliati come quelli delle barche di un tempo. Tanai battezzò *Manu-temiti-moana* (gabbiano-dell'altomare-profondo) la sua *pahi*; un tempo si dava un nome proprio a ogni parte della piroga: anche la vela, anche il bilanciere, la prua e la poppa, avevano un nome... io non ricordo quei nomi... ricordo solo che Tanai lasciò l'atollo con vento freddo. Un vento difficile,» mi spiega Tetoèa continuando il suo racconto «difficile, ma favorèvole per raggiungere l'arcipelago delle Isole Alte, a levante: Tahiti, o Moorea, o Huahine, le isole dove Tanai voleva raccogliere la terra.»

«Chissà quante avventure ha vissuto Tanai nel suo viaggio...» suggerisco a Tetoèa.

«Molte. Quella che a me piace di più, vuoi sapere qual è?... quella della *fafarua*.»

Le *fafarua* sono le mantas e, poiché Tetoèa è pescatore, è logico sia questo l'episodio che lo affascina più di ogni altro. Quando ha finito l'ultima sigaretta me lo racconta gesticolando con entrambe le mani, per imitare il movimento delle due grandi ali della più grande razza di tutti i mari.

«Sai, durante il suo viaggio di ritorno,» mi racconta «Tanai non trovava più la rotta di casa. Vagava tra le isole e non le riconosceva. Una notte la sua *pahi* rimase immobile, al largo, sull'oceano in bonaccia: come noi, ora. D'un tratto, all'alba, ode l'acqua sollevarsi come per l'uscita di un mostro o di un dio. Tanai ha paura, fissa lo sguardo dove sente il rumore. E vede sotto la sua canoa una *fafarua* enorme che muove le ali come una balena può muovere la sua immensa coda; e anche la canoa di Tanai si muove: perché la *fafarua*, sotto lo scafo, s'è impigliata nella cima di prua e ora trascina l'imbarcazione senza riuscire a liberarsene. E così l'uomo, la sua barca e quella bestia hanno corso un giorno intero sull'oceano. La *fafarua* puntava all'orizzonte: dal quale, a un certo momento, apparve un'isola bassa, un atollo. Io non so se questo che si racconta sia vero o no; ma potrebbe essere accaduto realmente... Infatti una *fafarua*, se si sente presa o impigliata a un corpo galleggiante, corre dall'alto mare verso un'isola: il suo istinto le suggerisce di raggiungere i coralli per infilarsi nel loro groviglio e liberarsi. L'ho visto accadere molte volte: esemplari anche grandi, appena colpiti da un arpione, nuotano veloci verso le scogliere, per strapparsi l'arma di dosso; sono piatti e forti, passano dove non può passare una barca, né una piroga. E così riescono quasi sempre a strapparsi dal corpo l'arma appuntita con la quale si tenta di catturarli... si rovesciano nei meandri del bassofondo, riescono a fuggire.»

«È accaduto così anche nella storia di Tanai?» chiedo a Tetoèa.

«Sì, la *fafarua* trascina la canoa in una grande corsa sulle onde, poi, esausta, s'infila tra i coralli, la cima si spezza, e la canoa galleggia immobile in una calma laguna: la bestia è fuggita. Tanai si guarda attorno e s'accorge che è la sua isola, quella. La *fafarua* l'ha condotto a casa...»

Di queste avventure di Tanai attraverso l'oceano sulle confuse rotte di un difficile ritorno avrei, poi, sentito infinite versioni in tante altre isole della Polinesia orientale. Vicende come pura favola e vicende reali vissute col semplice coraggio del pescatore;

ogni volta – come quella notte sulla motobarca, ascoltando Tetoèa – nell'udire di Tanai e della sua canoa, si ridestavano in me i ricordi delle imprese dei grandi navigatori polinesiani e si riaccendeva un mio antico desiderio: tentare la realizzazione di un film proprio su quell'argomento.

«*Navigavano da oriente a occidente, dal Nord al Sud del Pacifico senza l'aiuto né di stelle né di bussole, popolando gli arcipelaghi più lontani.*» Forse già nel mio primo viaggio in Oceania, nel 1956, avevo pensato a un film sulle grandi trasmigrazioni, quei viaggi dalla Nuova Zelanda alle Marchesi, dalle Hawaii a Bora-Bora, dalle Sottovento a Pasqua su imbarcazioni di fragile legno cucito spinte dal soffio costante dei venti regolari nelle vele di pandano intrecciato. Agli inizi degli anni Sessanta avevo già iniziato a raccogliere i dati, i testi, le ipotesi che poi – completati con pazienza e nel tempo – ho radunato nel capitolo precedente. Pagine con cronache di viaggi incredibili, su distanze paragonabili a quelle che corrono da Genova alla Florida o da Venezia a Città del Capo. Rotte tracciate attraverso orizzonti marini così vasti e sconfinati, da obbligarci a ridimensionare quelli celebri di un Colombo o di un Vasco da Gama; navigatori che affrontarono le loro imprese con riserve di viveri, armamento, strumenti di navigazione ed equipaggi al cui confronto le piroghe dei trasmigratori polinesiani erano poco più di semplici tronchi di legno.

Qualche corroso vecchio resto di scafo a bilanciere, i modelli al Bishop Museum di Honolulu, e l'incontro con le vele di piroghe polinesiane ancora «vive» al vento di Huahine di Tahà avevano poi, durante un mio secondo viaggio nel Pacifico nel 1961, rinnovato il mio desiderio di affrontare il racconto dell'epopea marinaresca della Polinesia. Un desiderio che doveva finalmente prender corpo ascoltando al largo di Rangiroa, durante una notte sull'oceano, la vicenda di quell'uomo chiamato Tanai e la sua ricerca di quattro sacchi di terra. Quel racconto mi suggeriva finalmente la chiave per realizzare quanto da tempo desideravo: una libera evocazione della storia di un pescatore capace oggi di rivivere l'esperienza antica dei suoi padri. D'isola in isola in una odissea primitiva da far rivivere in un film negli anni delle conquiste astronautiche, un uomo solo con la sua vela, e noi con lui per scoprire come si possa sopravvivere alla sete e alla fame, alla solitudine, alle tempeste e alle bonacce.

Le tappe della mia personale odissea nei Mari del Sud per raccontare di Tanai e del suo viaggio sono nomi che disegnano sulla carta del Pacifico la favola di un viaggio forse durato una vita, forse solo immaginato dai cantastorie delle isole: le Galapagos, l'Isola di Pasqua, gli atolli di Mangareva, le Marchesi, l'isola vulcanica di Hilo e le spiagge abitate dai papua nelle Wallis e nelle Trobriand.

Non penso di fare qui la cronaca ordinata dei miei mesi di lavoro sul mare per quel film, che è stato il terzo (ma non l'ultimo) del mio «ciclo polinesiano».

Avevo realizzato nel 1955-'56 l'*Ultimo paradiso* (titolo giustamente contestato, e che m'era stato imposto dai produttori del film), nel 1960-'61 *Tikoyo e il suo pescecane*, aiutato da Italo Calvino (ne narrerò più avanti). Quello che avrei poi intitolato *Oceano* fu il terzo.

Al quale nel 1976 ne seguì un altro (*Fratello Mare*) ove ho contrapposto scene di vita polinesiana filmate nel 1955 con altre datate 1975.

Ai quattro lungometraggi, in cui il documento filmato e la ricostruzione narrativa si innestavano volta per volta in un «*mio modo*» di narrare, si sono alternate altre esperienze di lavoro dedicato a soli programmi culturali per la televisione, come *I viaggi del Capitano Cook* del 1965 e *I mari dell'uomo* del 1973.

Insomma, molti temi, molti itinerari, tante isole, un bagaglio sempre più complesso di esperienze.

Ma in questo capitolo, avendo premesso tante annotazioni sull'epopea delle trasmigrazioni, è dell'esperienza vissuta di sequenza in sequenza nel film *Oceano* che vorrei scrivere. È la storia di Tanai che in alcuni momenti desidero ricordare così come essa è stata evocata davanti ai nostri occhi e ai nostri obiettivi.

Il primo problema che ebbi da risolvere per vivere questa avventura fu quello di trovare una grande canoa oceanica. Non ne esistono più in Polinesia, ma non riuscii a individuarne nemmeno l'ombra già nel 1970. Fortunatamente, vent'anni fa sopravvivevano ancora mastri d'ascia e carpentieri capaci di tagliare uno scafo, disegnare una vela, equilibrare un bilanciere e montare un albero e la sua attrezzatura di cime. Ne trovai uno a Tahiti; si chiamava Tehuirà Apoi e si disse disposto a costruire per me, con l'aiuto di due assistenti, l'imbarcazione di tipo ideale per navigare in oceano, governata da un solo marinaio (e quindi non eccessivamente grande ma particolarmente robusta).

La costruzione dello scafo, una volta d'accordo con Tehuirà sulle dimensioni e il prezzo, richiede un certo tempo; un arco di settimane durante le quali vedo riaffiorare, in filigrana, cento aspetti di un modo di vivere, di una mentalità ancora polinesiani: non tanto nel fatto che la canoa assomigli o meno a un modello antico, ma nei rapporti nati durante i vari momenti e di fronte ai vari problemi della costruzione.

All'ipotesi di abbattere un grande albero per scavarlo e ottenerne uno scafo dobbiamo rinunciare: tronchi della dimensione necessaria non ce ne sono ormai più a Tahiti, se non in zone inaccessibili delle montagne. Ma troviamo un vecchio scafo in legno tratto dall'albero del ferro. È della lunghezza giusta, anche se non sufficientemente profondo (a ciò si pone rimedio con due fiancate supplementari più alte, che vengono «cucite» con corda di *napè*). Albero, remo e pagaia, grande governale, le due vele, i tre arpioni e gli altri strumenti di pesca si trovano presso questa o quella famiglia, da questo o da quel pescatore. E qui, alla nostra prima sorpresa di scoprire in tante case della Tahiti più urbanizzata, anche quelle ove già è installato il televisore, pezzi diversi e rari usati nella vita quotidiana di un tempo, in apparente abbandono ma in realtà custoditi con molta cura, se ne aggiunge una seconda e maggiore: le famiglie interpellate per la raccolta delle parti necessarie a completare la nostra canoa oceanica ci prestano quanto occorre e accettano, o pretendono, in cambio un regalo; ma si tratta sempre, appunto, di prestiti: nessuno di loro pensa, nemmeno lontanamente, di *venderci* gli oggetti che abbiamo scelto.

Nasce così un'imbarcazione in «condominio»: a Paulò di Faa paghiamo una cifra per il vecchio scafo; e una a sua madre per una zucca vuota, specialmente adatta a conservare il pesce pescato; a Tehei si deve qualcosa per gli arpioni; a suo cugino, al nipote di suo cugino, a Marie Thérèse e a Vahiria e ai loro *feti* (parenti prossimi) un tanto per i pali del bilanciere e per gli occhialetti polinesiani, i *tiitia* usati nelle isole dei Mari del Sud per la pesca in immersione.

L'amico Jean Bodini, l'esperto nautico della nostra équipe, è ligure. È lui, sommando esperienze mediterranee a quelle polinesiane, ad aver coordinato tutto il lavoro; all'ultimo momento ha scovato a casa di una vecchia matriarca di Papeete, madame Terorotua, un fiocco di penne di gallo lungo circa tre metri: è stato cucito recentemente, ma l'idea è antica. Sventolava sulle cime degli alberi delle grandi piroghe da trasmigrazione per indicare forza e direzione del vento, come si vede nelle stampe e nei disegni dei primi viaggiatori europei giunti a Tahiti. Lo issiamo sull'albero della canoa di Tanai, quando l'imbarcazione è pronta a prendere il mare, il giorno del varo; quando vivivamo gli istanti magici in cui il passato si muta in presente, il racconto diventa realtà.

La piroga è appena entrata in acqua e già si apre la vela, il vento la tende. Un primo soffio, da poppa, le imprime una leggerissima spinta; poi un secondo, solo un poco più forte e la prua si rizza tra il filo delle onde e l'orizzonte. Questa presa di contatto è breve e delicata così come il gesto del piroghiere nell'afferrare il governale, la grande lama di legno con funzioni di timone, che si imbraccia e si tiene come fosse un remo. Il governale corregge la direzione dello scafo con semplici inclinazioni regolate dall'esperienza tattile della mano che l'impugna, quasi la pelle dell'uomo e il mare riescano a comunicare ritmo e modo di comportarsi attraverso vibrazioni continue; passa, dalla superficie marina al braccio del piroghiere, un fremito costante ma sempre diverso, lo stesso che tende le onde dell'oceano; conoscere il senso, il volere di quei messaggi significa possedere parte del segreto antico dei grandi trasmigratori.

Sono trascorsi pochi minuti dal suo varo e già l'imbarcazione esce dalla laguna, dove l'onda del Pacifico giunge gonfia e tesa anche nei giorni di calma e si infrange – ai due lati della *pass* aperta come un canale – sulla barriera corallina in una muraglia di spuma. È in quel punto che avviene il suo primo, rude contatto con l'oceano.

Dietro l'alta linea bianca dell'onda oceanica appaiono, a tratti, la vela e il fiocco. S'alzano e s'abbracciano nel ritmo del mare aperto che noi non riusciamo a vedere, coperto com'è dal confine spumeggiante che ci divide dal «largo».

Poi il timoniere vira sottovento, stringe di bolina e si riaffaccia nel canale della *pass*: è trascorsa un'ora, forse neppure.

La nostra *pahi* a vela, finalmente, è pronta alla sua lunga avventura.

Durante il periodo in cui il lavoro per costruire e montare la piroga aveva occupato gran parte delle nostre giornate, m'era capitato di visitare il «mercato del venerdì» di Papeete nella piazza dove nel 1970 sopravviveva ancora quanto è stato demolito per costruire orrendi edifici in cemento armato. Era un edificio a forma di capannone, con legni e lamiere ancora dipinti in celeste, bianco e giallo, con le grandi tende scucite e strappate, e pesanti cancelli in ghisa a dividere i vari settori delle contrattazioni per il pesce, la frutta, e gli altri prodotti portati al mercato dalle campagne e dai villaggi dell'isola e presentati in vendita ogni settimana, all'alba del venerdì.

A quel mercato, andavo spesso, nelle settimane di preparazione al film, per cercare volti, caratteri.

Mi servono per i diversi incontri che il protagonista del racconto avrà nelle varie isole dove lo condurrà la sua odissea. Ed è proprio Tanai che trovo, o quanto meno l'immagine del suo volto, non appena la luce del giorno inonda piazza e strada ove il mercato è già aperto dalle prime ore della notte. In fondo alla strada centrale, vicino a un magazzino cinese, si ferma una vecchia camionetta; ne escono tre tahitiani, che innalzano una specie di palchetto e issano un telone dipinto con le immagini di una vicenda che non tardo a riconoscere come quella del «mio» personaggio.

Un telone con la storia di Tanai dipinta; un cantastorie che la racconta: quanto ho davanti a me, mi ricorda subito qualcosa di analogo, l'incontro nel 1964, in un piccolo villaggio delle Sottovento, con un certo William, conosciuto in tutta la Polinesia centrale come un grande *tusitala* (narratore di storie) e come il più forte bevitore di birra di tutti i tempi. Anche da William avevo ascoltato raccontare – all'ombra di una casa a Huhaine, davanti a pochi paesani seduti a terra – la leggenda di Tanai.

Sono passati tanti anni da allora, e mi accorgo (ascoltando e paragonandolo) quanto il racconto di Tanai, pur restando sostanzialmente lo stesso, rispecchi in molti episodi i mutamenti di usi, costumi e gusti intervenuti in questi anni nel Pacifico orientale; il racconto udito nel '64 (così come quello udito ancor prima, da Tetoèa nel '61) era un tessuto di vicende destinate a pescatori, gente dello stesso mondo delle piccole isole ove la storia di Tanai era nata; il secondo; quello della Papeete negli anni Settanta, è invece un intreccio preparato per un pubblico già in parte smaliziato dagli spettacoli televisivi e cinematografici.

Accanto agli episodi il cui contenuto è immutabile – come le avventure in oceano del giovane trasmigratore, il suo errare di atollo in atollo, il suo sbarco alla lontana terra di Pasqua, la sua fame, la sua sete e infine la sua prigionia nell'isola dei papua – nell'agosto del 1969 ascoltai dal cantastorie di Papeete nuovi episodi, tutti «moderni». La variante che più mi sconcertò era nel finale: un disegno mostrava Tanai di ritorno alla sua isola con la terra per il prezioso *urù*; all'orizzonte si intravedeva l'isola di corallo sulla quale, con gioia, egli riconosceva la linea delle capanne del villaggio natale; verso quell'apparizione Tanai vagava felice, a bordo della sua canoa. Ma nel quadro successivo il narratore ci informava – e il disegno del suo cartellone lo confermava – che il villaggio non era più tale; i *farè* erano, sì, come Tanai li aveva lasciati tanto tempo prima, ma entro le fragili e fresche pareti di cocco intrecciato non abitavano più i pescatori puamutu e le loro famiglie; le capanne erano state trasformate in bungalow di un qualsiasi Club Méditerranée.

Le abitano turisti di ogni provenienza, dattilografe parigine e grassi californiani in vacanza esotica. I polinesiani locali non sono scomparsi; vengono chiamati aborigeni e servono i turisti guadagnando piacevolmente – e senza i rischi di un tempo – quanto occorre per vivere, anzi qualcosa di più. Suonano la chitarra, cucinano il pesce sul corallo, danzano, fanno l'amore a richiesta, infilano collane di denti di pescecane...; Tanai, secondo il cantastorie di Papeete, a quella nuova realtà si adatta subito, conosce una bionda nordica, dimentica l'albero del pane e vive felice e contento facendo l'istruttore di surf.

Un'altra variante del racconto si innestava nel ben conosciuto ordine cronologico delle vicende narrate; e riguardava l'episodio culmine di tutta la storia, quello in cui Tanai raccoglieva finalmente la terra per la quale aveva attraversato l'oceano; anche il racconto ascoltato a Papeete, a questo punto, divergeva profondamente dalla tradizione secondo la quale Tanai raccolse quella terra, dopo cento peripezie, in un'Isola Alta, aiutato da pescatori come lui. Nel racconto «cittadino» invece, la «sua» terra Tanai tenta di raccoglierla in un giardino pubblico; gli capita, infatti, di arrivare a Tahiti e di entrare con la sua canoa in un porto pieno di navi, anziché in una baia semideserta; dopo aver ormeggiato la sua imbarcazione tra yacht e golette, Tanai attraversa il lungomare, rischia d'esser travolto da auto e da pullman e raggiunge un praticello, fitto di alberi, punto eccellente per raccogliervi quanto fu lo scopo del suo viaggio. S'accinge così, con le mani, a scavare una buca al centro dell'aiuola – proprio sotto il monumento a Bougainville, scopritore di Tahiti – e con la terra estratta riempie i suoi sacchi. Secondo il racconto del cantastorie, quella strana operazione, il succinto *pareo* indossato dal ragazzo in una cittadina dagli abitanti tutti vestiti in camicia e pantaloni, sono elementi tali da attirare l'attenzione dei passanti. Tanai viene arrestato e, in attesa che lo si possa rispedire alla sua isola, vive l'esistenza dei carcerati di Tahiti, coltivando il giardino e i fiori del palazzo del governatore e degli altri edifici pubblici. Questo lavoro è certamente faticoso – disse al suo pubblico il cantastorie – ma gli offre, infine!, l'occasione di avere sottomano quanta terra vuole. Il che induce Tanai a riempirne quattro sacchi, a tentare (questa volta con fortuna) la fuga, recuperando la sua canoa, riaffrontando l'oceano, e tornando finalmente alla sua isola.

L'incontro con il cantastorie del mercato di Papeete e il confronto tra la sua narrazione e la versione ascoltata anni prima furono per me un'ennesima conferma di quanto siano mutati in questi anni i gusti, la vita, gli interessi nel mondo delle isole; ma mi aiutarono anche a scoprire che nei polinesiani d'oggi sopravvive, seppur a stento, l'amore per le proprie tradizioni, anche in chi abita ormai da diverse generazioni in città. Una storia come quella di Tanai subisce varianti di moda; ma continua a essere narrata per le strade, e un pubblico forse non più numerosissimo ma sempre attento la segue.

Nelle vie fragorose d'auto e di motociclette quei cantastorie, aiutati dal microfono e da qualche altoparlante a transistor, sono l'ultima ombra dei mitici *huarè-po* (coloro-che-ricordano-tutto-nella-mente), e personaggi della Polinesia antica che i primi navigatori vedevano ogni notte camminare lentamente attorno agli altari e ripetere ad alta voce le genealogie, le storie dei re, le vicende delle trasmigrazioni. Oggi l'*huarè-po* si muove con un camioncino, e s'aiuta con disegni che ricordano i racconti a fumetti o lo schermo televisivo; ma il personaggio è, in fondo, lo stesso.

E così come vive l'antico *huarè-po* nella figura del cantastorie in camionetta e camicia a fiori, altre ombre possono scoprirsi nel controluce di un lungo soggiorno in Polinesia, se si abita nei villaggi e si divide la vita quotidiana delle famiglie dei pescatori. È quanto abbiamo tentato noi – ogni volta che ci è stato possibile – alloggiando nelle capanne delle località più remote di ogni isola e dividendo la giornata con le famiglie divenute presto le nostre più preziose collaboratrici.

A Tahà, nelle isole Sottovento, ci ospita un gigantesco vecchio pescatore. Solo il suo nome è «importato»: Michel Garnier; per il resto sembra il leggendario Maui, «l'uomo-creatore-di-isole» della mitologia polinesiana. Da quando ci ha visti arrivare al suo villaggio portando al nostro seguito la canoa di Tanai, Garnier non ci lascia un momento; si informa, riesce a sapere le vicende del nostro film, discute, consiglia.

«Deve attraversare l'oceano, quello scafo?» mi aveva chiesto il primo giorno, osservando la nostra canoa.

«Sì, di isola in isola, così è la storia che vogliamo filmare.»

«Con la goletta certo è più facile... Ma con la canoa non è mai stato impossibile. Solo difficile.»

«Molto difficile?»

«*Grand-père* di mia moglie [lui andava a Papeete per vendere la *coprah*] diceva a tutti "è difficile l'oceano".»

«Lui, a Papeete, andava in canoa?»

«Sì, in canoa. C'eran già le golette, ma ancora molti navigavano a vela. E lui, *grand-père*, odiava la goletta; per via dei soldi. Diceva che a spedire la *coprah* con le golette tutto il guadagno andava al trasportatore; al coltivatore restava ben poco.»

«Allora?»

«Allora lui per Papeete partiva a vela. Aspettava il vento giusto, metteva in acqua un doppio scafo, sceglieva quattro amici e salpava.»

Qualche giorno dopo questa prima conversazione (nel frattempo siamo diventati inquilini della sua casa), abbiamo tutto il tempo di parlare con lui. Mangiamo assieme, ogni sera, sotto un gigantesco mango.

«Così, *grand-père* andava da qui a Tahiti in canoa a vela...»

«Sì, certo. Lui e i suoi amici. Tutti grandi marinai.»

«Sino a Tahiti non toccavano mai terra?»

«Dipendeva dal vento, naturalmente. Ma, se procedevano dritti dritti, non impiegavano molto tempo.»

«Una settimana, penso.»

«Talvolta meno. Se il tempo era cattivo occorreva invece di più, molto di più. Una volta si pensò addirittura che l'oceano avesse inghiottito *grand-père* e il suo catamarano a vela... Invece, dopo un mese, eccolo di ritorno al villaggio: si era fermato a Huhaine, dai cugini, in attesa di un vento favorevole.»

«Poteva telegrafare... o forse il telegrafo non c'era ancora?»

«Come? Certo che c'era. Quei viaggi lui li faceva una quarantina di anni fa, forse una cinquantina, non di più; a quell'epoca il telegrafo era già installato in tutte le isole. Ma lui non lo usava mai. Costava troppo. A spedire i telegrammi, diceva, s'arricchivano le poste e...»

Quel *grand-père* era certo una bella tempra di marinaio, ma anche un risparmiatore non da poco.

«Sai cosa mi diceva *grand-père*?» mi chiede Garnier un giorno in cui noi prepariamo senza fretta una scena in mare.

«Avrà detto di certo che era bene risparmiare denaro...»

«No, no. È morto poverissimo. Lui spendeva tutto quel che guadagnava. In banca non metteva nulla (come invece hanno sempre fatto tutti i coltivatori di *coprah*, da quando nella nostra isola c'è una banca). Lui diceva sempre: metter soldi in banca vuol dire arricchire i banchieri e impoverire i coltivatori...»

Garnier ride, pensando al bisnonno e mi chiede: «Quando il vostro eroe è in alto mare, solo, senza strumenti e cerca un'isola, un approdo, una terra ove riparare, come fa?».

Gli ripeto quanto ho letto a proposito dei navigatori polinesiani, e circa i loro vari sistemi d'orientamento. Tutto questo, Garnier lo conosce bene. C'è però qualcosa di più, e di diverso, che vuole spiegarmi: un «qualcosa» che gli insegnò, appunto, *grand-père*. A lui l'avevano detto i suoi nonni...

Mi attendo la descrizione di un sistema complesso, forse astronomico o cabalistico, oppure – chissà – esoterico, magico...

«Sai, coi maiali» mi dice.

«Maiali?»

«Maiali, sì, quelli piccoli delle nostre isole. Chi partiva per un lungo viaggio in oceano ne caricava sempre una decina in canoa; come riserva di cibo, naturalmente. Ma anche per trovar terra.»

Debbo aver la faccia certamente stupita, anzi incredula. Così Garnier insiste.

«I maiali servivano se il capopiroghiere era fuori rotta... Sai, i maiali hanno un particolare fiuto per "sentire" l'odore della terra: la sentono anche a decine di miglia di distanza...»

«E cosa fanno?»

«Nuotano» mi risponde Garnier. E mi ripete quanto aveva udito un giorno raccontare da «chi ricordava».

Sentendosi perduti e dopo aver tentato tutti i sistemi possibili per orientarsi – col sole, con le correnti, col volo degli uccelli o col guizzare di branchi migratori di pesci stagionali – gli uomini di un'antica canoa alla deriva decidevano di ricorrere a un'ultima speranza di salvezza, i maiali. Ne gettavano a mare uno; se l'animale, nuotando, mostrava di annaspare fra le onde a caso, muovendosi senza orientamento attorno alla canoa, l'equipaggio comprendeva di aver ben poche possibilità di trovare un approdo. Se invece il piccolo maiale, dopo un'inevitabile incertezza, puntava verso una direzione precisa, un filo di fiducia poteva subentrare alla disperazione: c'era da sperare che il maialetto avesse sentito «odor di terra» di un'isola lontana: era questione di seguirlo, contando sulle sue forze, augurandosi che lo potessero sostenere sino a quando, all'orizzonte, fosse apparsa una conferma, una certezza.

«Sai,» mi dice Garnier concludendo il suo discorso «molte volte, qui nel Pacifico, sei vicino a un'isola ma non la vedi, perché se si tratta di un atollo la linea della costa è più bassa della cresta delle onde. Perciò qui servono anche altri sensi, per esempio il fiuto oltre la vista, per trovare un approdo.»

Circa due mesi dopo navigavo in pieno oceano, in un tratto di mare tra i due atolli di Rangiroa e Apataki e ripensavo a quanto mi aveva detto Garnier.

Mi trovavo in alto mare con due barche a motore («Pura follia! sono troppo piccole...» aveva gridato dal pontile, vedendoci partire il «Delegato» di Avatoru, unica autorità ufficiale del paesino ove avevamo base). Osservavo il lento muoversi della nostra canoa protagonista. Avevo scelto quel tratto di oceano, perché unico a offrirci la possibilità di lavorare in mare aperto, con la relativa sicurezza di due rive non molto distanti, due atolli quasi a proteggerci da quella immensità d'orizzonte, fascino e angoscia di ogni navigatore con battelli di misura modesta, senza punti di riferimento. C'è subito da aggiungere che persino una petroliera gigante da duecentomila tonnellate è «misura modesta» di fronte alla dimensione innaturale di un oceano ove al ritmo regolare di onde gonfie come colline d'acqua s'alternano (anche nei giorni detti dai marinai di «calma piatta») onde «anomale» di cui non si può tacere lo sgomento che incutono con quel loro aspetto di muraglie violacee aggressive. Attraverso quelle onde, sfumate alla cima in ricami bianchi da un vento leggero, la nostra piroga, a vela spiegata, appare e scompare, mentre con lentezza tranquilla sale e scende lungo il suo cammino liquido; ogni tanto, attraverso quelle colline d'acqua tento di vedere le due «linee» emergenti degli atolli, uno a oriente e l'altro a occidente; e capisco quanto Garnier mi aveva asserito (e quanto ho letto nelle pagine di altri navigatori dei Mari del Sud di un tempo e di oggi) per quello che riguarda le difficoltà di scorgere le isole, appena d'un soffio emergenti dal mare. Facile il punto di riferimento con gli *amers* e le cime delle isole alte e con quelle vulcaniche; impossibile invece scorgere un atollo se non conoscendo quei segreti che sono propri dei marinai polinesiani.

Segreti di cui, forse, il più famoso è quello della «nuvola verde». Me l'ha svelato Mosè Salomon, armatore e comandante del *Maristella* di Papeete, grande conoscitore del Pacifico meridionale. Le acque delle lagune interne creano umidità con la loro continua evaporazione, per cui un atollo ha sempre la «sua» nube a sovrastarlo; quella nube si distingue dalle altre sospese sull'oceano perché ha un riflesso nella parte inferiore: la laguna specchia il verde smeraldo delle sue acque come un proiettore lucente su un immenso schermo opaco. E se questa «nube verde» indica un'isola riflettendone il colore nel cielo, è ancora il cielo il punto di riferimento di un terzo sistema per orientarsi: il volo degli uccelli migratori marini. Me ne parla Patrick Chenou, di Papeete, polinesiano da parte di padre, dal quale ha assorbito quanto un uomo delle isole conserva in antiche conoscenze nautiche: a Patrick, quell'eredità di cognizioni è molto utile perché il suo tempo lo passa tutto alla pesca d'altura. Per questa sua esperienza, unica, gli abbiamo chiesto di collaborare al nostro film, organizzandoci battute di pesca. Così succede che una volta, in alto mare, il discorso cade su come potrebbe orientarsi un pescatore senza bussola. Patrick mi mostra uno stormo di *sule* nere alte nel cielo e mi spiega:

«Un pescatore sperduto, senza bussola e senza indicazioni possibili per orientarsi verso terre emerse, è sul volo degli uccelli che si regola. Deve tener d'occhio tutte le evoluzioni dei suoi alati compagni di viaggio con i quali divide eguale solitudine nell'identica fatica: cercar cibo in alto mare. Il pescatore sa che durante tutto il giorno il volo degli uccelli marini è irregolare, è una continua perlustrazione in attesa di piombare su qualunque preda possibile, piccola o grande, apparsa alla superficie; ma quando comincerà il tardo pomeriggio, *sule* e gabbiani potranno molto chiaramente indicare la via di casa al pescatore solitario. Se si poseranno tra le onde, restandovi a galleggiare immobili, vorrà dire che di terre vicine non ce ne sono; se invece, interrompendo il loro volo basso e a cerchi concentrici tra le onde, saliranno alti nel cielo e voleranno precisi verso una direzione, vorrà certo dire che si dirigono verso una terra sulla quale sanno di potersi posare per la notte o dove, addirittura, hanno i loro nidi.»

Patrick m'indica una seconda volta le *sule* ad ali tese sopra le nostre barche.

«I loro lunghi colli tesi sono gli aghi dell'unica bussola dei polinesiani...» mi dice, e distogliendo lo sguardo da loro, ritorna a tener d'occhio la canoa che continua a navigare tra le onde alte; il ragazzo al governale di poppa è intento a mantenere la vela al vento.

«L'oceano è il padre di tutte le piccole barche e le ama e le protegge» continua Patrick, con un po' di retorica, perdonabile perché sincera. «Se non fosse così, in quale modo avrebbero agito i polinesiani come lui,» e mi indica, lontano sul mare, il nostro protagonista «per popolare tutte le isole di questo orizzonte?»

È la domanda che ci ripetiamo ogni giorno, quando prendiamo il mare a fianco della canoa di Tanai e la seguiamo minuto dopo minuto, ora dopo ora, per settimane intere.

Credi di conoscere un certo numero di testi, di studi, di ricerche storiche su questo argomento delle trasmigrazioni in oceano (e in questo libro cito di essi molti estratti che riuniscono le più diverse e attendibili teorie in proposito) ma, per quanto si possa aver letto e aver compreso questa o quella spiegazione, rimane sempre forte l'emozione, molte volte l'incredulità, nel vedere una canoa di legno tenuta assieme da fibre di cocco affrontare onde capaci d'intimorire una portaerei.

«Proprio questo è uno dei segreti delle nostre canoe» mi aveva detto Garnier «perché, vedi, contro una grande nave l'onda di grandi dimensioni provoca un vero e proprio scontro tra una prua in acciaio alta decine di metri e un muro d'acqua altrettanto alto, se non di più, e certo altrettanto veloce. Invece per una piccola piroga, l'onda è una massa liquida da salire e scendere come una montagna. Su e giù tra le onde: non per infrangerle da parte a parte, ma per seguirne dolcemente la curva...»

«Per questo le vostre imbarcazioni d'alto mare non hanno chiodi e sono "cucite"?»

«Certo!... così sono elastiche, quasi snodabili. Scafo e bilanciere, in questo modo, sono saldamente uniti, pur comportandosi come due imbarcazioni diverse...»

Tetoèa, Garnier, Salomon, Patrick: ho citato alcuni nomi. Ne potrei aggiungere altri; ognuno sul tema «oceano» mi ha dato un consiglio, svelato un segreto, aperto a un'ipotesi o a una curiosità. Uomini della Polinesia d'oggi, che vanno per mare con barche a motore, indossano blue-jeans, camicie a fiori, parlano più facilmente il francese o l'inglese dell'antica lingua isolana; a vederli bere una birra al banco di uno snack-bar, o rispondere al telefono o lavorare negli aeroporti o ai distributori di benzina, diresti che anche in loro, come nel paesaggio e nell'habitat naturale e umano dell'Oceania, ogni legame con il passato sia cancellato per sempre. Invece, proprio come un terreno anonimo può nascondere resti di tempi remoti attraverso i quali si riesce a interpretare senso, ritmo, strutture di culture scomparse, così nell'animo o nel carattere di molti polinesiani d'oggi si possono scoprire ricordi di un passato talvolta luminoso, spesso sconosciuto, sempre umanissimo e vivo. In questo, dunque, il mondo dell'Oceania non è del tutto morto; l'«archeologia nell'uomo», questo radiografare i caratteri, scandagliare i ricordi, stimolare i racconti nel tentativo di riportare al tempo presente quanto si riteneva ormai dimenticato per sempre, sembra finisca spesso col confermare una sensazione portandola a poco a poco al grado di certezza: nell'animo del più «cittadino» fra i polinesiani di oggi può sopravvivere, in varia misura e in differenti valori, il senso dell'antico rapporto tra la loro natura e la natura dell'oceano.

Ancora sullo stesso tema uomo-oceano, una delle mie maggiori sorprese è stata l'accorgermi quanto precisi e preziosi consigli mi vennero suggeriti al momento di affrontare, per il nostro film, il problema della sopravvivenza sull'oceano di un uomo solo.

Per una volta, mi veniva alla mente un paragone con il nostro mondo e la nostra gente; mi chiedevo come e cosa risponderebbero i nipoti di contadini emigrati da più di un secolo in città e quindi da tempo integrati in un meccanismo urbano implacabile, se venisse loro chiesto di risolvere un problema di semina o di potatura? Se dovessero dire con quale luna è bene imbottigliare il vino nuovo o come affrontare la siccità? Non saprebbero, credo, rispondere nulla; tutto quanto resta in loro a tre generazioni di distanza dall'ultimo nonno capace di vivere «sulla terra» è probabilmente solo un generico e quanto mai vago amore per la campagna, l'emozione di un paesaggio o di un sapore.

A distanza generazionale. ancor maggiore (sono almeno centocinquant'anni da quando in Polinesia non s'affrontano più, nemmeno in piccola scala, imprese trasmigratorie in canoa) la gente dell'Oceania mi pare invece conservi, almeno latente, il ricordo di un comportamento, di certe tecniche, di certe soluzioni d'emergenza: l'esperienza quotidiana, insomma, di un tempo tanto profondamente diverso da quello attuale. Ho scritto *ricordo latente*, perché può emergere d'un tratto, in caso di necessità.

Uturoa è squallida cittadina di cemento e lamiera nell'isola di Raiatea, dove si concentra il commercio di tutto l'arcipelago della Società; i polinesiani lavorano qui nei magazzini e nelle imprese di trasporto e sono dominati dalla comunità cinese. A Raiatea, i cinesi oltre a possedere la maggioranza degli stabili ed essere gli intestatari della quasi totalità del denaro depositato nella banca locale, gestiscono bar e locali ove ogni notte si consuma birra a casse in ambienti da piccola provincia europea, bigliardini e flippers compresi. Al porto arrivano quotidianamente decine di piccole golette – tutte di proprietà cinese – per scaricare le merci dell'arcipelago, e grandi navi per caricare quelle stesse merci e portarle presso mercati lontani. Al di là del molo, il mare di Raiatea credo sia il meno invitante del Pacifico meridionale: sporco, grigio, non tagliato dai colori di una vela, né punteggiato di canoe da pesca, o da qualunque altro segno di un rapporto diretto tra uomo e oceano.

Siamo a Raiatea quando, alla vigilia del Natale '61, due ragazzi di una ventina d'anni chiedono in prestito a un commerciante del porto una piccola motobarca con motore a nafta; un amico giunto da Tahiti ha portato loro in regalo due canne da pesca e i ragazzi vorrebbero provare se è vero che il mare, secondo quanto si dice, sia «al largo» tanto ricco di prede. E poiché quel giorno il tempo è tranquillo ottengono l'imbarcazione desiderata, con la quale di buon mattino si spingono al largo per il loro primo tentativo di pesca; hanno, in caso servisse, una latta di nafta di scorta per il ritorno. Ma né la sera stessa, come previsto, né l'indomani quel ritorno ha luogo. Benché sia il giorno di Natale e gli equipaggi, tutti a terra, siano difficilmente rintracciabili, una goletta salpa dal porto per ritrovare i due ragazzi alla deriva; e alla prima, se ne unisce una seconda, infine una terza.

Avvisato per radio, partecipa alla ricerca, il giorno dopo, anche un aereo militare francese e l'allarme viene segnalato a diverse navi in transito nella zona.

Intanto il tempo si guasta, l'oceano rinforza, s'ingrossa e le speranze da poche diventano nulle: i due non avevano imbarcato né cibo né tantomeno riserve da bere, e si suppone che un'imbarcazione così piccola non sia probabilmente in grado di reggere un oceano infuriato; è pertanto considerata perduta, dopo una settimana di ricerche. La cittadina è in lutto, non ci sono feste per Capodanno.

Partecipiamo anche noi a quel dolore collettivo; poi, lasciata l'isola alla fine di gennaio, l'episodio resta solo come un ricordo, un doloroso ricordo.

Passano i mesi di febbraio e di marzo. In aprile siamo a Tahiti, a Papeete. Stiamo attraversando la città quando vediamo d'un tratto la gente per le strade correre verso il porto. Non sappiamo cosa accade, ma a Tahiti, e in tutta la Polinesia, bisogna sempre lasciarsi portare dagli avvenimenti ponendosi il minimo possibile di domande; così corriamo anche noi nella stessa direzione. Giungiamo al porto nel momento in cui attracca una nave trasporto proveniente – ci dicono – da Tubuai e da altre isole Australi. A rimorchio trascina un piccolo battello, oggetto di quella tumultuosa curiosità.

Dai discorsi confusi attorno a noi comprendiamo trattarsi del battello perdutosi qualche mese prima al largo di Rangiroa.

Tocca terra dopo centoventisei giorni di deriva. I due ragazzi sono salvi, ma li intravediamo appena tra la folla, e solo a sera riusciamo ad ascoltare la loro vicenda. Ce la racconta Émile Goupil, nostro factotum di Papeete, testimone delle dichiarazioni dei due quasi-naufraghi, alle autorità portuali.

«Sai,» mi dice Goupil «stanno benissimo...»

«Dove li hanno trovati?»

«Al largo delle Australi... se non incrociavano la goletta arrivavano ai ghiacci del Polo Sud!... Non ci sono più isole, né navi dopo le Australi: solo oceano aperto sino ai ghiacci...»

«Un "fuori rotta" senza speranza.»

«E invece la speranza non l'hanno mai persa... dicono d'essersi salvati proprio per questo... A bordo avevano una chitarra; e hanno sempre suonato e cantato...»

A questa battuta di Goupil le nostre voci si accavallano e si confondono:

«Cosa mangiavano?»

«E cosa avevano da bere?...»

«Non avevano viveri di scorta, vero?»

Abbiamo aggredito Émile con domande concrete, vista la sua propensione, del tutto tahitiana, a voler credere e far credere che andando alla deriva per quattro mesi la salvezza possa venire dal saper suonare una chitarra.

Ma Émile ha ascoltato il racconto dei naufraghi e può rispondterci su tutto senza raccogliere il tono polemico delle nostre domande, e così abbiamo un riassunto diretto di quanto narrato dai due giovani alle autorità portuali e ai giornalisti.

Per mangiare se l'erano cavata con la pesca; avevano lenze e ami ma poiché inizialmente non sapevano pescare, gli ami li avevano perduti subito; ne hanno poi fatti altri, curvando e tagliando un coperchio di latta trovato a bordo.

«E cosa pescavano?»

«Di tutto, hanno detto. Ma soprattutto *bonitos*.»

«Li mangiavano crudi?»

«Certo, questo tutti i polinesiani lo fanno, anche noi in città.»

«Hanno pescato sempre?»

«Sì, e io credo di capire il perché...» ci spiega Goupil «...il loro battello andava alla deriva certamente portato da una corrente;

non so quale, ma immagino fosse calda. Infatti li ha portati dalle acque tropicali di Raiatea verso le Australi dove è sempre freddo. E quando si naviga nelle acque di una corrente calda si hanno buone possibilità di trovarsi in compagnia dei *bonitos*.»

«Perché?»

«Perché il plancton viaggia con le acque tiepide e con lui vanno i pesci piccoli e con i pesci piccoli vanno i *bonitos*, per mangiarseli...»

«Loro, questo, non lo sapevano, però...»

«No, ma è chiaro che l'hanno presto capito. Infatti hanno detto di essere riusciti, dopo qualche giorno di deriva, a mettere insieme uno straccio di vela e prendere il vento. Ma si sono accorti che appena l'imbarcazione sembrava essere portata da quel modesto panno teso fra i due remi, loro non pescavano più...»

«Evidentemente...»

«...Evidentemente il vento andava in direzione opposta a quella della corrente e li portava lontano dai branchi di pesci... E così tra andare lentamente verso nord, cioè verso casa, ma non mangiare, e andare verso sud, cioè sempre più lontano, ma con cibo, hanno scelto la seconda soluzione... È stata una intuizione giusta.»

Abbiamo ascoltato Goupil per l'intero tempo della colazione, e ci resta ancora da sapere come i due ragazzi hanno risolto l'altro problema di fondo di chi tenta di sopravvivere in oceano: riuscire a bere. Partendo per quell'odissea involontaria, i due avevano portato a bordo una bottiglia di birra (e già la sera del primo giorno di deriva quella bottiglia era vuota). Presto torturati dal desiderio, dalla necessità di bere, i due non tardarono ad accorgersi di quanto li poteva aiutare l'umidità notturna, quelle gocce d'acqua dolce che si depositano su ogni imbarcazione nelle ore precedenti il sorgere del sole. Così al terzo giorno di deriva tesero il cappuccio in tela impermeabile del motore di traverso allo scafo; e al mattino l'umidità, condensatasi e scivolata al centro dell'improvvisato serbatoio, formava una pozzetta di liquido potabile; all'incirca il quantitativo d'un bicchiere.

«Poco, se lo si deve dividere in due, per un intero giorno.»

«Sì, ma quanto basta per non morire, se si ha la costanza, durante le ore calde, di immergere continuamente il proprio corpo in mare... Comunque, è certo che con il caldo del Pacifico meridionale, un bicchiere d'acqua, per due, al giorno è poco» conviene Goupil. «Ma ci furono piogge, e in quei momenti loro riuscirono a riempire d'acqua ogni recipiente possibile... Infine, non dimentichiamolo, li ha aiutati lo *yoyò*.»

«Lo *yoyò*?» chiedo. Dopo tanti viaggi nelle isole, ancora non avevo mai sentito parlare di *yoyò*.

«È un pesce bianco, un grande cefalo d'altomare. Ne entrano, a volte, nelle lagune migliaia e non sanno più come uscirne. L'oceano ne è pieno, è una pesca facile... È ottimo da mangiare ma ancor meglio da bere.»

Ascoltiamo senza interrompere.

«A tagliarlo per lungo,» riprende «e a lasciarlo gocciolare, dal suo corpo, dopo il sangue, esce un liquido biancastro, dolciastro sufficiente a togliere la sete.»

«Chiamiamola acqua...»

«...Chiamiamola acqua che puzza di pesce, ma è pur sempre un liquido, capace di salvare la vita. E quando i due ragazzi se ne sono accorti...»

«Come se ne sono accorti?» interrompo.

«Dopo aver tagliato e appeso uno *yoyò* a un remo per farlo seccare al sole e conservarlo come riserva... Lo hanno visto gocciolare non sangue, ma qualcosa di diverso.»

Avevano così trovato un altro sistema di sopravvivenza; da mangiare e da bere con l'aiuto dell'oceano; oggi una preda all'amo, domani un acquazzone. Ascoltando le fasi di quell'avventura, mi son chiesto se il ricordare un'esperienza vissuta da altri avesse potuto infondere ai due naufraghi una fiduciosa speranza d'esser prima o poi salvati, la stessa fiduciosa speranza degli antichi migratori. Ma è una domanda che non si sarebbe comunque mai dovuta porre; loro, certamente, ne avrebbero riso; anzi non l'avrebbero nemmeno capita.

Eppure la risposta è positiva se si pensa a quel ritrovare in se stessi, a poco a poco, tante conoscenze da tempo ignorate; quel riscoprire come fare ami da una latta, una vela da due remi e due camicie; come conservare pesci pescati e acqua raccolta goccia a goccia; restando sereni, anche nei momenti peggiori.

«Sai quale fu l'unico giorno della loro deriva in oceano in cui rischiarono di lasciarsi morire?» mi chiede Goupil, concludendo.

«Quale?»

«Fu il giorno in cui l'idrovolante della marina partito alla loro ricerca passò molte volte a grande distanza e non li vide. Loro, invece, lo scorgevano in cielo, o ne sentivano il rumore... si avvicina, si allontana, si ripetevano; e per un intero giorno sperarono fino a quando il rombo si allontanò per sempre. Nel grande silenzio seguito all'ultimo volo, si sentirono veramente perduti.»

«E cosa fecero?»

«Piansero, credo. Loro però dicono di aver suonato la chitarra pensando di buttarsi in acqua e farla finita.»

Non c'è ricordo di viaggio in Polinesia che non si confonda con quello di una battuta di pesca. In particolare, la mia memoria ne conserva una vera antologia, dato che tutti i miei film «oceaniani» hanno avuto come sfondo il mare e come protagonisti dei pescatori.

Ricordo una battuta al grande *mahimahi*. Si svolse in un giorno senza sole, e fu bene; infatti quando il *mahimahi* esce dall'acqua è di un colore, poi mentre muore, le sue squame cambiano di alcune tonalità nel giro di pochi istanti. Alla luce violenta del sole questa metamorfosi cromatica non si riesce a percepirla appieno; infatti la condizione ideale per osservare questo fenomeno è che la pesca avvenga di notte e il *mahimahi* sia illuminato con una lampada; oppure che la pesca avvenga (come accadde a noi) in un giorno di cielo plumbeo. In questo caso non si perde nulla di quei mutamenti così stupendi.

Sul legno bagnato dei paiuoli, il nostro pesante *mahimahi* ebbe due guizzi di forza, di vita; e nel riflesso tra l'ombra e la luce del fondo della barca ci apparve argenteo, appena venato d'azzurro; appena giacque immobile (ma era ancora vivo: le sue branchie si aprivano e si chiudevano), le squame presero a colorarsi di un verde che si allargava a macchia come avviene quando gocce di petrolio cadono in acqua e si spandono in riflessi oleosi, cangianti.

Fu gettato a poppa, con altre prede. Quando fummo di ritorno, la sera, e venne scaricato a terra ci accorgemmo dell'ultima sua trasformazione: era diventato color oro: dalla coda lungo tutto il corpo brillava da lasciar interdetti.

Dopo il *mahimahi* e tanti *bonitos* vennero i momenti di pesca ai tonni (quasi sempre capaci di spezzare le nostre lenze e liberarsi) e a qualche isolato *barracuda* tirato fuori d'acqua con la bocca dilatata, all'amo, irta di denti come quella di un piccolo caimano. Ma i denti da metter vera paura in oceano non sono quelli dei *barracuda*; li ha visti molto da vicino, fra tutti noi, uno degli operatori del film, Vittorio: erano i denti di uno squalo-azzurro apparso un mattino a fianco della canoa attratto dalle prede catturate e ancora guizzanti.

Durante i giorni di pesca in oceano (o, per meglio dire, quando tentavamo di fotografare o filmare una battuta di pesca), avevamo l'abitudine, al momento del rientro all'atollo, di innalzare una bandierina sulla nostra motobarca, se la sortita in altomare aveva dato risultati positivi. Chi era restato a terra si rallegrava, così, in attesa di buone notizie; e questo serviva di volta in volta a tenerci su il morale. Un morale ogni giorno provato dalla vita dura che deve aspettarsi chi ha scelto d'installarsi in un seminterrato atollo; anzitutto nel piccolo villaggio, ove eravamo alloggiati, si viveva con l'assillo della mancanza d'acqua; e a quella angoscia quotidiana e generale si aggiungevano i guai di ciascuno: avevamo tutti ferite da coralli, ai piedi e alle gambe (tagli non rimarginati diventati piaghe dolorose, cause probabili di febbri incomprensibili, improvvise); qualcuno aveva sopportato attacchi gravi di dissenteria, e il nostro miglior collaboratore per le riprese subacquee era addirittura dovuto rientrare in Europa e farsi curare all'Istituto Pasteur; a turno, poi, avevamo tutti sofferto del «colpo di bambù», uno stordimento con febbre altissima dovuto a una inavvertita, troppo prolungata esposizione al sole. Questo per parlare solo delle nostre condizioni fisiche: ma è anche da aggiungere che eravamo tutti con i nervi tesi per le difficoltà di un film così semplice eppure tanto complesso per l'impegno d'affrontarlo tutto dal vero, senza artifici.

Quella «bandierina del buon risultato» era, di conseguenza, quasi un premio; e per questo chi rimaneva a terra scrutava l'orizzonte sin dal primo pomeriggio per vedere se il segnale sventolava sull'albero del battello a motore di scorta alla canoa, al suo primo apparire dal largo. E così, il giorno dello squalo-azzurro, appena apparvero dall'alto mare la canoa e la motobarca con la bandierina sulla coffa, già «sapevamo» che l'oceano aveva permesso una nuova avventura. Ci affollammo al piccolo pontile in legno; e non appena Vittorio Dragonetti – l'operatore da me incaricato, durante la lavorazione di *Oceano*, di realizzare le *sequenze difficili* del film – fu a portata di voce, cominciarono a incrociarsi le nostre domande e le sue risposte; subito sapemmo: ma solo molti mesi dopo, al nostro ritorno in Europa, trovammo nelle immagini filmate un termine di rapporto tra parole e realtà. E mi fu possibile comprendere non solo la grandezza dello squalo che Vittorio aveva filmato ma soprattutto la forza del suo attacco.

Motobarca e canoa – ci raccontò Vittorio appena a terra – avevano passato la notte all'esterno dell'atollo, in oceano, approfittando di una calma che permetteva di andare lentamente alla deriva senza essere trascinati né da correnti né da vento. L'attacco dello squalo, improvviso, iniziò quando i pesci cominciarono ad abboccare al primo chiarore del giorno, ancora tanto tenue da illuminare appena le prede guizzanti sul fondo della canoa. Il *paratà*, come i polinesiani chiamano lo squalo-azzurro, emerse dall'acqua tagliando di netto una superficie marina calma come olio e appena sfiorata dal sole obliquo e addentò una preda rimasta all'amo nel momento in cui era quasi salpata. Prima mossa aggressiva di una disputa durata, poi, più di due ore: l'uomo alla pesca e la bestia affamata, nel ruolo di eterni antagonisti d'ogni vicenda di mare, di fronte uno all'altro cercando ogni astuzia, impegnando tutte le loro forze. Lo squalo (audace sino al punto d'arrivar sottobordo non solo alla canoa ma anche alla motobarca, per mordere le esche quando una dopo l'altra venivano tratte a bordo) scandiva con i suoi attacchi quei momenti di violenza, durante i quali l'operatore riuscì a filmare la bestia così da vicino da riempire una inquadratura con i soli denti di quella rabbiosa bocca aperta e protesa.

«È proprio come raccontano» ci spiegò poi Vittorio, concludendo il racconto dell'attacco, «un pescecane quando morde orienta i suoi denti tutti in fuori... spalanca la bocca e, se vuole addentare, la sua mascella ha uno scatto e i denti si dispongono in verticale, fila contro fila, pronti a serrare, tranciare...»

Anche se non avevamo vissuto la scena né viste, ancora, le immagini filmate, un elemento preciso illustrava quelle parole: un tonnetto di rispettabili dimensioni, preda a lungo contesa tra lo squalo e il pescatore della piroga, e che Vittorio aveva riportato a riva, per provarci sino a che punto arrivava la forza di quella mascella. Con un guizzo il *paratà* l'aveva addentato verso la metà e, dove la sua bocca s'era chiusa, il tonno era tranciato, non come può essere il boccone di un carnivoro, anche feroce e anche grande, ma in ben diversa maniera. Il carnivoro di terra, un leone o una tigre, dilania; lo squalo invece taglia di netto; infatti il tonno sembrava fosse stato diviso a metà tra l'uomo e il *paratà*, come con un colpo di accetta.

«Non dimenticherò la fame cieca di quella bestia» ci disse Vittorio ritornando un giorno a parlarci di quell'incontro. «Pensate: quando in acqua non c'erano altre esche, perché il pescatore le aveva salpate tutte, il *paratà* (ancora sotto i nostri due scafi alla ricerca di qualcosa da addentare) fu attratto dal riflesso dell'elica, smaltata di bianco. Il colore l'aveva tratto in inganno e prese così ad assalirla a morsi, forsennatamente; se avessimo messo in moto il motore probabilmente avremmo dilaniato la sua bocca e il suo corpo, da ucciderlo...»

Il discorso sulla ferocia di certi squali del Pacifico non era ancora dimenticato quando un'avventura simile a quella di Vittorio toccò a un altro operatore del nostro film, Riccardo Grassetti; e fu l'occasione per filmare un attacco di un intero branco di pescecani alla canoa di Tanai ferma alla pesca in un bassofondo oceanico.

Il bassofondo oceanico: nel racconto dell'odissea di Tanai – così come essa viene narrata dai cantastorie – più volte si accenna alle soste della sua canoa in queste «acque chiuse», dove i pescatori polinesiani cercano rifugio durante i loro viaggi in alto mare. I grandi *reef*, le muraglie madreporiche che salgono dal fondo dell'oceano sino alla superficie, creano vere e proprie «barriere» a spezzare il movimento delle onde, anche quando non giungono a formare veri e propri atolli. Chiudendosi ad anello, le barriere riescono però a formare lagune di bassofondo, sempre in calma piatta assoluta; qui trovavano riparo e cibo, un tempo, i trasmigratori polinesiani; e qui ripararono le navi dei primi esploratori europei e vi si ancorano le golette, oggi, quando necessitano di una sosta e sono lontane dai loro punti di partenza e di arrivo. Lagune di rifugio e salvezza se si conosce o se ne indovina la loro posizione nell'oceano e si riesce ad attraversarne la barriera per passare dal mare aperto alle acque interne; pericolo estremo di naufragio o di morte se la manovra non riesce o se la rotta di una nave finisce, per errore di calcolo, proprio a portarla sopra l'atollo. Più l'imbarcazione è grande, più l'accostare, il manovrare e trovare il passaggio verso la laguna è difficile; per le piroghe – specie le antiche, a fondo piatto – la manovra invece doveva presentarsi meno drammatica, e la nostra canoa, costruita sul modello di quelle di un tempo, ha dimostrato l'esattezza di questa supposizione.

All'interno di queste lagune coralline si è al riparo, sì, dalle furie dell'oceano, ma il vento soffia con la stessa intensità dell'alto mare (non vi sono infatti coste né alte né basse a proteggere); l'acqua bassa non può ingrossarsi in onde pericolose, ma il basso-fondo è disseminato di *pitò*, come chiamano i polinesiani certe rocce affioranti di madrepora e che coperte di sostanze urticanti, in parte velenose, possono provocare gravi infezioni, in caso di graffi o di tagli. Sono loro, queste sostanze urticanti, a rendere i pesci delle lagune chiuse non commestibili: essi infatti, cibandosi delle madrepore dei *pitò*, diventano velenosi a loro volta, tanto da poter causare anche un'intossicazione.

Il fatto, infine, che queste lagune siano molto ricche di pesce comporta la presenza, in queste acque assai più che in alto mare, di squali grandi e piccoli.

E qui ritorniamo all'avventura del nostro operatore Riccardo e alle sue riprese dei pescecani attorno alla canoa di Tanai.

Questa, dunque, si trovava in una laguna, all'interno di una barriera (i polinesiani del centro Tuamotu più vicino, Tiputà, la chiamano «le lagon bleu» per il colore delle sue acque).

Quasi al centro di questo specchio d'acqua la piroga del nostro film è ferma, ancorata con una cima di *napè* a un masso di corallo.

Accanto alla canoa è, come sempre, la nostra motobarca con operatori e cineprese, fra cui anche quella subacquea maneggiata da un collaboratore che ho avuto vicino sin dalle prime riprese sottomarine: Masino Manunza (debbo a lui quanto ho imparato per risolvere al meglio ogni problema di ripresa filmata e di foto-grafia subacquea).

Mentre il nostro protagonista pesca, le cineprese seguono i suoi gesti, e si direbbe l'inizio di una giornata senza emozioni quando inizia l'attacco dei *rairà*. Sono squaletti insignificanti, comunissimi in tutte le acque tropicali; nelle lagune del Pacifico arrivano addirittura alla densità dei moscerini attorno a una lampada accesa nelle foreste del Congo; ma malgrado siano sempre in tanti (e anche se può accadere che mordano), a loro nessuno fa caso perché sono estremamente paurosi e, come ho detto, di piccole dimensioni.

Ma nel «lagon bleu» formano branchi talmente numerosi da lasciar stupiti; sono il doppio, il triplo del solito; hanno molto meno cibo da dividere e, di conseguenza, sono folli di fame.

Appaiono e attaccano la canoa: tanto velocemente che, pur vedendoli affiorare, il ragazzo non ha il tempo di portare in barca la preda sull'amo; e infatti, mentre in fretta recupera la lenza, già i primi *rairà* mordono. Le loro bocche (diversamente da quella del *paratà*, lo squalo-azzurro) sono, per la loro stessa misura, incapaci di tranciar netto; ogni *rairà* rimane così attaccato al boccone, istericamente mordendo. Intanto, già un secondo branco di dieci o quindici *rairà* appare accanto al primo e tenta a sua volta d'afferrare quel cibo, facile come può essere un pesce già sull'amo.

Per il pescatore non sarebbe impossibile salpare in fretta le lenze; ma ha capito quanto sia eccezionale la scena dal punto di vista delle nostre riprese e lascia quindi volutamente la sua preda in balia degli squali; intanto sulla motobarca a fianco della canoa prima una, poi due cineprese puntano la scena, per coglierla con obiettivi differenti, mentre anche l'operatore subacqueo si getta in acqua.

I tre diversi film registrano così la zuffa feroce di un branco di squali all'attacco e non solo mentre mordono una preda ma mentre si mordono fra loro; e quando esce dall'acqua il moncone sanguinante del pesce che era stato preso all'amo, alcuni tra i più accaniti *rairà* saltano in alto a seguire quel cibo che sfugge, e restano un istante come sospesi nel vuoto, spinti dal movimento vorticoso della loro coda sulla superficie liquida.

Altri *rairà* che si sono morsi fra loro durante la mischia e perdono sangue vengono finiti e divorati dai compagni di lotta. Intanto dalla motobarca viene gettato in acqua quanto di commestibile può trovarsi a bordo, per dar la possibilità agli operatori di continuare ancora a girare la scena; un tempo supplementare prezioso specialmente per Riccardo che riesce a passare, con la cinepresa in mano, sulla canoa, così vicino allo specchio d'acqua dove i *rairà* guizzano, da cogliere il particolare dei loro morsi frenetici nella spuma.

A bordo, tra le grida e nell'eccitamento generale, finiti tutti i possibili bocconi, viene gettata in acqua, per scherzo, anche una bottiglia di vetro vuota: e persino su lei si accaniscono gli affamati *rairà* tentando (ovviamente invano) di affondarvi i denti.

Nel raccontare, poi, quanto e cosa erano riusciti a filmare, gli operatori cercavano un termine di paragone con altre riprese analoghe. Masino Manunza mi diceva d'essersi sentito meno sicuro e tranquillo tra quelle piccole bestie, lunghe circa un metro e mezzo, di quando gli accadde di filmare uno squalo-tigre di quattro metri o nell'occasione in cui cercando di richiamare con varie esche un gigantesco squalo-martello intravisto nella laguna di Rangiroa gli capitò di vederselo arrivare dritto verso la barca, contro la quale il bestione finì col picchiare sulla fiancata e battendo contro la piccola cabina della timoniera con un colpo di coda così violento da spezzarne il vetro laterale.

«Quel branco di *rairà* è stato un'esperienza peggiore di ogni altra...» conclude Riccardo, dopo aver cercato un termine di paragone tra quella scena del «lagon bleu» e quanto aveva visto nel mondo selvaggio delle Galapagos, dove era rimasto a lungo (per filmare e fotografare) prima di iniziare con noi le riprese negli atolli centrali.

Nemmeno laggiù, pur essendo ogni isola dell'arcipelago un museo di animali marini allo stato primordiale, in continua e ben visibile lotta per l'esistenza e per il dominio di acqua e coste nella

ARCIPELAGO DELLE GALAPAGOS

90°

MARCHENA

GENOVESA

Equatore

0°

SAN SALVADOR

FERNANDINA

BALTRA

PINZON

PLAZAS

SANTA CRUZ

SAN CRISTOBAL

ISABELA

SANTA FE

San Cristobal

Villamil

Baquerizo Moreno

SANTA MARIA

OCEANO PACIFICO

ESPAÑOLA

km 0 12 24 36 48 60 72 84

totale assenza dell'uomo, gli era accaduto di assistere a scene di eguale violenza.

Ma non voglio evocare qui solo il lavoro negli atolli. Per narrare di Tanai fummo anche alle «isole di fuoco».

Il racconto degli *huarè-po* parlano infatti di terre vulcaniche ove Tanai giunge nel suo errare per l'oceano; per questa scena abbiamo scelto la costa est della grande Hawaii, sotto il vulcano di Mauna Loa e il cratere di Alemaumau. C'è un'autostrada che taglia quella costiera, e occorre evitare Hilo, sul lato nord dell'isola, e il suo aeroporto, i suoi grattacieli, i drug-stores e i pullman con turisti a grappoli. Ma lontani da quella città, nel triangolo meridionale dell'isola tra la baia di Kealakekua, ove Cook fu ucciso, e il punto del probabile primo insediamento polinesiano nelle Hawaii, autostrada e grattacieli sono distanti abbastanza da essere dimenticati.

Una costa e un entroterra di natura vulcanica completamente disabitati, dove lo smarrito Tanai non cerca più la rotta perduta di un'isola di corallo ma sembra esplorare territori oscuri dell'immaginazione; questa è almeno la sensazione che mi prende allorché vedo la sua figura, sul tavolato di basalto nero, lava vomitata dalla bocca dell'Alemaumau e colata lungo la montagna sino al mare. (Di tante isole vulcaniche del Pacifico, abbiamo scelto questa perché l'unica ove ci è stato possibile l'uso di un elicottero per filmare il nostro personaggio in una visione d'insieme con l'ambiente che lo circonda.)

Una figura sola sul tavolato di lava che si muove tra il pendio vulcanico e la costa contro la quale le onde, quasi viola, s'infrangono con violenza.

Il nostro protagonista visto in tal modo dal cielo, nella prospettiva di un oceano senza fine e di un'isola deserta e ignota, diventa il simbolo di un mistero; il mistero delle trasmigrazioni, e delle partenze verso l'ignoto, le quali hanno, forse, un'unica spiegazione: la ricerca di un fine, di un destino.

Quello di un uomo solo, come Tanai, o quello di un intero popolo, quando la partenza era epopea collettiva.

Altre genti, altre culture, hanno conosciuto un eguale desiderio

L'immagine classica dei Mari del Sud: la laguna di un atollo, la foresta di *cocotiers*, la capanna coperta con il tetto di *niau*. Un'atmosfera che si conserva solo nelle «isole minori» del Pacifico, come a Makemo (Tuamotu).

Così è un atollo: una sottile striscia di corallo (talvolta distesa nell'oceano anche per alcune centinaia di chilometri, come questa di Rangiroa; la macchiano di verde piccole, grandi e microscopiche isolette dette *motu* dai polinesiani (*pagina a fronte*).

Immagini di isole vulcaniche del Pacifico meridionale. *A sinistra,
in alto*: Deserto di cenere attorno al cratere di Alemaumau (Hilo, Hawaii)
e (*in basso*) la sua bocca di fuoco ritenuta dai polinesiani la sede della dea Pelé.
Gli spenti crateri che formano l'arcipelago di Palau (*sopra*), visti dal cielo,
in stagione delle piogge.

Le terre oceaniche di origine vulcanica sono ricche di acqua, e quindi, salvo rare eccezioni, coperte di un fitto manto di vegetazione; come l'area attorno alla «Montagna del Diadema», il cratere spento che domina Tahiti, segnata dall'imponente cascata di Fataua.

Per l'inventario di quanto sta scomparendo dalle isole dei Mari del Sud, ecco la *pahi* – la canoa a vela – e il *tehao* («granchio dei cocchi»), una specie endogena del Pacifico, in via d'estinzione.

Nelle pagine seguenti: Negli atolli ove l'uomo non vive più – ha preferito emigrare nelle «isole ricche» – la natura riprende il suo lussureggiante sopravvento.

Nell'area del Pacifico orientale, le isole Galapagos sono oggi tra
i maggiori centri oceanografici del pianeta; immenso laboratorio terrestre
e sottomarino intitolato a Darwin, che qui trovò importanti prove
a conferma della sua teoria dell'evoluzione (nella foto: una iguana anfibia).

Malaita, isole Salomone: piante e cespugli di mangrovie le cui radici si scoprono e si coprono d'acqua salsa a seconda dei movimenti di marea; esempio tra i più tipici di una forma di vita vegetale terrestre che il mare alimenta e fa rigogliosa.

Immagini «classiche» di vita quotidiana,
in una Polinesia ormai per sempre scomparsa.

In molte isole della Micronesia, scomparsi i sereni villaggi di *niau*, si vive in anonimi prefabbricati. Svanita ogni identità tradizionale, si registra qui la più alta percentuale al mondo di suicidi tra i giovani.

La tradizione *tuamotu* di ingentilire i rami di alberi morti s'è trasformata: non più «fiori di conchiglie» ma lattine e barattoli.

Hoena e *Aparima*, da tradizionali danze mimate polinesiane sono mutate in elementi di un folklore anonimo dedicato ai turisti in cerca «d'esotico».

Nella pagina a fronte: Quanto resta di una «casa nobile» di Rangiroa (Tuamotu) abbandonata dalla famiglia che un tempo governava l'isola.

Nel 1722 fu battezzata dagli europei «Isola di Pasqua» la terra più sacra
alla tradizione dei polinesiani. Vi avevano eretto gigantesche statue dette
moai, dedicandole agli antenati navigatori (alcune, incompiute, giacciono
nelle cave di pietra sui fianchi dello spento vulcano di Rano Raraku).

di trovare il senso della loro storia nella soluzione di incognite sempre diverse.

Per i polinesiani questa ricerca si identificò nella spinta verso l'orizzonte, verso il vuoto; il nulla e l'assoluto delle trasmigrazioni sono le componenti fondamentali della loro storia; tanto fondamentali da sopravvivere alla disgregazione delle tradizioni, oggi ormai fatto compiuto. La storia di Tanai che si ripete nel più popolare e semplice dei patrimoni culturali – quello del cantastorie di paese, di piazza e di città – ne è piccola ma significativa prova.

L'elicottero, sopra lo scosceso versante est dell'isola, volteggia a quote diverse sorvolando un paesaggio, un ambiente come non ne abbiamo mai visto di simili né io né Nanni, mio compagno di lavoro in tanti viaggi attorno al mondo.

Sorvoliamo insieme il grande cratere dell'Alemaumau, appena riconoscibile nel fumo e nel vapore e di lì raggiungiamo una foresta d'alberi bianchi, pietrificati dalla vampata di un'esplosione; e infine raggiungiamo la costa ove vegetazioni violacee (sembrano dall'alto un tappeto molle e umido) hanno coperto il magma impietrito e le sue gigantesche forme accatastate.

Al centro di quelle immagini, Tanai, nel suo smarrimento ormai assoluto, si muove in un ambito proprio, uno spazio di ansia privo di ogni fiducia, fuori dal tempo e dalla vita; il suo accanirsi con le forze del mare, le sue vittorie sui venti e sugli animali marini, i suoi abbandoni alle derive, come pure alle bonacce e le soste negli arcipelaghi amici, sembrano essere stati, per lui, pretesto e contrattempi, fino a trasformare il mito del suo ritorno in illusione vera e propria.

L'illusione del ritorno. La conclusione della lunga vicenda.

Cantastorie e *huarè-po* – come ho premesso, iniziando questo capitolo – hanno narrato la storia di Tanai con finali sempre diversi, da far credere che questa avventura non abbia, in realtà, mai avuto una reale conclusione.

Mi era piaciuta per la sua ambiguità la soluzione proposta dal cantastorie del mercato di Papeete, quel suggerire il confondersi di una vicenda nata dalla tradizione polinesiana più autentica nell'attualità quotidiana di un'Oceania ormai solo turistica; Tanai, Ulisse trasmigratore, mutato in bagnino di un club; poteva essere una conclusione emblematica, ma fino a che punto?

A poche settimane dalla fine del nostro lavoro mi ritrovo ancora indeciso su quale versione conclusiva scegliere; e intanto siamo sbarcati all'Isola di Pasqua, ove filmiamo, nel cielo grigio dell'autunno australe, la sequenza-chiave del racconto. Il confronto diretto tra l'uomo-simbolo Tanai e i *moai*, simboli-pietra dei suoi antenati. Lui smarrito, ma vivo di fronte alle statue dei grandi trasmigratori, coloro che non si smarriscono ma non sono più vivi. L'ultimo trasmigratore di fronte ai *moai* del tempo dimenticato, i sovrani dell'isola più perduta del mondo polinesiano. Un incontro come un ricordo, o quasi come un sogno: i sovrani infatti non sono più tali, l'isola non fa nemmeno più parte della Polinesia. L'odissea di Tanai non può concludersi qui, ma più lontano – nel tempo e nello spazio. Davanti alle statue che cadono a pezzi, nel cielo plumbeo dell'isola il nostro lavoro si svolge in un'atmosfera di tristezza. Ma forse, proprio per questo, sentiamo, in quei giorni così diversi dal resto di tutto il viaggio, che la sosta a Pasqua è qualcosa di differente da tutte le altre del nostro itinerario.

E questo m'aiuta a credere che in ultima analisi l'isola-madre della civiltà polinesiana – anche se ridotta a rovine, anche se per sempre tagliata fuori dal mondo di cui fu simbolo – ha ancora una sua forza, una sua autorità che né l'abbandono degli uomini né le forze della natura riescono ancora a distruggere.

Quando due settimane dopo il nostro arrivo all'«isola sacra» si conclude il mio lungo lavoro per il film, sono passati esattamente dieci anni da quella notte al largo dell'atollo Rangiroa quando Tetoèa per primo mi parlò di Tanai, del suo albero del pane e della sua odissea.

Ho risentito parlare dell'atollo di Rangiroa ascoltando, a Papeete, un notiziario sugli esperimenti nucleari francesi alle Tuamotu. Sdraiato su una piccola branda rigida, sono immobile, e attendo che la mia schiena possa riprendere a muoversi dopo essere stata accarezzata abbastanza rudemente dalla mano dell'oceano: mi ha colpito la forza di un'onda gigante, giunta dall'altomare per entrare con tutta la sua violenza nel canale di una laguna. E mi ha costretto all'immobilità, per alcune settimane. Portato via dagli atolli in aereo, sono stato «ricoverato» a Tahiti, dove mi curano, e cercano di rimettermi in sesto.

Ascolto la radio, anche perché non riesco a muovermi nemmeno quel poco necessario per tenere un libro in mano a sfogliarne le pagine. E così in quello scorcio dell'ottobre 1970 ascolto voci, musiche, notiziari. E un giorno, m'accade di sentire qualcuno parlare a lungo della «bomba».

Uno speaker francese racconta che gli abitanti degli atolli delle Tuamotu orientali, tutt'attorno a Mururoa (dove le esplosioni nucleari sperimentali erano già state più di quaranta), si trovano bene «nelle loro nuove località di residenza».

«Stanno bene» dice la voce anonima di radio Papeete, raccontandoci di come vivono quei profughi trasportati in altre isole o in nuovi quartieri alla periferia di Papeete. Il cronista parla di «trapianto sociale» e ci offre la cronaca diretta della visita di un ammiraglio alle comunità emigrate per lasciar posto agli «esperimenti» (per la «scienza» e il «futuro»...).

Ascolto, e intanto ricordo quando nel '61 vedemmo il cielo notturno illuminarsi nel chiarore di un'esplosione nucleare stratosferica americana sopra Christmas (e noi, che dormivamo in una capanna a quattromila miglia di distanza, fummo svegliati da quella inattesa aurora artificiale); mi ricordo i racconti di pesci contaminati e la paura di acque non più amiche. E ricordo (quando sono iniziati gli «esperimenti» nel Pacifico francese) l'angoscia degli uomini delle Tuamotu nell'apprendere che l'estremo lembo orientale del loro arcipelago era stato scelto come «poligono atomico» con epicentro nell'atollo di Mururoa.

Passate le mie settimane di immobilità, finalmente posso muovermi; e appena riesco a mettermi in circolazione, affitto un'automobile e tra semafori e stop mi muovo da un quartiere all'altro di Papeete: voglio riuscire a trovare i profughi di Mururoa. Chiedo, m'informo e m'accorgo che la ricerca non è facile ma riserva molte sorprese; durante le mie indagini e gli incontri nati dalle stesse, mi capita di trovarmi in un ufficio dell'Amministrazione francese dove, non appena parlo di esperimenti nucleari, un militare che mi conosce come fotografo mi dice: «Che ne pensa di queste?», e da una busta estrae, per avere un giudizio e senza forse pensare troppo al loro contenuto, una ventina di foto in bianco e nero. Le ha scattate nella zona degli «esperimenti» e sono immagini colte mentre le piccole comunità degli atolli venivano trasportate altrove; sullo sfondo di ogni laguna decine di navi formano vere e proprie città galleggianti: un innaturale paesaggio di isole impossibili.

«Negli atolli scelti per gli esperimenti» mi spiega «le navi sono alberghi, le navi sono laboratorio, le navi sono tutto per i cinquemila uomini che formano l'organico della base atomica... ecco: queste sono foto scattate proprio nella zona delle esplosioni...» E mi mostra mostruose deformazioni naturali di un atollo sconvolto, vere e proprie immagini da fantascienza; spiagge butterate di una sorta di escrescenze viscide e tondeggianti, sfere irregolari nate dal fondersi delle sabbie nella violenza dell'esplosione. Un oceano come nemmeno le apocalissi delle antiche cosmogonie polinesiane e melanesiane più angosciose riuscirono mai a evocare: immagini sulle quali si sovrappongono volti di giovani, di vecchi, di donne, di bambini: sorridenti o tristi, sono i profughi trasportati dalle zone «chiuse» a Papeete.

Qui, finalmente riesco a incontrarli, oltre Tiperui, quartiere periferico della città; non sono scontenti del loro nuovo stato: ed è proprio questo loro «esser contenti» l'aspetto umanamente più angoscioso della loro condizione; tutti, appena li ho interrogati, hanno detto d'esser felici di trovarsi là, a duemilatrecento chilometri dai loro atolli. «In fondo, perché lamentarsi?» mi hanno detto. «L'Administration ha pagato le spese per un viaggio che altre comunità, decise per diversi motivi ad abbandonare gli atolli, hanno dovuto sostenere da sole.»

Ci sono molti vantaggi nella nostra nuova condizione di «cittadini» mi spiegano uomini e donne: ad esempio, i nostri figli qui vanno a scuola («in belle scuole» ha aggiunto un interlocutore sorridente). E gli uomini guadagnano bene in vari impieghi, tutti garantiti dall'Armée.

«Cosa potremmo desiderare di più?» ha concluso una voce, dal gruppo riunito attorno a me.

«Le accoglienze sono state festose, riconoscenti...» aveva detto quell'anonima voce di speaker ascoltata alla radio giorni prima. «L'ammiraglio ha potuto constatare le condizioni d'ambientazione dei polinesiani che hanno abbandonato gli atolli destinati agli esperimenti nucleari; e con legittima soddisfazione, al termine dell'incontro, egli ha potuto affermare che l'operazione di "trapianto sociale" procede secondo il programma, senza incontrare nessuna difficoltà, anzi nella riconoscenza sincera degli isolani.»

Una vecchietta rugosa come la buccia di un pompelmo lasciato al sole ride mentre la inquadro tra i profughi, e mi chiede se potrà avere una copia di quella foto per spedirla a un nipote: «Siamo divisi in varie isole, sai... Lui è a Makatea» mi dice.

Le prometto la copia e mentre ci salutiamo: «Sembra anche a me una bella fortuna questo trasferimento in città,» mi dice stringendomi tutte e due le mani «ormai all'atollo eravamo rimasti in pochi e solo vecchi. Ora il nostro villaggio, tutto vuoto, non sarà così triste come negli ultimi anni. Sai che, ormai da tempo, una capanna era abitata e dieci no?...»

Nel ricordo del suo sorriso triste capisco di aver trovato il finale dell'odissea di Tanai. Un finale mai narrato né da cantastorie, né da *huarè-po*, con un protagonista più forte di Tanai stesso: la morte, quella stessa che noi «bianchi» abbiamo portato in quest'oceano. La morte provocata dagli esperimenti atomici, come quella causata un tempo dalle epidemie; la morte degli esodi forzati come quella che un tempo fu conseguenza delle deportazioni. Catena di eventi sempre presentati come l'aiuto di una mano civile al «povero» uomo primitivo; descritto di volta in volta come «l'uomo dei sacrifici umani» o il «cannibale», in ogni caso un «selvaggio» da salvare con Vangelo e luce elettrica, abiti lunghi e linee aeree. È un vecchio discorso, non val la pena di evocarlo, da due secoli lo ripete ogni ambigua autocritica (e poiché è stato dimostrato che, in taluni casi, eventi moralmente condannabili hanno avuto, qui, effetti benefici, l'autocritica è stata oltreché inutile, anche sciocca).

Riuscii così a riassumere il finale dell'odissea di Tanai in un'unica immagine.

La cinepresa bassa sul filo dell'acqua immota – oltre il quale la linea emersa dell'atollo è appena percettibile – coglierà il senso di quanto voglio narrare con tre obiettivi diversi: un «grand'angolo» per sentire lo spazio; un «normale» per contenere la proporzione dell'immagine nello stesso rapporto dei nostri occhi; e anche un «teleobiettivo» che ci avvicina al volto dell'uomo nel momento del suo approdo, i suoi piedi che calpestano la spiaggia di corallo, i suoi occhi smarriti in una sorpresa che non trova spiegazioni. Nella sua isola non vive più nessuno. Tutta la gente del suo villaggio è stata evacuata.

Nel silenzio di un pomeriggio senza vento, filmai così il finale della impossibile storia di Tanai: il suo ritorno con i sacchi di terra ormai inutili. Inutili, per un'isola deserta.

Tanai non ritrova più la sua gente, il suo villaggio.

È giunto all'ultimo approdo.

Quando remo, canoa e capanne non erano di plastica

Il villaggio primitivo – Il vino di palma e il forno nel corallo – L'amo magico – La caccia ai polpi giganti delle Gilbert – I fratelli-delfini – Le mille canoe di Kealakekua – Il *Wakasula*, rito per la velocità della canoa – I tabù di bordo – I poeti delle isole e gli *huarè-po* – I doni dei morti – L'anguilla innamorata della bella Tuna.

La società dell'Oceania non conosceva grandi agglomerati: tutt'al più il villaggio. Le era ignoto il concetto di città, ritrovo di artigiani, commercianti, sede del potere, regale o tribale che fosse. In varie isole aveva edificato centri religiosi, santuari o mausolei di capi ove si riunivano le popolazioni di villaggi o di isole per le loro celebrazioni annuali o pluriennali comuni. Ma anche in questo caso quanto sorgeva tutt'attorno non aveva mai un carattere duraturo e stabile.

Il villaggio degli arcipelaghi polinesiani e micronesiani non aveva una pianta prestabilita. Nel Pacifico occidentale, nelle isole papua, invece, alcune popolazioni hanno una topografia del villaggio che rivela ancora oggi una sua particolare struttura. Lo compongono due «quartieri» (uso impropriamente questa parola): quello dove sorgono le abitazioni delle famiglie (per le donne e i figli minori), in cui l'uomo si sente quasi un estraneo; e quello dove sorge la capanna comune degli uomini, quella del capo e quelle dei raccolti agricoli. L'immancabile spiazzo per le cerimonie e le danze è zona interdetta, mediante tabù, alle donne e ai bambini, salvo nelle celebrazioni festive.

Un esempio di villaggio a struttura sociale è quello di Omarakana, nelle isole Trobriand, in Melanesia, come ce lo descrive Malinowski: costituito da cerchi concentrici di capanne, la fila esterna per le donne, quella più interna con le capanne su palafitte dove si conservano i raccolti agricoli dell'annata, e un vasto terreno centrale, dove sorgono la capanna di riunione degli uomini, quella del capo e un'altra che serve come deposito, il cimitero degli antenati, e infine, ombreggiato da alberi, lo spiazzo per le danze e le cerimonie rituali collettive. Tutta la parte interna al circolo delle case-granai è considerata sacra; per cui la piazza del villaggio potrebbe essere indicata dalla via circolare tra queste e le case-abitazione delle donne.

La forma della capanna tradizionale polinesiana e melanesiana (prima che l'uniformità dei prefabbricati in plastica e alluminio togliesse ogni identità ai superstiti villaggi) è variatissima. Anche per l'adattamento alla diversità dei climi. Di solito è però rialzata dal suolo, specialmente nelle regioni ove si abbattono periodicamente grandi piogge; per questo la costruzione poggia su robuste piattaforme di pietra o su palafitte, anche se sorge lungi dal mare. In Nuova Zelanda, nelle comunità polinesiane dei maori, era invece leggermente infossata.

Ovunque, un tempo, e in alcuni villaggi ancor oggi – quelli che ho visitato tra i più primitivi – si costruiva con materiali lignei e fogliacei; tenuti insieme senza alcun uso di chiodi, cavicchi o incastri, ma soltanto mediante legature, che nelle capanne degli uomini giungono a essere elegantemente complicate, con fini decorazioni.

La cucina è distinta dalla capanna, in ricordo del tempo in cui gli uomini cucinavano i propri cibi nella capanna comune, in forza del tabù che vietava loro di consumare cibi confezionati da donne, e di mangiare insieme a esse. L'abolizione di tale tabù, nelle Hawaii, alla fine del sec. XVIII, quando il re Kamehameha I volle assimilare a quelli dei «bianchi» i costumi della sua gente, causò disordini gravi e fu l'inizio della dissoluzione della società polinesiana in quelle isole.

La capanna comune degli uomini, riservata alla vita anche organizzativa del gruppo, e luogo di cerimonie di culto, è grande, molto decorata. Vi si custodiscono gli oggetti del culto, maschere, strumenti musicali, i simboli degli antenati, le teste-trofeo (dove si pratica questo genere di caccia), le pietre sacre in cui s'incarnano le divinità (laddove queste non hanno un altro sacrario). Le capanne degli uomini sono le stesse case delle imbarcazioni, come

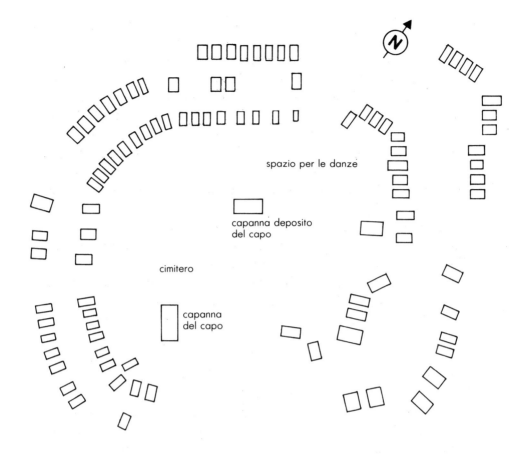

spazio per le danze

capanna deposito
del capo

cimitero

capanna
del capo

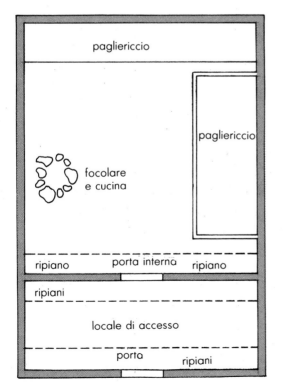

pagliericcio

pagliericcio

focolare
e cucina

ripiano · porta interna · ripiano

ripiani

locale di accesso

porta · ripiani

Pianta di una capanna e di un villaggio
(Omarakana) delle isole Trobriand,
in Melanesia, secondo
le descrizioni di Bronislaw Malinowski

ne ho visto ancora qualcuna nelle isole Palau, in Micronesia. Di solito sono di grandi dimensioni, rettangolari o circolari, talune lunghe anche duecento metri e alte venticinque. Quelle delle Palau hanno i frontoni, di forma triangolare, decorati con disegni a colori; quelle degli antichi maori (della Nuova Zelanda) avevano portali d'ingresso con intarsi in madreperla, travature e pali di sostegno intagliati finemente e qui gli uomini vivevano assieme, discutevano gli affari comunitari, preparavano acconciature, armi e la bibita più ricercata, la *kava*.

In Polinesia, altro genere di costruzione era la capanna sepolcrale, spesso sopraelevata, con una tettoia, in forma di piramide, di pietra per la sepoltura dei grandi capi.

I maori costruivano fortificazioni, per lo più in forma di palizzate, e sull'appuntita sua sommità esponevano teste di nemici uccisi durante questo o quello scontro come ammonimento.

Come viveva in questi suoi villaggi, in passato, l'uomo dell'Oceania?

A giudicare dalle notizie pervenute alla London Missionary Society, nel 1796, le nozioni igieniche dei polinesiani, quasi un secolo prima di Pasteur, erano molto progredite. Le relazioni dei missionari indicano che i nativi si lavavano con frequenza il corpo, sciacquavano dopo ogni pasto la bocca e i denti, per cui conservavano i denti bianchi; non sopportavano che una mosca si posasse sul cibo; se ciò accadeva, senza poterlo impedire, lo gettavano ai maiali. Se una mosca si posava sul loro corpo, con insistenza, si precipitavano subito al fiume per lavarsi. Per questo, prima dell'arrivo degli europei, in tutta l'Oceania si conoscevano poche malattie.

La repulsione per le mosche fa parte, ovviamente, del complesso dei tabù, per cui essi ritenevano che l'insetto li contagiasse del potere nefasto delle cose vietate. Per esempio, capi e sacerdoti maori non potevano portare da sé alla bocca cibi né bevande, e dovevano farsi imboccare; le bevande dovevano essere versate loro in bocca mediante una specie di imbuto.

Lo stesso Cook rimase meravigliato dell'igiene corporale dei tahitiani, per la pulizia nel mangiare, e per le cure del loro corpo.

«*Teniamo conto*» scrive de Bisschop «*che in quel tempo il "prendere un bagno" era in Europa una prescrizione medica.*»

Salvo nelle zone alte e in quelle extratropicali a clima temperato, il caldo non rendeva necessario il vestiario. In Melanesia si pratica ancor oggi la nudità completa, o, tutt'al più, ci si «veste» con un cordoncino attorno alla vita: un perizoma o un gonnellino di fibre intrecciate e legate insieme. Gli uomini usano una fascia intorno alla vita, che passa poi tra le gambe. Il busto è ricoperto eccezionalmente, per ragioni cerimoniali o quale distintivo del rango. L'indumento più in voga in Polinesia, il tradizionale *pareo*, in origine era un panno che avvolgeva le anche, in forma di gonna, costume usatissimo nel bacino dell'Oceano Indiano e nei suoi mari tributari (oggi è un «prodotto di moda» indossato più dai turisti che dai nativi).

Nell'Oceania autoctona s'ignorava l'uso della tessitura e quindi della filatura. Il panno veniva preparato sovrapponendo multipli strati di fibre, pressati e battuti insieme, che formavano come un feltro di spessore voluto. Il procedimento ricorda la preparazione del papiro egizio. La fibra per fabbricare questo *tapa* si ricava dal gelso cartaceo. Questo è un albero che non cresce in Nuova Zelanda; perciò i maori usavano le fibre di un lino selvatico, che legavano e intrecciavano insieme, formando una specie di tessuto; essi usavano inoltre mantelli di pelle di cane, e soprattutto di penne. Molto vistosi e riservati ai grandi capi erano i mantelli di piume di pappagallo, nelle Hawaii, con risultati policromi eccezionali.

All'arte plumaria si aggiungeva la lavorazione di disparate altre materie; e nel campo degli ornamenti, gli artisti delle Marchesi si dimostrarono dotati di straordinaria inventiva. Ancora pochi anni fa, alla fine dei Cinquanta, ho visto io stesso con quanta creatività ritagliavano orecchini di disegno e fattura squisiti dai denti del capodoglio; splendidi certi ornamenti che si portavano sul petto e le acconciature.

Braccialetti, ornamenti da caviglie e persino gonnellini erano fatti con ciocche di capelli umani abilmente attaccate a strisce intrecciate di fibra di cocco: ai capelli neri usati per questo tipo di ornamenti si faceva la «permanente» avvolgendoli intorno a una bacchetta di legno, chiudendoli in un involucro di foglie verdi e scaldandoli in un forno. Per fare ornamenti si usavano i peli della barba, ma in tal caso si preferivano quelli grigi. I tahitiani usavano ciuffi di peli grigi tagliati alla coda dei cani per formare frange e fiocchetti per ornamento da petto, e i maori adornavano con fiocchi consimili mantelli e armi. Gli abitanti delle isole Marchesi, non avendo cani, attingevano alla barba dei vecchi. Quando un vecchio riceveva la notizia che c'era in vista un nipotino, si lasciava crescere la barba per provvedere alla materia prima con cui sarebbero stati fabbricati gli ornamenti per il bimbo; ed esaminando campioni da museo, con ciuffi di ricciuti capelli grigi accuratamente legati con una sola fibra di cocco, non potei impedirmi di fantasticare sulla tenerezza con cui un vecchio doveva aver pettinato la sua barba, e sulla gioia che doveva aver provato nel vederla abbastanza cresciuta.[1]

L'ornamento del corpo era ottenuto anche mediante pratiche molto dolorose.

L'Isola di Pasqua si sarebbe potuta chiamare la «Terra degli uomini dalle orecchie lunghe» [ha scritto Métraux]. Gli indigeni descritti dai primi navigatori praticavano infatti sul lobo dell'orecchio un largo foro in cui facevano passare un pesante ornamento di legno o di vertebra di pescecane. Questa moda finì con la scomparsa della civiltà indigena, e gli ultimi vecchi, con le orecchie deformate da grossi fori, morirono al principio del nostro secolo.

È pure usata, in Melanesia, la perforazione del setto nasale, per tenervi introdotta un'asticciola. È tipica, infine, l'acconciatura con due zanne ricurve di porco, una per lato, uscenti dalle narici. Gli indigeni allevano questi animali con grandi sacrifici poiché per tradizione essi sono pescatori e agricoltori, mai allevatori.

L'agricoltura e la pesca erano un tempo e sono solo in minima parte oggi i due cespiti dell'alimentazione. In Nuova Zelanda si cacciava il *moa*, uccello terricolo, che raggiungeva i tre metri di altezza, estinto da oltre due secoli. Nelle grandi isole della Melanesia ho visto come ancora si dia la caccia al porco selvatico.

I frutti della terra costituiscono, comunque, il principale alimento. Senza la palma di cocco, che prospera sugli atolli corallini, dove altre piante non trovano abbastanza terreno, non si sarebbe forse avuta la colonizzazione di isolotti sperduti e improduttivi. Ma di pari importanza sono gli alberi del pane e il pandano, che

---

[1] P. Buck, *op. cit.*

fornisce tuberi succulenti. Vi sono poi i tuberi dell'igname, il banano, la canna da zucchero, l'arancio, dai frutti del quale si fa una specie di vino.

Malgrado oggi all'uso dei cibi locali si preferiscano i prodotti in scatola e preconfezionati (europei, americani e cinesi) in molte comunità sono ancora vive le leggende sulla trasmigrazione da un'isola a un'altra di alcuni animali e piante utili all'uomo. A un famoso capo, Kaha'i, si attribuisce l'introduzione dell'albero del pane a Kualoa, nell'isola Oahu, nelle Hawaii, probabilmente nel secolo XII; e ancora si riporta la rotta stellare che egli seguì in quel viaggio di oltre duemila miglia.

I pochi animali addomesticati non si diffusero parimenti in tutto il Pacifico. Il maiale non era conosciuto in Nuova Zelanda, all'arrivo degli europei. A Cook certi isolani chiedevano cani per allevarli. A volte furono gli isolani stessi, gelosi del loro patrimonio, che rifiutarono ad altri il possesso di certe specie di animali. Si ricorse perciò all'astuzia, come nel caso della diffusione del maiale, uscito dalle isole Figi con l'inganno, come narra Peter Buck:

Un viaggiatore proveniente dalle Samoa visitò le Figi, e vi fu festeggiato con un banchetto a base di carne di porco. Naturalmente, nacque subito in lui il desiderio di portare con sé, nel suo paese, quell'animale dalla carne saporita; senonché i figiani non permisero che nessun maiale vivo uscisse dalle loro isole; non fecero obiezioni però alla richiesta degli ospiti di portare con sé un paio di maiali morti, come provviste per il viaggio. I viaggiatori si procurarono due maiali molto grossi, li ammazzarono, li ripulirono delle interiora, e di nascosto dai figiani rubarono alcuni maialini e li chiusero nel ventre degli animali uccisi, che poi coprirono con foglie. Trasportando i due grossi animali appesi alle estremità di un palo riuscirono a eludere la sorveglianza dei figiani e così il maiale fece la sua comparsa nelle Samoa.

Varie leggende narrano come furono acquisite certe piante coltivate, e i miti risalgono all'origine prima delle piante basilari per l'alimentazione, come quella del cocco, che i polinesiani utilizzano in trentasei modi diversi. Il principale è l'intreccio delle foglie, il *niau*, con il quale si coprono ancor oggi i tetti e si chiudono le pareti delle capanne. Non si usa più, invece, trarre dal cocco

143

alimenti e bibite, stuoie, vele, e il *napé* per cucire le canoe, oltre ai cordami di bordo.

Importante per l'alimentazione, oggi come ieri, è l'albero del pane.

L'albero del pane, quand'è giunto al suo pieno sviluppo, è una pianta d'alto fusto, di aspetto imponente, altrettanto caratteristica e indispensabile, nel paesaggio delle isole Marchesi, di quanto lo sia l'olmo patriarcale nel panorama della Nuova Inghilterra. L'olmo in questione, anzi, ha in comune col primo l'altezza, l'ampiezza delle robuste ramificazioni e l'aspetto maestoso. [...]

Il frutto, per le dimensioni e l'aspetto, somiglia a un melone verde di media grandezza: solo che, al contrario di questo, non ha la superficie segnata da alcun solco longitudinale, ma è invece cosparsa di minuscole prominenze coniche, simili, per forma, alle borchie che ornano certi vecchi portali di chiesa. Tolta la scorza, che è spessa un ottavo di pollice circa, il frutto, qualora sia giunto a completa maturazione, si presenta come una sfera perfetta; la polpa è bianca, interamente commestibile, eccezion fatta per un piccolo torsolo, che però si lascia estrarre con estrema facilità.

Tuttavia, il frutto dell'albero del pane non lo si mangia mai, né del resto risulterebbe mangiabile, se non dopo averlo precedentemente sottoposto a cottura, secondo uno dei tanti sistemi in uso.

Il sistema più semplice, e credo il migliore, consiste nel mettere i frutti appena colti (non ancora perfettamente maturi) tra la brace, proprio come da noi si fa con le patate che si vogliono arrostire. Trascorsi dieci, quindici minuti al massimo la scorza verde acquista una tonalità bruna e si spacca; tra le fessure apparirà allora il bianco latteo della polpa. Si lascia raffreddare il frutto, poi si toglie senza fatica la scorza, e si ha a disposizione la morbida, rotonda palla di polpa, intera, mirabile a vedersi. Così mangiato, il frutto ha un sapore delicato e oltremodo gradevole.[1]

La bevanda oceaniana più frequente era ed è ovviamente l'acqua, raccolta in cisterne e contenitori dalla pioggia. Ovunque, poi, si consuma ancora il latte di cocco; e solo in minor misura la *kava*, bevuta specialmente in Polinesia, che si prepara e si consuma seguendo un cerimoniale ben preciso; si confeziona con la radice dell'arbusto dello stesso nome, spezzettata e masticata, lasciata in acqua a fermentare.

L'ottimo vino di palma, invece, si fa scolare salassando l'apice della pianta, da cui dovrebbero sbocciare le foglie novelle; questa,

---

[1] H. Melville, *Taipi*.

che può sembrare una bevanda voluttuaria, è al contrario complementare della dieta:

Alle isole Gilbert, in Micronesia, con protettorato britannico, i missionari puritani di origine americana (*Boston Mission*) erano scandalizzati, fin dal loro arrivo, dall'intemperanza degli indigeni, dal loro abuso di vino di palma ottenuto dalla pianta del cocco, che provocava una ubriachezza brutale.

In seguito alle loro insistenti pressioni, l'amministrazione locale finì col proibire l'uso di tale bevanda.

Ma non molto tempo era passato, che fu giocoforza ritornare sulla decisione presa, perché i medici s'erano accorti che, non bevendo più vino di palma, la gente presentava fenomeni di carenze pericolose; l'analisi dimostrò che la bevanda provocava, senza dubbio, ubriachezza, ma che possedeva un contenuto vitaminico elevato, cosa preziosa in quelle isole coralline, dove praticamente non esisteva vegetazione e gli abitanti erano quindi costretti ad alimentarsi quasi esclusivamente di pesci e di noci di cocco.[1]

L'Oceania degli atolli e delle isole vulcaniche orientali conobbe come unico sistema di cottura il forno a terra, essendovi ignota la ceramica, per mancanza di argille (i polinesiani non conoscevano l'acqua calda: per condensare le conserve di certi frutti, le esponevano al sole su lastre coralline). L'invenzione del forno a terra, o meglio il suo primo possesso, fu attribuito a quel maestro di astuzie che fu Maui, il pescatore di isole, che lo carpì al dio Tane, secondo il mito narrato a Peter Buck dai polinesiani di Mangareva:

Tane, continuando la lezione, scavò in terra una buca poco profonda, vi accese un fuoco e sulla legna accesa pose pietre grosse come un pugno chiuso: prima che la legna si fosse consumata, il calore del fuoco si era trasferito nelle pietre che erano diventate rosse e roventi. Tane le dispose l'una accanto all'altra, in bell'ordine, su di esse mise il cibo crudo, e coperse il tutto con uno strato di foglie; dopo qualche tempo, queste furono rimosse, e il cibo era cotto. Così, Maui aveva visto all'opera il semplice tipo di forno che si diffuse poi in tutta la Polinesia: il suo problema era ormai risolto.[2]

La descrizione di Métraux si riferisce all'uso del forno a terra nell'Isola di Pasqua:

Si facevano dapprima scaldare le pietre, ritirandole solo dopo che ave-

[1] A. Grimble, *op. cit.*
[2] P. Buck, *op. cit.*

vano raggiunto un'alta temperatura. Si tappezzava allora il fondo della buca con foglie di banano; quindi si riponevano i cibi coperti con uno strato di pietre prima, poi di foglie e infine di terra. Dopo qualche ora i cibi erano dissotterrati, ormai cotti senza che le carni avessero perduto nulla dei loro sapori originari. I forni antichi, numerosi nelle zone archeologiche, sono rivestiti di quattro o cinque lastre di pietra per evitare il contatto diretto del cibo col suolo.

Il sapore del cibo così stufato è eccellente e spesso è stato vantato dai viaggiatori. Ma la cucina pasquense, come quella di altre isole della Polinesia, risente della mancanza di condimento: gli indigeni, che assorbono il sale necessario all'organismo dall'atmosfera marittima che li circonda o dalle alghe marine mangiate crude, non sentono infatti più il bisogno di condire le pietanze.[1]

Queste «pietanze» – sembrerebbe inutile sottolinearlo – erano (e sono) in gran parte costituite da pesci, essendo la carne un cibo molto raro e limitato. I pesci sono, quindi, il prodotto base dell'alimentazione isolana d'Oceania, e la pesca è (o, per meglio dire, era sino a ieri) l'attività fondamentale degli uomini e delle donne che abitano le isole.

Ho raccolto in un capitolo a sé stante quanto ho visto, da testimone, del mondo della pesca nel Pacifico meridionale, prima che le trasformazioni profonde di molte zone non mutassero i pescatori polinesiani in cittadini inurbati, dediti ad attività terziarie. A lato di quelle cronache personali, mi è sembrato importante riunire altri documenti – sulla pesca e le sue tecniche – che ben aiutano a comprendere come questa attività, soprattutto per i polinesiani, fosse qualcosa di profondamente connesso alla loro propria natura.

La pesca era praticata sino a ieri, dai polinesiani, in ogni modo: dalla più usuale, alla pesca all'amo con l'aquilone, ma era comune anche la pesca sottomarina con l'arpione, anche allo squalo-tigre.

James Morrison, il marinaio «cronista» del *Bounty*, ci ha lasciato una serie di osservazioni (le prime, complete, dovute a un europeo) sulla pesca praticata dai tahitiani, con i quali egli visse dal 1789 al 1790:

[1] A. Métraux, *op. cit.*

Gli strumenti di pesca sono delle reti di grandi dimensioni, lenze e ami di tutte le misure, arpioni, nasse ecc. Ogni pescatore fabbrica i propri ami, lenze e tutti i suoi arnesi da pesca dei quali si serve con grande abilità. Le loro lenze sono fatte con la scorza del *roa*, che viene ritorta in due o tre fili e arrotolata sul fianco con grande abilità e regolarità; sono due volte più sottili delle lenze che noi adoperiamo per pesci delle stesse dimensioni.

I loro ami sono fatti di madreperla, di osso e di legno, la loro forma cambia secondo i pesci; alcuni hanno la forma di un amo con la sua esca; intagliano i loro ami sfregandoli su di una pietra con acqua e sabbia e con un punteruolo fatto con un dente di pescecane; ci fanno un buco che ingrandiscono con l'aiuto di una punta di corallo che serve come lima, staccando così la parte interna; questi ami non hanno «barba» ma la punta è incurvata verso l'interno, fino al basso, ed è raro che perdano un pesce.

Hanno molte maniere di pescare e tutte eccellenti. La prima è con sacche di reti che hanno da dieci a centoventi metri di lunghezza e da due a ventiquattro di profondità.

Le più grandi hanno nel centro una sorta di tasca o sacco che essi vuotano di tanto in tanto e rimpiazzano trasportando il pesce a terra con le piroghe. Prendono così molto pesce e anche qualche testuggine.

Quando pescano in questo modo, la sacca è sempre sorvegliata da tuffatori che sorvegliano affinché il pesce non scappi; succede che vengano chiusi nella rete dei pescecani e che li si costringa a riva; invece di essere considerato pericoloso, questo esercizio è giudicato uno sport (i pescecani non misurano mai più di due metri).

Hanno delle reti da lancio (giacchi), rotonde e quadrate che gettano con molta destrezza; quando il pesce si avvicina alla riva per deporre le uova, essi utilizzano le foglie del cocco, attaccate le une alle altre per il gambo e tese in modo da formare una lunga corda irta di foglie (che chiamano *raoere*) e raschiano il fondo, trascinando il pesce sulla spiaggia; utilizzano, qualche volta, delle reticelle per raccoglierlo, le stesse che servono anche alla foce di un fiume, ottenendo buoni risultati.

Prendono molti pesci di scoglio con le nasse e si tuffano con grande abilità per colpirli con l'arpione che essi chiamano *patia*.

Ho visto un tuffatore, in un'acqua calma e limpida, seguire un pesce da una tana all'altra, senza risalire.[1]

L'amo, quest'arma minuscola e insidiosa con la quale l'oceaniano si procura tanta parte della sua alimentazione, è per lui oggetto carico di forza magica. Per l'archeologo è una delle poche testimonianze sulla preistoria polinesiana; grazie ai suoi ritrova-

---

[1] In *Le journal de James Morrison* (1796), Société des études océaniennes, 1966.

menti in base alle forme e ai materiali, si sono potute ipotizzare influenze culturali tra i vari arcipelaghi, e con le regioni del Pacifico occidentale. Nella vita polinesiana essi hanno avuto una gran parte; e donare a un ospite ami della propria collezione, frutto cioè di lungo, paziente lavoro e d'inventiva, è manifestazione di grandissimo onore. Anche a me, come a Peter Buck è accaduto più volte di ricevere, con emozione, questo dono; ma lui – nelle sue lunghe peregrinazioni – ha avuto l'onore di questo regalo nel contesto di una solenne cerimonia con cui i polinesiani lo vollero onorare, insieme ad altri doni di artigiani isolani. Accadde, questo, all'atollo di Manihi; ove un *tavanà*, un capo, chiamava a gran voce, dinanzi alla folla raccolta, i doni che man mano dovevano essere recati, e al momento giusto gridò: «Gli ami da pesca!». Rievoca il Buck: «*Quattro uomini vennero verso di noi con una quantità di quei cucchiaini di madreperla che servono a pescare i bonitos. Io ebbi un extra, sotto forma di un grosso amo di legno*».

A proposito di ami-extra, occorre dire che così come la spada migliore per i tuareg è quella magica, la lancia migliore dei pigmei è quella stregata, per i polinesiani non c'è dubbio che l'amo da preferire sia quello «toccato dalla magia»; si chiama «Sussurro di Manuka» e il perché di questo nome è chiaro a chi conosca questa leggenda di Maui.

Per quanto gli dispiacesse separarsi dal suo amo magico, Tonga non poté mancare di mostrare i suoi ami ai visitatori e di lasciare che se ne scegliessero uno in dono. Sperava però che Maui-Kisikisi scegliesse male, perché tutti gli ami erano di madreperla, e solo quello magico era opaco e malamente legato: il più brutto di tutta la raccolta.
Invece Maui-Kisikisi, con l'astuzia che lo contraddistingue in tutti i miti polinesiani, aveva fatto all'amore con la volubile moglie di Tonga, e questa gli aveva confidato quale aspetto avesse l'amo magico (e perciò si guadagnò il nome di «Sussurro di Manuka»). Così Maui non ebbe difficoltà a mettere le mani su quello che cercava.[1]

Non solo nei tempi passati, ma anche oggi, quando un amo è «fatto a mano», la sua preziosità viene soprattutto da un motivo: chi lo taglia e lo leviga sa come «infondergli» – con antiche formule e pratiche magiche – un'*essenza* che attirerà e catturerà il

[1] P. Buck, *op. cit.*

pesce. Arthur Grimble, vissuto lunghi anni nelle isole Gilbert, ha narrato come vengono approntati con pazienza gli speciali ami di legno per la caccia allo squalo-tigre, prediletta da quegli isolani. I pescatori hanno da tempo cominciato a servirsi degli ami di acciaio, ma c'erano ancora, una trentina di anni fa, coloro che non conoscevano «*nulla di meglio per lo squalo-tigre dell'amo all'antica, lungo trenta centimetri, fatto di legno duro come il ferro e foggiato nella giusta forma sull'albero stesso, ancor vivo*».

Eccone il procedimento davvero imprevedibile, quanto indovinato: una radice di un grande albero (il *Pemphis acidula*) veniva curvata in modo che si ripiegasse su se stessa e lasciata crescere in quella posizione per un anno o due. Quando aveva raggiunto lo spessore di circa un centimetro e mezzo, la si tagliava e adattava allo scopo.

Il preminente vantaggio di questo gigantesco strumento, secondo i polinesiani, risiedeva nel fatto che «*si poteva farlo crescere con la magia, troncarlo con la magia, intagliarlo con la magia. Si poteva immettervi del buon augurio per il pescatore e del malaugurio per lo squalo in ogni fase della fabbricazione, laddove un amo d'acciaio acquistato nel negozio del villaggio non era influenzabile dagli incantesimi che una sola volta, in quanto oggetto già rifinito*». Secondo i vecchi, nessuno, tranne coloro che ignoravano gli opportuni incantesimi, si sarebbe mai sognato di adoperare altri ami all'infuori di quelli di legno.

Una novantina di centimetri di capelli intrecciati, provenienti dalla chioma della moglie o della figlia del pescatore, costituivano il setale di un amo all'antica, mentre la lenza era formata da una corda di fibra di noce di cocco spessa come l'indice di un uomo.

Ritorniamo al mare. Vediamo con gli occhi di chi – in un tempo anche non lontano – è vissuto in isole abitate da polinesiani, il cui sostentamento era ancora soprattutto affidato alle sorti della pesca. Leggiamo una cronaca solo di ieri su quanto accadeva nella laguna o in mare aperto in un mattino di lavoro alle reti e alle esche sugli ami. Fra i tanti testimoni e le infinite narrazioni e cronache di un tempo molto lontano, ho scelto una pagina di Paul Gauguin nella quale egli narra una caccia al tonno, su un'imbarcazione tahitiana agli inizi di questo secolo.

Un bel giorno gli uomini vararono una grande piroga a bilanciere, la quale reca a prora un lungo palo, che può essere sollevato con due canapi attaccati alla poppa. Con questo mezzo il pesce, quando abbocca, può essere rapidamente tirato a bordo. Uscendo da un varco aperto nella scogliera lasciammo la laguna e avanzammo verso l'alto mare. Una tartaruga ci guardò passare. Giungemmo in un punto dove il mare è molto profondo. Esso è conosciuto come la «buca dei tonni», perché laggiù, in profondità, i tonni passano la notte dormendo, fuori portata dagli squali. Un nugolo di uccelli marini era di guardia ai tonni e, ogni volta che un pesce arrivava in superficie, si tuffavano, alzandosi nuovamente con un pezzo di carne nel becco. Eravamo in mezzo a un bagno di sangue. [...]

Il capobarca ordinò a uno dell'equipaggio di gettare l'amo. Il tempo passava e nemmeno un tonno abboccava. L'incarico venne passato a un altro uomo. Questa volta abboccò un magnifico pesce, che incurvò il palo. Quattro robuste braccia cominciarono a tirar le corde da poppa e il tonno salì lentamente in superficie. In quel momento uno squalo s'avventò sulla preda. Pochi morsi delle sue mandibole e per noi, a bordo della barca, rimase soltanto la testa. La pesca cominciava male [...], poi presto prendemmo un grosso tonno. Un bastone e pochi colpi rapidi sulla testa furono sufficienti perché quel corpo iridescente e brillante si contorcesse negli spasimi della morte. Uguale successo avemmo una seconda volta.[1]

Arthur Grimble, entrato nel Colonial Office nel 1913, quale cadetto («qualcosa» gli aveva detto un suo superiore «di molto simile a un lustrascarpe, alle dipendenze di lustrascarpe più alti in grado»), quando poi crebbe di grado (vicegovernatore, e infine governatore) visse lunghi anni negli arcipelaghi della Micronesia. Congedatosi, ritornò alle Gilbert con la sua famiglia, incantato da quegli atolli e dall'esistenza di quegli isolani, che egli aveva imparato a conoscere da un punto di vista diverso da come glielo aveva prima imposto il codice sul trattamento dei colonizzati. Di quella esperienza egli ha lasciato testimonianze che ci documentano, fra l'altro, su sistemi di pesca oggi scomparsi completamente in Oceania.

Le avventure più frequenti da lui raccontate sono quelle con i pescecani, con i quali i polinesiani hanno sempre saputo convivere.

È sorprendente leggere, nei suoi scritti, come la pesca del pescecane fosse praticata da un uomo solo, su una piccola piroga non

[1] P. Gauguin, *Noa-noa*, 1990.

più lunga di lui. Il motivo era evidente e logico: era la piroga stessa a reggere gli strappi furiosi dello squalo alla lenza, e non la mano del pescatore. Per questo era un bene che la canoa fosse piccola per non opporre troppa resistenza alle galoppate del pesce impazzito: con una imbarcazione troppo grande, la cima che reggeva l'amo si sarebbe spezzata.

Il pescatore si porta al largo [narra Grimble], col suo guscio di noce, dispone l'esca sull'amo, sia esso di legno o d'acciaio, un'esca costituita di circa un chilogrammo di qualsiasi carne, la cala al centro dell'imbarcazione fino a due o tre braccia di profondità e si lascia andare alla deriva in attesa che la preda abbocchi, tenendosi il bastone a portata di mano. Un grosso pescecane abbocca all'amo. La canoa fino allora immobile si scuote improvvisamente e comincia a filare tutto intorno seguendo piccoli cerchi velocissimi; oppure sobbalza come impazzita su e giù; oppure procede a zigzag come un razzo mal diretto; o ancora corre in linea retta, avanti e indietro, a seconda dei casi, a spaventosa velocità, mentre il pescatore resiste cocciuto, qualsiasi cosa accada. [...] Ma la furibonda lotta dello squalo-tigre sfinisce ben presto il mostro; eccolo galleggiare inerte alla superficie, e allora giunge il gran momento nella giornata del pescatore.

Altri indigeni delle Gilbert vanno a caccia sott'acqua di squali-tigre, come altri cacciatori vanno dietro alla tigre, li affrontano cioè nello stesso loro elemento. Mentre veleggiavo un giorno con un amico di Taraua, additai una pinna dorsale che solcava la superficie del mare. «Quello è un *tababa*» disse: «Stai a vedere come lo uccido».

Ammainammo la vela e ci lasciammo andare alla deriva sulla corrente. L'indigeno scivolò col coltello e nuotò tutto attorno, aspettando di essere avvistato; e ben presto il pescecane si accorse di lui. La pinna cominciò a girare intorno all'uomo ed egli si rese conto che il mostro gli stava dando la caccia; percosse allora l'acqua e il pescecane si avvicinò a poco a poco, pigramente, fino a una quindicina di metri di distanza.

L'uomo impugnava il coltello con la mano destra, la lama all'ingiù, il manico appena sul pelo dell'acqua, il gomito destro ripiegato e puntato sempre verso la pinna lucente. Una volta iniziatasi la carica, non avrebbe avuto che una frazione di secondo per agire. Lo squalo si trovava ora a una decina di metri di distanza. Scorsi un guizzo spumoso; la pinna si precipitò innanzi con la velocità di una freccia. La testa e la parte anteriore del corpo del bruto affiorarono alla superficie, dondolando mentre balzavano innanzi. Il mio amico si gettò di lato proprio all'ultimo istante e affondò il coltello nel ventre inarcato dello squalo che gli passava accanto; lo slancio dell'avversario fece il resto. Vidi il ventre aprirsi come una chiusura lampo, perdendo sangue e visceri. Lo squalo-tigre scomparve per qualche tempo, ma tornò a galleggiare morto, un centinaio di metri più lontano.

I vecchi pescatori delle Gilbert solevano parlare, con evidente paura, di polpi giganti, dai tentacoli lunghi tre volte le loro braccia aperte, e grossi vicino alla testa quanto il corpo di un uomo. Ma il Grimble non aveva incontrato nessuno che ne avesse visti, sebbene la loro esistenza potesse essere reale, a giudicare da una mostruosa varietà di *Octopus*, alcuni esemplari del quale, pescati sulle coste nord-americane del Pacifico, hanno dimostrato, aperti a raggiera, una misura del loro diametro di ben otto metri e mezzo! Nelle Gilbert si poteva incontrare l'*Octopus vulgaris*, con tentacoli lunghi un metro e ottanta; temibili, come lo testimonia la pelle strappata via alla gamba di un pescatore, afferrato da un tentacolo e sforzatosi per liberarsi con uno strappo dalle ventose. Grimble aveva osservato il modo strano di pesca dell'*Octopus* mediante un'esca umana; e anzi aveva sperimentato a far lui da esca, riportandone un'impressione tutt'altro che gradevole. Tra le sue pagine più emozionanti in proposito, val la pena di ricordare un'avventura di pesca al polpo la cui cattura è resa possibile dal coraggio dell'uomo esca.

Gli indigeni delle Gilbert apprezzano molto come cibo determinate parti dei grandi polpi; e il loro metodo per catturare il mostro si basa freddamente proprio sul fatto che i suoi tentacoli non mollano mai la presa. I pescatori agiscono a coppie; uno dei due fa da esca, l'altro ha il compito di uccidere. Anzitutto, tenendo il viso sott'acqua, essi nuotano con la bassa marea lungo il margine esterno della scogliera e frugano con lo sguardo i crepacci della parete sommersa. Una volta individuata la vittima, tornano sulla scogliera per prepararsi alla seconda fase della caccia, fase che si inizia con l'intervento di colui che funge da esca umana. Il pescatore si tuffa e alletta la bestia in agguato nuotando di fronte al suo nascondiglio, dapprima fuori portata dei tentacoli, poi si volta e punta diritto verso la tana, per abbandonarsi all'abbraccio dei tentacoli in attesa. A volte non accade nulla; non sempre il polpo reagisce all'esca. Ma di solito colpisce.

Il compagno del pescatore, sulla sovrastante scogliera, spinge lo sguardo nelle acque trasparenti, in attesa del suo momento. La sola arma di cui disponga sono i denti; e la sua efficienza nell'uccidere dipende dal saper evitare ognuno di quei tentacoli strangolatori. Deve aspettare finché il corpo del compagno non sia afferrato dal polpo. La bestia, dentro al nascondiglio, sta allora premendo la cornea bocca contro le carni della vittima e non vede null'altro. Tale fase della caccia viene raggiunta in non più di trenta secondi dopo che l'uomo-esca si è tuffato; l'altro si tuffa a sua volta, afferra l'amico prigioniero tenendosi discosto da lui il più possibile e lo strappa via dal crepaccio. Il polpo viene staccato dall'ancoraggio delle grosse ventose e si avvinghia con forza maggiore alla preda. Nello stesso momento l'esca umana sferra un calcio che lo spinge, assieme al polpo, alla superficie. Qui, si stende sul dorso continuando a trattenere il respiro per stare meglio a galla, e ciò espone il corpo del polpo in modo da facilitarne l'uccisione. L'altro pescatore si avvicina, afferra dal di dietro la molle testa e la strappa dal pasto; voltandola verso di sé, affonda i denti fra gli occhi sporgenti e morde con tutta la sua forza. Questa è la fine; il polpo muore all'istante. Le ventose allentano la presa, i tentacoli si afflosciano.

Avventure e tecniche di pesca in Oceania potrebbero riempire libri. Ne ricorderemo altre, più avanti, che possono parere ancor più leggendarie di quella dell'uomo-esca. È certo, in ogni modo, che il pescatore dell'Oceania conosceva sino a ieri, come nessun altro, il mondo sommerso, perché là tutte le mattine scendeva e cacciava per procurarsi il vitto quotidiano per la famiglia.

La pesca è momento fondamentale della vita quotidiana delle isole, così come la magia. Era inevitabile, quindi, che nella Polinesia di un tempo questi due aspetti tanto importanti finissero ininterrottamente per incontrarsi, per confondersi;[1] tanto che è difficile all'osservatore poter distinguere – nel racconto di una particolare battuta, o di una avventura di pesca in oceano o in laguna – dove finisce la descrizione di una tecnica e dove inizia la fantasia del supposto intervento magico. Conturbante esperienza che ho avuto modo di provare personalmente in varie occasioni (per esempio, nell'assistere alla pesca delle tartarughe all'isola di Koro[2]); qui, per restare al testo di Grimble, vorrei riportare un altro brano da *Le isole delle anime* che mi sembra, in proposito, molto indicativo.

Nelle isole Gilbert – narra Grimble – era assai diffusa la diceria secondo la quale alcuni sciamani locali avevano il potere di chiamare a terra con la loro magia le focene, i piccoli delfini.

Fu il vecchio Kitiona che mise all'opera l'uomo che sapeva chiamare le focene. [...] Suo cugino in primo grado era un vero esperto in merito,

---

[1] Occorre annotare che questo «incontro» tra pesca e magia non è prerogativa solo polinesiana, ma fatto comune o quotidiano di tutte le genti di tutti i mari del mondo; e con una persistenza tenace anche oggi.
[2] Vedi pp. 302-303.

capace di sognare, a richiesta, i necessari sogni. Nel corso di tali sogni, lo spirito di lui si allontanava dal corpo; andava in cerca delle focene nelle loro dimore, al di là dell'orizzonte occidentale, e le invitava a una danza, con festeggiamenti, nel villaggio di Kuma. Se avesse pronunciato senza errori le parole dell'invito (e ben pochi ne conoscevano il segreto) le focene lo avrebbero seguito con grida di gioia alla superficie.

Dopo averle guidate fino all'entrata della laguna, egli volava avanti per rientrare nel proprio corpo e avvertire il popolo del loro arrivo. Si trattava di cosa semplicissima, per chi sapeva come comportarsi. Non accadeva mai che le focene non arrivassero. [...] Per favore, soggiunse in tono fermo, volevo essere così cauto da chiamarle, d'ora in poi, *soltanto* «i nostri amici dell'Ovest»? L'altro nome era tabù. Poteva darsi che non venissero affatto, se lo si pronunciava a voce alta. Parlando, mi condusse verso una capannuccia [...] situata accanto alla sua normale abitazione. Solo lì dentro, mi spiegò, avrebbe svolto il suo lavoro. Volevo onorare la sua casa, riposando mentre lui sognava? «Aspetta in pace, ora» disse, quando mi fui accomodato. «Io parto per il mio viaggio», e scomparve nella capannuccia schermata. [...]

Le quattro erano ormai passate; la mia fede cominciava a crollare dopo quella lunga attesa, quando un urlo strozzato si levò dalla capannuccia dell'uomo che sognava. Mi voltai di scatto e appena in tempo per scorgere il suo gonfio corpo sprizzare a testa avanti attraverso gli schermi di foglie sfondati. Cadde lungo disteso, si rialzò a fatica e barcollò all'aperto, con un filo di bava che gli luceva sul mento. Per qualche tempo rimase in piedi, artigliando l'aria e gemendo su una strana nota acuta, simile all'uggiolare di un cagnolino. Poi, interrotte parole gli scaturirono dalle labbra: «*Teirake! Teirake!* (levatevi! levatevi!)... Vengono, vengono!... I nostri amici dell'O-vest... Arrivano!... Andiamo ad accoglierli». E si avviò di gran carriera giù per la spiaggia.

Molti urli si alzarono dal villaggio: «Arrivano, arrivano!». E mi sorpresi intento a correre nelle acque basse, frammischiato a centinaia di altre persone, urlando con tutto il fiato che avevo in corpo che i nostri amici dell'Ovest stavano arrivando. [...]

Le focene erano assai vicine, ormai, e stavano capriolando verso di noi a una bella velocità. [...]

Si stavano dirigendo verso di noi in ordine sparso [...] fin dove poteva giungere il mio sguardo. E tanto lento era il loro moto che le si sarebbe dette in preda a una catalessi. Quella che le guidava sfiorò le gambe dell'uomo che aveva sognato; egli si voltò senza pronunciar parola e camminò accanto a essa che procedeva lenta verso i bassifondi. [...]

Si udì un chiacchierio di conversazioni sommesse. [...] Gli abitanti del villaggio davano il benvenuto ai loro ospiti, sulla spiaggia, con un cantilenar di parole. [...]

«Issate!» gridò l'uomo che aveva sognato, e le poderose forme oscure vennero – in parte sollevate, in parte trascinate – portate a riva senza che opponessero resistenza, là dove le onde lambivano la sabbia. Qui furono deposte, quelle forme bellissime, ricche d'una calma dignità, definitivamente in pace, mentre attorno a loro scoppiava un pandemonio. Uomini, donne e bambini, balzando e assumendo strani atteggiamenti con urla che giungevano al cielo, si strapparono di dosso le ghirlande e le gettarono sugli immobili corpi. [...]

Le lasciammo inghirlandate dove si trovavano e tornammo nelle capanne. Più tardi, quando la bassa marea le aveva abbandonate in alto sulle rive e all'asciutto, gli uomini si recaro a farle a pezzi con i coltelli.[1]

Fino a che punto questi racconti delle Gilbert di cinquant'anni fa sono cronaca vissuta veramente «sino in fondo», è domanda alla quale – dopo più di tanti anni di viaggi in Oceania – non saprei come rispondere. Sento di poter testimoniare in buona fede che quando la «pesca collettiva» si mutava in «festa collettiva» (se praticata ancora con la verità, ad esempio, della *taotai taora ofai* alla quale partecipai nel '56 a Bora-Bora[2]) lo spettatore perdeva, d'un tratto, la nozione della realtà.

Caratteristica, questa, e soprattutto *forza* di tutte le manifestazioni collettive, e non solo quelle di pesca e non solo in Oceania, poiché simile dimensione caratterizza analoghe manifestazioni in molte aree culturali primitive nel mondo. Pertanto, queste pagine sulla «vita quotidiana» in Oceania non apparirebbero complete senza un accenno a riti collettivi, ad esempio quelli nelle ricorrenze che scandiscono la successione delle stagioni.

I fenomeni stagionali, dai quali dipende il sostentamento della comunità, quali il fruttificare delle messi e degli alberi, il ritorno di certi uccelli, il passo di certi pesci riescono inspiegabili, misteriosi, per cui vengono attribuiti alle divinità che tali fenomeni impersonificano.

Per questo le cerimonie in onore – o per invocare – questi eventi coincidono, con un momento particolare dell'anno solare, desunto dal calendario dei raccolti o della pesca, il trapasso cioè da un passato ormai concluso verso un futuro appena all'inizio. Sono dette feste dell'anno nuovo, della nuova vita, o di Capodanno: le cerimonie esprimono l'idea di una rigenerazione, il bisogno di

[1] A. Grimble, *op. cit.*
[2] Vedi pp. 188-190.

assicurarsi la sopravvivenza del mondo in cui viviamo, per il successivo raccolto o stagione di pesca.

Sono pratiche, insomma, per la conservazione degli elementi della natura, senza i quali soccomberebbe tutto, il sole, la terra, gli uomini; hanno pure il fine di placare gli spiriti dei morti facendoli partecipare per qualche tempo alla vita rituale della comunità, ma respingendoli poi alle loro dimore lontane.

Di proposito, nelle pagine che seguono, ho evitato l'inserimento di mie note fra i testi prescelti; e questi testi raggruppano feste di contadini delle regioni interne della Melanesia e feste di pescatori della Polinesia; molte di esse non sono più praticate, altre lo sono ma hanno perduto il loro significato. Il documento è in tal caso trascritto come «testimonianza» (l'ennesima!) di una Oceania che non esiste più.

> I riti pubblici costituiscono effettivamente un vero spettacolo. [...]
> Tutti, il corpo lucente di olio di cocco profumato, avranno sottolineato i tratti del viso con svariati colori, avranno infilato fra i capelli fiori, pettini e piume, sulle braccia e sulle gambe anelli di conchiglie bianche, legacci rossi o chiari. Si vedono apparire costumi straordinari, per i quali sono state usate tutte le risorse della plastica, del «collage» e delle più varie combinazioni di [...] elementi marini: conchiglie, lastre di tridacna in forma di disco, di mezzaluna o di bastone. [...] e ragnatele, coleotteri dorati disposti a fregio, mucchi di fango colorato o dipinto esternamente, oltre a una quantità di fronde e foglie colorate.
> Chi assistesse a questi giochi collettivi dall'alto di un albero vedrebbe disegnarsi sul terreno, nel corso delle feste, motivi longitudinali, trasversali, circolari, ovali, a spirale, rigorosamente composti attorno a un punto centrale o a un asse. Si potrebbe anche scorgervi un simbolismo in stretto rapporto con i miti della vita e della morte o con le idee localmente diffuse sulla cosmologia. Il tornare degli uomini nella danza corrisponde a quello della danza sottomarina o sotterranea degli dèi, come agli atti degli uomini corrispondono, nel paese dei morti, atti inversi: di gente, per esempio, che si ciba di ciò che ai vivi ripugna.[1]

Negli anni Settanta, in Melanesia, ho avuto la fortuna di assistere a quella festa di *Milamala* che tanto ha interessato etnologi e antropologi, americani ed europei.

[1] J. Guaiart, *op. cit.*

La cerimonia d'apertura del grande ciclo festivo è una consacrazione dei tamburi cerimoniali, che prima di questa occasione è vietato usare. Il rito di chiusura consiste nell'espulsione dei morti ottenuta mediante la formula di scongiuro accompagnata da un pauroso rullio dei tamburi. Infatti i morti ritornano in occasione di *Milamala*, dall'isola di Tuma, che è la loro dimora posta a settentrione – nell'arcipelago delle Trobriand – e visitano il villaggio natio. [...] Per tutta la durata del mese *Milamala* il villaggio è trasformato in una grande pubblica mostra di frutti e prodotti: i magazzini di ignami sono resi ostentatamente visibili al pubblico e ornati a festa, mentre banane, taro, cocco e tutti i prodotti dell'anno sono simbolicamente riuniti sopra piattaforme speciali. [...]

Si fa anche un'offerta di cibi ai morti che vengono in visita al villaggio: vivande cotte si ostentano all'uopo sopra palchi speciali nello spiazzo centrale, fra i passaggi da una all'altra casa, dinanzi alle case e perfino ai margini del villaggio; i morti godranno allo spettacolo, si sazieranno dell'«essenza» dei cibi, saranno soddisfatti e pacificati. [...]

I morti o *baloma*, relegati nella loro isola, nella rappresentazione che di essi ci si fa sono tormentati dalla fame: usano apparire in sogno ai viventi e chiedere cibo. Inoltre la collera dei morti è grave per i vivi. Se non venissero soddisfatti nei loro bisogni, se un'inosservanza o una negligenza dei riti li offendesse, i morti riverserebbero il loro astio inesorabilmente, provocando malanni irreparabili per l'anno successivo, cioè carestia, assalti di cinghiali agli orti, marciume di tuberi: tutte piaghe sociali tra le più perniciose e più compromettenti per il benessere pubblico di una società di coltivatori. I morti esercitano, dunque, la loro continua potenziale minaccia.[1]

Una festa annuale dei morti è celebrata dagli indigeni *enga* nella regione di Mount Hagen (Nuova Guinea nord-orientale, zona interna). In essa si riscontra una forma particolare di culto delle pietre. Pietre sacre di forma differente, a seconda che simboleggino individui di sesso maschile o femminile, vengono di regola tenute nascoste sotto terra, in luoghi che solo individui devoti a tale culto e addetti al loro sotterramento conoscono. Le sacre pietre vengono dissotterrate solo in occasione della festa dei morti, a opera dei medesimi addetti al culto, e portate in un luogo detto *imbuand*, sorta di «orto degli spiriti» nel quale viene eretta una capanna in miniatura entro cui le pietre sono disposte in bell'ordine. Gli spiriti dei morti sono invitati a venire: a tale scopo un maiale prescelto viene ucciso e spartito, i pezzi di carne sono deposti sui rami di un albero appositamente ornato per raccogliere gli spiriti. Mentre una danza rituale è eseguita attorno al luogo sacro, agli spiriti viene rivolta un'invocazione: che essi diano un ricco e buon raccolto, che i maiali prolifichino abbondantemente.

[1] V. Lanternari, *op. cit.*

Le feste oceaniane di Capodanno, con le quali s'inaugura un nuovo ciclo stagionale e se ne chiude uno precedente, riaprono la pesca di determinati animali e concludono il raccolto agricolo. Sono collegate a un richiamo degli spiriti dei morti, dalle loro dimore lontane, per presenziare benevoli alle cerimonie e gustare delle primizie offerte dal villaggio, dopo di che essi saranno invitati a ripartire.

Fra le popolazioni di pescatori, la cattura della prima tartaruga è celebrata con riti particolari. Vittorio Lanternari scrive su tale argomento:

> Fra i pescatori delle isole Tuamotu vige un rito di Capodanno che sancisce la prima pesca di tartarughe dell'anno. La tartaruga è immolata in onore dei morti, i quali, sollecitati a «svegliarsi» mediante un canto rituale, in massa convergono a riva, montati sul caratteristico «battello dei morti», carico dei loro fantasmi.

> Tra i kiwai della Nuova Guinea [...] la prima pesca di tartarughe è sancita cerimonialmente dal rito Horiomu, con ritorno dei morti e offerta di primizie volta ai medesimi. Alle Hawaii, ove agricoltura e pesca sono attività preminenti come in tutto il Pacifico, il ciclo di Capodanno Matahiki, imperniato fondamentalmente sulla religione agraria, sancisce ritualmente anche l'inizio della stagione di pesca. Gli uomini scendono in mare con canoe, fanno la pesca e tornati a riva volgono un'offerta agli dèi o *atua* venuti a partecipare alla festa.

Anzi, alle Tuamotu, secondo quanto scrive Peter Buck, ogni tartaruga dava motivo a speciali cerimonie, nei templi all'aperto:

> Le principali cerimonie celebrate in queste corti avevano luogo in occasione di banchetti a base di tartaruga: ogni volta che si catturava una tartaruga di mare, un pezzo di sterno, immediatamente staccato, veniva offerto con accompagnamento di una formula magica al dio Tangaroa. Le donne non potevano partecipare alla festa, perché la carne di tartaruga era loro proibita.

Anche nell'Isola di Pasqua, le tartarughe dovettero avere grande importanza nella vita religiosa. Scrive Métraux:

> Le tartarughe sono diventate rare, ma parecchi petroglifi le rappresentano e di esse si parla in diverse leggende. [...] Quando venivano segnalate delle tartarughe al largo dell'isola, gli indigeni si lanciavano al loro inseguimento con i canotti, si tuffavano dietro di loro e le sospingevano verso una rete a maglie molto spesse. Ritenevano così pregiati questi animali che alcuni degli edifici di pietra secca, che sorgono sulla spiaggia, si dice fossero

delle vere e proprie torri di controllo, giorno e notte custodite da guardiani che vivevano nelle stanze annesse alle torri stesse.

Nel quadro di questa vita quotidiana dell'Oceania di un tempo, di cui tanto poco sopravvive oggi, un posto particolare occorre sia lasciato alla grande canoa oceanica. Strumento fondamentale, parte essenziale di una realtà e di una storia, così come lo fu il cavallo per i popoli indoeuropei o il carro nella conquista dell'Ovest americano.

La canoa vista in Oceania dai navigatori europei del XVIII secolo, viveva in quel tempo la sua epoca d'oro. Essa aveva compiuto le grandi esplorazioni e le trasmigrazioni polinesiane, e al dire delle guide e interpreti di Bougainville e di Cook, i famosi Atourou e Tupia, con essa si effettuavano ancora viaggi di quindici giorni o più senza scalo, su rotte di oltre mille miglia. L'arcipelago delle Tonga, famoso per i suoi marinai, i più audaci della Polinesia, aveva esteso un suo impero marittimo dovunque potessero giungere le sue linee per così dire «commerciali». La quantità, l'efficienza, la mole e la bellezza delle flotte incontrate dai navigatori europei, si può dire in ogni arcipelago, testimoniavano del grado di perfezione cui era giunta allora la marineria dei Mari del Sud.

Delle antiche canoe oceaniche non ce n'è pervenuta alcuna, perché, secondo la risposta del vecchio Pa a Buck,[1] le golette le avevano uccise; e su di esse non possediamo che i cenni degli stessi navigatori e le illustrazioni che ornano i loro libri di viaggio, oltre alle tradizioni e alle congetture degli studiosi.

Wallis e Cook accennano a flotte di duecento e trecento canoe (addirittura mille ne vide Cook, il giorno del suo ultimo approdo, nella baia di Kealakekua alle Hawaii), e ci danno misure sorprendenti, di settantacinque anche di centootto e persino di centodiciotto piedi, ossia di quasi trentasette metri. Potevano portare quaranta e anche cento armati; o anche duecento o trecento passeggeri. Descrizioni di manovre simultanee, di finte battaglie navali sono riportate spesso dai nostri esploratori; i quali annota-

[1] Vedi p. 80.

159

rono anche, nei loro «giornali di viaggio», che a eccezione della piroga da pesca o da viaggio familiare, le grandi canoe erano appannaggio dei soli grandi capi o dei re, per il loro forte costo; e venivano impiegate, nelle guerre o nei traffici collettivi.

Per le popolazioni dell'Oceania, la piroga – semplice, o a bilanciere, o doppia che fosse – non era legno soltanto, ma qualcosa di vivo[1] e di magico. Il fatto stesso di derivare da un potente ma rozzo tronco era un miracolo che il dio Tane compiva attraverso i suoi prediletti artigiani; esseri divini come lui presiedevano infatti a tutte le fasi della sua nascita, dalla scelta del tronco originario nella foresta al suo varo in mare. Rappresentava dunque una somma di sforzi e di perizia, insieme a un impregnamento di virtù e di poteri magici, per poter domare o propiziare le potenze occulte degli elementi da affrontare: onde, venti, gli ignoti orizzonti.

Numerosi studiosi hanno impiegato lunghi anni di ricerca e meditazioni sulla canoa dell'Oceania, per rintracciarne la genealogia e l'evoluzione nel tempo e nello spazio, nella sua varietà di tipi.

James Hornell, famoso investigatore dei misteri delle navi dei primitivi, si è preoccupato della tecnica costruttiva della canoa polinesiana; Peter Buck, invece, ne ha indagato i riti che conferivano una personalità vivente alla canoa; Henri Teuira è andato al particolare del sistema di cuciture, con il quale certi tipi evoluti di canoa venivano tenuti insieme; Bronislaw Malinowski si è occupato in prevalenza del rapporto tra canoa e mondo magico nell'Oceania occidentale. Il campo, malgrado i loro sforzi ammirevoli, è ancora in buona parte da scavare. Scrive Malinowski:

La piroga, strumento indispensabile per la sussistenza mediante la pesca, unico mezzo di trasporto fra le isole, potente macchina di guerra..., aveva raggiunto, con le grandi trasmigrazioni nel Pacifico, un grado di

[1] Anche in questo caso, occorre aggiungere che una credenza del genere non è particolare dell'Oceania, ma fa parte di una comune tradizione marina. L'etnografo Dick Dayala – specializzato in questo campo per l'area mediterranea – faceva notare in proposito che i due «occhi» dipinti sulla prora di tanti battelli dei nostri mari non avevano affatto una funzione decorativa o di generico portafortuna... ma sin dal tempo dei fenici, sino ai nostri giorni erano *occhi per vedere*; organi sensoriali *per un vero e proprio corpo vivo*, così come il marinaio di tanti mari considera la propria imbarcazione.

bellezza e di capacità nautica paragonabile a quello dei grandi velieri europei e americani del XIX secolo. Con mezzi dell'età della pietra, i tahitiani di un tempo realizzarono imbarcazioni ben studiate e veri battelli d'alto mare. Ci sarebbe da non credere che i polinesiani, con una cultura materiale tanto primitiva, abbiano scoperto i principi costruttivi delle grandi piroghe a bilanciere e a doppio scafo... i fasciami di tavole combacianti e legate fra loro, le vele di stuoie intrecciate.

In realtà, la genesi della canoa oceanica non è univoca né localizzabile. Come nella storia della nave in genere, anche la canoa dell'Oceania si valse di vari apporti, che elaborò col tempo, a essi aggiungendo intuizioni e perfezionamenti successivi: il miracolo consiste nel fatto che i polinesiani, in particolare, siano riusciti a dominare con scuri di pietra e succhielli di conchiglia la materia bruta, e con questa, infine, a dominare l'onda, e la vastità oceanica.

La nascita di una canoa passa per due fasi: quella costruttiva e quella animatrice. La prima comincia da lontano, dalla scelta di un tronco nella foresta, l'altra si proietta nel futuro, sul destino che l'attende fino all'ultimo istante in cui galleggerà.

Quando un capo progettava un viaggio per cui era necessaria una nuova canoa, comandava ai suoi sudditi di seminare messi più abbondanti [scrive il Buck] per nutrire gli artigiani di cui avrebbe richiesto il lavoro, e di preparare tessuti di scorza d'albero, di intrecciare stuoie, di raccogliere piume rosse, come doni di pagamento. Quando era stata raccolta una quantità sufficiente di provviste e di doni, il capo chiamava uno o più capi artigiani che si incaricassero del lavoro, e con loro andava nella foresta a scegliere gli alberi adatti per costruire le varie parti della canoa.

Infine si passava al taglio. Prima si compiva una serie di riti ben precisi, l'omissione dei quali sarebbe stata gravida di disgrazie (al mitico eroe polinesiano Rata, che li aveva trasgrediti, il giorno dopo il taglio l'albero già abbattuto si era ripresentato ritto e vegeto al suo posto di prima). Secondo Malinowski, negli arcipelaghi papua viene recitato un invito ai geni della foresta, perché cedano l'albero, loro dimora. Il *toliwaga* (padrone della futura piroga), il costruttore e qualche aiutante introducono un po' di cibo e una scheggia di noce d'areca in un foro praticato nel tronco, e con questa offerta invitano i *tokway* a sloggiare:

Scendete o spiritelli dei boschi, o *tokway*, abitatori dei rami, scendete. Scendete, voi che abitate i rami forcuti e i giovani germogli! Scendete, venite e mangiate!... Ecco qui un tronco di cattiva reputazione; un tronco coperto di obbrobrio, un tronco dal quale voi siete scacciati! All'alba e durante il mattino, ci aiuterete ad abbattere questo tronco; è nostro ora, o vecchi! Lasciatelo andare e cadere.[1]

[...] Seguiva, nei recinti del tempio, un banchetto riservato agli artigiani più esperti. Veniva ucciso un porco ingrassato, e, mentre lo preparavano per metterlo in forno, gli venivano strappati ciuffi di setole come offerta a Tane, mentre gli artigiani recitavano il loro motto:

> Lavora con occhi attenti
> con asce svelte...

Allo spuntare dell'alba le asce ancora dormienti erano svegliate immergendole nell'acqua del mare, l'elemento sul quale l'opera loro, una volta portata a termine, avrebbe dovuto galleggiare. Mentre la fredda acqua toccava l'orlo delle asce, risuonava l'esortazione:

> Svegliatevi a lavorare per Tane,
> il grande dio degli artigiani.[2]

Tale rito, secondo Malinowski, si riallaccia a un mito, quello detto della «piroga volante», localizzato nel villaggio di Kudayuri, nell'isola di Kitava. La formula magica diceva:

Impugnerò un'accetta, colpirò! Salirò sulla mia canoa, ti farò volare, o canoa, ti farò saltare. Noi voleremo come farfalle, come vento, spariremo nella nebbia, scompariremo!

Seguivano indicazioni geografiche, sugli stretti che la canoa avrebbe varcato, e le isole che avrebbe raggiunto. E ancora proseguiva:

Ti perderai nella lontananza, ti perderai con il vento, ti nasconderai nella nebbia.

Il carpentiere cominciava allora il lavoro dello svuotamento del tronco, che alla fine compiva da solo, data la delicatezza del lavoro di assottigliamento delle pareti dello scafo; quest'opera prendeva di conseguenza molto tempo.

---

[1] B. Malinowski, *Argonauts in the Western Pacific*.
[2] P. Buck, *op. cit.*

In Polinesia i grandi scàfi erano cuciti, cioè costituiti di tavole di fasciame tenute insieme da cordicelle passanti per appositi fori lungo i comenti: operazione quindi delicata per l'esattezza richiesta e impegnativa per le funzioni che tali legami erano destinati a compiere.

Prima di accostare l'una all'altra le tavole del fasciame, l'orlo della tavola inferiore veniva spalmato di fango: le imperfezioni, denunciate da macchie di fango sulla tavola superiore, erano corrette con cura, finché i margini delle due tavole non aderivano perfettamente.

Per calafatare le connessure si usavano gusci di noce di cocco ridotti in poltiglia e resina dell'albero del pane. Inoltre in prossimità dei margini delle tavole si praticavano, con bastoncelli appuntiti di legno duro o scalpelli di pietra, fori appaiati, attraverso i quali, per tenere insieme le varie parti della canoa, veniva fatta passare una corda costituita di una triplice treccia di fibra di cocco.

> Corda che ci viene dall'ospite del cielo,
> Corda che ci viene da te, o Tane!
> Se l'infili da dentro, sporge in fuori,
> Se l'infili da fuori, sporge in dentro.
> Legala ben dura, stringila ben forte.[1]

Imposto un nome alla canoa, il suo varo era avvenimento che richiamava gente da ogni luogo dell'isola; gli intervenuti vi giungevano inghirlandati di fiori o di erbe odorose, con i loro indumenti e ornamenti preferiti, affollando la spiaggia. Precedeva un sontuoso banchetto, in onore degli artigiani. Il capo dei carpentieri, dopo che sul tragitto tra il cantiere e l'acqua erano stati sistemati rulli di legno, quando gli uomini erano allineati lungo le fiancate per spingere la barca, una volta tolti i puntelli, «invocava l'aiuto dei numerosi dèi che potevano assistere lo sforzo degli uomini nello spingere l'imbarcazione verso l'acqua» scrive Peter Buck. Intanto gli uomini, nella fatica dello spingere, cantavano dandosi il ritmo:

> Un rullo è sistemato
> un rullo davanti per Atea...
> un rullo in mezzo per Atea!
> un rullo per lottare contro il vento!...
> Tane che regge i rulli,
> o Tane, adesso incantali.

---

[1] P. Buck, *op. cit.*

«Infine» prosegue Buck «fra le urla assordanti della folla, la canoa scivolava nella laguna e galleggiava con grazia sulle onde sollevatesi a salutarla.»

Fra i papua, secondo quanto riferisce Malinowski, erano in uso ancora altri riti preliminari; il *Wakasula*, cottura rituale della canoa, doveva donare velocità all'imbarcazione. Il suo padrone preparava «un vero calderone da strega e ingredienti che in seguito si fanno cuocere sotto il fondo della canoa, perché il fumo esercita una funzione purificatrice e "dona velocità"»; gli ingredienti erano ali di pipistrello, il nido di un uccellino *posisiku*, foglie di felci, peluria di cotone, e di erba *lalang*, indicanti volo, leggerezza. Anche la legna da ardere con tali ingredienti sotto la canoa doveva essere raccolta *al volo*, spezzando i rametti di alberi mediante sassate.

Il giorno dopo il varo si procedeva a completare la nuova imbarcazione, sistemando l'albero, la vela, e ogni altra attrezzatura. La legatura del buttafuori del bilanciere, in Polinesia, era operazione meticolosa e anch'essa regolata da riti. Il nodo stesso del buttafuori si rifaceva a una donna leggendaria, Lukia, per la quale, il marito geloso, aveva fatto confezionare una cintura di castità, tutta intrecci e nodi di cordicelle, detta appunto il «nodo di Lukia», indissolubile.

Finalmente la prova di velocità, ossia l'ingresso della nuova canoa fra le consorelle, fra le quali essa doveva dimostrarsi la migliore. Scrive Malinoswki in proposito:

La nuova canoa deve essere per forza la migliore e la più veloce. Vince sempre. Anche se non si distingue per velocità, gli altri cercheranno di restare indietro.

La corsa è piuttosto una specie di esibizione del nuovo scafo, fianco a fianco con gli altri. [...] Tre quarti di secolo fa,[1] la cerimonia rivestiva per gli indigeni un carattere molto più solenne e drammatico.

---

[1] Malinowski scriveva nel 1920.

Per i papua la navigazione fu sempre un fatto misterioso. Se il timore di finire, senza volerlo, su rive estranee atterriva la fantasia, i pericoli della navigazione in se stessa non erano immaginari. «Il mare che essi solcano è pieno di scogliere, di banchi di sabbia e di rocce a fior d'acqua; e anche se questi sono meno traditori per una canoa che non per un'imbarcazione europea, non sono tuttavia così inoffensivi» osserva il Malinowski.

Ciò che rende molto difficile la navigazione delle canoe indigene è che esse sono assai poco maneggevoli. Una canoa papua non può «stringere il vento», ciò che la rende incapace di bordeggiare. C'erano poi, oltre al rischio del naufragio, quello di approdare fra gente nemica.

C'era il rischio della prigionia, della schiavitù o peggio.

Esistono molti racconti di piroghe perdute, ed è straordinario che questi incidenti non avvenissero più spesso, se si tiene conto delle condizioni della navigazione...

Questi indigeni erano costretti ad andare su rotte obbligate:

Se sbarcavano in qualche parte abitata da una tribù non amica, correvano rischi non meno grandi di quello di finire su uno scoglio o di incontrare pescecani.

A ragione di tanti pericoli tra i papua l'utilizzare una piroga nuova impone numerosi divieti che vengono chiamati *bomala wayugo* («i tabù della scotta»). Per esempio, a bordo di una piroga nuova non si può né mangiare né bere, se non dopo il tramonto del sole; violare questo tabù renderebbe l'imbarcazione molto lenta. In realtà su una *waga* molto veloce si sorvola su questa ingiunzione, soprattutto se uno dei giovani ha fame o sete. In questo caso, il padrone della canoa attinge un po' d'acqua di mare, la versa sopra il nodo della scotta che lega la vela alla poppa della barca e dice: «Io bagno i tuoi occhi, o cavo *kudayuri*, perché tu non veda e i nostri marinai possano mangiare».

Oltre al tabù del bere e del mangiare, non è permesso su una nuova *waga* soddisfare i propri bisogni naturali. In caso di necessità, l'uomo si tuffa in mare e si aggrappa a uno dei bastoni che si incrociano sotto il galleggiante; quando si tratta di un ragazzo, un anziano l'aiuta a scendere in acqua.

Le donne non possono mai salire su una *waga* nuova prima della sua uscita in mare.

Ci sono, naturalmente, un buon numero di riti magici per far sì che il vento si alzi o cali.

Come molti altri riti di magia, quello del vento è appannaggio di alcuni villaggi. Gli abitanti di Simsim, il più grosso centro delle isole Luosançay, situato all'estremo nord-ovest di questo distretto, hanno la fama, senza dubbio per la loro posizione geografica, di poter controllare il vento. Si attribuisce per lo stesso motivo il potere di regolare il vento di sud-est ai nativi di Kitava, che si trova a est di Boyowa. [...]

È impressionante percorrere un villaggio durante uno di questi uragani devastatori che arrivano di notte e costringono gli abitanti ad abbandonare le loro capanne e a riunirsi negli spazi vuoti. Temono che il vento abbatta le loro dimore, o che sradichi un albero che potrebbe ferirli cadendo.

Al limitare di queste capanne, dai gruppi di persone strette le une contro le altre, si levano voci sonore, salmodianti con una ostinazione monotona: sono le formule suscettibili di rompere la forza della tempesta. In simili occasioni, mi sono sentito estremamente sensibile a questo sforzo, tutto della voce umana, che nonostante la sua fragilità affronta, sostenuta da una profonda fede, la potenza irresistibile e continuamente rinnovata del vento.[1]

Nelle relazioni dei viaggiatori europei s'incontrano spesso riferimenti allo stato di guerra fra talune isole, a operazioni navali, a parate navali dimostrative, cui assistette anche Cook; e anzi questo esploratore ricevette l'invito a entrare in alleanza per partecipare alla guerra imminente di Tahiti contro Moorea. Questi scontri armati (che si risolvevano per lo più in alto mare) nascevano per un nonnulla: la guida e interprete di Cook, il tahitiano Tupia, vedendo una cometa previde guerra imminente: bastava infatti un evento imprevisto a provocare lo scoppio di tensioni. Le flotte di grandi canoe erano quindi lo strumento principale dei combattimenti infrainsulari; e si può ammettere che l'ambita potenza navale, la «corsa agli armamenti» diremmo, fu causa fra le princi-

---

[1] B. Malinowski, *op. cit.*

pali dell'evoluzione tecnica della nave polinesiana o oceaniana in genere.

Malinowski accenna al modo in cui si svolgevano tali combattimenti, come si rileva dalle relazioni degli europei.

I due scafi delle canoe doppie, scostate fra loro di un metro circa, tenute insieme da un'armatura, travi e assi, avevano a proravia una specie di piattaforma sopraelevata dove si ammassavano i combattenti, che erano ben distinti dai vogatori, i quali badavano alle loro pagaie, vogando in piedi o seduti, col viso verso prora. Non c'erano scontri fra piroghe a vela. La tattica consisteva nell'affrontarsi, le opposte squadre, su linee di fronte, faccia a faccia, con le piroghe collegate da ormeggi fra di loro.

Queste due linee vogavano l'una contro l'altra, fino all'abbordaggio e i guerrieri, sulla piattaforma, combattevano senza pietà.

Tutto questo appartiene al passato. Dall'epoca d'oro della canoa dell'Oceania, e sommamente di quella gloriosa dei polinesiani, si è caduti nella fine repentina del ritrovato più classico e perfetto di quegli isolani. La canoa non seppe, e non poteva, reagire alla goletta, al trabiccolo a vapore, alla «grande barca» degli europei. Era, con la sua tecnica elaborata di costruzione, con gli artistici intagli delle sue polene, gli altissimi dritti di poppa dalle banderuole segnavento, i riti che ne regolavano la vita, il frutto di una società destinata a scomparire; in effetti non fu solo la concorrenza delle golette, incrocianti tra le isole per l'incetta dei prodotti, a uccidere le grandi piroghe, ma la decadenza generale degli arcipelaghi, con l'avvento dei primi protettorati, delle prime armi da fuoco e dei primi traffici con moneta sonante, in luogo dei venerati chiodi di Wallis e di Bougainville.

Nel 1774 Cook aveva stimato la popolazione di Tahiti in 240.000 abitanti; il censimento dei francesi, nel 1857, ne rilevò 7212 appena: in ottanta anni circa una ecatombe. Le cause? Le armi da fuoco fratricide, già nel 1789; le malattie (si disse che i balenieri di passaggio avevano trasformato le isole in lupanari); il sovvertimento dei regimi sociali antichi, con le nuove idee; l'economia di sfruttamento, senza dire delle prodezze degli schiavisti o dei reclutatori di lavoratori, che impoverirono di uomini i villaggi.

La canoa, espressione massima, insuperabile della cultura marinaresca dell'Oceania, seguì la sorte delle popolazioni che l'avevano generata e perfezionata.

Ma se è vero che non è sopravvissuto nemmeno un solo scafo dei grandi e famosi che vinsero l'oceano, è anche vero che qualcosa resta di quella gloria; resta la precisa tradizione dell'epica poetica marinara, soprattutto polinesiana; restano questi documenti in versi tramandati a voce, epopee del mare che sono parte essenziale di quella «letteratura oceaniana» la cui grandezza consistette soprattutto nella sua semplicità di fatto quotidiano. Un «fatto quotidiano» capace di trasmettere – di un tempo lontano come quello dell'*età d'oro* delle isole – vibrazioni come momenti di vita vissuta e come emozione di un sovrannaturale sempre immanente.

Canto e poesia in Oceania, infatti, non sono espressione del poeta, ma manifestazione corale di una fase culturale in cui la parola è carica ancora di potenza magica, il mito e la leggenda costituiscono la storia, e l'ordine sociale è regolato dal rito.

Canto e poesia tendono a soddisfare necessità pratiche della comunità: rievocare ritualmente – per la potenza del motivo, del ritmo, della parola – i grandi antenati, le divinità e gli eroi protettori.

In questi canti passa di tutto: teogonia, cosmologia, storia, epica, nautica, geografia, amore, per cui il rapsodo appare alla comunità come ispirato, quasi «conchiglia di tritone cui dà la voce un vento divino».[1]

Il poeta, infatti, non è un dotto o un sacerdote; più spesso è un marinaio che, in un lampo di rapimento, saluta con nobili epiteti l'isola appena scoperta. Frequenti sono le celebrazioni, diremmo campanilistiche, delle imprese dei propri dèi ed eroi, e della propria inconfondibile isola, impareggiabile per la sua forma, i colori, gli odori, i pesci, le pagaie.

---

[1] Erwin Maydell, studioso di costumi maori e polinesiani, Nuova Zelanda.

Vari canti sono cadenze tipiche di equipaggi in voga, orgogliosi del costruttore della piroga e della pagaia che ne governa la rotta, come della vigoria della cadenza della loro palata; o celebrazioni ritmate di altri celebrati navigli e navigatori; o cadenze di chi sgrossa un tronco con l'ascia, o di chi attende il vento, per veder sorgere infine l'isola attesa dall'orizzonte; o invoca il diradarsi delle nuvole, per scorgere le stelle della rotta, o invita o scongiura il dio dei venti; o declamazione di sentinella che sta all'erta.

Dalle letture che hanno preceduto o seguito i miei itinerari nei Mari del Sud, e dalle registrazioni che ho raccolto nelle Isole tra il 1955 e il 1991, ho tratto una vera e propria «antologia» della poetica oceaniana, che qui in parte trascrivo, con titoli puramente indicativi.

Canto del navigatore Kahu-Kora

Ora dirigo la prua della mia canoa
Verso la porta da cui appare il dio del sole,
Tama-nui-te-ra, Grande-figlio-del-sole.
Fa' ch'io non devii dalla mia rotta
Ma faccia vela diritto verso la terra, la Patria.
Soffia, soffia, o Tawhiri-matea, Dio dei Venti
Solleva il Vento occidentale che ci porti diretti
Lungo la strada del mare alla Patria, a Hawaiki.
Chiudi, chiudi il tuo occhio che guarda verso sud,
Così che quel tuo vento possa dormire.

Invocazione del pilota a Tangaroa, dio dell'Oceano

O Tangaroa nell'immensità dello spazio
Spazza le nubi nel giorno,
Spazza le nubi durante la notte,
Che Ru possa vedere le stelle del cielo
E ne sia guidato alla terra del suo desiderio.

Canto delle sentinelle sul promontorio di Kawhia

O soldati del forte, levatevi,
Se non volete sprofondare nella morte.
Alta, ben alta risuona
La fragorosa risacca sugli scogli di Harihari,

E il mare geme sommesso
Sulla costa di Mokau.
Ma io son qua, di sentinella,
E guardo, cerco, scruto,
Così come su quelle rocce scoscese
Il falco marino sta appollaiato
In attesa della sua preda.
Presto il sole si leverà
Fiammeggiando sul mondo.

Canto marinaio delle Tuamotu

Issate le vele
Le vele che ci porteranno lontano.
Dirigete la rotta verso una terra remota,
Partite con il favore di una corrente, con il vento in poppa.

Canto dei trasmigratori (Samoa?)

Come l'arcobaleno abbraccia gli orizzonti,
Così la canoa di Ui-te-rangiora solca i mari
Che fra essi si stendono.

Canto maori

Il mare ribolle
Il mare si ritira,
Ecco appare la terra
E su di essa è ritto Maui.

Canto maori («La pagaia»)

Aotea è la canoa,
Turi il capo,
Te Roku-o-whiti la pagaia.
Ecco la mia pagaia!
È posata lungo il fianco della canoa,
Ben vicina al fianco della canoa,
Ora è levata alta – la pagaia.
Ora che facciamo un balzo in avanti,
Guarda la mia pagaia, Te Roku-o-whiti!
Vedi come vola e riluce,
Freme come un'ala d'uccello,
Questa mia pagaia.

Sollevata lampeggia,
Rapida ricade nell'acqua, la getta indietro
La frusta,
L'ondata dalla bianca cresta, e la schiuma
Che si leva di sotto la mia pagaia.
Ascoltateci durante il nostro viaggio.

Preghiera dei navigatori di Tahiti

O dèi! Conduceteci
Fino alla terra con sicurezza
Che il nostro viaggio sia favorevole.
Senza cattivi avvenimenti.
Dateci una brezza,
Che essa ci segua,
Che il tempo sia bello e il cielo chiaro.
Ascoltateci, o dèi!

[Citato da P. Jourdan]

Canto maori

Alle onde dell'oceano, la canoa oppone la prua;
Alle onde degli uomini l'uomo oppone il suo coraggio.

Canti d'amore dell'Isola di Pasqua

Giovane Miru, sei bagnata fino al collo.
Ti ha bagnato la rugiada del Rano-Aroi.
Non sarai ancora asciutta
Quando sarai scesa sulla spiaggia
Per bagnare la scorza del gelso,
Con cui farai un nastro
Per i tuoi capelli.

Poesia d'amore di Bora-Bora

Quando l'ondosa risacca
e la luna nascente
e la svettante palma
e il volante uccello candido
e il pesce pigro
tutti parlano d'amore,
io grido nella notte:
dove sei tu, diletto?

Proverbio delle Samoa

I cieli ondeggiano
E toccano la terra.

Canto dell'isola di Aitutaki

Entro il cerchio del mare
c'è un pesce molto importante.
C'è un pesce
Sopra il quale s'incurva l'arcobaleno,
Che abbraccia l'immensità dell'oceano.
È la mia isola.

Canto maori di accoglienza

Tira in qua – la canoa!
Tira su – la canoa!
Al suo guanciale – la canoa!
Al suo letto – la canoa!
Al luogo dove riposerà – la canoa!
Benvenuto, tre volte benvenuto!

Canto maori

Mai si oscurerà la fama delle nostre canoe,
Le canoe che attraversano gli abissi dell'oceano,
Il mare di porpora, il grande Oceano-di-Kiwa,
Che si stendeva innanzi a loro.

Canto delle Sottovento

È Borapora; il suo motto sia
Borapora la grande, la primogenita,
Borapora cui il flutto si riversa da una e dall'altra parte.
Borapora dai remi silenziosi.
Borapora dalle rosse foglie,
Borapora la distruttrice di flotte.

[Citato da Peter Buck]

Canto d'addio di Mangareva

Raggiungete l'isola dei miei sogni,
cercate una riva meravigliosa,
dove il re possa porre la sua dimora.

Canto di Hawaii

Ecco gli dèi di Hawaii, dove sono nate le terre
di Hawaii, dove sono nati gli dèi
di Hawaii, dove sono nati i popoli.
Dèi all'interno, dèi all'esterno
dèi in alto, dèi giù in fondo,
dèi verso l'oceano, dèi verso la terra
dèi incarnati, dèi non incarnati
dèi che puniscono i peccati, dèi che perdonano i peccati
dèi divoratori di uomini, dèi uccisori di guerrieri
dèi salvatori degli uomini
dèi d'oscurità, dèi di luce
dèi dei dieci cieli
è possibile contare tutti gli dèi?
Innumeri sono gli dèi.

[Citato da Teuira Henry, in *Ancient Tahiti*]

Canto della canoa perduta

Schiuma, schiuma, onda che si frange, onda! Mi lancerò nell'onda
che si rompe, uscirò dietro ad essa. Da dietro mi ritufferò nell'onda
e uscirò di nuovo nella schiuma che produce, ricadendo.
Nebbia, nebbia crescente, nebbia avviluppante, circonda il mio
[albero!
Nebbia, nebbia crescente,... circonda la punta della mia barca!
Nebbia, nebbia, circonda la mia vela.
Nebbia, circonda il mio governale a poppa.
Nebbia circonda i miei attrezzi da pesca.
Nebbia circonda il mio ponte di bordo.
Io isolo i cieli con la nebbia; faccio tremare il mare con la nebbia;
vi chiudo la bocca, pescecani voi siete *bonubonu* [piccoli vermi], voi
siete *ginukwadewo* [altri vermi]. Andate sotto! e noi nuoteremo in
[superficie.

[Citato da B. Malinowski]

Coro per la pesca dei delfini con il sasso battuto

Batti forte il sasso
battilo forte
battilo sulla laguna e il grande mare
batti forte il sasso
battilo forte
e i pesci guizzeranno tra i tuoi piedi

balzeranno sulla spiaggia
saranno cibo e felicità per tutti.

Batti forte il sasso
battilo forte
battilo sulla laguna e il grande mare
nel grande mare saranno tutte
le prede grasse del dio Moana
i grandi pesci del mare veloce tra onde
gli azzurro-verdi delfini.

Batti forte il sasso
battilo forte
e anch'essi – pesanti e ricchi di sangue –
verranno docili a riva
e saranno tue prede.

[Raccolto dall'autore alle isole Marchesi]

Nella vita quotidiana dell'uomo delle culture autoctone del Pacifico, a lato della poesia altre forme di letteratura orale – favole, miti e leggende – riassumono in veste soprattutto simbolica l'intero scibile del sapere, in un voluto rifiuto di vedere un distacco fra realtà e immagine. Per questa mancanza di distinzione fra mondo tangibile e mondo irreale, la tradizione orale degli oceaniani ha finito per vestire d'aspetti favolosi o mitici alcuni fatti accaduti realmente, per esempio le esplorazioni marittime, presentate come «pesca di isole». Come questi, altri fatti, eventi, accadimenti, non sono stati celati volutamente dietro il simbolo; capaci, così, di stupire e di infondere il senso del sacro, per assumere forza di norma individuale o comunitaria di vita.

Purtroppo, avulsi dal loro contesto storico e ambientale, così come ci sono pervenuti, favole e miti appaiono frammenti di un mondo irricomponibile, anche perché ogni isola, nel suo duplice carattere di cosmo solitario e di meta fortuita di navigatori, è stata sempre campo di scontri indecifrabili tra mentalità anacronistiche, più che lo sia la terraferma. La lettura della favola o della leggenda può, quindi, apparire vuota in taluni casi ove se ne cercasse un significato preciso e chiaro; resta invece d'estremo interesse per scorgervi tracce di tradizioni scomparse e per avere un metro sul quale misurare l'estrema sensibilità poetica del mondo d'Oceania.

L'*ariki* Tangaroa disse: «Sto per gettarmi in acqua e mutarmi in foca, poi mi recherò in un'isola di cui diventerò signore». «Non partire,» gli consigliò il fratello «la morte ti attende su quella terra straniera.» «No,» ripose Tangaroa «posso approdare in quell'isola e fare ritorno nello stesso giorno.» Finirono così per bisticciarsi e venire alle mani. Tangaroa, che aveva avuto la meglio, nuotò alla volta dell'isola di cui voleva divenire re.

[...] Tangaroa arrivò sulla spiaggia di Tonga-Riki, e fu accolto da un grande clamore. La gente gridava: «Abitanti di questa terra, una foca è approdata a Tonga-Riki», e da ogni parte accorreva per vederla. Si diceva: «Ha le mani e i piedi di foca, ma la testa di uomo». Poiché qualcuno si apprestava a ucciderlo, Tangaroa disse: «Sono Tangaroa, il re, non una foca». E la gente allora commentò: «È una foca che parla».

Lo lapidarono e l'abbandonarono sulla spiaggia, poi scavarono vicino al mare un grande forno e ve lo rinchiusero. Aspettarono che fosse cotto, ma quando aprirono il forno si accorsero che la carne era ancora cruda. Finalmente capirono l'errore e dissero: «Sì, era veramente il re. Era Tangaroa e non una foca. La sua carne è rimasta cruda, benché messa a cuocere nel forno».

Il fratello, intanto, inquieto per la lunga assenza di Tangaroa, partì alla sua ricerca. Era tanto alto che con un solo passo poteva percorrere metà dell'isola. Andava di qua e di là domandando: «Dov'è il re Tangaroa?». Ma la gente spaventata non osava rispondergli, e così finì per andarsene: era un gigante immenso che toccava con i piedi la terra e con la testa le nuvole, e andava per il mondo alla ricerca del fratello.[1]

Anche i morti non sempre sono degli esseri temibili e nocivi; un tempo alcuni di loro si trasformavano in protettori della famiglia e la colmavano di doni, approfittando del potere proprio della loro condizione di spiriti; spesso mandavano in regalo ai figli tartarughe o alberi galleggianti, cioè carne e legno, due materie di cui l'Isola di Pasqua era poverissima.

Un uomo di nome Rano, sentendosi prossimo a morire, disse al figlio: «Otto giorni dopo la mia morte, vedrai arrivare dal mare un tronco d'albero con i rami e le radici». Detto questo morì. Il figlio lo seppellì in un *ahu* (mausoleo), accese un forno (*umu*) e diede una solenne festa funebre.

L'ottavo giorno, mentre si recava alla grotta di Ana-havea, trovò sulla spiaggia un albero con dei grossi rami. Alcuni uomini stavano dividendoselo in vari pezzi. Allora il giovane gridò di non toccare l'albero perché gli apparteneva; ma gli uomini, con un gesto osceno, gli risposero: «Eccolo il tuo albero, ragazzo».

[1] Citata da A. Métraux, che ha raccolto il mito all'Isola di Pasqua.

Il giovane se ne tornò a casa, prese una gallina bianca e fece ritorno ad Ana-havea. Qui giunto, brandendo il volatile, gridò: «Padre, alzati». L'albero cominciò a muoversi e poi si raddrizzò completamente.

Gli uomini che se ne erano impadroniti dissero al ragazzo di lasciare in pace l'albero, ma il ragazzo, senza dare loro ascolto, gridò ancora: «Padre mio, alzati e cammina».

L'albero si allontanò rapidamente verso il mare. Allora i parenti vennero a implorare il giovane di richiamare la pianta. Il giovane promise. L'albero infatti tornò e si abbatté sulla spiaggia. La famiglia del ragazzo con i pezzi ricavati costruì delle statuette, degli ornamenti di vario genere, dei remi e delle mazze.[1]

Tempo fa viveva nell'isolotto di Miok Wundi un vecchio che aveva la pelle tutta grinze per l'età, e il corpo coperto dalle piaghe; dal che gli veniva il soprannome di *Manamakeri*, ossia «Colui che prova pudori». Manamakeri gustava molto il vino che riusciva a ottenere incidendo i fiori di un grande frangipane. Tanto gli piaceva tale bevanda, che egli ogni giorno, nonostante la tarda età, saliva sull'albero a cambiare i recipienti di bambù, quei recipienti che via via, durante il giorno, si beveva all'ombra della sua capanna. Ma si accorse che un ladro gli rubava una parte del liquido. Al fine di prendere in trappola il ladro, egli una notte vegliò ai piedi dell'albero, aspettando che quello venisse. [...]

Poco dopo ecco apparire il ladro, e Manamakeri lo afferrò. Figuratevi chi era! Niente di meno che la Stella del Mattino in persona, Kuméseri! La stella era tutta vergognosa e terrificata. Supplicò Manamakeri di lasciarla andare, poiché il sole andava sempre più avvicinandosi ed essa ne temeva il bruciante potere. E diceva: «Se mi lasci andare, ti compenserò per le ruberie».

Manamakeri era d'accordo; ma voleva prima sapere che cosa mai essa gli offrisse per essere rilasciata.

Dapprima, la Stella gli offrì una bacchetta che poteva procurare pesce in abbondanza. Ma Manamakeri disse che la bacchetta non lo interessava, poiché i suoi parenti gli fornivano pesce a sufficienza; sicché rifiutò di lasciare andare Kuméseri. [...]

Intanto la luce cresceva sempre più; e la Stella andava facendo offerte sempre più seducenti. Adesso diede al vecchio un frutto, dicendogli che qualora egli lo lanciasse al petto di una fanciulla, questa diventerebbe incinta, e le donne sarebbero da lui attratte. Manamakeri prese il frutto sdegnosamente, ma non lasciò ancora libera la Stella. Kuméseri gli diede ora un pezzo di legno, dicendo: «Qualunque cosa tu disegnerai con questo bastone, essa diventerà reale quando vi sovrapporrai il piede». Allora il

---

[1] A. Métraux, *op. cit.*

vecchio lasciò libera la Stella, sia pure malvolentieri, e fece ritorno a casa sua.[1]

Tuna, l'anguilla maschio, innamorato di Sina, fu ucciso da alcuni gelosi corteggiatori della sua bella; ma durante il loro ultimo convegno le aveva rivelato quale sorte incombesse su di lui, e le aveva ordinato di piantare nel terreno la sua testa: ne sarebbe cresciuto un albero il cui frutto le avrebbe fornito cibo e bevanda, e sul quale lei avrebbe visto gli occhi che l'avevano adorata, le labbra che le avevano sussurrato tenere parole. Sina obbedì; e dalla testa di Tuna nacque infatti la palma di cocco.

Il mito è diffuso in tutta la Polinesia; la bella di Tuna, Sina, nelle Samoa, altrove si chiama Hina. Ancor oggi il polinesiano che apre una noce di cocco per dar da bere allo straniero si compiace di fargli notare le tre depressioni alla sommità del guscio: gli occhi e la bocca di Tuna. La depressione rappresentante la bocca è l'unica che attraversi tutto lo spessore del guscio e cresce in albero, per provvedere di cibo e di bevanda i discendenti di Sina.

L'origine delle piante commestibili che hanno avuto una parte importante nella vita economica dei polinesiani è sempre avvolta in un alone mistico.[2]

[1] P. Worsley, *The trumpet shall sound*; trad. it. M. Salvadori, *La tromba suonerà*, Einaudi, Torino 1961.
[2] P. Buck, *op. cit.*

Pescatori, squali e perle dell'Oceania: pagine di diario

Patià-titià: caccia sottomarina con l'arpione – La sfida agli squali – La pesca «col sasso lanciato» – La grande avventura dei pescatori di perle – Manì e la casa nella laguna – Gli «squali di famiglia» e una lettera a Italo Calvino – Lo squalo tigre e Tikoyo – L'ultima cernia gigante – Re Punuà e Tepoè regina – Vent'anni dopo, il cane solitario di Kauehi.

Queste pagine sono state scritte in momenti diversi durante differenti periodi di lavoro presso comunità di pescatori dell'Oceania centrale, negli arcipelaghi delle Tuamotu e della Società. Sono il racconto di momenti che mi sono parsi irripetibili: vicende rare a viversi oggi non solo in questo, ma in tutti i mari del mondo.

Avrei voluto – a ognuna di queste cronache – porre a fronte una foto, immagine per un ideale catalogo di volti e di situazioni che il lungo andare fra i polinesiani mi ha permesso di raccogliere; purtroppo questo *muro di immagini* a confronto con il *muro di parole* che si edifica per costruire un racconto di viaggio, non è di possibile realizzazione; lo ostacolano – in un libro – il carattere della collana, il limite pratico di impaginazione. Che mi permette di offrire qui solo una limitata selezione del mio archivio.

Da sempre, per me, testo e immagini sono qualcosa di indivisibile. Quando mi trovo a osservare i raccoglitori ordinati nel grande scaffale che dai miei primi viaggi sino a oggi ho destinato al materiale raccolto nei diversi itinerari attorno al mondo, sento le pagine delle foto e quelle fitte di appunti come qualcosa di unitario. Non vorrei mai separare le une dalle altre: sono *il* viaggio in un'unica testimonianza.

In questo caso sono il *viaggio* nell'Oceania centrale, dal 1955 al 1991. Lo narro trascrivendo fogli di appunti e di diario, presentandolo al lettore qualche volta in voluto disordine cronologico;

181

per accostare esperienze simili ripetute a distanza di anni. Come, ad esempio, s'è avvilito il rapporto tra l'uomo e lo squalo in Polinesia: da mitico, favoloso, a tassello del mosaico d'attività turistiche nelle isole. Oppure s'è trasformata – da avventura corale a impresa commerciale – la grande epopea dei raccoglitori di perle.

QUANDO IL *PATIÀ-TITIÀ* ERA LA PESCA DELLE TUAMOTU

Atollo di Rangiroa – Arcipelago delle Tuamotu – Settembre-ottobre 1956

5 settembre '56

Il comandante del *Maristella* m'ha svegliato stamane dicendomi: «*Voilà les Tuamotu!...*», e mi ha indicato una sottile linea di costa che appena si distingueva nel viola del mare e nel grigio dell'alba.

Poi mi ha gridato: «*Et voilà la pass*» mentre la attraversavamo e così ho conosciuto il canale tra oceano e laguna ove per settimane sarei sceso sott'acqua con gli uomini di queste isole, i migliori cacciatori sottomarini del Pacifico secondo chi li conosce.

11 settembre '56

Nel mare degli atolli, salvo in certi punti, gli uomini possono pescare con le reti solo a costo di grande fatica e superando molteplici difficoltà: il fitto intrico di corallo sul fondo le strappa e impedisce di manovrarle; e non è facilmente praticabile la pesca con l'amo perché quando un pesce abbocca, quasi sempre gli squali – che in queste acque pullulano – sono più veloci dell'uomo e strappano la preda al pescatore prima che questi abbia potuto tirarla a galla.

Gli uomini delle Tuamotu hanno quindi imparato a scendere direttamente sul fondo per procurarsi il cibo.

Nuotano sott'acqua con un'arma che solo loro sanno maneggiare, un lungo arpione di tre metri, il *patià*. Davanti agli occhi hanno piccoli occhiali di legno che fissano nelle orbite, come quelli dei pescatori giapponesi, inventori – si dice – di questa tecnica d'immersione: qui la chiamano *titià*.

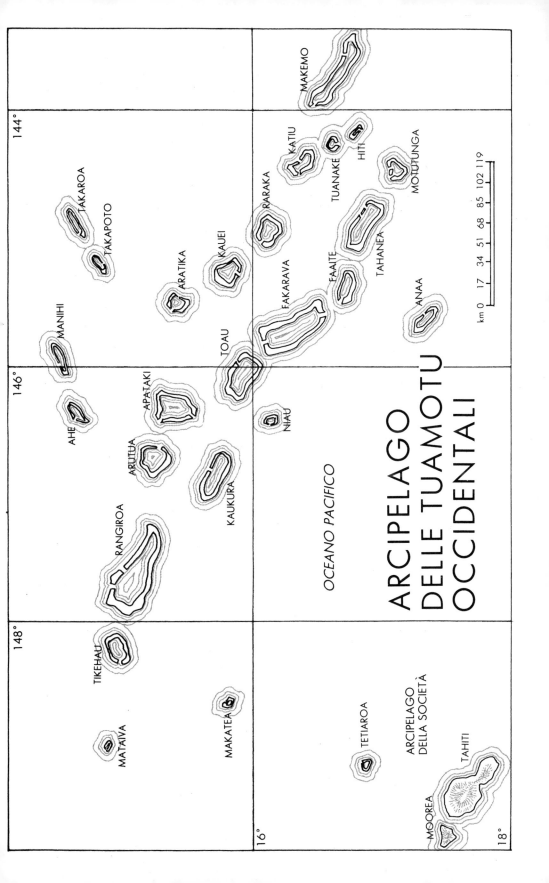

ARCIPELAGO DELLE TUAMOTU OCCIDENTALI

Patià-titià è il nome della pesca sottomarina delle Tuamotu.

Ogni sera, quando le correnti dovute alle maree si equilibrano, i pescatori a gruppi di cinque o sei entrano in acqua. Di preferenza scelgono il canale d'acqua che unisce l'oceano all'interno della laguna perché essendo un punto di passaggio è il più ricco di pesce. Non di rado pescano anche in mare aperto, se le acque sono calme.

16 settembre '56

Dopo una settimana di allenamento e di affiatamento, scendiamo oggi sott'acqua a fianco di un gruppo di pescatori, nella *pass* del villaggio di Tiputa. Entriamo in mare con le attrezzature per le immersioni sottomarine che la nostra tecnica ha messo a punto per resistere sul fondo a lungo: bombole, profondimetri, maschere, lampade, pinne, mute; attorno a noi così bardati i seminudi pescatori guizzano, invece, nel blu dell'alto fondo a corpo libero. Sono completamente a loro agio, le labbra serrate, gli occhi attenti dietro i piccoli occhiali, tra le mani la lunga asta del *patià*. Noi, al confronto, siamo *terrestri* artificialmente immersi in un altro mondo: loro sono pesci tra i pesci.

All'avvicinarsi di un branco, si rannicchiano dietro i coralli per non impaurirli. Poi, quando questo è a tiro, i loro corpi si tendono in un guizzo, gli arpioni colpiscono una volta, qualche volta due.

Quando è infilata nel *patià* la preda si dibatte disperatamente; nell'acqua «l'eco» di questi sussulti dei pesci feriti crea vibrazioni che si propagano come onde di richiamo; gli squali non tardano ad avvertirle, anche se sono lontani. È questo l'aspetto drammatico del *patià-titià*: infatti in brevi istanti, attorno all'uomo e alla sua preda, guizzano i pericolosi incursori, decisi a strappare dall'arpione la preda «vibrante» che ha segnalato la sua presenza. Perché questa è la caratteristica degli squali di tutto il mondo, cui evidentemente questi dell'Oceania centrale non fanno eccezione: raramente attaccano esseri – grandi o piccoli – che siano nelle loro condizioni abituali; ma assaltano e ferocemente addentano l'animale (pesce o uomo) che si trovi in difficoltà o peggio ancora ferito. E si tratta sempre di attacchi in forze: sia nei canali come nelle *pass*, sia soprattutto in mare aperto, le acque del Pacifico sono il regno di un infinito numero di squali, di specie e famiglie diverse: i *mao-rii*, i più comuni e quasi innocui; i *rairà*, squali-scuri non molto grandi né pericolosi; gli *aravà*, squali grigi; gli *ohié*, simili alle nostre verdesche; e i *paratà*, gli squali azzurri nemici giurati degli uomini immersi. Temibilissimi, ma rari, sono il *tigre* e il *martello*. Per esperienza tutti questi squali sanno che l'uomo che risale verso la superficie con la preda sulla punta del suo arpione, può difendersi male, al limite com'è delle sue energie per la prolungata immersione. Ed è allora che lo attaccano.

Ho fotografato questi momenti e li ho impressi nella memoria.

Uno, due, cinque pescecani di tutte le dimensioni – dai piccoli di un metro a quelli di tre metri e mezzo, quattro – nuotano veloci attorno all'uomo. Gli contendono la preda tentando di addentarla sul *patià*; se l'uomo non si difende non v'è alcun pericolo per lui; i pescecani si limitano ad afferrare il pesce colpito e si allontanano disputandosi il boccone. Ma se l'uomo non vuol perdere la preda faticosamente strappata al fondo del mare, mentre risale vibra violenti colpi col suo *patià*, difficile da manovrare quando una preda ancora viva è infilata sulla sua punta.

Molte volte un colpo a segno nel dorso dell'aggressore più coraggioso mette in fuga tutto il branco, altre volte gli squali raccolgono la sfida e assalgono l'uomo con rapide e numerose «cariche» che possono metterlo in pericolo. In quel caso tutti gli altri pescatori immersi, anche a costo di perdere le loro prede, si stringono attorno al compagno in difficoltà, difendendolo con una barriera di arpioni, come a formare una sorta di riccio dalle punte d'acciaio.

18 settembre '56

Il capo di tutti i pescatori di questo atollo di Rangiroa è Punuà. Mi ha mostrato le sue ferite di tanti anni di pesca e mi ha fatto conoscere questo e quel vecchio villaggio. «Se da giovani sono stati pescatori al *patià*,» mi ha detto «li riconosci subito dalle cicatrici... come me, vedi?»

Molti hanno avuto scontri con un *aravà* o con un *paratà* e ne parlano mostrandone i segni (non di rado molto profondi); mutilazioni di una mano, di un piede, di un polpaccio. Il *tavanà* stesso del villaggio, una sorta di sindaco della comunità, cammina aiutandosi con le stampelle: un *aravà* gli ha tagliato di netto una gamba, dieci anni fa.

20 settembre '56

Ieri si pescò con gli uomini del *patià*, ma oltre la barriera, verso il mare aperto; le condizioni dell'oceano, infatti, ci hanno permesso di lasciare per un giorno la *pass* e tentare l'avventura delle «profonde acque blu».

Pronti a iniziare la battuta, gli uomini con il *patià* fra le mani aspettavano in piedi sui coralli il momento di rottura dell'onda oceanica sulla barriera per tuffarsi oltre il suo dorso verdastro e farsi portare dalla corrente verso il largo.

Tutto questo per loro è abitudine; per noi è ancora nuova e sconosciuta esperienza. Quando anche l'operatore con il pesante ingombro della cinepresa e io con la macchina fotografica sottomarina, vinto il gioco delle correnti siamo arrivati sul fondo, abbiamo finalmente toccato quel gradino di roccia madreporica che è lo zoccolo di tutto l'atollo.

Dal fondo abbiamo guardato lo specchio luminoso della superficie, venticinque metri sopra di noi.

Come sospesi nel vuoto di quell'acqua limpidissima, gli uomini del *patià* iniziavano in quel momento l'immersione, con estrema lentezza.

Giunti, dopo circa un minuto, accanto a noi si sono appostati tra i coralli e le madrepore.

Qualunque altro subacqueo, per quanto allenato, sarebbe potuto rimanere a quella profondità solo per qualche istante, poi avrebbe cominciato la risalita.

Invece, per loro, l'immersione era appena cominciata.

Sul fondo, si muovevano lentamente su loro stessi; gli occhi sbarrati per la pressione dell'acqua sui piccoli *titià* cercavano la preda. Le aste si muovevano, seguendo gli sguardi.

Nuotammo adagio sullo zoccolo di madrepora e di alghe fino al punto in cui questo finiva. Davanti a noi era l'abisso oceanico. Sembrava d'essere affacciati a un balcone aperto sulla fine del mondo, nel vuoto.

Lenti, isolati e a branchi, i pesci passavano accanto a noi, ci venivano incontro, ci giravano attorno.

Avevo perso la nozione di quanto quell'immersione stesse durando.

Gli uomini dai lunghi *patià* intanto s'erano stesi tra i coralli mentre passava un branco di *orii*, i «pesci balestra». Li lasciarono avvicinare, poi vibrarono il colpo, guizzando fulminei. Molti *orii* furono colpiti.

Gli uomini diedero altri due o tre colpi a vuoto, nell'acqua: l'*orii* che ciascuno di loro aveva sulla punta del *patià* rimase allora ancora più profondamente infilato nell'asta dell'arpione; non poteva fuggire dibattendosi e lasciava libera la punta dell'arma per un secondo colpo, che gli uomini subito vibrarono, mettendolo a segno. Poi cominciarono a salire, lentamente. Ognuno di loro aveva due prede da riportare alla superficie.

Gli squali – che subito erano giunti numerosi e s'intravedevano sul fondo – non s'erano avvicinati; gli *orii*, pesci di carne scura, evidentemente non li attiravano. Talvolta, se non sono particolarmente affamati, per spiegare all'attacco gli squali e renderli così audaci da tentare di strappar le prede sugli arpioni degli uomini immersi, occorre che questi abbiano colpito pesci che perdono sangue a fiotti e si dibattono molto.

Proprio com'è accaduto alla seconda immersione di oggi.

Sul fondo abbiamo visto una massa scura venirci incontro: era una cernia maculata di rispettabili dimensioni. Non scappa davanti all'uomo ma, anzi, incuriosita, lo avvicina come per vedere di che si tratta. Nuota con la bocca semiaperta, mostra denti aguzzi e seghettati; non è pericolosa, ma ha un aspetto feroce. Per il suo peso e la sua forza non può essere catturata con un sol colpo di *patià*; e infatti per vincerla ci sono volute cinque arpionate con il relativo rischio dovuto al fatto che cinque ferite gettano sangue a non finire.

Benché i pescatori, appena inferti i loro colpi, abbiano tentato di portar subito alla superficie la preda, l'inevitabile accade: non sono passati più di cinque secondi da quando la cernia è sull'arpione, e già un primo *aravà* giunge per contendere all'uomo la sua cattura.

Ne arrivano altri, e le bestie, scatenate, cominciano a girare veloci fra noi e la preda, finché il più coraggioso, il più piccolo, s'avvicina alla punta dei *patià* e strappa il corpo della cernia dagli arpioni. Ma il boccone è grosso e lo squalo non riesce a ingoiarlo completamente; la cernia continua a perdere sangue, stretta tra i suoi denti, e tutti gli squali gli sono addosso. Il piccolo *aravà* sentendosi braccato, dopo una indecisione punta verso una roccia corallina, vi giunge col muso contro, spalanca la bocca e agitando spasmodicamente la coda, spinge con il boccone di forza contro l'ostacolo per riuscire a infilarselo in gola. E ci riesce.

Scomparso il boccone torna la calma. L'*aravà* soddisfatto nuota lentamente verso il largo; gli altri squali continuano ancora per poco a incrociare nelle scie di sangue sospese nell'acqua, le bocche aperte, i piccoli occhi fissi in uno sguardo giallo (un colore che nel blu viola del fondo sembra acceso, luminoso), poi a loro volta s'allontanano verso il largo.

TAOTAI TAORA OFAI: LA «PESCA COL SASSO LANCIATO»
Bora-Bora - Gruppo delle Sottovento - Autunno 1956 e 1964

14 novembre 1956

Finalmente il cielo ha avuto una schiarita e abbiamo detto «sì» al *tavanà* Joseph, il capopesca pronto già da molti giorni a dar inizio alla battuta che coinvolgerà circa seicento persone, novanta canoe e bloccherà l'intera laguna di Bora-Bora. Poiché non è certo l'esito «pratico» della battuta – da oltre vent'anni non ne sono state più organizzate di così grandi – il *tavanà* vuole una cifra a forfait per pagare uomini e donne a prescindere da quello che sarà il risultato della pesca; e noi abbiamo accettato, chiedendo però che l'«operazione» avvenga in un giorno di buon tempo.

Stamani alle quattro, dopo due settimane di cielo nuvoloso e pioggia, al primo limpido chiarore dell'aurora, abbiamo detto: «È ora di andare!». E ha così avuto finalmente inizio la fase conclusiva di una battuta la cui organizzazione era iniziata già da dieci giorni, quando il *tavanà* della pesca aveva annunciato che l'epoca era propizia e i ragazzi di Bora-Bora erano saliti sulle palme altissime del *motù* Tapù (un isolotto piantato nel mezzo della laguna) e avevano tagliato le larghe foglie a decine, a centinaia, lasciandole cadere sulla spiaggia, una dopo l'altra come grandi farfalle verdi. Le ragazze del villaggio prospiciente il *motù* avevano poi intrecciato tutte quelle foglie – c'era voluta una settimana – sino a farne una rete in vari segmenti, che uniti avranno la lunghezza di un paio di chilometri: tanto quanto sarà l'apertura del semicerchio da disporre in laguna all'inizio della battuta.

Dato il «via» oggi alle quattro, sono bastate poco più di tre ore e già la lunga rete vegetale è tesa nell'acqua bassa. La mattinata è così solo al suo inizio, e già tutto è pronto; anche il grande semicerchio formato dalle piroghe dei pescatori di Bora-Bora, di Raiatea, Maupiti, Tahaa e Huahine.

Fra l'arco delle donne con la loro rete vegetale e l'arco degli uomini in piroga, lo specchio immobile delle acque è mosso ogni tanto da un fremito, da un brivido argenteo: sono i branchi di pesce tra i coralli del fondo e la superficie della laguna.

Il *tavanà* attende che ciascuno abbia preso posizione sul lungo fronte della laguna; poi osserva con attenzione se al centro dei due semicerchi si è radunata una quantità sufficiente di pesci, e finalmente dà il segnale d'inizio. La *taotai taora ofai* (come è chiamata questa battuta) comincia allora, con un tonfo sordo. È un primo sasso che cade nell'acqua: ha disegnato in cielo la traiettoria obbligata della fune di *niau* che lo lega.

Immediatamente dopo, altri cento, duecento, trecento sassi cadono in mare con un ritmo incalzante lungo l'arco delle piroghe che formano, macchia dopo macchia, una sottile linea nera nella luce della laguna.

Sulla prua di ogni piroga un uomo in piedi – la fronte coperta di una corona di fiori per proteggersi dal sole – getta in mare all'unisono con tutti gli altri il sasso legato alla sua mano con il *niau*; dopo ogni colpo lo ritira, lo fa roteare e lo rilancia. A ogni colpo il suo compagno a bordo, con il remo, spinge avanti la piroga e così, lancio dopo lancio, le piroghe stringono in un anello sempre più piccolo i pesci che sotto il pelo dell'acqua percossa ritmicamente dai sassi fuggono terrorizzati e finiscono nella zona chiusa dalle reti di foglie tese in acqua dalle donne, una accanto all'altra. Le donne gridano, e altre incitazioni agli uomini presi dalla furia del battere vengono dalle rive della spiaggia di Matirà, ove si è ammassata la popolazione dei villaggi costieri.

I sassi cadono insieme nell'acqua, poi brillano in alto roteanti, poi ripiombano nell'acqua. La laguna ribolle per i branchi impazziti: i tonfi creano echi sempre più fitti e vicini.

I gabbiani e le sule volteggiano sopra la zona perché non appena il cerchio delle canoe si stringe essi si tuffano con uno stridio acuto e afferrano col loro lungo becco i pesci che balzano fuori dall'acqua, resi folli dal panico collettivo che ha sconvolto il fondo della laguna.

E intanto le canoe sono già a riva: il bottino stretto alla spiaggia è chiuso nella rete di foglie. La battuta è finita.

Grida delle donne, richiami di pescatori, stridii degli uccelli e risa dei ragazzi si inseguono e si mescolano alle voci forti e chiare dei capibattuta, attenti a organizzare l'ultima fatica della giornata: dividere in parti uguali quel tappeto guizzante di prede che copre la spiaggia. Il più bravo «a far le parti» dicono a Bora-Bora è Joseph, il *tavanà*.

Bora-Bora, 27 settembre 1964

Sono sbarcato da un DC4 per una veloce ripresa filmata dell'isola (mi serve per l'apertura della serie sui viaggi di Cook e per la sequenza del suo sbarco, qui, alla ricerca di un'àncora perduta da Bougainville).

Sulla pista mi è venuto incontro un bell'uomo, camicia di popeline e scarpe inglesi «da deserto». È Joseph, il *tavanà* della *taotai taora ofai* di otto anni fa. Ci abbracciamo, e mi accompagna in albergo prima con il motoscafo, poi con la sua Land-Rover.

All'arrivo a Matirà evochiamo insieme il grande finale della pesca collettiva conclusa anni or sono proprio sulla spiaggia dove adesso sorgono i bungalow dell'albergo.

Qui c'era il tale... qui finì lo squalo... qui c'era il mucchio di *perroquets*... qui le donne con gli *avai*... E lì, sotto gli alberi, i due pescatori di Maupiti si picchiarono per dividersi un *mahimahì*, l'unico catturato quel giorno in laguna.

«Ti ricordi?... ti ricordi?...» intrecciamo nel parlare tante immagini, precise ancora nella nostra mente come la grande pesca appena finita.

«Sai,» mi ha detto Joseph lasciandomi «la "tua" pesca con i sassi fu l'ultima. Da allora non ne sono state più organizzate.»

Volevo chiedergli perché, ma mentre aprivo bocca mi son reso conto che la domanda era quanto meno ridicola: ho fatto appena in tempo a salutarlo invitandolo, stasera, a bere un drink. «Non alcolico!» mi ha gridato Joseph scomparendo oltre la curva.

I PESCATORI DI PERLE: DA AVVENTURIERI A MERCANTI

Quattro soggiorni tra i plongeurs aux nacres *della Polinesia centrale, a distanza di trentacinque anni*

Laguna di Takaroa – Maggio-giugno 1956

Gli atolli e le lagune delle Tuamotu sono ottantacinque; e a rotazione, ogni anno, la pesca della conchiglia perlifera avviene in una e sempre diversa laguna. Solo ogni ottantacinque anni la pesca si ripete, così, nelle stesse acque, e le *nacres* hanno tutto il tempo di riprodursi.

Quando giunge la stagione, tutti i *plongeurs* della Polinesia centrale confluiscono all'atollo scelto dai tecnici dell'Amministrazione; con loro sbarcano le donne, le piroghe, i viveri, le suppellettili più svariate.

A fianco del villaggio preesistente nasce una disordinata, provvisoria metropoli di capanne; e le spiagge deserte della laguna diventano approdo fitto di piroghe e di barche.

Al seguito dei pescatori arrivano sulle rive dell'atollo i cinesi che fanno mercato ogni sera al rientro delle piccole flottiglie per acquistare le *nacres* pescate nella giornata. Oltre ai grandi commercianti vengono i piccoli, quelli che si accontentano di guadagnare quattro soldi vendendo bibite e quelli che organizzano cucine all'aperto pomposamente battezzate *restaurants*. Vengono anche strani tipi che si spacciano per medici, e sbarcano da ogni goletta sempre diversi chitarristi e intraprendenti *vahinè*. (Ogni domenica sera è bandita una gran festa, e gran festa si scatena anche quando qualcuno trova una perla. In quelle occasioni di chitarre e di *vahinè* ne servono molte.)

Di perle se ne trovan pochissime da cent'anni a questa parte. Ma non importa, perché anche la madreperla (il guscio delle *nacres*) ha un suo considerevole valore, a peso. Dopo aver visto quanto gli uomini hanno raccolto nei giorni della nostra permanenza in questo atollo, e quanto i cinesi hanno pagato al chilo quelle *nacres*, abbiamo potuto stimare quel valore calcolando il guadagno medio di un pescatore nei tre mesi in cui dura la «stagione»: quattrocentomila franchi-Pacifico: più di seimila dollari.

Fatto questo conto ci siamo chiesti dove finisse tutto quel denaro; e abbiamo compreso come nemmeno un soldo di quel capitale resti nelle mani dei pescatori che se lo sono guadagnato. È la più patetica, toccante storia delle isole, questa delle *nacres*: non una romantica, avventurosa vicenda che si conclude quando la perla miracolosamente arricchisce il suo scopritore, ma vicenda di un lavoro estenuante, di denaro troppo facile e di una mentalità ingenua.

In sintesi: durante i tre mesi della pesca il mercante cinese, sera dopo sera, paga al pescatore una parte dei quattrocentomila franchi per le conchiglie che l'uomo ha raccolto sul fondo. E, sera dopo sera, se la riprende.

Il pescatore non possiede nulla e si trova in un'isola che non è la sua; durante la raccolta delle *nacres* non avendo il tempo di procacciarsi il cibo pescandolo in laguna, deve acquistarlo, per sé e per chi è con lui. Ha pagato il viaggio dal suo atollo a quello dove avviene la pesca anche per la moglie, i figli, le mercanzie e la piroga. Deve pagare gli acquisti di ogni stagione (tutto il materiale da *plongeur* nuovo: occhiali di profondità, sessanta metri di sagola per l'immersione col piombo e sessanta metri per calare e salpare il grande cesto per la raccolta, la *teeté*). Deve infine pagare i debiti che ha contratto durante l'anno con altri mercanti, quando ha ordinato a Tahiti qualche cassa di carne in scatola, arpioni o chissà quale altra merce, volta per volta indispensabile.

A questo punto, dati i prezzi dei mercanti cinesi, ha già ipotecato metà del suo guadagno. Per perdere il resto è sufficiente l'ingranaggio da fiera allestito da cinesi e bianchi attorno alla laguna della pesca.

Una birra costa l'equivalente di cinquecento lire,[1] una zuppa calda in scatola costa cinquecentocinquanta lire; l'ingresso a un

---

[1] Prezzi del 1956, come gli altri di queste pagine di diario.

cinema 16 millimetri montato all'aperto costa quattrocento lire (per avere un'idea comparativa di questi prezzi annoto il costo della nostra casa dove abbiamo abitato in quattro, affittata nello stesso arcipelago, completa di mobili e suppellettili e pozzo dell'acqua: *quindici franchi al giorno*).

Il cinema dell'atollo della *plonge* è astutamente organizzato: proietta il film più lungo, credo, fra tutti quelli mai prodotti da Lumière in poi: *La croiseur de la jungle*, storia di un'auto blindata carica di banditi in corsa sfrenata attraverso foreste più o meno tropicali, attraversate da comode strade asfaltate; l'auto è seguita perennemente da poliziotti montati – ahimè – a cavallo e che non riescono quindi – per quel *gap* tecnologico – a raggiungere mai gli antagonisti montati sulla macchina infernale. L'intero film è diviso in sedici episodi, proiettati per sedici sere, l'uno dopo l'altro; e chi è nell'ingranaggio del primo resta preso dall'intera serie. Sedici giorni, sedici biglietti, totale: seimilaquattrocento lire. Mi chiedo in quale cinema al mondo, che non sia quello per i *plongeurs aux nacres* si paghi una tale cifra per vedere un film.

Le piroghe vanno e vengono dalle spiagge alla laguna; i grandi cesti scaricano ogni sera montagne di *nacres*. E noi vediamo ogni sera il denaro guadagnato con l'affannosa fatica dell'immersione passare dalle mani piccole e nervose dei cinesi alle mani grosse dei pescatori polinesiani, incrostate di sale, scavate dalle piaghe. Obbediscono a una troppo generosa ingenuità quelle mani: ogni sera distribuiscono franchi-Pacifico senza calcolo, guidate da una mentalità per la quale quel denaro altro non è se non carta sporca, meglio cambiarlo in bicchieri di *lemonade*, perderlo nell'ingranaggio dei mercanti e continuare a spenderlo fin che si finisce col cascare vinti dal sonno, nel letto di foglie di cocco del piccolo *faré*; nel sonno scomparirà la stanchezza, si dimenticherà l'abbrutimento del freddo sofferto per le lunghe immersioni; quanto basta per immagazzinare l'energia necessaria a ricominciare il giorno dopo.

È la pesca delle *nacres*.

Gli uomini continuano ogni giorno a calarsi dalle piroghe le cui ombre, dal fondo, s'intravedono minuscole e confuse nella luce intensa e lontana della superficie. Si aiutano nella discesa con una cima e un piombo. La loro immersione è diversa da quella di qualunque altro uomo che scenda sott'acqua a corpo libero; il *plongeur* non nuota ma cala in verticale, equilibrando la pressione soffiandosi aria nelle orecchie e tappando il naso; a portarlo giù immobile, è quella cima che si srotola lenta nel peso del piombo. Arrivato sul fondo il *plongeur* lascia l'appiglio e librato nel liquido mondo sottomarino, si muove lento.

Accanto alla sagola con la quale è sceso nella zona di lavoro attorno ai blocchi di corallo, è calata la *teeté*, la grande cesta della pesca, dove l'uomo porta la *nacre* strappata dal fondo con un gesto difficile, che richiede una tecnica particolare.

A questo punto egli è sott'acqua da un minuto, a più di trenta metri. Si muove adagio per non sprecare energia, per non affannarsi. Anche sul fondo, come durante l'immersione, non nuota nel senso letterale della parola; il suo corpo, teso ma elastico, è un gioco armonioso di movimenti. Per la pressione, i piccoli occhiali gli premono gli occhi, dilatati e enormi.

Con un'altra *nacre* e poi un'altra ancora, va e viene alla *teeté*; e solo quando si sente all'estremo limite della resistenza risale lungo la sagola, a veloci bracciate come arrampicandosi.

Prenderà fiato, si ritufferà, raccoglierà.

Risalirà per prender fiato, si ritufferà e raccoglierà ancora. Finché la *teeté* non sarà piena: solo allora si isserà a bordo della piroga per riposare al sole, ritrovare energia e calore.

In questi giorni, ho visto i *plongeurs* al lavoro. Ognuno ha il suo stile, ha il suo tempo.

Ognuno scende su quel fondo di mare come nel proprio campo, al sole. E lavora, fatica, raccoglie.

Hikueru - Ottobre 1961

La stagione quest'anno è in quest'atollo «periferico»: e io ci sono arrivato alla fine. Non devo filmare, ma solo cercare i protagonisti[1]

---

[1] Per il film *Tikoyo*, raccontato da Italo Calvino dall'omonimo romanzo del francese Clément Richer.

del mio film, i dodici fratelli: dodici grandi, bravissimi, espertissimi pescatori.

Alla fine della stagione restano solo i più bravi ed è per questo che io sono venuto adesso; le lagune degli atolli sono come dei catini: più fondi man mano che si va verso il centro. Tutti sono capaci di pescare ai margini, pochi sono capaci di pescare al centro, sui quaranta metri di fondo. E quei pochi sono i migliori, i più belli fisicamente, i più furbi, quelli che hanno saputo risparmiarsi. È il momento più emozionante, perché laggiù ci sono le *nacres* migliori ma c'è anche il pericolo delle embolie, tali da inebetire chi ne è colpito (qui l'effetto dell'embolia è chiamato *taravanà*) e l'angoscia dell'incontro con gli squali-tigre. Sull'isola ormai semideserta, punteggiata di bottiglie vuote e capanne abbandonate, c'è una strana atmosfera e la senti subito, appena ci sbarchi.

Gli uomini, bravi, sono spavaldi ma come smarriti: quella solitudine improvvisa, dopo tanto chiasso e tanta festa, li impaurisce più del pericolo delle immersioni profonde, e la spavalderia, la consapevolezza vanitosa d'esser fisicamente capaci di tutto gli fa correre i rischi più grandi. Perché sono capaci tranquillamente di scendere a quaranta metri e di risalire ma se trovano un campo di *nacres* dimenticano ogni prudenza e affannosamente ne raccolgono il maggior numero possibile restando sul fondo sino al limite fisico di ogni loro possibilità; e quando debbono poi nuotare ancora quaranta metri per risalire, il più delle volte arrivano scoppiati, svenuti, e sono i compagni di piroga che li raccolgono, afferrandoli letteralmente per i capelli. Ed è nella lunga e ripetuta permanenza sul fondo il pericolo dell'embolia, del diventare *taravanà*. Un uomo di Ahe è diventato di colpo *taravanà*: è tornato a riva, s'è spogliato nudo e s'è messo a regalare tutte le *nacres* che lui e il suo compagno avevano accumulato nei sacchi durante i tre mesi. E quando il compagno è tornato dalla laguna s'è trovato di colpo povero e con l'amico che stava correndo per tutta l'isola contando uno dopo l'altro i crocchi che crescevano in riva al mare. Minacciando gli è corso dietro. E dopo di lui un gendarme sudato e in divisa, che controlla per tutti e tre i mesi la *plonge* proprio in vista di questi incidenti, è saltato in bicicletta e via di corsa sotto il sole a inseguire l'inseguitore. A sera sono tornati dall'altra parte – gli atolli sono circolari – tutti e tre sottobraccio, il *taravanà* in mezzo che cantava la *Marsigliese* a squarciagola, il socio sorridente perché il gendarme gli aveva assicurato la restituzione delle *nacres* regalate, e lui, il gendarme, in mutande (la divisa se l'era levata pezzo per pezzo sotto il sole per non morire d'un colpo di calore).

Alla sera lungo la spiaggia si accendono i *morigaz* e tutti siedono in circolo raccontando le avventure del giorno, esagerate e smisurate come le ombre che le lampade proiettano sulla sabbia. E noi fra loro a guardarli in faccia, uno dopo l'altro, mentre ridono, mentre sono seri, mentre si immedesimano nel racconto che fanno. Le luci di taglio e l'eccitazione della compagnia che rende vivissima la mimica di ognuno ti fan sembrare già seduto al cinema davanti ai primi piani eccezionali, e vorresti poterli filmare così e fare un film di quelle facce, con quei racconti in una lingua impossibile, che ti sembra però di capire dai movimenti delle grandi mani e dalle espressioni degli occhi, chiusi a fessura, ora, poi spalancati per dir la sorpresa e poi duri e fissi raccontando del pericolo e sorridenti alla conclusione di ogni storia.

Quando gli ultimi giorni della stagione di Hikueru sono finiti, e le ultime *nacres* sono state pescate, nella cisterna comune dell'acqua dolce sono rimaste appena due dita d'acqua, sugli alberi non c'è più una noce di cocco né una bottiglia di birra nelle casse.

È arrivata l'ultima *goélette* e tutti hanno protestato, è la *Haupeaterai*, di Papeete, la più piccola e lenta di tutto l'arcipelago e una volta che tutto e tutti furono caricati – e noi con loro – s'era in centoundici passeggeri su uno scafo lungo ventuno metri e largo quattro, velocità massima tre nodi.

E fino a Rangiroa, la maggiore delle isole dell'arcipelago, dove il viaggio ha avuto termine, la traversata è durata sei giorni e cinque notti, e tutti e centoundici passeggeri, stretti tra la prua e il piccolo ponte del timoniere, sono rimasti serrati gli uni agli altri, i pescatori, il gendarme, le donne dei pescatori e noi in mezzo. Immobili sotto il sole e la notte dormendo con la testa sulla spalla del vicino, mossi solo ogni tanto dall'ondeggiare dei corpi quando una delle donne doveva raggiungere il gabinetto, un abitacolo di legno legato fuori bordo, e tutti cercavano di aprire cavallerescamente un passaggio.

Proprio davanti a Makatea una donna di Takopoto debordante grasso da ogni lato è stata addirittura spinta dentro il piccolo casotto: non riusciva a entrarci con quel sedere immenso che ondeggiava ai colpi di mare e i seni che sobbalzavano per le risate; rideva lei assieme a tutti e continuò a ridere nel gabinetto, più forte del motore della *Haupeaterai*. Quando si accorse che non poteva più uscire di là dentro, da sola non ce la faceva, le risate gorgoglianti son diventati patetici singhiozzi e poi un lungo silenzio per due giorni. Ogni tanto qualcuno le passava da bere e la rassicurava, annunciandole che il comandante aveva ordinato di passare due cime attorno a tutto l'abitacolo sporgente e di legarlo così ancora più saldamente al bordo dello scafo. S'erano sentiti degli scricchiolii e lui forse temeva di perdere improvvisamente, in un sol colpo, tutti i suoi servizi igienici e un passeggero.

Costa nord di Raiatea e di Tahaa - Agosto 1964

Le piroghe sono partite per la pesca delle *nacres* mentre era ancora notte. Alle prime luci dell'alba sono piccoli punti neri all'orizzonte della laguna, macchie lontane, confuse.

Al sorgere del sole, gli occhi dei pescatori hanno cominciato a scrutare il fondo dell'acqua, a venti, trenta, quaranta metri sotto di loro per individuare i banchi corallini sui quali crescono quelle *nacres* che ho visto già pescare da uomini come questi, negli atolli delle Tuamotu. Apparentemente la scena davanti a me è la riproduzione identica di quella vista a Takaroa e Hikueru. Ne ha la medesima staticità, dovuta al rapporto tanto sproporzionato tra l'infima misura degli uomini e delle loro imbarcazioni, e l'immensità di laguna e cielo attorno a loro.

Le prime differenze tra questa flottiglia al lavoro e quella vista alle Tuamotu sono visibili quando canoe e barche si accostano alla nostra e noi cominciamo a distinguere certi dettagli; le vele sono tutte scomparse per lasciar posto ai motori; e cambiati sono i sistemi di *plonge* e di pesca. Sono scomparsi i *titià* – gli occhialetti da immersione – e le *teeté* sul fondo; il *plongeur* scende sott'acqua con maschera e pinne, come i subacquei nel resto del mondo. Vige ancora l'interdizione di usare apparecchi d'autorespirazione per evitare una corsa sfrenata alla *plonge* e limitarne la partecipazione a chi è nato con questo mestiere: infatti l'uso libero degli autorespiratori, permettendo a chiunque di raccogliere *nacres* con l'aiuto delle bombole, favorirebbe i ricercatori ricchi ai quali sarebbero accessibili tutte le attrezzature più moderne, e di conseguenza danneggerebbe i poveri, cioè i pescatori locali. Niente bombole, quindi. E niente cinesi.

L'assenza di mercanti cinesi al seguito dei ricercatori e raccoglitori di *nacres*, mi aveva già insospettito ieri, a terra. Oggi il non vederli nemmeno nelle barche di scorta e di appoggio (né su quella di controllo), mi fa supporre che debbono essere mutati molto i termini economici di questa impresa subacquea.

È una giornata splendida, acqua piatta come marmo. Brace e piroghe galleggiano immobili, mentre gli uomini lavorano senza sosta. Nel primo pomeriggio con la nostra motobarca raggiungiamo un gruppo di pescatori al riposo: rispondono al nostro saluto, sorridendo. Capiscono le domande, parlano sufficientemente il francese (alle Tuamotu lo conoscevano solo alcune donne e i bambini delle scuole). Quando riprendono il lavoro in acqua, desiderano che li osservi dalla superficie: vogliono farmi vedere di essere ancora capaci d'immergersi (malgrado la sostituzione dei *titià*) sino a quaranta metri restando sul fondo sempre oltre due minuti per raccogliere le conchiglie.[1]

Più tardi mi mostreranno le loro *nacres*, pulite. Sono più piccole di quelle dei fondali delle Tuamotu. Anche loro ridono quando chiedo delle perle. «Non ce ne sono più» dicono, e questa è l'identica risposta che mi diedero a Takaroa nel '56.[2]

Due *plongeurs* mi parlano della *nacre* e del valore del suo guscio a prescindere dall'eventuale perla contenuta nel suo interno.

La *nacre* ha perso gradatamente il suo valore: è meno richiesta per la presenza sul mercato di prodotti plastici, simili e di gran lunga meno costosi. E quindi il suo prezzo è dimezzato. Non le

---

[1] È questa un'eterna discussione tra chi ha visto e crede, chi non ha visto e non crede, e chi crede senza aver visto. Il limite di profondità raggiunta a corpo libero dai *plongeurs* tocca livelli tali da irritare da sempre i tecnici dell'immersione sottomarina; così, in mancanza di ogni possibilità di controllo ufficiale, chi si è immerso con questi uomini testimonia di averli seguiti con autorespiratori sino a trenta, quaranta talvolta sessanta metri; ma i tecnici non ci credono. Al testimone oculare non resta altro che *confermare*; e aggiungere un'osservazione fondamentale: queste profondità sono raggiunte dai *plongeurs* non in una competizione, ma per un lavoro da svolgere sul fondo.
[2] Più sovente nelle lagune delle Sottovento che in quelle delle Tuamotu, i *plongeurs* trovano un embrione di perla, protuberanza cresciuta nel lato interno della conchiglia. Le hanno dato un nome francese: *gigot*. Ma vale poco.

resta altra utilizzazione se non quella per oggetti-ricordo lavorati e come materia prima di bottoni *di lusso*.

Mi domando come mai, per risultati economici tanto aleatori e bassi, i *plongeurs* continuino la loro nomade esistenza spostandosi di stagione in stagione da questa a quella laguna. La risposta, credo, non è difficile: è la mancanza d'alternativa. Cosa mai potrebbe fare un uomo esperto solo in questo mestiere e attaccato alla tradizione con la stessa forza della *nacre* agli scogli corallini del fondo?

I *plongeurs* si trasmettono il mestiere da generazioni, e quello dell'andare sott'acqua a guadagnarsi la vita è parte stessa del loro essere, una ragione di vita. Non ammetterebbero mai di smettere, nemmeno se le loro isole mutassero ancor di più; scomparirebbero piuttosto di diventare uomini *di terra* disposti a un lavoro qualsiasi, anche se ben retribuito.

I padri e i figli: qualcosa salta agli occhi a chi osserva le due generazioni al lavoro insieme (molte volte sono sulla stessa barca): la bellezza e la forza fisica dei più giovani contrasta crudelmente con l'aspetto misero, malato, quasi ebete dei vecchi. Le lunghe immersioni, le piccole paralisi da emboli, le infezioni agli occhi e cento altri malesseri hanno ridotto così i *taravanà*, i vecchi pescatori pieni di acciacchi.[1] I *tamarii* sono invece i giovani ancora validi. Tra gli uni e gli altri non corrono più di dieci, quindici anni: questo mestiere fino a un certo punto sviluppa il fisico, poi improvvisamente diventa pericoloso. Superati i trent'anni (e centinaia, migliaia di ore d'immersione a grande profondità), accade come per gli alberi troppo grandi, troppo alti, troppo al di sopra degli altri; basta un colpo di vento a spezzarne anche i rami più robusti. Nonostante ciò, essi non hanno il coraggio di smettere; e sanno di essere gli unici capaci di praticarlo. Questo dà loro un certo legame di casta, di corporazioni, forse quasi di setta. Conoscono i fondali, sanno restare sul fondo, hanno la certezza di un guadagno, anche se sempre più misero. E resta sempre la remota speranza della perla che può cambiare il corso della loro vita. E

---

[1] *Taravanà* significa anche «ebbrezza da profondità», che è lo strano malore che prende i pescatori per una lunga permanenza nel fondo, a causa di scarsa ossigenazione del cervello.

così non trovano il coraggio di fermarsi. Continuano e sono condannati: il fisico non regge e cede di schianto, d'improvviso.

Oggi, quando la flottiglia è tornata a riva, le canoe erano a rimorchio delle motobarche più potenti e veloci. Tutte le imbarcazioni navigavano alla stessa velocità, insieme; e noi con loro, per le ultime fotografie.

Sulle barche e sulle piroghe il materiale per la *plonge* è stato sistemato in buon ordine; le *nacres* pescate subiscono già un primo lavaggio.

La brezza della sera è, come sempre, fresca. Forse addirittura fredda, per chi è stato otto, dieci ore in acqua e sott'acqua.

Tutti i *plongeurs* si coprono: con vecchi giacconi di tela cerata, come i marinai in tutti i mari del mondo, con qualche maglia stinta di lana, come quelle di tutti i pescatori del mondo.

Alcuni però indossano magliette di cotone, bianche. Hanno grandi scritte sulla schiena.

«Sai, tutti le hanno perché a Raiatea negli altri paesi dell'isola le distribuiscono gratis» mi dice il mio timoniere e motorista. Una delle scritte è nera: «POLYNÉSIE FRANÇAISE»; un'altra, invece, è rossa: «AUTONOMIE INTERNE». Sono gli slogan dei due fronti politici delle isole, oggi.

Su una maglietta isolata, un'asserzione categorica: «POMPIDOU, OUI».

Toau - Febbraio 1991

Quando scrissi le mie prime pagine di diario, appena sbarcato agli atolli delle Tuamotu più di trenta anni fa, le *nacres*, le ostriche perlifere, si raccoglievano secondo una legge stabilita dalle autorità coloniali francesi, che erano, e quel tempo, gli amministratori di queste isole. Regolamentazione certamente saggia, perché prevedeva che i pescatori di *nacres* potessero mettere a frutto la loro singolare predisposizione fisica per raccogliere le preziose conchiglie. Osservando però una norma: dovevano riunirsi, per la raccolta, tutti in un unico atollo, scelto a rotazione, ogni anno, fra gli ottantacinque che formano l'arcipelago. Sicché per quella legge i raccoglitori tornavano nello stesso luogo a strappar *nacres* dal fondo solo dopo un lungo periodo; dopo un ciclo vitale che dava tempo alle *nacres* di riformarsi e tornare a crescere. Il sistema aveva funzionato.

Infatti quando assistei a quella «stagione» di raccolta, vidi con i miei occhi quanto eran ricche di *nacres* le lagune di Takaroa e Hikueru, gli atolli «di turno» in quei due anni.

Narrai allora dei villaggi provvisori, creati per chi giungeva da qualsiasi parte all'atollo prescelto, e lì restavano per i tre mesi della stagione dedicata alla raccolta. E scrissi che le imbarcazioni usate dai polinesiani, nel '56, erano ancora solo canoe a vela; nel '60, la maggioranza degli scafi aveva già un motore. E le canoe cominciavano a essere sostituite da battelli in plastica.

Sostanzialmente, però, il sistema di raccolta era ancora lo stesso. Così come erano abituati da generazioni, gli uomini si immergevano senza pinne e a corpo nudo; sugli occhi si calavano piccoli occhialini, i *titià*, che permettevano loro di trovare le *nacres* sul fondo.

Scendevano sempre più in profondità, a mano a mano che le zone di raccolta si restringevano verso quelle «più difficili», al centro della laguna. I raccoglitori infatti avevano cominciato le immersioni dal bordo del grande specchio, dove l'acqua è bassa, e avanzavano verso il centro dove il fondo scompariva nel blu; sicché la fatica delle loro immersioni aumentava via via, così come la resistenza e l'allenamento. Narrai, allora, che dopo un mese da quando la raccolta era iniziata ero stato testimone di immersioni a oltre trenta metri di fondo con punte sino a quaranta. Laggiù l'uomo – senz'altra riserva d'aria se non quella dei suoi polmoni – si muoveva tra i coralli per circa un minuto, cercando con calma la preziosa conchiglia. Quando la localizzava la strappava dal fondo tagliandone con forza il robusto muscolo.

All'estremo della sua resistenza, l'uomo riemergeva issandosi con veloci bracciate lungo una corda tenuta in tensione – tra fondo e superficie – da un pesante piombo. Il tutto, come allora non solo scrissi nel mio diario[1] ma riuscii anche a mostrare in vari miei film,[2] era motivo non solo di grande fatica, ma anche di

---

[1] Pubblicato nel volume *Oceano*, De Donato, Bari 1971.
[2] Soprattutto in *Fratello Mare*, del 1975; nella sequenza ove un uomo anziano ricorda la sua infanzia, inserii preziose riprese che avevo filmato nel 1956.

numerosi incidenti. Se ne verificarono di gravi, infatti, sia perché molti degli uomini, troppo sicuri di sé presumevano di andare al di là delle loro possibilità fisiche; sia a causa di incursioni, all'interno della laguna, di pescecani che potevano rappresentare un pericolo mortale per l'uomo immerso. Un giorno riuscii a filmare l'arrivo dell'intruso. Stando ben protetto dall'interno di una gabbia metallica assieme all'operatore subacqueo Manunza, vidi uno «squalo-tigre» volteggiare minaccioso tra gli uomini immersi su un banco di *nacres*; e documentai, in quel film, com'essi vennero salvati dai compagni in superficie: per distrarre lo squalo, gettarono in acqua dalle imbarcazioni pesci appena pescati. Lo squalo si mise ad addentarli e di questo approfittarono gli uomini immersi, che risalirono dal fondo completamente stremati.

Pochi anni dopo, nel 1970, quando mi recai in Polinesia per un altro film e per una lunga serie televisiva,[1] tutto era cambiato. L'introduzione degli autorespiratori ad aria aveva tolto agli straordinari pescatori abituati a quella vita anfibia sopra e sotto il livello del mare, l'*esclusiva*, per così dire, di quelle immersioni.

A loro si erano infatti uniti – nelle immersioni –, raccoglitori subacquei francesi, americani e australiani, che si davano alla raccolta delle *nacres* perlifere usando le loro bombole, e immergendosi negli atolli in cui nessun controllo era possibile, data l'esistenza vastissima dell'arcipelago. E così una sorta di pirateria rastrellava dal fondo tutte le *nacres* indiscriminatamente mettendo in crisi il sistema instaurato settant'anni prima.

Fu probabilmente anche per il diffondersi di questa attività, che gli atolli delle Tuamotu cominciarono a spopolarsi. Persa o ridotta quella fonte di guadagno, la gente dai piccoli villaggi cominciò già allora a emigrare verso Papeete, Moorea e Bora-Bora, dove le occasioni di lavoro, date dallo sviluppo turistico, offrivano di che vivere con meno fatica e senza rischi.

Ritornando ora – trentacinque anni dopo le mie prime immersioni con i *plongeurs*, e vent'anni dopo le ultime – ho visto, con sorpresa, come il commercio delle *nacres* sia tornato in mano ai

---

[1] La serie *I mari dell'uomo*, del 1973.

locali e si sia sviluppato in misura impensabile. E come gli atolli ove la *plonge* è ripresa si stiano ripopolando.

In alcune lagune si è sperimentata con successo una forma di «allevamento artificiale» delle *nacres*, che però del tutto artificiale non è, come ho potuto osservare visitando la «piantagione di perle» di Toau.

Mi sono immerso nel fondale ove l'*impianto* già funziona da alcune stagioni. Superato il canale, che unisce l'oceano all'interno dell'atollo (è la *pass* di Tumakohua, un budello di acque che scorrono aprendosi un varco nella barriera corallina per entrare nella laguna), ho raggiunto una piccola isola corallina appena emergente, il *reef* di Papahonu. Su quella piattaforma naturale, dall'incerta superficie, sono piantati pali solidi di una palafitta che sostiene una grande capanna, costruita secondo gli schemi tradizionali polinesiani, cioè tutta con tronchi di cocco come scheletro e foglie intrecciate – il *niau* – a formare pareti e tetto. Una casa in mezzo al mare, che, Teù, la mia guida polinesiana, in questo viaggio, definisce senza mezzi termini «la casa delle perle». Vi abita, e lavora, un *plongeur* di nome Manì, che non mi è stato difficile incontrare dato che raramente s'allontana dalla zona ove ha intrapreso la fatica di «coltivare», una «piantagione subacquea» di *nacres*.

«I primi a importare nel Pacifico meridionale questa tecnica» mi ha detto «sono stati i giapponesi; vero o no questo dato, fatto è che ora sono soltanto i polinesiani a saper come destreggiarsi in questa attività e a renderla molto fruttuosa. L'abilità di uomini anfibi permette loro più che a chiunque altro di seguire quotidianamente l'evoluzione della «piantagione» e di far tesoro d'esperienze dirette. Prima fra tutte quella di essersi accorti – e averne approfittato – di una impensabile coincidenza: su pezzi di plastica portati – ahimè, anche qui! – dalle correnti e depositati dalla stessa tra i coralli, piccole *nacres* si formano su di loro più rapidamente che non sui coralli stessi.

Un caso credo unico per classificare come «amica» quella materia ovunque vista – da chi si occupa di ecologia marina –, come una maledizione. In questa parte del mondo, invece, gli oggetti di plastica in mare si sono resi utili. Un esperto in materia mi ha chiarito come il fenomeno sia spiegabile con il fatto che la plastica usata in Polinesia per stampare sandali, scarpe e contenitori è di un tipo scadente, di «bassa qualità tecnica»; sicché è composta da molecole «molto larghe», e questo permette l'infiltrarsi al suo interno di acqua e aria consentendo alle microscopiche radici delle *nacres*, le cui spore sono portate dalle correnti, di fissarsi. E di svilupparsi poi su quella superficie artificiale con maggior velocità di quanto non sia possibile su un nudo corallo.

Manì, creatore e proprietario della fattoria sommersa alla quale Teù mi ha guidato – e dove poi mi sono immerso – mi ha detto che le «sue» *nacres*, radicate su fogli di plastica, crescono di un centimetro al mese: nel giro di due anni hanno il diametro all'incirca di un palmo di una mano. Quindi, a prescindere dalla possibilità o meno che contengano una perla, esse rapidamente raggiungono misura e peso tale da renderle «commerciali». Il loro rapido ritmo di crescita sulla plastica non va a scapito della qualità: nelle fattorie sommerse, oggi (così come ieri quando crescevano spontaneamente – ma con lentezza – sui *reef* corallini) la madreperla delle Tuamotu è di straordinaria bellezza. È di un grigio molto scuro, capace di accendersi nei colori dell'arcobaleno quando vi si riflette la luce del sole. È un «*nero che brilla*» tanto magico e abbagliante da render preziosa come gemma tra le più ricercate la perla nata e cresciuta in quel guscio. Rarissima, un tempo; ora invece è prodotta in serie.

Le *nacres* quindi, oggi più di ieri, continuano a mantenere un loro elevato valore anche se non contengono la bramata perla. Rendono bene solo come materiale madreperlaceo; i laboratori che lo lavorano richiedono particolarmente proprio il guscio di *nacres* delle Tuamotu, dalle venature grigio-nere con riflessi dorati di grandissima qualità.

È questo a rendere attivo il bilancio di ogni «fattoria» sommersa. Se poi s'aggiunge il plusvalore delle perle, l'affare diventa tale da cambiare non solo il destino di un uomo, ma forse anche quello dell'isola dov'è creata una «fattoria» e la si sappia far rendere bene. Ovvero, si sappiano coltivare filari che producono perle nere come dalle parti nostre si curano quelli ove maturano grappoli d'uva. Paragone semplicistico, ma efficace che non riesco a cancellare dalla mente quando emergo dai fondali dell'atollo di Toau, al centro della sua laguna. Siamo scesi nelle sue acque là dove sembra galleggiare la grande capanna su palafitte di Manì.

Proprio lì ha inizio la visita alla «fattoria» sommersa dove si «coltivano» ostriche perlifere. Il mio ospite, nell'invitarmi alla visita, mi ha spiegato d'averla divisa in due zone: quella destinata soltanto alla riproduzione e alla «maturazione» delle ostriche madreperlacee; e quella in acqua profonda dove solo una piccola parte delle ostriche «coltivate» vengono predisposte all'operazione che le porterà a essere «portatrici» di una perla.

Quando abbiamo indossato le bombole e ci siamo immersi con Manì, siamo stati inghiottiti da un'acqua calda, di una trasparenza appena velata da foschia lattiginosa, per quel plancton che rende rigogliose le infinite forme di vita marina presenti nelle lagune interne di ogni atollo.

Nel controluce luminoso ho visto lievemente flottare tra i coralli un'architettura elastica e ondeggiante: cime, reti, griglie tenute in sospensione da galleggianti fissati – tra superficie e fondo – con complicati e ingegnosi sistemi. L'insieme forma l'elastico supporto sul quale crescono le *nacres*. Disteso in fondale marino, il flottante supporto è creato secondo un disegno quale solo un «autodidatta» può immaginare accumulando esperienze. Tali e tante da permettergli di calcolare (ed equilibrare) benefici e pericoli derivanti dal costante afflusso della corrente oceanica (dal mare aperto all'interno della laguna) e il ritmo delle maree.

Nel fondo ondulato della laguna, su queste strutture che mi ricordano i filari delle vigne collinari che si disegnano in tanti nostri paesaggi, non maturano però chicchi d'uva carichi di zucchero ma conchiglie piatte come il palmo di una mano. Il cui chicco, se c'è, è una perla.

Mi muovo in labirinti tortuosi, sempre diversi.

Sfioro centinaia e centinaia di *nacres*; ondeggiano con le due parti del loro guscio socchiuse. Come labbra di una bocca semiaperta.

Appena lo spostamento dell'acqua avverte il mollusco all'interno della *nacre* dell'avvicinarsi di un essere estraneo, le due valve si serrano per evitare un'eventuale aggressione.

Le osservo e mi vengono alla mente altre fantasie; mi sembra di essere al centro di una scenografia «da cartone animato», là dove i disegnatori attribuiscono «reazioni umane» a oggetti animati – una roccia, un tronco d'albero – facendo apparire volti ed espressioni su quelle forme pietrificate.

La scogliera di *nacres* sembra infatti una quinta rocciosa del fondo marino; invece si muove e palpita quando ogni *nacre* reagisce serrando la sua «bocca» in istintivo moto di paura. Proprio come fosse reazione umana.

Percorrendo questo giardino delle meraviglie non c'è però tempo da perdere, in queste fantasie; bisogna arrivare sul fondo, alla nostra meta, prima che termini la riserva d'aria delle nostre bombole.

Manì, con un segno, mi invita a seguirlo verso la zona profonda della sua «fattoria»; là dove si cela il suo scrigno di *nacres* fecondate per generare perle. Non che a percorrerla, questa parte della laguna «coltivata», appaia molto diversa dall'altra. Anche qui i «filari» di conchiglie sono irregolarmente distesi tra fondo e superficie, e palloni di varie dimensioni tengono in sospensione grappoli di *nacres* là dove la corrente è più costante, e meglio nutre queste ostriche, *stimolate* artificialmente a produrre perle.

Stimolate «come»? Una volta selezionate le migliori e dopo averle sistemate nella zona profonda della laguna, l'«allevatore» di *nacres*, dall'atollo dov'è la sua «fattoria», spedisce un messaggio radio al centro organizzatore più vicino; in questo caso a Papeete (Tahiti). Informa d'esser pronto ad accogliere il tecnico del centro stesso: l'«impollinatore». Uso un termine errato, lo so: sto riferendo qui d'attività nel mondo sottomarino; «impollinatore», invece, è termine esatto se lo si riferisce al mondo vegetale che cresce alla luce del sole. Ma non saprei come definire diversamente uno specialista che giunge all'atollo su chiamata di un cliente ed è lautamente pagato per il suo lavoro, che consiste nello stimolare artificialmente centinaia di piccoli molluschi, mutando una parte del loro sterile guscio in perfetta, preziosa sfera: per renderla una perla. Ottiene questo inserendo nelle *nacres* microscopiche conchiglie della grandezza di poco superiore a quella della testa di un chiodo. Sono state raccolte nel fango del fiume Mississippi; e nessuno m'ha saputo spiegare come – pochi anni fa – si sia scoperto che esse sono particolarmente adatte a provocare la crescita di una perla all'interno di una *nacre*. Tutti ben sanno, invece, come nasca per via naturale una perla all'interno di una ostrica delle *nacres*: accade quando un grano di sabbia, o comunque un elemento di disturbo, casualmente entra in quella «bocca» di cui ho appena detto. Quando il corpo estraneo penetra all'interno della conchiglia, il mollusco reagisce perché soffre, e può persino morire a causa di quell'intruso. Per sua (e nostra) fortuna, assai spesso riesce, invece, a espellerlo dal proprio corpo, a esiliarlo in una cavità del guscio, sulla superficie della madreperla. Là avviene il fenomeno che darà vita al prezioso gioiello: quanto ha infastidito il mollusco irrita anche l'apparentemente fossile corpo madreperlaceo della conchiglia. Le sue cellule, per neutralizzare la irritante presenza, avvolgono l'intruso della loro stessa materia; formano qualcosa paragonabile a un neo sulla pelle umana. Quell'escrescenza della madreperla, infatti, è la perla.

Detto in questi termini, il fenomeno può sembrare semplice, la reazione regolare e senza problemi. In realtà, proprio per la capacità del mollusco di chiudere le valve della conchiglia prima che un corpo estraneo vi entri, è raro che uno di essi riesca a penetrare per via naturale. (Si è calcolato che solo una *nacre* su un milione produce al suo interno una perla per mutazione naturale; con sistemi artificiali, invece, la percentuale è ben diversa.)

L'«impollinatore» si immerge e con l'aiuto di un apposito strumento, una sorta di siringa, introduce in ogni *nacre* il corpo estraneo preparato; vale a dire quella piccolissima conchiglia del Mississippi di cui ho detto. L'«inseminazione» (è anche questo termine troppo inesatto?) richiede pazienza, è operazione complessa – per questo assai costosa – ma garantisce al trenta per cento una certezza. Se la casualità della natura rendeva infatti aleatoria la possibilità di trovare una perla dentro una *nacre*, l'operazione artificiale garantisce che quasi ogni *nacre* oggetto dell'operazione sarà portatrice del prezioso prodotto. Non tutte, è ovvio: accade che alcune non sopravvivano alla forzata introduzione dell'agente provocatore e muoiano; o che altre sopravvivano, ma non riescano a reagire a eventuali infezioni portate dal granello introdotto. In altri casi, può verificarsi che ci siano *nacres* capaci di espellere dal guscio quanto le disturba, e l'operazione fallisca. Si arriva così a una buona percentuale di *nacres* sopravvissute e «portatrici» di perla: e a loro sono affidate le sorti dell'intero allevamento.

Sorti incerte, perché anche quando le *nacres* cominciano a produrre la perla all'interno delle due valve, i rischi dell'allevatore non sono finiti. Vi è quello su cui molto si racconta – in toni romanzeschi – nei villaggi degli atolli delle Tuamotu: le furtive incursioni subacquee nei fondali delle «fattorie» sommerse, le rapine di quanto vi sta crescendo.

A fine immersione ascolto nella capanna sulle palafitte di Manì racconti di vere e proprie battaglie notturne, combattute sul fondo della laguna nello sciabolare di raggi di luce proiettati da lampade subacquee, e dall'incrociarsi di arpioni scagliati da fucili «da caccia grossa sottomarina». Lotte mortali tra rapinatori e difensori con bottini, in certe occasioni, di molte migliaia di dollari. Racconti – quelli che ascolto – perfettamente aderenti al classico repertorio della narrativa avventurosa che ha per sfondo i Mari del Sud; quell'alone che rende indimenticabili le pagine di Stevenson, Melville, London. Racconti, tutti, dall'inconfondibile finale: sempre sorprendente.

Così com'è sorprendente il finale dei racconti di Manì. Il mio ospite, infatti, mi narra cosa accade alle Tuamotu, al concludersi di una stagione di raccolta. Poiché di anno in anno la produzione «artificiale» cresce e poiché molte perle artificialmente prodotte presentano impurità, gli «allevatori» hanno concordato un «codice» di comportamento per far sì che il mercato non crolli per troppa abbondanza. O per qualità scadente del prodotto.

Tutti loro, quando si incontrano alla fine di ogni stagione di raccolta, selezionano quanto i sub hanno portato in superficie. Delle perle conservano solo gli esemplari più perfetti, più belli, dal colore più regolare (quel nero *fumé* ove si riflettono i colori dell'arcobaleno per cui le perle delle Tuamotu sono uniche al mondo).

Tutte le imperfette sono scartate. Sono da gettare in mare, letteralmente.

Alla presenza di un gendarme e di un notaio, alcune barche si allontanano dal punto in cui i raccoglitori si sono riuniti per il confronto. Raggiungono un punto dove l'oceano sprofonda per molte migliaia di metri. Là, alla presenza di tutti, cesti ricolmi di centinaia (anzi – da alcuni anni – di migliaia e migliaia) di perle nere vengono rovesciati in mare. Ed esse scompaiono in un abisso dove nessuno potrà mai più raccoglierle.

AMI DA PESCA E FEDELTÀ DI UNA *VAHINÈ* IN UN RICORDO DI GAUGUIN

Bora-Bora (Isole Sottovento) - 7 agosto 1961

Siamo andati a pesca con il gruppo del vecchio Rehau. Gente della costa occidentale dell'isola, zona di Bora-Bora ove non esistono ancora né alberghi, né ristoranti o spiagge per turisti. Anche qui i giovani a pesca non ci vanno più; ci hanno guardati partire alle prime luci del giorno, poi sono andati a lavorare al cantiere del *motù* dove s'allarga, tra gli alberi di cocco, la pista dell'aeroporto che sarà presto agibile non solo ai vecchi DC4 provenienti da Tahiti, ma anche ai jet dei charter dalle Hawaii e da Samoa.

Anche per noi, in barca e in piroga, quel *motù* (bassa isola estranea al corpo centrale roccioso di Bora-Bora, distesa tra la laguna e l'oceano) è punto di riferimento per la nostra giornata di lavoro. Ci hanno spiegato che con l'alta marea i *bonitos* entrarono nella laguna proprio sul lato nord di quell'isola, portati dalla corrente, e ne pescheremo decine, centinaia; è la stagione, ormai. Infatti, a luce piena del giorno, i loro branchi sono giunti. Li filmiamo fino a quando la luce è alta, poi ci uniamo anche noi ai vecchi e peschiamo.

È una raccolta miracolosa. Il fondo delle barche, tra i paiuoli, è coperto di uno strato di lenze e ami, simultaneamente, in acqua; e ognuna sale e scende dal fondo senza un attimo di sosta. Pesca anche l'operatore venuto con me nel Pacifico meridionale per la seconda volta; non sa nuotare, e partecipa a quest'impresa in alto mare con il corpo ben salvaguardato da un salvagente.

È un ragazzo che ama le contraddizioni: pur non sapendo nuotare, viene sempre con noi in oceano; e pur essendo timido e silenzioso, instancabilmente corteggia le ragazze dell'isola. E infatti una delle belle di Bora-Bora vive con lui: la *vahiné* Bolimhì, figlia di un pescatore che già lavorò con noi nella *taotai taora ofai* del '56.

Questo timido amico si rivela, dunque, molto diverso da come sembra; tanto che i polinesiani l'han battezzato Epitì, che vuol dire «due».

«Perché?» chiedo.

Mi risponde Bolimhì: «Perché per noi lui non *è* uno, lui *è* due persone: una diversa dall'altra».

Oggi il grido «Epitì!... Epitì» è stato improvviso e generale, da tutte le barche: il timido che non sa nuotare, il timido che ha la più bella *vahiné* dell'isola, improvvisamente ha catturato all'amo un pescecane! In mezzo a tanti *bonitos*, quella è la cattura più importante della giornata; le barche si chiudono a cerchio attorno a noi e tutti i pescatori aiutano Epitì a mettere in barca il lungo corpo grigio, ancora guizzante, del *toriré*.

La bestia, appena in barca, viene uccisa con una mazzata e subito dopo Tihei, fratello di Rehau, gli toglie l'amo di bocca. Il pescatore alza la mano, mostra l'amo a Epitì e, indicando il pescecane: «*Attention vahiné*» grida metà in francese e metà in polinesiano, il che, alla lettera, vuol dire «attenzione alla ragazza». Tutti, nelle barche attorno, scoppiano in una generale risata, udendo la battuta e guardando la preda catturata; e anche noi ridiamo benché di quella frase approssimativa non si sia capito l'esatto significato. Solo ho compreso che esiste un rapporto tra la cattura di quello squalo e la vita amorosa del mio amico operatore, ma non più di questo.

Intanto, tutti, sulla barca, fanno coro a Tihei: «*Attention! Epitì! Attention à ta vahiné Bolimhì*».

Questa sera ho raccontato l'episodio a Marc Dergue, giovane etnologo belga da tempo qui nelle isole.

«Non sai cosa significa?» mi chiede; e mi parla della radicata credenza polinesiana di un destino comune di ogni vicenda di pesca e d'amore; quasi ogni azione o gesto o accadimento della prima si riflette nelle altre. «Non ti darò un testo scientifico sull'argomento,» mi dice «ma un libro che non t'aspetti. Tieni: leggi quest'episodio raccontato da Gauguin in *Noa-noa*. Ci ritroverai l'Epitì di oggi, e capirai il perché di tanto ridere...»

Ho letto, e ora trascrivo. È la cronaca di una «battuta» in alto mare durante la quale il pittore (stabilitosi in un piccolo villaggio della costa est di Tahiti) era riuscito a prendere all'amo due tonni.

Pescammo fino a sera. Il sole aveva già acceso di rosso l'orizzonte, quando il nostro rifornimento di esche cominciò a esaurirsi. Ci accingemmo a rientrare. Dieci bei tonni riempivano la piroga. Mentre gli uomini erano affaccendati a sistemare una specie di argano, chiesi al giovane perché tutti avessero riso così, bisbigliando tra loro, quando erano stati tirati a bordo i miei due tonni. Non rispose; sapendo però che un polinesiano, messo alle strette, offre solo una debole resistenza, insistetti. Allora egli mi disse ridendo che se l'amo si fissa nella mascella inferiore del pesce vuol dire che la tua donna ti è stata infedele mentre eri lontano a pescare. Sorrisi scettico.

Rileggendo il testo e ripensando a stamane, mi accorgo di non ricordare nulla della posizione dell'amo nella bocca dello squalo pescato dal mio amico; i vecchi polinesiani – a giudicare dalle loro risate – dovevano però aver visto qualcosa di preciso e tratto presagi e supposizioni in merito alla possibilità che la *vahiné* del nostro amico avesse tradito il suo uomo mentre questi era a pesca con noi. Se così è stato, dovrebbe consolarlo (domani glielo dirò) il sapere che anche a Gauguin, in quella sua giornata di pesca davanti alla costa di Raiatea nel 1892, la *vahiné* non fu fedele. È lui stesso a narrarcelo, nelle righe che seguono del già citato brano di *Noa-noa*.

Rientrammo. La notte scende veloce ai tropici. Ventidue robuste braccia tuffavano in rapida successione i remi nel mare, accompagnando la vogata con grida eccitate. La nostra scia luminosa luccicava come neve, io ebbi la sensazione di far parte di una razza selvaggia, vegliata solo dalle misteriose creature dell'abisso e da banchi di pesci curiosi che, seguendoci, di tanto in tanto affioravano alla superficie. Dopo due ore di voga giungemmo alle fenditure della scogliera, dove le onde si frangono con grande violenza. Il passaggio è pericoloso, per via del basso fondale formato dalle scogliere. Bisogna entrarci con la prua della piroga volta verso i frangenti. I nativi sono molto più abili, ma non fu senza paura che osservai la loro manovra, eseguita del resto molto bene.

La riva davanti a noi era illuminata da luci in movimento, grosse torce fatte con foglie di palma essiccate. Le nostre famiglie ci attendevano in quel fluttuare di luce, che illuminava il mare e la terra. Alcuni sedevano immobili, altri, in particolare i bambini, correvano avanti e indietro saltellando e lanciando in continuazione acute grida. Con uno sforzo possente la piroga scivolò sulla spiaggia sabbiosa.

Adesso l'intero bottino veniva scaricato sulla sabbia. Il capo lo divise in parti uguali tra tutti quelli che avevano partecipato sia alla pesca d'alto mare che alla cattura delle piccole esche, senza distinzione tra uomini, donne e bambini. Si fecero trentasette parti.

La mia *vahiné* fu pronta ad afferrare una scure, tagliare la legna e accendere il fuoco. Intanto io mi ripulivo e indossavo qualche indumento caldo, per proteggermi dal freddo della notte. Il mio pesce era arrostito, ma lei mangiò il suo crudo. Dopo mille discorsi sulla pesca, venne l'ora di coricarsi. Bruciavo dalla voglia di informarmi su una certa faccenda.

Sarebbe servito a qualcosa? Infine le domandai: «Sei stata buona?».

«Sì»

«Hai avuto un amante simpatico, oggi?»

«Non ho avuto amanti.»

«Bugiarda. Il pesce ha parlato.»

Il suo viso assunse un'espressione che non avevo mai visto prima. Sembrava pregasse e con le lacrime agli occhi, disse: «Battimi, colpisci forte».

Ma il suo volto sottomesso e il suo magnifico corpo mi ricordarono una statua perfetta e sentii allora che se avessi alzato le mani su tale capolavoro della creazione sarei stato dannato per sempre. Per me lei era un meraviglioso fiore giallo-oro, fragrante del *noa-noa* tahitiano e io l'adoravo come artista e come uomo.

«Battimi, ti dico. Altrimenti resterai arrabbiato per molto tempo e la tua ira ti farà male.»

Invece l'abbracciai. Dopo la notte tropicale, si alzò un mattino radioso. La suocera ci portò alcune noci di cocco fresche. Guardò maliziosamente Tha'amana. Conosceva il suo segreto. Astutamente disse: «Ieri sei andato a pescare. È andato tutto bene?». Risposi: «Spero di poter andar presto a un'altra partita di pesca».

A PROPOSITO DELLO SQUALO DI FAMIGLIA
CHE SALVA BAMBINI E PROTEGGE FIDANZATE

Tiputa (atollo di Rangiroa) - 4 settembre 1961

Sono qui da più di un mese per preparare le riprese del mio nuovo film in Polinesia. La sua storia – ispirata solo parzialmente a un romanzo francese – è scritta da Italo Calvino, che l'ha intitolata *Fratello pescecane*.[1]

È un racconto che s'innesta nella tradizione fiabesca e fantastica di Calvino, come un «Barone rampante» del mare (così fra noi si diceva, scherzando, durante i mesi dell'inverno scorso, quando si stendeva insieme il *treatment* del film).

Per meglio aderire a quel tono, a quella chiave «calviniana», avevo deciso con Italo di ambientare la vicenda non nelle Antille – là dove il libro dal quale abbiamo liberamente tratto la trama del film era stato scritto – ma in Oceania; perché qui *veramente* i bambini giocano con i pescecani; qui veramente ogni famiglia ha... un «suo» pescecane come mitico protettore.

Italo è stato subito d'accordo su questa mia scelta. E ora, per rassicurarlo, debbo subito scrivergli una lettera. Dovere che mi accingo a compiere, a macchina, con una «Lettera 22» sistemata su uno sgabello, sotto una grande palma.

Caro Italo,
quando arricchirò il diario che da cinque anni redigo, con il racconto di questo mio ultimo itinerario, qui, e il racconto dei giorni vissuti ora in Oceania, preparando «il nostro» film, intitolerò le pagine che narrano di queste esperienze con una frase che faccia comprendere come qui tutti si vantino di avere uno *squalo di famiglia*; e sostengono che questo loro «protettore» *salvi i bambini e protegga le fidanzate*.

Leggi, e mi darai ragione.

Siamo, come sai, a Tiputa nell'atollo di Rangiroa.

Su uno degli ami messi ieri dai pescatori che lavorano per il mio film è rimasto questa notte uno squalo-tigre di tre metri.

Portato a galla, il suo corpo verdastro tagliato dalle righe giallastre sul dorso che gli hanno, appunto, valso il nome di «tigre», incute ancora paura.

Tutto il villaggio è sulla riva quando attracchiamo con la nostra preda a rimorchio. Uomini e donne si avvicinano all'animale ucciso con un misto di paura e di ammirazione. Lo squalo-tigre è, qui, un nemico ma è anche il protagonista di tanti episodi della locale mitologia marina; è ritenuto un essere sovrannaturale, forse in rapporto con il mondo delle anime: da temere, come abitante del mare, ma – come spirito – da venerare e da considerare «supremo protettore».

In questa prospettiva la vicenda del nostro film – storia dell'amicizia fra un uomo e uno squalo – mi sembra trovi qui, proprio come noi due si

---

[1] La società produttrice del film avrebbe poi preferito – purtroppo! – imporre il titolo di *Tikoyo e il suo pescecane*.

sperava, la sua sede ideale: sia dal punto di vista pratico (per quanto riguarda la possibilità di riprese marine e sottomarine) sia – e soprattutto – come ambientazione umana. Qui la favola diventerà «documentario-morale», chiave narrativa per dare a quella incredibile amicizia il significato ideale della fedeltà di un uomo al mare, alle sue isole, a una certa maniera di vita.

Quella familiarità, quella amicizia tra un uomo di nome Tikoyo e uno squalo – affascinante come idea – ci aveva molto preoccupati. Come tradurla in immagini filmate? Malgrado la mia sicurezza di poter raccontare il film usando pescecani veri, sono partito dell'Italia con i tuoi auguri... e con un grande squalo finto (corpo di plastica, motorino elettrico per le pinne, abitacolo per due sub: un vero e proprio piccolo sommergibile). Giunto qui, però, mi sono reso conto che le lagune delle Tuamotu ci offrono la possibilità di realizzare un film di verità assoluta, con squali reali e non... di plastica. Usiamo piccoli pescecani *maori* (quando Tikoyo bambino trova la bestia appena nata e la nutre): squaletti *nutrice* quando la bestia comincia a crescere e Tikoyo si fa trainare attaccato alla sua coda; e tenteremo di filmare un vero squalo-tigre vivo e libero per le scene di Tikoyo già grande, nel momento in cui ritrova, dopo tanti anni, il suo amico diventato un temibile gigante del mare.

Oggi ti scrivo nel momento in cui mi rendo conto di trovarmi – per una felice serie di circostanze ambientali – nella possibilità di realizzare il film che noi due si desiderava, sospeso tra la realtà delle immagini e la fantasia dell'argomento: e aggiungo subito che questa possibilità mi è offerta non soltanto dalla natura di questo mare e dei suoi fondali attorno agli atolli, ma dai pescatori locali, gli stessi che collaborarono alle mie riprese del '56, per il film *Ultimo paradiso*.

Sono loro che mi permettono di conoscere quel rapporto uomo-mare, alla base di questa cultura; loro che ancora «sanno» del mare, dei suoi abitanti, degli squali, delle correnti, degli accorgimenti di pesca segreti e astuti. Punuà, Potinì, Madame Teopoé, il capopesca Aperà, Titirià, Hinaro e Tamà sono – con noi due – altri coautori del film. Senza il loro aiuto sarei perduto.

Da loro, oggi (ascoltandoli mentre erano riuniti attorno al grande «tigre» catturato) ho capito fino a che punto è ancora qui radicato l'antico timore e l'antico rispetto verso i grandi squali. E con loro, con il loro aiuto, ho potuto raccogliere sull'argomento altre note e osservazioni. Mi hanno così involontariamente confermato sino a che punto pescatori come loro, vivendo nel costante incubo di questi eterni nemici delle battute di pesca e di raccolta dell'ostrica perlifera, la *nacre*, abbiano fatto dei grandi squali una familiare divinità. È un *transfert* psicologico tipico: hanno divinizzato ciò che temono, come accade in altre parti del mondo (e in epoche e tempi diversi) con i vulcani, le folgori, i terremoti, i leoni o le pantere. La forza più temibile della natura, l'assoluta nemica dell'uomo, la più crudele, è da venerare. È una divinità.

Qui alle Tuamotu, ove le conversioni dei locali alle chiese cristiane di varie confessioni sono rimaste alla superficie, resta vivo in molti un particolare animismo naturalistico; quello che fu proprio degli antichi polinesiani. Per loro lo squalo era (ed è ancora per alcuni) «il corpo» ove sopravvive lo spirito di pescatori e di marinai scomparsi in mare. È «reincarnazione» feroce ma divina dell'anima di un antenato defunto.

Molti dei pescatori che oggi vivono alle Tuamotu sono certi di avere in mare un «proprio» squalo di famiglia, tutelare; ciascuno, qui, a cominciare da Punuà, parla dello squalo suo «amico»; al quale si dice sia possibile rivolgersi dalla riva del mare, parlando a gran voce come a un confidente, a un fratello.

Sull'argomento fioriscono nell'arcipelago mille racconti, in bilico tra favola, leggenda e cronaca; e con l'aiuto di un interprete, quando sento di averne sottomano di buoni passo due o tre ore – dopo il lavoro – a farmi raccontare storie, favole e cronache da chi ancora ricorda (o dice addirittura di conoscere).

Ieri, ad esempio, ho raccolto due testimonianze sul tema uomo-squalo.

La prima è la leggenda di un ragazzo caduto in mare proprio al centro della *pass*, aggredito da molti squali ma salvato dallo squalo «di famiglia» che lo ha addentato alla vita, delicatamente, portandolo lontano dal pericolo, e depositandolo poi a riva, incolume. Pavinà di Avatoru mi ha narrato l'episodio e giura d'esserne stato testimone quand'era bambino (ha ora una settantina d'anni); dice anche di ricordare che il padre del ragazzo restò molte ore sulle rive della *pass* ringraziando a gran voce «lo squalo salvatore» nel quale «aveva riconosciuto il cugino Rikà».

La seconda vicenda è quella di una fanciulla, Veherì, tradita dal fidanzato quando questi per lavoro si recava in un'altra isola. Veherì fu avvisata da un pescecane-amico del tradimento; non solo, ma venne trasportata, dallo squalo stesso, fulmineamente, attraverso un largo braccio di mare fino alla spiaggia lontana dove si stava consumando l'atto d'infedeltà. E a Veherì fu così possibile vendicarsi...

Se questo film, caro Italo, avrà successo, ne potremo forse scrivere un altro: su Veherì e il fidanzato... che ne dici?

Ti abbraccio, saluto, e torno agli squali. Spero di trovarne anch'io uno «di famiglia» che mi aiuti a realizzare bene il magnifico racconto che mi hai scritto.

Un abbraccio dal tuo

Folco

CACCIA GROSSA AL GIGANTE DELLA LAGUNA

Avatoru (Rangiroa) - 21 ottobre 1961

Il *tonù*, la grande cernia (abbiamo calcolato sia oltre due quintali e misuri circa due metri di lunghezza), è chiusa in un canale tra le rive coralline, dove l'acqua è profonda da sei a sedici metri e dove rocce e ammassi madreporici s'accatastano disordinatamente.

Il capopesca Potinì e otto suoi aiutanti hanno teso una rete metallica lunga cento metri da una secca di corallo a un'altra. La grossa bestia, pur avendo la più ampia libertà di movimenti, non può sfuggire ai suoi cacciatori; e noi vanamente imploriamo che non venga colpita dai loro arpioni. Mi viene solo concessa un'ora di tempo per filmarla e fotografarla, in cambio di una tanica di cinquanta litri di miscela per fuoribordo.

In un primo momento vorrei filmarla mentre si muove. Piazzato con la cinepresa sul fondo, Masino Manunza che è l'operatore per le riprese subacquee anche di questo mio secondo film nei Mari del Sud, mi fa cenno: è pronto. Con un bastone avvicino la bestia e la tocco più volte sulla schiena per obbligarla a lasciare le rocce ove s'è nascosta, e a muoversi; ritengo il *tonù* innocuo, malgrado la sua mole, e mi muovo sul fondo comportandomi come un *cornak* che cerca di farsi ubbidire dal suo elefante.

La cernia evoluisce lentamente. È nera, con alcune macchie bianche: le pinne lungo la sua spina dorsale sono dritte e le danno l'aspetto di tozzo animale preistorico. La bocca è socchiusa, ma benché sia preoccupantemente grande, ancora non ci fa paura: in questa prima immersione nessuno di noi può supporre cosa accadrà tra poco. Forse i polinesiani – che ne hanno incontrato e cacciato altre – lo sanno; ma non ce ne parlano, per non apparire impauriti.

Il *tonù*, toccato dal mio bastone, si muove lentamente, nuota verso di noi, come attratto dal ronzio della cinepresa, confermandoci che a differenza dei pescecani, quel rumore costante attira le cernie. Intanto arrivano qui, dove siamo immersi, due ragazzi di Avatoru: stavano pescando e in una grotta hanno trovato un grosso polpo. Hanno pensato di portarcelo e vendercelo, nel caso volessimo filmarlo; non è un'idea sbagliata, penso possa proprio servirci e lo faccio calare in acqua accanto alla cernia, intanto nuovamente immobile.

Il polpo ci dà spettacolo: forse scambia il dorso nero della cernia per una roccia e vi si muove sopra a cercare un rifugio; con i tentacoli copre gli occhi del *tonù* e per qualche istante il bestione è completamente cieco; subito dopo il polpo trova una fessura soc-

ATOLLO DI RANGIROA

Pass di Avatoru

Avatoru

Pass per piroghe

Pass di Tiputà

☐ PALO

Tiputà

·15°

Zona disseminata
di banchi di corallo

△ PIRAU PIRAU
(L'isola delle
rondini di mare)

NAO NAO
☐

Motu Kaveka

△ TIARARI

Zona disseminata
di banchi di corallo

10°

OCEANO | PACIFICO

Punto di naufragio
della goletta *Wanderer*

km 0 3 6 9 12 15 18 21

50°

40°

chiusa (è la bocca del *tonù*), la reputa una piccola grotta e, cambiato fulmineamente colore, vi entra per intero. Certo a causa di qualche brusco movimento, il polpo non tarda a rendersi conto, però, di quanto quel rifugio sia sconsigliabile; e con un guizzo e uno spruzzo d'inchiostro, esce dalla bocca-grotta e fugge lontano.

Scappato il polpo, termina il preludio innocente. Comincia l'avventura drammatica.

L'ora concessa è scaduta. Siamo obbligati a cedere il campo ai cacciatori polinesiani, i quali, dal momento in cui hanno chiuso in laguna la cernia, attendono sempre più impazientemente di ucciderla e non ascoltano ragioni; rifiutano un ulteriore mio compenso in cambio della preda *viva*. Vogliono il «trofeo» (quella grande bocca) perché sperano di poterlo vendere a Tahiti per una cifra assai superiore a quella che mi è possibile offrire. Mi concedono solo il permesso di restare in acqua con loro, assieme all'operatore e alle nostre attrezzature.

Entrano in acqua con gli arpioni in mano nuotando verso la bestia che, in confronto a loro, sembra ancor più grande. Gli uomini cercheranno di colpirla con i *patià*; con quelle armi così poco maneggevoli la cattura di una cernia gigante è particolarmente difficile. Non ci possono certo riuscire i normali *arbaletes* o altri fucili subacquei, i cui colpi non potrebbero nemmeno perforare le scaglie del *tonù*, veri e propri scudi naturali.

Dopo alcune evoluzioni dei quattro uomini attorno alla cernia, due si preparano a colpirla. Anche noi siamo pronti a filmare. Al segnale del capo battuta Potinì, i cacciatori hanno un guizzo e la cernia è raggiunta dai due *patià*; ma la spinta non sembra sufficiente: gli arpioni rimbalzano sul dorso della bestia riuscendo appena a scalfirlo.

La cernia come stupita da quei due colpi si muove incerta sul fondo, finisce davanti all'operatore che la sta filmando e si ferma a pochissima distanza da lui; Masino, dopo averla ripresa in primissimo piano, vuole allontanarla, la tocca con la cinepresa, leggermente, sul dorso. Un guizzo e il bestione gira su se stesso; prima ancora che ci se ne renda conto, apre la bocca e la richiude *addentando la cinepresa*. Non è un morso «a strappo» come quello di altre bestie: è un colpo pesante; qualunque cosa rimanga schiacciata da quella tenaglia non ha certo molte possibilità di sopravvivere.

Questa volta il violento morso ha colpito un oggetto metallico, resistente. Dopo averlo addentato e subito mollato, la cernia sembra sicura d'essersi liberata di ogni fastidio. Ritorna tra i coralli, mentre l'operatore tiene sempre pronta la grossa macchina come scudo per se stesso e per me, nel timore di un secondo attacco.

Tutti siamo rimasti sorpresi dall'improvvisa violenta reazione del bestione; più di tutti è scosso e interdetto Masino. Osserva la sua cinepresa in acciaio dove due solchi profondi hanno intaccato il colore e messo a nudo il metallo, visibile segno del morso. La piccola sbarra d'acciaio sulla quale poggia l'esposimetro è spezzata di netto: prova della forza di quelle mascelle.

Intanto il *tonù* si è nascosto fra due alti massi corallini. Tamà – uno dei migliori tra quelli scelti per dargli la caccia – lo tocca con il *patià* e l'obbliga a uscire in acque libere. Il ronzio della cinepresa ci rassicura: la macchina, malgrado il colpo, funziona ancora: la puntiamo a inquadrare altri due uomini che s'immergono a fianco di Tamà e puntano verso la cernia. Appena tutti e tre sono in posizione, si raccolgono e scagliano i lunghi arpioni, la forza delle braccia raddoppiata dal guizzo del corpo che si distende. Questa volta gli arpioni perforano le scaglie del *tonù*.

Ricevuti i tre colpi, la bestia rimane immobile per un istante; poi si rovescia con una codata e nuota verso il punto più fondo del canale. Al suo scatto le aste di ferro dei *patià* si piegano, come bastoni di gomma. E si sfilano dal corpo dove erano profondamente penetrate.

La cernia è di nuovo immobile e gli uomini risalgono alla superficie. Osserviamo la loro preda ferita, fra i massi, gonfia, irta di spine, pinne, branchie: un tutto compatto e ostile.

Tamà, in superficie nuota per recuperare il suo *patià*, piegato e portato a galla dalla parte in legno. Ondeggia proprio sulla verticale del *tonù*. Questi, come vede Tamà nuotare verso l'arma, si appoggia alla sabbia del fondo per dare slancio a un nuovo scatto, si alza in verticale, muso in alto: ed è la coda a dargli la forza di un veloce, aggressivo guizzo verso la superficie.

La bocca si spalanca. La bestia è all'attacco dell'uomo, come mai ho visto un animale marino.

È addosso a Tamà.

La bocca sembra ingoiare tutta la testa del pescatore sino alle sue spalle e si richiude di colpo. L'istinto da uomo-pesce salva Tamà: malgrado sia già urtato dal bestione riesce a tirar indietro la testa. La mascella della cernia, chiudendosi, afferra così solo la sua maschera sottomarina e la spezza. Tamà è ferito superficialmente alla fronte e al petto, con lunghi tagli verticali; se la sua reazione avesse tardato di un decimo di secondo, l'animale gli avrebbe stritolato la testa. Ora l'istinto gli dà un altro consiglio: non muoversi. Infatti, appena chiusa la bocca e sfiorato l'uomo, la cernia preferisce ritornare sul fondo. Il polinesiano solo dopo aver visto il suo aggressore rintanarsi si allontana dal punto dell'aggressione nuotando lentamente; ora risente dello choc e delle ferite. Quando lo vedo montare faticosamente a bordo di una canoa vorrei risalire alla superficie per aiutarlo: ma il *tonù* non me ne dà il tempo. È ancora all'attacco, con un nuovo guizzo, a bocca aperta: è scattato contro di me e contro l'operatore. Usiamo ancora la cinepresa come scudo e ancora le mandibole della cernia si chiudono a maglio attorno al voluminoso apparecchio.

La pressione delle mascelle segna di nuovo profondamente la vernice, ma trova un ostacolo (certo doloroso!) in ciò che resta del perno d'acciaio dell'esposimetro; la bocca non riesce a chiudersi fino in fondo: il perno è come un arpione. Allora la cernia lascia la presa. Con movimenti convulsi, guizzi veloci e ciechi, sgretola ammassi corallini nei quali urta e più volte si graffia profondamente nella rete metallica che chiude il canale. Ci sfiora e ci sposta con la massa d'acqua che muove; solleva una nube di sabbia. Ma è alla fine delle sue energie: evitando di misura questi suoi ultimi guizzi, la vediamo perdere come d'un colpo le forze. Gira su se stessa, sembra allungarsi piegando la cresta di aculei che le ornano il dorso, apre e chiude le branchie come boccheggiando. Nuota sempre più lentamente; di tanto in tanto si ferma, e di nuovo si gonfia, erge le pinne.

Tamà è stato intanto portato a riva e ha ricevuto le prime cure.

Io e Masino, al momento di un ultimo scatto della cernia, ci eravamo issati su un masso di corallo affiorante. Ora siamo di nuovo in acqua, e Potinì, accanto a noi, studia come chiudere la partita.

Mostra ai suoi uomini il punto migliore per colpire definitivamente la preda, che adagiata sul fondo offre un bersaglio meno protetto. L'ordine è subito eseguito, i *patià* dei cacciatori polinesiani raggiungono la preda, la colpiscono in pieno, e questa volta nelle branchie.

Gli uomini, scagliato il loro *patià*, si sono rapidamente portati fuori tiro e infatti ancora una volta, seppur debolmente, la bestia li ha seguiti sino alla superficie. Ed è proprio quest'ultima reazione a perderla. Appena emerge, viene colpita da altri arpioni scagliati con forza dalle barche: la «mossa conclusiva» preparata dal capopesca.

Il *tonù* si dibatte per spezzare ancora una volta gli arpioni; sono gli ultimi suoi sussulti. Poi cala senza vita fra i coralli, rigido e gonfio. Le sue pinne dorsali sono rimaste ritte: sembra più grande che mai.

TECNICA DI UNA CACCIA PER UCCIDERE IL «TIGRE»

Papeete - 2 dicembre '61

Dopo i vari incontri di questi giorni per raccogliere notizie sulle zone migliori per fotografare e filmare squali d'alto mare, oggi ci hanno consigliato di recarci alla chiesa della Missione cattolica di Papeete e chiedere del campanaro. Da quando siamo a Tahiti abbiamo imparato a non meravigliarci più di niente, e dieci minuti dopo aver ricevuto l'informazione abbiamo fermato l'auto sotto il campanile della Missione.

Il nostro uomo, un tahitiano di pelle rossiccia, alto e generoso, si chiama Alphonse; appena capisce il mio interesse per i pescecani, si accarezza la testa con aria pensosa, una testa completamente calva e dalla pelle stranamente arricciata, come una buccia d'arancia: «Questo me lo ha combinato un *aravà*, uno squalo bruno, dieci anni or sono, sott'acqua» mi dice. E racconta che l'*aravà* gli aveva addentato la testa e gliela avrebbe staccata di colpo se, proprio mentre chiudeva la bocca, lui non fosse riuscito a levargliela dai denti lasciandogli in pasto solo i capelli. Alphonse era riemerso salvo ma completamente scotennato.

«Comunque, lasciamo perdere gli *aravà*. In fondo sono squali piccoli. Se volete incontrarne di grandi, andate da Garnier, a Tahaa, alle isole Sottovento» mi dice il campanaro scotennato.

Ho seguito il suo consiglio: partiamo domani.

Tahaa (Isole Sottovento) - 21 dicembre '61

Tre settimane di preparazione, di incontri, di discussioni; ricerca di uomini, di ami, e raccolta delle esche (altre se ne pescheranno durante la caccia). Ora finalmente c'è tutto; e per giunta la luna è piena, la qual cosa sembra sia elemento fondamentale per la pesca degli *avaii*, che costituiranno il richiamo principale per il «tigre». «Da oggi» dice infatti Garnier «possiamo pescare quanti *avaii* vogliamo. E con gli *avaii* pescati chiameremo il "tigre".»

È questo lo squalo che vogliamo; il più grande e, secondo i polinesiani, il più temibile.

Già da qualche giorno Garnier e i suoi pescatori mi avevano annunciato che tutto era a posto e si aspettava solo il plenilunio, per dare il via alla caccia e alle riprese.

Garnier ha chiamato a raccolta – qui a Tivà, il villaggio sul mare ove la sua famiglia vive dai tempi di Cook (è lui a dircelo) – i più anziani pescatori di Tahaa; e questi hanno portato con loro, per farsi aiutare, una schiera di fratelli e cugini. Tutti assieme hanno studiato la tecnica migliore per la buona riuscita della battuta. Garnier vuole che la nostra pesca del «tigre» sia regolata sul gioco delle due correnti costanti di queste isole: quella «uscente» – cioè dall'isola verso l'oceano – e quella «entrante», cioè dall'oceano verso l'isola. Inizieremo la battuta quando più forte è la corrente d'uscita dalla laguna verso l'oceano. Gli uomini sulle barche, in quelle ore, pescheranno il più gran numero possibile di *avaii* e le loro prede saranno tagliate a pezzi e gettate in mare, come pastura.

Quando, ieri, le operazioni preliminari erano finite uno dei pescatori ha affermato:

«Verrà domani, alle nove.»

A sentirlo così sicuro, ho avuto quasi voglia di ridere; meno male che non l'ho fatto.

Tahaa - 22 dicembre '61

Stamane, dalle tre del mattino in poi, gli uomini sono in azione; pescano, come stabilito, *avaii* da una ventina di piroghe e barche e gettano in acqua – secondo il piano di Garnier – tutto quello che le lenze salpano. Per sei ore la corrente «uscente» ha portato questa pastura dalla laguna all'oceano, un fiume di *avai* tagliuzzati e sanguinanti particolarmente appetitosi. Il tutto si è riversato nelle acque dell'oceano antistanti l'isola e ha funzionato da richiamo. Un richiamo sicuro e efficace, a giudicare dal fatto che, appena è finita la corrente «uscente», alle nove, puntuale, è giunto dall'oceano con la corrente «entrante» un affamato squalo-tigre di cinque metri.

Una grande ombra striata, sgradevolmente vicina. Come tutti i pescatori, ci siamo acquattati nelle barche per non spaventarlo con movimento o rumore, e abbiamo aspettato che entrassero in azione gli uomini delle seconde esche. Con le prime Garnier ha attratto lo squalo. Ora, con le seconde (altri pesci tagliati a pezzi ma legati «a grappolo» alle barche) tenterà di trattenere lo squalo nella zona, cercando di farlo muovere tranquillo anche accanto a noi e permettendoci così di filmarlo da vicino.

Sotto il sole a picco, gli uomini nudi, sudati, iniziano questa nuova fase dell'operazione e sempre nel massimo silenzio e con movimenti lentissimi gettano in acqua le esche e le recuperano con le cime.

Oltre ai pesci, si cala in acqua un maialetto. Gli uomini della piroga accanto alla nostra lo avevano sgozzato in un lampo, per offrirlo al «tigre» come boccone particolarmente appetitoso. E il «tigre», infatti, non tarda un istante a scorgere l'invitante preda. Lo vediamo riapparire a mezz'acqua e avventarsi sul corpo della bestia, dritto e violento. Mentre l'ingoia, gli uomini incaricati dell'operazione «cinema» entrano a loro volta in azione. Garnier ci aveva promesso lo «squalo-tigre» in cambio del preciso impegno di andar sott'acqua non allo sbaraglio, ma protetti da una grande gabbia in acciaio. Lui sa fin troppo bene che con i «tigre» non si scherza e lo scendere in mare sprovvedutamente quand'è segnalata la sua presenza può costare la vita. Per obbedire al consiglio che con una certa perentorietà ci era stato dato, da Tahiti avevamo fatto venire una gabbia; e ne avevamo predisposto l'uso legandola fra due barche: grosse cime che funzionavano come un rudimentale ma efficace sistema di imbragaggio e di calata in acqua. L'unico problema era quello di far scendere la gabbia fino a dieci metri sott'acqua senza impaurire e mettere in fuga lo squalo.

Bisognava distrarlo con cibo, molto cibo.

Oltre al maialetto sacrificato come esca, in ogni piroga erano stati preparati i corpi di numerosi piccoli pescecani, pescati precedentemente con l'arpione.

Come tutti gli squali anche il «tigre» è ghiotto della carne dei suoi simili. Sapendo di questa sua preferenza, i pescatori getteranno in acqua, come ultimi e più appetitosi bocconi, i pescecani morti che hanno a bordo. Si inizia con un primo lancio, e dopo qualche passaggio il «tigre» si avvicina e gli uomini lo lasciano mangiare.

Da un'altra piroga viene gettata un'altra esca. Più sicuro di sé, avendo inghiottito il primo boccone senza difficoltà, il «tigre» si avvicina per addentare di nuovo; questa volta gli uomini approfittano della sua ingordigia tirando l'esca più vicino alle piroghe.

Il «tigre» passa e ripassa sempre più vicino mostrando come chiaramente la fame lo condizioni. Legati a «grappolo» con una cima più corta altri pezzi più sanguinolenti di pescecane, anche questi volano fuori bordo a un ordine di Garnier, che, a questo punto, ci permette d'iniziare a calare la nostra gabbia.

Lo squalo, sempre meno diffidente, non si occupa per nulla dell'operazione, anzi si avvicina sempre più alla nostra imbarcazione. Le gira intorno due o tre volte, punta a destra per una trentina di metri, poi a sinistra, e finalmente con le mascelle aperte addenta un nuovo «grappolo» di pesci offertogli così vicino alla barca che sembrerebbe possibile accarezzarlo.

Ormai il «tigre» si avvicina alla preda con tanta disinvoltura da sembrare addomesticato. Ed è passata meno di un'ora da quando è giunto dall'oceano!

Gli uomini a bordo, vista la sua buona disposizione recuperano svelti altri metri di cima per «tenerlo» sempre sotto la nostra barca.

Seguendo le mosse della bestia, ogni volta che l'abbiamo vista mordere abbiamo calato di qualche metro la gabbia per le riprese; ora è sospesa a mezz'acqua, dieci metri sotto, come desideravamo; e con lei, cineprese e operatore per filmare lo «squalo-tigre» da un punto abbastanza al sicuro; l'obiettivo lo punta mentre guizza da

Lungo l'estremo confine orientale del Pacifico, giungono – durante
la loro migrazione in stagione invernale – le balene dirette verso le acque
temperate del Sud. Una «grey-whale» è qui ritratta mentre emerge
al largo della costa americana.

Immagini-documento del
mondo che fu realtà
quotidiana di ogni
arcipelago dei Mari del Sud:
la cattura di pesci, squali,
cernie giganti e tonni «di
passo»; momenti della sfida
all'oceano di comunità
che nella pesca avevano
la principale, indispensabile
fonte di nutrimento.

Il rapporto «primitivo» dei *puamutù*
con i pescecani: la pesca col sacco
intriso di sangue, l'esca offerta
a un gigantesco «tigre», e il gioco
dei bambini di Manihi con gli squali
noipirii. *In alto, a destra*: La luce
del sole sul retro, e quella del flash
a fronte, contribuiscono a rendere
evidente la trasparente bellezza
di un crinoide fiorito
sul *reef* esterno di Malaita.

Giganti del mare all'esterno del *reef* di Avatoru: una *manta birostris*, avvicinata da un operatore cinematografico (*in alto*); una immersione per lo studio del comportamento di squali pelagici (*sopra e a destra*); se attirati con cibo se ne radunano in gran numero (*doppia pagina seguente*).

A sinistra, in alto: Sifone nella roccia madreporica, al *Blue Hole* dell'isola di Peleliu (Palau). *In basso*: Un fitto banco di pesci corallini dell'Uchelbelu *reef*, nello stesso arcipelago. *Sopra*: Un primo piano di acanturide colto mentre l'operatore cinematografico emerge dalle profonde acque antistanti Tahaa, nelle isole Sottovento.

Quanto resta della plancia-comando della nave arsenale giapponese *Yamagiri*, uno dei relitti più grandi tra gli oltre sessanta che giacciono nella laguna di Truk dopo l'attacco aeronavale americano detto *Operation Hailstone* («Operazione Grandine») del febbraio 1944.

In alto: Resti di un marinaio giapponese fotografato nel relitto della *Shinkoku Maru*, colata a picco nella laguna di Truk. Tutto – di ogni nave – viene protetto e conservato come al momento dell'affondamento. *Sopra*: La cabina della mensa della *Fujikawa Maru*.

Un carro armato giapponese fotografato sul ponte della *Nippo Maru*,
una delle navi da carico di quella «flotta fantasma» che riposa nei fondali
di Truk; e fa di queste acque il più grande «Museo sommerso» oggi esistente
della marineria del ventesimo secolo.

La raccolta delle perle è resa molto redditizia da nuove tecniche d'allevamento delle *nacres* perlifere. *In alto*: L'immagine di una «piantagione» artificiale nelle calde acque dell'atollo di Toau.
Sopra: Su palafitte, la casa dove «il coltivatore» vive senza *allontanarsi* dalla sua subacquea fattoria.

una canoa all'altra e a ogni suo morso alle esche; sembra tutto troppo facile. A ricordarci la sua forza e la sua ferocia – anche in questi istanti in cui pare mansueto – è la sua grande coda: a ogni movimento, solleva montagne di spuma. Gli uomini di Garnier non sembrano però minimamente intimoriti né da quella coda né dallo squalo tutt'intero; forse perché si sentono padroni di quella volontà annullata sin dai primi bocconi di incoraggiamento.

Per un istante la testa del pescecane emerge a un palmo da Garnier; vediamo un occhio grosso come fosse di un bue; è come spento, quasi non ci incute paura. Il corpo invece (ora che lo vediamo per la prima volta intero a fior d'acqua e così vicino) impressiona ancor più dei colpi di coda: è lungo due volte la nostra piroga!

Un pescecane del genere sarebbe troppo imprudente, oltreché difficile, cercare di catturarlo con un sistema tradizionale. Per questo Garnier adotta in questi casi un sistema di pesca tutto suo. In una frazione di secondo getta un'ultima esca sanguinante in acqua, vicino alla piroga; e subito la grande bocca si spalanca per addentarla. Dopo il morso il corpo di inarca e in quell'istante le fessure delle branchie attraverso le quali il «tigre» respira, affiorano dall'acqua, dilatate, palpitanti. Garnier fa scattare rapida e sicura la mano armata di un ancorotto d'acciaio lungo un palmo. Le due punte si infilano tra una fessura e l'altra delle branchie, ficcandosi profondamente nel tessuto delicato attraverso il quale ogni pesce respira. Lo squalo a quel lancinante dolore salta dall'acqua in un balzo, in due, tre. È il momento del pericolo per le nostre piccole imbarcazioni. Ma anche il «tigre» – come tutti i pesci grandi e piccoli quando sono arpionati o all'amo – appena si rende conto di non riuscire a liberarsi pensa solo a fuggire verso l'alto fondo. E questo, facendogli conficcare ancor più gravemente l'ancorotto nelle branchie, causa una inarrestabile emorragia. Malgrado il dolore e la perdita delle forze, il «tigre» dopo il primo spasimo, punta dritto verso il centro della laguna tirandosi dietro quaranta metri di sagola, la nostra barca e le due che sostengono la gabbia subacquea con l'operatore immerso. Per mezz'ora siamo trasportati come sugheri, ma intanto possiamo filmare – sopra e sott'acqua – quella corsa disperata. Poi, a un ultimo sussulto, il «tigre» si arresta di schianto sulla corda tesa. L'intravediamo sul fondo, immobile: a ogni strappo la sua ferita si è allargata, a ogni spasimo le sue forze sono diminuite. Ora è morto.

Garnier ha vinto la sua battaglia. La battuta è finita.

TECNICA DI UNA CACCIA PER CATTURARE VIVO IL «TIGRE»

Tivà (Isole Sottovento) - 8 gennaio 1962

Davanti al villaggio di Tivà, nella laguna di Tahaa, c'è un molo che si spinge molto al largo, dove l'acqua è fonda; serve d'attracco per le golette dirette alla Sottovento per caricare vaniglia.

A destra e a sinistra del molo (dove questo è vicino a riva) costruiamo, con l'aiuto della nostra équipe polinesiana, due grandi recinti chiusi da trecento metri di rete metallica tenuta in tensione dal fondo alla superficie da bidoni di benzina vuoti.

Mi occorre filmare un grande squalo vivo, prigioniero; tenteremo quindi di far entrare in uno dei due recinti a lato del molo di Tivà un grande «tigre», vivo. Ed è stato scelto il molo di Tivà perché qui Garnier è convinto di poter catturare vivo uno squalo come quello richiesto, basta che gli si dia come esca un cavallo. Un cavallo morto da gettare in acqua, di notte, proprio sulla punta del molo.

Ne troviamo uno vecchissimo, già condannato. I cinesi, proprietari della bestia, ci chiedono una cifra astronomica e occorre mezza giornata di discussioni per ridurre il prezzo a cifre accessibili.

Al termine della trattativa, Garnier ha il suo cavallo: lo uccide, e lo getta in mare accanto a molti ami le cui sagole fanno tutte capo alla punta del molo dove lui, gli altri pescatori e noi passiamo la notte attendendo che qualcosa abbocchi.

Alle prime luci dell'alba due strappi fortissimi alle sagole ci scuotono dal torpore dell'interminabile attesa. Due bestie sono sull'amo. Garnier attende qualche istante prima di salpare: vuol giudicare – dalle ombre che intravede muoversi sotto il pelo dell'acqua – quale sia la preda da portare a galla per prima. Sceglie una delle due sagole e lascia la seconda.

«Quello è un "martello",» grida mentre corre da un lato all'altro del molo, aiutato dai suoi «lasciamo che si ammazzi da solo.»

Ha ragione; e per di più sulla sagola buona ci accorgiamo presto che – come lui aveva previsto – c'è un «tigre».

Con pazienza, evitando strappi violenti che potrebbero ucciderlo o staccarlo dalla sagola, i pescatori di Tivà portano l'animale lentamente sotto il molo. Poi lo trascinano (sempre in acqua) sino al recinto chiuso della rete metallica. Ve lo spingono dentro con lunghe pertiche e usando le stesse riescono a immobilizzarlo nel basso fondale, premendolo. Garnier entra allora in acqua a due passi dalla bestia. A un suo ordine, gli uomini recuperano ancora qualche metro di sagola e il «tigre» viene tirato fin quasi a riva. La sua bocca è fuor d'acqua.

La luce dell'alba tinge di un aspetto irreale la prova di coraggio di Garnier: con un bastone, facendo perno fra i denti dello squalo, riesce ad aprirgli la bocca; nello stesso istante, due uomini sul molo che avevano fra le mani l'estremità della sagola, danno uno strappo e l'amo infilato nella mascella dello squalo salta via. Garnier con un balzo è subito fuor d'acqua, s'arrampica sul molo, grida: ordina di lasciare libero anche della pressione dei pali che lo tenevano immobile il corpo del «tigre».

La bestia, dopo qualche attimo di immobilità rotola sul dorso, e con un colpo di coda guizza nell'acqua più fonda del recinto, ove subito nuota veloce; è imponente, dietro la rete metallica, sfondo della scena sottomarina.

Appena sorge il sole, entriamo in acqua e lavoriamo per sei ore: immagini di un grande «tigre» in una rete; dei suoi tentativi per uscirne; di sue reazioni a passaggi di barche a motore alla superficie; e infine (creato un varco nella rete stessa) il momento della sua fuga, guizzo conclusivo a portarlo in salvo, di nuovo verso l'alto mare.

Prima di liberarlo, abbiamo dovuto trasferirlo dal primo recinto al secondo, perché il passare delle ore del giorno ci aveva a poco a poco posti in cattive condizioni di luce. Anche questa operazione era prevista e benché fiducioso sulle qualità di Garnier mi ero domandato tra una ripresa e l'altra, durante tutta la mattinata, come sarebbe stato possibile trasportare viva una bestia di tali dimensioni e così pericolosa.

Ma Garnier sa bene cosa deve fare. Con l'aiuto di tutti i suoi uomini innanzitutto sgancia dal fondo e trascina verso riva, lentamente, la grande rete metallica del primo recinto sottomarino, obbligando così a nuotare fin quasi sulla spiaggia il «tigre» prigioniero; poi, con uno strappo finale della rete, porta il pescecane all'asciutto, sulla sabbia; è un istante, e già tutti gli uomini gettano addosso a quel gigantesco corpo rimasto all'asciutto sacchi bagnati, per tempo accumulati nei pressi. I sacchi seppelliscono letteralmente il «tigre»; lo immobilizzano, gli impediscono di balzare a destra e a sinistra come aveva tentato mentre lo traevano a riva; di quella forzata immobilità subito approfitta Garnier. Accanto allo squalo, prima che possa rendersene conto, riesce a passargli un cappio attorno alla coda e a stringerlo con forza. Il gioco è fatto: tutti gli uomini aguantano la cima e corrono verso la zona chiusa del secondo recinto subacqueo, trascinando il pescecane che per qualche istante scivola sulla sabbia.

L'operazione (da quando il «tigre» è stato tirato a riva a quando è stato riportato in acqua) non è durata più di due o tre minuti. E non appena la sagola è stata tagliata, la bestia ha ritrovato la sua forza (la coda è libera) e nuota veloce riprendendo subito confidenza e sicurezza.

CACCIA ALLO SQUALO DI LAGUNA CON L'*URU* BOLLENTE

Atollo di Manihi (Tuamotu) - 19 dicembre 1964

Abbiamo vissuto, tre anni dopo l'avventura con il «tigre» di Garnier, altre scene di caccia grossa sottomarina nell'Oceano Pacifico. Ci avevano detto, giurando che era vero, come i pescatori polinesiani catturino squali con sistemi ancor più curiosi di quello che avevo filmato nel '56 e nel '61; non l'ho mai creduto possibile fino a oggi, quando abbiamo assistito a una battuta basata su una «tecnica» che è propria dei polinesiani, da sempre alla ricerca di sistemi tali da permettere la cattura di pescecani senza rovinar loro la pelle (un tempo preziosa per farne i grandi tamburi da cerimonia).

Sono di nuovo tornato alle Tuamotu,[1] e con me sono tornati agli atolli alcuni protagonisti delle avventure passate. Punuà ha

---

[1] Per la realizzazione della serie televisiva in più puntate, *I mari del Capitano Cook*.

lasciato Rangiroa per seguirci qui a Manihi, e lavorava con noi come capopesca; e con lui – oltre ai suoi uomini – sono due subacquei italiani che hanno pescato e cacciato squali in tutti i mari del mondo: Jean Bodini e Flondar Brunelli.

Con il loro aiuto, montiamo la scena, troviamo i personaggi adatti a interpretarla, il luogo migliore per ambientarla.

Da una scogliera corallina dell'atollo di Manihi i pescatori gettano in acqua esche di carne di cavallo per chiamare in questa zona gli squali. Basta aver pazienza, e dopo un paio d'ore squali ne giungono in gran numero ad addentare quanto gli uomini gettano loro in abbondanza. Tra i massi rocciosi di quella scogliera, un grande fuoco è stato intanto acceso da alcune donne del villaggio; in questa pentola sono stati gettati *urù* (i verdi frutti dell'albero del pane).

Quando i pescecani – resi folli dalla carne che gli uomini gettano loro in acqua – addentano i bocconi sanguinolenti senza nemmeno la precauzione di «sfiorarli» per sentirne la natura prima d'inghiottirli, uomini e donne, con grandi forche di legno, tiran fuori dalle pentole gli *urù* messi a bollire e li gettano in acqua tra le altre esche di carne; la voracità spinge i pescecani (che si disputano ormai l'un l'altro i bocconi di carne) ad addentare sempre più veloci qualunque cosa; quando gli *urù* cadono in acqua, le bestie li inghiottono così in un sol colpo anche se sono bollenti.

«Vedi,» mi grida Punuà nel clamore che donne e pescatori hanno cominciato a levare al cielo non appena gli squali addentano le prime false esche «l'acqua raffredda la buccia delle zucche d'*urù* e loro, così, le mangiano! Non s'accorgono della trappola, le scambiano per pezzi di carne...».

È proprio così: in quel «diffuso sapore» di sangue, i pescecani inghiottiscono gli *urù*. Il loro stomaco sempre affamato non li fa nemmeno riflettere: hanno cominciato a mangiare e non smettono. Ma è una ingordigia mortale; perché se la buccia dell'*urù* si raffredda subito quando cade in acqua, dentro, però, la polpa è rimasta rovente. Una volta nello stomaco questo calore violento – al quale l'organismo di uno squalo è impreparato – uccide la bestia in pochi istanti.

Aveva ragione Punuà: pochi minuti dopo il forsennato banchetto molti squali affiorano inerti alla superficie, morti, il ventre dilatato dal calore.

Seppi poi perché quel tipo di caccia era rimasta in uso, anche quando la necessità delle pelli per farne tamburi era tramontata per sempre. Per oltre cinquant'anni, sino al 1940, i pescatori polinesiani avevano continuato a catturare i pescecani senza rovinarli con colpi di arpione perché quella pelle grigia e ruvida era richiesta da mercanti che la spedivano a ditte tedesche specializzate in abbigliamento di alti ufficiali: la pelle grigia dei pescecani serviva a completare certe divise, impugnature di rivoltella o di sciabola, bastoni da maresciallo, e a far gambali e soprabiti grigi e ruvidi. Crollato l'esercito tedesco, la richiesta era continuata per i militari sudamericani. Oggi la domanda è ancora alta perché i turisti, a Tahiti, trovano bellissimi gli oggetti souvenir, e piuttosto Kitsch, che l'artigianato locale crea con la pelle di pescecane: borse, gambali, paralumi. E così la «pesca con le zucche di *urù*» continua.

OONÙ CHIAMA TAMATAROA

Mangareva - Arcipelago delle Gambier

10 ottobre 1961

Un battito d'acqua molto lontano da riva disegna forme spumeggianti attorno a qualcosa apparsa sulla laguna. «*Oonù... Oonù!*», il grido viene dalla costa, e lo sentiamo ripetersi sino al villaggio. Comprendiamo il significato di quel grido appena vediamo meglio cosa si muove nell'acqua: una grande tartaruga.

Vicino alle capanne del villaggio, a circa mezzo chilometro dal punto dove siamo, c'è una barca a motore ancorata dalla quale tre uomini stanno scaricando qualcosa; forse pesci raccolti in uno di quei vivai che qui chiamano *parc-à-poissons*. Da dove siamo sino al villaggio, la spiaggia disegna una larga ansa; ci separa, quindi, da quegli uomini una certa distanza, a piedi; in realtà, in linea d'aria siamo abbastanza vicini da comprendere facilmente quel che accade laggiù. Due pescatori al grido «*Oonù!*» sono arrivati correndo al gruppo vicino alla barca e concitatamente indicano il punto della laguna dove la tartaruga è apparsa. L'effetto della notizia è immediato: il motore della barca è subito avviato, e l'imbarcazione prende il largo a tutta velocità.

La tartaruga è ancora lì, al centro della laguna, tranquilla. emerge, scompare, riemerge; e intanto, per darle la caccia, dalla riva partono anche alcune piroghe: la notizia dell'avvistamento è ormai generale.

La barca a motore non tarda ad avvicinarla sino a pochi metri; la bestia per ora inspiegabilmente non fugge; la vediamo restare in superficie mentre i suoi cacciatori le son già quasi addosso; e due di loro si gettano in acqua prima ancora che la barca si sia fermata. Schizzi d'acqua e schiuma ci impediscono di comprendere cosa accade. Poi sulla barca l'uomo al motore, in piedi, gesticola: la preda è scappata. I due troppo precipitosi pescatori non avevano atteso che il capobarca fosse pronto per gettarsi a sua volta sulla bestia e tentar di catturarla; volevano esser certi di guadagnare una parte della preda e s'eran buttati in acqua troppo presto; e l'azione di cattura era diventata così una gara per riuscire ad afferrare la bestia a qualunque costo, con il risultato prevedibile di mettere in fuga l'animale. Anzi, *gli* animali perché non tardiamo a essere informati che la tartaruga... erano due, in amore. Esemplari di grossa taglia, tanto strettamente uniti da sembrarci, da lontano, una sola bestia; e presi talmente dal loro impegno amoroso da non fuggire all'avvicinarsi del pericolo. Per questo la barca era riuscita ad accostarli così da vicino; in casi del genere, agendo con prudenza, è possibile avvicinarsi alle bestie tanto da catturarle legandole per una zampa con una cima e agganciandole con un amo tra il guscio e il corpo.

Abbiamo appena finito di commentare la fuga dei due animali quando, trecento metri a poppa del battello, le due tartarughe riemergono improvvisamente; avevano nuotato sul fondo per portarsi lontano dal pericolo, e invece se lo trovano di fronte: perché sono salite in superficie a respirare proprio davanti alle piroghe staccatesi da riva dieci minuti dopo la motobarca.

In un attimo, sulla piroga più vicina un uomo, con il *patià*, si bilancia, raccoglie le forze, scaglia il lungo arpione. Da riva abbiamo appena percepito il fulmineo riflesso della punta d'acciaio dell'arma e già questa si conficca sullo scudo della maggiore delle due tartarughe. L'asta ha volato da una decina di metri: solo un pescatore polinesiano può colpire con tanta precisione un bersaglio in movimento lanciando a quella distanza un'arma lunga tre metri.

Mentre la seconda tartaruga fugge, l'altra resta con l'arpione nel corpo, a galla, morta.

A terra, sono quasi cento chili di carne per l'intero villaggio... Carne: il cibo più raro, qui alle Gambier, perché la carne la si conosce di solito solo in scatola.

11 ottobre 1961

Tagliati in quattro pezzi i resti non commestibili della tartaruga uccisa ieri (il pescatore ce li ha venduti volentieri), li abbiamo legati a una cima e li abbiamo gettati oggi nel pomeriggio nella *pass*. Sapevamo quanto il suo sangue attiri i pescecani: ma non immaginavamo con quale immediatezza! Prima ancora di darci il tempo di essere pronti a filmare, una grande ombra passa veloce sotto la barca e addenta una delle esche. Tutti vorremmo gridare per la sorpresa, ma, a un gesto del capobarca, taciamo e ci immobilizziamo perché l'ombra si sta muovendo in un giro più lento e più vicino. «*Tamataroa!*» (squalo-martello) sussurra una voce accanto a me.

La nostra immobilità dura minuti interi, per non spaventare con un'ombra nell'acqua o un rumore nella barca il sospettoso animale che potrebbe tornare. Almeno così speriamo: ma non è quello che poi accade.

Lo squalo si allontana e il nostro polinesiano scuote la testa. Il *tamataroa* ha addentato il primo boccone, certo perché affamato; ma non torna a mangiare gli altri bocconi attaccati alla cima perché evidentemente conosce gli ami, le lenze e li teme. Bisognerebbe lasciar liberi quei resti della tartaruga, allora certo riapparirebbe per divorarli; ma con la corrente della *pass*, se lasciamo libere le esche, non le vedremo più in meno di mezzo minuto.

Vale ancora la pena di aspettare.

Restiamo nella *pass* l'intero pomeriggio e la nostra pazienza è finalmente premiata. Non dal ritorno del sospettoso squalo dalla testa a martello, ma di un suo simile di misura più ridotta che ci permette di essere testimoni di un emozionante momento di caccia sottomarina.

A forza di attendere il grande *tamataroa* qualcuno, a bordo della barca, s'è stancato e ha pensato di entrare in mare per catturare qualche *avaii* in acqua bassa. Questo qualcuno è un certo Tamà; avrà vent'anni e dice che pesca sott'acqua da quindici! È il migliore, quando caccia con il *patià*: il lungo arpione nelle sue mani è arma perfetta e infallibile. È stato lui a colpire al volo, ieri, la grande tartaruga.

Scomparso sotto il pelo dell'acqua, Tamà non lo vediamo per un paio di minuti; il sole è così basso da togliere ogni trasparenza dalla superficie al fondo, e l'acqua attorno a noi sembra una tavola nera. Poi, ancora una volta, quel giorno, uno stesso grido è ripetuto concitatamente: «*Tamataroa! Tamataroa!*».

È l'uomo che era sott'acqua ad aver gridato un istante dopo essere emerso. Un lungo corpo nero è infilato nel suo *patià*, si dibatte debolmente e lo riconosciamo subito: un «martello» di un paio di metri di lunghezza, e forse mezzo metro d'apertura fra un occhio e l'altro. Più piccolo di quello passato sotto la nostra barca, ma sempre di rispettabili dimensioni. Evidentemente, attirato dal sangue della tartaruga, nella *pass* oggi ne era entrato un branco.

Nella semioscurità di un fondale di venti metri al tramonto, la caccia di Tamà era stata fulminea. La ricostruisco dal racconto dello stesso protagonista.

Tamà aveva visto – appena immerso – un branco di *avaii*, ne aveva colpito uno e l'aveva preso; il piccolo pesce era riuscito a sfuggire all'arpione, s'era allontanato vibrando e perdendo sangue. Mentre Tamà girava su se stesso per colpire ancora, dal fondo della *pass* è apparso il «martello». Tamà l'ha subito puntato con l'arpione mentre la bestia gli volteggiava attorno. Un carosello circolare: a ogni giro, il movimento della bestia attorno all'uomo immerso è diventato sempre più veloce, mentre la lunghezza dell'arpione impediva a Tamà di girare su se stesso con eguale rapidità e non gli permetteva di far sempre fronte all'aggressore. Perciò il cacciatore ha appoggiato l'asta in legno del *patià* sul ginocchio destro e l'ha spezzata. Ha stretto poi fra le mani quanto rimaneva dell'arpione (la parte con la punta d'acciaio) e con l'arma così raccorciata, più libero, può girare su se stesso velocemente, faccia allo squalo, restando in difensiva.

Al termine dell'apnea, per levarsi d'impaccio, è costretto a fingere di attaccare l'aggressore. Stende il corpo di scatto e si lancia con tutte le sue forze verso il pescecane. Solo per impaurirlo: ma in quell'istante il *tamataroa* ha un guizzo, proprio verso di lui, così le velocità di quei due corpi in rapido movimento subacqueo si sommano; questo raddoppia la forza dell'arpione nel momento in cui tocca il corpo del «martello». Tutta la lunga punta d'acciaio penetra lo squalo proprio sotto le branchie. Lo uccide sul colpo.

Nessuno, qui, prima di Tamà, aveva mai catturato un *tamataroa* con l'arpione subacqueo; e così stasera lo festeggiamo con un'intera cassa di preziosissima birra.

12 ottobre 1961

Ancora una vicenda di tartarughe. Ce l'hanno narrata dopo la conclusione delle vicende di ieri e del giorno precedente. Questa sera il padre di Tamà ha raccontato che i ragazzi dell'atollo di Reao vanno a pesca in laguna con una cintura di zucche vuote legata al corpo. Le zucche servono per appendervi le prede, senza aver la necessità di dover tornare a riva a ogni cattura o di farsi seguire in canoa.

Durante le loro lunghe nuotate i ragazzi colpiscono il bersaglio dalla superficie: si tratta quasi sempre di piccole tartarughe (questa laguna ne è la più ricca, si dice, della Polinesia), legate poi dai ragazzi stessi — che non avrebbero la forza di tenerle a galla – alle zucche vuote allacciate le une alle altre. Colpo dopo colpo i ragazzi, a volte, se ne tirano dietro una lunga fila e la pesca continua finché ogni zucca è piena (otto, dieci, e perfino venti piccole tartarughe).

Quel lungo carniere galleggiante è un irresistibile richiamo per i pescecani. Per questo è adottato quel sistema di appendere le prede alle zucche legate in fila una dopo l'altra: gli appetitosi bocconi così sono *lontani* dal corpo del pescatore che li trascina; non c'è pericolo che lo squalo, nel tentativo di addentare una tartaruga, morda invece le gambe del pescatore; questi nuota tranquillo. E solo se gli attacchi dei *rairà* e *toriré* si fan troppo insistenti (e c'è il pericolo che tutto il risultato della pesca finisca nel loro stomaco), i ragazzi allontanano gli aggressori con qualche colpo d'arpione, usando però il *patià* alla rovescia, cioè dalla parte del legno e non della punta.

234

Il nostro Tamà ha commentato così questo racconto, osservando da un buon tecnico: «Colpir di punta uno squalo è consigliabile solo se si è sicuri di ucciderlo; se non lo si è, bisogna impaurirlo sfiorandolo ma senza ferirlo, con un bastone, per esempio... Proprio come fanno i ragazzi di Reao che sanno di non aver la forza per trafiggere il loro aggressore e tentano, così, solo di allontanarlo.

INCHIESTA PER UNA REGINA
Atollo di Rangiroa, ottobre 1971 - Isola di Pasqua, novembre 1971

Ritornando dopo un'assenza di anni a Rangiroa, abbiamo trovato detronizzata colei che fu un tempo la «regina» di questo atollo: Madame Tepoè. La regina, però, non ha perso il suo potere: essendo molto ricca ha costruito una sorta di bar-ristorante in bambù e lamiera tra gli alberi di cocco e la laguna, ha un gruppo elettrogeno e diverse barche a motore. Così è sempre lei la padrona della situazione, e non c'è foglia che si muova nell'isola senza il suo consenso.

La conosco dal '56, l'ho rivista nel '61 e nel '64.[1] Suo marito Punuà è il pescatore tante volte ricordato come compagno in tante avventure di pesca. Sia Tepoè che Punuà sono due polinesiani tra i più autentici che io abbia mai incontrato in tutti i miei viaggi in Oceania. Dico questo perché si possa comprendere il senso di un episodio che mi sembra indicativo per parlare dell'importanza dell'Isola di Pasqua in questo mondo sparso su distanze enormi, eppur così profondamente legato a una comune matrice unitaria.

Sono al bar-ristorante dell'ex regina e a voce alta rispondo alla domanda di un amico polinesiano che mi ha chiesto cosa c'è di vero nella voce udita nell'isola, secondo la quale stiamo per partire per raggiungere la più lontana fra tutte le terre della Polinesia.

«Sì, di qui ci muoveremo presto e andremo a Rapa Nui, l'isola di Pasqua» gli dico. E mi accorgo che Tepoè ha sentito la frase e mi fissa interrogativa.

---

[1] Quando l'ho rivista nel '91 era l'ultima superstite della «vecchia Rangiroa». L'ex regina, ormai matriarca, non si era arresa al tempo e alle mutazioni ma vi si era adattata; e si era fatta eleggere «députée» al primo Parlamento semi-indipendente della Polinesia francofona.

«È la prima volta che qualcuno raggiunge l'isola partendo da qui» mi dice dopo aver riflettuto.

«Ti stupisci?» chiedo.

«No, ma finalmente posso sapere qualcosa della mia grotta.»

Apprendo che la nobiltà di Tepoè e della sua famiglia è così antica da risalire al tempo dei grandi trasmigratori, e che in quel tempo una parte della sua gente giunse a Pasqua; e poiché ogni famiglia polinesiana aveva una grotta ove seppellire i propri defunti, anche la famiglia di Tepoè ne ebbe una.

I tempi di *quella* trasmigrazione erano attorno al XIII o XIV secolo; da allora mille e mille eventi si sono abbattuti sull'isola e ne hanno dilaniato il tessuto sociale e comunitario. Ogni famiglia ha avuto la sua odissea; molte sono state annientate, altre deportate. I nonni lontani di Tepoè furono fatti schiavi nell'Ottocento, portati in Sudamerica, poi salvati, trasportati a Tahiti, infine mandati a popolare un atollo allora semideserto, dove ora regna Tepoè.

Tra Tepoè e la grotta dei suoi antenati corrono cinquemila chilometri e cinque secoli di storia; eppure ancora è in lei vivissimo il ricordo del luogo e del nome ove un sacro antro aveva accolto, per generazioni i defunti di famiglia. E del nome e del luogo mi scrive un appunto su un tovagliolino di carta che troviamo sul bancone del suo bar. Foglio prezioso che proteggo con attenzione fino al mio arrivo a Pasqua; lo immagino una sorta di lasciapassare di prova: se quel nome e quel luogo scarabocchiati confusamente hanno un riscontro reale avrò una sorta di conferma, diretta e personale, di quanto ho letto e udito da sempre da quando studio la Polinesia e la sua civiltà: e cioè che Pasqua è l'isola madre legata indissolubilmente a tutti i polinesiani che ancora hanno un rapporto con il passato.

Dopo un mese dal mio colloquio con Tepoè, sbarco a Pasqua; passano due o tre giorni di formalità, in problemi organizzativi, logistici. E quando siamo pronti a iniziare il nostro lavoro di ricerca, per prima cosa sbandiero il foglietto di carta scarabocchiato alle Tuamotu, leggo i due nomi polinesiani, quello della grotta e quello del luogo ove la grotta dovrebbe trovarsi. La nostra guida si stupisce: sì, c'è un luogo con quel nome, a Pasqua; e c'è una grotta laggiù, «scoperta» da poco. Come mai lo sapevo?

Non c'è bisogno di rispondere. L'importante è che la grotta di

Madame Tepoè esista a Pasqua e sia esatto il nome e il luogo ove erano stati seppelliti, mezzo millennio prima, gli antenati di una famiglia da tempo lontana dall'isola. Ho la misura, ora, del valore sacrale di questa terra: Rapa Nui, da noi bianchi chiamata Isola di Pasqua.

CACCIA AL «LUNGA CODA» COME IN UNA CORRIDA

Lato sud e lato nord dell'atollo di Rangiroa - Arcipelago delle Tuamotu - Autunno 1970

7 novembre 1970

Una volta, qui, di uomini capaci di *parlare con gli squali* ce n'erano parecchi, e ho scritto e parlato più volte di loro. Il migliore era il vecchio Tianì, il nano con un dente solo. Aveva cominciato ad andare sott'acqua a cercar *nacres* quando ancora non era scoppiata la prima guerra mondiale; quando l'ho conosciuto nel '56 di tuffi in apnea ne aveva già accumulati per una quarantina d'anni. Suo fratello Punuà (che ho già ricordato come l'amico di tutte le odissee oceaniche) era, fino a ieri, di coraggio e bravura pari certo a Tianì, ma quando quest'anno siamo tornati alle Tuamotu ci siamo accorti che sia Tianì che Punuà non sono più in grado di scendere sott'acqua ad affrontare gli squali (a «parlare con gli squali», si dice qui).

Li abbiamo, naturalmente, ancora al nostro fianco, per guidarci e controllarci; e per andar sott'acqua non ci resta che cercare tra i giovani; ma i giovani in mare, al *patià*, a pesca, oggi non sono più capaci d'andarci; anzi *non vogliono* più andarci; non ne vedono lo scopo e non ne hanno desiderio. È il solito motivo: preferiscono il lavoro quotidiano regolarmente retribuito (basta mettere insieme quanto serve per acquistare un biglietto di goletta per Papeete, e laggiù si è subito salariati negli impianti turistici o in quelli militari).

Mi sembrava una situazione senza uscita, quando ieri ho incontrato Teramai, e di lui Punuà mi ha detto: «È un giovane che ci sa fare. Ha ucciso uno squalo *noipirii* con un sacco di tela. A lui la pesca piace. Prova a parlargli...».

È sui venticinque anni, magro, e indossa un blue-jeans che non si toglie nemmeno quando si getta in acqua.

Ha una sorta di continuo sorriso nervoso sulle labbra e parla molto, specialmente se ha bevuto «un paio di birre» (nel senso della frase, alle Tuamotu per «un paio» si intendono *casse*, non *bottiglie*).

La storia della caccia col sacco me la sono fatta raccontare proprio da lui, ieri sera al bar di Tepoè. È stato un racconto metà in francese, metà nel suo dialetto; un racconto aiutato dalle mani, dagli occhi, dalle pause e da qualche grido; un racconto durante il quale Teramai ha mescolato, come sempre fanno i narratori polinesiani, presente e passato.

«Ero andato sottovento alla costa sud, alla laguna di Tipiipì, dovevo raccogliere la *coprah* che avevamo riunito in mucchi e preparato due settimane prima. Sulla barca ho molti sacchi vuoti, per riempirli, appunto.

Sono quasi arrivato, quando vedo che mi segue un *noipirii*, un "lunga coda". Poi vedo che non è solo, ma sono quattro, e tutti grossi. Uno solo non mi avrebbe preoccupato, perché il *noipirii* è uno squalo sonnacchioso, timoroso e ha la bocca piccola.[1] Il *noipi-*

---

[1] Parlando dello squalo a «lunga coda» (il cui nome polinesiano *noipirii* significa «occhi piccoli») mi riferisco a un tipo facilmente riconoscibile, della specie detta «nutrice». Il «nutrice», si sa, non ha mai fatto paura a nessuno, e questo in un certo senso ridimensiona i termini dell'impresa di Teramai. Io, confesso, non mi intendo in maniera particolare di famiglie e specie di squali come i veri specialisti dell'argomento; parlo quindi solo con l'aiuto di una limitata esperienza personale, frutto di una ventina d'anni di immersioni in vari mari del mondo. Quest'esperienza mi ha insegnato che non sempre uno squalo innocuo in un mare, lo è anche in un altro: mutate condizioni ambientali cambiano profondamente il suo carattere e la sua aggressività. E non solo: ma ho anche imparato che uno squalo innocuo *oggi* non è detto che lo sia altrettanto un altro giorno. Ad esempio, per quanto riguarda il *noipirii* delle Tuamotu, ricordo che uno di essi (e nemmeno di grandi dimensioni) un giorno staccò di netto il polpaccio di quel vecchio pescatore Tianì di cui parlo in queste pagine; e diverse volte ho visto pescatori sottomarini esperti, polinesiani, considerare l'incontro con un *noipirii* degno della massima considerazione e attenzione.

Per finire, aggiungo che il timore che gli squali a «lunga coda» incutono ai pescatori isolati su canoa, in Polinesia, viene soprattutto dalla forza del suo colpo di coda (da cui il soprannome), causa sovente di ribaltamenti dell'imbarcazione e relativi pericoli. Si sa che lo squalo, anche non eccessivamente aggressivo, lo può essere e in maniera preoccupante nell'accanimento con cui può cercare di impossessarsi di prede già pescate, o nell'attaccare un uomo in mare che si trovi in difficoltà. Così è certo che un pescatore caduto dalla sua barca nelle acque della laguna con tutte le sue prede che porta a bordo, si trova in condizioni migliori per farsi aggredire non solo dai *noipirii* ma anche da altri squali (anche se «bonaccioni») che possono incrociare nelle vicinanze, e che per l'occasione possono diventare pericolosi. «Chi casca in acqua con quel che ha pescato, da queste parti, è come se fosse morto» mi disse un giorno Punuà con quel sorriso sulle labbra che i vecchi polinesiani sfoggiano quando dicono qualcosa di grosso e di vero, e sanno di non esser – chissà perché – creduti fino in fondo.

rii si deve temere di notte perché lui ci vede, gli altri pescecani no. Per questo non ho alcuna paura dei *noipirii*, di giorno; ma questi sono quattro, e hanno fame. L'ho capito perché mi vengono dietro dopo che in acqua ho messo la traina e, navigando, ho cominciato a pescare: le prede che hanno abboccato alle mie esche sono state evidentemente un richiamo invitante, per loro.

Queste bestie resteranno sotto la barca – mi sono detto – e non mi lasceranno, mi seguiranno anche quando arriverò alla costa di Tipiipì. Non hanno paura dell'acqua bassa, molte volte li ho visti anche in mezzo metro di fondo, la coda tutta fuori, alla superficie; quindi non potrò scendere dalla barca per tirarla a riva. Debbo trovare il sistema di mandarli via prima.

Ed ecco il mio errore: getto in acqua un paio di pesci da me pescati, pensando che se li sfamo, gli squali se ne vanno. Invece divorano il boccone e subito diventano più aggressivi. Hanno *sentito*; hanno capito che nella barca c'è da mangiare. Non mi piace che sappiano questo, e ci penso sopra ancora.

Intanto sono arrivato. Alla costa ad aspettarmi non c'è nessuno, e questo lo sapevo. Debbo cavarmela da solo.

Butto il sasso con la cima, come àncora, e la barca s'arresta dondolando. Loro si muovono lenti proprio sotto l'ombra dello scafo; il tonfo del sasso che ho gettato in acqua non li ha spaventati affatto. Considero la possibilità di armare una specie di arpione con un remo, e frugo tra i sacchi vuoti cercando qualcosa di appuntito da usare allo scopo. Non trovo nulla, e intanto sento la prima codata del *noipirii* sul fianco della barca. La barca è di legno compensato e ha una decina d'anni: non so quanto sia ancora solida. L'ha costruita mio padre, l'ha usata mio fratello: che mi ricordi, non è mai stata sostituita una sola parte del suo fasciame. Potrebbe resistere ai colpi del *noipirii*, ma potrebbe anche cadere a pezzi. In vista di questa ipotesi non c'è tempo da perdere.

I sacchi vuoti: mi viene in mente un gioco, un nostro gioco da bambini, quando infilavamo la testa degli squaletti *rairà* in una stoffa di pareo, piegato a sacco. Lui, lo squalo, ci restava impigliato e guizzava come un ubriaco perché non ci vedeva. E qualche volta moriva perché la stoffa aderendo alle branchie lo soffocava.

Il ricordo mi suggerisce un'idea, e non penso nemmeno se è buona o cattiva: debbo agire in fretta perché anche subito i "lunga coda" potrebbero cominciare il loro attacco e demolire la barca.

Prendo uno dei sacchi vuoti, lo inumidisco d'acqua poi lo inzuppo con quel po' di sangue che riesco a "spremere" da uno dei pesci catturati con l'arpione.

Mi sporgo fuori bordo attento a non sbilanciare lo scafo; immergo il sacco insanguinato in acqua, e vedo subito l'ombra degli squali avvicinarsi. Agito nell'acqua il sacco: il sangue si spande. E subito un *noipirii* si avventa.

Io, con uno strappo, lascio la stoffa non appena sento la bocca della bestia chiudersi su quella specie di preda. Lo squalo ha un guizzo, e picchia verso il fondo sabbioso. L'acqua è trasparente: così vedo tutto.

La bestia si dibatte, ma non riesce né a inghiottire né a lasciare quella stoffa che si impiglia nella sua mascella sempre di più e si apre come un cappuccio, sino a infilarsi sulla testa del *noipirii*, che non ci vede più ed è terrorizzato; quando il sacco copre le due branchie per lui è la fine, il soffocamento.

I suoi movimenti diventano lenti mentre si rovescia sulla sabbia del fondo. La lunga coda ha un guizzo e resta immobile. Immobile sono anch'io, come di pietra: e gli altri *noipirii*? I guizzi di quello rimasto impigliato nel sacco mentre soffocava forse li hanno spaventati. Almeno lo spero.

Vedo la laguna intorno vuota e non perdo tempo. Spingo con i remi la barca verso riva, balzo nell'acqua bassa, ormai al sicuro (o quasi) e riesco a prender terra. L'avventura è finita...»

Terminato il carico di *coprah*, Teramai ritornò nella laguna. Erano passate due ore dallo «scontro» e dello squalo morto soffocato restava ben poco: altri *noipirii* e forse anche *rairà* o *paratà* lo avevano divorato. Sul fondo la carcassa ondeggiava alla corrente, facendo fluttuare il sacco ancora impigliato nella sua bocca.

10 novembre 1971

Tre giorni da quando abbiamo ascoltato il racconto di Teramai: tre giorni di discussioni serali su una mia proposta: sarebbe

240

capace Teramai di ripetere per noi (che vogliamo filmarla e fotografarla) quella strana caccia col sacco allo squalo?

Teramai si è alla lunga convinto. Ieri ci ha finalmente assicurato che sarebbe stato pronto a ripetere la sua corrida non appena
il vento ci avesse permesso di tornare alla laguna di Tipiipì (dove
maggiori sono le probabilità d'incontrare squali a «lunga coda» di
grandi dimensioni).

Oggi è stato il giorno propizio. Con due cineprese subacquee e
l'equipaggiamento fotografico abbiamo atteso «il momento della
verità» entro le due vecchie gabbie metalliche che anni fa ci servi-
rono per le riprese del «tigre». Dall'isola di Tahaa (ove erano
rimaste al *faré* di Garnier che le usava come pollaio) le gabbie ci
sono giunte qui alle Tuamotu portate da una goletta. Rimesse più o
meno in ordine, dopo tanto tempo ci sono di nuovo utili; questa
volta non appese alle barche, ma appoggiate sul fondo, dato il basso
livello della laguna nel punto prescelto, proprio sotto la barca dalla
quale Teramai cerca di attirare i *noipirii* gettando in acqua esche
sanguinolente. Per non impaurire gli squali, e far sì che si avvici-
nino a noi il più possibile, abbiamo camuffato le gabbie con ciuffi
d'alghe, rami di corallo, blocchi di madrepore. Sembra che funzioni: un *noipirii* di grandi dimensioni giunge infatti dopo un po' di
attesa. La tela di sacco sporca di sangue è calata in acqua. Ma il
programma, all'ultimo momento, presenta alcune varianti; negli
istanti in cui lo squalo si prepara a mordere (e questo lo capiamo
dai suoi scatti nervosi, così anomali rispetto al suo lento muoversi
di sempre) Teramai, sicuro della sua bravura, del suo coraggio e
della bontà del suo sistema, lo sfida gettandosi in acqua proprio
davanti a lui, stringendo tra le mani i bordi del sacco sporco di
sangue. Gesto che non mi attendo, fuori programma; e che rende la
scena ancora più simile a un modello certo da Teramai non conosciuto: quello del torero nell'arena con la cappa rossa da agitare
davanti agli occhi di un toro. Anch'io debbo variare il mio programma; abbatto con un colpo delle pinne il mascheramento della
gabbia, e esco nuotando in acqua libera; seguo Teramai e lo squalo
che si fronteggiano, porto la cinepresa a pochi metri da loro; a un
guizzo del *noipirii*, la sua coda colpisce la cinepresa, senza danneg-
giarla anzi rendendo ancor più efficace la scena. E questa è già di
per sé veramente emozionante nel guizzo dell'uomo immerso e nei

suoi movimenti a portare le maglie della stoffa insanguinata sino alla bocca dello squalo, come invitandolo a mordere.

Accade tutto come Teramai ci aveva narrato. Il *noipirii* addenta il sacco, poi, inarcandosi di scatto, tenta in guizzi disperati di liberarsi, ma invano. La sua stessa bocca trattiene quella stoffa fluttuante che lo soffoca, lo uccide.

Smettiamo di filmare e fotografare quando vediamo lo squalo morto sul fondo, ancora inarcato dalla testa alla coda quasi per un ultimo, furioso slancio.

Teramai ha guadagnato i cinquemila franchi pattuiti.

FINE DI UN DIO

Tiputa (Rangiroa) - Ottobre 1970

L'atollo di Rangiroa dista circa millecinquecento chilometri da quello di Mururoa, ove hanno luogo gli esperimenti nucleari francesi; questi esperimenti hanno causato un vero sconvolgimento nella vita degli atolli meridionali delle Tuamotu e hanno prodotto anche qualche novità qui a Rangiroa, a poche centinaia di metri dalle case di quella che fu la comunità dei pescatori di Tiputa. Una stazione di rilevamenti sismici, per il controllo degli effetti di ogni esplosione, è stata costruita dai francesi e funziona giorno e notte da ormai due anni. Vivendo qui un buon numero di settimane (divenute poi tre mesi), non abbiamo tardato a renderci conto che una discreta «impronta» polinesiana scalfisce, almeno in superficie, questo prodotto periferico della *grandeur* gaullista del poligono nucleare del Pacifico. Malgrado un reticolato, le antenne radar e radio, il continuo borbottio di gruppi elettrogeni, e altri aspetti militareschi nell'insieme, galline e maialetti neri convivono con gli strumenti più perfetti della tecnologia sismologica. E malgrado rigidi regolamenti da «007», tra le costruzioni *top secret* circolano mogli polinesiane e cino-polinesiane a consolare – anche con l'arrivo di qualche moccioso figlio dell'atomica – la solitudine dei tecnici (le cui divise, sia detto per inciso, sono sostituite da gaie camicie multicolori o addirittura dal *pareo*). Naturalmente è vero anche il contrario: ho ritrovato infatti i miei amici pescatori influenzati, e non poco, da quelle costruzioni in cemento e lamiera.

Giorno dopo giorno, vivendo qui, ho sentito quant'è forte, oggi, in tutta la comunità polinesiana l'ambizione di buttare all'aria le confortevoli case in legno o in *niau* (i famosi *farê*) e costruirne di nuove in cemento e lamiera; ho compreso l'invincibile desiderio, in tutti, di sostituire con un gruppo elettrogeno i lumi a petrolio e a gas. E sono stato, infine, quotidiano testimone della «follia degli orologi»: nella «base» ce ne sono otto, uno accanto all'altro, tutti giganteschi, regolati su diversi fusi orari, di un modello di estrema precisione, elettronico. Dal momento in cui il primo pescatore ha pensato di controllare l'ora del suo vecchio, arrugginito quadrante su quelle apparecchiature tanto perfette, tutti nell'isola hanno sentito l'identica necessità. A ogni «mezzogiorno» possessori di orologi da polso o da parete, di apparecchi da taschino e di sveglie vecchie e nuove, contagiati dalla frenesia dell'ora esatta, lasciano precipitosamente il villaggio, interrompono le occupazioni del momento, arrivano alla base, entrano nella «saletta orologi» e s'accalcano nell'affanno d'avanzare o ritardare vetuste lancette capaci fino a ieri di fermarsi o anticipare, o saltare ore intere, segnandone una sì e una no, senza che nessuno avesse mai trovato da stupirsene.

Tiputa (Rangiroa) - 8 ottobre 1970

Il «turbamento» portato dalla tecnica in questa Rangiroa ritrovata dopo sette anni, l'ho riscontrato riflesso persino nel nostro vecchio, grande Punuà. Stamane all'alba eravamo sulla laguna per le nostre riprese filmate, delle quali Punuà è il nostro «consigliere», diciamo così, tecnico. Il tempo era bello, ma davanti alle nostre barche avanzava l'ombra di una pesante nube nera, bassa sull'acqua. C'era da prevedere lo scroscio di un violento acquazzone e l'abbiamo più volte ripetuto a Punuà, al quale oggi abbiamo affidato l'organizzazione di una scena di raccolta di murene, con una decina di ragazzi-pescatori in acqua ai suoi ordini.

Con quella nuvola di pioggia in arrivo era forse il caso d'interrompere il lavoro e tornare al villaggio? No, mi ha risposto Punuà;

e mi ha fatto subito capire che la nuova dimestichezza con la scienza moderna, che contraddistingue la vita del suo atollo nel 1970, ha influenzato anche lui. Ci tiene a passar sopra all'evidenza dei fatti naturali così come gli si presentano (dei quali una volta era tanto buon interprete) e preferisce affidarsi agli «strumenti». Nel caso di stamattina, comunque, non si trattava di una particolare «interpretazione» perché era evidente anche a un bambino l'imminenza di un piovasco. Ma Punuà guardava la nube e scuoteva la testa: quella non era pioggia, diceva; e mi spiegava d'aver ben visto stamane, prima d'imbarcarci, che gli apparecchi della base indicavano «bel tempo». Non si è arreso all'evidenza nemmeno quando siamo entrati in un acquazzone così fitto da impedirci di veder la prua della barca.

Fra uno scroscio e l'altro ho incontrato il suo sguardo e indicando il cielo gli ho gridato: «Hai visto? Questa è pioggia, no?».

Ha cercato bene le parole esatte e mi ha gridato in risposta: «*C'est ne pas la pluie, Folco, c'est "l'athmosphère"*».

Una risposta misteriosa? O solo una gran confusione di parole nella confusione delle idee che si sovrappongono (idee-tradizione vinte dalle idee-novità)? In ogni caso è evidente, come un simbolo, che Punuà, maestro dell'Oceano, padrone della laguna, erede della tradizione più vera delle Tuamotu, mai nemmeno superficialmente interessato ai primi mutamenti profondi del suo mondo (l'arrivo dei turisti, ad esempio), posto di fronte a una nuova magia, quella tecnologica, non è più lo stesso. Non è più capace di giudicare il suo cielo, il suo mare, la sua laguna; preferisce interpretarli secondo il segno di uno strumento lucente dal quale è stato completamente soggiogato.

Rangiroa - 10 ottobre 1970

Punuà aveva quotidianamente un suo mattutino colloquio con gli elementi del creato; un tempo – voglio dire nel '56, nel '61, nel '64, durante gli altri miei soggiorni qui, a Tiputa – era lui a svegliarmi quand'era ancora notte; aveva già scaldato una tazza di caffè, la bevevamo insieme e dalla capanna ci portavamo in una zona di costa aperta, ove fosse possibile vedere il mare e il cielo tutt'attorno l'atollo. Nel tempo di quella breve passeggiata e di qualche parola (Punuà allora non parlava il francese) la prima luce dell'aurora schiariva acque e orizzonte: bastavano, poi, pochi minuti, e già il pronostico di Punuà era pronto. Sapeva dove e come avremmo potuto spostarci con le barche a lavorare, quale vento sarebbe stato più forte o più debole nel corso della giornata, quale spiaggia o *reef* corallino sarebbe stato protetto e di facile accesso. Non erano ancora le cinque, e già s'era di ritorno ai *faré* per preparare tutto, svegliare l'équipe, cercare nelle varie capanne i pescatori, e finalmente prendere il mare. In genere, partivamo quando ancora non s'era alzata la brezza delle sette, quella che increspa la laguna e la muta da specchio perfetto (capace di riflettere le nubi e il cielo con una chiarezza da miraggio) in un braccio di mare mosso da onde e correnti come un grande golfo o insenatura di una qualunque isola.

Punuà non voleva assolutamente partire con le barche dopo l'arrivo della brezza; lo considerava un cattivo augurio, un eventuale ritardo era presagio di una giornata certamente tutta sregolata. E poiché i desideri, gli ordini, i consigli e anche i malumori di Punuà erano per noi legge, si faceva sempre il possibile – almeno in questo – per accontentarlo.

Anche quest'anno ero pronto a regolare gli orari dell'équipe su quella norma che credevo immutabile, quando, sin dal primo giorno di lavoro, ho visto che l'appuntamento mattutino era ritardato sull'orario consueto, e di molto.

Solo ieri, a quasi due settimane dal mio arrivo, ne ho capito la ragione. Mi ero già accorto di una inconsueta abitudine del Punuà degli anni Settanta: quella, cioè, di lasciare ogni mattino il piccolo gruppo di *faré* dove si trova la sua abitazione (e dove sono anche le nostre) per dirigersi a passo rapido verso il bosco che ci separa dalla base dei tecnici francesi. Punuà non porta orologio al polso, avevo quindi escluso un suo interesse per il controllo dell'ora sugli apparecchi della base; ma per la verità non m'ero chiesto il perché di quel quotidiano pellegrinaggio. E ieri, finalmente, ho capito. Sono i sismografi, visti, però, da lui come apparecchi destinati a interpretazioni completamente diverse da quelle per le quali sono stati installati.

Per Punuà, la grafia misteriosa tracciata da quegli apparecchi serve per sapere «che tempo farà». E su questo – ce ne siamo accorti subito – non ammette discussioni.

«*C'est le sismographe qui a dit ça!*» afferma categorico quando cerchiamo di controbattere certe sue asserzioni sul futuro meteorologico di una giornata.

Il sismografo, secondo lui, ha detto pioggia, e pioggia sarà, anche se c'è il sole; ha detto bonaccia e bonaccia sarà, anche se soffia il *maramù*, e le cime degli alberi ondeggiano paurosamente.

Tiputa (Rangiroa) - 29 dicembre 1970

Debbo ricredermi sulla mia precedente affermazione nei riguardi di Punuà?

A conti fatti, mi sono accorto che durante tutti i due mesi in cui ci ha guidato, non ha poi sbagliato più di una media accettabile. Superato il primo choc nel vederlo succube delle lancette dei sismografi, debbo ammettere che ora come un tempo Punuà riesce a prevedere pioggia, vento, bonaccia e tempesta con quasi assoluta esattezza.

E allora?

Abbiamo riso nell'accorgerci che guardava ai sismografi credendoli dei barometri. Abbiamo riso nell'accorgerci che l'ago del sismografo gli sembrava una lancetta infallibile capace di dire «bel tempo» o «brutto tempo». Ma ora siamo perplessi nell'ammettere che, salvo qualche madornale errore come quello dell'acquazzone il giorno delle murene, per il resto le sue previsioni si sono tutte avverate.

Senza saperlo, un pescatore di una perduta isola corallina come lui ha scoperto un nesso segreto fra gli impercettibili movimenti della terra e del mare (che i sismografi segnalano, momento dopo momento) e le condizioni del tempo? Forse Punuà ha scoperto una regola ignorata dalla scienza? O invece tutto è stato un caso, una serie di combinazioni?

Avrei voluto chiederglielo, oggi, mentre lasciavamo Rangiroa. Poi ho taciuto.

Preferisco restare nel dubbio, e nel dubbio crederlo ancora il padrone degli elementi, tutt'attorno al suo atollo, al centro del suo oceano.

IL RITORNO, VENT'ANNI DOPO

Tiputa (Rangiroa) - Dicembre 1990

Sembrerebbe, quello che ho scelto, un titolo che voglia echeggiare il famoso «seguito» dei *Tre moschettieri*. In realtà, l'ho scritto invece perché suggerisce subito l'esatta misura del tempo tra il mio penultimo viaggio e l'ultimo agli atolli delle Tuamotu. Dopo questo ritorno non sbarcherò mai più in questi atolli. E il mio diario nelle isole orientali si concluderà con queste pagine.

Anche perché, se dovessi riferirmi ai *Tre moschettieri*, non potrei andare al di là di una semplice citazione. I «miei» tre moschettieri di quest'isola sono morti, Punuà e suo fratello Tianì, qui a Rangiroa. E anche Masino Manunza – mio fedele operatore subacqueo, loro inseparabile compagno d'immersione tra squali e coralli – è scomparso già da molti anni.

Appena messo piede a Rangiroa, sono andato a portare un saluto alla tomba di Punuà. E mentre sostavo qualche minuto accanto all'ingenuo e commovente cippo funerario coperto da tettoia di latta che protegge una sua foto e la scritta «Papà Punuà», non sono riuscito a evitare che – invece di una preghiera: ma per quale religione? – il ricordo dell'amico scomparso si intrecciasse con una disordinata sequenza d'immagini evocative. Schegge di momenti vissuti assieme lungo le coste, e sotto le onde, di quest'atollo ove ho trascorso quelli che sono stati forse i giorni più avventurosi e intensi (e forse per questo felici) della mia vita e del mio rapporto con il mare e con gli uomini che del mare avevano fatto «il loro elemento». Punuà e la sua gente, appunto.

Due ore dopo sono al largo dell'isola.

Finiamo d'indossare le mute, di fissarci sulle spalle le bombole. Il canotto gigante nel quale siamo imbarcati ha il motore in folle, sale e scende sull'onda lunga dell'oceano.

Guardo la costa di Rangiroa, sei, settecento metri alle nostre spalle. E la sequenza evoca gli istanti di quando da quella riva, guidati da «papà» Punuà ci gettavamo in acqua per fotografare gli squali dalla *pass*. Allora *lui* non ci avrebbe mai suggerito, nemmeno per ipotesi, di immergerci *al largo* dell'atollo, in oceano.

Sembrava un'immersione impossibile, quella. Sia perché allora non eravamo attrezzati per immersioni lunghe e a grande profondità, sia perché i pescatori di squali del gruppo di Punuà «lavoravano» sott'acqua in un ambiente ben preciso: tuffandosi sul precipizio della *pass*, subito fuori della riva; ma non pensavano proprio a immergersi in mare aperto. Ne avevano un giusto e sacro terrore.

D'altra parte la *pass* e le sue acque non ci avevano certo lesinato emozioni, paura, sorprese. Dal giorno in cui mi ero immerso per la prima volta con Punuà e suo fratello e avevo visto e filmato (credo di esser stato il primo) «come» quella gente nuotava sott'acqua; solo gli occhi protetti dai piccoli occhiali di legno, i *titià*, e difesi da un'arma subacquea che solo loro sapevano maneggiare, un palo appuntito di tre metri, il *patià*.[1]

Il *patià*, ovvero l'arpione che tutti i pescatori sapevano maneggiare perfettamente sino a venti metri di fondo, e di cui ora non è possibile rintracciare nemmeno un esemplare da esporre assieme ai *titià*, sulla parete di un ipotetico museo antropologico delle Tuamotu. Un museo capace di evocare, se non altro con foto e film, il tempo in cui i pescatori a gruppi di cinque o sei, entravano in acqua quando le correnti dovute alle maree si equilibravano. E all'avvicinarsi di un branco di pesci si nascondevano tra i coralli per non impaurire le potenziali prede. Quando poi erano a tiro, il corpo di ogni uomo si tendeva in un guizzo, il suo arpione colpiva una volta, qualche volta due.

Guardo Tiriirià, l'uomo che maneggia il motore fuoribordo del grande canotto sul quale siamo quasi pronti all'immersione al largo dell'atollo ove un tempo, e ora non più, si pescava al *patià-titià*. È un nipote di Punuà; ed è l'ultimo polinesiano di Rangiroa ancora appassionato alle battute in mare; allora era il più giovane del gruppo a immergersi con noi, avrà avuto quindici o sedici anni. Tiriirià, adesso, ha i capelli bianchi, e il segno di un gran morso di squalo in una gamba.

S'accorge del mio sguardo e ride. Indica la ferita e mi grida:

---

[1] In questo stesso diario, l'ho narrato nelle pagine scritte nel settembre '56; e qui riportate da pagina 182 a pagina 188.

«Aità pea pea...», esclamazione che in polinesiano, grosso modo, vuol dire: «... e che ci vuoi fare?...».

A ricordarmi la forza dell'aggressore che l'aveva ferito, Titiirià muove braccio e mano – ridendo – per ricordarmi i colpi di coda del grande squalo-tigre che avevo filmato con lui, con Punuà e con Masino.

Poi Tiriirià, con un'altra risata, spalanca la bocca e imita il movimento di una mascella che morde; e m'aiuta a ricordare quando quella del «tigre» era a pochi metri da noi, e si era spalancata per addentare l'esca preparata da Punuà: sei file di denti si erano allora «girate» verso l'esterno, per serrarsi in un istante. Taglienti come perfette macchine dalle lame d'acciaio.

È a quelle «lame» che penso – rivedendomele davanti agli occhi come se non fossero passati più di trent'anni – quando, sul nostro canotto, il capo del gruppo pronto all'immersione ci fa segno di gettarci in acqua.

Vale a dire in quel «blu profondo» dal quale veniva fin sotto costa il «tigre» che i pescatori polinesiani sapevano come chiamare. Tiriirià proprio oggi, prima dell'immersione, m'ha detto che ormai da anni di quei giganti del mare nel Pacifico meridionale non se ne vedono più. Come gran parte dei *pelagici*, vale a dire i predoni sempre a caccia in oceano aperto, sono stati praticamente sterminati dai pescherecci giapponesi e coreani con le loro reti distese per miglia e miglia tra gli atolli.

«Vedrai solo gli squali che, allora, pescavamo con gli arpioni» mi ha detto Tiriirià.

Tento di credergli mentre, dopo il tuffo, scendiamo in gruppo verso un fondale che non vediamo. È quasi sera e attorno a noi, già a poche decine di metri dalla superficie, è molto profondo l'azzurro dell'oceano. Una penombra dalla quale vedo arrivare uno, cinque, dieci squali.

Scendiamo a candela, loro ci volteggiano attorno a spirale. Da dieci son presto venti. Arriviamo alle rocce del fondo. Ci guida Patrick, un australiano. Ormai sono personaggi come lui, che si definisce «un organizzatore del brivido», a guidare sott'acqua i sub che visitano Rangiroa. Prima di immergermi ci ha consigliato di restare vicini, sul fondo; e tenere le schiene ben poggiate alla scogliera, per evitare attacchi di squali alle spalle. In effetti ne abbiamo molti tutt'attorno, e sempre più vicini.

Li osservo come mai avevo potuto prima. In maggioranza sono *mako*, ovvero nervosi *Isurus*; ma ci sono anche i *raira* e i *Chardiarinus melanopterus*.

Per quel che si sapeva degli squali solo pochi decenni fa, e per la paura che incutevano, un sub in queste condizioni d'accerchiamento si sarebbe sentito perduto. Anche perché le bestiacce gli si fanno sempre più sotto. Patrick, infatti, ha preso l'abitudine di offrir loro un pasto, a ogni sua immersione in alto fondale.

Ed essi – sempre così di buon appetito! – si fan sotto. Pretendono il dono.

Malgrado la loro pelle sia quasi una corazza, vedo su molti esemplari che ci passano accanto segni di profonde ferite. Cicatrici dalle forme più diverse.

Guardo Patrick, e lui mi fa segno di «sì» con la testa, confermandomi quanto mi ha raccontato prima dell'immersione. Ovvero un'osservazione importante, raccolta da lui e dai suoi amici. I loro «tuffi nell'avventura» non sono – fortunatamente! – soltanto fini a se stessi e al *mestiere* di «accompagnatori turistici subacquei».

Certo, per guadagnare quanto serve a lui e al suo gruppo per vivere alle isole, le «immersioni pericolose», vengono vendute da Patrick a caro prezzo. I suoi clienti sono turisti in cerca di emozioni (purché siano esperti) e fotografi o realizzatori di film, come è oggi il caso mio e di Luca Tamagnini sceso con me (lui fotografa mentre io filmo).

Ma altre immersioni di Patrick e del suo *Sub Sea Club* non sono solo mirate al «turismo avventuroso»; ma consentono di registrare molte osservazioni «in loco» e contribuiscono a portare avanti alcuni «studi diretti» sul comportamento degli squali. Patrick è più volte riuscito a vederli – caso rarissimo – mentre s'accoppiano.

Atto che può durare da pochi secondi a più ore, ma che sempre ha una caratteristica: il maschio brutalizza con i suoi denti – e fa sul serio! – la sua partner; «morsi d'amore» a far comprendere alla femmina non solo che il maschio «è pronto», ma lo stringere con i denti è *a lui* «indispensabile durante l'accoppiamento» come mi spiega Patrick «a tenersi ben stretta *lei*, per il tempo necessario a introdurre *uno dei due* pterigoidi che ogni squalo maschio ha a disposizione – beato lui! – per deporre nel seno della futura madre il suo liquido spermatico».

Le bestie che ci sfiorano mostrando sul corpo profonde ferite son dunque tutte femmine. E più cicatrici ostentano, più son state corteggiate, possedute; e più di altre hanno messo al mondo centinaia di nuove creature.

Kauehi (Tuamotu centrali) - 8 gennaio 1991

Sono al centro dell'arcipelago ove tante volte ho navigato (e sono approdato) nell'arco di oltre tre decenni. Ma ora navigo nella sua zona più desolata. È quasi un deserto, qui, il Pacifico meridionale.

Ancora una volta, oggi ho misura di come sia questo rapporto uomo-natura (o meglio e più semplicemente quello uomo-mare, uomo-oceano) a essere unico, qui; e a suscitare uno stato d'animo particolare nel viaggiatore che si muove oggi come ieri in quest'area del Pacifico meridionale. Da racconti che ho sentito da amici alpinisti, unico paragone possibile, credo sia quello dello stato d'animo di chi risale massicci come quelli himalaiani o delle Ande e si trova al cospetto dell'immensità di montagne inabitate e dei loro ghiacciai, delle loro vette; e alle nubi che le sovrastano e agli improvvisi temporali che si scatenano.

Solo questo – credo – è paragone possibile con il mare e le isole che i Mari del Sud, nella loro estrema frontiera orientale, offrono a chi riesce a giungervi e a navigarvi per qualche settimana.

Vela solitaria, la nostra, tra isole ormai quasi tutte disabitate. È questo, d'altra parte, un «quadrante», immenso e sconfinato perché dall'Isola di Pasqua all'arcipelago delle Tonga parliamo di un'estensione pari all'incirca a due volte quella dell'Europa.

In tale vastità proprio la mancanza, o quantomeno la rarità degli incontri con la gente delle isole, permette di non avere diaframmi, di non avere specchi deformanti tra «l'io che osserva» e il mare o gli atolli tutt'attorno.

Qui si può dimenticare la «corruzione» – oltreché sociale ed etnografica anche naturale – delle isole divenute meta turistica, come Tahiti, Bora-Bora e Rangiroa. Nelle Tuamutu centrali e occidentali, invece, la presenza umana ha subìto un fenomeno di rarefazione. Proprio al contrario di quanto è accaduto altrove; *altrove*, ovvero in quella parte del mondo dove l'aumento della densità umana ha negativamente influito sull'ambiente, sul paesaggio. E indirettamente su usi e costumi tradizionali, sul rispetto di radici culturali, troppo spesso tagliate di netto.

Sto scrivendo queste note mentre continua la mia navigazione attraverso una parte – quella «centrale» appunto – degli atolli Tuamotu, anelli di corallo sparsi su una zona d'oceano paragonabile in estensione – tanto per continuare con paragoni di «casa nostra» – a quella che si potrebbe tendere dal Marocco alla Danimarca, dalla Grecia alla Bretagna. Qui, nel corso dei secoli, la lunga e continua migrazione polinesiana dall'Ovest verso l'Est aveva creato «colonie» stabili di molte comunità; sulle superfici emerse degli atolli erano sorti microvillaggi di poche decine di abitanti; che avevano come punto di riferimento il capoluogo – per così dire – di tutto questo immenso settore marino e insulare: l'«isola grande» di Tahiti e la sua capitale, Papeete. Ma si trattava di riferimento puramente amministrativo: da lì giungevano, infatti, alle Tuamotu le disposizioni, le leggi, i divieti; da lì partivano le golette che alle Tuamotu portavano il minimo indispensabile alla sopravvivenza dei villaggi. In cambio caricavano *coprah*, ovvero polpa di noci di cocco disseccata, il principale prodotto degli atolli; e anche – quand'era stagione di raccolta – si caricavano le *nacres*, le ostriche madreperlacee.

Agli atolli l'uomo viveva tra cielo e mare, in una fascia sottilissima emergente e circolare; era una vita dura ma tale da potersi definire *serena* (e qui uso malvolentieri un termine «occidentale», e quindi in parte inesatto).

La gente anche quando i contatti con Tahiti si interrompevano per mesi, tavolta per anni, non si lamentava. Né fuggiva, né emigrava. Viveva il suo tempo senza porsi molti problemi, e senza particolari velleità: da generazioni, un'esistenza sempre eguale. Sino a un punto di rottura con la tradizione che mi auguro queste pagine abbiano fatto comprendere sia situabile all'incirca intorno agli anni Sessanta. Ma aggravatosi, poi, in epoca recente: da quando a Papeete, a Tahiti e nelle altre isole della Società si è sviluppato un turismo estremamente dissacratore, un vero boom urbanisticamente dovuto anche al rafforzamento delle basi militari francesi in Oceania, tutt'attorno al poligono nucleare di Mururoa.

Per questa doppia ragione a Papeete è aumentata la richiesta di manodopera; e stagione dopo stagione i *puamutù* – gli abitanti delle Tuamotu – hanno lasciato i loro atolli. Hanno abbandonato il loro villaggio. Sono andati a fare i muratori, i camerieri, i tassinari, i commessi a Papeete e dintorni.

Continuando il nostro itinerario, oggi abbiamo gettato l'àncora nella laguna interna dell'atollo di Kauehi. Dove si apre il canale della *pass*, che unisce la laguna interna all'oceano, è rimasta ancora in piedi – ma senza tetto – una delle capanne che un tempo ospitavano una comunità di pescatori.

Un vecchio cane – ben conosciuto dai pochi navigatori che vanno a vela tra gli atolli e fanno tappa qui – vive ormai da parecchi anni solo, accanto alla casa che fu dei suoi padroni da tempo partiti. Sceso a terra, sono stato accolto dai suoi latrati di gioia (vive nell'attesa di una barca che venga ad approdare a ridosso della *pass*). Dai resti sparsi tutt'attorno alla sua cuccia (o sarebbe meglio dire la sua «tana») ho capito di cosa si nutre: polpa delle noci di cocco che il vento fa cadere dagli alberi; o pesci che addenta quando con la bassa marea qualcuno di essi rimane intrappolato tra i coralli accanto alla riva; e questo accade ogni giorno. Non di rado restano in secca anche piccoli squali, e pare che il cane eremita non abbia paura – se ha fame – d'ingaggiare vere e proprie battaglie con loro; li afferra per la coda, li tira in secca, attende che muoiano e poi ne divora le parti più commestibili.

Kauehi - 10 gennaio 1991

Case scoperchiate e un cane eremita: non potrei citare un simbolo più struggente di una solitudine così totale. Restando qui due giorni, e muovendomi nell'atollo deserto, ho potuto però registrare il «lato positivo» di questo abbandono. Ed è quanto può interessare particolarmente chi ama la natura; e si augura di poter dire che ha trovato – almeno in qualche area di questo pianeta – un punto dove essa ha avuto una sua rivincita sull'uomo.

Nelle Tuamotu centrali e occidentali, negli atolli dai quali l'uomo è fuggito, la natura riconquista il suo dominio. Le isole sono tornate a essere il regno incontrastato di cento diverse varietà di uccelli marini.

E i fondali tutt'attorno, le coste, dove ormai non pesca più nessuno, brulicano di vita: branchi di pesci «di passo» e nubi di quelli corallini, sembrano voler aumentare ogni cupa previsione negativa sul destino degli oceani.

È certo un'eccezione che – ahimè! – non contraddice il quadro generale dei mari del mondo; ma permette per qualche giorno di dimenticare angosce e timori di tante disastrose – e quotidiane – notizie «ecologiche».

Qui – per una breve parentesi – è permesso essere ottimisti, fiduciosi. Ed entusiasti.

Ma abbiamo appena il tempo di godere di una così emozionante sensazione e serenità. E già le notizie dall'altra parte del pianeta ci raggiungono, e ci obbligano a dimenticare ogni ottimismo.

IL GIORNO DELLA GUERRA
(VISTA DALL'ALTRA PARTE DEL MONDO)

Fakarava - 20 gennaio 1991

Ci avviciniamo a vele spiegate all'atollo di Fakarava, verso la sua *pass* a nord. Là ove sopravvive uno dei villaggi delle Tuamotu centrali. Uno dei pochi ancora abitati.

Molte scorte stanno esaurendosi sull'*Alpha Centauri II*, la barca che ci porta da tre settimane attraverso questa zona dei Mari del Sud, di atollo in atollo.

Al villaggio intendiamo far rifornimento: quello di Fakarava è l'unico scalo ancora praticabile in questa zona delle Tuamotu centrali. Ha un piccolo ospedale, una stazione di radiotelefono via satellite, e alcuni empori dove chi ancora vive nell'arcipelago (o chi vi naviga) trova quanto di essenziale potrebbe servirgli: dalla benzina ai biscotti, dalle pile allo zucchero, dai ricambi dei motori più in uso alla birra; e *parei* colorati, scarpe di plastica, cibi in scatola, ami e lenze per la pesca.

Certo, scesi a terra per rifornirci, non ci attendiamo – entrando in uno dei magazzini del porto – di trovarci di fronte all'abbondanza di un supermercato. Ma con i miei compagni di navigazione resto, comunque, di stucco: quando un primo, un secondo e un terzo emporio ci appaiono sconsolatamente vuoti.

Ai nostri sguardi interrogativi, eguale risposta: «È la guerra: non lo sapete?».

Certo che lo sappiamo. Anche noi, da «quel giorno» – il 15 gennaio – siamo perfettamente al corrente di cosa è esploso in Medio Oriente: appesi alla radio di bordo, avevamo ascoltato – con trepidazione – notizie dal lontanissimo Golfo che s'infiammava.

Quelle stesse trasmissioni radio, più altre informazioni e servizi televisivi ricevuti in quel perduto atollo via satellite (malissimo ma intelligibili, comunque) erano stati ascoltati e visti da chi accanto alla sua capanna ha montato un'antenna parabolica (non pochi, anche se il livello economico delle comunità isolane è ovviamente assai basso). Sicché il crescendo drammatico delle notizie da quel giorno in poi aveva creato, nel minuscolo centro di Fakarava, la stessa reazione isterica delle grandi città europee e australiane: in molti si erano affrettati a fare incetta di prodotti che potevano diventare introvabili, accumulando in casa riserve «per ogni evenienza».

Su quell'atollo poche decine di abitanti si erano comportate come quelle centinaia di migliaia di individui del cui panico quella sera stessa avremmo saputo, ascoltando notizie radio dall'Australia, dall'America, dall'Europa.

La reazione alle «notizie di guerra» provava come sia ben vero l'assioma che ci invita a considerare il pianeta come «villaggio globale». In questa remota periferia del Pacifico la reazione è stata infatti eguale e simultanea al resto del mondo, là ove ci si era impauriti per le conseguenze di quanto andava accadendo a causa della «crisi del Golfo».

Ho evocato «la paura», ed è di questa che mi parla un'anziana capovillaggio: «Ti meravigli del nostro timore per una guerra, anche se così lontana? Ma sai cosa accadde, qui e nelle altre isole del Pacifico meridionale, nel 1939? In Europa e poi nel mondo tutti presero a combattersi, e tutti si dimenticarono di noi. Non giunsero più golette e rifornimenti sino al 1944; sicché quelli furono anni di fame. Avevamo solo pesci e noci di cocco, per nutrirci».

Un *instituteur* – il maestro della scuola elementare dell'isola – aggiunge: «Se per cinque anni ci fu poco da mangiare, per sette non ci fu nulla da studiare, qui; e nelle isole non s'imparò più a leggere né a scrivere». Alza le braccia al cielo e spiega: «Quando nel 1938 la Francia – che ci governava – delegò il potere al Fronte popolare, una delle prime decisioni della sinistra fu quella di chiudere (ovunque sventolasse la bandiera francese) le scuole gestite dai religiosi; tassativa disposizione che giunse sin qui, dove le scuole, tutte!, erano state create e tenute in vita da missionari di varie congregazioni religiose. L'ordine giunto ai gendarmi per radio – già da allora ce n'era uno per ogni isola – fu scrupolosamente eseguito. Per tener buoni gli isolani, venne loro promesso: "Al posto dei preti arriveranno *instituteurs* laici". Arrivò invece la guerra, tutti si dimenticarono di noi sino al 1946, e questa fu la ragione per la quale chi oggi ha sessant'anni è un incolto: venne su nella più completa ignoranza».

Il villaggio di Fakarava è piccolo; e come ovunque, alle Tuamotu, appare incombente, sconfinato l'oceano tutt'attorno.

Sensazione d'immensità resa ancor più sconvolgente qui, come in tutti gli atolli dove sono sbarcato, da quella «natura particolare» della quale così spesso ho accennato in questo diario e in tanti altri miei scritti sui Mari del Sud: quell'essere – un'isola corallina – piatta e sottile come anello etereo poggiato precariamente tra mare e cielo. Di questo, nelle pagine che sin qui avete letto, ho scritto più volte. Ma debbo ripetere la descrizione ambientale; dire ancora dell'azzurro cinerino della laguna interna, chiusa dall'anello verde dei *motù*, le dune di sabbia corallina sulle quali crescono boschi di palme di cocco: piccole selve che riescono a essere rigogliose anche in questo clima d'aridità totale (l'unica acqua dolce degli atolli è – lo ricordo – quella rara delle piogge).

Ancora una volta, e forse più intensamente di quanto in altre occasioni m'era accaduto, godo dello spettacolo di queste luci del cielo, dell'oceano, delle lagune. Variano con straordinaria varietà, cerando come sempre contrasti di colori, di prospettive, di temperatura. Brezze fresche – nei giorni del gennaio australe – s'alternano, con soffi improvvisi, all'afa bruciante del Tropico.

In questa atmosfera, delle cui magie la natura è l'unica regista, sembrerebbe difficile che possa rimbalzare e impressionare l'immagine di un remoto scenario di guerra, l'esplodere, il ribollire di una follia collettiva, ricevere l'eco dolorosa di eventi lontani non solo geograficamente (l'Iraq è a 22.000 chilometri da qui) ma anche politicamente, socialmente, culturalmente.

Quello degli atolli periferici Tuamotu è un mondo ancora «fuori dal mondo», si vorrebbe affermare con uno scherzoso gioco di parole. Ma oggi lo scherzo non ha più senso. Da quando l'intero pianeta è *un unico villaggio*, Fakarava non è microscopica, dimenticata entità ai margini del pianeta. È parte del tutto; tant'è vero che i suoi piccoli emporii tra gli alberi di cocco sono stati presi d'assalto come i grandi magazzini nelle città di aree ben più vicine all'epicentro degli eventi.

Fakarava - 23 gennaio 1991

Con la radiolina a onde corte in mano, la lunga antenna tesa verso il cielo, ascolto – camminando sul *reef* corallino dell'isola – le folate di notizie diffuse sul pianeta dalla Bbc, dalla radio francese, da quelle americane. Voci concitate che incalzano, con la cronaca delle notti di guerra che si susseguono (a undici ore di fuso orario di differenza, io sono invece in pieno giorno). Mi trovo lontano dal villaggio; e mi sorprende vedere, nelle luce accecante, un pescatore *puamutù* muoversi lentamente nell'acqua che gli arriva alle ginocchia. Raccoglie granchi, che afferra con mosse rapide – anche se è molto anziano – e infila in un sacco. È un raro polinesiano «d'altri tempi». Mi avvicino e lui s'accorge di me. Sente il gracidare della radiolina.

«La guerra?» mi chiede, in francese.

Accenno di sì con la testa. Mi guarda a lungo, probabilmente ha identificato la bandiera della barca dalla quale sono sceso; galleggia sulla laguna, poco distante.

«Italia?» domanda. E senza attendere risposta mi dice: «Mio fratello ha fatto la guerra nel tuo paese, andò volontario con la "brigata polinesiana" che combatté con De Gaulle, dal '41 al '45. È caduto laggiù, il suo nome è inciso da qualche parte in un cimitero dei *poopa* francese vicino a Roma, assieme ad altri tre di queste isole». Tace per un istante, poi scuote la testa e conclude: «Lui e gli altri sono dall'altra parte del mondo».

«L'altra parte del mondo» ripeto fra me. E mi rendo conto che ormai, quando si parla di guerra, «l'altra parte del mondo» è un modo di dire senza significato. Da mezzo secolo in qua «l'altra parte» non c'è più. Siamo tutti, per così dire (e purtroppo) da una parte sola.

Navigando nel vento del mito, quello di ieri (e oggi?)

La solitudine del Pacifico – Magellano, Cook e chi rivive oggi le loro imprese – Drake il pirata – Strage alle isole Marchesi – L'introvabile *Terra Australis* – Realtà e interpretazioni sulla morte di Cook e su come venne divorato – L'ammutinamento del *Bounty* e altre avventure – Melville, Stevenson, Loti e London – Naufragi, cicloni; e, ancora una volta, i pescecani.

È ridicolo, ovviamente, usare la parola «esplorazione» in un racconto di esperienze e di avventure nei Mari del Sud di oggi; un mondo dove all'isola ancora deserta e poco (o per nulla) conosciuta è vicina un'altra ove sono sorti centri turistici e vere e proprie cittadine, ove si preferisce l'aria condizionata alla fresca ombra di un *cocotier*. Nel Pacifico meridionale si naviga assai più nelle acque incerte e mutevoli delle contraddizioni, che non in quelle tempestose di un quadrante oceanico, la cui meteorologia tanto preoccupava i primi navigatori.

A loro va attribuita a pieno titolo la definizione di esploratori, ma certo non solo quella. A differenza dei loro omologhi che per primi attraversarono – descrissero e disegnarono – aree ignote d'Africa, d'Asia e d'America, e poi le zone polari, agli «esploratori» dei Mari del Sud va attribuito qualcosa di più: sono loro ad avere creato quanto ha composto uno dei più favolosi miti del *nostro* «immaginario» esotico (ove *nostro* sta per occidentale).

Il *mito dei Mari del Sud*, appunto.

Ai suoi autori, diretti e indiretti, ho dedicato questo capitolo; che è da leggersi in diretta antitesi con quello precedente: là ho narrato le mie esperienze, e ho voluto mantenere la loro forma di diario, proprio a sottolinearne la natura di cronaca diretta. Qui riferisco, riassumo e cito invece estratti di diari, resoconti, libri di «ieri», scritti da esploratori che furono senza saperlo anche scrittori e poeti; è da scrittori e poeti che finirono con l'essere a loro volta esploratori, perché quanto essi pubblicarono completò il quadro globale del mondo dei Mari del Sud. Quale appariva a chi giungeva – dopo i primi contatti nei due secoli precedenti – nel Settecento e Ottocento; e quale non è più, dato che credo che si possa affermare che questo mondo, più di ogni altro, appena veniva «scoperto» da noi occidentali, iniziava a mutare, decomporsi e svanire.

Era un miraggio che, appena intravisto e osservato con stupore, si dissolveva.

Per questo sui Mari del Sud, più che in ogni altra parte del mondo, è sorto un mito che non cessa di ammaliarci.

Dalle emozioni dei primi navigatori europei, affacciatisi per primi alle isole sconosciute dell'Oceania, si può aver idea leggendo le loro relazioni di viaggio che coprono un periodo di due secoli e mezzo, fra il 1520 – prima traversata del «grande oceano» da parte di Magellano – e la fine del Settecento, anni dell'esplorazione scientifica del Pacifico da parte di Bougainville e di Cook. Sono prese di contatto eccitanti, meravigliose, talune cruente, come quelle di Magellano e di Cook, talune sfortunate, come quella del d'Entrecasteaux, morto di scorbuto e altre tragiche, come quella di La Pérouse scomparso, forse vittima di un massacro, sulle scogliere delle Nuove Ebridi.

Tutte queste traversate si svolgevano in un fondo di solitudine assoluta, la solitudine del Pacifico:

È una solitudine [ha scritto Durmayer, navigatore solitario olandese] che non ha riscontro altrove. Una solitudine che pare segregare l'uomo dal resto dell'umanità; se l'hai sperimentata una volta ti fa meraviglia che qualcuno abbia avuto il coraggio di spiegare le vele e tuffarsi alla cieca in quel deserto d'acqua senza aver la minima idea di ciò che il fato gli riserva.

Magellano, per primo, conobbe nel Pacifico il vuoto: attraversandolo in tutta la sua ampiezza non seppe nulla dell'esistenza della Polinesia: trovò un orizzonte senza terre dinanzi a sé fino alle Marianne, ormai sotto le coste dell'Estremo Oriente.

Sette anni prima, nel 1513, Vasco Nuñez de Balboa, affacciatosi dall'istmo del Darien, aveva contemplato affascinato il Mare del Sud, ignoto agli europei. Nei ventun anni precedenti, dalla scoperta di Colombo, si erano infittite nell'Atlantico le ricerche di un passaggio, di un canale, verso il Mar della Cina, scopo del viaggio di Colombo; i navigatori seguitarono a frugare, scoprendo il contorno atlantico delle Americhe, senza riuscire a capire come si potesse pervenire al paese del Gran Can e alla «Cipango-dai-tetti-d'oro». Dopo la scoperta di Balboa dovevano passare altri sette anni, prima che un europeo veleggiasse attraverso quel Mare del Sud. E l'impresa magellanica nel Grande Oceano non fu meno ardita di quella di Colombo, poiché anch'egli affrontò l'ignoto di una nuova rotta, e i patimenti (forse maggiori) e una fine tragica. Egli scoprì le Filippine dal lato oceanico; una scoperta maggiore di quella, pagata con stenti inauditi, fu l'aver «misurata» l'ampiezza inattesa di quelle acque; una vastità che rivelava finalmente l'errore fondamentale di Colombo sulle reali dimensioni del globo, non avendo egli immaginato che tra le coste della Spagna e il Mare della Cina, oltre l'Atlantico, si estendessero un mondo nuovo e l'oceano maggiore della Terra.

Magellano era già stato in India, a Malacca e nell'isola di Sumatra, al servizio di quell'effimero impero portoghese delle spezie che stava sorgendo; poi, deluso, era rimpatriato. Un giorno, una lettera di un vecchio commilitone rimasto laggiù lo informava dell'arrivo delle prime navi portoghesi alle preziose Molucche, le isole dei chiodi di garofano e della noce moscata; facendogli intendere che, in base al cammino percorso, quelle isole sospirate giacevano molto più a oriente di quanto si era pensato. Fatti i suoi calcoli, Magellano, folgorato da un'intuizione, s'accorse che anziché cercare di risolvere l'enigma dei ventisette anni precedenti (un passaggio marino verso il Cipango o la Cina) era affare molto più lucroso il trovare una via per le Molucche, raggiungendole per ponente, anziché per il Capo di Buona Speranza. Tutto stava nel trovare un passaggio attraverso il Nuovo Mondo, per uscire nel Mare del Sud che aveva scoperto Balboa. Pensando alla realizzazione del progetto, si rivolse alla Spagna, lui portoghese, convinto a priori che le Molucche dovevano appartenere di diritto alla Spagna, non al Portogallo, in base alla vera posizione geografica e alla loro distanza dal meridiano già concordato tra Spagna e Portogallo per spartirsi quanto l'una o l'altra avrebbero scoperto nei nuovi oceani. Così Magellano, passato in servizio da un re a un altro, poté salpare nel 1519 verso le Molucche.

Da allora, durante quasi tre secoli, tutte le marine europee che detennero a turno la signoria dei mari esplorarono il Grande Oceano: dopo gli spagnoli, che fecero qualche traversata esplorativa partendo dal Perù verso occidente, fu la volta dei mercantili olandesi, nella ricerca di una terra di nessuno, il mitico Continente Australe, dopo la parentesi piratesca di Drake e di altri pirati inglesi; quindi fu la volta dei francesi e degli inglesi, sino alla vigilia della Rivoluzione francese, anche essi alla ricerca del Continente Australe; benché Cook, alla vigilia del suo massacro nelle Hawaii, avesse già sfatato per sempre questa favola, dopo i suoi tre viaggi diventati classici nella storia della marineria del Pacifico meridionale. Intanto, le molte esplorazioni avevano tratto dal nulla, come vedremo, la maggior parte degli arcipelaghi dell'Oceania; per tutti i navigatori c'erano state avventure, gloria, gioie e sofferenze; e tante scoperte, nel coacervo insulare, restano ignorate, o non identificabili, o dimenticate (come avvenne per le scoperte del Torres, per esempio, rimaste per secoli nell'archivio di un convento di Manila).

Con James Cook cominciarono le esplorazioni scientifiche, che aprirono le rotte alle navi dei mercanti e dei marinai, cui fecero presto seguito quelle di balenieri e di avventurieri.

Insieme alle esplorazioni si affermarono gli accaparramenti politici delle nuove terre; queste troppo povere, in verità, al confronto di quelle americane sottratte agli inca e agli aztechi, per sollecitare subito gli appetiti. Furono quindi timide prese di possesso: per citare due date, ricorderemo la fondazione nel 1788 della base inglese della baia di Sydney che sarebbe poi diventata una colonia penale; e l'avvento del protettorato francese su Tahiti, cui fu testimone un baleniere allora sconosciuto di nome Herman Melville.

Si deve giungere alla metà del secolo scorso per poter dire che l'Occidente prenda davvero possesso e *conosca* il grande oceano, tra le coste americane e i festoni insulari che contornano l'Asia e l'Indonesia fino all'Australia. E ancor oggi, nell'età dei satelliti artificiali, nessuno potrebbe giurare che non ci sia ancora una scogliera da scoprire.

La storia geografica del Pacifico comincia dunque dal vuoto. Magellano, quel vento, se lo trovò di fronte appena doppiato il Capo chiudente lo stretto che da lui prese poi il nome. Lasciata quell'estrema punta meridionale d'America alle spalle, Magellano risalì per una quindicina di gradi la costa cilena, come avrebbe poi fatto chiunque avesse seguito le sue orme, e quindi si lanciò nella traversata del Pacifico, con rotta a nord-ovest, verso le Molucche. Riprese terra centodieci giorni dopo, nelle «Isole dei Ladroni», in Micronesia, patendo la fame e lo scorbuto, e senza essersi accorto del mondo insulare polinesiano, pur attraversandolo. Antonio Pigafetta[1] ci ha lasciato la cronaca dei malanni che accompagnarono la prima presa di contatto europeo con il Pacifico:

Mercore a 28 novembre 1520 ne disbucassemo da questo stretto ingolfandone nel mar Pacifico. Stessemo tre mesi e venti giorni senza pigliare refrigerio di sorta alcuna. Mangiavamo biscotto, non più biscotto, ma polvere di quello con vermi a pugnate, perché essi avevano mangiato il buono: puzzava grandemente de orina de sorci, e bevevamo acqua gialla già putrefatta per molti giorni, e mangiavamo certe pelle de bove, che erano sopra l'antenna maggiore, acciò che l'antenna non rompesse la sartia, durissime per il sole, pioggia e vento. Le lasciavamo per quattro o cinque giorni nel mare, e poi se metteva un poco sopra le brace e così le mangiavamo, e ancora assai volte segatura de asse. Li sorci se vendevano mezzo ducato lo uno e se pur ne avessemo potuto avere. Ma sovra tutte le altre sciagure questa era la peggio: crescevano le gengive ad alcuni sopra li denti così de sotto come de sovra, che per modo alcuno non potevano mangiare, e così morivano per questa infermità. Morirono diciannove uomini e il gigante con uno Indio de la terra del Verzin. Venticinque o trenta uomini se infirmorono, chi ne li bracci, ne le gambe o in altro loco, sicché pochi restarono sani. Per la grazia di Dio, io non ebbi alcuna infermitade.

In questi tre mesi e venti giorni andassemo circa quattro mila leghe in uno golfo per questo mar Pacifico (in vero è bene pacifico, perché in questo tempo non avessimo fortuna) senza vedere alcuna, se non due isolette disabitate, nelle quali non trovassimo altro se non uccelli e arbori; le chiamassemo Isole Infortunate.[2]

Sono lunghi l'una dall'altra duecento leghe. Non trovavamo fondo appresso de loro, se non vedevamo molti *tiburono*.[3]

Eric de Bisschop, che ha rivissuto personalmente l'avventura di

[1] *Relazione del primo viaggio intorno al mondo*, Alpes, Milano 1929.
[2] Forse atolli delle Tuamotu.
[3] Squali! Questo confermerebbe trattarsi, appunto, dei sopraddetti atolli.

viaggiare a vela nel Pacifico, ha notato, in una sua breve sintesi delle esplorazioni del grande oceano che per molti decenni le navi europee attraversarono il Pacifico senza toccar mai un'isola polinesiana:

Magellano [egli scrive in *Vers Nousantara*] giunse in Micronesia e dopo aver attraversato tutto il «triangolo polinesiano» senza vederlo; e come a lui accadde lo stesso con altri navigatori: a Saavedra, nel 1527, salpato con tre navi; a Grijalva, dieci anni più tardi, che doveva finire assassinato dal suo equipaggio; ad Alvaredo che scopre qualche atollo disabitato appartenente probabilmente al gruppo delle Gilbert. Nel 1543 ha inizio dal Perù il viaggio di Villalobos, che dopo trenta giorni di mare, scopre un gruppo di atolli «popolato da povera gente nuda», che egli battezza «de los Reyes». Terre probabilmente a est della Caroline, non certo isole polinesiane, che tanto meno vengono scoperte da Miguel Lopez de Legazpi fondatore, nel 1565, della colonia delle Filippine.

Nnel 1559 Filippo di Spagna ordinò che fossero imbarcati preti su tutte le navi del Pacifico, «per scacciare il diavolo delle isole più lontane, e di toglierle a lui, dopo lungo tempo che usurpava, a suo profitto, l'adorazione di questi popoli». Purtroppo per la Spagna, mentre Filippo si occupava di questi problemi inutili, non era più la sola a muover navi nel Pacifico: erano entrati in scena gli inglesi, con Drake.

Drake, «prototipo degli sfruttatori delle altrui conquiste», come fu chiamato, segue pressoché la scia magellanica, sinché questa non si distacca dall'America, puntando poi verso ponente; uscito nel Pacifico nel settembre del 1578, lo abbandona nel novembre dell'anno successivo, dopo aver saccheggiato centri costieri e galeoni spagnoli, nella sua scorribanda verso il Nord; tra un assedio e un genocidio scoprendo la California; una terra che sarà parte di quanto riporta alla sua regina come bottino piratesco: sette milioni di dollari, al valore di oggi. Prosegue de Bisschop:

Altri filibustieri (Cavendish, nel 1581, e Richard Hawkins, nel 1593) penetrano nel Pacifico e gettano la confusione nelle linee spagnole di navigazione. [...] Nemmeno a loro va la gloria di aver scoperto qualcosa della Polinesia. Sarà solo nel 1595 che la prima terra polinesiana verrà toccata da un navigatore europeo: Alvaro de Mendaña, salpato da Callao in Perù il 9 aprile e giunto il 28 luglio di fronte a un'isola alta stagliata all'orizzonte.

Quel giorno era la festa di Santa Maddalena (l'isola venne infatti battezzata Magdalena) e quel giorno veniva sollevato un lembo del velo che aveva nascosto la Polinesia. L'Occidente aveva un'altra grande scoperta di cui vantarsi.

Settanta piroghe con bilanciere vennero incontro agli spagnoli. Portavano noci di cocco, *poipoi*, banane, acqua contenuta nei bambù.

Uno degli indigeni viene issato a bordo; gli si dà una camicia e un cappello. Una quarantina fra i suoi amici salgono allora sulla *Capitana*, cantando, ballando, con scoppi di risa come i bambini, ma non certo bambini timidi.

Fanno tanto baccano che Mendaña, trovandoli molesti, ha l'assurda idea di far partire a salve un colpo di colubrina. I visitatori, spaventati, si gettano in acqua; tuttavia, uno di loro ritorna, aggrappato a una manovra; allora un soldato spagnolo gli fa lasciare la presa con un selvaggio colpo di spada. Incomincia un massacro.

La civiltà europea aveva avuto il suo primo contatto con la Polinesia; e quel contatto era stato una strage. Ma ci voleva ben altro per un discendente dei *conquistadores*; Mendaña ne conosce «lo stile» e vuole imitarlo: in onore del viceré del Perù, «battezza» con il nome di Las Marquisas de Mendoza il gruppo delle quattro isole della strage.

Gloria e sangue: com'era, appunto, nella tradizione.

Il 5 agosto la flotta leva l'àncora non prima di aver piantato qualche croce e aver lasciato sulle spiagge dell'isola un totale di due o trecento cadaveri; fu l'ufficiale pilota della spedizione, il famoso Quiros, che narrò questi avvenimenti e a lui dobbiamo le prime osservazioni in certo senso «etnografiche» sulla razza polinesiana.

Egli scrisse, a proposito di quei massacri, e sulla condotta del suo capo in quelle circostanze che:

Simili brutalità non sono, né da farsi, né da lodarsi, né da essere autorizzate, né da rifarsi, né tantomeno rifiutarsi di punirle se l'occasione si presenta.

Dieci anni più tardi il viaggio alle isole Marchesi, nel 1605, egli prese il mare, a sua volta deciso a trovare la terra misteriosa del Sud. Non la trova, ma trova molte isole polinesiane. Le sue relazioni di viaggio non lasciano dubbi in proposito: egli è passato per Marutea, Taharunga, Vahanga, Tenararo. Il luogo ove approda il 12 febbraio 1606 non può essere che il grande atollo di Hao.

Nel 1595, alle isole Marchesi, Quiros aveva scritto:

Gli abitanti di queste isole sono di pelle quasi bianca, hanno lunghi capelli che alcuni lasciano sciolti, altri riuniscono in crocchia sulla testa. Molti di questi indigeni hanno i capelli rossi. Hanno una bella statura e sono di forme così perfette che, fisicamente, sono molto superiori ai nostri spagnoli.

Era un primo riconoscimento delle «qualità polinesiane», cui se ne aggiunsero altre; e non solo fisiche. Da Quiros in poi si dovette infatti ammettere, poco per volta, che queste genti delle isole del Sud erano gli eredi di una grande cultura materiale e spirituale. Quale? È un interrogativo che le tappe successive della scoperta della Polinesia avrebbero non risolto ma reso ancor più misterioso, almeno sino ai viaggi di James Cook che seguono quelli degli olandesi Schouten e Le Maire (navigano nel Pacifico meridionale nel 1615); di Tasman che scopre nel 1615 la Nuova Zelanda e le Tonga; di Roggeveen che visita per primo la misteriosa Isola di Pasqua, e scrive stupito, anche lui, dell'incontro con indigeni, «la cui pelle bianca non è in nessun modo differente da quella degli europei».

Ma nessuno affronta il problema scientificamente, pone domande, trova risposte. Il primo a farlo è appunto James Cook, che nelle sue rotte attraverso il Pacifico ebbe sempre vicini gli scienziati che egli aveva voluto come compagni nell'esplorazione dell'oceano compreso tra le due opposte regioni polari; esplorazioni che si conclusero con la scoperta delle Hawaii *e la certezza che il Continente Australe era stato soltanto un sogno.* Quelle sue rotte hanno quasi cancellato quelle dei suoi immediati predecessori: Tasman, Boungainville e Wallis, quest'ultimo scopritore dell'«isola felice» per antonomasia: Tahiti, e dell'arcipelago poi detto da Cook «della Società».

Nelle pagine d'antologia che seguono, ho raccolto alcuni echi delle impressioni provate da quegli scopritori di cui ho appena evocato le vicende, nel mettere piede su terre mai prima calpestate da altri «uomini bianchi». Espressioni spesso entusiaste, anche se le loro conoscenze dei luoghi e delle popolazioni furono talvolta superficiali e affrettate. Su tutte queste manifestazioni, per quanto di nuovo si va scoprendo, eccelle – in molte pagine di molti autori – la descrizione di Tahiti.

Dal momento della sua scoperta a oggi, sono due secoli che si continua a scrivere su Tahiti (fino a oggi si contano oltre tremiladuecento pubblicazioni). Persino Cook, sempre misurato, alieno da entusiasmi, arrivò a scrivere: «Tahiti, una delle contrade più beate della terra».

Il comandante Samuel Wallis, con il suo *Dauphin* e il comandante Filippo Carteret, con la *Swallow*, salparono nel 1766 da Plymouth, inviati insieme, ostinatamente!, a cercare nel Pacifico l'allora introvabile *Terra Australis Incognita*.

Quando sbucarono nel Pacifico, le tempeste separarono le due navi per sempre. Wallis, invece di staccarsi dall'America all'altezza dell'isola Juan Fernandez, a 400 miglia dal Cile (l'isola del vero Robinson Crusoe, tappa obbligata per i velieri che uscivano dallo Stretto di Magellano) risalì fino al 20° parallelo sud, e quindi piegò diritto a ponente. Fu così che alla fine s'imbatté nell'arcipelago delle Isole Basse, le Tuamotu. Aveva a bordo molti malati di scorbuto gravi, e aveva bisogno di prender ristoro. Cercava perciò qualche baia riparata, in qualche isola non cinta dall'invalicabile barriera corallina, e proseguendo finì nell'arcipelago poi detto «della Società» ove avvistò un'isola non bassa come le altre: Tahiti. Appena a ridosso si vide circondato da centinaia di canoe, con un migliaio di uomini che portavano doni di frutta e di animali.

Il clima sembra ottimo [scrive Wallis nel suo diario[1]] e l'isola è uno dei paesi più sani e gradevoli della terra: noi non vi abbiamo veduto alcuna malattia. Le montagne sono coperte di boschi, le vallate di verdura, e l'aria in generale vi è sì pura che, malgrado il caldo che fa, la carne ci si conserva sana due giorni, e un giorno il pesce. Non vi osservammo né rane, né rospi, né scorpioni, né millepiedi, né serpenti, e pochissime sono le formiche le quali pure sono l'unico insetto incomodo che ivi si trovi. Il soggiorno che noi facemmo in Tahiti giovò eccellentemente alla salute di tutta la nostra gente, e quando salpammo non avevamo più verun ammalato.

---

[1] Ne citiamo qui una traduzione edita da Sonzogno nel 1816. È tratta dall'edizione francese del 1774, pubblicata a Parigi «*chez Saillant et Nyou*». Il titolo dell'opera nell'edizione originale, era: *Voyages* (1770).

Gli abitanti di quest'isola sono grandi, ben fatti, agili, e di gradevole figura. La taglia degli uomini in generale è di cinque piedi e sette fino a dieci pollici: ve n'ha tra essi pochissimi che siano o meno o più alti. La taglia delle donne è all'incirca di cinque piedi e sei pollici. Bruno è il colore degli uomini, e più carico quello di essi che vivono costantemente a terra. [...] Tutte le donne sono graziose d'aspetto, e alcune sommamente belle. Non pare che riguardino la continenza come virtù. [...]

Tutti i naviganti ricevettero doni nelle isole dove approdarono, quando non furono ricevuti ostilmente; ma essi avevano anche bisogno di provviste, e queste le pagavano. I chiodi erano la «moneta» preferita dalle popolazioni oceaniane che, pur ignare del ferro, avevano capito quanto quegli oggetti durissimi potevano servire come ami da pesca. E così i chiodi furono sempre oggetto di baratto in tutti gli arcipelaghi. Ma molto spesso i nativi li rubavano, persino schiodando qualche parte della carena (per aver ferro, fu rubato anche un fucile a Cook, e persino un'àncora, nelle isole Tonga; e anche i campanacci del bestiame sbarcato perché pascolasse). Si dovette ricorrere alle frustate, per punizione, e infine alla rasatura del capo dei colpevoli, condanna severissima per loro. Col tempo il valore dei chiodi ribassò, specialmente per l'introduzione, sullo scorcio del secolo XVIII, delle armi da fuoco, le quali, a cominciare dalle Hawaii contribuirono, con l'alcool e le malattie, anch'esse introdotte dagli europei, a decimare i nativi.

Ma nei primi tempi il valore dei chiodi era stato inestimabile, tanto che con essi si poteva avere in cambio di tutto: porci, galline, cocchi, igname, e altri generi commestibili, nonché farne dono alle donne.

E comunque il prezzo fosse modico [prosegue il Wallis] era non ostante tale che i nostri non erano sempre in istato di pagarlo. Perciò furono nella tentazione di rubare quanti chiodi e quanto ferro potessero distaccare dal vascello. S'incominciò dunque a portar via tutti i chiodi, che qua e là servivano per attaccarvi qualunque cosa: donde nacquero tosto due inconvenienti gravissimi, uno de' quali fu che il prezzo delle cose portate al mercato s'alzò notabilmente; mentre non più erano contenti, come in principio, per esempio di un piccolo chiodo per un maiale, ma ne volevano de' grandi. Accadde pure, che alcuni marinai non potevano aver chiodi veri, rubarono del piombo, e con esso fecero de' chiodi, che ben presto furono dagl'isolani conosciuti per falsa moneta; e vennero reclamando contro tale frode. Oltre ciò la licenza crebbe ne' marinai pel commercio delle donne; e molta insubordinazione nacque, che mi obbligò a prendere risoluzioni severe. [...]

Chi celebrò da un altro punto di vista le bellezze di Tahiti e la generosità dei suoi abitanti fu il francese Louis-Antoine de Bougainville (1729-1811) che l'anno dopo Wallis «riscoprì» Tahiti nel suo viaggio intorno al mondo, che egli ribattezzò, con immagine tolta dai classici, «Nuova Citera». Si narra che gli inglesi, ricevendo i doni tradizionali a bordo, donne e maiali, avessero trattenuto soltanto i suini. Bougainville invece non fu insensibile, con il suo equipaggio, alla bellezza delle tahitiane, non mercenarie né sentimentali, ma libere di sceglersi la compagnia al pari degli uomini. Dal suo viaggio non riportò in Europa solo una pianta rampicante di fiori rossi, battezzata poi col nome di *buganvillea* in suo onore, ma un pregevole saggio; infatti, oltre a esser brillante ufficiale, era anche uomo di salda dottrina, imbevuto delle idee degli Enciclopedisti. Della sua opera[1] cito qui un brano tra i più significativi:

Al due aprile del 1768 noi vedemmo verso la tramontana un'alta e scoscesa montagna. [...]
L'aspetto della costa, che formava una specie di anfiteatro, ci presentava uno spettacolo bellissimo. Le montagne vi sono altissime, e dappertutto coperte di boschi. Fra gli altri vi si vede un picco carico d'alberi fino alla sua cima isolata, la quale si alzava a livello delle montagne. Pareva che quel picco non avesse che trenta tese di diametro, e aveva sembianza di una piramide ornata di ghirlande fatte di frondi. Le terre poi meno elevate sono interrotte da praterie e da boschetti e una striscia di terra bassa e piana coperta di piantamenti seguiva lungo il mare. Ivi in mezzo agli alberi pieni di frutta le case di quegli isolani. [...]
Tutti ci gridavano *tavo, tavo*, che in loro lingua vuol dire *amico*: tutti ci domandavano de' chiodi e de' pendenti da orecchie. Le piroghe erano piene di donne, le quali per la beltà del corpo potrebbero contrastare con tutte le europee: per la maggior parte erano nude affatto; imperciocché era stato loro tolto d'attorno il pannó, di cui si avviluppano. Ci fecero esse molte smorfie, nelle quali malgrado l'aria di assai naturale ingenuità appariva dell'imbarazzo; gli uomini o più semplici di esse, o più liberi ci pressavano a prendere una donna, e ad andare con essa in terra. Una di loro restò fra noi, e trascinò a sé tutti i marinai. Il mio cuoco scappò dal vascello, scendendo a

[1] *Voyage autour du monde en 1766 jusqu'au 1769*, Parigi 1772.

terra con una bella che si era scelta; e dacché fu colà, si vide circondato, svestito e spogliato in mezzo a un profluvio di acclamazioni a modo.

Egualmente festoso, nel marzo del 1769, fu il saluto amichevole dei tahitiani a Cook. Questi veniva a Tahiti con un gruppo di scienziati che desiderava osservare un'eclisse di Venere sul Sole, con l'aiuto di un osservatorio. Doveva quindi mantenere i migliori rapporti con la popolazione, evitando ogni motivo di sospetto o di risentimento, ignorandosi usi e lingua dei nativi, per cui ogni cautela era indispensabile. Cook nel suo primo viaggio era accompagnato dallo scienziato Sir Joseph Banks e dai famosi Forster: il padre intento a raccogliere testimonianze sulle genti delle isole e le loro usanze, il figlio diciottenne incaricato di curare le raccolte naturalistiche.

Al 12 marzo 1769 [scriveva il navigatore più famoso del Pacifico[1]] molte piroghe partirono da Tahiti, all'incontro. Queste si accostarono a noi; ma gl'isolani che ne erano portati non vollero nel momento venire a bordo. Essi ci presentarono prima de' giovani platani, e de' rami d'un albero da loro chiamato *e-midho* pegno di pace e di amicizia che ne arrecavano. Ci fecero altri segnali che nell'istante non furono compresi: ma credemmo ch'essi esprimessero il desiderio che i suddetti rami fossero da noi posti in vista sul vascello; di fatto vennero infissi fra i nostri attrezzi, e dal contento che essi dimostrarono vedemmo che non ci eravamo ingannati. Furono da noi comprate le loro frutte, e navigando a basse vele venne a gettar l'àncora nella baia di Porto Reale, ch'essi chiamano *Matavai*.

Gli approdi furono considerati da Cook momenti indispensabili dei suoi viaggi per fornirsi di acqua, di legna e, potendo, di viveri freschi per combattere lo scorbuto (una precauzione, questa, che Cook non trascurò mai, tanto che in vari anni di lunghe navigazioni non ebbe un sol morto per questa causa, mentre sulle altre navi le perdite si aggiravano tra il quindici e il trenta per cento dell'equipaggio).

Ma non tutti questi sbarchi a terra (di James Cook come di altri esploratori dell'Oceania) furono pacifici e amichevoli. Ve ne furono nati tra la diffidenza, altri addirittura accolti con ostilità che cagionarono vittime e non soltanto fra i nativi. I maori, polinesia-

---

Le opere di Cook furono pubblicate tra il 1770 e il 1784; la traduzione qui riportata è tratta dall'edizione italiana del 1816, edita da Sonzogno.

ni della Nuova Zelanda, furono sempre difficili da avvicinare: violenti e sospettosi. I papua furono anche peggio: da loro, il francese La Pérouse venne massacrato con il suo equipaggio alle Nuove Ebridi. Nemmeno gli hawaiani furono spontanei e amici come i tahitiani e il loro tumultuoso rapporto con Cook si concluse infatti con l'uccisione del comandante inglese. Viceversa, aperti e generosi furono tongani e samoani (Polinesia occidentale) accoglienti e di buona indole come i tahitiani.

Sempre bellicosi e pronti a difendere le proprie isole i papua della Melanesia.

Le apparizioni di navi e di uomini così diversi dal normale suscitarono nei papua paure irrazionali, talvolta apocalittiche, quando, al contrario, i nuovi arrivati non vennero salutati come dèi reincarnati.

Nell'isola di Tanna, Cook s'imbatté nell'ostilità dei nativi:

Feci segno ai locali di deporre le armi, al che mi fecero intendere, ch'io prima ne dessi loro l'esempio; né per vero dire condanno io queste genti se trovavano assurdo ed ingiusto che un pugno d'europei venisse a dar leggi nelle case loro, e pretendesse di disarmare più di novecento uomini. Le due divisioni d'indigeni ricusarono del pari di tirarsi addietro, e lasciarci uno spazio maggiore pel nostro sbarco; né alcune scariche di moschetteria, che si eseguirono all'aria, valsero in ultima analisi che a renderle più ardite, cosicché uno di essi ci mostrò le natiche che si percoté colle mani, segno di sfida fra tutte le nazioni del Mare del Sud. Diedi allora i convenuti segni agli artiglieri del vascello, i quali corrisposero così bene alle mie intenzioni nelle grandi scariche da essi eseguite che furono queste imponenti quanto bastò per far sentire agl'indigeni la necessità di abbandonare il terreno, senza che veruno di essi rimanesse ucciso.

Il programma di Cook, nel suo primo viaggio, non si limitò all'osservazione dell'eclisse di Venere, ma si mosse attraverso il Pacifico come da ordine segreto, alla ricerca del Continente Australe: questo sfuggente paese del quale sembrava di costeggiare di continuo qualche lembo e che poi si rivelava parte di isole, come fu per la Tasmania, la Nuova Zelanda e la Nuova Guinea.

Cook, rientrato in Europa senza aver scoperto il continente fantasma, fu presto rispedito alla sua ricerca; e nel secondo viaggio (1772-1775) ritornò a far scalo a Tahiti.

In questa rada, il nostro soggiorno fu impiegato nel calafatare i vascelli, che d'uopo grandemente ne avevano per le vie d'acqua formatesi nell'ultimo tragitto, nell'esaminare le provviste, e separarle da ciò che di esse sofferto aveva corrompimento, nel procurare acqua, e nel far pascolare a terra i nostri quadrupedi. Ozioso non fu in questo mentre il nostro commercio; in proposito di che non è da tacersi, essere a quell'epoca caduti di pregio i grani di vetro, e molte altre bagattelle europee: le sole accette mantenersi in alto prezzo; e quanto alle stoffe rosse delle Isole degli Amici, la quantità grande di esse poste in circolazione da ciascuno dell'equipaggio che delle medesime soltanto aveva formato il suo piccolo fardello, fu motivo di prezzo scemato, ma non per questo, che ne fosse meno incessante lo smercio.

Cook fu entusiasta anche delle altre isole della Società, in particolare di Bora-Bora, dove poté apprezzare la lealtà di re Opuny, col quale trattò la restituzione dietro compenso dell'àncora perduta da Bougainville.

Alla mattina del 7 dicembre facemmo vela per Bolabola, alla qual isola mi traeva soprattutto la voglia di acquistare l'àncora del sig. Bougainville.

Fu questa un'àncora che il predetto viaggiatore perduta aveva nelle acque di Tahiti, e che raccolta dagli abitanti venne spedita in dono al re di Bolabola. Il ferro pel commercio cominciava a mancarmi, tanto distribuito se n'era ne' doni e cambi cogl'indiani fino a quest'epoca visitati, e la predetta àncora poteva essermi del più rilevante compenso. Oreo, e molti principali d'Ulietea vennero a bordo del mio vascello accompagnandomi a Bolabola, e mi avrebbero seguito fino in Inghilterra, se io avessi a ciò acconsentito. [...]

Mi feci tosto a esporgli [al re Opuny] il motivo del mio sbarco, e a porgli sott'occhio gli oggetti in contraccambio dell'àncora che da me veniva richiesta. Consistevano questi in una veste da camera di tela, in alcuni fazzoletti da spalle di velo, in uno specchio, in granelli di vetro, e in sei accette, che eccitarono l'ammirazione dei circostanti. Nulla oppose quel re, che fosse contrario ai miei desiderii: e unicamente ricusò a qualsiasi patto di toccare i miei doni, finché io non avessi ricevuta l'àncora: non tardai ad accorgermi derivare da delicatezza tale sua ritrosia.

In virtù della venerazione che egli seppe suscitare, Cook fu ammesso a visitare i monumenti polinesiani, fra i quali i recinti funebri dei grandi capi, dove i cadaveri venivano lasciati a seccare sotto tettoiette sopraelevate, per poterne poi estrarre le ossa da inumare.

Vedemmo un grande *marae*. Le sue muraglie erano di corallo, alte otto piedi. L'area di circa venticinque verghe quadrate era ricoperta di picciole pietre; stavano attaccate alla parete delle tavole scolpite, e da una parte un altare, sul quale trovavasi un porco recentemente arrostito, ultimo olocausto che vi era stato collocato.

A poca distanza, molte *case di Dio* simili a quella veduta in Uaena. Il sig. Banks mise la mano entro una di esse, e gli parve di sentire qualche cosa di lungo avvolto da diverse stuoie; ma non poté continuare le sue indagini, perché si avvide di far dispiacere agli indiani. E in questo *morai*, e in diversi altri luoghi si videro delle mascelle umane attaccate, e ci fu detto essere quelle un segno della discesa fatta dai guerrieri di Bolabola.

Permettendo a un esploratore europeo la visita ai luoghi tabù i polinesiani degli arcipelaghi centrali rivelarono che nei loro riti magico-religiosi non mancavano cerimonie in cui il sacrificio umano evidenziava l'esistenza di pratiche antropofaghe. Il sacrificio umano e il cannibalismo trovano, oggi, negli studi più avanzati di antropologia e di socio-antropologia interpretazioni di varia forma e misura, visti come sono non tanto nel fenomeno in sé ma «storicizzati» nel loro ambiente e nella cultura che li ha prodotti. Ma era inevitabile che i primi viaggiatori ed esploratori fossero stati tutti «inorriditi» nel constatare che tali «costumanze» venivano praticate dalle popolazioni locali. Unico a restar perfettamente freddo e testimone senza emozione davanti alla conferma e alla prova che una gente da lui conosciuta (e tenuta nella massima considerazione) praticava cannibalismo e sacrifici umani fu James Cook; dando così ancora una volta prova dell'attendibilità delle sue osservazioni, nelle quali il giudizio moralistico, l'indignazione ipocrita non trovan mai posto. Salvo le forme del tutto umane di una sua reazione alla notizia che gli era giunta secondo la quale «sacrifici di vittime umane formavano parte delle istituzioni religiose di Tahiti», Cook non si chiude nello sdegno dell'«uomo civile» di fronte alle barbarie dei selvaggi ma accetta, per dovere di testimone, l'invito a una di quelle cerimonie. Premesso che «non potendo salvare la vittima che già era stata uccisa, non mi restò partito migliore che di pormi io pure fra gli spettatori del rito» così prosegue nella sua relazione, lasciandoci un testo d'estrema importanza sull'antica ritualità tahitiana:[1]

---

[1] Il sacrificio di cui Cook dà notizia nella cronaca del suo secondo viaggio fu atto di propiziazione in vista di una guerra tra Tahiti e la prospiciente isola di Eimeo, oggi Moorea.

Non può questo compirsi che alla presenza del re, e le cerimonie del medesimo durano due giorni. Nel primo di questi, i signori Anderson, Webber, e io ci trovammo ad Attauru nel *morai* destinato al sacrifico, ove pure recossi il re, che raccomandò a noi di tenere il cappello in mano per tutto il tempo. Era posto il *morai* sulla riva del mare, e il cadavere dell'infelice che prescelto per vittima, steso era sopra una piccola piroga ritirata sulla spiaggia, e in parte esposta all'azione de' flutti. Seduti presso il medesimo ritrovavansi i sacerdoti, e gli altri di ordine minore addetti al tempio. [...]

Le prime cerimonie eseguite dai sacerdoti si ridussero a coprire la vittima di foglie, e rami di cocco e banano, a tirarla dalla piroga, e stenderla per terra coi piedi rivolti verso il mare. Venne in seguito scoperta dalle foglie, e mentre recitavansi certe preci, un sacerdote le strappò alcuni capelli dalla testa, e le cavò l'occhio sinistro. Quest'occhio e questi capelli involti in una foglia verde presentati furono al re da un sacerdote, il quale raccomandògli di aprire la bocca, dopo di che il sacerdote medesimo tornò al primo posto con la sua offerta, e di più con un mazzo di penne, che il re vi aggiunse. La predetta parte di rito viene denominata in lingua taithiana *mangiar l'uomo*, o *dono del capo*; ed è secondo tutte le apparenze, il figurato di costumanza più antica, per cui il re cibavasi effettivamente della vittima. Poco dopo il cadavere fu portato a piccola distanza e collocato sotto di un albero, presso al quale erano tre pezzi di legno grossolanamente intagliati: deposto venne ai piedi del cadavere il mazzo di penne donato dal re, e il gran sacerdote lo prese, indi arringò il morto per ben un quarto d'ora, e lo rimproverava, e lo blandiva a vicenda, e gli fece diverse interrogazioni, tra le quali si fu la più curiosa, se veramente non si aveva avuto ragione di sacrificarlo, poi si fece a pregarlo (quasi che così purificata la vittima divenisse potente presso la divinità) affinché cadessero in potere del popolo di Tahiti Eimeo, il capo della terra, i maiali, e le donne che vi esistevano. [...]

Merita attenzione particolare un ammasso di pietre,[1] che ritrovasi in vicinanza al terreno de' sacrifizii. Stanno sopra esso esposti i crani di tutti que' che sono stati immolati alla divinità, e che a tal fine vengono dissotterrati alcuni mesi dopo seguito il sacrificio. Noi contammo fino a quarantanove crani, che parevano assai recenti, e ponno far giudicare della frequenza di queste religiose stragi.

Di grande importanza, nel campo della religiosità polinesiana così come egli la conobbe, è un brano che ci illumina su quel culto dei morti che gli studi più approfonditi ci confermano essere alla base di tutta la metafisica di questa cultura.

[1] Il *marae* o altare sacro.

In una delle mie corse a Oparro vidi il *Tuapapau* sacro di Tee, uno dei capi da me conosciuto nel precedente viaggio, e morto da quattro mesi. Sono i *Tuapapau* luoghi dove depongonsi i cadaveri di quegli individui che avendo ottenuta qualche celebrità si vuol salvare dalla putrefazione con l'imbalsamarli. Il *Tuapapau* è cinto di palizzate, oltre le quali non si può penetrare dai profani, e il cadavere imbalsamato vi sta entro avvolto di stoffe. Ebbesi per me il riguardo di svolgere delle stoffe il corpo di Tee, e di porlo sopra una bara onde meglio potessi vederlo.[1]

Le citazioni dei testi dell'esploratore inglese potrebbero continuare; note, appunti, studi, descrizioni aggiunte e documentazione geografica e grafica dei suoi tre viaggi d'esplorazione, formano una tale massa imponente di materiale di studio che solo a duecento anni dal primo viaggio di Cook se ne è potuta pubblicare *in extenso* l'opera; si tratta della monumentale edizione della Cambridge University Press del 1961.

È in questa edizione, critica e storica, che le parole di Cook giungono al lettore senza le deformazioni delle precedenti edizioni. Davanti alla semplicità e chiarezza di quelle pagine, Bengt Danielsson, direttore del Centro Polinesiano di Scienze Umane, ha scritto:

Non c'è dubbio che Cook avesse la stoffa del vero scienziato. [...] Un esempio è sufficiente a provare questa sua attitudine; quando egli si ferma al famoso *marae* del tempio di Mahaiatea, a Tahiti, nel 1769, non si mette a divagare a vuoto sul sistema religioso dei tahitiani, né li condanna con la bigotteria che i navigatori del tempo dimostravano per la loro «idolatria». Si accontenta di misurare attentamente l'altare e l'intero luogo sacro, e ne disegna una mappa. Anni dopo – al secondo e terzo viaggio –, conoscendo meglio la lingua e sentendosi in grado di porre domande e comprendere le risposte, scrive sull'argomento facendo però una netta distinzione tra le *informazioni* e le *sue interpretazioni*. È questo il metodo con il quale un etnologo moderno conduce oggi un'inchiesta sul posto scelto per una ricerca scientifica.[2]

Prima di chiudere l'antologia delle citazioni di Cook varrà forse la pena di ricordare, con sue brevi osservazioni, come la curiosità dell'esploratore inglese sulla vita dei polinesiani investisse anche

---

[1] Anche questo brano è tratto dal diario del secondo viaggio; e la versione è sempre tratta dal testo in italiano del 1816.
[2] B. Danielsson, *La découverte de la Polynésie*, Société des Amis du Musée de l'Homme, Parigi 1972.

l'area della loro vita quotidiana, sino a descriverne i giochi, i divertimenti; quasi a voler ben dire alla imparruccata scienza del tempo che conoscere un popolo vuol dire anche – e soprattutto – vivere con lui il momento d'ogni giornata.

Fu già osservato che la passione dominante degli isolani dell'arcipelago della Società è l'amore. Sono quindi prediletti loro intrattenimenti tutte le cose che contribuir ponno ad alimentarlo. Quindi amano e la musica e il canto a cui commettono i propri affanni, le storie delle loro peregrinazioni. [...]
Assistemmo in un villaggio di Tahiti a una delle cerimonie, che consisteva in due giovani di diverso sesso, i quali soddisfacevano pubblicamente alle amorose loro inclinazioni, senza che l'atto avesse per essi verun'idea d'indecenza. [...]

A metà del suo terzo viaggio,[1] al ritorno dal Mare di Bering e dalla vana ricerca di un «passaggio di nord-ovest in senso contrario», Cook decise di svernare alle Hawaii, in attesa di riprendere l'esplorazione del Nord artico. Egli e i suoi uomini, come pure le navi, avevano bisogno di ritemprarsi delle fatiche e dei rischi corsi nel Nord. Benché deluso della vana ricerca, Cook registrava di suo pugno, e furono le ultime sue note, sul giornale di bordo, due risultati confortevoli di quel terzo viaggio: la scoperta e la ricognizione appunto dell'arcipelago delle Hawaii e una definitiva *conclusione* sul problema del Continente Australe: era quella una teoria da porre per sempre nel campo delle fantasie. Alle Hawaii fu confortato da un'accoglienza che mai in nessun luogo aveva avuto, sebbene ormai abituato a onori solenni dappertutto. Oltre mille canoe gli vennero incontro, mentre egli si dirigeva a vele spiegate verso l'ancoraggio nella baia di Kealakekua, nell'isola oggi chiamata «La Grande Hawaii».

Tosto che si diede fondo, i navigli furono circondati da piroghe, riempiute d'isolani. Io non avevo veduto in tutti i miei villaggi una quantità così grande di piroghe, attruppate intorno a noi: i loro gruppi parevano un letto di grossi pesci a fior d'acqua, spettacolo per verità singolare. Ciò mi consolò in parte di non aver trovato quest'anno il passaggio nel mare del norte; altrimenti non avremmo avuto occasione di dar fondo alle Isole Sandwich

---

[1] Il terzo viaggio di Cook ebbe inizio nel 1776 quando le sue due navi, la *Revolution* e la *Discovery* lasciarono l'Inghilterra.

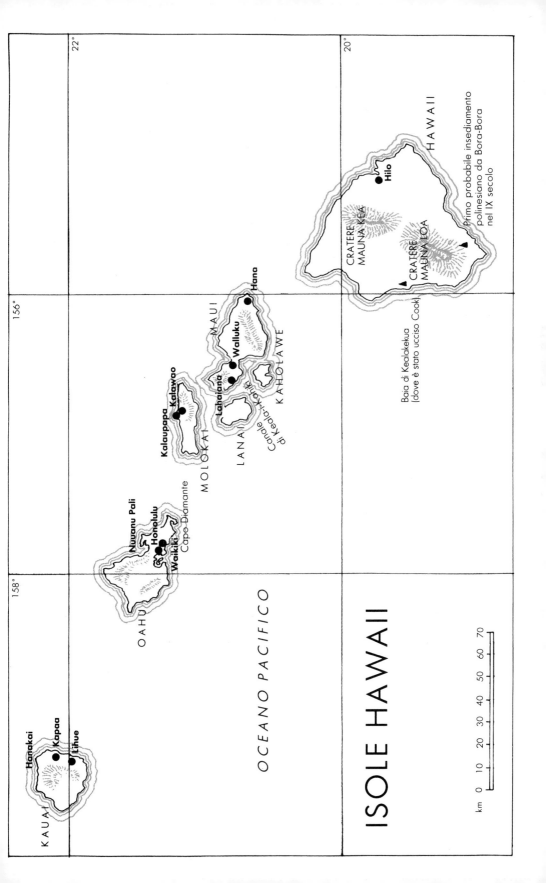

ISOLE HAWAII

KAUAI

Hanakai

Kapaa

Lihue

OCEANO PACIFICO

OAHU

Nuvanu Pali

Honolulu

Waikiki

Capo Diamante

MOLOKAI

Kalaupapa

Kalawao

MAUI

Wailuku

Lahaiana

Hana

LANAI

Canale di Kealaikahiki

KAHOLAWE

HAWAII

CRATERE MAUNA KEA

CRATERE MAUNA LOA

Hilo

Primo probabile insediamento polinesiano da Bora-Bora nel IX secolo

Baia di Kealakekua (dove è stato ucciso Cook)

km 0   10   20   30   40   50   60   70

158°   156°

22°

20°

[le Hawaii] e di arricchire il nostro viaggio di una delle scoperte più interessanti fatte finora nella immensa estensione dell'Oceano Pacifico.

Era il suo addio. In realtà quegli onori quasi divini non erano rivolti all'esploratore bianco trionfatore di tanti misteri, ma al dio Lono, o Atuna, che gli hawaiani avevano creduto di ravvisare nell'uomo venuto su una nave grande tanto quanto aveva promesso una vecchia profezia (così era capitato a Pizarro tra gli inca; l'avevano scambiato per l'atteso dio Viracocha). Cook fu venerato come una divinità familiare scesa tra gli hawaiani, venerazione che si tradusse in una continua offerta di doni: tutti frutti di quelle isole, di cui i nativi si privarono con sacrificio ogni giorno maggiore.

Quando Cook salpò, cercando un altro ancoraggio per la sosta invernale e per i lavori alle sue navi, le genti della grande baia furono al contempo addolorati – un dio se ne andava! – ma certo anche lieti: cessava finalmente per loro l'impegno di nutrire e servire gli stranieri venuti dal mare. Ma le tempeste impedirono a Cook di proseguire, soffrì di avarie, e fu costretto a rientrare a Kealakekua. Fu allora che la situazione precipitò.

Cosa sia realmente accaduto non è del tutto certo. La fine imprevista è stata ricostruita e interpretata in diverse maniere, non riuscendo lo storico a spiegare il diverso atteggiamento contro l'esploratore da parte di quei nativi che egli aveva sempre trattato con umanità, e dopo che essi lo avevano deificato. La versione ufficiale della tragedia è stata redatta dal capitano C. Clerke,[1] comandante della *Discovery*, succeduto a Cook.

Ecco il testo del suo rapporto:

Nel gennaio 1779, il re di O-why-e[2] rivestì Cook con un mantello simile a quello di cui egli ricopre di grande Ea-thu-ah-nu-eh (Auta Nui). Lo condusse al *marae* con tale vestito. Gli fu posta sul capo una ghirlanda di foglie di banano; lo si fece assidere su una specie di trono. Discorso di un prete e canti. Poi tutti gli isolani si prosternarono. Il re gli dice a gesti: questo *marae* è vostro e voi ormai sarete nostro *Ea-thu-ah-nu-eh...* I marinai dicevano del *marae*: è l'altare di Cook.

Poi in febbraio furto di canotto. Cook esige il re come ostaggio. È nell'an-

---

[1] Il rapporto è contenuto nella cronaca del terzo viaggio di Cook, apparsa a Londra nel 1871.

[2] Nell'isola Hawaii, presso la baia di Kealakekua.

dare a cercare questi e nel condurlo a bordo che egli viene ucciso (14 febbraio) con un colpo di clava e di pugnale inglese. Ne portarono via il corpo. La notte, un indigeno venne a portare il resto di una delle cosce di Mr. Cook che egli aveva visto tranciare; dice che i guerrieri avevan mangiato il Comandante. [...] Il 21, tregua. Si ottenne dal capo A-nu-a che radunasse le ossa di Tutee [così Cook era chiamato dai polinesiani. *N.d.A.*]. Il giorno seguente, egli reca tutte le ossa, salvo la spina dorsale e i piedi. La testa non era più riconoscibile. La mano era stata tranciata e salata. Dice A-nu-a che il resto non era stato mangiato. Infine il 23 il corpo fu completo.

Più di vent'anni dopo il tragico scontro, un missionario protestante, W. Ellis (che ci ha lasciato una notevole relazione sui sui viaggi in Oceania[1]), raccoglieva sul suo diario queste scarne notizie sulla fine Cook:

Morte di Cook: 14 febbraio 1779, baia di Kealakekua sulla costa occidentale dell'isola di Hawaii. In realtà, il suo corpo non fu divorato, ma bruciato con un grande rispetto. Noi tutti – dicono i polinesiani – abbiamo pianto la sua morte; abbiamo separato le sue ossa, distaccato e bruciato la carne, come usiamo fare per i nostri capi quando muoiono. Lo consideriamo come nostro dio Rono, lo adoriamo come tale, e dopo la sua morte abbiamo venerato le sue ossa.

Un altro viaggiatore, il francese Vedel[2], ci fornisce un'altra versione, a suo dire raccolta dalla viva voce degli ultimi testimoni dei fatti di Kealakekua, ancora viventi quarantatré anni dopo il loro accadere:

Cook arrivò di notte e noi all'alba ci stupimmo della sua nave. Cos'era quel grande tronco con tutti quei rami? «È una foresta che galleggia sul mare» disse qualcuno. Nella nave vediamo del ferro. Qualcuno di noi vuole prenderne. Viene ucciso: era un capo.
La notte seguente Cook spara colpi di cannone, gli indigeni lo riconoscono per il dio Atuna del quale si compie la predizione del ritorno dal mare. Gli vengono offerti cibi e donne. Quando ritorna l'anno successivo, lo si conduce al *marae*, lo si issa sull'altare e lo si veste con la stoffa degli dèi.
Il fratello del capo ucciso l'anno precedente gli domanda vendetta. Cook non risponde.
Un sacerdote lancia una pietra che lo colpisce alla testa; Cook ha un grido di dolore, il sacerdote esclama: «Egli ha sentito dolore, allora non è il dio Atuna! Gli dèi non sentono dolore».

---

[1] *Relazione sui viaggi di W. Ellis*, 1803.
[2] Nel suo volume *Lumières d'Orient*, edito nel 1822 a Parigi.

Allora gli uomini uccidono subito Cook, poi lo fanno a pezzi, bruciano la sua carne e conservano le sue ossa per farne degli ami da pesca.

Così morì un capo straniero che noi amavamo molto.

È molto difficile, anzi è letteralmente impossibile, decifrare la verità da tante e diverse versioni. Quel che è certo è l'improvviso cambiamento di stato d'animo dei locali verso Cook; e questo lo si può spiegare facilmente pensando alla gelosia che la sua ritenuta personalità divina suscitò certo nella classe sacerdotale dell'isola. È quindi molto probabile che da quella parte sia stato alimentato un fermento contro il capitano inglese. Comunque, a gettare una luce particolare sull'episodio, resta il fatto che sia accaduto malgrado i polinesiani abbiano sempre e in ogni isola riaffermato la loro ammirazione, il loro amore per l'uomo di cui non sapevano pronunciare esattamente il nome e che avevano battezzato Tutee.

A parte il dichiarato dolore per la sua morte espresso dal gruppo stesso che aveva partecipato all'uccisione, la notizia della sua fine fu motivo di lutto in isole e arcipelaghi di tutto il Pacifico meridionale, a mano a mano che vi giungeva portata dalle navi che s'avventuravano attraverso l'oceano.

Interessante testimonianza di questo dolore è la cronaca della cerimonia in memoria di Cook nell'isola di Tahiti, narrata[1] da un marinaio di una nave destinata a restare famosa: il *Bounty*.

Il primo febbraio [1790] venimmo distratti dal nostro lavoro da una *heiva* che secondo l'uso veniva eseguita davanti al capo del distretto vicino a noi; tutti gli abitanti del distretto si erano riuniti per assistervi.

Quando fu tutto pronto, venne portato il ritratto del Capitano Cook da un vecchio che lo aveva in custodia e che lo depose davanti a tutti, togliendo la stoffa che lo ricopriva; a questo punto tutti i presenti gli resero omaggio, togliendosi i vestiti, gli uomini mettendosi nudi fino alla cintola e le donne scoprendosi le spalle.

Il direttore della cerimonia presentò, quindi, un *utu* [offerta abituale], indirizzando un lungo discorso al ritratto, riconoscendo il Capitano Cook come capo di Matavai e mettendo davanti al ritratto un maialetto attaccato ad un giovane banano.

Il discorso era press'a poco questo:

«Salute! Salute da parte di tutti a Cook, capo dell'Aria, della Terra e

---

[1] Il brano è tratto dal volume *Le Journal de James Morrison* scritto nel 1796 ed edito in veste critica nel 1966 della Société des études océaniennes.

dell'Acqua, noi ti riconosciamo capo, dalla spiaggia fino alla montagna, capo degli uomini, degli alberi, del bestiame, degli uccelli nell'aria e dei pesci nel mare [...].»

Venne poi eseguita una danza da due giovani donne elegantemente vestite con belle stoffe, e da due uomini, il tutto eseguito con molta regolarità e ritmo al suono dei tamburi e dei flauti per circa quattro ore.

A un segnale, le donne si tolsero i vestiti e si ritirarono, e tutte le stoffe e le stuoie sulle quali si era danzato vennero arrotolate e posate vicino al ritratto; il vecchio guardiano ne prese possesso in nome del Capitano Cook.

Lo stesso Morrison ci ha tramandato la cronaca dell'ammutinamento del *Bounty*, così ampiamente rievocata nella letteratura e nel cinema.

Nel 1831 sir John Barrow ne ha pubblicato la versione più conosciuta e tradotta con il titolo *L'ammutinamento e la cattura piratesca della nave di Sua Maestà Bounty*. Com'è arcinoto, la nave aveva lasciato Tahiti, con un carico di frutti dell'albero del pane, ed era diretta all'Oceano Indiano, attraverso l'Indonesia, per proseguire alla volta del Mare delle Antille, dove gli inglesi volevano acclimatare quella pianta così utile. Ma il capitano Bligh (uno psicopatico, un sadico) odiava e martirizzava i suoi uomini; i quali d'altronde non riuscivano a cancellare dalla mente le delizie godute a Tahiti. All'altezza dell'arcipelago degli Amici, gli ufficiali Fletcher Christian e Alexander Smith (che poi mutò il nome in John Adams, e divenne patriarca della colonia meticcia di Pitcairn) s'impossessarono della nave, e abbandonarono il comandante e parte dell'equipaggio su una barca (Bligh narrò poi le sue disperate avventure per salvare i suoi fedeli). James Morrison era uno dei marinai ribelli. Dell'avventura tenne un diario in cui l'incontro con gli indigeni è così descritto:

Trovammo nell'isola di Tubuai[1] indigeni molto amichevoli e che sembravano essere un popolo diverso dagli altri; vennero a bordo pacificamente, senza armi e senza conchiglie, senza la minima traccia di ostilità, ciò che convinse Mr. Christian a far sbarcare la vacca e duecento maiali nell'isola (questo impaurì gli indigeni molto più che non le armi).

---

[1] Tubuai, fra le isole Australi, giace sul tropico del Capricorno, sul 149° meridiano Est; è lunga sei miglia da est a ovest e misura circa 22 miglia di perimetro.

Il resto del bestiame fu sbarcato sugli isolotti dove sarebbe stato più facile sorvegliarli, essendo stati gli altri lasciati allo stato brado nell'isola.

Fletcher Christian non tarda a capire – testimonia Morrison – che gli indigeni non li volevano tra loro. Nell'isola scelta come rifugio la situazione diviene, conseguentemente, molto pesante. Agli ammutinati, e ai loro compagni e compagne tahitiani, non rimaneva che reimbarcarsi con scorte e animali e proseguire verso est; sapevano della scoperta fatta nel 1767 dal Carteret, di un'isola che questo aveva battezzato col nome del figlio dell'ufficiale che l'aveva avvistata per primo, Pitcairn, e la raggiunsero. Era disabitata, ma si vedeva che non lo era da sempre, poiché c'erano statue e alberi del pane. «Fu allora» prosegue Morrison «che Mr. Christian cominciò a parlare di asportare gli alberi della nave e di disarmare quest'ultima, con l'intenzione di costruire delle case e di vivere a terra.» Ma la vita sull'isola fu un inferno, perché tra gli ammutinati nacque in breve un sordo odio, e finirono tutti con l'uccidersi a vicenda, meno Alexander Smith (detto Adam) capostipite dell'attuale comunità anglo-polinesiana di Pitcairn.

Sorte egualmente drammatica perseguitò un altro gruppo di ammutinati, quelli che avevano scelto di rimanere a Tahiti: furono catturati dalla nave *Pandora* inviata apposta per ritrovare il *Bounty* e quasi tutti impiccati.

Peraltro, tutte le relazioni lasciateci dai navigatori e dagli esploratori dell'Oceania non potevano non creare e alimentare quel mito del mare che essi avevano scoperto. Esso non fu, fortunatamente, terreno fertile solo per le opere degli «scrittori d'avventure» che per un secolo hanno immaginato o anche hanno visitato quei luoghi o sono vissuti laggiù e ne hanno tratto opere tanto popolari al momento quanto ignote oggi; ma lo fu anche e soprattutto per personaggi di grande statura letteraria, a cominciare da Melville, Stevenson, Conrad.

Questo Oceano, sereno e forte, è il mondo adottivo di ogni uomo di mare. Con le sue tempeste e bonacce amalgama le acque miste del mondo. Le stesse onde lavano America e Asia, mentre tra tutto galleggiano i profili di isole corallifere e le onde lambiscono le alte scogliere di arcipelaghi sconosciuti. Così questo misterioso, divino Pacifico, è una parte del mondo e fa, di tutte le coste, una baia: su ogni isola il fruscio della marea è il respiro stesso della nostra terra.[1]

Dalla sommità dei grandi scogli ricoperti di verde limo, sparsi qua e là nella corrente, i locali si lasciano andare nell'acqua, a testa in giù e le ragazze nuotano mettendo in mostra i loro corpi nudi fino alla cintola, con le lunghe chiome ondeggianti nell'acqua gli occhi brillano nel sole come gocce di rugiada, tra un continuo echeggiare di risa. [...]

La bellissima Faiauhei, la mia prediletta, era la perfezione, la grazia, la bellezza femminile fatta carne; la carnagione era di un colore oliva caldo e delicato e, quando ne ammiravo le morbide guance, avrei giurato che la pelle trasparente fosse soffusa di un lievissimo color di rosa; il volto era di un ovale quasi perfetto, i lineamenti di una purezza tale, che cuore o mente d'uomo non avrebbe potuto desiderare maggiore, le labbra carnose, quando si schiudevano in un sorriso, mettevano in mostra denti di un candore abbagliante, i quali se la sua bocca rosea si apriva in un trillo di gioia, parevano proprio i semi di un bianco latteo dell'*arta*, un frutto della valle che, spaccato a metà, li mostra perfettamente allineati su ambo i lati della ricca polpa zuccherina; i capelli di un bruno scurissimo, spartiti in due bande irregolari, le scendevano sulle spalle in morbide onde naturali, e quando Faiauhei si chinava, piovevano in avanti, celando alla vista il suo delicato seno. [...]

Erano grazie che non conoscevano l'artificio, quelle di questa figlia della natura, nata e cresciuta in una perenne estate.[2]

Il fatto di essere bruni è per un uomo [di queste isole] segno di forza fisica e morale.

Dice infatti un detto locale:

> *Se bruna è la guancia della mamma*
> *il figlio suonerà la conchiglia di guerra;*
> *se essa invece è chiara, egli detterà leggi.*

Con questa concezione che i tahitiani hanno della virilità non meraviglia poi che essi considerino gli europei pallidi e molli alla stregua di gente debole ed effeminata; mentre un marinaio con le guance brune come il petto d'un tacchino arrosto e i bicipiti di acciaio è tenuto nella massima considerazione e viene chiamato «taata tona», cioè «torre di ossa».[2]

Melville non ci lascia solo testimonianze delle «meraviglie» sparse a piene mani nei Mari del Sud, ma narra con sgomento e

[1] H. Melville, *Moby Dick*, 1851.
[2] H. Melville, *Taipi*, 1846.

vergogna di come questo «paradiso» fosse stato dissacrato, ferito, contagiato già pochi anni dopo la sua scoperta.

Intorno all'anno 1777, secondo calcoli fatti dal Capitano Cook, la popolazione di Tahiti ammontava a circa 200.000 persone, mentre, secondo un censimento regolare fatto quattro o cinque anni fa, si sarebbe ridotta a sole 9.000. Questa spaventosa diminuzione della popolazione è dovuta principalmente a influenze esterne. Per tacere degli effetti della ubriachezza e delle stragi fatte dal vaiolo, basterà alludere a un morbo virulento che ora ha infettato il sangue di almeno due terzi della popolazione dell'isola e che, in una forma o nell'altra, si trasmette ereditariamente di padre in figlio.

L'orrore e la costernazione che gli indigeni provano al primo manifestarsi del male è quanto di più pietoso vi possa essere. Oppressi dalle atroci sofferenze, i familiari ancora sani, conducono i loro ammalati dai missionari, poi mentre sembrano assorti nella preghiera, a un certo punto si mettono a gridare: «Ci parlate di salvezza e invece moriamo; nessun'altra salvezza desideriamo, se non di vivere in questo mondo. Dove sono quelli che avete salvato con le vostre parole? Pomaree è morta; e noi stiamo tutti morendo delle vostre maledette malattie. Quando la finirete di dire menzogne?». [...]

Interessante può essere la predizione fatta da Tearmoar, la più alta autorità religiosa di Paree, vissuto oltre cento anni fa. L'ho sentita spesso cantare a bassa voce, tristemente, dai più vecchi tahitiani:

La palma crescerà
Il corallo fiorirà
Ma l'uomo morrà.[1]

Stevenson fu chiamato dai polinesiani Tusitala «il narratore» prima che, quarantaquattrenne appena, la morte lo cogliesse all'improvviso. Il suo *Nei Mari del Sud*, postumo, offre un senso umanissimo del mondo che egli raffigurò, invece, nei suoi racconti, così misterioso e magico (come nell'*Isola delle voci*):

Le acque cupe che ci portavano verso l'isola si trasformarono d'un colpo in masse di colori, viola, grigi, gialli; sorprendenti. Attraverso quella trasparenza si vedeva il corallo aprirsi nei suoi rami fioriti, mentre i pesci della laguna, un vero mare interno, vengono ben visibili sotto di noi. [...]
Soprattutto a bordo, all'ore morte, quando avrei fatto meglio a dormire, l'incanto di Fakarava mi ripigliava e teneva. La luna era tramontata. La lanterna del porto e due de' maggiori pianeti segnavano la laguna di riflessi

[1] H. Melville, *Omoo*, 1847.

multicolori. Dalla riva, la sveglia gioconda dei galli squillava a intervalli sulla nota dell'organo della risacca. E quella capitale spopolata, nell'isola come un sottile giro d'anello con il suo pettine di «dattolieri» e la frangia di scogli, e quel mare sereno che sconfinava fino alle stelle, mi occupavano il pensiero deliziosamente, lunghe ore. [...]

In cima ai palmizi [...] il vento fa gaudioso tumulto; e guardate dove vi pare, in alto o in basso, non c'è anima viva. Ma proprio sul vostro capo il canto di un cantore invisibile rompe tra il denso fogliame; più in là una seconda cima risponde: e ancora oltre, in mezzo ai boschi, un rapsodo lontano oscilla lassù appollaiato e canta. Così per tutta l'isola: i raccoglitori di noci di cocco, sulle vette dei palmizi, cullati dal vento che va all'Equatore, guardano la gran distesa del mare, spiano l'apparizione d'una vela, e simili a uccelli enormi levano i loro canti mattutini.[1]

Keola era sposata con Lehua, figlia di Kalamake, il mago di Molokai, e abitava col padre di sua moglie. Non esisteva uomo più furbo di quel profeta. Egli sapeva leggere nelle stelle e indovinare il futuro, sia attraverso i cadaveri, sia per mezzo degli spiriti maligni; poteva recarsi, solo, nelle parti più alte della montagna, nella regione degli spiriti folletti, e disporvi trappole per farvi cadere gli spiriti degli antenati.

Per questa ragione, in tutto il reame di Hawaii non c'era uomo più consultato di lui. Le persone prudenti acquistavano, vendevano, si sposavano, arrischiavano la vita in base ai suoi consigli e il Re l'aveva fatto andare due volte a Kona per ricercare i tesori di Kamehameha. D'altra parte, non c'era uomo più temuto. Dei suoi nemici, alcuni, per virtù dei suoi sortilegi, erano stati logorati dalla malattia, altri si erano dileguati, corpo e anima, così che la gente non aveva mai potuto ritrovare nemmeno un osso dei loro corpi. Si diceva che possedesse l'arte, o, per dir meglio, le doti, degli antichi eroi. L'avevano visto, di notte, sulle montagne, passare da un picco al picco vicino: l'avevano visto camminare nella foresta e la testa e le spalle di lui ergersi al disopra degli alberi.[2]

Nato a Parigi da una nobile peruviana, educato in Francia, dove abbandonò gli studi per imbarcarsi su una nave qualsiasi, Gauguin navigò sei anni. Visse a Lima per qualche periodo, poi vagabondò sulle rotte alla ventura tra arte, miseria e rancori interminabili, finché approdò in Polinesia ove trascorse, oramai disancorato dalla famiglia, il resto dei suoi anni, a parte una breve e

---

[1] R.L. Stevenson, *Nei Mari del Sud*, 1888.
[2] R.L. Stevenson, *L'isola delle voci*.

deludente visita a Parigi. Nel 1903 morì dopo due anni di solitudine a Hivaoa nelle isole Marchesi.

Gauguin tenne un diario, *Noa-noa*, pubblicato nel 1900, che ci presenta il paese e i costumi di una Tahiti da tempo scomparsa. Tehura, la sua *vahiné* è una tredicenne tahitiana il cui ritratto è di disarmante verità nella sua idolatria infantile e profonda.

Oltre la veste, di mussola rosa troppo trasparente, si vedono spalle e braccia dalla pelle dorata. E i seni spuntano con forza. Nel suo bel viso non ritrovo il tipo, comune nell'isola, a me finora noto e anche i capelli sono assai curiosi, cresciuti a siepe e appena crespi. Al sole è tutta colore. [...]

Acceso qualche fiammifero, vedo immobile, nuda, a ventre piatto sul letto, gli occhi troppo aperti dalla paura, Tehura che mi guarda e pare non mi riconosca. È un momento di strana incertezza anche per me. Il suo terrore mi suggestiona. Una fosforescenza pare emani dallo sguardo fermo dei suoi occhi. Mai è stata tanto bella, mai soprattutto di una così eccitante bellezza. [...]

È tanto semplice: dipingere come vedo, senza calcolo tradurre sulla tela un blu, un rosso! Nei fiumi forme dorate m'incantano; esiterò ancora a cogliere tutta questa luce, questa felicità di sole?[1]

Prima di Gauguin, un altro francese aveva iscritto il suo nome nella storia del mito letterario dei Mari del Sud. Ha un suo peso che non si può ignorare: fu probabilmente proprio lui, infatti, a contribuire in maniera determinante a rendere quel mito caramelloso e falso; e non è colpa di poco. L'autore, Pierre Loti, era ufficiale di marina a Papeete.

Tuttavia, pur nei limiti romantici del suo talento, non potendosi negare la validità di alcune sue descrizioni, vorremmo ricordarlo, citando una sua immagine dell'interno di Tahiti:

Nei profondi di questi gorghi la scena era qualcosa di puramente incantevole. A Fataua, l'acqua polverizzandosi nella sua caduta viene giù come un torrente di pioggia, in basso spumeggiando fieramente nei bacini che la paziente mano degli anni ha scavato nella roccia levigata, e poi di nuovo lontano danza nella corrente facendosi strada sotto il verde.[2]

In Jack London, il mito si veste di un carattere ben diverso per

---

[1] P. Gauguin, *op. cit.*
[2] P. Loti, *Rarahu*, 1780.

la personalità dell'autore, ovviamente, e per la scelta e il carattere dei suoi personaggi. Anche lo «sfondo» delle vicende cambia: non la Polinesia, ma la difficile Melanesia abitata da papua e canachi dal capo lanoso, fra i quali London pesca tutti i suoi protagonisti, se si eccettuano quelli de *Il dissidente di MacCoy*, che si svolge fra Pasqua e Mangareva. Eroi della pazienza, i suoi; e dell'amicizia: in questo tema il «Pagano» narra di Mapuhi, il pescatore di perle e del «bianco» che egli salvò.

Lo incontrai per la prima volta durante un uragano e, benché fossimo tutti e due sulla stessa goletta, non fu che quando la goletta andò in pezzi sotto la violenza dell'uragano che la prima volta posi gli occhi su di lui. Si chiamava Otoo ed era *kanak*.

Senza dubbio lo avevo visto insieme agli altri *kanak* di ciurma a bordo, ma non mi ero particolarmente accorto della sua esistenza perché la *Petite Jeanne* era piuttosto affollata. Oltre ai suoi otto o dieci marinai *kanak*, al capitano, al secondo, al sopraccarico bianco e ai suoi passeggeri di prima classe, essa aveva levato l'ancora da Rangiroa con qualcosa come ottantacinque passeggeri delle Tuamotu e di Tahiti, uomini, donne e fanciulli, che non avevano diritto a cabine ma che dormivano in coperta, ciascuno con la sua cassetta, le sue stuoie per dormire; le coperte e i fagotti di vestiario.[1]

Nel suo racconto, London narra della tempesta e del naufragio della goletta sulla quale il suo protagonista «bianco» era imbarcato; e di come si adoperasse per aiutarlo Otoo finito sulla stessa copertura del boccaporto che funzionava da zattera e andava alla deriva sull'oceano. È Otoo a insegnare al suo compagno di sventura come non morire di sete, immergendosi continuamente nell'acqua di mare «benché quella e il sole» nota London «riducessero i corpi dei due naufraghi a qualcosa fra l'aringa affumicata e quella sotto sale».

Infine è Otoo a salvare il «bianco» che si ritrova dopo giorni di delirio su una spiaggia a sei metri dall'acqua, riparato dal sole da un paio di foglie di cocco; due naufraghi, unici sopravvissuti della *Petite Jeanne*. Otoo entra in contatto con la gente del posto, cura notte e giorno l'ammalato – che a poco a poco si riprende – e con lui trova finalmente imbarco su una nave di linea che si trova a far scalo a quell'isola. Otoo devoto amico «che conosce le isole» di-

---

[1] J. London, *Racconti dei Mari del Sud*, 1911; trad. it. T. Novi, CEI, Milano 1963.

venta a poco a poco un vero fratello. Tanto da far scrivere al protagonista:

Non ho mai avuto un fratello ma, per quel che so dei fratelli degli altri, dubito che vi sia un fratello che sia per il fratello suo quello che Otoo fu per me. Egli mi fu insieme fratello e padre e madre, e posso dire questo: che a causa di Otoo sono diventato più giusto e migliore. Mi curavo poco degli altri, ma dovevo rimanere giusto agli occhi di Otoo. [...] Rimanemmo insieme diciassette anni; diciassette anni egli rimase al mio fianco, vegliando mentre dormivo, curandomi nelle mie febbri e nelle mie ferite, sì, e ricevendo ferite combattendo per me. Si imbarcò sulle navi su cui m'imbarcavo io, e insieme traversammo il Pacifico da Hawaii al Capo Sydney, e dallo Stretto di Torres fino alle Galapagos, ed errammo dalle Nuove Ebridi fino alle isole dell'Equatore a ovest, attraverso le Louisiade, la Nuova Britannia, la Nuova Irlanda e la Nuova Hannover.

Il racconto, attraverso tutte queste vicende, scorre di anno in anno sino al suo episodio finale che è ambientato nelle Salomone, dove i due hanno compiuto le imprese più temerarie negli avventurosi giorni della loro giovinezza:

[...] Eravamo fermi a Savo dove eravamo andati per comprare alcune curiosità del posto. Savo è piena di pescecani. L'abitudine che hanno quelle teste lanose di gettare in mare i loro morti non tendeva certo a scoraggiare i pescecani dal frequentare quelle acque.
Il destino volle che tornassi a bordo in una canoa indigena, piccola e sovraccarica, e che questa si rovesciasse. Eravamo quattro indigeni e io sulla canoa – anzi aggrappati a essa, e la goletta era un cento metri lontano. Stavo appunto urlando perché ci mandassero una barca quando uno degli indigeni cominciò a gridare di spavento: si teneva stretto ad un'estremità della canoa ed io vidi sia lui sia quella parte della canoa andar sott'acqua diverse volte finché egli lasciò andare la sua stretta e scomparve. Lo aveva portato via un pescecane. [...] Abbandonata la canoa, cominciai a nuotare verso la goletta sperando che mi avrebbero mandato una barca per trarmi su [...], guardai ancora sott'acqua e vidi un grosso pescecane passare proprio sotto di me. Era lungo cinque metri, lo vidi benissimo. [...]
Abbandonai ogni speranza di salvezza. La goletta era ancora lontana sessanta metri e io stavo con la faccia sott'acqua a spiare i movimenti del mostro che si preparava a un nuovo attacco, quando vidi un corpo bruno passare fra me a lui: era Otoo.
«Nuota verso la goletta, padrone!» disse, con tono gaio, come si trattasse di un semplice scherzo. «Io li conosco i pescecani. Il pescecane è mio fratello.»
Obbedii e continuai a nuotare lentamente mentre Otoo nuotava intorno

a me, tenendosi sempre fra me e il pescecane, sventando i suoi attacchi e incoraggiandomi. [...]

Il pescecane, rassicurato perché non aveva ancora ricevuto nessuna ferita, si faceva più ardito. Già diverse volte stava per prendermi, ma ogni volta Otoo giungeva proprio un momento prima che fosse troppo tardi. Naturalmente Otoo avrebbe potuto salvarsi le mille volte, ma restava al mio fianco. «Addio! Non ne posso più!» ansai con gran fatica. Sapevo che era giunta la fine e che un istante appresso avrei sollevato in alto le braccia lasciandomi andar giù. Ma Otoo, mi rise in faccia, dicendo:

«Ti mostrerò un nuovo espediente. Vedrai che farò restare male quel mostro.»

Egli si tuffò dietro a me dove il pescecane si preparava a slanciarsi addosso.

«Un po' più a sinistra!» gridò poi. «C'è un cavo in acqua! A sinistra! a sinistra!»

Cambiai direzione spingendomi avanti ciecamente quasi senza coscienza di ciò che avveniva intorno a me. Mentre la mia mano si chiudeva sul cavo udii un'esclamazione a bordo: mi volsi e guardai: non vi era più traccia di Otoo. L'istante appresso egli riapparve: dai polsi senza mano zampillava il sangue.

«Otoo!» chiamò dolcemente, e nel suo sguardo potei leggere l'affetto che tremava nella sua voce.

Allora, e solo allora, al termine di tutti i nostri diciassette anni, egli mi chiamò con quel nome.

«Addio Otoo!» disse, poi fu tratto sott'acqua.

Io fui issato a bordo, dove svenni fra le braccia del capitano.[1]

Joseph Conrad, da quel navigatore che era stato, aveva descritto quello che può capitare a una vecchia «carretta», investita da un tifone con la stiva ricolma di lavoratori cinesi.

Jack London, che a sua volta di ire oceaniche ne conobbe non poche, ci narra di una famigliola, quella di un certo Mapuhi, quando un ciclone tropicale si abbatté sull'atollo di Hikueru nelle Tuamotu:

[...] durò dalle undici di sera alle tre di mattina; e appunto alle undici l'albero a cui erano attaccati Mapuhi e le sue donne si spezzò. Mapuhi riaffiorò alla superficie della laguna tenendo stretta sua figlia Ngakura. Solo un isolano dei Mari del Sud avrebbe potuto resistere a tanto; il pandano a cui stava ancora attaccato si voltava e rivoltava nelle acque schiumanti e ribollenti, e solo tenendo duro un momento e aspettando, e un momento

---

[1] J. London, *op. cit.*

dopo spostando rapidamente la presa, egli riusciva a tenere la propria testa a quella di Ngakura alla superficie a intervalli abbastanza vicini per continuare a respirare. Ma l'aria era più che altro acqua, un po' per la spruzzaglia volante, un po' per la pioggia che scrosciava dirottissima.[1]

London descrive quel naufragio nelle poche miglia quadrate di laguna dell'atollo, sulla cui estremità opposta tronchi, relitti di barche e di casse uccidevano «nove su dieci» gli sciagurati sopravvissuti al volo sulla laguna: «semiannegati, esausti, venivano scagliati in quel pazzo mortaio degli elementi e maciullati in una massa informe di carne».

Alle tre del mattino di quel giorno narrato da London, la spina dorsale del ciclone si spezzò; alle cinque non soffiava più che una brezza ostinata. Anche in queste notizie, il racconto cita dati e avvenimenti realmente accaduti alle Tuamotu. Quel ciclone non è un'invenzione letteraria, né è fantasia che delle milleduecento persone vive la sera prima a Hikueru non ne restassero l'indomani che trecento. Un missionario mormone e un gendarme di cui a Tahiti ancor oggi si conservano le «relazioni» fecero il censimento: la laguna era ingombra di cadaveri, non rimaneva più né una casa né una capanna; solo una palma di cocco su cinquanta era ancora eretta. In questo ambiente descritto con la fedeltà di un giornalista, London muove i suoi personaggi superstiti.

Afferrata a una rozza tavola che la feriva e l'ammaccava e le empiva il corpo di schegge, era volata al di là dell'atollo, e il mare se l'era portata via [...] vecchia di quasi sessant'anni, aveva trascorso sul mare tutta la vita. Mentre nuotava nelle tenebre, strangolata, accecata, lottando per respirare, venne colpita violentemente a una spalla da una noce di cocco. In un lampo formò il suo piano e afferrò la noce. Nell'ora seguente ne catturò altre sette: formarono una cintura di salvataggio che la tenne in vita. [...] Riprese i sensi quando fu scagliata da un'onda sulla spiaggia: vi si attanagliò con le mani e i piedi escoriati e sanguinanti.[2]

Non resta, alla vecchia polinesiana, che nutrirsi con le stesse noci di cocco che l'avevano tenuta a galla; ma quando le provviste finiscono e la sete comincia a straziarla, essa si convince di essere ormai morta. Invece è salvata, per caso, da un battello giunto con i soccor-

J. London, *Racconti dei Mari del Sud*, trad. it. B. Boffito, Rizzoli, Milano 1955.
Ibidem.

si e riportata all'isola ove Mapuhi e la figlia vivevano come profughi in un buco nella sabbia coperto con frammenti di lastre di zinco.

A quel ciclone che sconvolge la Polinesia orientale agli inizi del secolo, doveva seguire più di mezzo secolo di «quiete» meteorologica. Poi, nella seconda metà degli anni Ottanta, due tremendi uragani hanno sconvolto – con furia crescente – i piccoli e i grandi atolli delle Tuamotu sparsi nell'oceano.

Hanno abbattuto foreste di *cocotiers*, sollevato le acque delle lagune, investito villaggi e porticcioli. Hanno portato una devastazione che è stata – per le comunità di molte isole – il colpo di grazia: rimasti senza casa, soccorsi e trasportati a Tahiti, non hanno più fatto ritorno ai loro atolli. Accettano di buon grado l'assegno mensile di assistenza che distribuisce l'autorità centrale, e così abbandonano – oltre alla loro patria d'origine – anche l'abitudine a una propria atavica forma di vita. Certo avevano già da tempo sostituito la vela con il fuoribordo, l'*ukelele* con la radio a transistor; ma erano comunque rimasti fedeli a una «cultura isolana» che li vedeva ottimi pescatori, buoni navigatori e attenti curatori dei raccolti di *coprah* elargiti con generosità dai loro *cocotiers*. Oggi anche questi ultimi «ricordi» sono stati cancellati. A sradicarli è stato un uragano dalla forza e dalla violenza degna delle pagine più leggendarie scritte nel gran libro sui miti dei Mari del Sud. Tanto forti e tanto violenti da strappare – di quel libro – anche l'ultima pagina. Finita a pezzi, non potremo mai più leggerla.

Proprio per evocare il tempo intercorso tra l'età «d'oro» vissuta dagli uomini che videro il mondo del Pacifico meridionale qual era, e da chi ha avuto la fortuna di poterne vivere gli ultimi anni autentici, nei capitoli precedenti ho raccontato le mie esperienze andando d'arcipelago in arcipelago nel Pacifico orientale e occidentale. Nelle pagine che seguono ho raccolto i racconti di approdi e navigazioni, di entusiasmi e di paure, insomma di quanto vissuto e documentato andando verso il Pacifico occidentale.

E li ho intitolati, appunto, «D'isola in isola, verso Micronesia e Melanesia».

D'isola in isola, verso la Micronesia e la Melanesia

Da Tahiti alle Figi – Tartarughe catturate con il canto – Sulla rotta di Capitan Bligh – Samoa e *Tusitala* – Cicloni e pirati – Le golette scomparse – L'abisso di Ramapo e la Micronesia – Palau e le meduse gialle – La nippofobia – Amelia Erhardt dove si è inabissata? – La flotta fantasma della laguna di Truk – Una seconda esplosione sugli scafi delle navi morte.

«E gli altri arcipelaghi?» mi chiede l'australiano, appena finisce di bere una enorme spremuta di pompelmo. Siamo al *Vaemà*, il bar «sempre-aperto» di Papeete.

«Vuoi dire...»

«Voglio dire che voi europei quando viaggiate nel Pacifico gravitate sempre nelle isole orientali... qui a Tahiti, alle Tuamotu, qualche volta sino a Pasqua o alle Marchesi; oppure ve ne andate a giocare «il gioco degli esploratori» nelle isole papua nel Pacifico occidentale, alla ricerca dell'età della pietra, dell'uomo primitivo: Nuova Guinea, le Trobriand...

«È vero» convengo. «Ma è anche vero che tu hai ora nominato le isole più interessanti del Pacifico.»

«Perché?»

«Per noi, forse, esiste un mito dell'autenticità. E nelle zone papua di cose e fatti autentici ce ne sono...»

«Posso essere d'accordo. Ma non crederai sia ancora autentica la Polinesia?» e con un largo gesto il mio interlocutore accenna alla Papeete attorno a noi, fragorosa di auto, chiassosa in quella sua aria di boutique alla St. Tropez.

«No, la Polinesia non è più autentica» convengo. E intanto penso all'esperienza vissuta negli anni Cinquanta e ancora nei Sessanta, penso ai personaggi conosciuti nelle piccole isole, ai loro racconti, alle tradizioni nautiche e di pesca affiorate durante le lunghe settimane, i mesi del mio andare d'arcipelago in arcipelago. «Certo, in Polinesia è rimasto poco di autentico, ma forse è possibile cercare tra le auto e i supermercati i suoi "resti" ancor vivi sotto le ceneri della distruzione.»

«Un viaggio da archeologi...»

«Sì... In fondo noi europei abbiamo tutti la mania dello scavo. Viviamo in una civiltà tutta archeologica, anche se costruiamo il *Concorde* e le autostrade.»

«Queste sono tutte chiacchiere e intanto non rispondi alla mia domanda.»

«Sulle altre isole, gli arcipelaghi centrali?»

«Sì.»

«Su quelle isole, a mio parere, è abbastanza difficile, o comunque noioso, scrivere. Sono quelle che nel passato ebbero meno storia e nel presente vivono nella incolore realtà dei missionari neozelandesi...»

«... e australiani» aggiunge l'amico, ridendo dei suoi connazionali in abito scuro e panama bianco, parte inscindibile del panorama di tanti arcipelaghi.

Mi sento in colpa, dopo quel giudizio forse troppo scortese sulle aree neozelandesi e australiane d'Oceania, gettato là durante quella conversazione al pompelmo finita con una risata. Ma sono abbastanza convinto di quanto ho detto. Convinto da sensazioni mie personali, quindi forse troppo soggettive, psicologiche. Nate quando fui una volta alle Figi, tappa iniziale del mio primo viaggio nel Pacifico.

Era, se ricordo bene, il maggio del '56. Viaggiavamo in goletta, ed eravamo giunti in una rada per metterci alla fonda. Si sarebbero potuti udire i passi di uno degli indigeni scalzi sul legno del ponte, tanto era il silenzio.

Non un alito di vento, né il grido di un gabbiano, né il rombo lontano dell'oceano sulla barriera di corallo.

«Bene,» disse una voce dietro di noi «ora ci siete. Questa è un'isola dei Mari del Sud, sapete.»

Avevamo fatto la traversata di notte, aiutati da un gran vento di levante.

«È un bell'ancoraggio, questo, non c'è mai un cenno di vento. Bello e sicuro...»

Il grasso comandante dell'*Anna del Mar*, d'origine tahitiana, si consacrava alla birra e alla sua chitarra. Nei porti, o negli approdi, faceva in modo che gli altri si occupassero del carico della *coprah*; alla rotta, in navigazione, ci pensava il pilota cinese; al motore stava suo fratello di nome Natale.

Tutti gli altri, i marinai e i passeggeri, erano parti dell'*Anna del Mar* che si sarebbero potuti confondere con il fasciame e la soprastruttura della goletta. I marinai erano elementi come i due alberi, le vele, il timone e il motore; e i passeggeri (le donne soprattutto) facevano, da quando erano saliti, corpo unico con il pavimento del ponte coperto: forme e colori immobili sulle stuoie di pandano.

«Bene...» continuò il comandante (era in canottiera, felice d'aver in testa una corona d'erba e di fiori intrecciata per lui a terra dai marinai sbarcati a cercar frutta) «...appena sarà giorno lasceremo l'ancoraggio. Bisogna fermarci qualche giorno qui alle Figi, per riprendere al più presto il viaggio; la rotta verso est sarà dura in questa stagione. A Suva caricheremo acqua e petrolio, a Levuka la *coprah*... C'è sempre da perdere un sacco di tempo a Levuka con quei figli di un cane della B. & P.»

Tornò il silenzio che durò fino alla notte; dietro le cime dell'isola s'allungava il buio, e noi eravamo immobili nel chiarore della baia.

Dormii poco e male e, appena desto, cercai la mia sacca, frugai in fondo sotto le carte, i biglietti, le macchine fotografiche e trovai una agenda con la copertina blu, che aprii alla prima pagina.

Cominciavano, a prua, a salpar l'àncora. La catena si arrotolava adagio sul fondo metallico della prima stiva. Andai dal pilota cinese e, sotto la lampada della timoneria, lo trovai intento a scrivere sul libro di bordo: «Diciotto maggio – Lasciato ancoraggio ore 20.10, vento moderato di S.E., rotta per 242°...». Presi una matita e copiai sulla mia agenda quella frase; forse andava bene, come inizio di un diario (comunque, il giorno dopo a Viti Levu persi subito l'agenda, e quella annotazione non ebbe mai più un seguito: l'unico diario «nei Mari del Sud» che sono riuscito a tener sempre aggiornato – e a non perdere – per più di trent'anni è quello dei miei soggiorni alle Tuamotu; e un altro, assai breve, scritto nei luoghi dove americani e giapponesi si scontrarono nella seconda guerra mondiale e mutarono il paradisiaco atollo di Truk in un inferno.

Gli indigeni dell'isola di Beqa, una delle più piccole fra tutte le Figi, camminano a piedi scalzi su pietre roventi; lo fanno quando lo stregone lo comanda, e dopo aver cantato una preghiera. Si nascondono prima per una settimana nelle selve, raccolgono massi di pietra basaltica, li accumulano in una grande buca, la stessa da secoli. Vi accatastano, di fianco e sopra, legna da ardere e il fuoco brucia per giorni e giorni.

Le donne s'occupano dei costumi per la cerimonia dei loro uomini – fibra di pandano colorata di viola – e si dispongono poi durante l'intera cerimonia sui due lati della radura, tutta circondata dagli alberi della foresta. In silenzio, osservano i loro uomini camminare uno dopo l'altro su quelle pietre divenute bianche per essere rimaste sul fuoco tanto tempo.

Uomini e donne, quando la cerimonia era ancora sacra, pregavano, durante lo svolgimento, le divinità della foresta e del fuoco; chiedevano loro i doni elementari della forza, del coraggio, della virilità, e fortuna nella caccia e nella pesca. Oggi, forse, chiedono nella preghiera l'arrivo di sempre nuovi turisti desiderosi di assistere allo spettacolo in cambio di una ventina di buoni dollari; e poiché anche questa è una grazia si continua a camminare su quelle pietre per ottenerla; e così, in fondo, il fenomeno resta identico. A chiedere come mai sul fuoco i loro piedi non bruciano essi rispondono oggi probabilmente allo stesso modo con cui devono aver risposto i loro antenati ai primi esploratori europei che giunsero qui; e cioè che le preghiere li aiutano a trovare una «forza» che li rende del tutto resistenti alla prova; anche se quelle pietre sono tanto roventi che a lasciarvi cadere una foglia, questa subito brucia.

Per confermare poi che, malgrado il contatto rovente, le piante dei loro piedi non si sono ustionate, gli uomini chiudono la cerimonia con un ballo di ore: anche questo è un rito antico che continua a ripetersi eguale.

A meno di cento chilometri da Beqa – ma forse a un secolo di distanza dalla danza sul fuoco – nell'isola di Viti Levu, si trova Suva, capitale dell'arcipelago.

Viti Levu è la maggiore delle Figi, e Suva è uno fra i porti più importanti del Pacifico centrale.

La nostra *Anna del Mar* – siamo sempre nel maggio del 1956 – si è ormeggiata alla banchina, dietro un lungo sommergibile Usa. A terra, nelle strade del porto e della città i figiani vestono alla moda del cappello di feltro come nelle grandi città africane, o nelle Antille o nei piccoli centri del Brasile; e camicie colorate e vecchi pantaloni lunghi. Le guardie che regolano il traffico, conservano – capriccio di un governatore – il gonnellino figiano.

C'è il sole tiepido del primo mattino, le ombre sono fonde e i colori sono vivaci e caldi; siamo appoggiati alla porta spalancata della nostra cabina, investiti dal frastuono corale delle camionette e dall'odore dei sacchi di *coprah* sparsi al suolo.

«Si fa presto a dimenticare il chiasso delle danze di Beqa, sentendo il fragore di Suva, eh?» dice Natale. «Eppure non è lontana la costa di Beqa,» indica la punta dell'isola oltre il porto « è subito lì, a poche ore... È così il Pacifico oggi. Ci sono isole con case di cemento armato e altre isole con i villaggi di paglia e lo stregone ancora potente.»

Una musica comincia a sentirsi al di là del molo, verso i giardini: la banda figiana in gonna scozzese prova gli inni da suonare con le cornamuse nei giorni di festa nel prato antistante il Palazzo del Governatore. È la Royal Fijan Band, che ritroviamo a sera nell'unico night di Suva; ci sono alcuni marinai nordamericani, qualche ragazza inglese, due turisti neozelandesi con le lentiggini; un gruppo di figiani «bene» in un angolo. Tre lunghe file di sedie di legno chiudono lo spazio per le danze come fossero una parete; il pavimento è polveroso. Da bere, solo aranciata; è un triste saluto all'isola che lasciamo.

Con l'*Anna del Mar* giungiamo a Levuka il 30 maggio '56. Ci guida un pilota figiano i cui capelli sono così tanti e fitti da parere un copricapo.

Levuka è tra le «piccole» dell'arcipelago; l'intera isola è come oppressa da un gran dente di roccia; alcune palme, poche case di legno e una lamiera sono l'unica alternativa alla pietra basaltica. Ma il suo porticciolo è importante per le isole vicine, prive di un ancoraggio altrettanto sicuro. Per questo l'*Anna del Mar* è venuta qui a caricare sacchi e sacchi di *coprah*.

«Puzza!» grida indignato Natale, benché quello scalo sia per lui, chissà, il milionesimo e dovrebbe essere abbastanza abituato agli effluvi del prodotto «base» di tutte le isole. «A me fa schifo perché è dolciastra; odio la *coprah*. E poi, qui ci mettono giorni per caricarla. Avessero almeno tanta voglia di lavorare quanti capelli hanno in testa...»

Conosciamo un missionario cattolico, che pare ritagliato nella cartapecora (ottant'anni), e il suo giovane assistente irlandese. Dispongono di due chiese, e si tengono in collegamento percorrendo più volte al giorno gli unici tre chilometri di strada dell'isola a bordo di una Ford nuova fiammante (spettacolo tale da ridurre livido di rabbia il missionario concorrente, anglicano, che possiede solo una bicicletta a motore).

Fu il vecchio missionario cattolico a consigliarci di andare a Koro, un atollo vicino. «E mi direte se là sentirete la magia dei Mari del Sud o no» ci disse.

All'*Anna del Mar* occorreva ancora tempo per finire il carico; i figiani del porto lavoravano ogni ora più lentamente perché il comandante era molto di malumore a causa di quel ritardo, e loro evidentemente si divertivano molto a vedere un comandante tahitiano perdere la calma.

Avevamo quindi il tempo di visitare Koro; il braccio di mare tra le due isole era calmo e potevamo andarci con la piccola motobarca di un indiano. Il missionario irlandese si mise i blue-jeans e lasciò la Ford dietro la chiesa; l'indiano proprietario della barca, per andare a Koro, ci chiese dieci sterline e lui gliene offrì una; si accordarono per tre, e si mise lui stesso al timone per accompagnarci.

«Vedrete,» diceva «vedrete a Koro. Lui, il missionario vecchio, è qui da sessant'anni e dice di non aver mai visto una pesca più straordinaria di quella di Koro. Vedrete.»

Alcuni uomini, due o tre, stavano nascosti tra le rocce di lava nera, piantate sulla spiaggia bianca di corallo. Cantavano una nenia triste, lenta, insistente.

Passarono alcune ore, il sole salì alto e gettò nella laguna la sua luce a lame guizzanti. Qualcosa si mosse nell'acqua, emerse: la testa triangolare di una tartaruga.

La bestia stette immobile qualche minuto – il canto si fece più forte e più acuto – poi si diresse verso riva. Prese terra e cominciò ad avanzare a fatica sulla spiaggia. La vedevamo venire avanti e sembrava veramente *attratta dal canto*: infatti se il canto si interrompeva, la tartaruga si fermava; e non appena riprendeva, ricominciava a trascinarsi verso il masso dietro il quale l'uomo della nenia era nascosto. Più volte si ripeté, identica, questa sua reazione: il ritornello finiva e lei si fermava, poi il canto ricominciava e lei di nuovo strisciava adagio sulla sabbia calda. Fino a quando, veloci, due ragazzi sbucarono alle sue spalle con un bastone, lo infilarono nella sabbia sotto l'enorme massa della sua corazza, usandolo come leva e sollevarono la bestia di scatto, rovesciandola.

Lei rimase senza scampo agitando le zampe contro il cielo, vanamente tentando di raddrizzarsi.

Catturata da una nenia.

«Tartarughe catturate cantando a Koro?» mi chiede stupito il figiano dell'aeroporto, addetto al *bureau* turistico.

Scuote la testa. A Koro, che lui sappia, non ci abita più nessuno.

«Sono passati sedici anni, da allora» borbotta il mio compagno di viaggio, contando sulle dita la differenza, a ritroso, dal 1971 al '56.

«Sia, e non son pochi» convengo. «... Ma la noia di questo arcipelago mi sembra la stessa. E se non si pescan più tartarughe col canto e non si danza più sul fuoco, cosa siamo venuti a filmare, qui?...»

All'aeroporto internazionale di Viti Levu siamo in attesa di un pullman per spostarci in città. Intorno a noi, sui muri, il centro abitato pare ingombro – se così posso dire – dei multicolori resti di una grande festa. È quella dell'Indipendenza, protrattasi per settimane nell'autunno del 1970. I proclami e i manifesti strappati sui muri di legno ondeggiano al vento a ogni decollo e atterraggio di jet – una decina al giorno a Viti Levu.

Il *free-shop* espone cartelli nei quali si garantiscono i prezzi più bassi del mondo per i prodotti giapponesi in vendita qui ai turisti (più bassi che a Hong Kong, più bassi che ad Aden). Questo per «incentivare l'economia dell'isola» il cui problema, come tutti sanno, è l'espandersi della colonia indiana immigrata. I giornali locali non parlano d'altro. «Le Figi ai figiani o le regaliamo a Indira Gandhi?» dice un titolo. E il sottotitolo spiega – per chi ancora non lo sapesse – che tutti i soldi in banca sono degli indiani, e le iniziative industriali ed economiche sono loro anch'esse.

Corriamo finalmente verso la capitale; e l'occhio scopre meno mutamenti di quanti la sosta all'aeroporto e dintorni ne avesse suggeriti. Identifico il paesaggio, rarissime le nuove costruzioni; sempre le stesse buche sulla King-road che circonda l'isola (ma in onore di quale King?)

A Suva nel viaggio precedente avevo perso l'inevitabile visita al Museo che conserva la Bibbia e l'àncora del *Bounty*; ci vado questa volta, anche per riprendere in mano gli appunti già da tempo riuniti in un lavoro collettivo di ricerca e di preparazione su queste isole.

«È mia intenzione dirigermi ovest-nord-ovest per avvistare quel gruppo di isole chiamate Figi, se si trovano in quella direzione» aveva scritto nel suo giornale di bordo il 3 maggio 1789 il tenente William Bligh, ex comandante del vascello armato *Bounty* di Sua Maestà Britannica, dal quale era stato sbarcato in seguito a quell'ammutinamento che nella storia del tempo doveva restare una pagina indimenticabile. Il 7 maggio nel quaderno che portava con sé sulla piccola scialuppa a remi sulla quale avanzava nell'oceano alla ricerca di un approdo sicuro per sé e i suoi compagni, così ancora scriveva Bligh:

> Abbiamo avvistato due grosse canoe procedenti lungo la costa delle Figi finalmente da noi raggiunte. Le canoe vengono verso di noi, ed essendo in allarme sulle loro intenzioni nei nostri riguardi, ci siamo dati a remare il più velocemente possibile. Verso le tre del pomeriggio, solo una delle due canoe si era avvicinata, arrivando a due miglia di distanza, ma a quel punto rinunciava all'inseguimento.

Bligh e gli altri diciotto uomini di quella barca lunga ventitré piedi sbarcarono poi nell'arcipelago scegliendo l'isolotto di Tofua; raccolsero acqua e viveri, ma persero un uomo in un attacco dei guerrieri figiani sbarcati sulla loro terra. Fu allora che Bligh prese l'incredibile decisione di navigare senza più concedersi una sola tappa – e sempre a remi! – verso Timor a 3600 miglia nautiche di distanza, attraverso tutto il quadrante occidentale del Pacifico.

Un giornalista inglese, trovatosi un giorno in un ufficio della Marina, alle Figi, osservava una vecchia mappa che un cartografo governativo gli mostrava per indicare il percorso di Bligh attraverso le isole. Mentre i due parlavano, li ascoltava un *turanga*, un capo figiano. E quando il cartografo ricordò l'incidente delle due canoe che avevano inseguito Bligh, l'inglese chiese al figiano:

«Che cosa sarebbe successo se le canoe avessero raggiunto Bligh?»

«Oh, di certo i guerrieri l'avrebbero mangiato!» rispose ridendo il *turanga*. E ricordò che loro, i figiani, praticavano tutti il cannibalismo, e chi naufragava sulle loro coste era secondo la tradizione *una preda legale*. Specialmente se i naufraghi erano quei violenti bianchi incursori e invasori chiamati *gli uomini con acqua di mare negli occhi*. Per quanto crudele fosse questa consuetudine, era comunque giustificata ritualmente e fisicamente; e per di più era certo comprensibile quando a subirne le tragiche conseguenze erano i marinai europei, dai quali gli isolani avevano subìto flagelli altrettanto inumani: malattie, violenza, alcolismo e tratta.

Tornando agli uomini della scialuppa di Bligh, essi navigarono attraverso il centro dell'arcipelago figiano senza fermarsi finché raggiunsero – come avevano deciso – la base portoghese di Timor. Morendo quasi di fame e di sete e non avendo altro che li guidasse se non un orologio, un compasso e un quadrante, erano riusciti a segnalare la posizione di ventitré isole con una accuratezza sorprendente. Tre anni dopo, Bligh navigò nuovamente (con una grande nave, questa volta) lungo il percorso che aveva coperto con la piccola barca e confermò e amplificò le sue precedenti osservazioni mentre andava cercando i superstiti del *Bounty* per impiccarli poi, appena presi, a uno a uno con la stessa freddezza e lucidità che aveva dimostrato come geografo.

Dopo la sua morte, le isole Figi vennero chiamate dai marinai «le isole Bligh». Sono più di trecento, sparse come una manciata per 2500 miglia quadrate dell'Oceano Pacifico a cavallo del 180° meridiano, fra la Nuova Zelanda e l'Equatore. Circa un centinaio è abitato e la loro grandezza varia moltissimo. La maggiore, Viti Levu, ha esattamente la stessa grandezza delle Hawaii; e la seconda in grandezza, Vanua Levu (Grande Terra), è esattamente la metà della prima. Sono entrambe di origine vulcanica e hanno coste ricoperte di folte foreste a sud-est. Durante la stagione delle piogge, da aprile a novembre, tonnellate e tonnellate di acqua cadono dal cielo su tutto l'arcipelago, di certo il più umido di tutto il Pacifico centrale, e quelle piogge sono un'altra componente della sua invincibile noia.

In una cronaca di viaggio in lingua inglese, pubblicata per quei turisti che gli abitanti delle Figi sperano veder giungere sempre di più numerosi, si legge: «Sotto le palme di cocco, s'intravedono dalla strada gruppi di capanne di legno con tetti di paglia, disposte a circolo intorno a uno spiazzo d'erba rasato. Sulla costa di Singatoka crescono tutti i migliori materiali per la costruzione di abitazioni in giunchi, bambù, palme e felci. I figiani costruiscono le case migliori di tutto il Pacifico, e le elaborate costruzioni che ospitano i capi tribù, costruite su piattaforme di corallo roccioso, sono veri capolavori».

I figiani – ben piantati, generalmente altissimi – sono di ceppo etnico melanesiano, hanno pelle scura e capelli ispidi ritti sulla testa, ma si vede in loro una forte componente polinesiana: le Figi sono proprio sulla linea di divisione tra questi due grandi ceppi etnici del Pacifico.

La gente, nei villaggi, si muove con la grazia di grossi gatti; la maggior parte delle donne portano ancora la capigliatura unta di olio di cocco, sollevata alta sulla nuca. Per gli uomini, questa moda è passata dal tempo del loro servizio militare durante la seconda guerra mondiale (quando furono obbligati a tagliare le loro chiome per portare il basso elmetto inglese). I figiani restano comunque molto orgogliosi delle loro capigliature tradizionali, anche se ne sopravvivono ben poche, ed è da loro considerata ancor oggi estrema maleducazione toccare i capelli di un'altra persona. In tempi più antichi un simile modo d'agire avrebbe causato una morte sicura.

Alle Figi del «problema di fondo» si parla da sempre e – mi

pare – con le stesse parole. Eppure è un problema grave che investe la realtà politico-sociale, culturale dell'arcipelago: l'immigrazione, alla quale poco sopra mi riferivo, di indiani e pakistani. Tanti da essere oggi (negli anni Novanta) la maggioranza.

I primi erano stati trasportati a Suva nel 1879 come manodopera e, quando nel 1917 l'immigrazione in grande scala ebbe termine, essi ammontavano già a sessantatremila. Il governatore inglese, accorgendosi di quanto la loro presenza mutava la realtà dell'arcipelago, offrì di rimpatriarli, ma naturalmente più di tre quarti rifiutarono. Da allora, si sono perfettamente adattati, al clima e all'ambiente, sposandosi giovanissimi e mettendo al mondo – dicono le statistiche – dieci, dodici figli per coppia; e così in meno di un secolo gli indiani hanno superato (e di molto) la popolazione figiana.

Oggi essi non sono solamente i principali agricoltori, ma anche i maggiori investitori bancari delle isole. «I figiani non sono pigri,» ha scritto un sociologo di Suva «ma in questa terra dove sono sempre stati padroni non riescono ad assuefarsi a vivere lavorando per altri; trovare da mangiare è sempre stato facile per loro ed è comprensibile che non riescano a imparare a combattere per il loro benessere. Con una filosofia di vita basata sul *Kerekere*, cioè l'equa divisione dei beni tra i membri di ciascuna famiglia, non è facile per un figiano inserirsi in quella che è "l'ideologia" della società moderna: la lotta per affermarsi, la lotta per sopraffare. È a questa lotta che li obbligano gli indiani; ed è per questo che ogni figiano odia *per principio* il suo vicino di casa indiano.»

Abbiamo lasciato Viti Levu su un piccolo aereo, verso le isole Samoa. Dopo il decollo, per quasi un'ora sorvoliamo l'arcipelago che stiamo abbandonando. Dall'alto (stiamo sfiorando una montagna) vivo l'esperienza di sempre, quando osservo un paesaggio dal cielo; tento di leggerlo come un grafico, un geroglifico, un ideogramma: la misteriosa scrittura della terra, come un libro, racconta le opere dell'uomo e il rapporto tra lui e l'ambiente naturale. In Italia come in Africa, nelle zone più industrializzate come in quelle agricole; in Oceania come altrove. Il linguaggio della terra vista dal cielo è lo stesso, ovunque. Anche alle Figi.

Tagliando di traverso Viti Levu, le divisioni del terreno parlano di piccole proprietà collettive dei villaggi montani; di quelli ancora vivi e di quelli morti (gli abitanti sono ormai tutti nelle città!). Di questi ultimi restano solo gli spiazzi di terreno vuoto dove esistevano in anni passati capanne, piccole e grandi, e sentieri e granai e le case dei capi.

Sorvoliamo Ovalau, e anche qui s'indovina un grande villaggio semiabbandonato, alle radici di montagne che arrivano sino al mare; poi puntiamo a nord-est attraverso un piccolo gruppo di isole, le Lomaiviti; qui a Wakaya, si ricorda un'altra pagina d'avventure di mare, quasi epica come quella del *Bounty*; in quella baia fu catturato il prussiano Felix von Luckner, il Conte-corsaro della prima guerra mondiale. Appena il tempo di scattare una foto ed eccoci sulla verticale di Makongai, isola-lebbrosario del Pacifico.

Al di là di queste terre appare Taveuni, a forma di pantofola; un'unica, vasta piantagione di cocco.

«Famiglie europee possiedono qui le più grandi coltivazioni di *coprah*» mi dice un figiano seduto accanto a me. Non ha parlato per tutto il volo, questa è la prima sua battuta che sento; aggiunge: «Dove non sono gli indiani, sono ancora i bianchi a dominarci... è questa la nostra indipendenza!». Mi guarda sorridendo, e nuovamente mi indica il paesaggio che continua a scorrere sotto le nostre ali, misura del vasto impero privato il cui potere è evidente in quella sorta di mappa catastale vista dal cielo.

Ancora un'isola «grande»: Vanua Levu. Gli altipiani che circondano il Monte Vittoria erano dominio dei *Kai-tholos*, le «grandi teste» delle colline. Dall'alto distinguo le antiche strade che collegavano un villaggio all'altro; nella «lettura del cielo» anche questa immagine parla chiaro: i sentieri corrono proprio sulla cresta delle colline evidentemente perché i viandanti fossero obbligati a incontrarsi per forza, e potessero procedere tranquilli senza temere il pericolo di agguati. Dalla grande Vanua Levu è poi breve il volo sulle isole Yasawa, di origine vulcanica, in verticale sul mare. Queste Figi sembrano non aver mai fine.

Una immensa roccia a strapiombo e sotto la sua ombra, il villaggio di Yalombi, sull'isola di Waya. Qui, nel '56, mi fecero bere la prima volta il *kawa*, blanda droga di acqua con polvere di una pianta pepata che ricorda la liquirizia: è una bevanda senza alcol ma il suo effetto è quello di paralizzare ogni sensazione della lingua e del palato. «Se bevuto in grandi quantità» m'aveva detto uno dei miei ospiti «sembra bloccare anche le gambe». Un effetto che non ho provato, essendomi stato allora sufficiente quello – quasi altrettanto paralizzante – di bere il *kawa* da un unico recipiente, dove i miei ospiti, dopo ogni sorsata, sputavano con disinvoltura quella parte di liquido che non avevano inghiottito perché *non è educato bere tutto un sorso.*

Diamo l'addio alle Figi sorvolando un piccolo isolotto, non più grande di una ventina di miglia quadrate: si chiama Mbau.

Mbau era, una volta, la dimora dei più temuti guerrieri di tutte le isole; il loro capo Rato Thakoubau estese in pochissimo tempo la sua potenza sulla maggior parte dell'arcipelago ed era temuto da tutte le Figi come un Attila locale. A Mbau oggi non ci sono più guerrieri; c'è solo un missionario metodista.

Quando sbarcai in quell'isola, un ragazzo della missione mi indicò una roccia basaltica isolata da un prato, simile a una statua di Moore. «Vedi» mi disse «su quella pietra i miei antenati guerrieri spaccavano le teste dei loro nemici prigionieri; oggi è diventata il nostro fonte battesimale.»

Addio guerrieri vinti da un missionario metodista; e addio mille Figi dalle mille noie.

Ancora un'ora di volo sull'oceano e saremo alle Samoa.

Le Samoa, per me, restano le isole della *date line*, una linea che permette, se si vuole, di vivere due Natali nello stesso anno; ma permette anche, se si è allergici alle festività, di evitarle spostandosi in senso contrario alla data del calendario.

Questa della *date line* è una convenzione, come quella dei fusi orari per la quale i viaggiatori in transito dalle Samoa perdono oppure guadagnano un giorno, a seconda della direzione del loro viaggio.

Mi capitò di sorvolare le Samoa mentre, provenendo da Tahiti, stavo andando verso l'Australia. Era il 9 aprile, proprio il giorno in cui compio gli anni. Da Papeete eravamo partiti alle undici di sera del giorno 8; l'indomani mattina eravamo a Sydney dove il calendario del bar, all'aeroporto, segnava già la data del 10. Il 9 non era esistito, era stato cancellato sorvolando le Samoa e la loro famosa *line* (non sapevo cosa pensare: durante due anni avrei avuto la stessa età? Sarei stato più vecchio o più giovane?... e nel dubbio decisi che la *date line* è una macchina mangiatempo applicata alla geografia, qualcosa per confondere date e memorie).

Per questo, forse, il mio ricordo delle Samoa, ove giunsi anni fa e sono tornato di recente, è giustificatamente coniugato sia al presente che al passato; è ricordo del tempo-senza-tempo ove anche il paesaggio sembra voler confondere il succedersi degli avvenimenti vissuti. Un paesaggio simile, certo, a quello di tutti gli altri del Pacifico meridionale, ma, a tratti così oniricamente diverso; da parer quasi sospeso nello spazio.

Come il monte di Vailima, dove ero salito un giorno a trovarvi la tomba di Stevenson.

Ero uscito dalla cittadina di Apia, capitale dell'isola di Upolu e delle Samoa occidentali e andavo verso quel monte, sotto i boschi di cocco.

Era un tardo pomeriggio, il caldo stava diminuendo e cominciava a spirare dal mare una brezza lievemente fresca.

Le case si aprirono allora tutte, le pareti erano stuoie che si arrotolavano e si appendevano in alto e il tetto restava sospeso sui pali che ai lati disegnavano la costruzione. E così le case non erano che verande, o, meglio, parti di quel bosco dove stavo passando. Avrei potuto attraversarle, le case, e forse le immobili figure che intravedevo all'interno (sdraiate su tappeti di corteccia di albero conciata, i *tapa*) non si sarebbero nemmeno mosse.

Intanto ero giunto sotto le pendici del monte. Nella foresta che lo attornia, il 3 dicembre 1894 i tamburi avevano annunciato: «*Tusitala* è morto». *Tusitala* era il nome polinesiano dello scrittore inglese Robert Louis Stevenson; l'avevano così battezzato quei capi locali che sapevano quanto Stevenson aveva desiderato riposare per sempre su quella montagna selvaggia, ma salita da un uomo, alle pendici della quale egli aveva vissuto gli ultimi due anni della sua esistenza. *Tusitala* era un grande amico; per lui

smossero la roccia, sradicarono gli alberi e tagliarono il fitto sottobosco tropicale per tracciare un sentiero sino alla cima affinché
potesse essere sepolto dove aveva desiderato.

Iniziai a salire adagio la china ripidissima del monte. Mi ar-
rampicavo, mi facevo strada nel groviglio del sottobosco, e intanto
evocavo fra me l'immagine di quei mille uomini vestiti di stoffe
bianche, in segno di lutto, che alla luce delle torce avevano lavora-
to senza riposo per aprire un sentiero sino alla cima dove si domina tutta questa isola delle Samoa e l'oceano; un quasi festoso
funerale.

Sulla vetta coperta di verde, la tomba di Stevenson è una superficie di cemento grezzo, in parte coperto da arbusti, oltre i quali
s'intravede l'orizzonte da cui sale il rombo dell'onda oceanica
sulla barriera di corallo.

Sotto il cielo vasto e stellato scavate la tomba e lasciatemi dormire: lieto
sono vissuto e lietamente muoio e volentieri mi sono qui disteso. Questo sia
il verso che inciderete per me: Egli riposa qui dove bramava riposare, dal
mare è tornato alla sua casa il marinaio, dalle colline è tornato il cacciatore.

Così è scritto sulla tomba di Stevenson in inglese e in polinesiano. Frase finale del racconto di una vita iniziata davanti a un altro
orizzonte, quello del plumbeo Mare del Nord della Scozia dove
Stevenson nacque. Un lungo cammino aveva portato quell'uomo a
morire in una terra tanto lontana da quella d'origine; una vita di
vicende meravigliose la cui conclusione, così drammatica, avrebbe
contribuito in maniera determinante, a creare il «mito dei Mari del
Sud», ipoteca romantica che ancora pesa sulla realtà del Pacifico.
R. L. Stevenson aveva vissuto un'infanzia dominata dalla affascinante, affettiva presenza del padre, ma alienata – per la sua malferma
salute – dalla vita e dai giochi in comune con i compagni di scuola.
Fantasioso, sensibile, ma troppo spesso costretto a letto, cominciò a
leggere avidamente di tutto, la mente eccitata dalle appassionanti e
tragiche leggende scozzesi. Fallì come studente di ingegneria, fallì
come avvocato, ma a venticinque anni era già scrittore e pubblicava il
suo *Viaggio nel continente*, primo di quella lunga serie di avventure nel
mondo che si sarebbe conclusa alle Samoa.
Isole che ha scelto soprattutto per il suo clima: Stevenson, infat-

ti, a soli trentacinque anni, anche se la fortuna letteraria ormai lo guida, è tisico e debole di cuore: e poiché i suoi libri registrano incassi favolosi egli ha deciso di stabilirsi in una località adatta al suo stato, fosse pure la più sperduta. Il viaggio nelle isole dei Mari del Sud è così, insieme, tentativo di riacquistare salute e desiderio di conoscere anche questa parte del mondo prima di lasciarlo.

Visitare, studiare, analizzare l'esistenza quotidiana delle isole del Pacifico sembra guarirlo. Nelle Samoa, le abitudini, il lavoro, le fatiche dei polinesiani insieme alle loro credenze, alla loro mentalità – fantastica e pratica al tempo stesso – lo affascinavano; passa lunghe ore del giorno nel porto di Apia a vedere arrivare dall'oceano e ripartire, e caricare e scaricare golette, carghi, le navi di linea ancora a vela. Nascono così i *Racconti dei Mari del Sud*, *L'isola delle voci*, *La spiaggia di Falesa*, *Bassa Marea*, *Il diavolo nella bottiglia*.

Contemplando l'oceano ha scritto:

> Nell'estasi del silenzio,
> un misurato respiro...

E non c'è giorno in cui alle Samoa egli non ricordi la Scozia; riesce a trovare nelle leggende locali similitudini e analogie con leggende della sua terra; visita i villaggi, osserva i bambini polinesiani (i loro giochi, la loro felice libertà e comunanza con la natura) e li paragona ai coetanei delle sue terre brumose e fredde, condizionatrici di infanzie senza sole.

> Un ragazzo del nostro paese vede il mare – plumbeo e ostile [scrive in una lettera alla madre] come un'entità mostruosa, da temere. Qui invece il mare è compagno di giochi. Lo avrei voluto avere anch'io: e forse oggi la mia salute sarebbe diversa... [e ancora:] I bambini delle isole sono – per i polinesiani – quel che per noi sono i quadri delle più belle gallerie: qualcosa da non stancarsi mai di rimirare, di mettere in mostra.

Dei re dell'isola, i grandi capi famiglia chiamati *matai*, R. L. Stevenson fu confidente e amico. E alla sua casa di Vailima si incontravano con visitatori europei e americani sbarcati dalle navi all'àncora in Apia. Questi «bianchi» di passaggio alle Samoa chiedevano tutti di far visita a Stevenson allora al massimo della sua fama. Raggiungevano Vailima a cavallo, lo pregavano di raccontare dei suoi viaggi a vela negli atolli o la magia di un diavolo chiuso in bottiglia, il suo racconto più conosciuto nel mondo.

Fu un periodo felice, che durò due anni. Un periodo di cui ho visto, nella sua casa diventata museo, alcune immagini ingiallite, di quando appunto i re dell'isola si facevano fotografare con lui sulla veranda, con l'ospite di turno e il grande cerchio familiare a poco a poco riunitosi alle Samoa. E proprio a uno di loro, Lloyd Osbourn, figliastro di Stevenson, dobbiamo la cronaca della sua fine:

Accadde la sera del 3 dicembre 1894. La morte ha un suo accento particolare, e quando udii gridare Fanny compresi che Stevenson non era più. Era stato un embolo cerebrale, poco dopo il tramonto.

Quando le luci si accendono lungo il porto di Apia, gruppi di ragazze e ragazzi, con fiori nei capelli e dietro le orecchie, incominciano a cantare nelle strade mentre le loro ombre allungate tremano sotto gli alberi di *pulu*. I loro canti svaniscono nella notte verso le barche illuminate alla fonda, verso il relitto di una nave in rovina su un letto di corallo a pochi metri dalla riva.

Quel relitto è tutto ciò che rimane della nave da guerra tedesca *Adler*, distrutta durante la tempesta che si abbatté su queste rive nel 1889. A quel tempo le Samoa occidentali erano appunto colonia germanica; poi se le divisero i neozelandesi e gli statunitensi, sotto mandato. Le Samoa occidentali sono ora indipendenti, con una Costituzione democratica di stampo occidentale mista alla «democrazia tribale» che pare fosse una caratteristica dell'arcipelago ai suoi tempi d'oro. Il tutto verte sull'importanza della *aiga*, famiglia (che può consistere di pochi membri o di centinaia); la «famiglia» elegge il *matai* (un capo) il quale ha il diritto e il dovere di parlare per tutti, ed è oggi, secondo la Costituzione, il solo a poter votare.

La «famiglia», come unità sociale, dovrebbe essere quindi l'aspetto principale della vita comunitaria delle Samoa. Ma benché questa istituzione presenti notevoli vantaggi (nessun membro dell'*aiga* lascerà morire di fame un altro membro della stessa famiglia, questo sarebbe un disonore per tutti), i giovani, anche qui, contestano; trovano ingiusto che solo i *matai* possano votare e conseguentemente legiferare. Hanno certamente ragione, ma la loro protesta cade nel silenzio in una società dove è così facile vivere, o quantomeno sopravvivere: tutti possono costruirsi il proprio *faré*, case di *niau*, foglie di cocco intrecciato (diritto sancito dalla Costituzione) e chiunque può sposarsi senza dote (diritto sancito dalla tradizione polinesiana locale); il vestiario può anche consistere solo di un paio di metri di cotone colorato, quel che basta per fare un *lava-lava* o per uomo o per donna (a parte s'intende un abito bianco da portare la domenica per andare in chiesa, ma chi contesta, in chiesa non ci va); il cibo, infine, non manca, perché la «famiglia» mantiene per tradizione anche i figli che la contestano.

E così, anche la protesta giovanile finisce con l'essere assorbita in una realtà troppo tranquilla; e il tempo resta immobile in queste isole.

La mia sosta alle Samoa nel '56 doveva essere brevissima, e lo fu. Non potendo più resistere a tutti gli scarafaggi dell'*Anna del Mar* e alle canzoni che il comandante continuava ininterrottamente a suonare con la sua chitarra (sempre le stesse), andai a sistemarmi in uno degli alberghi di Apia, il White Horse Inn, dove si mangiava male ma si dormiva deliziosamente bene e una ragazza polinesiana grassoccia e sonnacchiosa suonava, con la chitarra, un repertorio un po' diverso da quello del comandante del battello sul quale ero ormai da un mese.

Per un paio di giorni vagai nella zona del porto, gettando ogni tanto un'occhiata alla vecchia goletta che avevo tradito perché mancante di lenzuola pulite. Fotografai le superstiti chiese e case in architettura tedesca; conobbi le ragazze della missione mormone e fotografai anche loro, finché non sentii il ridicolo e patetico fischio della nostra sirena di bordo: l'*Anna del Mar* stava per ripartire.

Corsi al White Horse Inn, infilai spazzolino da denti e pigiama nella valigia, promisi alla ragazza grassoccia di spedirle una delle foto che le avevo scattato con un fiore rosso nei capelli, e poco dopo ero a bordo.

Le cime, da tesate che erano, caddero in lasco; subito gli ormeggi furono lasciati e il motore si mosse «avanti adagio». Lasciavamo Apia.

Natale spalancò le braccia.

«Tutto bene» disse «il carico è aumentato e adesso, per arrivare sino alle Cook, c'è l'oceano, quello vero, da attraversare...»

Tre ore dopo, in mare aperto la goletta saliva e scendeva le onde, avanzando lentissima.

«Un ciclone?» mi chiede sorpreso il comandante fermando di colpo le dita sulle corde della chitarra.

«Sì, un ciclone» insisto. «Si scatenano spesso tempeste e cicloni, nel Pacifico, no?»

«Eccome si scatenano!»

«Be', se l'*Anna del Mar* incrocia in un ciclone come ce la caviamo?»

«Come sempre.»

«Come sempre, come?»

«Le situazioni difficili s'affrontano di petto, io dico, e finora i fatti m'han dato ragione. C'è un ciclone? Chi scappa ci rimette, tanto quelle bestiacce son più veloci di tutte le golette del mondo... E se c'è un rischio, è di esser presi di poppa da un ciclone o di essere sfiorati dai lati. Bisogna andarci dritti dentro.»

«Dentro?»

«Sissignore, io nel ciclone mi butto dritto come una spada. Si chiudono le vele e, con l'aiuto di Dio s'affrontano di prua onde e vento. È questione di poco, perché andando verso il centro, il peggio del ciclone (che è fatto come una ciambella, in mezzo non c'è niente) è presto passato... all'interno di quell'inferno c'è una zona calma, quasi di bonaccia completa...»

Rifletté un poco su quanto aveva detto, poi gridò: «*Mahu!*» al pilota cinese, e si rimise a toccare le corde della chitarra; non a suonare, ma solo ad accarezzarle, adagio, in scala, con quelle sue mani grosse e piene di peli neri.

Pensava ai cicloni, il comandante, e ci pensavo anch'io; con paura, vedendo le onde immense a cui andavamo incontro. Il tempo era buono, non c'era molto vento, brillava il sole, e mi dicevo: «Se questo mare è così quand'è calmo, quando si infuria cosa diventa?».

Il primo atollo, lontano, me lo indicò Natale perché non era facile distinguerlo; emergeva d'un pelo dall'oceano: una sottile linea bianca appena disegnata sul filo dell'orizzonte.

Era Palmerston, a metà strada tra le Samoa e le Cook. Riuscii a osservarlo meglio quando fummo più vicini e capii che la terra era disegnata dalla spuma dell'onda bianca, rotta sulla barriera di corallo, anello esterno a difesa della sottile striscia emergente ove a mano a mano che ci si avvicinava si scorgevano le case di un villaggio e ciuffi folti di *cocotiers*.

Natale mi narrò di Palmerston. Mi disse della sua gente, di incerta origine, non bruna come la polinesiana, non bianca come l'europea; uomini e donne quasi tutti con cappelli o biondi o rossi e gli occhi chiari. Una comunità nata, per così dire, da un naufragio, all'inizio dell'Ottocento: una nave inglese finì su quella scogliera di corallo e gli scampati, rimasti prigionieri dell'isola, senza speranza di poterne ripartire, si unirono ai pochi polinesiani e diedero vita a una comunità mista che, a quanto si dice, parla un inglese settecentesco, lingue e accento dei naufraghi di due secoli fa.

Ci lasciammo alle spalle Palmerston e continuammo ad avanzare.

Venne la notte, ritornò il giorno, il cielo da sereno si rannuvolò fino a diventare nero. Natale e il comandante non parvero preoccuparsene – infatti nel pomeriggio venti misteriosi, alti nel cielo, dispersero ogni minaccia di maltempo – e venne ancora la notte e dalla cucina di bordo uscì pane croccante e caldo. All'alba Aitutaki, una delle isole Cook, non era molto lontana. Sul ponte, alla prima luce, trovammo pesci volanti saltati dalle onde e finiti in coperta nella notte; li raccogliemmo a uno a uno prendendoli per le loro ali trasparenti (indurite dalla morte sembravano di vetro) e li ributtammo in mare: i gabbiani che ci venivano incontro da terra li afferrarono immediatamente, tuffandosi nella grande onda di poppa.

Finalmente attraccammo ad Aitutaki. E dalla stiva dell'*Anna del Mar* sbucarono, per esser scaricati a terra, una macchina da cucire Singer modello 1911, due biciclette, un letto matrimoniale con le molle, alcuni sacchi di semi, un carretto a stanghe e con le ruote di bicicletta, alcune capre della cui presenza a bordo non m'ero mai accorto, e tre passeggeri.

Mi gustavo la scena di quello sbarco, scattando qualche foto.

«Non hanno nulla, sai, sugli atolli» disse Natale vedendomi vicino. «Non hanno nulla, tutto deve venire da lontano. Pensa che l'atollo è alto solamente ottanta centimetri sul livello dell'oceano e se venisse, come venne nel 1903, una grande onda di maremoto, tutto scomparirebbe sott'acqua. E non c'è una fonte o uno stagno o un ruscello; se la pioggia non riempisse ogni tanto i pozzi, tutti morirebbero di sete.»

«Pronti laggiù?» gridò qualcuno.

«Sì!»

Il suono della chitarra s'interruppe. Il comandante stava per occuparsi di qualche manovra.

«Via!... È tardi... dobbiamo uscire dalla *pass* prima di notte.»

«Leva!»

La catena dell'àncora cominciò a salire e io, indossato un impermeabile contro l'umidità della notte, mi distesi sui sacchi di *coprah*. Ormai m'ero abituato a quell'odore.

Fra poco sarebbe stato buio, avrei visto apparire a una a una quelle stelle di un cielo che non era il mio, e avrei seguito con lo sguardo l'albero della goletta dondolare avanti e indietro a ogni onda, finché non mi sarei addormentato.

Anche se dal '56, data di quel viaggio sull'*Anna del Mar*, al '91 corrono gli anni dei grandi mutamenti (il cemento, il turismo, gli aeroporti), alcune, superstiti golette, nel Pacifico meridionale navigano ancora.

E in goletta l'oceano è ancora eguale, eternità garantita dal perennemente identico respiro delle onde.

E così anche durante il mio ultimo viaggio nel Pacifico, ancora una volta compiamo uno spostamento in goletta; stavolta però dalle Samoa non abbiamo puntato a est verso Palmerston e Aitutaki, come con la vecchia *Anna del Mar*, ma dritti al nord verso la Melanesia.

Due settimane con vento in poppa per conoscere qualche isola di questa zona del Pacifico e trovar poi la coincidenza con un piccolo aereo per le isole occidentali del gruppo papua, gli arcipelaghi meno facili da raggiungere, come la Nuova Britannia.

In attesa di imbarcarmi – con gli immancabili compagni di lavoro degli anni Settanta, Riccardo Grassetti, Jean Bodini, Massimiliano Sano – sul primo mezzo volante disponibile, ci avvicinammo agli arcipelaghi centrali della Melanesia via mare. Con una vecchia goletta ancora in servizio bordeggiamo le collane di piccole isole esterne alle Salomone, aiutati da vento favorevole e oceano calmo; apparentemente, sono isole simili in tutto e per tutto a quelle polinesiane, specie «le basse». I loro abitanti vivono di stenti commerciando la *coprah* con un reddito annuo medio, per ciascuno, non superiore ai dodici dollari.

Anche per questo, il fenomeno di tutti gli arcipelaghi dei Mari del Sud è qui più pronunciato che altrove; gli abitanti delle isole «esterne» abbandonano laguna e villaggi e vanno nei centri maggiori, dove sono attratti come falene dallo squallore rumoroso dei capoluoghi.

All'isola di Liredo approdiamo a un pontile in legno, davanti a un villaggio dominato da una grande costruzione in *niau*; la casa «degli uomini», che non molto tempo fa serviva alle prime imprese erotiche degli scapoli del paese; adesso ha solo funzione di «circolo», ove si passa il tempo probabilmente parlando delle città nelle quali si vorrebbe emigrare. A lato della casa «degli uomini» è il cimitero; anche questo è una novità. In queste isole, una volta infatti si usava mettere il defunto in una canoa che veniva poi spinta alla deriva. Ora invece i morti si sotterrano come nei «paesi bianchi».

Il capo villaggio, vecchio, con le gambe tatuate, mi racconta del tempo dei giapponesi e della guerra; una guerra ancora presente nelle carcasse di navi sulla spiaggia e di aerei nella boscaglia; (sono talmente tanti i residui di guerra sulle isole, che il ferro – per vent'anni dal '45 al '65 – ha costituito il secondo prodotto di esportazione, dopo la *coprah*).

Dei settemila giapponesi che nel '45 erano ancora sparsi in

quest'area del Pacifico, solamente millecinquecento tornarono a casa, dopo ripetuti assalti degli americani per riconquistare le isole diventate tutte importanti basi militari e porti strategici.[1] L'unico «bianco» di Liredo, nell'anno di grazia 1975 era un austriaco, proprietario di una piccola segheria; ci invita a bere una birra; gli chiediamo come vanno gli affari, e risponde che non vanno mica tanto bene:

«Le schegge,» e qui lancia una bestemmia «le schegge ci mandano in rovina. Le schegge delle grandi battaglie... Ogni albero di queste isole ne è pieno. E così la guerra continua: fra noi e gli alberi. Qui son scoppiati milioni di proiettili, grandi e piccoli. Ognuno ha lasciato il suo ricordo nei tronchi della foresta... e quando vogliamo abbatterli, le lame dentate delle seghe elettriche incontrano, nella polpa dolce del cocco o in quella compatta dell'albero, del ferro, schegge che ormai da trent'anni fanno corpo unico con la fibra vegetale. E ci spezzano di colpo la lama della sega. Una al giorno, due, tre: sono foreste d'acciaio, non di legno, queste...»

L'austriaco vive qui da cinquant'anni, di storie ne conosce tante. Si è imbarcato sulla nostra goletta, e gli ho chiesto che cosa pensa dei pirati. Perché qui, ai margini estremi del Pacifico, quasi nelle acque filippine, malesi, indonesiane, si corrono gli stessi rischi d'aggressione che ormai caratterizzano tutti i mari di Oriente.

«I pirati? beh, è una storia complicata: una volta esistevano, poi sembravano scomparsi per sempre; solo te li ricordavi quando ti capitava di vederli nelle avventure dei film e in quelle dei fumetti. Ma ora sono ricomparsi, si dice...»

A poca distanza da noi, appare e scompare tra le onde calme dell'oceano un vecchio peschereccio d'alto mare.

«Sarebbero quelli, i pirati!» borbotta l'austriaco.

«Così dicono tutti, vero?»

«Sì, tutti... Nessuno li ama i pescatori giapponesi; né quelli filippini; e tantomeno quelli coreani, i più poveri fra tutti...»

---

[1] L'ultimo superstite, nascosto nella foresta di una delle centoventinove isole dell'arcipelago di Palau, si è «arreso» all'inizio del 1972: non sapeva che la guerra era finita.

«Sono loro il nuovo terrore dei mari?»

«Certo, non tutti. Ma io credo, che buona parte di quei pescherecci siano vere e proprie navi-pirata...»

Si ripete quanto ho visto e ascoltato navigando nell'arcipelago delle Sulu e nelle Filippine; incontro di cui ho narrato in uno dei miei racconti raccolti nel volume *L'avventura e la scoperta*.[1]

Qui come laggiù, e in altre zone «povere» dell'oceano orientale, vagano pescherecci di cui scrissi: «motobarche alla ventura sull'oceano, lontane per mesi dai porti d'origine; senza prendere terra se non dopo aver imbarcato, sino al limite di galleggiamento, tanto pesce salato quanto la stiva del loro battello può contenere; un carico conservato sotto sale, perché questo genere di imbarcazioni ha raramente un impianto frigorifero; e quindi lo si vende a prezzo bassissimo, malgrado la fatica nel pescarlo sia enorme.

Sulla loro miseria e sul loro aspetto, prima ancora di fatti concreti, è nato il mito del «peschereccio-corsaro», un luogo comune come quello che vuole gli zingari, in Europa, rapitori di bambini e sempre pronti al furto o all'imbroglio; e non a caso ho sentito in molti porti chiamare *sea-gipsy*, «zingari del mare», gli uomini di quei battelli di oscura provenienza e di ancor più oscura destinazione. Di loro, a mio parere, solo un dato è certo: la condizione di assoluta miseria degli equipaggi e la durezza del loro lavoro che sembra ininterrotto giorno e notte; e non trova sosta nemmeno nei rari approdi ai porti, perché questi battelli, generalmente, non attraccano alle banchine, ma si mettono all'àncora al largo, in rada. «Per sfuggire ai controlli» si dice; ma più probabilmente per non pagare la tassa d'ormeggio, i diritti doganali di transito e per non spendere denaro a terra. Ma quale denaro?

Continuando la nostra navigazione, accostammo un giorno uno di questi pescherecci nelle acque a nord della Nuova Britannia, verso la quale puntiamo, facendo rotta sull'isoletta di Long Island.

I volti dei marinai e l'aspetto dell'imbarcazione ci lasciarono

Mondadori, Milano 1989.

interdetti; mancava la benda agli occhi del comandante o la gamba di legno al timoniere e l'immagine di maniera della nave-pirata era pronta, davanti a noi, per testimoniare la sua presenza nei mari del XX secolo. Ma non c'era da sorridere: quella gente – erano coreani – aveva raggiunto un tal punto di degradazione, dal lavoro cui era costretta, da giustificare, davvero, un suo ipotetico esser pirati.

Ci venne chiesto un poco di zucchero (avevano foglie di tè che bollivano in un'acqua salmastra, impossibile a bersi allo «stato naturale»). E se quel liquido era l'unica bevanda con cui potevano dissetarsi a bordo, l'unico cibo era lo stesso pesce che pescavano; sempre della qualità più scadente, ché il resto andava messo sotto sale per aumentare il valore del carico.

Pensammo a chi li mandava per mare in quelle condizioni; e sentimmo di odiare quel loro lontano padrone capace di sfruttare un pugno di uomini sino ai limiti della bestialità.

Quando si lesse, alle Samoa, della goletta *Tiaré*, la gente di mare del Pacifico meridionale non facevano che ripetere: «Sono stati i pescatori giapponesi». E l'identica accusa si sentì ripetere quando sparì il *Southern Cross* in Micronesia e quando il *Vailima* fu trovato alla deriva (come il *Tiaré*) tra le Figi e le Tonga.

Racconti e discussioni si accavallavano, e si incrociavano le ipotesi sul destino delle golette scomparse in oceano: «Sono state attaccate dai *sea-gipsy*, gli ultimi pirati del mondo» ripetevano le varie fonti d'informazione «locali».

«E chi se non loro?» mi diceva a Noumea il comandante di un piccolo cargo, «soltanto di loro non si sa mai dove siano, come si spostino. E solo essi sono spinti dalla fame e dalla necessità a cercare in altri battelli acqua e cibo...»

«E la radio? Perché chi è "assalito" non la usa?...» chiedo.

«Perché non ne hanno il tempo, se l'incontro è iniziato tranquillamente; infatti sono proprio le golette, sovente, ad accostare quei pescherecci per acquistare pesce salato.»

Un elemento è comune a tutti i casi di supposta «pirateria»: non ci sono mai superstiti. O le golette scompaiono per sempre (e allora potrebbe anche trattarsi di avarie, naufragi, tempeste: ma come mai non giunsero Sos dalle imbarcazioni in difficoltà, prima dell'affondamento?) o le golette vengono ritrovate alla deriva *deserte*. È questo il punto più inspiegabile delle cronache ripetute e riascoltate ogni giorno in tutti i piccoli porti del Pacifico.

Un caso può servir d'esempio per tutti quelli accaduti negli ultimi anni; il mistero del *Vailima*.

Il *Vailima* è una goletta in servizio tra le Figi e le Tonga; casualmente, un idrovolante neozelandese la sorvola in alto mare e si stupisce di vedere il battello a motori spenti, quasi fosse alla deriva; s'abbassa per veder meglio, e si accorge che il ponte è deserto, e l'intero battello sembra sia stato abbandonato. Dall'idrovolante parte subito un messaggio d'allarme e si segnala la posizione dell'incontro. Una vedetta militare raggiunge il *Vailima* in poche ore da Viti Levu. Un'altra poco dopo.

E subito si ha conferma di quanto visto dal cielo: a bordo non c'è nessuno. Cabine, ponti, stiva sono vuoti; non ci sono né bagagli, né viveri. Oltre all'equipaggio, quattro uomini, sono spariti i passeggeri: ventisei persone in tutto. C'è solo un cane che accoglie i marinai della vedetta militare figiana con un latrare disperato. Ad aumentare «l'atmosfera» i soccorritori trovano una larga e profonda padella sul fuoco della cucina, a poppa; contiene olio e resti di cibi che ancora sono caldi.

L'idrovolante, intanto, segnala nella zona ove il *Vailima* è ritrovato, numerose imbarcazioni da pesca al lavoro. Vengono tutte raggiunte dalle vedette militari, perquisite da cima a fondo; quattro sono giapponesi, due filippine, una malese, una di Taiwan. Non viene trovato, a carico di alcun battello, il minimo indizio; ma solo volti impenetrabili, come vuole la tradizione.

Abbiamo impiegato tre settimane dalle Samoa alla Melanesia bordeggiando le Salomone; ora finalmente siamo nel cuore del mondo papua; una sosta a Guadalcanal, un'altra a Lae; e finalmente il nostro gruppo si ricostituisce. Siamo pronti a iniziare una nuova serie di riprese filmate in questa zona e io, intanto, voglio vedere l'isola chiamata «Isola». Era questa la mia meta.

La storia di questo mio desiderio inizia il giorno in cui guardai un atlante in lingua inglese di queste zone, e, cadutomi l'occhio su una piccola macchia scura nell'oceano, vidi che i cartografi a quella piccola macchia scura avevano dato il nome di Long Island; un nome che in tutto il Pacifico papua, tra la Nuova Guinea e la Nuova Britannia, nei porti e lungo la costa, s'è raccorciato in Island, dimenticando l'appellativo di *Long*.

Ma a Isola non voglio approdare solo perché mi attrae il suo nome (che da sempre, lo confesso, da quando ho cominciato ad amare le carte nautiche del Pacifico mi ha incuriosito, così presuntuoso e assurdo: come si può chiamare un'isola «Isola» in un oceano punteggiato di isole?), ma voglio approdare a quella terra minuscola, soprattutto per il suo vulcano spento diventato lago interno.

Nel disegno delle carte più particolareggiate, Isola mostra tutta la sua singolarità: è una ciambella rotonda, il cui «buco» è colmo d'acqua; certo, nel Pacifico, non ci sarebbe nulla di particolare (tutti gli atolli, più o meno, hanno questa forma), se non fosse da segnalare un fatto: lo specchio liquido interno di Isola si trova almeno un centinaio di metri più in alto dell'oceano circostante, in quanto la «ciambella» di terra emersa è formata da una montagna circolare di roccia vulcanica a picco sul mare; e quelle rocce tengono chiuse, come una diga, le acque del lago. Per di più, al centro di quel lago per così dire «alpino» (salato? dolce?) spunta un isolotto di cenere rossa, ultimo resto del cono eruttivo del grande vulcano che formava un tempo l'intera isola.

«Sei sicuro... è proprio spento?» mi grida all'orecchio il compagno di volo, indicandomi il cratere.

«Sembra in eruzione» convengo.

Vapori si alzano al centro del lago e salgono al cielo a dare quella impressione. Il mio compagno di volo è Jean; è lui ad aver organizzato questo volo.

«L'isola misteriosa...» borbotta il pilota nell'interfonico.

Voliamo bassi, a gran balzi nella nuvolaglia tra la quale giocano correnti d'aria calda e fredda. I vapori contribuiscono, in effetti, a farci credere che tra qualche crepaccio il vulcano continui a fumare; ma non è vero, ovviamente; e ce ne convinceremo tornando a Isola dal mare.

Ma non è tanto facile tornare a Isola dal mare. A Lae ce lo

sconsigliano tutti, anche i piccoli armatori del porto dove cerchiamo d'affittare un'imbarcazione.

«Isola è deserta, da qualche anno» mi dice un capobarca dopo aver pazientemente ascoltato il mio inglese approssimativo, con cui ho cercato di spiegargli da dove e perché voglio dirigermi là.

«Isola è deserta, se ne sono andati tutti...» mi ripete, e aggiunge: «Molti di Isola sono qui, a Lae... altri a Biak... altri non si sa».

Sembra una vicenda eguale a quelle di sempre. La gente delle isole piccole lascia i villaggi per cercar lavoro e denaro e distrazioni nelle città delle isole grandi. Qui, però, la storia dell'esodo da Isola ha un elemento in più, ed è quello che mi ha fatto giungere fino a lei: il «culto del cargo» vi era praticato sino a pochi anni prima; e ne ho avuto conferma da chi ci ha guidati dal primo giorno del nostro arrivo nel TPNG (Territory of Papua and New Guinea); un ossuto neozelandese che si qualifica «bianco delle isole». Si chiama Philip; è alto, leggermente claudicante per chissà quale incidente o malattia.

«A Isola comandava un uomo molto amato dalla sua gente... non più di duecento o trecento persone, divise in cinque o sei villaggi.»

«Pescatori...» suggerisco.

«No, tutti agricoltori: radici di manioca, di cocco, di papaia. gente povera, molto povera. Le coste troppo alte di Isola hanno sempre impedito alle canoe di prendere con tranquillità il mare e offrire qualche possibilità di pesca.»

«Il lago interno...» suggerisco.

«Solo anguille nere, ma non da pescare. Per i papua sono tabù; fanno paura, quelle anguille; si diceva, a Isola, che avessero due corni velenosi sulla testa...»

Come al lago Vahiriahà sulle montagne di Tahiti, ricordo; lo stesso timore, reale e metafisico, e la stessa leggenda. E anche là si tratta di acque alte di un lago di montagna: un'identica componente nella paura di genti così profondamente diverse quanto possono esserlo i papua e i polinesiani.

Intanto il discorso è caduto su colui che fu il capo villaggio più importante di Isola. Un uomo per due volte già recatosi nella «terra grande», cioè in Nuova Guinea, dove aveva visto città, automobili, le grandi navi, gli aerei.

«Perché molti nelle isole, vedi, hanno più volte scorto sul filo dell'orizzonte grandi navi da carico o, altissimi, gli aerei in cielo. Ma pochi hanno visto le navi nei porti, all'attracco per lo scarico delle merci o gli aerei sulle piste commerciali... Quello spettacolo lascia stupito l'uomo del villaggio, quando ha l'occasione di trovarsi in un grande porto sull'oceano o di vedere un aeroporto.»

«Oggi un fatto del genere mi sembra comune.»

«Sì, per quasi tutti. Ma con qualche eccezione; e fra queste eccezioni è necessario includere la gente di Isola, dove i giapponesi non erano sbarcati durante la guerra. È impossibile creare una base in un'isola tutta roccia a perpendicolo sul mare e sempre nella foschia, né vi sbarcarono poi americani o australiani quando la guerra del Pacifico si concluse nel '45.»

Come poi ho visto con i miei occhi quando vi ho posto piede, a collegare Isola con le terre vicine era un servizio saltuario destinato a far scalo all'unico e precario approdo possibile, una piccola baia nebbiosa. Con quella motobarca dai servizi irregolari giunge all'isola qualche prodotto in scatola, qualche episodico missionario, qualche radiolina a transistor; non «abbastanza» da causare mutamenti nella piccola società papua di Isola che resta sempre eguale, in quell'ambiente tagliato dal mondo, dove tutto è morto come il grande vulcano annegato in piogge cadute per millenni.

«Quel che mi interessa è la storia del *cargo*» rammento a Philip, mentre ci muoviamo tra le misere capanne, osservati con passiva curiosità.

«Sì, certo: la storia di un uomo vissuto qui a cui capitò per due volte di lasciare il suo villaggio e venire in città, qui a Lae; ove vide un porto, osservò che dalle navi veniva scaricato ogni ben di Dio e sentì parlare del *cargo*. Quel *culto del cargo* di cui egli, subito, si sentì partecipe; anzi, protagonista. In effetti appena tornato al suo villaggio se ne dichiarò Profeta.»

«Predicendo l'arrivo dei beni dal mare, scaricati da navi inviate dal dio Atuna...»

«No, non dal dio Atuna... quello è nel mito polinesiano. Per i papua non c'è un dio nella fede del *cargo*; ma solo un destino. Il destino del millennio felice.»

Posso immaginare confusamente gente di Isola ascoltare il suo profeta mentre narra di casse e casse di ogni bene uscire dal ventre di navi immense ferme nel porto di Lae. Come tutti i profeti del *cargo*, avrà detto: «Bisogna pregare! Bisogna preparare lo scalo per la grande nave! Giungerà qui e ci porterà ogni bene...».

Restiamo due settimane sull'isola, percorrendola passo passo quasi tutta. A livello del mare e sin sulla cima del suo cratere spento. Una terra capace di tener sospeso un lago alto sull'oceano è soggetto che val la pena di visitare a fondo. Anche se del molo del *cargo* è rimasto assai poco; il vento, qualche mareggiata e i cinque anni ormai passati hanno causato il crollo di gran parte dei pali di legno del pontile, quel lungo, folle, commovente trampolino verso la felicità che testimonia la fede della comunità di Isola in un mutamento profondo di vita, l'arrivo dal mare del *cargo* miracoloso.

Poco lontano, dietro i resti delle capanne di quello che fu il centro del Profeta s'indovina che un incolto groviglio verde doveva essere un tempo una piantagione di papaie. Nell'abbandono si riconosce una lunga striscia tagliata al centro della vegetazione; la cosiddetta «pista» sulla quale il Profeta aveva annunciato la discesa di aerei; anch'essi carichi, come le navi, dei beni favolosi di cui tutti avrebbero beneficiato.

Saliamo al lago, filmiamo e fotografiamo le immagini desiderate. Non sembra d'osservare un paesaggio d'Oceania, ma di trovarsi di fronte a una immaginazione d'altri mondi, morti all'uomo e vivi solo per forze invisibili, nascoste tra acqua e rocce; e anche queste sembrano non naturali nel senso comune di questa parola: il colore di questo specchio d'acqua è di un plumbeo, immobile nero tagliato da cordoni ombelicali di nebbia e foschia, distesi in disegni geometrici spezzati eppur regolari; la costa attorno al grande catino immobile è di lava, una lava di ere perdute il cui trascorrere è tutto inciso, segnato, nelle screpolature aperte in un impossibile ghiacciaio di neve nera, opaca come l'acqua nel quale si specchia. Eppure, in certi punti, la roccia di lava conserva ancora il segno d'una colata tumultuosa e rovente e sembra si sia appena raffreddata. E c'è, infine, quello squilibrio di piani tra la superficie dell'oceano, lontano, e quella del lago, vicina, a dare un senso d'irreale precarietà alla visione d'insieme: quelle due super-fici d'acqua quasi confinanti, ma assurdamente distese su due livelli diversi; e il cielo stesso sembra spezzarsi là dove i due orizzonti non coincidono.

Abbiamo appena colto queste immagini e già una foschia gri-gia, fitta e umida ci avvolge. Dobbiamo in fretta scendere dalla montagna e raggiungere l'ancoraggio.

Sotto di noi, appena un centinaio di metri, l'oceano si getta con violenza sulle scogliere dell'isola detta «Isola» dove il *cargo* non giunse mai.

«Peccato,» mi dice la nostra guida «se restava una discreta visibilità, t'avrei mostrato la valle dove il Profeta venne sepolto quando morì. Sai, di solito attorno a una tomba come la sua se ne vedono altre a decine: tutti vogliono esser sepolti accanto a chi predisse la felicità, anche se questa non è mai giunta. Ma accanto alla tomba del Profeta di Isola non c'è nessuno: la gente fedele al suo culto è andata a morire altrove...»

Quando mi imbarcai sulla goletta che ci riportava a Lae – era l'ottobre del 1975 – non me ne resi conto; e me ne dispiace perché se ci avessi pensato avrei scattato una foto ricordo con il coman-dante e il suo equipaggio: era quello il mio ultimo viaggio su una puzzolente, lenta, sovraccarica goletta «dei Mari del Sud». Quan-do sarei tornato nelle isole non ne avrei trovato in servizio nemme-no una.

Ho seguito il balzo migratorio di una grande gru nera. Anzi, ho volato con lei, seduto fra le sue ali, per più di seimila miglia.

La gru azzurra è dipinta su fondo giallo nell'impennaggio dire-zionale del B747 della Lufthansa che mi riporta – luglio 1991 – verso «i Mari del Sud». Un nuovo itinerario verso nuovi approdi, dispersi lungo il suo confine incerto tra orizzonti e arcipelaghi; quello detto *the edge of paradise*; oltre i mari che toccano l'Asia del Sud-est; e formano il mondo evanescente della Micronesia.

Volo verso questo *edge of paradise* con un aereo proveniente dalla Germania perché quest'itinerario, particolarmente, toccherà alcu-ne isole del Pacifico che furono tedesche. Furono «colonie» e l'impronta di quel tempo è rimasta anche qui in superstiti e ormai cadenti cittadine, che in clima tropicale ostentano ancor alcune case e chiese di legno, dai tetti spioventi come quelli di Baviera; quasi fossero destinati anche in questo clima tropicale a resistere al peso di una nevicata improvvisa. In questo quadrante del Pacifico sono altre le «impronte» della storia coloniale particolarmente emozionanti. E dovrò cercarle e scoprirle sott'acqua.

Non so se le splendide gru azzurre raffigurate nel simbolo della Lufthansa abbiano mai migrato tra queste isole. Non so nulla d'ornitologia e sull'argomento mi è gradito poter fantasticare a piacimento. Certo è che i coloni tedeschi d'Oceania giungevano ai «loro» approdi di Micronesia e Melanesia seguendo la stessa direzione (verso oriente) del mio volo odierno; ed era la loro rotta inversa a quella (verso occidente) dei loro antagonisti francesi e inglesi. Questi puntavano ai Mari del Sud navigando di preferenza dall'Atlantico al Pacifico via Capo Horn; i tedeschi invece preferirono, un secolo più tardi, le rotte – via Capo di Buona Speranza – disegnate attraverso l'Oceano Indiano. Francesi e inglesi diedero il via all'esplorazione e poi alla conquista delle loro basi nei Mari del Sud portati dalle vele della prima marineria transoceanica, alla fine del XVII secolo; i tedeschi invece sbarcarono in Occania oltre un sccolo dopo, quando già il fumo delle navi a vapore si disegnava sull'orizzonte del Pacifico; e lasciava la sua nera traccia su quel particolare azzurro che i polinesiani chiamano *moana*; ovvero il colore dove si confonde il blu del cielo con quello del mare.

Quando nel Pacifico meridionale si installarono francesi e inglesi, questi fecero giungere alle isole, al loro seguito, una prima migrazione asiatica: dalla Cina all'India. I discendenti di quei miserabili *coolies* deportati, oggi sono non solo tanti, più degli autoctoni, quasi ovunque; ma hanno in mano le chiavi economiche di tutte le isole dove solo ieri erano schiavi: i cinesi negli arcipelaghi attorno a Tahiti, indiani e pakistani soprattutto alle Figi.

Nel quadrante opposto del Pacifico, invece, la marea umana asiatica d'importazione è giapponese: in parte della Melanesia e nelle isole della Micronesia la presenza nipponica inizia solo in questo secolo; e non è migrazione miserabile, di manodopera servile, ma di espansione – e per di più brutale – di una grande potenza: economica e militare.

Per ripercorrere alcune tappe, ho iniziato il mio nuovo itinerario dal cuore stesso del Giappone. Ad ali spiegate la gru azzurra della Lufthansa è calata nelle congestionate piste dell'aeroporto di Haneda-Tokyo; e lì sono sceso dal rassicurante, comodo ventre del B747 per affrontare il più avventuroso e molto meno comodo viaggio che m'attende per mare sulle stesse rotte della migrazione nipponica: dal Giappone alla Micronesia. Ovvero dal mondo super affollato, soffocante, frenetico di quella che è oggi una delle più grandi e congestionate città del mondo, alla vastità silenziosa dell'oceano; dallo smog pungente e irritante che soffoca con la sua cappa allo 0,063 per cento di biossido d'azoto – dieci volte di più del limite teorico di sopportazione – alle ben più sconfinata, e tanto infinitamente più pura distesa di nubi e onde che sono la cornice e il quadro del Pacifico. Che mi accoglie con un fresco, teso, vigoroso vento di nord-est.

Da fresco, il vento dell'oceano si fa di giorno in giorno in più caldo e umido – volgendo da sud-est a ovest – via via che l'Asia e la Micronesia s'avvicina.

Superato «l'abisso di Ramapo», uno dei punti più profondi del Pacifico (− 10.340 metri) ed entrato nell'area delle isole Marianne, navigo sulla stessa rotta lungo la quale mosse la flotta d'invasione del Sol Levante durante le due guerre mondiali di questo secolo. Nella prima, dal '14 al '18, riuscendo a sostituirsi – in arcipelaghi e isole – alle guarnigioni coloniali tedesche che avevano facilmente sconfitto; nella seconda, tra il '41 e il '45, attaccando l'area degli ex alleati anglo-australiani-americani e infliggendo loro una serie di clamorose umiliazioni nella travolgente avanzata del 1941.

Lungo una di quelle direttrici, scelgo d'andare da Saipan a Guam a Yap a Palau; e arrivo in *questo* quadrante dei Mari del Sud, nel cuore della Micronesia (se di «cuore» si può parlare:

dove mai batterà in un corpo frantumato in mille, microscopiche schegge verdi? isole e atolli la cui consistenza sembra inesistente, al confronto con la vastità del mare che le circonda e le separa le une dalle altre?).

Approdo a Palau. I ricordi del periodo germanico sono anche qui superstiti tetti di alcune case cadenti e in un profondo canale tagliato tra i coralli, ancora utilissimo per unire le aree settentrionali e meridionali dell'arcipelago. Altri reparti sono – come dire? – affettuosi: ingiallite fotografie «d'epoca» (ove troneggiano distinti signori con baffi a manubrio e caschi di sughero stretti e lunghi) volutamente ostentate sulla parete di alcuni alberghi gestiti ancora da famiglie che a quanto si dice sono vagamente d'origine tedesca.

I ricordi del Giappone guerriero e aggressore sono invece ovunque; e subito avanti agli occhi. Carcasse di navi emergono nelle lagune, cannoni arrugginiti da grotte artificiali e caverne naturali; e scheletri di aerei avvolti – ma non nascosti – dalla vegetazione. Immagini di una potenza che dopo esser stata vittoriosa, fu totalmente distrutta nel giro di pochi mesi, dal '44 al '45.

A specchio di quelle immagini, la realtà attuale è esattamente l'opposto. È di nuovo quella di una potenza vincitrice. Tutto quanto si muove a terra – qui, come in ogni isola – è giapponese. Lo sono gran parte delle barche da pesca e da diporto (tutte a motore, non si vede una vela); lo sono le insegne dei due o tre empori che non solo inalberano le famose insegne commerciali che ormai fan parte del paesaggio urbano del mondo intero (e qui *sono le sole*); ma basta oltrepassare le loro porte, così come quelle degli edifici più moderni e dei migliori alberghi, per rendersi conto di come, al loro interno, dal cacciavite al trattore, dagli stuzzicadenti al menù, dai cartellini con i prezzi in yen ai gruppi elettrogeni, dagli impianti stereofonici alle antenne paraboliche e ai frigoriferi dai cento scomparti, via via attraverso mille prodotti – dai più essenziali ai più inutili – *tutto è giapponese.*

Sto cercando una spina elettrica a tre punte che si raccordi con la mia a due, e mi permetta di farmi la barba. Accanto a me un altro viso pallido sta acquistando le bacchette di legno indispensabili a ogni tavolo ove si consumino piatti della cucina locale... «Ormai qui, in casa e nei ristoranti si mangia solo alla giapponese» mi dice sconsolato il suddetto viso pallido; e aggiunge, con un tono che rivela quanto ci tenga alla precisazione: «Sono neozelandese...».

Ci ritroviamo dopo dieci minuti alla cassa e lui con la testa mi indica un ordinato gruppo di turisti dagli occhi a mandorla intento all'acquisto di cartoline postali e di altre bacchette da tavolo: «Ne consumano centinaia di milioni ogni settimana, rifiutano quelle di plastica... un lodevole attaccamento alla tradizione; come quella – altrettanto lodevole, ovviamente – per l'ecologia. A onor della quale non tagliano un solo albero delle loro pregiate foreste, ma in compenso pelano tutto il manto verde dell'Indonesia: con la loro moneta forte, da quel paese dalla moneta debole, acquistano il diritto a radere al suolo tutte le sue foreste tropicali, per farne bastoncini da tavola. Ne consumano circa cento milioni al giorno. Ovvero dieci ettari di selva...».

Mentre lui conclude mormorando «razza di bastardi» fra i denti, vorrei osservare che noi occidentali – per fedeltà ad altra, ben diversa ma egualmente radicata tradizione – stiamo «pelando» grandi spazi d'Amazzonia e d'Africa equatoriale per garantirci il nostro, sacrosanto fabbisogno quotidiano di carta igienica; purtroppo, però, non mi vengono prontamente alla lingua – in inglese! – adeguate parole per la risposta; e debbo tacere. Ancora una volta pentendomi per non aver seguito alla lettera remoti consigli materni, quando (in evidente polemica con la scuola del tempo, ufficialmente filo-germanica) mi ripeteva: «Impara l'inglese, se non vuoi trovarti, un giorno, in difficoltà...». In questo momento, in uno sperduto supermarket di Palau – Micronesia – ho l'ennesima prova della saggezza di quel consiglio (come diamine si dice in inglese «carta igienica»? e come si traduce l'aggettivo «pelato» riferendolo a una foresta?).

Ho divagato, e debbo farlo ancora; ma pertinentemente, spero. Ricordando come in quei lontani anni – mi riferisco a quelli dal '41 al '45 – nelle nebbie di una Val Padana, sottoposta ogni giorno allo spavento di bombe che cadevano dal cielo e di tedeschi che rastrellavano scuole e case, si ascoltava con spasmodica attenzione Radio Londra.

Certamente era a quel tempo che mi sentivo ripetere con crescente insistenza «perché non studi l'inglese?»; e certamente era in quel tempo, in quelle stagioni di guerra in cui si ascoltano ore e ore di trasmissioni, cronache, bollettini di combattimenti, battaglie, vittorie che ascoltai per la prima volta i nomi esotici di Yap, Saipan, Truk, le Caroline, e Ponape, e Palau; gli stessi delle isole ove ora mi trovo.

Pochi anni dopo, appena finita la guerra (e noi ci si era stabiliti a Roma), cominciò la mia passione per i film documentari. Andavo ogni giovedì pomeriggio in una saletta dell'Usis – sorta di «Centro Propaganda» dell'Ambasciata Usa – dove si proiettava ogni genere di cortometraggio americano. In particolare quelli realizzati quando noi, in Europa, non avevamo potuto vederli; come la già famosa serie di Frank Capra, *Perché combattiamo*; e il piccolo capolavoro intitolato *Memphis Bell* del quale ora si fa un gran parlare. E tanti altri filmati in quello che era stato il teatro delle operazioni nel Pacifico meridionale.

Cinquant'anni dopo mentre sorvolo le isolette del gruppo di Palau e le immagini viste sullo schermo dell'Usis mi tornano nitide alla memoria: piccole isole verdi con navi alla fonda, i proiettili traccianti degli aerei in attacco, linee rette, fosforescenti dal cielo alla terra visti dal *cockpit* di un «Corsair» americano, la laguna azzurra macchiata d'esplosioni, uno «Zero» giapponese, colpito, che s'abbassa sul mare, lo impatta e cala nel bassofondo.

È lo stesso che ora osservo, sott'acqua, praticamente ancora intatto? Non lo posso certo dire, tutto questo mare è un cimitero di aerei e di navi. Di varie guerre, di diverse bandiere.

Palau era stata una colonia tedesca. La perla del Kaiser nei Mari del Sud; principale base navale germanica, durante il primo conflitto mondiale. Quando vinsero i giapponesi la Società delle Nazioni affidò a loro tutta la Micronesia tolta alla Germania sconfitta.

Per ventisei anni essi ne furono amministratori perfetti. Me lo dice uno dei rari testimoni diretti, un gesuita dalla pelle nera, occhiali spessi, dietro i quali si muovono occhi giovanissimi; eppure tanto giovane non è, Padre Felix Yaoch, se lo si può qualificare, appunto, «testimone oculare» degli avvenimenti succedutisi durante la dominazione nipponica; e lo è da uomo giusto, imparziale. Infatti non è certo tenero verso i giapponesi; tuttavia sa distinguere.

Con parole ancora accentate da dolore e rabbia mi indica la foto di quattro Padri – spagnoli e portoghesi; neutrali, dunque – trucidati dai nipponici nel '44, poco prima della loro sconfitta.

«Eppure,» mi dice «per vent'anni ci avevano amministrato con serietà, con ben maggior rispetto di quanto da queste parti non avessero dimostrato – prima e poi – neozelandesi, australiani e inglesi. Tutto è cambiato con la guerra. Inutile osservare che questo è ovvio, violenza chiama violenza; ma qui – negli ultimi mesi d'occupazione – è stato un vero inferno. Centinaia d'azioni aeree americane al giorno, e la rabbia cieca di un contingente ancora poderosamente armato, e non rassegnato al destino di una sconfitta. In quello stato d'animo, con quella furia in corpo, soldataglia e ufficiali hanno commesso crimini orrendi: alcuni praticarono il cannibalismo su prigionieri di guerra, tutti sparavano agli aviatori americani che riuscivano a saltar con il paracadute da aerei in fiamme; la polizia militare crocefisse e poi uccise a colpi di baionetta due marines sorpresi mentre tentavano di fuggire dal campo ove erano racchiusi e bestialmente trattati i prigionieri di guerra. Infine trucidarono anche i miei fratelli gesuiti, che non erano in guerra con nessuno, è ovvio, ma anzi si prodigavano a curare i feriti, qualunque divisa essi indossassero; e soccorrevano le donne e i bambini di Palau per quasi due anni costretti a vivere come bestie nelle caverne che si aprono nei fianchi delle montagne più alte dell'arcipelago.»

«In quelle caverne alcuni reparti giapponesi hanno continuato la guerra per conto loro per oltre un anno dopo la resa del loro imperatore...» mi dice un australiano dall'aria triste che mi trovo accanto al bar del *Pacific Resort* di Koror, capitale della (futura) Repubblica di Palau.

Non ho ben capito come abbia iniziato a chiacchierare con me, probabilmente ha dato il via ai suoi borbottii così come lo avrebbe fatto con chiunque gli si fosse seduto accanto; è già un miracolo se alla seconda battuta non mi ha offerto il suo biglietto da visita, chiedendo il mio in cambio; stupito, poi, nel rendersi conto che non l'avevo pronto, in tasca.

Questa è l'abitudine, qui (regola sociale degli americani e degli altri occidentali di lingua ed educazione sociale inglese, assimilata come costume, dai giapponesi; che del biglietto-da-visita-mania, hanno fatto una liturgia; e del suo scambio immediato con qualsiasi interlocutore una regola inderogabile; come gli americani, appunto).

Americani e giapponesi. Di loro parla, borbotta, bestemmia il mio triste vicino di tavolo al bar dell'albergo; si definisce «professore d'economia dell'Università di Brisbane» e si affretta a precisare d'esser qui, in lunga vacanza, per godere del suo anno sabbatico. A prima vista potrebbe anche essere uno steward della Qantas (la compagnia aerea australiana) in vacanza o un esportatore di carne di canguro o chissà chi; la qualifica non ha grande importanza, dato che quanto mi dice (cercando di farmi ammettere che sono d'accordo con lui) è opinione diffusa fra non pochi «bianchi» in quest'area condannati ad assistere impotenti alla perdita progressiva di potere e d'influenza, mentre cresce quella dei figli del Sol Levante che solo ieri avevano sconfitto.

«A tua opinione» mi chiede sottovoce «quanto sono stupidi gli americani?»

Sorride al mio imbarazzante silenzio; ma è una smorfia, quel sorriso, che non muta minimamente l'espressione lugubre del suo volto.

«Beh, se non ne hai misura,» e giù una manata sulla mia spalla «ti aiuto a tirare le somme.»

Si guarda ancora intorno (ci saranno venti americani e altrettanti giapponesi ai tavolini vicino a noi) e conseguentemente abbassa ancor più la voce: «Hanno fatto la guerra a Saddam Hussein, l'hanno vinta... e poi? E poi hanno lasciato quel satrapo orientale, quell'assassino, al potere; con la sua cricca, le sue armi nascoste. E così hanno ripetuto l'errore del '45, quando misero a terra l'impero giapponese con una vittoria tanto netta da ottenere dai loro orgogliosi nemici la resa senza condizioni; e poi? e poi ecco il Giappone che dopo pochi decenni non solo si riconquista l'Asia, ma si compera pezzo a pezzo gli Stati Uniti. E fra poco toccherà anche a voi in Europa...».

Cerco di fermare il torrente di parole indicandogli col dito il bicchiere Bodweiser che stringe in mano. «La sua birra diventa calda» osservo, ma lui non mi ascolta e continua, quasi senza perder fiato.

«Sono stupidi, e la storia non perdona agli stupidi. Tu sei italiano, vero? vieni da Roma?»

Confermo annuendo tacitamente, e lui giù un'altra risata (sempre triste, è ovvio).

«Roma, eh? Te lo immagini, tu, se i tuoi antenati dopo tre secoli di guerra con Cartagine, quando finalmente riescono a vincere il loro implacabile nemico, anziché distruggere la loro capitale e cospargerne le rovine di sale rimettono sul trono quel tal Annibale, che, se non sbaglio, era giunto sino alle porte di Roma, e gli dicono: "Beh, ora fai il bravo, mi raccomando". E Cartagine, vent'anni dopo, non solo è di nuovo padrona dei suoi mercati di Spagna, di Sicilia, di Sardegna, ma ha aperto una dozzina di uffici commerciali nell'Urbe, e sta trattando con i Cesari per l'acquisto del Colosseo?»

È un australiano che conosce bene la storia del Mediterraneo, questo signore, dico tra me cancellando la mia prima impressione (certo non è né uno steward della Qantas né un mercante di canguri se mi parla – in Micronesia! – delle basi commerciali cartaginesi in Sardegna). Intanto lui beve, finalmente, la sua birra, e io ne approfitto: lo saluto per andar a cena.

«No, caro amico» mi fa, prendendomi per un braccio, «fermati ancora un momento... e supponi, con me una radiosa ipotesi e chiediti: se l'America avesse fatto con Saddam e l'Iraq quel che Roma ha fatto con Annibale e Cartagine non ci sarebbero assai meno angosce in Medio Oriente, ora? Sarebbe ancora necessario, oggi, minacciare un nuovo "inevitabile" conflitto?»

«Beh, il problema è complesso» tento di obiettare. Ma è impossibile interromperlo, ora è arrivato al punto voluto, non tenta nemmeno di sorridere, anzi alza anche un po' la voce, malgrado gli odiati giapponesi siano alle sue spalle.

«Dopo Hiroshima gli americani dovevano annientare il Giappone, spartirne le spoglie: ogni sua isola doveva esser affidata a un *Daimo*, come al tempo del loro medioevo. Con una novità: ovunque una commissione alleata avrebbe dovuto controllare che tutto andasse come la loro sconfitta totale richiedeva: tutti i giapponesi a casa, buoni, costretti a occuparsi solo di agricoltura e pesca. Invece... [gran segno circolare] eccoli qua i nuovi padroni del Pacifico. Dilagano d'isola in isola costruiscono hotel, vendono automobili, barche, radio, motori, investono in ogni campo. Ogni giorno ce ne sono di più: in pianta stabile e di passaggio. Turisti, a sciami.

«Tu conosci bene, immagino, l'abitudine dei turisti giapponesi, quelli che si incontrano in tanti aeroporti, hall di alberghi, davanti alla Tour Eiffel, in Piazza della Signoria o in cima all'Empire State Building: si muovono "in gruppo", stretti stretti, seguendo ciecamente il capofila che inalbera una banderuola o uno stendardo. Beh, se deciderai d'ammirare le bellezze subacquee della Micronesia, avrai una sorpresa...»

Anche nel paradiso subacqueo degli atolli e dei *reef* corallini dei Mari del Sud – secondo il mio ossessivo interlocutore australiano – i *tourist-divers* giapponesi in queste acque «così attraenti» giungono a sciami; e s'immergono seguendo un istruttore-guida, il quale in una mano stringe una lampada con la quale illumina questo o quel corallo; nell'altra ha ben stretta un'asticciola con bandierina di plastica, in genere bianca e gialla, ma a segni diversi. I bravi sub giapponesi lo seguono in fila indiana, senza deviare di un metro. Un motivo ben preciso spiega la «diversità» di quelle bandiere subacquee; lo capisco quando mi immergo in due dei più frequentati *reef* dell'arcipelago delle Palau, uno detto *Blue Corner*, l'altro *Blue Hole*. Debbono la loro fama, il primo alla presenza di branchi di pesci predatori – soprattutto barracuda e squali a caccia di piccoli pesci d'ogni specie che qui pascolano in nubi fittissime, argentee; nutriti da correnti cariche di plancton; al contempo essi stessi nutrimento per gli affamati aggressori che sfrecciano dal largo sino a sfiorare il bassofondo. E poiché questo luogo è protetto da una vera e propria muraglia di massi corrallini e madreporici, i turisti-sub come fossero sulla balconata di un grande teatro, assistono tranquilli, al *Blue Corner*, a quanto l'oceano offre come emozionante spettacolo di vita e di morte.

La fama del *Blue Hole* è invece dovuta al gioco di luci, veramente magico, che all'interno del *reef* si crea per riflessi, l'un nell'altro evanescenti che illuminano una caverna vasta come navata di cattedrale gotica. Nella sua volta si aprono due grandi squarci, verso il cielo: di lì penetrano – a fasci dorati – i raggi del sole, quelli che producono, appunto, quel gioco di luci e ombre, attrattiva senza paragoni per una immersione in queste acque.

Le due particolarità del *Blue Hole* e del *Blue Corner* sono, in effetti, così affascinanti da spiegare come qui convergano tanti visitatori (assai di più di quanti ne possa contare – nei giorni più fortunati – la visita alla grotta azzurra di Capri!); poiché sott'acqua tutti i sub si assomigliano e un gruppo potrebbe confondersi con un altro, ecco perché le previdenti agenzie di turismo giapponesi hanno dotato ogni sub-capofila di asta e bandierina diversa da quella di un altro sub-capofila. Encomiabile idea che suscita in chi – non giapponese – assiste a queste «visite guidate» irrefrenabile ilarità; la quale è fonte di problemi: infatti a rider troppo sott'acqua, si può anche affogare, o correrne il rischio.

Forse sono stato involontariamente contagiato dalla nippofobia del mio logorroico interlocutore australiano, anche se dopo la prima sera passata ad ascoltarlo sono riuscito a evitare con cura altri incontri e altri sfoghi. Ma ho ripensato a lui e alle ondate d'invasione giapponesi – militari prima, commerciali poi – quando mi sono immerso in un altro luogo famoso della Micronesia: nel *jelly-fish lagoon* (la «laguna delle meduse») a Rock Island. È un'isoletta vulcanica dell'arcipelago delle Palau il cui cratere, al tempo di primordiali assestamenti geologici, s'è riempito d'acqua di mare, creando un piccolo lago salato; un *lagoon*, appunto. Microcosmo liquido che offre la possibilità di osservare un fenomeno unico al mondo: milioni di minuscole e gialle meduse del genere *Mastigias* popolano queste acque salse chiuse dall'anello di roccia lavica del defunto vulcano; sul quale cresce, fittissima, la foresta pluviale tipica delle isole alte equatoriali del Pacifico. A portarmi in capo al mondo per osservare questo spettacolo era stato non certo la nippofobia – alla quale torno fra breve – ma la mia curiosità nei confronti di ogni fenomeno relativo al mare; essendo *questo* unico al mondo e non da molto tempo conosciuto, avevo iscritto un'immersione a Rock Island – in Micronesia – nella lista dei miei desideri; ovvero delle esperienze «assolutamente da vivere».

E l'esperienza non mi ha certo deluso.

Infatti, è emozionante nuotare in uno specchio d'acqua ove da tempo non calcolabile una sterminata colonia di «particolari» esseri viventi riesce a sopravvivere benché sia completamente isolata dal suo naturale habitat, l'oceano. A renderla indimenticabile, quest'immersione, è innanzitutto la sensazione di trovarti in una calda e minuscola bolla d'acqua al centro dello sterminato Pacifico; senti le sue acque spumeggianti, spesso irate, gonfie per tempeste e correnti tutt'intorno; ma sai bene che esse sono «chiuse fuori», al di là della invalicabile barriera circolare di rocce che chiude la laguna del cratere spento. Un isolamento, questo della bolla d'acqua all'interno di Rock Island, non da intendersi, però, in senso assoluto, immaginando le rocce vulcaniche dell'isola come un contenitore impermeabile; gli studiosi hanno spiegato in qual misura un certo flusso di correnti salse raggiunga e si mescoli con quelle interne; le «nutre», per così dire, in quantità sufficiente da rendere possibile la sopravvivenza della «colonia» delle meduse.

Sono fessure sotterranee a rifornire la laguna con costante ricambio del mare aperto; per questo le sue acque sono sempre vive.

Come lo prova, appunto, la vivace presenza di quel milione e seicentomila *jelly-fish* (calcolo approssimativo, che si deve ai locali idrobiologi) in perenne movimento sul fondo (di notte) e in superficie (di giorno) in acque sempre fresche e rigenerate.

Muovendosi, le meduse ricavano di che nutrirsi.

Raccolgono il loro «cibo» nottetempo, traendolo dalla simbiosi con alghe distese come prateria sul fondo della laguna; da loro assorbono il nitrogeno.

Poi, di giorno, ricevono altra energia vitale dal sole. La sterminata, gelatinosa marea vivente delle *jelly-fish*, infatti, non appena si fa luce sale alla superficie e migra con lenta fluttazione da un capo all'altro del suo microsistema, cercando di muoversi il più vicino possibile alla superficie; necessitano, infatti, di molte ore di calore per metabolizzare quanto hanno nottetempo assorbito dalle alghe.

Per raggiungere la laguna e assistere a questo spettacolo ho dovuto scalare la ripida, scivolosa costa dell'isola, seguendo un sentiero individuabile a fatica nell'intrico della foresta; poi sono sceso lungo il versante opposto, sino alle immobili acque che Rock Island gelosamente ha chiuso e protegge.

Dopo essermi tuffato, mi sono allontanato dalla riva deciso a incontrare la migrazione delle *jelly-fish*. Non mi hanno deluso.

Circondato dalla loro palpitante presenza attraverso a nuoto nubi formate dai trasparenti esseri che la popolano; mi sfiorano, mi toccano, ma non causano alcuna fastidiosa reazione alla pelle, come invece accade quando per disgrazia si ha contatto, in mare, con una loro velenosa «sorella»; queste meduse, fortunatamente, sono innocue. Non hanno – come altre – fluttuanti e pungenti appendici, né lunghe code irte, a migliaia, di minuscoli pungiglioni carichi di sostanze tossiche (e per restare in argomento, ma per citare un caso opposto, vorrei ricordare come, là ove le acque del Pacifico toccano l'Australia, sia *mortale* la puntura della minuscola e trasparente *Chironex flecherii*, medusa che concede – in chi colpisce – non più di due minuti di vita).

Le *jelly-fish* di Rock Island sono pacifiche, amabili; e questa particolarità, questa differenza tra loro e le altre consorelle (tutte – a vario livello – velenose) gli studiosi la sanno perfettamente spiegare. Nella laguna vulcanica di Rock Island – ci ricordano gli scienziati – le *jelly-fish* sono isolate dal resto del mondo marino. Sono sole, nessun tipo di pericolo, di aggressione, le minaccia; e così, nel trascorrere di milioni di anni e migliaia e migliaia di generazioni, esse hanno obbedito alle ineluttabili regole dell'evoluzione; e lentamente i loro sistemi offensivi-difensivi si sono atrofizzati, sono scomparsi. A cosa sarebbero serviti in un piccolo universo senza pericoli?

Interrogativo, questo, che mi permette di tornare al punto iniziale; al poco sopra ricordato sentimento antigiapponese diffuso come germe contagioso in tutto questo settore del Pacifico; a quella nippofobia alla quale debbo ancora una volta riferirmi, pur se solo per poche righe. Per confessare come la visione di quella moltitudine gialla di meduse in migrazione così continua e regolare da apparire implacabile; e quel vedermi venir incontro – in numero sterminato – tante infinite entità viventi (minuscole ma capaci per il loro numero, appunto, di angosciare, suggerendo paure di possibili soffocamenti) abbia evocato in me un involontario paragone con l'espansione giapponese in quest'area oceanica.

Ove i nipponici fecero da padroni tra la prima e la seconda guerra mondiale; ne furono poi ricacciati, ma ora vi tornano, vincitori della «madre di tutte le battaglie», quella commerciale. L'immaginarli come una massa avanzante di entità vive, inarrestabili, insomma il paragonare la loro migrazione in Micronesia come quella delle *jelly-fish* a Rock Island è una fin troppo facile figurazione; ed è paragone, oltretutto, anche irritante perché razzista, forse, ma di certo banale. Purtuttavia esso è abbastanza convincente (forse proprio perché banale) da finir con l'essere difficilmente rifiutabile. Sicché, qui lo confesso, quel confronto ha finito con il convincermi, se non altro per scherzarci sopra e per notare che calza bene anche per un altro motivo. L'onda gialla delle meduse avanzanti e l'onda umana giapponese dilagante in Micronesia hanno infatti in comune – oltre a quantità e colore – anche il fatto di aver perso – col tempo – ogni loro «equipaggiamento aggressivo»; di essersi mutate in «individui» pacifici (se mai posso permettermi di definire «individui» le meduse). Insomma, sono uno sterminato esercito, un'armata dilagante, sì; ma inerme. Non è anche in questo raffigurabile il simbolo dell'espansione giapponese, prima armata, ma ora pacifica e solo commerciale?

Per tornare al tempo paragonabile a quello durante il quale le meduse della laguna vulcanica avevano potenti e temibili pungiglioni – ovvero a quando i giapponesi si espandevano in tutte le direzioni con le loro vincenti forze armate navali e aeree ancor più che terrestri – ho lasciato l'arcipelago di Palau.

Passando da Guam sono giunto al grande atollo di Truk; per vivere qui l'esperienza d'immergermi là ove giace la più famosa «flotta fantasma» di tutti i mari.

Potrò così evocare il momento in cui il susseguirsi di vittorie e di conquiste giapponesi nel Pacifico subì un violento colpo d'arresto. Drammatico e sanguinoso; dal quale l'armata del Sol Levante, nei Mari del Sud, non si sarebbe mai più ripresa.

Ebbe un nome, quel momento, nato dalla mania degli americani di battezzare tutte le loro operazioni militari con un titolo da film western. Recentemente abbiamo seguito le vicende del *Desert Storm* in Iraq; nel febbraio del '44 si mise in moto, si sviluppò e vittoriosa-mente si concluse – in Micronesia – la cosiddetta *Operation Hailstone* ove la parola *hailstone* evoca quella «grandine» di fuoco che cadde dal cielo – nel '44 – sull'atollo più fortificato dei giapponesi in tutti i Mari del Sud da loro occupati: Truk, appunto.

La portò, quella grandine, una forza d'attacco Usa forte di sei corazzate, dieci incrociatori, nove portaerei e trenta torpediniere di scorta che mise in fuga, e per sempre, la superstite flotta da battaglia giapponese in Micronesia. E subito dopo colò a picco, nella baia di Truk, sessanta navi e distrusse quasi trecento aerei.

Quasi fosse stata fotografata, o incisa in materia capace di conservare nel tempo un momento della storia, il riverbero di quella battaglia continua ad abbagliare.

Infatti, se ci si immerge nelle acque di Truk, dell'«operazione-grandine» se ne può rivivere la violenza osservando resti di navi affondate che, in certa misura, si conservano – là, sul fondo – come se eventi di quasi cinquant'anni fa fossero appena accaduti.

Per questo a Truk ho vissuto un'avventura sotto il pelo delle onde particolare ed emozionante come poche altre; e tale da suggerirmi di riferirne qui in forma di diario; nella successione di esperienze accumulate con immersioni ripetute giorno dopo giorno. Dal momento del mio approdo a Truk sino alla partenza.

Mentre – io che racconto e voi che mi leggete – sbarchiamo a Truk (ribattezzata Chuuk dal neo-governo indipendente di quella che si è autodefinita Federazione degli Stati di Micronesia), compiamo insieme un breve passo indietro. Riandiamo al tempo della prima guerra mondiale.

Sconfitta nel 1914 la flotta e la guarnigione tedesca nelle isole micronesiane, i giapponesi si installano anche nell'atollo di Truk come nuovi dominatori. Stringono un patto segreto con gli inglesi («noi vi cediamo le colonie germaniche a sud dell'equatore, voi ci aiutate a farci attribuire dalle altre potenze alleate quelle a nord dell'equatore»); accordo che diviene definitivo con la Conferenza di Versailles del '22. Da quell'anno in poi queste isole (e in particolare Truk), che per la Germania avevano un minimo valore militare, per il Giappone diventano una catena difensiva-offensiva di enorme importanza; uno scudo, nei Mari del Sud, a difesa del fianco sud-orientale della madre patria; una protezione da eventuali attacchi provenienti dal Pacifico dell'Est. Ma anche base di partenza per l'eventuale spinta d'espansione, in quella stessa area del Pacifico, ai danni degli Stati Uniti e dell'Australia.

E così, malgrado «il mandato» della Conferenza del '22 vietasse ai giapponesi ogni installazione militare nelle isole e negli atolli loro affidati, l'Imperial Esercito, e la Marina e l'Aviazione del Tenno – l'Imperatore – chiudono le isole a ogni contatto e le fortificano al punto da far definire una di esse, Truk, la «Gibilterra dei Mari del Sud». Isola destinata a divenir famosa anche per un altro motivo.

Al Museo dello Spazio e dell'Aviazione dello Smithsonian Institute di Washington, assieme agli aerei più famosi dell'età d'oro dei raids intercontinentali – da quello di Lindbergh, ai modelli delle squadriglie di Balbo – è esposto un monoplano rosso, ad ala alta; accanto al quale è la foto del suo pilota, giovane e sorridente: la miliardaria americana Amelia Erhardt. Con quell'aereo lei divenne un eroe popolare per alcuni record attraverso il Pacifico. Con un altro aereo – un bimotore *Electra*, interamente metallico – Amelia progettò e condusse quasi a termine nel '38 il giro del mondo più rapido fino ad allora mai tentato. Non lo concluse perché durante il suo penultimo balzo, la traversata del Pacifico, Amelia, il suo aereo e il copilota scomparvero. Non giunsero mai a destinazione.

In quella tappa, la rotta dell'*Electra* tagliava al traverso l'immensità occidentale dei Mari del Sud; là ove atolli e isole della Micronesia sono granelli di polvere sparsi in una vuota vastità ancor oggi tale da impressionare chi la sorvola, anche se imbarcato su un potente jet.

In quello spazio tra cielo e oceano, la Erhardt svanì nel nulla.

Ci fu, allora, chi offrì – senza alcuna prova – una particolare interpretazione dell'evento che non aveva mancato di commuovere l'opinione pubblica mondiale: altro che eroina, quell'Amelia: era una spia! E che spia! Il suo aereo – sosteneva quella voce – era equipaggiato con macchine da ripresa e fotografiche d'alta precisione; la mascheratura del raid sportivo, in realtà copriva una delicata missione militare. Nessuno era riuscito a violare il segreto dei giapponesi di Palau, Guam e Truk: lo avrebbe compiuto, quell'atto di coraggio, la patriota Amelia; avrebbe sorvolato le basi militari riportandone immagini rivelatrici e preziose.

Piano ingegnoso, scoperto però dai giapponesi, che abbatterono l'intruso apparso tra le nubi nel cielo di Truk uccidendo la coraggiosa aviatrice; o catturandola, come molti sperarono sino al 1945 quando il Giappone sconfitto restituì all'America i suoi prigionieri. Ma non l'aviatrice.

Né si saprà mai con certezza se il bimotore di Amelia Erhardt sorvolò il guarnitissimo atollo. Sappiamo invece che su Truk volò, il 4 febbraio 1944, un supercarmato ed equipaggiato monomotore della *U.S. Air Force*, un *Marine* PB4Y. Volava a 20.000 piedi d'altezza e sfuggendo alla reazione giapponese, riportò all'ammiraglio Nimitz la prima foto della «Gibilterra dei Mari del Sud».

Immagine rivelatrice di una potenza marina ancora pronta a dar del filo da torcere agli americani, anche se dopo le sconfitte del '41 e del '42, essi erano già – nel '44 – in piena controffensiva; potevano però esser colpiti sui fianchi da quella flotta giapponese – e dalla sua aviazione – pronte a intervenire sulle forze Usa non appena il generale MacArthur avesse tentato – come infatti tentò, riuscendoci – di sbarcare alle Filippine e liberarle dai giapponesi.

Venne decisa, quindi, un'azione congiunta aeronavale.

Il 10 febbraio '44 mossero verso Truk tre *Task-force* americane, con le relative navi da battaglia, incrociatori, e navi scorta e da rifornimento. Entro il loro scudo navigavano «veterane del Pacifico», le portaerei *Enterprise*, *Yorktown*, *Essex*, *Intrepid* e *Bunker Hill*; più altre quattro di recente costruzione.

Dai loro ponti di volo si alzarono, prima dell'alba, settantadue «gatti dell'inferno», gli *Hellcats*, i famosi cacciabombardieri F6F. Sorpresero i giapponesi e ne misero fuori uso tutta la forza aerea, distruggendola in gran parte a terra, e abbattendo quella che – disperatamente, e in ritardo – s'era alzata in volo.

Subito dopo ebbe inizio l'operazione «Pioggia-di-grandine»: bombardieri, cacciabombardieri, aerosiluranti, in ondate successive, per due giorni, riuscirono non solo a demolire ogni fortificazione, le centrali operative e di comunicazione, ma tutta la flotta all'àncora tra le isole che emergono all'interno del grande atollo.

Quelle quarantott'ore segnavano l'inizio di una nuova tecnica di battaglia nel quadro generale delle operazioni del Pacifico durante la seconda guerra mondiale: gli americani avevano compreso a quale costo di vite umane e di mezzi essi andavano incontro tentando sbarchi nelle isole-roccaforti dov'erano annidati i loro nemici. E adottarono la diversa tattica dell'*Operation Hailstone*: là ove era possibile, occorreva distruggere ogni potenziale offensivo e difensivo giapponese, con azioni combinate dal mare e dal cielo. Una volta resa inservibile, «quella base» non valeva il costo di una sanguinosa operazione anfibia di sbarco e di conquista.

E così accadde per Truk: completamente distrutta, non venne occupata se non dopo la sua resa e la vittoria sul Giappone.

Ma dall'operazione «Pioggia-di-grandine» doveva nascere un'altra ispirazione... Tattica anche questa; ma di pace, non di guerra. A pochi anni dalla fine del conflitto – quando alcuni *divers* della Marina Usa narrarono dello spettacolo assieme macabro e grandioso, pauroso ma affascinante di quei fantasmi di navi poggiate nel fondo, squarciate dalle bombe e dai siluri ma in complesso ancora intere, con il loro carico di morti e di merci e di esseri – gli amministratori dell'isola proibirono la demolizione delle navi affondate. Con successivo atto legislativo si stabilì che tutte le acque interne di Truk erano «un parco storico» intoccabile; i relitti di quelle navi e degli aerei – e i loro carichi, equipaggiamenti e resti – erano «un patrimonio» prezioso per conoscere, in futuro, com'era formata e cosa trasportava una flotta militare degli anni Quaranta. E così oggi la laguna di Truk è meta di studiosi, di fotografi, di operatori cinematografici e televisivi. Sotto il pelo delle sue onde si vuole capire, scoprire, conoscere la realtà di quella «flotta fantasma» passata dalla vita alla morte in poche ore; come era nel 1944, essa è visibile adesso. Uno dei «musei del mare» più straordinari del nostro pianeta.

Nelle sale di questo museo, ovvero tra le ombre della «flotta fantasma» di Truk, mi sono immerso per una settimana raggiungendo sul fondo grandi e piccoli relitti.

Per dire di loro e di cosa offrono come «patrimoni d'immagini ed emozioni» a ogni esploratore subacqueo che scende sul fondo a percorrerne i ponti e a visitarne le stive, ne riferisco trasferendo qui il nudo diario che ho redatto tra una immersione e l'altra.

LA SECONDA ESPLOSIONE DELLA *YAMAGIRI MARU*

Lunedì mattina, 29 luglio 1991

Ci siamo mossi dall'ancoraggio di Moen – la cittadina capitale di Truk – alle 7.00. Dopo un'ora siamo sulla verticale del relitto di questa grande nave passeggeri di 6432 tonnellate, usata come trasporto munizioni dalla Marina imperiale giapponese. Ancorata a nord-est di Fefan, era pronta a trasbordare proiettili di grosso calibro alle navi da battaglia all'àncora accanto a lei. Colpita da siluro, è affondata senza esplodere.

Ci immergiamo col mio compagno di lavoro in questa avventura, Andrea. Siamo gli ultimi del gruppo a saltar in acqua perché l'umido in superficie grava come cappa che penetra ovunque; anche all'interno delle attrezzature, tanto da aver bloccato i comandi elettronici della telecamera. Faremo solo fotografie, oggi.

Alle 9.00 iniziamo una immersione che sarà di 34 minuti, sino a 30 metri di fondo (e io uscirò dall'acqua con l'ultimo soffio d'aria del respiratore).

Raggiungiamo lo scafo a −18, la fiancata è enorme. Un muro d'acciaio inclinato (la nave è adagiata a 45 gradi) al quale m'avvicino con un minimo d'emozione. Intravedo l'ombra mostruosa dello squarcio, la slabbratura nella carena che ricorda il siluro aereo lanciato all'alba del 16 febbraio e la mortale ferita inferta. L'acciaio è deformato, le paratie interne sono contorte, il manto di ruggine copre uniformemente fiancata e cicatrice; allo stesso tempo, però, quello squarcio, visto dal suo interno, sembra ormai una grotta naturale tanto è ricoperto di coralli e madrepore. È una seconda esplosione, quella che sta cancellando anche l'ombra di questa nave morta da quasi cinquant'anni; il rigoglio della vita subacquea tropicale la sta trasformando in un *reef* corallino.

A poppa le due eliche non si riconoscono, tanto sono addobbate da gorgonie, spugne, coralli, anemoni. Trovo un passaggio per entrare in una delle stive, la presenza di una montagna di bidoni di nafta (o benzina?) arrugginiti e accatastati mi ricorda l'incidente di Peter San nel mio racconto *Cacciatori di navi*; dalla finzione alla realtà, scatto alcune foto cercando di vedere nel controluce la silhouette di alcune strutture metalliche, sperando così che le immagini da me colte siano in grado di trasmettere l'emozione di questo immenso corpo artificiale, tragicamente finito in fondo al mare. E che il mare fa di tutto per metabolizzare, tanto da renderlo irriconoscibile come opera dell'uomo e solo da ammirare come creazione della forza biologica della Natura e della sua sfrenata fantasia creativa.

NEL VENTRE D'UNA NAVE CORSARA

Pomeriggio del 29 luglio 1991

Dopo esserci spostati di poche miglia ci immergiamo su un secondo relitto: il *Kensho Maru*. Le note che il nostro monitor ci legge prima dell'immersione ci hanno preventivamente informati che penetreremo all'interno di un cargo di 4862 tonnellate, dall'incredibile autonomia di 21.600 miglia alla velocità di 15 nodi. Questo dato induce a immaginare il *Kensho Maru* come ideato per servire da nave corsara; il che sarebbe provato anche dalla presenza – a poppa e prua – di due cannoni a caricamento rapido, brandeggiabili su due torrette, mobili su 360 gradi; tipo di armamento abbastanza sorprendente per una nave mercantile, seppur usata in teatro d'operazioni.

Eccolo, ora, davanti a me, uno di quei cannoni. Da arma temibile s'è mutato in contenitore fiorito; ed è così una immagine che evoca quella cara ai pacifisti, i poster con la canna di un arma da fuoco nella quale è stato infilato un garofano, una rosa, un mazzolino di mimose. Qui tutto questo è «dal vivo», in versione marina: fiori di corallo, con aggiunta di una farfalla – pardon, un pesce-farfalla – con sfoggio di altri colori in aggiunta a quelli dell'infiorata.

Dall'acqua, tutt'altro che limpida, vedo sbucare Andrea con la telecamera (che finalmente funziona); nuota tra il doppio albero del *Kensho Maru* dal quale pendono – inerti – i bracci delle gru di carico; ombre contro il cielo d'acqua, appena un po' più luminoso là ove si indovina battere il riflesso del sole.

Torniamo verso il centro del piroscafo, ove alcuni sommozzatori hanno lasciato ben in evidenza quanto trovato nelle cabine e nei ponti sottocoperta: piatti e altre stoviglie in ceramica, lampade ad

acetilene, persino un paio di scarpe, cucite con cuoio evidentemente di buona qualità se dopo esser rimaste immerse dal febbraio 1944 al 29 luglio del 1991 appaiono ancora per quel che
sono. Scarpe, appunto.

Due compagni d'immersione escono da una larga fessura dietro
il ponte di comando; mi diranno, poi, d'esser stati all'interno della
Kensho Maru sino alla sala macchine ove ancora troneggiano i due
motori diesel di cui disponeva la nave. Sembrano intatti, a parte
la patina depositatasi con gli anni.

Durante la decompressione – necessaria a ogni nostra risalita
verso la superficie – sono immobile a mezz'acqua. Prima a −12,
poi a −9 e poi a −3 per lunghi, eterni minuti. Sono solo c così ho il
tempo e anche la condizione per rimuginare tra me due riflessioni.
Una riguarda quei «reperti» curiosi esposti all'attenzione di chi
esplora il relitto; sono là da anni, a poco più di venti metri di
fondo, e a nessuno è mai venuto in mente di raccoglierne un
esemplare come souvenir: per quanti giorni – mi dico – una tentazione del genere, nel nostro Mediterraneo, resisterebbe alla visita
di gentlemen subacquei? È un calcolo presto fatto, se si considera
con quanta velocità furono devastate dai *tombaroli sottomarini* –
eufemisticamente autobattezzatesi «archeologi volontari» – aree
«protette» ove giacciono relitti di navi greche, romane, fenicie,
etrusche: depredate del loro carico sin dal momento in cui vennero alla luce in questo o in quel fondale.

La seconda riflessione è di tutt'altro ordine, anche se anch'essa
è suggerita da queste prime immersioni tra i relitti della *ghost fleet*
di Truk. La parola *flotta* induce a immaginare nelle acque di
questa laguna le ombre – una accanto all'altra – delle navi qui
affondate; la suggestione di racconti e cronache lette nei reporta-
ges di chi fu già sott'acqua a Truk, induce a questo errore. Perché
di errore si tratta: nella foschia di queste acque ogni nave è un
mondo a sé; non solo: ma ogni sua parte è separata dall'altra; la
dividono buio, silenzio, e nubi di plancton. Si tratta di scafi molto
grandi, tanto che, nel caso dei due oggi visitati, non è nemmeno
possibile vederli per intero, in un unico colpo d'occhio.

Solo l'immaginazione – e non la realtà – può suggerire l'immagine di un quadro globale della «flotta perduta»; così come me la
figuravo prima di immergermi a Truk; e come continuerò in futu-

ro a rappresentarmela. Come tessere di un mosaico, sommerò, fra me, immagini e colpi di flash, cannoni, motori e lampade, prue, ancore, eliche, interni di stive e sale macchine; e tante, tante ombre maestose, gigantesche. Lentamente mutanti da navi costruite e poi distrutte dall'uomo in scogliere coralline.

GLI *ZERO* DELLA *FUJIKAWA*

Martedì, 30 luglio 1991

Vento forte tutta la notte, due spostamenti della nostra barca per trovar riparo. Anche in una laguna il maltempo è fastidioso.

Alle 8.00 si sceglie l'ancoraggio a sud-est dell'isoletta di Eten dov'era la pista degli aerei da caccia che avrebbero dovuto difendere Truk e la sua flotta; colti di sorpresa dal primo raid del 16 febbraio, furono quasi tutti distrutti al suolo. Il sistema d'allarme organizzato dai giapponesi con le loro apparecchiature radar evidentemente ancora molto imperfette, non aveva segnalato per tempo le squadre aeree americane in avvicinamento alle prime luci del giorno. Per di più, l'ottusa mentalità militare nipponica aveva organizzato gli acquartieramenti dei piloti non accanto alla pista di decollo degli *Zero* e ai loro hangar, ma nella propisciente isola di Dublon; seppur minimo, tuttavia lo spostamento via mare da un pontile all'altro, causò il fatale ritardo nell'alzata in volo dei caccia giapponesi contro gli attaccanti.

Nelle sue stive, la *Fujikawa Maru* era carica di parti di ricambio per gli *Zero* di Eten; e venne affondata prima di poterne effettuare lo sbarco. Da come è organizzata l'immersione di oggi, in una delle sue stive (a 90 feet di fondo) andremo a vedere ali, eliche, motori e bombe preparate per azioni di guerra che non sarebbero mai state combattute. Siamo ancorati sulla prua del relitto, e dopo il tuffo con le nostre attrezzature, Andrea e io raggiungiamo la *Fujikawa* in pochi minuti. Un cannone montato a prua del cargo è ben visibile, anche se le colorate incrostazioni del tempo lo hanno mutato in una sorta di monumento al Carnevale corallino dei Mari del Sud. Così come il grande albero doppio da carico, verticale sulle stive che si intravedono tra le strutture metalliche del ponte.

La attraversiamo, raggiungiamo la profondità prevista, Andrea accende le lampade e io lo filmo mentre lui si muove accanto alla carcassa perfettamente riconoscibile di uno *Zero* (nella semioscurità delle stive la sovrappopolazione di corallo e madrepore è inferiore a quella delle aree esposte alla luce del sole; sicché le parti del carico così come le strutture stesse della nave sono ben riconoscibili).

Irriconoscibile, invece, è la prua della *Heian Maru* quando, nel tardo pomeriggio – trascorse le dovute ore in superficie per uscire dalla «saturazione» da azoto, «dono» delle ripetute immersioni di questi primi due giorni –, ci immergiamo su questo relitto.

L'acqua di Truk, qui, mi sembra meno torbida del solito (anche se il plancton fluttua a banchi fitti, quasi come nebbia). Era già tardo pomeriggio quando siamo entrati in acqua, con la luce del sole in rapido calo; in quel chiaroscuro, mentre guadagnavo i quaranta metri che separano – qui come in tutte le lagune di Truk – la superficie dal fondo, ho visto veniri incontro l'ombra maestosa del cargo colato a picco da un bel mirato lancio di siluri degli aerei americani alzatisi dalla portaerei *Enterprise*. Ho continuato a scendere mentre dentro di me mi rallegravo e dicevo «questa volta potrò inquadrare un'intera nave affondata, o quanto meno una sua parte ben visibile e il resto come fantasma chiaroscuro».

E così ho scelto la prua per inquadrare «la parte» e «l'insieme». Ma non tardo a deludermi: quando ho la prua nel visore della telecamera e poi nel reflex della macchina fotografica, quel che vedo è – in realtà – uno sperone di *reef*; quanto al resto, l'ombra alle sue spalle potrebbe essere una grande scogliera, e non quello di una nave affondata.

Mi soccorre un colpo di flash. L'ha scattato Andrea a non grande distanza dalla prua. Lo raggiungo, e vedo quanto ha attratto la sua attenzione: tra madrepore e spugne fiorite sull'acciaio dello scafo, si intravedono alcune lettere con il nome della nave.

E così, di questa, ho raccolto se non altro il biglietto da visita. Simile anche questo a tutti quelli che ogni giapponese all'estero distribuisce a chi incontra, è descritto in due caratteri: in latino e con idrogrammi.

IL MISTERO DEL *FUMITSUKI*

Mercoledì, 31 luglio 1991

Prua verso l'esterno della laguna. Sotto una pioggia torrenziale puntiamo al tratto di mare ove è colato a picco il *destroyer Fumitsuki*; ove *destroyer* sta per il nostro termine di «torpediniere».

Ancoriamo sulla sua carcassa a nord-est dell'isoletta di Udot.

Entriamo in acqua alle 10.00, dopo aver saputo dalla nostra guida che il *Fumitsuki* è l'ultimo – in ordine di tempo – tra i relitti individuati ed esplorati nella laguna di Truk. Si sapeva della presenza di questa piccola nave da guerra: nelle foto dal cielo del primo giorno d'attacco degli aerei Usa era stata identificata, ma non si poteva affermare con certezza che fosse stata colpita. Nelle foto del secondo giorno dell'operazione «Pioggia-di-grandine» il *Fumitsuki* era scomparso. Dove? Fuggito nottetempo dalla laguna?

Il mistero è stato svelato solo quarantatré anni dopo quel febbraio del '44. Il merito va a uno storico giapponese della seconda guerra mondiale, Tomoyuki Yoshimura. Pur visitando più volte Truk e immergendosi con il miglior sommozzatore dell'isola e forse di Micronesia, Kimo Asek (tra i primi a far sapere al mondo l'esistenza della «flotta-fantasma», e averne disegnato una mappa, abbozzato un inventario), Tomoyuki non riusciva a trovar soluzione dell'enigma del *destroyer* scomparso. Fin quando ebbe un'idea tanto semplice quanto geniale: sui principali quotidiani giapponesi mise un annuncio: «C'è qualche onorevole superstite dell'imperial torpediniera *Fumitsuki* che ha la buona volontà di mettersi in contatto con me?».

L'appello ebbe risposta: quattro membri dell'equipaggio scrissero a Tomoyuki; e come risultato dai successivi contatti, su una mappa della laguna di Truk, ricercatore e superstiti riuscirono a indicare il punto d'affondamento del *Fumitsuki*; e la conseguente, probabile posizione del relitto.

Il 14 aprile dell'87 il mistero era risolto. E anche questo «pezzo» – forse uno dei più preziosi – è entrato a far parte del Museo sottomarino di Truk.

Il «perché» della preziosità di questo *destroyer* mi appare chiaro tirando le somme della mia immersione. Innanzitutto è una delle rare navi da guerra che giacciono in questo fondale disseminato di cargo, petroliere, navi officina e da trasporto truppe. (Dove siano la corazzata e la portaerei qui segnalate *prima* dell'attacco aereo è un altro mistero. Affondate dopo la loro fuga? Giacciono *oltre* la barriera corallina dell'atollo-laguna là ove il Pacifico precipita in un abisso di circa seimila metri? Oppure riuscirono a eludere il blocco, ma furono affondate in altra zona del Pacifico?)

Prezioso il *Fumitsuki* è anche per le sue «armi da guerra», tutte in posizione di combattimento, cannoni, mitragliatrici pesanti; i bossoli dei colpi sparati sono sparsi ovunque, sul ponte. E tutti i lanciasiluri e i siluri stessi sono come pronti a essere lanciati.

Per di più, è la prima volta, oggi, che posso godere della visione d'insieme di un intero scafo; c'è poco plancton in acqua; e inoltre questo relitto è ben conservato e riconoscibile. Coralli e forme di vita subacquea tropicale hanno fatto anche qui ovviamente sfoggio di prolificità e di fantasia. Ma non sono riusciti a cancellare il profilo del battello sommerso.

Meno drammatici, ma non per questo meno interessanti sono altri reperti: le stoviglie della mensa, che nel contraccolpo del bombardamento, dell'urto subito e dell'affondamento, giacciono sparsi nel deck centrale.

La visita alle torrette armate, poi ai lanciasiluri, le foto e le riprese hanno fatto valere il tempo. Per fortuna, mentre scatto alcuni flash là ov'era la mensa, quella visione mi fa risuonare all'orecchio un campanello d'allarme. Alla cui eco, il mio occhio non corre al profondimetro, né al minicomputer sub dal quale traggo tutte le informazioni e le conseguenti cautele per il sommarsi di tante immersioni. Ma all'orologio, le cui lancette luminose segnano le dodici e mi ricordano – assieme alla visione della mensa e dei suoi piatti – che a bordo della nostra barca-alloggio, in superficie è già ora di colazione.

Inizio così, subito, la risalita in superficie; ed è tempo! La bombola che mi permette di respirare è già così scarica d'aria da obbligare Andrea a nuotarmi vicino, alternando le mie boccate d'aria alle sue, attingendo entrambi alla bombola d'aria ancora carica, sulla sua schiena. Insomma, gli chiedo più volte di respirare con l'aiuto del suo erogatore; e così finiamo tranquillamente con lo scambiarcelo – una boccata a te, una a me – sino a trovarci sottobordo alla nostra base galleggiante. Dalla cui poppa pende un lungo boccaglio collegato con una bombola in superfice, ovvero quanto permette di esaurire anche oggi – prima a 12 poi a 19 poi a 3 metri – una tranquillizzante decompressione.

IL TESCHIO DELLA *SHINKOKU*

Mercoledì, 31 luglio 1991

Sono giunti a Truk, dal Giappone, nel 1985, decine di congiunti dei marinai e degli aviatori nipponici morti qui durante gli attacchi aerei Usa del '44.

Precedentemente, sommozzatori locali e altri (giapponesi, americani, australiani) s'erano impegnati per varie settimane nel raccogliere all'interno dei relitti resti dei caduti che il mare aveva reso, ovviamente, irriconoscibili; ma tuttavia aveva conservato: ossa consistenti dello scheletro; e teschi a centinaia.

Radunata su una spiaggia di Moen questa macabra collezione, i familiari dei defunti hanno preparato una pira di legname; i monaci shintoisti, qui giunti con loro, hanno pronunciato le tradizionali parole del loro rito funebre, poi con gran rogo è stata data pace ai corpi pietosamente trovati e raccolti; ricordando al contempo gli altri, a migliaia rimasti per sempre in fondo al mare.

Non tutti e non per sempre, invero. Di tanto in tanto altri resti vengono individuati e segnalati. Ma non più raccolti e portati a terra, per esplicito desiderio delle famiglie: riposeranno per sempre nei relitti che giacciono sul fondo della laguna di Truk.

Oggi, al momento di immergerci sulla verticale della grande petroliera *Shinkoku Maru*, la nostra guida ci ha detto: «Remains of the ship's crew still be found on the *Shinkoku*». E io non ho capito se i resti cui alludeva erano stati appena ritrovati da lui, o da altri nei giorni precedenti (ah! se avessi studiato *bene* l'inglese...). Ha poi aggiunto, a mia richiesta, che m'avrebbe accompagnato – sul fondo, nel relitto – là ove quei resti giacevano. Si tuffa in acqua, io lo seguo; ma subito lo perdo di vista. Appena raggiunto il ponte

Approdo a un'isola delle Trobriand. Sulla riva, un villaggio papua;
una delle tante comunità in un rapporto vivo con le sue tradizioni, protette
da condizioni climatiche che hanno limitato gli insediamenti di coloni
europei, e sconsigliano oggi ogni speculazione turistica.

A sinistra: Le case su palafitte della gente papua insediatasi da migliaia di anni sulle rive e le lagune del fiume Sepik, in Nuova Guinea.
I micronesiani, genti del Pacifico meridionale che paiono un incrocio (etnico e culturale) tra i papua dell'ovest e i polinesiani dell'est.
Sopra: Bambini a Fefan, isola sotto mandato Usa sino al 1992.

Sopra e a lato: Nuova Guinea centrale. Momenti di una pantomima di guerra: qui vediamo ritualizzati – con armi e costumi – momenti di lotta, di sfida e di morte.

Sopra e a sinistra: Maschere rituali di fango policromo sul volto di papua che vivono nella zona del lago Tchambuli, in Nuova Guinea.

Nella doppia pagina seguente: Guerrieri dell'alta Valle dell'Asaro in «tenuta da combattimento»; le acconciature di conchiglie non sono ornamentali ma costituiscono, in certa misura, una corazza di protezione al viso e al ventre.

A sinistra: Dettagli di uno scudo «umanizzato» di Karau. *Sopra*:
Due bastoni di comando, l'uno dell'isola Karkar (Mare di Bismarck),
l'altro di Ambunti (Medio Sepik).

Sopra: Da una foresta di bambù giganti appare un gruppo di «notabili» di villaggio, a Mount Hagen, nel cuore della Nuova Guinea. Si presenta ai visitatori in tutto lo splendore dei suoi costumi. Alcuni di essi (*in alto a destra*) riportano direttamente ad acconciature dell'età della pietra.
In basso, a destra: Una rara immagine del 1970 della *malimala*, festa dell'abbondanza alle isole Trobriand, oggi non più celebrata.

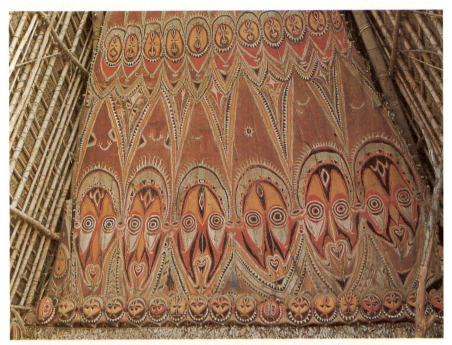

A sinistra: Un «monumento» unico del mondo papua: la grande
capanna cerimoniale per uomini a Kalebu (Nuova Guinea, valle del Sepik).
Sopra: Le sue raffinate decorazioni.

All'interno della capanna cerimoniale di Kalebu, maschere e statue
come «oggetti-testimoni»: memoria singola o collettiva di ispirazione,
creatività, tecniche e forme per onorare divinità e defunti.

In alto: Nuova Guinea, Roka Valley. Un bambino è morto: la vibrazione vertiginosa prodotta da un frenetico movimento di canne e il soffio d'aria che essa produce sono elementi di un rito che mira a far tornare, in un corpo che l'ha perduta, il soffio della vita. *Sopra*: Lo scheletro di un capo cannibale *puka-puka* onorato nel villaggio che fu di suo dominio.

Nuova Guinea, Roka Valley. Uccisione sacrificale di un maiale nel corso
di una cerimonia di villaggio. Il fango bianco del fiume Asaro – presso cui
risiede questa comunità papua – è usato nella complessa ritualità
di questa come di altre feste iniziatiche.

Una «maschera di fango» durante il rito del «ritorno dei morti», nella Roka
Valley (Nuova Guinea montana). Qui colte, anche, le immagini molto
rare della *sanguma*, una «fattura» stregonesca (*in alto, a destra*);
e dell'allattamento simultaneo di un bambino e di un cucciolo di maiale,
due beni preziosi per una previdente mamma papua (*in basso, a destra*).

Fotogrammi tratti dal film del 1955, eseguito nell'isola di Pentecôte
(Nuove Ebridi) in occasione dell'ultimo *kgöl*, salto da una torre delle liane
di oltre trenta metri. Prova di coraggio oggi proibita; solo permessa,
su ben minori altezze, in occasione della visita all'ex colonia dei sovrani
inglesi, negli anni Settanta.

Nell'isola di Koror, un padre
gesuita locale, Padre Felix,
davanti alla sua chiesa – nello stile
tradizionale – e tra i suoi più
giovani fedeli.

Antichi dèi della Melanesia,
nuova fede in Micronesia: una
statua in onore degli antenati
(*pagina a sinistra*), tipica della
ritualità di Korevori (Alto
Sepik): sommità di capanna
cerimoniale (*a lato*) nella Nuova
Britannia, dominata da uno
spirito-vampiro.

In alto: Nelle isole papua, oggi: il raccolto del caffè asciuga sulla plastica nei pressi di Goroka, in Nuova Guinea. *A lato*: Il mercato della frutta, di legumi e degli inami ai margini di un villaggio delle isole Trobriand.

Donna delle comunità urbanizzate, al mercato di Port Moresby, capitale della Repubblica Papua Nuova Guinea; la cui unità è resa difficile non solo dal contrasto tra città e zone primitive, ma dalla babele delle lingue: qui se ne incrociano ben settecentodiciassette differenti, ovvero il quarantacinque per cento di quelle parlate nel nostro pianeta.

A sinistra, in alto: Danza di propiziazione a Washkuk. *In basso*: Un rito
di iniziazione a Mount Hagen (*in basso*), tra i melanesiani della Nuova Guinea.
Sopra: Una superstite capanna comunitaria micronesiana, nell'isola
di Koror (arcipelago di Palau), con accanto i resti di una postazione
da combattimento abbandonata sul posto dai giapponesi nel 1944.

Reperti della dominazione e della
sconfitta dell'Impero del Sol Levante,
dal 1914 al 1944: (*a destra*) una
buca per lettere a Koror (Palau)
e (*in alto*) un relitto a Peleliu, dove
la conquista della piccola base aerea
nipponica costò ai Marines americani
oltre mille morti e cinquemila feriti;
ai giapponesi diecimila morti
e molte migliaia di prigionieri.

A bordo di un cacciabombardiere Mitsubishi G4M3 (arma vincente
dei giapponesi all'inizio della seconda guerra mondiale). Il famoso
ammiraglio giapponese Yamamoto venne abbattuto mentre atterrava
con un aereo come questo nelle isole Salomone. Qui il Mitsubishi G4M3
è fotografato in un fondale di circa venti metri: visibili le cabine
di pilotaggio (*in alto*) e le postazioni per le mitragliatrici laterali (*sopra*).

Nuova Guinea, Snake Valley (zona di Orokolo). L'ossario di un popolo cannibale ove le ossa dei sacrificati venivano ordinate – dopo i banchetti antropofagi – e onorate perché la forza «benefica» dei morti non andasse dispersa. Secondo l'antropologo olandese Wielens che ha scoperto il luogo, pitture e graffiti, dedicati sia ai divorati che ai divoratori, testimoniano quello «scambio» di forza vitale tipico delle culture animiste.

superiore del relitto, a venti metri dal fondo, cerco di capire in quale anfratto della grande carcassa sia andato a infilarsi (di regola, dovrebbe esser vicino a me e ad Andrea) e non so come e dove dirigermi. Perché continuo a non vederlo. Con lui avrei dovuto penetrare all'interno dello scafo, là dove mi doveva mostrare questi *remains of the schip's crew*; ma dubito che da soli, Andrea e io, potremo muoverci nel labirinto della petroliera affondata.

Sono solo pochi minuti di incertezza, poi la nostra guida appare. Tra le mani ha un teschio che con attenzione appoggia sul ponte; mi fa intendere che posso fotografarlo, il che mi provoca un certo fastidio; il tutto mi appare irriverente; comunque inquadro e scatto, mentre Andrea filma. Lui intanto attende con pazienza; poi, dopo aver visto lampeggiare i flashes, riprende in mano il teschio e con la stessa velocità con la quale era apparso, scompare di nuovo nel ventre della *Shinkoku*.

Quando emergiamo, mi spiega. Per principio lui non guida nessuno nel vano interno del relitto, là ove tempo addietro ha ritrovato resti umani; perché sa che c'è chi, senza alcun ritegno, li raccoglie e li porta via, come macabri trofei di guerra.

Quel vano – a suo avviso – deve restare sconosciuto. Ammette che di quei «resti» si possa scattare qualche foto; ma non offensiva, come potrebbe esserlo, ad esempio, un teschio in mano a una bella sommozzatrice, magari semisvestita (c'è chi ha provato a farla, una foto simile).

A me ha permesso di scattare foto, e di girare una scena del mio film; ma non all'interno, nel «suo» luogo segreto.

I morti giapponesi i cui resti non furono cremati, hanno qui i loro guardiani. Attenti e fedeli.

IL TANK DEL «NATIONAL GEOGRAPHIC MAGAZINE»

Giovedì, 1° agosto 1991

Vento, maltempo e pioggia sulla laguna. Il relitto che visitiamo è quello della *Nippo Maru*. Abbiamo avuto un onorevole predecessore, il Comandante J.Y. Cousteau; a lui e alla sua subciurma va il merito di aver individuato questo cargo, che nessuno aveva più visto da quando alle 8 e 15 del 16 febbraio '44 era stato colpito dalla prima ondata di cacciabombardieri *Hellcats* decollati dalla portaerei *Essex*, scortata dalla *Task-force 5*, della Marina americana. Accadeva questo tra le isolette di Eten e Dublon, esattamente ove gettiamo l'àncora oggi.

La *Nippo Maru* e altre cinque navi da trasporto avevano scelto lo stesso nostro ancoraggio il 10 febbraio, solo sei giorni prima dell'attacco aereo; e stavano scaricando a terra armi, munizioni e rifornimenti quando furono tutte colate a picco in pochi minuti.

Tra il materiale già sul ponte della *Nippo Maru*, pronto allo sbarco a terra per contribuire alla difesa dell'atollo in caso d'invasione dei marines americani (che invece non era prevista e infatti non avvenne mai) vi erano cannoni di vario calibro e carri armati.

Verso uno di questi *tank* – caricato sulla tolda della *Nippo*, un piccolo mostro di ferro arrugginito – mi muovo per più di mezz'ora. L'ho individuato appena giunto a livello del ponte, a trentasei metri di profondità. Riconoscendolo subito come il soggetto che mi aveva colpito e fatto sperare di immergermi un giorno nella laguna di Truk, quando vidi la sua tozza forma troneggiare nella copertina del «National Geographic Magazine».

Quando un progetto a lungo preparato giunge al momento in cui viene realizzato, *quel* momento si identifica con la prima idea, la prima impressione registrata nella sfera dei desideri (e delle ambizioni); è allora che io mi sento in stato d'animo di indefinibile incertezza e quasi sempre di leggera, amara delusione. Il tempo, infatti, non manca di caricare un'attesa di tensione, speranza; di ingigantire il valore o l'importanza di un evento cui si dovrà assistere o la bellezza o la rarità di un'immagine della quale spero di riuscire a cogliere l'essenza, la verità.

Riferendomi al *tank* giapponese ridotto a ferro vecchio sul ponte della nave che lo trasportava, non posso certo parlare di «bellezza». Ma di rarità e suggestione, sì; perché altri manufatti evocatori della grande battaglia aeronavale qui combattuta, evidentemente più fragili, come gli aerei, il mare li propone alla nostra attenzione come preziosi ma disintegrati ricordi; specchio solo parziale di quella che fu la loro forma e forza. E altri reperti ancora – i cannoni e le mitragliatrici – per le loro forme appuntite sembrano aver stimolato all'eccesso fantasia e prolificità di madrepore, coralli, gorgonie, alcionarie; sotto il loro mantello lussureggiante, si fatica ormai a riconoscere «quella» forma così come essa era un tempo.

Il carro armato della *Nippo Maru*, invece – compatto, solido, gigantesco scarafaggio rosso-bruno – è subito riconoscibile per quello che è; o meglio: quel che fu.

Sembra aver rifiutato il destino di vaso-da-fiori. Niente coralli, né colori fluttuanti sul suo tozzo corpo. Ha accettato (come non avrebbe potuto?) solo la ruggine, ma questo non impedisce di distinguere bene i cingoli, le ruote dentate, la torretta semovente. Il *mio* soggetto (anche se tanti l'hanno già fotografato e filmato, ora è solo *mio*, per i minuti di questa immersione) è davanti ai miei occhi, all'obiettivo della mia Hasselblad subacquea; e io posso girargli attorno, ritrarlo da varie posizioni e angolature. Ma finalmente una sola è quella che mi piace: frontale e dal basso. Come se stesse venendomi addosso.

Lì per lì non me ne rendo conto, ma vi è un motivo per cui quell'inquadratura mi piace: è la stessa, identica, della prima fotografia che ho visto – quella sulla copertina del «National Geographic Magazine» – tra le altre che ho avuto sotto gli occhi tra le cento e cento scattate nella laguna di Truk.

Non mi resta che dedurre una conclusione: animalescamente, son soggetto anch'io al fenomeno dell'*imprinting*. Come le oche di Konrad Lorenz.

UNA DATA DI MORTE È IL GIORNO DI FONDAZIONE
DEL LABORATORIO SUBACQUEO PIÙ GRANDE DEL MONDO

Giovedì, 1° agosto 1991, pomeriggio

Un relitto semidistrutto da un colpo di siluro, le sue strutture metalliche dilaniate, contorte, irriconoscibili.

Siamo alla consueta quota di fondo di questa laguna, a −35 metri circa; la carcassa è davanti a me, coperta più d'ogni altra sin qui visitata, da un manto di vita sottomarina. Sono sul *Sanki-San*, cargo che trasportava munizioni nello sfortunato (per lui) giorno dell'*Operation Hailstone*. Colpito, esplose come un fuoco d'artificio drammatico, infernale: quale lo documentano le foto scattate dall'aereo americano che lo aveva centrato con le sue bombe da duemila chili. Un fuoco d'artificio, non più drammatico ma gioioso perché policromo e allegro, è esploso poi sul *Sanki-San* pochi anni dopo il suo affondamento: l'impressionante fioritura corallina in tutti i suoi aspetti.

A proposito della quale, ecco un altro motivo di grande interesse per la laguna di Truk e i suoi relitti; non solo nei confronti di quanti studiano dati, situazioni, reperti relativi alle battaglie aeronavali nel Pacifico; ma per i biologici del mare. Infatti, per la scienza, è di grande interesse seguire la progressiva crescita del manto naturale sottomarino sulle morte sovrastrutture delle navi qui affondate. Si sa, infatti, la data esatta alla quale far riferimento nel calcolare il tempo necessario alle più diverse forme di vita stanziali per attecchire sul supporto ove esse hanno posto le loro «radici». Come fosse *reef* roccioso, o scogliera di lava, quel supporto artificiale diventerà, per le forme di vita subacquee coralligene, una sorta di spina dorsale sulla quale svilupparsi, stagione dopo stagione. È un caso unico, ed è su vasta scala; per questo motivo oltre agli appassionati immersionisti alla ricerca dell'emozione, dell'avventura, del brivido, gruppi sempre più numerosi di specialisti in biologia marina tropicale da ogni parte del mondo si spostano ogni anno per analizzare l'avanzata e/o il regresso – dal 1944 a oggi – delle madrepore, dei coralli, delle alcionarie, degli anemoni e di quante specie e sottospecie formano la palpitante copertura di un *reef*. Le centotrenta miglia di mare racchiuse entro l'anello della laguna di Truk sono così diventate – oltre al più grande museo storico marinaro del mondo – anche un preciso orologio di «tempi naturali» per le analisi e il calcolo degli specialisti al lavoro in questo che si può considerare il più grande laboratorio di ricerca dal vivo. E ogni relitto ne è una particolare sezione; è una lancetta del grande cronografo che ha cominciato a scandire secondi, minuti, ore, giorni, anni dal febbraio 1944.

La scienza della vita si prende così la sua rivincita, qui, sulla follia distruttiva e annientatrice dell'uomo.

COMPLIMENTI, ONOREVOLE PORTUALE

Venerdì, 2 agosto 1991

Chissà se ancora sopravvive, in una delle maggiori città riviera-sche del Giappone, l'uomo che pose catenelle e bloccaruote ai camion caricati sul cargo *Oki Maru* destinato a trasportare armi, munizioni, automezzi alla guarnigione arroccata nell'imprendibi-le, fortificatissimo atollo di Truk, ai confini tra i Mari del Sud orientali e quelli occidentali.

Ovunque, nel mondo, quello dello «stivatore» è stato mestiere di tutto riguardo; da secoli, direi da almeno tre millenni, se ponia-mo come inizio di quest'attività il commercio di prodotti contenu-ti in anfore, e quelli dei primi metalli, a cominciare dall'epoca della nascente marineria mediterranea (XVI, XV secolo a.C.?); certo già allora era stimato, apprezzato e ricercato l'uomo che con cura, diligenza ma soprattutto intelligenza sapeva disporre un carico all'interno di uno scafo destinato ad affrontare il mare. I pesi dovevano essere ben equilibrati tra poppa e prua, tra una fiancata e l'altra. Solo così, in caso di tempeste, nulla si sarebbe mosso, e la tenuta del battello non sarebbe variata.

Questo nobile, ancorché umile, anzi miserabile mestiere – lo stesso, identico, in un porto del nord o del sud del pianeta, in occidente come in oriente; perché sono invariabili le leggi dell'e-quilibrio e le conseguenze del moto ondoso del mare – è finito da quando l'uomo, nei porti del nostro pianeta ha a che fare con navi da carico ormai completamente diverse da quelle tradizionali; quelle che riempiono le loro stive con i containers; e il calcolo del loro peso e della loro disposizione a bordo è rapidamente eseguito – anche nel più remoto porto commerciale, anche per una piccola nave da trasporto – da un maneggiabile computer.

Il portuale-stivatore, oggi, non serve più a nessuno.

All'ignoto stivatore giapponese – e ai suoi compagni di lavoro – ho pensato quando sono giunto sul fondo della seconda stiva del-l'*Oki Maru* e Andrea ha acceso di colpo i due grandi fari subacquei che aveva nelle mani. Il buio del relitto è stato tagliato dai fasci luminosi, la luce è tornata là dove da anni e anni – a parte la momentanea accensione di qualche altro flash di fotografo sub – era bandita sia dalla profondità sia dal labirinto di acciaio contorto e arrugginito creato dal crollo delle sovrastrutture della nave, ferita dalle bombe piovute dal cielo e dilaniata dall'esplosione dei suoi serbatoi.

I due potenti raggi di luce impugnati e mossi da Andrea inquadrano prima uno, poi due, poi tre camion stivati uno accanto all'altro. Sono perfetamente allineati, non si sono spostati dalle posizioni nelle quali l'ignoto portuale giapponese e i suoi compagni con scrupolo, nel '44, li avevano sistemati per il viaggio.

Prima di filmare, un colpo d'occhio mi permette di vedere le ruote dei camion e noto – oltre i pneumatici, gonfi e perfetti da sembrare nuovi – come dopo quasi mezzo secolo passato sott'acqua i ganci di fissaggio degli automezzi siano ancora nella loro posizione di tenuta.

Congratulazioni, vecchio stivatore giapponese! Questa nave ha attraversato un oceano con le sue alte, lunghe onde, è stata bombardata, colpita ed infine è esplosa. S'è inabissata, poi – con contraccolpo certo violento se si calcola le ottomila tonnellate della sua stazza – è arrivata sul fondo, dopo una caduta di cinquanta metri; tutto, a bordo, s'è scomposto, ammucchiato, disperso, o rovinosamente contorto; ma nella stiva della *Oki Maru* i camion caricati e ben fissati ai pianali d'acciaio (quanti? io e Andrea ne abbiamo visti tre, ma forse sono assai di più) sono invece rimasti perfettamente immobili. Al loro posto. In quello che tu, vecchio stivatore giapponese, gli avevi assegnato.

Congratulazioni, ripeto fra me.

Ma già Andrea mi fa cenno che dobbiamo risalire, a questa profondità l'aria delle bombole l'abbiamo respirata di fretta.

IL BIMOTORE DI YAMAMOTO

Sabato, 3 agosto 1991, mattino

La mia ultima immersione a Truk è nel relitto dell'aereo giapponese che aveva semidistrutto la base aerea americana di Pearl

Harbor nel '41, e poi cancellato l'aviazione Usa dalle Filippine, affondando le corazzate inglesi *Prince of Wales* e *Repulse* al largo di Singapore: era un aereo invincibile, quello, agli inizi degli anni Quaranta. È il *Mitsubishi G4M3*, il bimotore «familiarmente» chiamato dai piloti americani *Betty*.

Poi, alla fine del '42, la tecnologia aeronautica Usa ha dotato l'aviazione alleata di aerei più veloci, più armati e più corazzati di lui; lo ha messo in condizioni di non nuocere.

Nell'aprile del '43 trasportava il famoso ammiraglio Yamamoto verso Bougainville, in Melanesia, dove gli alleati affrontavano i giapponesi nella partita decisiva per la salvezza dell'Australia. Aerei da caccia a lungo raggio americani, intercettato il messaggio radio del comando aereo giapponese che comunicava ora e rotta del volo di Yamamoto, piombarono sul bimotore dell'ammiraglio mentre stava per atterrare nella zona delle operazioni; abbatterono la scorta (erano solo quattro, contro i ventisei attaccanti) e poi colpirono a morte la loro preda; che cadde in fiamme nella foresta dell'isola. Da quel momento le sorti del conflitto nel Pacifico volsero definitivamente a sfavore dei giapponesi.

Il *G4M3 «Betty»* che ho davanti agli occhi – lo stesso di Yamamoto – fu abbattuto mentre decollava dall'isola di Eten. Ora giace sul fondo a non più di venti metri dalla superficie, in linea retta sull'asse della pista, dalla cui testata – oggi coperta di vegetazione perché l'aeroporto è in disuso dalla fine della seconda guerra mondiale – dista nemmeno un miglio.

Il relitto è impressionante, sia perché la parte anteriore rivela con tragica chiarezza la violenza dell'impatto in acqua, sia perché il resto dell'aereo è perfettamente riconoscibile. Sull'alluminio delle ali e della fusoliera, infatti, solo in minima quantità hanno attecchito fiori, muffe, rampicanti del mar tropicale. La natura coralligena dell'atollo non ha avvolto con la sua rete mimetica multicolore il *Betty* adagiato sulla sabbia.

Si può entrare nella carlinga. E, di lì, se si osserva l'azzurro del mare all'esterno dei due vani laterali dov'erano poste le mitragliatrici di difesa, l'illusione di essere in volo e non in fondo al mare per un istante è magica.

Basta però riportare lo sguardo all'interno della fusoliera, e ogni fantasia svanisce nella crudezza di uno spettacolo di morte.

Pinneggio nella carlinga con lentezza, avanzo tra cavi e telai sconnessi e certamente taglienti; arrivo là dove la cabina di pilotaggio s'è schiantata sul letto di sabbia del fondo.

Qualche strumento è ancora riconoscibile. I seggiolini dei due piloti e del navigatore che sedeva tra loro sono scomparsi, se ne intravedono solo gli attacchi al pavimento.

Mentre cerco di sgusciare all'esterno, continuo ad avere davanti agli occhi quell'ammasso di metallo accartocciato. E ricordo d'aver letto che il primo sommozzatore sceso all'interno di questo relitto, che per anni nessuno aveva visto, trovò sotto il sedile del pilota – che era ancora al suo posto – una confezione di cognac francese, consumata a metà.

Forse quell'aviatore poco più che ventenne ne beveva un sorso a ogni volo, per farsi coraggio. Ma non riuscì a terminare la bottiglia.

LASCIANDO LA MICRONESIA

Lunedì, 5 agosto 1991

Sulla rotta che mi allontana da queste isole e atolli, rileggo gli appunti che ho scritto.

Li confronto con libri e fascicoli che ho acquistato a Guam, relativi a navi, battaglie, esplorazioni, relitti: nomi, date, mappe di *reef*.

Mi rendo conto – caso mai vi fosse bisogno di questa conferma! – che quanto ho visto, fotografato, filmato – l'esperienza vissuta, insomma, in questi giorni di immersioni e sensazioni – è un nulla; è insignificante rispetto alla quantità di altre esperienze che quest'area del Pacifico offre a chi vi approda con la curiosità di scoprire un mondo tanto poco conosciuto.

Nella laguna di Truk ho visto i resti della flotta fantasma giapponese; a Guam mi sono immerso dove una nave tedesca, il *Cormoran* e una giapponese, la *Tokyo Maru*, giacciono una sull'altra, e collegano eventi della prima e della seconda guerra mondiale, incastrando l'un nell'altro i loro relitti e le pagine di due capitoli di storia.

Storia che è antica, qui – come in tutto il Pacifico – per vicende che risalgono a migliaia di anni fa, se ci si riferisce all'inizio delle migrazioni di nomadi del mare dell'Asia verso l'Oriente; di cinque secoli se il calcolo del tempo parte dall'apparizione, in questo orizzonte marino, delle prime vele europee.

Se passassi qualche mese con chi sta cercando i resti dei piccoli galeoni spagnoli che alla fine del Cinquecento già si spingevano dalle Filippine verso il grande oceano e le sue isole per esplorare, commerciare, sbarcare missionari gesuiti (che furono poi uccisi), se mi dedicassi a seguire chi studia quel periodo e investiga nei fondali attorno ai *reef*, o nelle foreste delle isole maggiori, forse potrei cogliere immagini relative a quei primi navigatori che sfidarono le incognite del Pacifico. In particolare in quest'area.

Altri mesi potrei viverli con chi desidera una risposta al «mistero» sulla sorte di Amelia Erhardt e la ricerca nelle probabili aree dove il suo *Electra* cadde in mare.

E altri mesi ancora potrei trascorrerli sulle navi oceanografiche che studiano le migrazioni delle ultime balene azzurre dal Pacifico settentrionale sino alla vasta «area protetta», là creata per loro dalla generosità del re di Tonga.

Insomma non basterebbero, dieci cento vite per raccogliere, in una sola, esperienze minimamente rapportabili alla vastità di quest'ambiente oceanico. E alle possibilità di ricerca e alle avventure che esso offre.

Altri le compiranno, queste ricerche; altri vivranno queste esperienze, emozioni a non finire. Ne leggeremo cronache e relazioni.

Ma tutto quanto s'aggiungerà alla nostra conoscenza sarà sempre relativamente *nulla*. Polinesia e Melanesia emergono con isole e atolli nello stesso oceano dov'è distesa la Micronesia. Ma quelle terre oceaniche sono in gran numero alte ed estese; la Micronesia, invece, è solo un pulviscolo di minute schegge emergenti, separate le une dalle altre da centinaia, talvolta migliaia di miglia di vuoto. Per questo motivo la sensazione di spazio-deserto, di vastità incolmabile – in certi momenti angosciosa – è limitata in Polinesia ad alcuni quadranti nautici del suo oceano, come alle Tuamotu; qui è invece una caratteristica comune di tutta l'area.

Mentre osservo da novemila metri di quota l'azzurro cupo del Pacifico interrotto solo da evanescenti macchie candide di nubi che paiono poggiare sulle onde (da due ore volo verso la Melanesia, e nessuna terra emergente è apparsa nel quadro monocolore che si staglia nel riquadro dell'oblò), mi torna alla mente una chiacchierata con il comandante della motobarca con la quale si andava da un relitto all'altro della laguna di Truk.

Una sera dopo un temporale osservavo – ancora una volta estasiato – l'accendersi in cielo e sul mare di un tramonto «di proporzioni cosmiche» come disse qualcuno fra noi.

Fu l'inizio di una chiacchierata durante la quale non si parlò della «flotta fantasma» sepolta nelle acque su cui si galleggiava in quei giorni; ma della vastità marina che ci circondava; e come essa ci appariva nel paesaggio aperto all'infinito attorno all'atollo, per trecentosessanta gradi.

Il vecchio marinaio al timone della motobarca – americano d'origine greca – ci teneva a sfoggiare la sua memoria, «di qui alle Marshall sono più di mille miglia... di qui all'America quasi novemilacinquecento... di qui a Guam novecentotrentasei...»; non so se queste distanze fossero citate con esattezza; ma ricordo che quella sera azzardò un paragone, che nella sua semplicità mi parve di chiarezza conturbante. «Vedete,» disse rivolgendosi a me e ad Andrea, che sapeva entrambi d'origine «mediterranea», «quest'area del Pacifico, detta Micronesia, copre una superficie pari a cinque volte quella del vostro Mediterraneo; ma le sue isolette, se le si unissero le une alle altre sino a formare un'unica terra, formerebbero una superficie pari solo alla metà di quell'isola del vostro mare che mi pare si chiami Sardegna...»

Un Mediterraneo cinque volte più vasto e al suo centro una sola piccola terra. Non credo ci sia una maniera più chiara e semplice per suggerire un'immensità marina.

Introduzione alla Melanesia, ovvero «gli altri Mari del Sud»

Ultimi primitivi, quelli veri – Il *cargo* che porterà ricchezza e felicità a tutti – La grandezza dell'arte oceaniana – L'avventura etnografica di Malinowski – I bambini nascono da gocce d'acqua di mare – Gli argonauti del Pacifico orientale – Il traffico della *kula*, il commercio dei regali che portano alla rovina – Denti di cane come monete – Margaret Mead, lo spazio e il tempo.

Gli «ultimi primitivi» di questo pianeta? *Veri?* Fedeli ad ancestrali modelli di vita?

Certamente gli *unici* a esserlo, sul pianeta Terra, sono i superstiti gruppi papua.

Per questo, non si può approdare nelle isole melanesiane – in alcune delle quali sopravvivono, appunto, queste micro-unità – senza una adeguata preparazione; «per non stupire a bocca aperta davanti ai selvaggi» come mi dice il mio amico etnologo Pier Giovanni D'Ayala mentre mi elenca una serie di suggerimenti e consigli prima di un mio viaggio tra i papua – agli inizi degli anni Settanta – più impegnativo dei precedenti. Ai quali consigli, aggiunge una riflessione: mi ricorda che uno studioso d'etnografia ha cento o mille chiavi da scegliere per forzare la porta segreta che lo esclude dalla conoscenza di società e culture diverse dalla sua. E infatti ogni etnologo approdato in Melanesia ha adottato un suo diverso sistema di ricerca e di analisi. Per questo mi consiglia di riunire in un dossier (quello che ora qui riporto) un ventaglio di argomenti, e di autori, per poter disporre di un quadro sufficientemente vasto – e da punti di vista diversi – relativo agli studi in questo campo.

Una scelta che m'è sembrato potesse iniziare con il tema del *cargo-cult* non solo perché s'allaccia direttamente all'episodio di Long Island che ho narrato nelle pagine precedenti, ma anche perché questo è un fenomeno così precipuo dell'Oceania «nera» – quella papua, appunto – da sembrarmi quasi inevitabile aprire queste note su questo argomento.

Tra i tanti studiosi del *cargo*, Peter Worsley, con il suo già citato volume *La tromba suonerà*, è stato la guida di chi si è interessato a questo straordinario fenomeno del mondo papua (e solo lui può esserlo, dato che solo lui ha dedicato una vita a un solo grande studio etnografico; quello sul *cargo-cult*, appunto).

Nella sua introduzione all'argomento Worsley spiega che le «merci» (o *cargo*, come esse vengono chiamate nel Pacifico, in gergo anglo-cinese) secondo i papua non siano «*oggetto di scambi e di commerci*», ma siano prodotti magici, creati da antenati dell'uomo bianco. Il quale li ottiene tramite un rito così come esso è richiesto dagli spiriti. Nello stesso modo un papua dovrebbe ottenere a sua volta un *cargo* se potesse seguire un giusto e analogo rito religioso.

Ogni culto del *cargo* – aggiunge Worsley nel suo studio – ha avuto un *profeta* che ha anche regolato i riti e predetto date d'arrivo del *cargo*; e anche il mezzo che lo consegnerà. Una nave, un tempo; oggi invece può trattarsi di un aereo, una nave da guerra oppure (come nelle isole della Nuova Britannia) si attende un *cargo* trasportato da un gigantesco uovo dipinto di giallo che dovrebbe discendere dai cieli.

In molte isole (noi l'abbiamo visto a «Isola») i «cultisti» hanno costruito terreni di atterraggio, nell'attesa di ricevere merci per via aerea, e anche dighe sui fiumi per permettere il passaggio di navi da guerra e hanno tagliato interi boschi e giungle per creare eliporti. Un aspetto curioso del culto è che pur se il profeta si rivela menzognero non sembra che nessuno dei suoi adepti perda la fede in lui; la colpa del mancato arrivo del *cargo* è sempre dell'uomo bianco.

Naturalmente, il culto del *cargo* ha aspetti e sviluppi, in Oceania, ben diversi d'isola in isola; e sulla falsariga dello studio che ho scelto come guida, possiamo analizzarne i principali, oggi tutti scomparsi.

Il movimento *tuka* alle isole Figi nasce dall'inquietudine indigena, in queste isole sin dalla seconda metà del XIX secolo. In tutte le Figi, nel 1885 si diffuse la notizia che bande di uomini, i volti dipinti di nero, si addestravano «militarmente» nell'alta valle del fiume Rewa. Si trattava di un movimento i cui componenti, conosciuti come «soldati», erano comandati da «sergenti», *rokos* e *mbu-*

lis, e da «scribi» (titoli tutti ispirati da quelli degli ufficiali coloniali e dalla polizia; e anche dalla Bibbia: infatti gli alti ufficiali erano chiamati «angeli della distruzione»).

Il capo, che si richiamava a profetiche e occulte potenze, assicurava che entro un periodo di tempo molto breve l'ordine del mondo sarebbe stato rovesciato, tanto che i bianchi avrebbero servito gli indigeni. Nel primo capitolo del suo studio, Worsley ci dà notizie delle informazioni storiche avute sull'argomento:

I credenti seguivano un addestramento che comprendeva danze ed esercitazioni le quali imitavano il corpo di polizia, anche nelle parole di comando; il che avveniva poiché in mezzo ai fanatici della setta *tuka* si trovavano numerosi ex membri della polizia. Lo stesso Navosavakandua [il Capo, N.d.A.] si faceva salutare militarmente. Per entrare a far parte del movimento e per ottenere la «bottiglia dell'acqua attinta alla Fontana della Vita» conferente secondo i *tuka* l'immortalità, gli aderenti pagavano dai 10 scellini alle 2 sterline. Il successo del profeta lo si può giudicare dalla ricchezza accumulata: in una sola festa egli mise in mostra 400 denti di balena, un riscatto da re, nelle Figi. Nei luoghi di culto, egli compiva «miracoli»: al di là di una tenda dove sedevano i suoi «preti» e donne inservienti, era possibile udire discendere Dio con un basso suono sibilante.

In breve, in tutte le Figi si cominciò a temere che scoppiassero disordini nella zona in cui predominavano i *tuka*.

«L'ingrassamento di un porco bianco, simbolo dei bianchi, in vista del suo sacrificio in onore degli avi nel Gran Giorno, determinò uno stato di vero allarme», scrive Worsley; e aggiunge che indigeni ostili al movimento furono i primi a chiederne ufficialmente la dissoluzione.

Genitori che avevano visto le proprie figlie assunte fra i *tuku* informarono la polizia del fatto che il profeta aveva delle relazioni sessuali con queste fanciulle, cui prometteva che, malgrado tutto, sarebbero rimaste vergini finché bevessero l'acqua santa.

Finalmente il profeta fissò il giorno in cui il *cargo* sarebbe giunto. E subito:

[...] il profeta e alcuni suoi «angeli della distruzione» vennero arrestati da elementi della polizia nonostante una certa resistenza. [...] La voce popolare disse che il carceriere aveva tentato di tagliare i capelli del profeta, ma che le forbici si erano avvolte all'indietro rifiutando di tagliare la sede del potere spirituale. Egli non era stato condannato a morte, correva voce, perché il governo non poteva ucciderlo.

Il profeta fu inviato nell'isola di Rotuma, situata trecento miglia a nord delle Figi, dove si sposò e morì, dopo aver vissuto una normale vita privata. Ma questo evento «naturale» non concluse la vicenda dei *tuka*; loro leggende dissero che il governo aveva cercato invano di uccidere il profeta, gettandolo fra gli enormi rulli di un mulino per zucchero. Uno dei suoi «angeli della distruzione» asserì d'aver da lui ricevuto «lettere cadute dal cielo. [...] Ricominciò la vendita dell'acqua santa; l'addestramento militare riprese vigore, e si ripredisse l'arrivo di un *cargo* e la fine della dominazione inglese». Questo favorì la consueta «reazione» colonialista in quanto turbava l'ordine entro il quale doveva svolgersi la vita indigena; gli inglesi decisero di radere al suolo il villaggio di Ndrauni-vi, ove era nato Navosavakandua, e deportò la popolazione a Kadavu; nel paese evacuato di forza si stabilì di stanza un reparto di polizia: solo dopo dieci anni di continue petizioni si permise agli esiliati il ritorno.

Ma quello dei *tuka* alle Figi non fu il solo caso di quegli anni; Worsley racconta che nel 1893, R.J. Kennedy, della magistratura indigena di Samarai, in Nuova Guinea, riferì di un giovane indigeno di nome Tokerua del villaggio Gabagabuna (a nord della Milne Bay), che diceva di essere ispirato da uno spirito «incarnato», per così dire, in un albero tradizionalmente sacro. Secondo le sue parole, Tokerua proclamava di aver visto lo *Hiyoyoa* (l'altro mondo) e al suo ritorno profetizzò un grande uragano,

il quale con un'onda gigantesca avrebbe sommerso l'intera costa. I villaggi esistenti, compresi quelli di Wagawaga e di Gabagabuna, sarebbero stati sommersi da quest'onda, che avrebbe causato l'emersione di una nuova isola nel mezzo della baia. Solo i credenti si sarebbero salvati, [...] i beni dei bianchi venivano messi al bando: erano proibite le scatolette di latta per fiammiferi, i coltelli a serramanico, eccetera; gli indigeni dovevano tornare all'uso degli utensili di pietra.

Fu un missionario a scoprire l'esistenza del movimento quando una domenica s'avvide che alla sua predica della mattina erano presenti solo bambini. Egli scoperse che tutti erano emigrati sulle rive della Milne Bay; a Tavara, dove viveva Tokerua; per cui partì immediatamente con un collega per Wagawaga, dove si trovava un centro missionario con un «insegnante» indigeno, Biga. Ma solo Biga con sua moglie e la famiglia diedero il benvenuto alla comitiva; anche là uomini, donne e bambini erano fuggiti nell'interno coi loro maiali e coi cani.

Uno spirito aveva annunziato al profeta che dopo l'uragano il vento di sud-est, il vento cioè della bella stagione del racconto, avrebbe soffiato di continuo; [...] una vela sarebbe apparsa all'orizzonte, annunziando l'arrivo di un immenso vascello con gli spiriti dei morti a bordo; e così i fedeli si sarebbero riuniti ai loro congiunti morti e Tokerua avrebbe formato un governo, con a disposizione un piroscafo molto più grande di quello del governo, il *Merrie England*; il cibo sarebbe stato abbondantissimo e tutti i maiali sarebbero stati uccisi e mangiati, e il cibo consumato nei campi.

Worsley ci assicura che la gente ascoltò la profezia, non svolse alcun lavoro, e centinaia di maiali vennero uccisi e mangiati in attesa del «miracolo».

La profezia ovviamente non s'avverò; e l'ira dei delusi fu di grande violenza. Però non si rivolse verso Tokerua, ma verso chiunque rappresentava l'*ordine costituito*; per questo il profeta della Milne Bay e i suoi seguaci furono a lungo perseguitati, e la loro setta dispersa; ma, con loro, il culto del *cargo* era giunto in Nuova Guinea e quando alle grandi navi s'aggiunsero altri mezzi di trasporto, il mito si adeguò al processo tecnologico dei bianchi. Quando negli anni Trenta nei cieli della Melanesia cominciarono a volare i primi aerei, alcuni «profeti» della Nuova Guinea si adattarono alla novità; e questo benché il solo rumore degli aerei gettasse nel terrore più cieco la gente dei villaggi. È divertente leggere in proposito la testimonianza di un pilota: J. L. Taylor, uno fra i pionieri del volo in Nuova Guinea.

Ogni volta che l'apparecchio si abbassava sulla radura per lanciare soccorsi alle nostre pattuglie in esplorazione nell'interno delle *Highlands*, riso, farina, asce e beni di ogni genere cadevano a terra, la gente del posto stava sbigottita e meravigliata, gli occhi sbarrati. Per loro, l'aereo era un messaggero del cielo che portava cibo a spiriti in difficoltà... Ricordo che osservando le radure dei «lanci» vedevamo spesso dei vecchi che ci facevano capire a segni che erano pronti a partire con noi per «il mondo di sopra».

Date queste premesse, non è poi molto stupefacente che i primi papua capitati nei pressi di una pista d'atterraggio, nel vedere uomini bianchi uscire dal ventre dell'«uccello», credessero di trovarsi di fronte a reincarnazioni magiche degli spiriti dei morti, provenienti dal cielo. E questo «desiderio di rapporto col cielo» è un'altra delle più tipiche manifestazioni del *cargo*. Nel novembre del 1932 si ebbe notizia in Nuova Guinea (è ancora Worsley a raccontarlo) di un movimento semi-religioso che faceva capo a un certo Pako, il quale affermava d'essere in relazione diretta col cielo e parente del Sole e della Luna. Egli profetizzava una marea mostruosa e l'arrivo di una nave con un *cargo* composto di armi da fuoco, ferro, cibo, tabacco, scuri, autocarri.

Il movimento di Pako era chiaramente antieuropeo; si decidevano stragi, si attendevano armi e intanto in tutti i villaggi aderenti al movimento ci si esercitava con finti fucili e con bastoni.

La parola d'ordine [riferisce ancora Worsley] era «i bianchi a mare!», e si aspettava con fiducia la vittoria. Pesava sugli europei l'accusa di celare una parte della dottrina e del rituale dei cristiani: essi nascondevano il fatto che erano gli antenati degli indigeni a produrre i beni che poi gli europei ricevevano. La prova era l'incapacità dimostrata dagli europei nel riparare i congegni meccanici quando questi si rompevano; incapacità per cui dovevano spedirli gli spiriti degli antenati per la riparazione. [...]
La crisi finale sopraggiunse con l'arrivo dei giapponesi. Quando le autorità australiane abbandonarono il paese, i depositi governativi vennero saccheggiati da una folla eccitata di indigeni. Non più i tedeschi, ma i giapponesi erano ora gli attesi portatori del *cargo*; sicché vennero accolti con pazza gioia.

L'episodio citato introduce il discorso sul rapporto tra la guerra nel Pacifico fra americani e giapponesi e il *cargo*. Quella guerra aveva colto le varie potenze coloniali impreparate, l'avanzata giapponese era stata quindi travolgente. In Nuova Guinea, Rabaul cadde il 4 gennaio 1942, la Nuova Britannia e la Nuova Irlanda poco dopo e così altre regioni costiere del mandato conquistate. L'avanzata giapponese causò la partenza dei più alti funzionari australiani; e così venne a cessare in tutto il mondo papua il controllo esercitato dalle autorità amministrative. Questa partenza precipitosa coincideva con molte profezie riguardanti il *cargo* e i giapponesi tentarono di strumentalizzare per i propri scopi il movimento profetico dei papua.

Nell'isola di Karkar [scrive ancora Worsley] un ufficiale giapponese disse agli indigeni che i giapponesi avevano cercato di venir prima, ma che solo adesso erano riusciti nell'intento. I giapponesi, diceva, lavoravano; mentre gli europei, no. Gli indigeni dovevano lavorare duramente per i bianchi, ricevendone in cambio una miseria. A differenza dei bianchi, in cambio ne avrebbero ricevuto auto, cavalli, scialuppe, case e aerei. A questo discorso fece seguito una generosa distribuzione di bottino.

Ma questo idillio tra i papua e i soldati del Tenno durò poco; Worsley narra le nefandezze degli occupanti e conclude:

Fu con immenso sollievo e gioia che la popolazione salutò l'attacco americano contro Biak del 1944. I 5000 soldati giapponesi furono disarmati in breve tempo; poi cominciarono le operazioni che, probabilmente, fecero più impressione sugli isolani che non la vera e propria vittoria militare: lo sbarco del materiale bellico. Proprio come profetato, navi e battelli da sbarco di tutti i tipi riversarono il loro *cargo* sulle spiagge. L'aria era piena di rumori: navi immense arrivavano in un numero sempre maggiore. Biak, che non era mai stata una zona di grande produzione di sago, era a corto di viveri. Gli americani rifornirono gli indigeni di viveri e consegnarono loro delle armi per riceverne aiuto nella caccia ai combattenti giapponesi. Per ogni testa di giapponese si offriva un fiorino olandese; in un secondo tempo fu solo necessario produrre due orecchie.

Quei beni e depositi costituivano una certezza di future ricchezze; la popolazione papua cantava: «Quando gli americani se ne andranno, tutto sarà nostro».

Ma quali, invece, furono le conseguenze del periodo bellico? Da un lato la delusione perché ovviamente quel «tutto sarà nostro» dei papua non s'avverò mai. D'altro lato s'erano prodotti mutamenti, causa di reazioni irreversibili, che avevano minato la struttura della società indigena. Un esempio fra mille potrebbe essere quello delle isole Salomone che, quando le armate giapponesi furono sconfitte, presentavano uno spettacolo di «distruzione sociale» quale mai comunità primitive avevano offerto prima di allora nei Mari del Sud. «Vi si erano prodotti dei mutamenti di tale profondità e con effetti così sconvolgenti da poter definire giustamente il risultato di tutto questo come rivoluzionario» scrive Worsley; e sottolinea che anche il culto del *cargo* aveva subìto trasformazioni assai curiose. Nella valle del Markam, alla fine della guerra, si scoprì che influenzato da quattro anni di esperienza militare nell'isola, il culto del *cargo* s'era adattato all'organizzazione strategica e logistica dei giapponesi e degli americani. Esistevano laggiù «stazioni radio», in cui erano piazzati dei cilindri di bambù, con «fili» che andavano da questi cilindri a un «isolatore», anch'esso di bambù, fissato al tetto, e di qui a una fune che faceva da «antenna» tesa di fuori fra due pali. Quando si scoprì questo «impianto», si sospettò per un istante la presenza di giapponesi superstiti; ma fu un'idea che cadde quando si vide, la mattina dopo, una strana adunanza degli abitanti del villaggio che si allenavano esercitandosi militarmente con canne al posto di fucili.

Interrogati i locali, si seppe che la radio avrebbe dato loro in anticipo la notizia dell'imminente venuta di Gesù. E allora gli indigeni addestrati avrebbero avuto i fucili, avrebbero scacciato i bianchi, e avrebbero avuto al loro fianco, per aiutarli, gli spiriti dei morti tornati finalmente in vita.

Nel centro delle «stazioni» c'erano dei pali con piuoli; questi pali dovevano servire a Gesù per scendere a terra, oppure agli indigeni per salire a lui. Inoltre gli indigeni disponevano di «canne» che *facevano* «lampi al magnesio», con cui «scoprire», al buio, Gesù. L'ufficiale australiano incaricato di questa indagine non volle contraddire quella fede cieca e si limitò ad informare gli indigeni che *Gesù avrebbe annunciato la sua venuta per prima cosa al governatore... ma che questo sarebbe accaduto solo fra molti anni; e che, se questo fosse mai successo, la notizia dell'arrivo sarebbe stata data dallo stesso governatore... e da lui solo.*

Dagli anni sessanta in poi si registrarono solo alcuni episodi sporadici. Nell'isola di Nuova Hannover (arcipelago di Bismarck) nel 1964, la maggior parte dei papua si rifiutò di votare alle elezioni generali perché tra i candidati non si trovava il presidente degli Stati Uniti Lyndon Johnson. I «neocultisti» spiegarono all'Amministrazione come un giovane di nome Bosmailik fosse stato visitato dagli spiriti e avesse annunciato che se gli abitanti dell'isola avessero votato per il presidente Johnson, questi sarebbe giunto a Nuova Hannover con una nave carica di ogni bene, avrebbe liberato l'isola dagli «oppressori» australiani, avrebbe preso in mano le redini del potere e ridotto immediatamente le tasse. Dopo questo annuncio, e dopo essersi conseguentemente rifiutati di votare, i cultisti decisero di sfidare il Governo non pagando le tasse.

Mentre l'Amministrazione cercava affannosamente il consiglio degli etnologi per decidere come reagire, l'influenza del culto continuò ad accrescersi. Bosmailik predisse l'arrivo del presidente non più via mare ma con aerei militari; e destino volle che per una strana coincidenza nel giorno stesso predetto da Bosmailik un bombardiere volasse sopra l'isola. Ovviamente non atterrò, ma questo fatto e il conseguente mancato arrivo del presidente Johnson non scosse il profeta Bosmailik, il quale asserì ai suoi fedeli che erano stati gli australiani a deviare l'aereo.

Un altro episodio fu causa, per un equivoco, di una grave minaccia di rivolta. La radio locale annunciò, un giorno del 1966, la visita all'isola del direttore del Dipartimento per l'educazione L. W. Johnson. L'annuncio che «proprio lui» avrebbe prossimamente visitato il Nuova Hannover, trasmesso per radio, fu sentito da migliaia di «cultisti» che equivocarono sul nome; certi che il presidente degli Stati Uniti sarebbe presto veramente, e finalmente!, giunto, cominciarono a fare piani di feste per accoglierlo. Furono uccisi maiali, i villaggi furono decorati e gran quantità di frutta e verdura furono raccolte. Quando fu chiaro che tra il presidente Usa e il signor Johnson, professore australiano, c'era una bella differenza, poco mancò che la sede centrale dell'Amministrazione australiana venisse data alle fiamme; la reazione violenta si placò solo alla notizia che nelle vicine isole Tsoi e nella Nuova Irlanda (dove altri «cultisti» di Johnson avevano creato «gruppi d'attesa del *cargo*») si era dato inizio a una sottoscrizione per raggiungere i 2200 dollari necessari a «comprare» il presidente americano.

Quando visitai quelle isole, negli anni Settanta, potei vedere con i miei occhi come la colletta «pro Johnson» fosse ancora in corso; e amici locali mi dissero che quel particolare «culto» era fonte di continue scaramucce con le autorità australiane incaricate della riscossione delle tasse e che ormai da anni si vedevano opporre un netto rifiuto alle loro «legali» richieste perché «il denaro serve per l'acquisto di Johnson», il quale, una volta «comprato», verrà finalmente a portare il *cargo* custodito dai morti.

Al di là della cronaca di questo o quell'evento, di queste o quelle assurdità, il *cargo-cult* e le sue sopravvivenze sono indicative per comprendere come questo mito del *cargo*, malgrado le sue *varianti*, dovute al mutare dei tempi, resti pur sempre una *forma particolare* del culto dei morti.

In Oceania, è bene ricordarlo, la morte non corrisponde mai a una nozione di annientamento. «Essa» ha scritto Jean Guaiart[1]

---

[1] *Op. cit.*

«rappresenta una diversa qualità di vita. I vivi trovano appoggio ed aiuto nei morti, che sono costantemente presenti intorno a loro.» Guaiart cita in proposito un mito antico dei papua che spiega la differenza «materiale» esistente fra gli europei e la gente dell'Oceania; secondo questo mito, che anche noi abbiamo ascoltato in Nuova Guinea, con qualche variante, un antenato capostipite comune a tutte le genti violò un giorno un tabù causando la partenza di un «fratello bianco» con quelle ricchezze che ora sono degli europei, degli americani e degli australiani, mentre un altro fratello, quello papua, aveva conservato la verità fondamentale della vita.

Del fratello partito con tutte le ricchezze comuni, il mito promette un ritorno escatologico: quello, appunto che i profeti del *cargo* hanno promesso ai loro fedeli. Tra l'altro, questo mito dei due fratelli spiega come sia stato accettato facilmente dalle genti locali l'insediamento degli europei in Oceania; [...] la delusione generale nel «non ritorno» del fratello ricco è stata poi spiegata con un nuovo mito, secondo il quale il famoso *cargo* sarebbe stato rubato dai bianchi, i quali inoltre avrebbero cambiato gli indirizzi sulle casse dei doni, impossessandosi sacrilegamente di quanto era stato inviato dai morti ai loro discendenti.

Il «culto dei morti» è quindi fondamentale nella vita di ieri, ma anche di oggi, delle genti che abitano isole e arcipelaghi dei Mari del Sud. Questo è vero, lo sappiamo, per tutte le culture («evolute» e «progredite») create dall'uomo sin dalla più lontana preistoria.

In Oceania[1] ne restano, però, poche *fisiche* tracce per la «demolizione» delle tradizioni locali compiute con cieco fanatismo dai missionari protestanti nel XIX secolo.

Nel 1826 [narra Peter Buck, e questo episodio vale a illustrarne chissà quanti analoghi fra quelli noti e quelli sconosciuti] un'imbarcazione inviata dal quartier generale della London Missionary Society in Raiatea tornò da Rurutu con un carico di «dèi pagani» che furono mostrati al pubblico

---

[1] Nel suo saggio *Les réligions de l'Océanie* delle Presses Universitaires de France, l'etnologo Jean Guaiart dice testualmente: «La ricerca di questo campo, da tempo balbettante malgrado le sue ambizioni, è ora a uno stadio modesto ma più efficace della raccolta "regionale" dei fatti. E così fra qualche anno i vasti lavori in corso, opere di équipes etnografiche di americani, australiani, inglesi e francesi, permetteranno nuove "sintesi" oceaniane» (1962).

dall'alto di un pulpito. Uno di essi, di nome Aa (Ha), il dio principale di Rurutu, era rappresentato da una statua di legno alta un metro e venti, di forma umana e con corpo e testa cavi, chiusi sul dietro da un coperchio. Sollevato quel coperchio, si trovò là dentro una folla di piccoli dèi: non meno di ventiquattro, secondo il missionario John Williams, furono cavati fuori l'uno dopo l'altro e mostrati al pubblico. Facile indovinare la sorte che toccò a quella straordinaria scultura: come le anime dei malvagi bruciano all'inferno, così gli idoli di legno dei pagani bruciarono nel mondo. Per quanto ne so io, si salvò soltanto la grande immagine di Aa, che ha oggi il suo santuario nel British Museum, dove è venerata col nome di Tangaroa-upao-vahu.

Questa citazione da Peter Buck ci permette di collegare il discorso sulla religione, il culto dei morti e i suoi simboli, a quello sull'arte dell'Oceania che nella ritualità sacra sembra aver trovato, un tempo, la sua principale ragione d'essere.

Zona luminosa del passato, l'estetica dell'Oceania, oggi, è invece completamente assorbita dalla necessità di aderire a una realtà mutevole e sempre più complessa. Polinesiani e papua, all'oriente come all'occidente del grande oceano, non hanno più tempo di dedicarsi, come una volta al concludersi d'ogni stagione agricola o di pesca, ad attività «creative». Sopravvive l'arte cosiddetta minore: stuoie, cestini, *tapa*. La scultura, per esempio, è scomparsa o è sul punto di scomparire. I pezzi più belli superstiti sono finiti, lo sappiamo, nelle collezioni private o nei musei d'Europa o d'America. Un tempo, erano oggetto di venerazione, simbolo di riti collettivi, ornamento della vita quotidiana; oggi, secondo lo studioso Guaiart

essi [gli oggetti d'arte] sono divenuti gli elementi essenziali di determinati circuiti speculativi. [...] Pochi si preoccupano delle condizioni sociali, di luogo e di tempo che definiscono ciascuna di tale opere. [...] Così le grandi forme dell'arte oceaniana sono divenute oggetti morti, segni vuoti ai quali ognuno vuole riferire le proprie emozioni, il proprio sistema di valori. E tanto più sono oggetto di speculazione intellettuale quanto più è ignorato il loro valore reale. È stato il surrealismo a crearne per primo la moda, credendo di ritrovare in essi i propri fantasmi.

È lo stesso Jean Guaiart a ricordarci che non si può, comunque, parlare dell'arte d'Oceania senza ricordarne un aspetto che le fu così tipico e che, seppur conosciuto da altri popoli, solo nelle isole del Pacifico raggiunge le dimensioni, appunto, d'arte: il tatuaggio.

Il tatuaggio, in Oceania, era una funzione sociale essenziale. E poiché rimane incancellabile, almeno come traccia, è il risultato di un rito, il cui compimento è la creazione artistica stessa; e di questo rito «estetico» le isole della Polinesia sono il luogo di elezione. La tecnica del tatuaggio si basava su varianti di un unico procedimento: fissaggio di linee o di fasce di colore ottenuto introducendo sotto la pelle una sostanza scura; disegno sottocutaneo ottenibile usando «punte» d'osso o di avorio, a denti aguzzi, fissate a un manico quasi ad angolo retto, un po' come un'accetta;

lo strumento [spiega Guaiart] spalmato di pigmento, veniva posato sul corpo al punto voluto, e vi si affondavano le punte con un colpo secco battendovi con un pezzo di legno come una mazza; con tamponi di *tapa* si fermava il sangue. Le punte essendo fitte, si otteneva in superficie un effetto di punteggiatura. [...]

Per ragioni di prestigio e perché l'operazione costava molto, i tatuaggi totali del viso erano un segno di appartenenza a classi elevate. Le teste dei capi, pertanto, venivano accuratamente svuotate, dopo la morte, poste a cuocere in un certo modo nel forno, quindi fatte seccare col fumo. Sono quelle di cui numerosi musei posseggono qualche esemplare. [...]

Il risultato del lavoro si riteneva dipendesse dalla rigorosa astinenza sessuale imposta a chi operava, ai suoi aiutanti e al paziente, prima e durante l'operazione.

La religiosità ispirava dunque profondamente l'estetica dell'Oceania d'un tempo; l'estetica, come ogni altra azione dei papua, dei polinesiani e dei micronesiani che non sfuggivano alla regola comune di tutte le popolazioni primitive: nulla accade o *non accade* senza un motivo, una causa o una giustificazione magico-religiosa.

Uno dei precursori dell'etnografia oceaniana moderna, Rivers, ha parlato di gerontocrazia, governo tenuto dai vecchi, notando che esiste *soprattutto e in gran parte dell'Oceania* una tendenza generale a riservare agli uomini di una certa età (profondamente iniziati ai riti, possessori delle tecniche di magia capaci di garantire il buon esito delle attività economiche, caccia, pesca, raccolto, agricoltura, e ricchi per la cumulazione di beni tradizionali) il possesso delle fanciulle, lasciando ai giovani la sola possibilità di avventure irregolari, rischiose o punibili con ammende da pagare in maiali, in attesa di aver raggiunto a loro volta una posizione sociale che permetta a essi di procurarsi una o più di una sposa e di creare una famiglia.

Nel tema della «famiglia» in Oceania, la citazione d'obbligo è quella di Malinowski. Un nome troppo noto nel campo dell'etnografia perché si debba ricordare il suo lungo lavoro attorno agli anni '20 nell'arcipelago delle Trobriand.

Nell'organizzazione della famiglia papua studiata da Malinowski, il ruolo della madre è alla base d'ogni rapporto. Qui la società è *matrilineare*, cioè è un sistema nel quale la parentela viene considerata attraverso la madre, e ogni «eredità» si trasmette solo in linea femminile; ogni figlio o figlia «appartengono» alla madre e solo a lei e alla sua famiglia. Un figlio succede nelle cariche e nella posizione sociale *al fratello della madre* ed eredita la proprietà non dal padre ma dallo *zio o dalla zia materna*. Fatta questa premessa, Malinoswki nel suo saggio già citato *Sex and repression in savage society*[1] così scrive sul rapporto fra uomo e donna nelle comunità da lui studiate:

> Ogni uomo o donna delle Trobriand passa a matrimonio dopo un periodo infantile di giochi sessuali, seguito da una generale licenza nell'adolescenza e poi da un periodo nel quale gli amanti vivono insieme in maniera più stabile, abitando in comunità con due o tre coppie una «casa da scapoli». Il matrimonio, che è in genere monogamico, eccetto fra i capi che hanno più mogli, è un'unione permanente, che richiede esclusività sessuale, comunanza economica e vita domestica indipendente. A prima vista, un osservatore superficiale potrebbe credere che si tratti di un tipo di matrimonio del tutto simile al nostro. In realtà, invece, esso è del tutto differente. Per cominciare, il marito non è considerato il padre della prole nel senso da noi dato a questa espressione; fisiologicamente egli non ha nulla a che fare con loro nascita, secondo le idee degli indigeni, che ignorano la paternità fisica. I figli, secondo la credenza indigena, vengono introdotti nell'utero materno sotto forma di spiriti piccolissimi, generalmente dallo spirito di una parente della madre. Il marito deve allora proteggere e amare i piccoli, «riceverli nelle braccia, quando nascono», ma essi non sono «suoi», nel senso che egli abbia partecipato alla loro procreazione.

[1] Trad. it. *Sesso e repressione sessuale tra i selvaggi*, Boringhieri, Torino 1969.

Il padre è, così, un amico benevolo e amato, ma non un parente riconosciuto del fanciullo. Parentela reale, cioè identità di sostanza, «identità fisica», esiste soltanto attraverso la madre, ed è il fratello della madre che è investito di autorità sui figli. [...]

Il padre, perciò, viene considerato dai figli *solo per le cure affettuose e per la tenera amicizia che li lega.* Il fratello della madre rappresenta il principio di disciplina, autorità e potere esecutivo della famiglia.

Proseguendo in questa sua analisi, Malinowski anzitutto fa notare come il paragone tra la maternità in queste isole e la nostra sia interessante perché lo «svezzamento» del bambino ha luogo molto più tardi che da noi (quando esso sa camminare, è già indipendente, mangia ogni cibo, è già stimolato da vari interessi); un momento in cui, insomma, egli non ha desiderio assoluto né bisogno reale «della mamma». E così il primo «strappo» è eliminato, con grande vantaggio per il suo equilibrio psichico. Malinowski, poi, precisa che questo matriarcato, questo diritto della madre, non deve certo intendersi come un potere duro, terribile di madri-virago. Le madri delle Trobriand come quelle di tutto il mondo, amano teneramente i loro bambini, li vezzeggiano, giocano con loro in un legame più stretto di quello esistente tra donna e uomo; alle Trobriand *i diritti del marito sono inferiori a quelli dei figli.* Altra differenza fra le nostri madri europee e quelle papua, è il fatto che le prime sono *molto più indulgenti*: nessuna educazione morale si richiede tra i papua per i bambini; e quel poco che qui si dà, comincia molto tardi ed è fatto da altre persone. C'è quindi, per forza, scarsa possibilità di rigore in una assenza di disciplina materna che impedisce fortunatamente l'aberrazione di un'eccessiva severità e dall'altra rende inutile l'*interesse*, nel bambino, di essere gradito alla madre per meritare la sua approvazione.

Così descritta la posizione della madre, l'etnologo ci illustra quella del padre:

Un uomo delle Trobriand raramente litigherà con la moglie, quasi mai si proverà ad essere brutale con lei, e non sarà mai capace di esercitare una tirannia permanente. Persino la coabitazione sessuale non viene considerata dalla legge e dalla tradizione indigena quale dovere della moglie e privilegio del marito, come accade nella nostra società. Gli indigeni delle Trobriand ritengono, secondo quanto stabilisce la tradizione, che il marito è in debito verso la moglie per i rapporti sessuali: deve meritarli e deve pagarli.

Un'analisi che ci dà la misura di quanto le società cosiddette primitive possano essere in tanti casi *più umane* di questo nostro mondo e della nostra società occidentale che riteniamo, anche se ipocritamente lo neghiamo, perfetta.

Più umana anche nell'ambito della libertà assoluta che godono i bambini e gli adolescenti delle Trobriand; dove i bambini e le bambine giocano insieme in una specie di repubblica giovanile; una libertà che può lasciar sconcertato un occidentale abituato a ben altre regole: si tratta, infatti, di una libertà che trova il suo sfogo soprattutto in «passatempi sessuali».

Fin dalla prima età [scrive Malinowski] i fanciulli si iniziano alle pratiche sessuali reciprocamente, o talvolta per mezzo di un compagno di poco più grande. Naturalmente in questo stadio non possono eseguire gli atti veri e propri, ma si contentano di ogni sorta di giochi nei quali sono lasciati completamente liberi dagli anziani; e così possono soddisfare le loro curiosità e la loro sessualità direttamente e senza finzioni.

Nel caso di un'importante veglia funebre, gli abitanti dei villaggi vicini arrivano in massa per partecipare alle lamentazioni e ai canti. Secondo l'usanza, le ragazze del gruppo «visitante» devono consolare i giovani del villaggio del morto.

Un altro grande etnologo, Havelock Ellis,[1] ci dà un giudizio sereno e interessante sullo studio compiuto in quest'area così delicata della vita quotidiana. Per Ellis

la vita sessuale dei selvaggi ha atteso a lungo lo storico che la studiasse dal punto di vista naturalistico. A causa dei tabù sessuali, i quali pesano con eguale forza sulla mente civilizzata e su quella selvaggia, questo argomento è sempre stato velato di mistero; mistero affascinante o tenebroso, a seconda dell'atteggiamento generale che prevaleva nei confronti dello stato selvaggio. Nel diciottesimo secolo fu affascinante. Quel secolo specialmente nella sua moda francese, scoprì virtualmente ciò che viene chiamato erroneamente e genericamente «l'uomo primitivo» e trovò la sua più perfetta incarnazione nel nuovo e paradisiaco mondo dell'America e dell'Oceania. [...] Nel diciannovesimo secolo prevalse il punto di vista più tenebroso. Gli esploratori erano quasi tutti inglesi e si portavano appresso il puritanesimo anglosassone secondo il quale tutti i costumi sessuali non familiari erano disgustosi o sconvenienti. «Osceno» era la parola comunemente usata, e si lasciava all'immaginazione del lettore figurarsi ciò che essa poteva significare. Il comportamento sessuale dei selvaggi era cosa di cui non si poteva

---

[1] Cfr. introduzione a Malinowski, *Sesso e repressione*, cit.

parlare. L'incisione uretrale praticata da alcune tribù australiane venne misteriosamente chiamata «il terribile rito». Una simile mutilazione del naso o dell'orecchio e in qualsiasi posto un po' più in su o un po' più giù non veniva considerata terribile, ma in quel punto particolare dava luogo a un brivido e a un atteggiamento di sgomento colmo di vergogna.

Ed è esattamente in questa linea di «aperta e franca» analisi, che Malinowski ha impostato il suo lavoro.[1]

I reni [scrive Malinowski] sono considerati come la parte o il tronco (*tapwana*) principale o centrale del sistema. Da essi altri dotti (*wotuna*) vanno all'organo maschile. Questo è l'apice o la punta (*matala*, letteralmente occhio) di tutto il sistema. Di modo che quando gli occhi vedono un oggetto di desiderio, si «svegliano», comunicano l'impulso ai reni i quali a loro volta lo trasmettono causando l'erezione. Quindi gli occhi sono la causa principale di ogni eccitamento sessuale: essi sono le «cose dell'accoppiamento»; sono «quello che ci fa desiderare di accoppiarci». La prova di questo è che l'indigeno dice: «Un uomo con gli occhi chiusi non può avere erezione»; anche se poi precisa ulteriormente questa asserzione ammettendo che certe volte il senso dell'olfatto può sostituire gli occhi, perché «quando una donna toglie la gonna nell'oscurità, il desiderio può venire stimolato».

Nel riferire delle credenze papua di queste isole in relazione al concepimento e alla nascita, si potrebbe dire che tra i papua *ogni nuova vita comincia con la morte*; tesi che deriva dall'aver osservato quanto la tradizione trobrianda insegna in proposito: al momento della morte lo spirito d'ogni uomo vola a Tuma, Isola dei Morti, dove vive un'esistenza molto simile, anzi più felice di quella terrestre. Ma ci sono defunti che hanno desiderio di ritornare e ad essi è concesso un balzo indietro nel tempo così che si mutano in spiriti di bambini non ancora nati.

Questi bambini «preincarnati o spiriti-bambini» sono l'unica fonte dalla quale l'umanità trova una sua «vita di ritorno». Nel ringiovanimento finale, che li fa tornare allo stato di infanti, gli spiriti devono bagnarsi nell'acqua di mare e quando diventano di nuovo bambini, vanno nel mare e si lasciano trasportare dalla corrente. Di questi spiriti di bambini preincarnati si parla ancor oggi alle Trobriand come se essi stessero galleggiando su pezzi di legno, o foglie, rami, alghe marine morte, schiuma di mare e altre sostanze leggere sparse sulla superficie del mare.[2]

[1] *The Sexual Life of Savages in North-Western Melanesia*, New York 1929; trad. it. di E. Campi, *La vita sessuale dei selvaggi nella Melanesia nord-occidentale*, Feltrinelli, Milano 1968.
[2] Malinowski, *op. cit.*

Ogni nuova vita alle Trobriand galleggia sul mare, si potrebbe dire, quindi, citando i racconti dei pescatori locali che quando vanno al largo, in oceano, alla pesca dello squalo, sentono il gemito caratteristico degli spiriti bambini – *wa, wa, wa* – nel lamento del vento e delle onde: «Ogni bambino galleggia su un pezzo di legno,» dicono i trobriandesi «uno spirito vede che è un bel bambino. Lo prende. Lo spirito è lo spirito della madre o del padre della donna incinta (*nasusuma*). Allora lo spirito mette il bambino sulla testa e sui capelli della donna incinta che soffre di mali di testa e vomita e ha male alla pancia. Poi il bambino s'infila nella pancia e a questo punto la donna è veramente incinta. Dice: "Già mi ha trovata; già gli spiriti mi hanno portato il bambino"».

Nei villaggi della costa del nord, c'è la consuetudine di riempire d'acqua di mare un recipiente di legno che viene lasciato di notte nella capanna di una donna che desidera concepire, con la speranza che un *galleggiante-spirito-bambino* sia rimasto imprigionato nell'acqua del recipiente e che durante la notte si trasferisca nel corpo della donna.

Se nel rapporto «nascita-mare» era il concetto stesso della vita che si rinnova a essere mitizzato, il rapporto con il mare di un'altra tradizione papua – quella della *kula* – è anch'esso d'estrema importanza, investendo la realtà sociale quotidiana d'intere comunità, in operazioni che non dobbiamo assolutamente vedere come transazioni puramente commerciali; la *kula* non risponde a un calcolo utilitario, di profitto e di perdita, ma è un fenomeno volto a soddisfare aspirazioni emotive ed estetiche d'un ordine diverso dal soddisfacimento di bisogni elementari. Su questa *kula* Malinowski scrive un lungo saggio *Gli argonauti del Pacifico occidentale*[1] nel quale egli analizza tutte le fasi e gli aspetti, anche avventurosi e magici. Un'odissea nera, la cui vicenda va vista nel generale quadro di un mondo marino, quello del Pacifico meridionale, le cui popolazioni costiere, tranne rare eccezioni, sono o erano,

---

[1] Da noi letto nella versione francese a cura di André e Simonne Devyver, nella collana «L'éspèce humaine» di Gallimard (1963). Tutte le citazioni in questa antologia sul fenomeno della *kula* sono tratte da questo volume.

prima di estinguersi, composte da marinai e commercianti accorti (sempreché si parli dei gruppi detti *salt-water-men* da tempo immemorabile a contatto col mare; ché la maggioranza dei papua quello detta *bushmen* vive, invece, all'interno delle isole occidentali, e teme il mare). Questi navigatori coraggiosi, artigiani attivi, e abili mercanti hanno creato «forme precise di scambio» scrive Malinowski «lungo vie commerciali ben definite». Su queste rotte si è inserito il fenomeno della *kula*, un sistema di scambio molto diverso da quello tradizionale, ma egualmente esteso e complesso; con le sue ramificazioni, interessa non solamente le isole vicine alla Punta Est della Nuova Guinea ma anche le Luoisiades, l'isola Woodlark, l'arcipelago Trobriand e il gruppo di Entrecasteaux[1] ed esercita un'influenza indiretta su molti distretti lontani come l'isola Rossel e certe regioni della costa settentrionale e meridionale della Grande Isola.

Questi arcipelaghi sono disposti in un ampio cerchio, sicché la rotta commerciale che li unisce forma un circuito chiuso. Per la *kula*, lungo questo itinerario due specie d'articoli, e solamente questi due, circolano senza sosta in direzioni opposte.

Il primo consiste in una lunga collana di conchiglie rosse, chiamata *soulava* e «si muove» in un percorso nel senso delle lancette dell'orologio. Il secondo, un braccialetto di conchiglie bianche, chiamato *mwali*, va nella direzione contraria.

Tutti e due questi tipi di merce seguendo, così, la propria strada nel circuito chiuso, sono fonti di transazioni, fissate e regolate da un insieme di convenzioni e di principi tradizionali che formano appunto la *kula*.

In ogni isola, un numero ristretto di individui riceve gli oggetti in questione, li tiene per un certo periodo di tempo e li passa poi ad altri.

La *kula* [nota Malinowski, dopo le premesse che abbiamo riferito] non è affatto una forma di scambio precaria e clandestina. Essa è, al contrario, radicata nel mito, sostenuta dalla legge tradizionale e contornata da riti magici. Tutte le sue principali transazioni sono pubbliche e solenni, e vengono eseguite secondo regole ben precise. Queste transazioni non vengono fatte sotto l'impulso del momento, ma hanno luogo periodicamente, in date

[1] Vedi cartina nella pagina accanto.

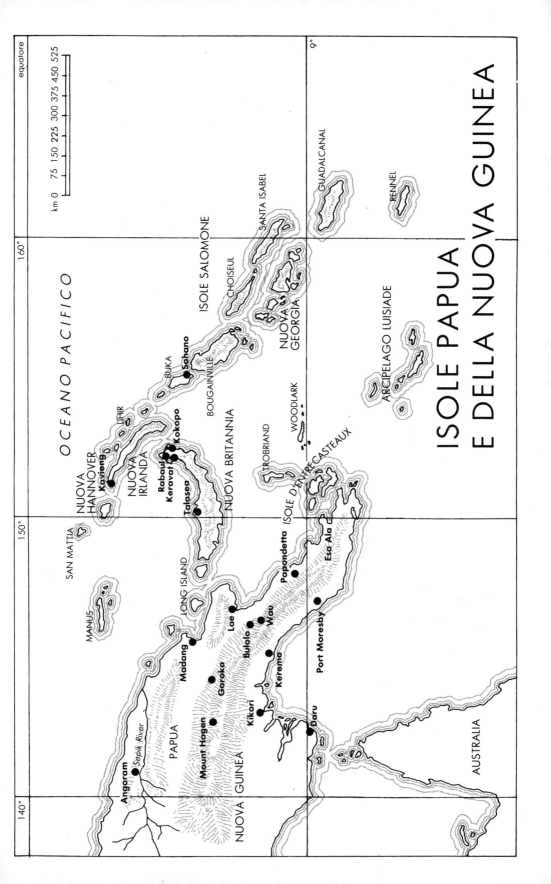

ISOLE PAPUA E DELLA NUOVA GUINEA

stabilite in anticipo, ed esse scorrono lungo vie commerciali ben definite, che portano a incontri fissi.

I due principali articoli *kula* (i braccialetti di conchiglie da una parte e le lunghe collane di spondilo dall'altra) sono ornamenti che non vengono portati se non in occasione di danze cerimoniali, grandi feste, e riunioni collettive dove molti villaggi sono rappresentati.

Oltretutto [scrive stupito Malinowski] la maggioranza di questi braccialetti sono di misura piccola anche per un bambino, e altri sono così grandi e preziosi da essere portati una volta ogni dieci anni circa e solo da personaggi importantissimi. Nonostante che tutte le collane siano, invece, portabili, alcune sono considerate troppo ricche e scomode per poterne fare un uso frequente.

Ma una descrizione della *kula* non è sufficiente a intenderne il fenomeno nella sua completezza, se manca una testimonianza diretta di un protagonista del grande scambio.

Non sarà la mia, essendo purtroppo da alcuni decenni scomparsa la tradizione della *kula* quando io ho cominciato a disegnare i miei intinerari tra le isole dei Mari del Sud e gli arcipelaghi papua. Come «testimonianza» non posso non citare ancora il testo di Malinowski; là dove descrive il commovente momento d'una partenza per un viaggio di scambio e durante il quale la *kula* sarà praticata.

Gli abitanti della comunità si riuniscono tutti sulla spiaggia; fra loro, ci sono le donne, i bambini, i vecchi e i pochi uomini di guardia al villaggio. Il capo della flottiglia si alza e pronuncia pressappoco queste parole, indirizzandosi alla folla: «Donne, noi partiamo, voi restate al villaggio per occuparvi degli orti e delle case, dovete rimanere caste. Quando andrete nella foresta per cercare legna, fate in modo che nessuna di voi resti indietro. Quando andrete negli orti a lavorare, cercate di restare tutte insieme. Ritornate in gruppo con le vostre sorelle più giovani».

Egli scongiura poi gli abitanti degli altri villaggi vicini, perché non infastidiscano le donne rimaste sole; sentendo ciò, un uomo dell'interno di alza e prende la parola: «Non dite questo, o capo, voi partite e il vostro villaggio resterà come voi lo lasciate. Poiché andate sul mare, noi saremo i guardiani del vostro villaggio. Al vostro ritorno, ritorneremo alle nostre case; forse ci darete un po' di noce di betel, del sagu, della noce di cocco. Forse praticherete la *kula* con noi per qualche collana di conchiglie».

Scambiate queste raccomandazioni e promesse, le imbarcazioni si allontanano tutte insieme. Succede che qualche donna pianga al momento della partenza ma è tabù piangere dopo.

Viaggiando per paesi lontani, provvisti di risorse naturali sconosciute nella loro patria, i navigatori *kula* ritornano, ogni volta, abbondantemente carichi di prodotti d'ogni genere; per poter offrire dei regali ai compagni che sono restati, i partenti si caricano al momento del ritorno di oggetti che sanno essere molto apprezzati dagli abitanti dei loro villaggi rimasti al di là dei mari.

Qualche oggetto serve come regalo per i compagni, ma la maggior parte di essi è destinata a pagare le merci che interessano.

Infine sulla strada della *kula*, oltre agli oggetti di cultura materiale del commercio sussidiario viaggiano anche costumi, canzoni, motivi artistici e influenze culturali. La *kula* quindi è, per citare testualmente il suo studioso, «una ampia rete di relazioni intertribali, una grande organizzazione che interessa migliaia di persone».

Di Margaret Mead, l'antropologa americana direttrice del reparto etnologico dell'American Museum of Natural History e professore di antropologia alla Columbia University, celebre soprattutto per le sue ricerche nel Pacifico meridionale, nell'arco degli anni che vanno dai Trenta ai Sessanta, soprattutto mi ha interessato leggere quanto più mi ha aiutato ad affrontare il tema di fondo di questo libro: la trasformazione delle isole e delle società indigene che le abitano.

In *Crescita di una comunità primitiva*[1] la Mead ha steso il resoconto di un ritorno, dopo venticinque anni, a un villaggio (Peri), in cui vive la popolazione detta dei *manus*, nell'isola omonima. Una esperienza che ha stimolato l'etnologa a compiere il lavoro d'indagine necessario a scoprire cosa fosse realmente «accaduto» per trasformare «quel piccolo gruppo di cacciatori di teste, rimasti a una forma di civiltà da età della pietra, in una comunità che domandava di avere un posto nel mondo moderno».

Quel villaggio, posto sulla costa meridionale della più grande

[1] Edito nel 1962 da Bompiani, in traduzione di G. Griffini, dalla versione inglese *New Lives for Old*, pubblicata a New York nel 1956.

delle isole dell'Ammiragliato, fu scelto, ci spiega la Mead, perché era pressoché «vergine» da ogni contatto con gli occidentali; *condizione* fondamentale questa per il tipo di ricerca che si voleva compiere laggiù:

Per la prima volta da quando la scienza aveva cominciato a svilupparsi, il mondo scientifico occidentale era pronto a servirsi costruttivamente e spiritualmente del comportamento, così prezioso e così labile, di quelle popolazioni ancora «non civilizzate». Invece di meditare, seduti in poltrona, sulle narrazioni di viaggiatori, missionari o ufficiali coloniali, ora si poteva porre un problema al quale dare una risposta non trasformando gli esseri umani in animali da esperimento scientifico, ma mediante osservazioni controllate scientificamente sulla materia viva della storia.

E così nel 1928, il suo studio ebbe inizio, e la Mead si trovò a vivere *all'interno* di quella comunità.

Avevo imparato a parlare con loro, a prestare attenzione ai tabù, a fare le domande adatte quando un adulto si ammalava: «Quale spirito lo tormentava? e perché? Lo aveva già confessato? Aveva già fatto la sua espiazione?». Avevo imparato a interpretare gli improvvisi periodi di silenzio imbronciato o gli scoppi d'ira violenta della virtù offesa. Fintanto che parlavo il loro linguaggio e che pensavo nella loro stessa maniera, mi comprendevano. Ma non avevano però modo di capire le mie idee, i miei valori, né di fare la più semplice congettura sul perché, per esempio, volessi medicare le loro ferite; tanto meno potevano comprendere perché avessi lasciato un paese lontano e fossi venuta a vivere nel loro villaggio, se non per ragioni di vile guadagno. Quando partii, in ogni casa del villaggio venne suonato il tamburo di morte, ed era la cosa più appropriata da fare, perché io, per loro, stavo morendo.

Quei tamburi, invece, avevano suonato «a torto» se così si può dire: alla Mead, infatti accadde di ritornare dopo venticinque anni in quel luogo perduto del mondo.

Nel 1953 ritornai a Peri, un nuovo villaggio costruito sulla terra ferma con case in «stile americano», tutte eguali, disposte accuratamente in fila. [...]
Qualche giorno dopo il proprietario della casa che era stata messa a mia disposizione mi portò un quaderno, sul quale aveva scritto un lungo elenco di regole per l'allevamento del bambino, la nutrizione, il sonno, la disciplina, ecc. Mi disse che non avevano ancora emesso queste ordinanze, ma che esse costituivano quanto di meglio erano riusciti a raccogliere, basandosi sui ricordi delle spiegazioni avute e di quello che avevano visto fare dalle mogli degli australiani nelle città delle «isole grandi».

Davanti a tanto profonde trasformazioni, e pur rallegrandosi di quanto di positivo esse significassero, nel ricordo della Mead restassero l'immagine del villaggio *manus* così come le era apparso la prima volta, *parte integrata* di una natura nella quale si inseriva perfettamente, case a specchiarsi in quella laguna i cui canali scorrevano tra una casa e l'altra, costruite in modo da resistere agli improvvisi «colpi di vento»; canali sui quali scivolano piccole canoe, ognuna costruita «con uno scalmo sporgente che mantenga l'equilibrio, una piccola piattaforma su cui portare all'occorrenza viveri o persone, e qualche volta una polena scolpita con una testa di coccodrillo che divora un uomo»,

[...] popolo che lottava senza sosta, sostenuto in questo da un sistema religioso rigido e inflessibile, contro la povertà e l'incertezza di un'esistenza nella quale essi non possedevano niente, nemmeno la capacità di compiere lavori impegnativi, a eccezione di quelli ancora rozzi della costruzione di barche e della carpenteria, della pesca e del commercio. Le piattaforme erano costruite sulle palafitte per erigervi le case, fuori, nella laguna, perché fossero sicure dagli attacchi delle popolazioni della terraferma; ma i tronchi che servivano da pali per le case, o per le canoe, le foglie per la copertura dei tetti, la *rubber nut* per calafatare, l'occorrente per le gonne di erba, la corteccia per le lenze e le cinture degli uomini, le pentole, i vasi, i recipienti di guscio di cocco, e i cibi amidacei, il *sagu* e il *taro*, loro nutrimenti principali, tutto ciò proveniva dalla terraferma. Ed essi vivevano, così, costretti a un lavoro continuo, diligente, a viaggi lunghi, scomodi, pericolosi, a notti intere di pesca per raccogliere qualche manciata di pesce da portare al mercato all'alba, e a un complesso sistema economico per cui ogni uomo era invischiato in una rete tale di impegni che ogni debito pagato ne apriva contemporaneamente uno nuovo.

Ritratto di un popolo poveramente ma perfettamente ambientato nel mondo che lo circondava, in cui sapeva «muoversi» basandosi, come dice la Mead, «su un'immensa fiducia in se stessi e nelle proprie abilità nel trattare con ogni persona e con ogni situazione, e su un assoluto coraggio di fronte al vento e al mare».

Una fiducia [aggiunge la studiosa] che nasceva tra quella gente sin dalla prima età. Già i bambini più piccoli sapevano come destreggiarsi in quell'elemento sul quale il villaggio galleggiava come fosse una grande zattera: l'acqua della laguna. Quasi prima che a camminare, veniva insegnato ai bambini, con una pazienza inesauribile e con ogni cura, a destreggiarsi sull'acqua.

Da annotazioni come queste la Mead dedusse, in quel lontano

viaggio del 1928, che i primitivi *manus*, erano un piccolo popolo che faceva molto affidamento sui propri occhi e sui propri muscoli, nella più completa fiducia delle proprie forze, e nella sicurezza che sarebbe sempre stato possibile fabbricare ciò che era necessario, in parte con i loro corpi in parte con quanto si aveva sottomano, magari facendo a pezzi la trave di una casa per ricavarne un palo per la canoa. E tra i loro scarsi beni materiali, la Mead ci dice che essi avevano, però, una specie di moneta:

> Essi conoscevano il denaro: i denti di cane e le conchiglie, nel modo in cui venivano adoperate, possedevano tutte le qualità necessarie alla definizione moderna del denaro. Erano oggetti piccoli, resistenti, con singole unità intercambiabili; ma erano di scarso valore e rispondevano anche a un uso ornamentale; si trattava di un tipo di *denaro liquido* che poteva essere usato per qualsiasi necessità.

In questa realtà fatta di miserie e di astuzie i primi *manus* si muovevano senza dare alcun significato alla nozione del tempo.

> Gli avvenimenti reali del passato e quelli che si dicevano accaduti nella sfera degli spiriti [ci dice la Mead] venivano trattati in qualche maniera dai *manus*. La memoria di ognuno di essi si offuscava man mano che si allontanavano nel tempo gli altri eventi che ne convalidavano l'esistenza: il debito da saldare, l'ornamento di ossa che era stato indossato per una cerimonia funebre, l'amuleto che era stato legato alla trave centrale della casa, la memoria dei lamenti che erano stati composti per le morti avvenute in famiglia, il nome dei loro bambini che erano morti senza discendenza, i lunghi viaggi che avevano compiuto, le battaglie vinte, i banchetti offerti. [...] La vita intensa, piena di esperienze, di ogni generazione *manus* scorreva tra due nozioni del nulla; si supponeva, per tacito accordo, che il passato fosse sempre stato simile al presente e che il futuro non sarebbe stato diverso.

L'etnologa ci dice che la stessa assenza di misura del tempo esisteva per i *manus* riguardo allo spazio. Solo mondo conosciuto, per loro, era il mondo stesso in cui vivevano. L'oceano che li circondava da ogni parte, era un orizzonte non definito, senza limiti e senza nome. «Abitati dai serpenti di mare mitologici e dagli dèi dell'oceano,» come la Mead dice testualmente concludendo «*questo piccolo universo, avrebbe potuto anche galleggiare sul nulla, non ancorato né allo spazio né al tempo.*»

Dopo venticinque anni la Mead torna nel villaggio e lo trova trasformato.

La differenza non è, ovviamente, solo nella struttura delle cose: e questo la Mead ci tiene a ripeterlo.

Un altro importante mutamento era stato causato dalla nuova nozione del tempo che il calendario europeo aveva apportato sostituendosi al vecchio sistema genealogico.

Così la loro vita era come se fosse cominciata nel 1946; prima del 1946 i *manus* non sapevano che giorno fosse; vivevano in un tempo differente, in cui gli uomini di una generazione contavano il tempo in avanti o indietro, partendo da se stessi, senza preoccuparsi se c'era mai stato un principio e se ci sarebbe stata una fine.

La conclusione di questa esperienza è, in fondo, non solo la conclusione di queste pagine nelle quali vedo riflesse e analizzate, così come io non avrei mai potuto, tante situazioni delle quali sono stato testimone dal '56 al '91, ma dell'intera avventura umana narrata in questo volume:

Se la cultura di ogni uomo costituiva una parte irrevocabile della sua umanità, appresa una volta per non essere mai più respinta, e se essa era essenziale alla sua dignità di essere umano, *occorreva proteggerla e risparmiarla da parte di coloro che hanno il potere di studiare o di trasformare la cultura di altri esseri umani.* [...] Una serie di avvenimenti storici li trasformò, come avrebbe potuto essere trasformato qualsiasi piccolo gruppo di individui in questo nostro mondo. [...] Che essi sopravvivano, che l'inconsueto esperimento di superare in un quarto di secolo un lasso di tempo di duemila anni sia destinato al fallimento o al successo, dipende da quell'incredibile concatenarsi di avvenimenti che rende estremamente rischiosa l'esistenza di ogni individuo.

Re cannibali, uomini volanti e tanti fantasmi di fango

Nel cuore selvaggio della Nuova Guinea – Gli spiriti dei *pangunas* – La babele delle lingue – La valle dell'Asaro e le paludi del Sepik – *Kgöl*, ovvero il salto nel vuoto per guadagnare una moglie – Processo per stregoneria – La *sanguma* è magia contagiosa – Il ritorno dei morti è un ricordo di stragi – Il miracolo di Langa Langa.

I resti dei due capi *puka-puka* dominano ancora il villaggio e le comunità che furono sotto il potere del loro gruppo tribale, nel verde fitto delle montagne dell'Asaro, al centro della Nuova Guinea. Pur essendo ridotti da tempo a ossa calcificate («Era finita da poco la guerra con i giapponesi» precisa, in pessimo inglese, la nostra guida), impugnano ancora l'asta di comando e indossano i *talêk* di cuoio, simbolo del loro prestigio di guerrieri; e ancora portano sul petto due piccoli contenitori entro cui sono racchiuse le ceneri dell'ultimo nemico da loro ucciso in combattimento. Sia il *talêk* sia l'asta di comando, sia i contenitori delle ceneri ornano i loro scheletri che due strani troni di bambù tengono insieme in posizione eretta.

Ci ha guidato a vedere quei resti un *lapuna*, parola che significa «saggio che conosce il sentiero». Il nostro *lapuna* pare abbia assai più di settant'anni (ricorda il tempo in cui la Nuova Guinea era colonia tedesca) e quest'età – in un mondo ove a trent'anni si è vecchi e la vita ha una durata media inferiore ai venticinque – lo fa sembrare un patriarca fuori del tempo agli occhi dei suoi fratelli papua più giovani di qualche generazione. Lo abbiamo scelto anche per questo: gode di un rispetto assoluto ovunque si rechi e noi – con lui – siamo accettati in ogni villaggio e possiamo ascoltare, sapere, documentare.

Nell'alta valle dell'Asaro, oggi percorsa da una strada camionabile fino al suo passo più alto (quasi a duemila metri), il *lapuna* ci ha guidato agli inizi degli anni Settanta lungo una pista che raggiunge i più isolati villaggi montani. Quando lui «era giovane» –

ci dice – la valle era molto pericolosa per chi non abitava quelle montagne; l'abitavano i *puka-puka*, gli ultimi cannibali del mondo. Essi formavano un gruppo numeroso e articolato in una vera e propria «società»: «ultimi» solo in questa dimensione collettiva, dato che si conoscono casi isolati d'antropofagia successivi ai *puka-puka* sino ai nostri giorni, non solo in Nuova Guinea ma in altre zone primitive del mondo.

Il nostro *lapuna* ci ha raccontato di agguati, imboscate, pericoli continui. Nella zona (ancor oggi impervia a causa di foreste impraticabili, gole, canaloni) i cannibali erano sempre pronti a tendere un agguato, un attacco improvviso.

Le esigenze della guerra '41-'45 tra alleati e giapponesi mutarono profondamente le condizioni di isolamento della valle. Piste, aeroporti, ponti e strade vennero costruiti. E i cannibali furono sterminati.

«Dai giapponesi?» chiedo, e non ottengo risposta. «Dagli alleati allora?»

Il *lapuna* mi guarda e mi indica gli scheletri dei capi *puka-puka*, al centro del villaggio.

«Loro hanno voluto morire quando la gente dell'Alto Asaro ha deciso di non essere più antropofaga.»

Guardo gli scheletri, i loro simboli di guerra e di magia ancora intatti (le donne ne ungono le ossa e gli oggetti ogni giorno, con grasso di capra) e ascolto dal *lapuna* la storia di questo villaggio ove si decise d'un tratto di non mangiar più i propri simili. Vicenda emblematica in un itinerario nel mondo papua; introduzione precisa a un ambiente umano sino a ieri chiuso in un tempo suo, e oggi di colpo, nel giro di una generazione, di fronte all'impatto violento col tempo contemporaneo. Nelle altre società abitanti le isole di questo oceano (Polinesia e Micronesia) il livello culturale era assai diverso al momento dell'incontro con l'Occidente: l'acculturazione delle varie società è stato per loro fenomeno lentamente maturatosi attraverso due secoli e giunto «all'oggi» attraverso un susseguirsi continuo di cause ed effetti. Per le società papua dell'Oceania occidentale, il trapasso è stato invece di una brutalità senza precedenti: l'uomo di queste terre isolate, chiuse in se stesse si è trovato all'improvviso davanti all'alternativa di mutare vita e costumi, o di perire.

«Quando iniziò la "campagna" contro il cannibalismo» mi dice il *lapuna* «nella vallata i *puka-puka* venivano uccisi, sterminati; interi villaggi furono incendiati, rasi al suolo. Chi si voleva salvare doveva accettare di essere sottomesso, rinunciare alla propria tradizione...»

A seguire questa procedura, era stato costretto anche il villaggio dove il *lapuna* ci ha guidati perché potessimo vedere gli scheletri di due capi *puka-puka*. Per paura di rappresaglie e di sterminio e per convenienza quel villaggio, un giorno del lontano '45 o '46 non volle più essere cannibale. Decisione non gradita ai due più forti guerrieri che, nel villaggio, univano il potere di capi guerrieri a quello di intermediari con il mondo magico e sovrannaturale. L'abbandono del cannibalismo toglieva loro la doppia autorità: quella di condottieri in guerra con diritto all'incursione contro il nemico, allo scopo ultimo di procurarsi cibo umano; e quella religiosa. Per i papua, come per tanti altri popoli primitivi, l'antropofagia infatti era non solo motivata dalla fame, ma anche dalla convinzione che essi mangiando un essere umano ne avrebbero assimilato virilità, coraggio, astuzia, eventuale saggezza.

Un popolo non più antropofago sembrò ai due guerrieri-stregoni ingovernabile e forse insopportabile. E così decisero di morire. «Di loro volontà» assicura il *lapuna*.

Il loro atto finale – gravato di pesante maledizione nel caso di disobbedienza – fu un comando esplicito alla comunità: «Noi moriremo e voi dovrete mangiarci, per essere eredi della nostra forza e della nostra esperienza». Quell'ordine fu eseguito. I due capi *puka-puka* vennero divorati nell'ultimo banchetto sacro del loro villaggio per l'ultima volta antropofago; le loro ossa, pulite e raschiate, furono poi composte e i due scheletri sistemati in quella posizione eretta in cui li avevamo visti all'ingresso della «Casa del Comando»; là dove ancora vengono onorati ogni giorno in un veloce e semplice rito che abbiamo potuto filmare e fotografare.

«Nessun europeo prima di voi è stato qui» ci dice il *lapuna*. «Nessuno ha ascoltato questa storia, sino a oggi» aggiunge poi, mentre lasciamo il villaggio. Intanto ci ha chiesto se possiamo portare con noi a valle, con la camionetta, tre anziani della comunità.

Acconsentiamo, naturalmente, e il *lapuna* ce li presenta uno dopo l'altro come fossimo in un salotto.

Il più vecchio dei tre si chiama «maiale ridente», un altro «sole», il terzo «ananas». Il *lapuna* ci spiega (mentre duecento bambini volonterosi cercano di far uscire il nostro automezzo dal fango) che questi nomi hanno a che fare con i risparmi che i tre hanno alla Banca Nazionale d'Australia.

In quel villaggio ove gli scheletri ancora comandano, l'immaginare un *puka-puka* intento a operazioni bancarie mi lascia interdetto. E così non so come guardare i tre che stiamo trasportando. A quello seduto accanto a me vorrei chiedere a quanto ammonta il suo conto in banca, ma alla fin fine preferisco lasciarlo al suo silenzio.

Dal cannibalismo ai conti correnti il salto è notevole e non ne capisco, oltretutto, la meccanica: lo comprenderò solo molti giorni dopo quando un funzionario di una banca di Port Moresby mi spiegherà che un papua che non sa né scrivere né leggere sceglie un simbolo a lui noto e lo usa – come nome proprio – nel suo libretto di risparmio.

Per tornare al nostro rientro in camionetta dal villaggio *puka-puka*, e ai racconti sui «tempi antichi» che con l'aiuto del *lapuna* intrecciamo con i nostri passeggeri, è proprio uno di loro a interrompere due ore di silenzio e a narrarci dell'ultimo «banchetto cannibale» cui assistette; quello appunto in cui i due capi si fecero divorare. Così ci traduce il *lapuna*:

«Dice che lui fu fortunato; infatti ebbe in sorte di mangiare le dita della mano di uno dei due capi; il punto della saggezza, le dita. Con esse l'uomo fa tutto: l'uomo saggio, con le dita, governa le cose del mondo.»

Il vecchio che aveva mangiato le dita sorrideva alla conclusione del suo racconto; e vedendo i sui denti appuntiti ci ricordiamo quanto ci avevano riferito a Port Moresby e a Goroka: quelli con i denti appuntiti sono proprio *puka-puka* autentici. La stessa fonte d'informazione aveva poi aggiunto, per tranquillizzarmi, che comunque di gente simile ne avrei vista poca; non sopravvivono molti discendenti dei *puka-puka*, nella Nuova Guinea d'oggi.

Il racconto del nostro compagno di viaggio riprende, ispirato dalle strade che stiamo percorrendo: «Quando fu costruita la prima pista militare in questa valle dell'Asaro, gli abitanti dei villaggi che non dichiaravano pubblicamente d'abbandonare l'antropofagia venivano tutti sterminati: uomini, donne, bambini». «Quel che è più stupido di tanta strage» aggiunge, di suo, il *lapuna* «è che quei bianchi sparavano e ammazzavano per niente. I *puka-puka*, è vero, assalivano e uccidevano. Ma sappiamo perché lo facevano: per loro era rito... era fame. Soprattutto fame.»

Il *lapuna* mi ha parlato guardandomi negli occhi, a esser certo che io capisca bene il suo strano inglese. E quando ne è certo, conclude: «Uccidere senza necessità di cibo: una cosa senza senso... Ma d'altra parte molto di quanto fate, voi bianchi, non ha proprio senso».

La deferenza che i tre uomini trasportati nella camionetta e gli altri incontrati durante il cammino hanno mostrato verso il nostro *lapuna*, m'ha confermato ancor più quanto avevo saputo di lui al primo incontro, e quanto s'era manifestato nella visita al villaggio dei *puka-puka*: è uomo che gode di grande autorità e le sue parole sono ascoltate con attenzione. Nessuno, credo, avrebbe il coraggio di disobbedire a un suo ordine. Eppure non è un *capo*; così come in fondo, non erano due capi assoluti i due ultimi re di quel villaggio sul quale si continua a vegliare a vent'anni dalla loro morte. In un caso come nell'altro (e in tanti ancora nel mondo papua che ho potuto controllare), alla deferenza e all'ossequio profondo che la popolazione ha per chi è investito di un certo grado di potere (sia religioso che civile) fa riscontro una diversa anzi opposta impossibilità di questo stesso «potere» di imporsi con autorità. Ed è proprio questa *mancanza d'autorità* in un gruppo, nella comunità, nei villaggi, la prima sensazione di differenza che ho avvertito tra le società melanesiane e quelle polinesiane. Là il *tavanà* può essere rimosso o disobbedito, in certi casi; ma la sua autorità è certa e indiscussa (e vi si sente un'origine marinaresca, quella del capobarca, del capopesca, del timoniere, dell'«uomo-che-fa-la-rotta», tipico della gente abituata alla disciplina dell'imbarco). Invece qui, nelle isole della Melanesia, pochi gruppi riconoscono un capo o una guida; un uomo può godere di un certo prestigio per la sua età o le sue ricchezze, il numero delle mogli, dei maiali o di altri simboli di benessere; là dove sono ancora in corso lotte tribali – ma ce ne sono ancora? – un uomo può raggiungere una posizione di preminenza nella sua comunità per la sua abilità di guerriero; è chiamato in quel caso, «capo-lotta»: titolo – oggi come ieri – di grande prestigio. Al punto che il governo australiano ha scaltramente nominato suoi «agenti» un certo numero di «capi-lotta», sfruttando il loro ascendente per mantenere il controllo delle popolazioni.

La seconda differenza di carattere sociologico che avverte il viaggiatore giunto alle isole melanesiane provenendo da quelle polinesiane riguarda il rapporto tra l'uomo e il mondo che lo circonda. Anche qui siamo tra genti che abitano isole del grande oceano; eppure sembra che nessun legame unisca il papua all'orizzonte liquido che circonda le sue terre; nessuna inquietudine lo prende davanti a quello spazio vuoto, né desiderio di cercare sul mare quanto potrebbe bastare per nutrire se stesso e la propria famiglia.

In compenso, fortissimo è il senso dell'attaccamento al territorio del proprio gruppo tribale, al campo coltivato, al luogo «sacro ai morti», come a quello ove sorge la capanna per l'intera famiglia; e questo anche se ogni papua può godere del «suo terreno» solo durante il periodo in cui è in vita. La terra appartiene, senza eccezioni, alla tribù. In molte zone una famiglia ha la possibilità di scegliere dove coltivare mentre in altre l'assegnazione del terreno è decisa con discussioni collettive. Questo attaccamento alla terra non è certo indebolito con le mutate condizioni di vita degli ultimi anni; mi sembra ne sia prova un episodio clamoroso accaduto nella foresta di Bougainville. Qui, in seguito a ricerche costate milioni di dollari, il gigantesco complesso minerario australiano *Conzinc Rio Tinto* ha scoperto ricchissimi depositi di rame e ne ha deciso l'estrazione. Durante tutto il periodo delle ricerche i papua di quella zona, le tribù dei *pangunas*, si sono opposti con ogni tipo di resistenza alle attività della Compagnia, impedendo ai geologi l'accesso alla valle e ai corsi d'acqua e arrivando persino a distruggere gli accampamenti degli studiosi. E ancora oggi s'oppongono all'estrazione del minerale.

I funzionari dell'amministrazione australiana hanno cercato di spiegare ai «notabili» che il sottosuolo delle isole è proprietà del governo; hanno promesso un compenso per ogni albero tagliato o qualsiasi altro danno alla loro terra. Ma malgrado questo e le spiegazioni sui vantaggi che sarebbero loro venuti dalla presenza di un centro minerario, la gente del posto si è ostinata – sino al limite di una resistenza addirittura armata – a opporsi al lavoro della Conzinc. Un'opposizione che ha costretto l'amministrazione australiana all'impegno di versare ai proprietari dei terreni il dieci per cento del tributo totale ricevuto al momento in cui la Compagnia iniziava gli scavi. Ma perfino di fronte alle possibilità di diventare ricchi i *pangunas* si rifiutano di cedere la loro terra.

Hanno cominciato a raccogliersi in gruppi organizzati mettendo insieme i fondi per combattere l'opera della Compagnia, la quale ha allora tentato di rispondere con il consueto atteggiamento dell'autoritarismo coloniale di tutti i paesi e di tutti i tempi: ottusità e repressione. Ha inviato pattuglie di polizia a controllare i villaggi e a salvaguardare i periti nel corso del loro lavoro; e ha imprigionato coloro che tentavano di ostacolare la loro opera.

Malgrado tutto questo, è risultato chiaro che i *pangunas* non intendevano ad alcun prezzo rinunciare alla loro terra. Non solo, ma invitavano altri gruppi papua a fare altrettanto, inviando loro «missioni» per spiegare che la Conzinc avrebbe scavato una voragine di 600 metri di profondità al centro dell'isola, attraverso la quale l'acqua avrebbe inondato tutti i villaggi. La notizia, propagatasi rapidamente, ha consolidato il sentimento di avversione dei nativi contro i bianchi. I quali hanno cominciato a mormorare che quando fosse venuto il momento dell'indipendenza gli avi delle diverse comunità sarebbero risorti dalla terra per cacciare ogni invasore, ma se si fossero venduti i terreni ove gli spiriti giacevano accanto a quei resti che furono i loro corpi, chi sarebbe risorto a guidare la rivolta e la lotta per la libertà?

La domanda chiarisce, con sicura evidenza che agli occhi dei *pangunas* non esiste nemmeno teoricamente una qualsivoglia disponibilità del loro terreno; a nessun costo e a nessuno scopo. E questo non solo perché i loro avi riposano nella terra dove erano stati seppelliti (e ciò doveva essere facilmente capito) ma anche perché vi erano i «non-ancora-nati» da considerare: se la Conzinc avesse scavato le sue gallerie e buttato all'aria villaggi e foreste, i futuri *pangunas* avrebbero perduto la loro legittima eredità di quelle terre.

Attaccamento basato non solo sull'economia agricola tribale, ma ancor più su una precisa struttura sociale, con forti accenti religiosi.

Un episodio significativo, che ci invita – prima di proseguire il nostro viaggio in questi arcipelaghi – a ripercorrere in breve la storia di questo mondo papua.

«Circondata da mare pericoloso alla navigazione, ancora popolata da feroci cannibali e da tagliatori di teste, insalubre nelle regioni costiere, scarsa di animali commestibili e apparentemente priva di risorse naturali»: così Villeminot, etnologo belga che visitò la Nuova Guinea solo trent'anni fa definì, certo senza adulazione, un paese ancora in parte alle soglie della preistoria che è divenuto una delle nazioni più giovani della terra.

E con le sue stesse parole la evoca in un suo testo Giovanni Verusio, viaggiatore italiano; leggo il suo scritto mentre torno, nel 1991, da un itinerario che ha ripercorso i luoghi dove sono stato – e a lungo – nel '55, nel '69 e nel '71.

Verusio cita nobili nomi di concittadini che ci hanno preceduto; come quello in onor del quale è stata battezzata una delle ottanta tra specie e sottospecie di uccelli del paradiso: lo *Eteridophora Alberti*, in onore del nobiluomo genovese Luigi Maria d'Albertis che per primo risalì il fiume Fly, nel 1875, con la *Neva*, una lancia a vapore lunga sedici metri senza ponte o cabina ma con «una tettoia di zinco su due terzi della sua lunghezza». «Doveva essere fresca!» annota Verusio; e aggiunge che d'Albertis era un patriota: dette il nome del suo sovrano, Vittorio Emanuele, a una montagna e di Torricelli a una catena di monti e offrì la Nuova Guinea a Casa Savoia «che, per una volta saggiamente, rifiutò». Di lui si dice che nelle sue esplorazioni sparasse a tutto quello che vedeva muovere, indigeni compresi.

Altri italiani in Nuova Guinea furono naturalmente i missionari: la Papua-Nuova Guinea è terra di conquista dei missionari, cattolici e di tutte le sette protestanti, che da circa cento anni cercano o credono di convertire e di educare la gente che sembrava più convinta della bontà della carne umana che degli insegnamenti della Bibbia.

«Sono intelligenti?» ha chiesto Verusio a una missionaria che da otto anni è responsabile di una scuola ad Ambunti sul medio corso del Sepik.

«Diciamo che qualcuno capisce» è stata la diplomatica risposta.

Il che è già un miracolo, se si pensa che in questo paese (che occupa poco più della metà dell'isola; l'altra metà appartiene all'Indonesia) più grande dell'Italia, con 3.300.000 abitanti si parlano 717 lingue differenti (il 45 per cento di tutte le lingue conosciute, annota Verusio con pignolo sarcasmo).

Una proliferazione di lingue in casi totalmente differenti da rendere inutile – me ne accorgo ben presto – il viaggiare nell'interno con un interprete: appena lascio la Asaro Valley e restituisco il *lapuna* alla quiete del suo villaggio ogni pochi chilometri incontro gente che parla un linguaggio del tutto diverso da quello usato da chi ho appena lasciato.

Le isole della Melanesia giacquero dormienti lungo i millenni come reliquie dell'età della pietra tra i confini occidentali dell'Asia sud-orientale e l'Oceania.

Di tanto in tanto i *rajas* di Ambom e Celebes inviavano i loro *prahos* a far razzia di schiavi sulle coste della Nuova Guinea e delle Salomone. Una vela portoghese o spagnola appariva brevemente all'orizzonte per poi sparire nell'ignoto dopo aver lasciato su rive apparentemente ospitali missionari che venivano regolarmente uccisi e divorati appena la sopracitata vela svaniva alla vista.

Nelle isole, le cui terre centrali sono dominate da montagne (nelle parti alte perennemente tra le nubi) vivevano tribù il cui mondo terminava sulla cresta successiva di montagne. La stregoneria e la legge dell'ascia di pietra lavorata regnavano sovrane.

Gli scontri di civiltà e il sorgere, il decadere o il mutare delle culture che hanno scosso il mondo, non sfiorarono gli arcipelaghi papua. Remote al flusso e riflusso delle storie conosciute, le isole del Pacifico occidentale avevano però vissuto e continuato a vivere una loro vicenda umana «diversa» ma non per questo meno complessa. *Fuori della storia* ma non per questo *senza storia*.

Vicissitudini di genti le cui origini sono probabilmente una somma di varie componenti cui si sovrappone un esodo forzato di popoli dalle giungle dell'Asia meridionale, e che – spinte verso Sud e verso Occidente da popoli più forti – si sparsero, per trovare rifugio, nella catena di isole dell'Indonesia sino al Pacifico occidentale. Il risultato di quelle lontane, successive e sempre diverse sovrapposizioni e migrazioni è chiaramente visibile oggi: genti sconcertanti nella loro varietà, separate da quelle lingue completamente diverse fra loro e da circa duemila dialetti derivati.

Inclusi sotto lo stesso nome di melanesiani, o papua, sono gruppi di chiara origine asiatica e i *negritos*, piccoli e dai capelli lanosi (testimonianti antropologicamente e culturalmente il loro legame con gli aborigeni australiani); sono i *kiwais*, dell'estuario del Sepik (dei quali un po' troppo fantasiosamente si dice che potrebbero essere una delle tribù disperse d'Israele); sono i *bukas*, belli come i somali; e sono gruppi d'origine polinesiana che parlano una lingua simile al samoano e vivono negli arcipelaghi più orientali.

Nelle paludi del Sepik occidentale abbiamo visto pigmoidi la cui vita ha una durata media superiore ai vent'anni, e ci è stato affermato che in certe montagne della stessa immensa isola vivono gruppi che sembrano in certa misura discendere dallo stesso ceppo degli *ainu*, i «primitivi» del Giappone.

A parte queste dubbie curiosità etnografiche, alcune certezze etniche permettono di osservare che la maggior parte degli abitanti della Melanesia migrò, secondo gli antropologi, dall'Asia attraverso il ponte delle isole indonesiane in un lento e continuo processo durato 50 o 60.000 anni; un paletnologo australiano ha intrapreso studi nell'area di Woitape (a nord-ovest di Port Moresby) ed è dell'opinione che vi fosse gente organizzata in comunità, in quelle montagne, ventiseimila anni fa. Lo provano test al carbonio.

In attesa di chiarire – anche qui – il mistero delle origini, le genti papua del Pacifico sud-occidentale sono state divise in tre gruppi: melanesiani, micronesiani e polinesiani. La schiacciante maggioranza degli autoctoni è rappresentata dai melanesiani, mentre i micronesiani e i polinesiani sono disseminati sull'area periferica. I micronesiani che vivono nelle isole papua sono concentrati nell'arcipelago di Manus e atolli adiacenti; e i pochi polinesiani occupano le isole di Nukumanu e Tauu, a est delle Bougainville.

Più grande della diversità fisica è quella – s'è detto – dei gruppi linguistici: nelle zone costiere i gruppi linguistici sono raramente composti di più di cinquemila individui. Nelle zone di montagna si trovano gruppi maggiori, ma anche qui, dove la popolazione è più densa, tre gruppi soli annoverano una infinità di dialetti. In vari arcipelaghi gli studiosi hanno trovato comunità isolate di persone composte da non più di cinquanta individui, gli unici a parlare una certa lingua; e a sole poche miglia un altro villaggio, anch'esso di pochi abitanti, depositario di una lingua altrettanto unica e profondamente diversa; gli uni e gli altri nell'assoluta incapacità di comunicare senza l'aiuto di un interprete. Questa frantumazione linguistica ha impedito ai papua – nel passato remoto e prossimo – di avere una dimensione unitaria sul piano culturale, come nello stesso oceano hanno saputo crearsi i polinesiani.

Prime notizie di queste terre del Pacifico occidentale cominciarono a essere raccolte in Europa dai navigatori portoghesi nel Cinquecento (Antonio d'Abren, 1511). Poi il portoghese Meneses continuò le ricerche intorno al 1526 (fu lui a chiamare questa gente dalla pelle scura *papua*, da una parola malese il cui significato è «nero dai capelli ricciuti»[1]). Nel 1545, un altro navigatore spagnolo, Inigo Ortis de Retes, navigò in questi mari lungo la costa settentrionale di una grande isola e credendo di scoprire una somiglianza tra la gente che l'abitava e quella della Guinea africana, chiamò l'isola Nuova Guinea. Essa, nel Seicento, venne rilevata dagli olandesi, e nel 1700 dal navigatore inglese William Dampier, che per primo ne disegnò il periplo. James Cook vi approdò nel 1770. Durante il diciassettesimo e diciottesimo secolo, a parte qualche esplorazione e un tentativo degli inglesi di fondare una colonia (Nuova Albione, nel 1793), solo gli olandesi mostrarono qualche interesse nella colonizzazione del mondo papua. E infatti dopo le guerre napoleoniche, il governo olandese riorganizzò i suoi possedimenti nel Pacifico con particolare interesse alla Nuo-

---

[1] Annoto che fra i papua si contano molte decine di gruppi che presentano diversi aspetti etno-culturali, quali i *chimbu*, i *big nambas*, i *puka-puka*, ecc.

va Guinea; e nel 1824 i Paesi Bassi e la Gran Bretagna firmarono un accordo secondo il quale tutta la grande isola, a occidente della longitudine 141°47' est, veniva assegnata ai Paesi Bassi.

Anche nel diciannovesimo secolo le spedizioni di osservazione ed esplorazione europee nel mondo papua furono scarse; dal 1871 in poi venne stabilito un certo numero di missioni religiose, e si aprì un'altra pagina di storia, ben diversa: quella delle deportazioni, di cui parleremo più avanti.

Intanto una nuova potenza s'era affacciata nel Pacifico. Una potenza che intendeva accaparrarsi anch'essa la sua parte di colonie: la Germania che, arrivando per ultima, doveva accontentarsi di quanto gli altri avevano rifiutato.

Nel 1884 vennero dichiarati protettorato tedesco numerose zone costiere e un arcipelago ebbe il nome, come ho già ricordato, «di Bismarck». Nel 1885 la Germania occupò un territorio interno della Nuova Guinea costringendo nel 1888 la Gran Bretagna a fare altrettanto. Nacque così la Nuova Guinea inglese che venne affidata ai «cugini» australiani, il 1° settembre 1906. Furono essi nel 1914, immediatamente dopo lo scoppio della guerra con la Germania, a occupare la Nuova Guinea tedesca, la Nuova Britannia e Nuova Irlanda e l'arco di isole dell'Ammiragliato e delle Salomone settentrionali. Nacque così una Amministrazione australiana del «territorio» (Tpng) che dal 1921 agì sotto mandato della Società delle Nazioni.

Dopo la seconda guerra mondiale, l'Australia pose volontariamente il «Territorio» sotto mandato delle Nazioni Unite quale zona amministrativa, e il 13 dicembre 1946 un accordo tra l'Australia e le Nazioni Unite fece, di quella, l'Autorità Amministrativa. Dagli anni Ottanta in poi, il Tpng è Stato autonomo e apparentemente sovrano (gli australiani, in realtà fungono sempre da tutori).

La maggioranza della popolazione, più di tre milioni di abitanti, ha ancora vive radici nell'età della pietra; ma l'ultima generazione elegge un parlamento a suffragio universale; ed i suoi rappresentanti più impegnati politicamente agiscono sia per riunire tutta la Nuova Guinea sotto un'unica bandiera («liberando» quindi la parte del paese *occupata* dai colonialisti indonesiani di Giakarta), sia per scuotere dal loro governo l'ipoteca del pesante controllo australiano.

Avvenimenti, questi, tutti riferibili agli ultimi trent'anni; tutti precedenti al mio primo viaggio in questo mondo sperduto nel più remoto Pacifico. Quando qui approdai alle «più melanesiane» fra tutte le isole del mondo papua: le Nuove Ebridi.

Era il dicembre del 1956. Nel Mediterraneo si combatteva attorno al canale di Suez; noi non ne sapevamo nulla e navigavamo a vela tra Vila ed Espíritu Santo.

Durante un giorno e una notte interi era caduta una pioggia violenta di gocce fitte, veloci, calde. Poi era stato come se quella violenza avesse condensato e spezzato le nubi in tanti blocchi, simili a immensi solidi geometrici rimasti a galleggiare in un cielo chiarissimo, concreti come isole volanti.

Sotto la loro foresta, bagnata e illuminata lungo la costa ove eravamo approdati non era verde ma quasi nera.

«*Novelle Ebridi tra 9° e 20° di lat. sud e 163°-168° long. est*»: così si legge, ma non si immagina che cosa voglia dire «*tra 9° e 20° sud*».

Lo si sente ancor prima di arrivare, quando dopo aver avanzato nell'oceano per giorni e giorni, lasciando alle spalle il soffio fresco e leggero dell'aliseo, si entra in un forno acceso tra mare e terra. Si sbarca in isole grigie per un sole che non esiste, nascosto com'è nel groviglio immobile di nubi basse a sfiorare le cime dei monti di cui non si indovina la forma né la misura.

«*163° e 168° est, 9° e 20° sud*»: così è scritto e si vedono sulla carta del Pacifico, cioè sulla distesa blu del mare, le macchie di Vate, Ambrim, Pentecôte, Tanna, Malekula, le isole dell'arcipelago.

Solo arrivando si scopre che la parola «caldo» traduce in termini concreti quel dato geografico dei «*tra 9° e 20° sud*». Caldo senza scampo.

La pioggia a scrosci aveva inzuppato tutto: noi, il tetto di foglie della casa dove c'eravamo riparati dopo lo sbarco, la terra intorno e il bosco vicino. Persino il mare mi era sembrato inzuppato d'acqua, e qualcosa del genere, laggiù, è forse possibile.

Col ritorno del sole tutto aveva preso ad asciugarsi velocemente, e, nel silenzio di quella capanna, ricordai un giorno in cui si fece una gita in Abruzzo, e per le ore trascorse sulla neve bagnata avevamo i maglioni intrisi d'acqua e noi stessi ne eravamo inzuppati, tanto che alla fine, riparatici nella casa del guardiano di una diga, stavamo raccolti vicino alla stufa mentre l'acqua dei vestiti, dei capelli, del corpo si asciugava evaporando veloce, bianca e calda.

In quell'angolo delle Nuove Ebridi, dalla terra e dalla foresta e da tutti noi il vapore si levava leggero e l'aria – rimasta per pochi istanti dopo la pioggia come di vetro – si appannava sotto i nostri occhi per una nebbia prima impercettibile poi chiaramente visibile nel sollevarsi dalle cose e nel condensarsi a mezz'aria dove restava immobile. Dalla pioggia al sole, e dal sole alla nebbia: pochi minuti.

Nella luce pallida e gialla riprendemmo a sudare, tutto fu di nuovo madido e zuppo e sembrava che forze, volontà, memoria svanissero e fossimo mutati in ombre di piombo.

Guardai in alto e vidi il sole: nella foschia gli si era disegnato tutt'attorno un arcobaleno rotondo, pallido, senza vita.

Un tale, in divisa, giunse alla capanna dalla quale non ci eravamo mossi dopo lo sbarco, guardò i nostri passaporti e vi stampò. al centro di una pagina, il timbro PERMITTED TO LAND più grande del visto d'ingresso negli Stati Uniti. Cercò d'intavolare un discorso in inglese, ma, per quanto mi riguardava, sentivo solo caldo. Così, in attesa del Residente e degli altri che ci dovevano portare all'interno, restai in silenzio.

Ripenso alle ore passate ad aspettare e cerco di ricordarmi se fu allora che lessi gli appunti sulle Nuove Ebridi; le pagine di quel taccuino sono ancora arricciate dall'umidità; e mi pare sia stata proprio l'aria di quel giorno ad averle ridotte così. Comunque le note segnate con biro rossa e biro blu sono ancora oggi ben leggibili.

In blu avevo scritto informazioni utili ma non determinanti per il mio lavoro in quelle isole; in rosso avevo sottolineato gli spunti a mio parere più interessanti per le riprese che avevo in animo di realizzare per il film *Melanesia* (1956) che era lo scopo del mio viaggio.

L'arcipelago delle Nuove Ebridi – avevo segnato in blu – fa parte del gruppo delle isole di cultura papua e gode della particolarità di essere il più tagliato fuori dalle linee di navigazione fra tutti quelli del Pacifico; finendo così per essere assai poco conosciuto.

La sua struttura è un sistema di isole disposte longitudinalmente su un asse di circa 900 chilometri. L'isola maggiore, Espíritu Santo, copre 500 chilometri quadrati (ancora oggi praticamente inesplorati). La abitano tribù primitive dette *big nambas*. Le isole sono tutte vulcaniche e sono punteggiate di coni e crateri spenti o attivi, qualcuno alto sino a 1600 metri. I due più famosi per la loro attività eruttiva, sono il vulcano Benbow, dell'isola di Ambu, e il vulcano Yasur di Tanna.

In tutto l'arcipelago vi sono complessivamente sessanta coni vulcanici e il più strano è quello spento e semisommerso di Ureparapora, che somiglia a un piccolo atollo. Di veri atolli non ve n'è nemmeno uno, in questo arcipelago; ma tutte le isole hanno una corona madreporica sul lato sottovento, chiamata qui come nel resto del Pacifico *reef* o *recif*, a seconda della lingua occidentale più conosciuta nel posto.

Ma se i *recifs* sono comuni a tutte le isole del Pacifico, nelle Nuove Ebridi ce ne sono di particolari: quelli che, per eruzioni vulcaniche, sono emersi dall'acqua a molti metri sul livello dèl mare; alcuni di essi, proiettati quattrocento metri sopra le onde, si alzano sull'oceano come torri e sono abitati unicamente da migliaia e migliaia di gabbiani e rondini di mare.

La presenza di sessanta vulcani nell'arcipelago provoca ineluttabilmente frequenti movimenti tellurici; tra i più recenti due sono rimasti famosi nella storia delle isole, quello del 1907 e quello del 1943.

Nel 1907 venne rasa al suolo la piccola Vate, unico centro che può essere definito *urbano* dell'arcipelago, sede dell'amministrazione coloniale franco-inglese. La popolazione trovò scampo nelle navi all'àncora e sui battelli per molti mesi, per cui Vate divenne una specie di città galleggiante.

Nel 1943 gli americani allestirono un'immensa base aeronavale nell'isola di Espíritu Santo, forte a un certo momento di quasi duecentomila uomini; base operativa per la loro guerra contro i giapponesi, a Guadalcanal. Costruirono tre piste in cemento per le loro «fortezze volanti» e per i loro caccia, che erano continuamente in volo.

Un giorno centinaia di aerei partiti in missione si accingevano a rientrare quando una fortissima scossa di terremoto fece tremare paurosamente l'intera isola e profonde crepe spezzarono le piste in cemento. Gli aerei trovarono il campo semidistrutto, e, ormai al limite delle loro riserve di benzina, furono costretti a una drammatica scelta: o scendere in mare o tentare comunque l'atterraggio sul campo devastato. Quasi tutti rimasero distrutti (poiché nelle isole ci trasferiamo di pista in pista con un vecchio DC3, questa notizia la sottolineo in rosso...).

All'angoscia per le imprevedibili scosse telluriche, a rendere più dura la vita nelle Nuove Ebridi, s'aggiunge il supplizio continuo delle piogge. Su queste isole piove in media duecentoquaranta giorni all'anno; e può cadere tanta acqua dal cielo in un giorno quanta a Parigi in un anno.

Questa incredibile umidità ha coperto le Nuove Ebridi di una densa foresta tropicale, intrico verde di alberi d'alto fusto, liane, cespugli ed erbe altissime. In questo groviglio, dove dovremo muoverci, vivono circa quarantacinquemila melanesiani abitanti i dodicimila chilometri quadrati di inferno che copre l'insieme di tutte le isole. Parlano dialetti tutti di diverso ceppo tribale; ma una specie di «esperanto» sui generis permette loro di comunicare con i propri fratelli di altri villaggi e con i «bianchi». È una lingua nata dai contatti fugaci degli isolani con i primi navigatori e colonizzatori. Si chiama *bishlamar* (dallo spagnolo «bicho del mar») ed è una fusione eterogenea dei dialetti melanesiani con l'inglese e con lo spagnolo.

Da quanto ho poi potuto constatare direttamente, il *bishlamar* lo conoscono in egual misura i due gruppi umani delle Nuove Ebridi, i *bushmen*, «abitanti della foresta», e i *mensalwater*, «abitanti della costa salata». Questi ultimi – per ragioni che conosceremo più avanti – sono stati più volte indotti a lasciare le coste e a stabilirsi nelle foreste: è a causa di ciò che fra loro e i *bushmen* esiste un perpetuo stato di ostilità, motivo sino a ieri di lotte sanguinose per il possesso delle rare zone abitabili.

Per i bianchi, d'altra parte (sino all'inizio di un'epoca di serio interesse culturale ed etnografico), le Nuove Ebridi hanno avuto una attrattiva sempre molto limitata.

Nella corsa alla conquista del Pacifico (tra il 1800 e il 1900) quest'arcipelago rimase escluso; nessuno ne sentiva il richiamo. Solamente nel 1906, Francia e Inghilterra decisero di amministrarlo in condominio: una forma politica unica al mondo che ha generato, qui, una serie ininterrotta di grandi e piccoli problemi; il Residente francese Antonioz, che ci ha ospitati e guidati per alcuni giorni nelle zone più impervie di Tanna e del suo vulcano, di «problemi minori» dovuti a una gestione coloniale in condominio, ce ne ha elencati di curiosi.

Il primo, veramente ridicolo, fu quello nato al momento di regolare la «circolazione» nelle isole; quando, pochi anni fa, venne costruita a Port Vila la prima unica strada dell'arcipelago (tre chilometri dal porto alle case della cittadina), i bianchi dell'amministrazione si chiesero: «In quale modo debbono circolare le "auto", a mano destra come in Francia o a sinistra come in Inghilterra?».

Per trovare una soluzione, fu deciso di stabilire se inglese o francese fosse stato il primo veicolo importato nelle Nuove Ebridi. Risultò che il primo veicolo sbarcato laggiù era stata una bicicletta Peugeot nel 1908; e pertanto venne ordinato di regolare il «traffico» secondo gli usi francesi.

Un altro problema nacque al momento di dare il nome al battello dell'amministrazione: dargli un nome inglese o francese? Nel dubbio fu battezzato in spagnolo *Sancho Pancha* e non se ne parlò più.

Altri racconti del Residente-Governatore delle Nuove Ebridi nascevano dalla sua esperienza di amministratore di quella strana giustizia (in bilico tra codici anglosassoni e giurisprudenza francese, con un pizzico di esotica influenza di costumi tradizionali) che gli europei hanno importato ed adattato.

Ai diversi racconti di queste isole, come a quelli delle Salomone e delle Wallis o della Nuova Guinea facevano eco, nelle parole del nostro narratore, sempre identici accenti di stupore «europeo» per i delitti dei «selvaggi», quasi che le nostre buone società d'Europa, d'America e d'Australia non conoscano la piaga del furto, del delitto, dell'omicidio in misura proporzionalmente tanto superiore a quella del mondo primitivo, da sfuggire a qualsiasi paragone.

Fra i racconti sentiti, ho raccolto note di alcuni «casi» che aiutano, secondo me, a comprendere la meccanica di certi comportamenti umani primitivi; non per trarne un giudizio moralistico ma piuttosto per conoscere l'uomo papua anche nei suoi lati d'ombra, nei suoi aspetti meno nobili, di cui, tra l'altro, siamo sovente responsabili noi, i bianchi, per la violenza con la quale abbiamo assalito le strutture sociali di gruppi etnici «diversi».

Un caso che può interessare come esempio tipico, è quello che vide imputati un certo Wimo e altri quattro componenti della sua tribù. Il loro caso è stato giudicato da una corte coloniale di Lae in Nuova Guinea; un processo al quale assistette colui che poi divenne Residente-Governatore delle Nuove Ebridi, e che ce lo ha riferito. Era un caso centrato sull'assassinio di una donna di nome Iyam.

Come avevano compiuto il loro «delitto» quei cinque papua?

«Si sedettero sotto l'abitazione su palafitte di Iyam e puntarono un osso di opossum in sua direzione, attraverso le assi del pavimento, augurandosi che morisse,» ci ha raccontato il Residente «seppellirono l'osso e dissero a Iyam che avevano ordito una magia contro di lei. Iyam cercò l'osso nella terra, lo trovò e si rese conto della stregoneria ormai in atto. Nei giorni seguenti una sua gamba cominciò a ricoprirsi di piaghe e la donna si ammalò seriamente: in poco tempo si aggravò e morì...»

Il procuratore del processo narrò che qualche tempo dopo entrambe le sorelle di Wimo caddero malate e morirono.

«Il loro fratello, l'imputato Wimo, immediatamente pensò che una stregoneria di "rappresaglia" era stata compiuta contro di loro. Nella propria convinzione, Wimo, per vendicarsi, decise di uccidere qualcun altro per pareggiare il conto. Scelta la vittima, una donna della famiglia nemica, Wimo si recò alla capanna dove lei abitava e le scagliò una freccia per ucciderla; poi la colpì con un legno da ardere e mentre essa tentava di fuggire le scagliò un'altra freccia nel dorso. La donna cadde urlando, ancora viva, e il vendicatore Wimo con i suoi quattro complici la trasportarono nella foresta dove ognuno la trafisse con un'altra freccia. I cinque tornarono poi al loro villaggio.»

Un uomo aveva però visto tutto, e si recò dal marito dell'uccisa. Gli disse: «Mi dispiace, fratello, ma tua moglie è stata assassinata.

Dobbiamo trovare una "pattuglia" di bianchi e dirglielo, non possiamo uccidere gli assassini perché i loro parenti ucciderebbero a loro volta i nostri».

Il marito della morta inviò due donne nella boscaglia alla ricerca del cadavere; disse loro di tagliare una mano da portare all'ufficiale della «pattuglia», come prova, e di estrarre le frecce dal suo corpo. Le donne andarono e tornarono con la mano tagliata e cinque frecce. Fu chiamata una «pattuglia», ed esse spiegarono che avevano reciso la mano della morta con un coltello fatto di osso di cinghiale e mostrarono le frecce che le avevano strappato dal corpo.

Lo sviluppo della storia è quanto di meno logico si possa immaginare. Con la sua parrucca settecentesca sul capo, il giudice bianco decretò per i cinque assassini una sentenza di morte; ma questa venne commutata in prigione perché la zona era solo «superficialmente» sotto controllo dell'amministrazione coloniale, e si temeva che una impiccagione multipla potesse creare nei papua uno stato d'animo ostile verso i bianchi.

In prigione i cinque assassini si trovarono bene: impararono l'inglese, a mangiare con la forchetta ed ebbero pantaloni e camicie. Furono, poi, amnistiati e liberati; e per quel loro contratto con il mondo esterno, oggi sono personaggi influenti nel loro villaggio d'origine.

Un altro caso recente nel quale la stregoneria fu causa di omicidio avvenne a Wewak. Dinenyeng, abitante di un villaggio papua «età della pietra» nella zona di Telefomin fu accusato dell'omicidio di una donna di nome Foias.

Aiutata dalla sua bambina, Foias stava lavorando nei giardini del villaggio, quando Dinenyeng si avvicinò e disse: «Sei stata scoperta! Sei una strega! Lo dicono i "bastoni magici"[1]».

Dinenyeng, impugnato il suo lungo arco, colpì allora la donna con tre frecce e l'uccise.

Un ufficiale di pattuglia narrò che Dinenyeng, per spiegare il

---

[1] Rami sfrondati, a cui, dopo la cerimonia particolare, si attribuivano poteri sovrannaturali, e in particolare la capacità «infallibile» di scoprire la verità.

sua feroce omicidio, gli aveva detto che una giovane si era impiccata e che lui e altri abitanti del villaggio avevano usato i «bastoni magici» per individuare la casa della persona che l'aveva stregata e spinta al suicidio.

«Foias con la sua stregoneria aveva già fatto morire sette uomini, per questo l'ho uccisa» concluse Dinenyeng.

Uno degli accusati «spiegò» alla corte come dopo che la giovane era stata trovata impiccata gli uomini del villaggio «si munirono di "bastoni magici" e si avviarono alla ricerca della strega... Ogni "bastone", ricavato dall'albero *kilimdara*, avrebbe diretto il suo possessore alla casa del colpevole. Alcuni rinunciarono alla ricerca perché i loro "bastoni" non si appesantivano; altri sentirono il loro "bastone" appesantirsi mentre si avvicinavano alla casa di Foias...».

L'uomo aggiunse poi che era compito di Dinenyeng fare qualcosa, essendo lui stesso il parente più vicino di Foias: non era compito di un estraneo uccidere una strega. Anche il giudice bianco ritenne che questa fosse una comprensibile attenuante; e Dinenyeng fu così condannato a meno di due anni di prigione.

La «rappresaglia» è praticata dalla maggior parte dei gruppi tribali come forma di giustizia tradizionale; si crede che lo spirito di una vittima di morte violenta continui a vagare senza requie sulla terra supplicando i propri congiunti di vendicarne l'uccisione perché possa riposare in pace.

La rappresaglia non chiede che i vendicatori trovino e uccidano l'assassino: può essere «fatta giustizia» ammazzando un membro qualunque dello stesso clan. Ciò porta spesso all'uccisione di una persona innocente, forse di qualcuno che si era pronunciato contro il primo omicidio.

Un caso nel quale un innocente fu vittima di un assassino che praticò la «rappresaglia» avvenne all'ospedale di Port Moresby; episodio che me ne ha ricordato un altro analogo[1] di cui fui testimone a Brazzaville.

---

[1] Cfr. *I mille fuochi*, Bari 1964, pp. 324-326. L'accostamento dei due casi potrebbe indurre in una troppo facile ricerca di «parallelismi» tra popolazioni lontane e diverse, ma di simile livello etnologico; l'operazione è sconsigliabile, se non affrontata con le dovute cautele del caso.

La vicenda ebbe inizio quando un trattore che operava in una piantagione di gomma, vicino a Port Moresby, investì e uccise un lavoratore *goilala* della piantagione. Il giudice istruttore trovò che l'uomo era deceduto in seguito a incidente, ma la sua spiegazione non soddisfece il fratello. Questi rintracciò il nome del conducente del trattore e decise che invece di uccidere lui, avrebbe tolto la vita al fratello. L'uomo prescelto era degente all'ospedale di Port Moresby, dove si recò l'assassino. Questi vide uscire la vittima in barella dalla camera dei raggi X, si avvicinò e senza una parola gli affondò il coltello nel petto. Non oppose in seguito quasi alcuna resistenza all'arresto: aveva ucciso il fratello dell'uomo, che, secondo lui, gli aveva ammazzato il fratello.

A Port Moresby, si ricorda un altro caso di vendetta familiare: è la storia di Obura chiamato Teitendau.

Per anni credette che suo fratello (il quale era morto di cause naturali) fosse stato ucciso da un papua del gruppo tribale *chimbu* mentre lavorava come operaio in una piantagione nei pressi di Madang, e si era prefisso di vendicarlo.

Un giorno del 1963, Teitendau e sette uomini del suo clan s'imbatterono in un gruppo di cinque *chimbu* arrivato nel territorio di Obura per vendere piume di uccello del paradiso. Teitendau e i suoi compagni si gettarono sui *chimbu* e li assassinarono con le loro accette. Le procedure legali si tennero a Kainatu al limite del territorio di Obura. Alla fine del terzo giorno di processo, mentre Teitendau e gli altri accusati venivano scortati dalla polizia, due *chimbu* si precipitarono su Teitendau e lo fecero a pezzi a colpi di accetta. Poi gli assassini si presentarono con le loro armi, ancora grondanti sangue, alla stazione di polizia. Dissero che non essendo soddisfatti del modo in cui si era svolto il processo e temendo che Teitendau sarebbe stato proclamato innocente, avevano deciso di vendicarsi quando si trovava a portata di mano; anche perché non volevano addentrarsi nel territorio di Obura per cercarlo.

Rinforzi di polizia si recarono in DC3 a evacuare i lavoratori della piantagione teatro della vicenda, dopo aver ricevuto informazione a Kainatu che centinaia di uomini di Obura si stavano dirigendo sulla città alla ricerca di *chimbu* da uccidere. Gli ufficiali dell'amministrazione riuscirono, dopo lunghe trattative, a persuadere i vendicatori a ritornare ai loro villaggi e fu evitata un'ulte-

riore strage; e così il processo ai sette detenuti complici di Teitendau continuò senza ulteriori violenze in una corte circondata da
polizia armata. Ma un anno più tardi un gruppo *chimbu* pareggiò il
conto; e pochi mesi dopo quelli di Obura contraccambiarono: una
«rappresaglia» a catena che sembra, ancora oggi, non aver mai
fine.

Ho narrato questi episodi non solo perché illustrano il meccanismo reattivo dell'individuo papua nelle sue massime espressioni
di violenza; ma perché ancora una volta mi accorgo con il loro
aiuto di quanto l'uomo tuttora vestito di penne e pelli e l'uomo in
calzoni e cravatta si assomigliano profondamente, nel bene come
nel male; si identificano in certi casi in maniera assoluta, benché
sia l'uno che l'altro rifiutino con ostinazione di ammetterlo.

Quanti, fra gli episodi di «rappresaglia» ascoltati, non trovano
un immediato parallelo in altri accaduti nella nostra società? A
parte la diversa tecnica di questi delitti e il movente «magico» di
taluni di essi, non basterebbero solo i casi di vendetta, singoli o di
gruppo, per trovare una casistica *bianca* assai più ricca di quella
nera?

I «bianchi» delle amministrazioni ancora coloniali che mi narrarono gli episodi di «ferocia indigena» sopra citati, intendevano,
coscientemente o no, illustrare quanto basso era a parer loro il
livello umano delle tribù locali.

«E noi dovremmo portare all'indipendenza queste isole e queste genti?» mi hanno ripetuto tutti, a conclusione dei loro racconti,
ponendomi, con uguale tono e intenzione, la stessa domanda che
ho sentito per dieci anni, dal '50 al '60 in Africa, in insistente
monotona polemica. È la domanda che si ripete ora, da altri dieci
anni (dal '60 al '70) in Oceania; o perché *troppo buoni* («veri bambini») o perché *troppo feroci* («restano in fondo tutti cannibali») ai
polinesiani dell'Est così come ai paupa dell'Ovest si è tentato e si
tenta ancora di negare il diritto di essere considerati uomini a pari
condizioni d'ogni altro; e d'esser quindi liberi d'affrontare autonomamente il loro destino in un mondo ove il colonialismo – nelle
sue forme più diverse e più occulte – deve scomparire per sempre,
senza trovare giustificazioni o ritardi.

Certo, la persistenza di forme esasperate di ritualismo legano ancora molti gruppi tribali a un passato di tenebre e ferocia; ma una delle tante colpe del colonialismo in Oceania è proprio quella – in quasi quattro secoli di «storia» – di non essere riuscito a mutare certe condizioni di vita, adoperandosi affinché certe strutture societarie interne venissero a poco a poco modificate. E non solo questo è stato raramente tentato, ma l'esempio della continua violenza offerta dai «bianchi» – in Oceania, così come in Africa e in tutte le altre terre «colonizzate» – ha contribuito a imporre i lati peggiori anziché i migliori delle popolazioni locali.

Ma se tra i cosiddetti «amministratori» delle isole e i «coloni» bianchi la mentalità ottusa del colonialismo è ancora una componente fondamentale, occorre aggiungere che fortunatamente qualche eccezione esiste, soprattutto tra coloro che non hanno ricoperto cariche «ufficiali».

V'è, tra i «bianchi» che hanno vissuto negli arcipelaghi del Pacifico occidentale, chi ha studiato a fondo la società familiare papua, in modo da citarla come esempio di convivenza civile e di educazione dei figli quale il mondo occidentale non conosce.[1] V'è chi ha collezionato oggetti d'arte melanesiana molto tempo prima dell'attuale moda; e possiede collezioni non solo per il gusto di raccogliere opere rare e di straordinaria espressività artistica, ma anche perché di molte di esse, conoscendo l'origine e l'importanza, può servirsene per aiutare a spiegare a se stesso, e agli altri, il livello altamente evoluto di un'estetica così diversa dalla nostra, non solo nei risultati ma anche e soprattutto nelle sue componenti d'origine.

E infine ci sono coloro che hanno avvicinato le genti delle isole non con l'accanito intendimento di trovarvi quella «degradazione» umana che serve a giustificare personalmente e storicamente il persistere di una politica coloniale, ma per studiarvi a fondo le linee di una evoluzione che, anche dove profondamente diversa da quella occidentale, riconduce sempre a un'unica matrice originaria della storia dell'uomo.

[1] Vedi da p. 377 a p. 385 la parte antologica dedicata alla straordinaria opera in Melanesia di Malinowski.

Fu proprio da uno studio in questa direzione che venimmo a sapere, alle Nuove Ebridi, della «prova del salto».

Nelle isole di Pentecôte una tribù papua provava il suo coraggio gettandosi nel vuoto di un'alta torre di liane: l'informazione ci veniva da due straordinari conoscitori del mondo papua, due autentici amici di quelle popolazioni, di cui conoscevano i problemi e le angosce ma anche lo splendore raffinato d'una cultura dal gusto sicuro e dotata del coraggio di affrontare il mistero dalla vita con un rito che difficilmente può trovare paragoni nel mondo, primitivo e no.

I nostri informatori – due coniugi inglesi che vivevano, unici bianchi, a Tanna – ma parlarono, per primi, nel 1956 di quel rito come di una straordinaria «prova di coraggio», simile a tante altre praticate dalle culture europee in altre epoche.

Una «prova di coraggio» ancora autentica, e (a quanto sembrava) di particolare violenza e drammaticità; nulla di meglio per un gruppo di ricerca documentaristica in Oceania.

Non c'era da perdere tempo; e, pur essendo stati informati anche di quanto sarebbe stato problematico convincere quella popolazione a compiere la prova davanti a noi, decidemmo di partire al più presto per l'isola indicataci, distante tre giorni di navigazione da Port Vila, unico punto possibile di partenza per l'arcipelago delle Nuove Ebridi.

Un francese, proprietario di una piccola goletta e conoscitore dell'arcipelago, offrì i suoi servigi alla nostra missione; radunammo le necessarie scorte di viveri e di carburante, caricammo il nostro materiale cinematografico e fotografico; e prendemmo il mare aperto verso il Nord.

Fu un viaggio tanto avventuroso da essere banale per quanto riusciva a coincidere con certi schemi della letteratura più ovvi dei Mari del Sud. Il padrone della goletta era sempre ubriaco; i marinai a bordo erano indefiniti e indecifrabili; il motore ogni tanto si inceppava e ripartiva per motivi a noi rimasti sempre misteriosi.

Infine giungemmo a Pentecôte. Ce l'avevamo fatta: ognuno di noi s'era improvvisato motorista, timoniere o mozzo, e tutti insieme coalizzati eravamo riusciti ad attraversare felicemente quelle trecento miglia di Oceano Pacifico; eravamo riusciti persino a cucinare un pentolone di spaghetti, che sarebbe poi rimasto come unico pasto «serio» di un mese abbastanza «difficile».

Trovammo un ancoraggio il secondo giorno di navigazione lungo l'isola, e guidati da uno dei marinai (in funzione di interprete) sbarcammo. Ma se fu facile il contatto, a riva, con i gruppi di papua già da tempo abituati agli incontri, con i gruppi dell'interno la vicenda fu assai ardua[1]. Passarono molti giorni prima che riuscissimo a entrare in contatto con loro; poi quando, finalmente, fu stabilito in quale villaggio potevamo essere accolti come «ospiti», ci mettemmo in marcia.

Un cammino faticoso, seguendo passo passo il corso di un torrente. Sopra di noi il tetto verde di una foresta fittissima ci impediva la vista del cielo, e un calore asfissiante ci perseguitava per tutto il tempo della nostra marcia (anche questo, pensavo, è come il viaggio in goletta con il padrone ubriaco e i marinai infidi: una situazione da racconto a fumetti. Ma come tale dovevamo accettarla, e viverla).

A mezza giornata di marcia dalla costa (pochi chilometri ma in continua ripidissima salita) sulla riva di un secondo corso d'acqua incontrammo un solo uomo: era un *bushman*. Non si voltò nemmeno per vederci passare: pescava con una rete da lancio (in Toscana e in Liguria chiamata «sparviero») e pur avendo udito le nostre voci, non si girò; raccoglieva la rete, la preparava e poi la lanciava stendendo i muscoli forti di tutto il suo piccolo, agile corpo. Noi non lo interessavamo.

Nella marcia verso il villaggio più alto nelle montagne di Pentecôte, ci accompagna il proprietario della goletta con la quale abbiamo viaggiato da Port Vila sin qui; dapprima è stato molto incerto se seguirci o no a terra, poi ha deciso di sì.

«Ci vuole coraggio da parte mia,» ha borbottato il francese «qui il mio nome, Gabriel Des Granges, lo conoscono tutti...»

Sempre per continuare l'atmosfera «di maniera», nell'atteggiarsi a vero e proprio «bianco insabbiato nei Mari del Sud», Des Granges beveva whisky caldo e liscio a ogni sosta lungo il cammino e parlava fitto fitto di tutto e di tutti. Con la lucidità degli

---

[1] Ci accorgevamo per la prima volta della differenza tra *mensaltwater* e *bushmen*.

ubriachi, narrava ogni sera, quando ci accampavamo sotto le stelle, dei primi sbarchi su queste isole delle Nuove Ebridi, di Pedro Fernandez de Quieros, di Torres nel 1606, e di Carteret, Bougainville e Cook centocinquanta anni dopo. Non perché amasse la storia: ma perché cercava radici lontane per giustificare la sua vita nelle isole.

«I primi esploratori,» iniziò a dirci la prima sera «sostanzialmente, si comportarono bene con gli indigeni. Dopo cominciarono i guai... Quando altri bianchi presero ad approdare a Tanna, a Malekula, a Pentecôte...»

«Erano negrieri, quei bianchi» riprende Des Granges l'indomani, mentre ci fermiamo per mangiare qualcosa e per riposarci; i piedi nell'acqua fresca del torrente ci aiutano a sopportare il calore, che nell'ora del mezzogiorno è quasi insopportabile.

«Voi conoscete la mia casa, vero? Io sono un uomo che ha una certa cultura, vero? La mia casa di Port Vila è piena di quadri di ottimi autori moderni e dei migliori libri di tutte le letterature, no?... Ho una bella barca, molti soldi... E sapete perché? come?» Des Granges non aspetta una nostra risposta e continua con enfasi, sembra che reciti. Un fondo di verità nelle sue parole rende quel discorso qualcosa di più di un soliloquio ispirato dal whisky e dalla stanchezza; è una confessione, un documento.

«Erano negrieri i bianchi che per cent'anni, dopo i primi esploratori, hanno infestato per più di un secolo la Melanesia; e io sono stato l'ultimo di loro. Ecco perché ho soldi, una bella casa, eccetera, eccetera. Non ci chiamavamo negrieri, naturalmente, ma *reclutatori*. In teoria noi non violavamo nessuna legge. Il *reclutatore* con il suo battello arrivava a un villaggio della costa o si spingeva sino a quelli dell'interno e reclutava gli uomini che *volontariamente* accettavano di seguirlo per andare a lavorare nelle piantagioni di canna da zucchero degli altri arcipelaghi o del Queensland. Non violavamo nessuna legge, in teoria, ma in pratica pochi erano i "i volontari" propriamente detti che ci seguivano. La maggioranza non capiva cosa accettava... o veniva attratta dal desiderio di aver subito il piccolo premio di ingaggio offerto... In qualsiasi caso nessuno di loro avrebbe mai rivisto il villaggio da cui era partito, perché il *reclutatore* "vendeva" ai padroni delle piantagioni di canne da zucchero il suo carico umano, e là i *reclutati* sarebbero rimasti per sempre...»

Anche se il racconto di Gabriel Des Granges fosse terminato con una lacrima di coccodrillo, non ci sarebbe mai stato possibile vederlo; alle sue ultime parole il cielo s'era aperto nell'inevitabile acquazzone del pomeriggio e lo scroscio della pioggia sulle foglie del bosco era così assordante da impedire non solo una conversazione ma qualunque nostra parola a meno che non fosse gridata.

Ma conoscendo meglio, poi, la storia della Melanesia, ho ripensato sovente a quel suo racconto e ho capito la sua paura di accompagnarci al villaggio nostra meta. Infatti dopo la seconda guerra mondiale, i papua di tutte le isole, compresi i gruppi più primitivi, hanno «preso coscienza» d'essere stati per un secolo oggetto di scambio e di commercio. Il contatto coi bianchi fu temuto ed evitato al massimo, e così molti gruppi papua, specialmente i *big-nambas* più bellicosi, sono stati raggiunti solo saltuariamente e superficialmente da chi li cercava non più per razziarli, ma per conoscerli e studiarli. E a causa di questo stato di inimicizia, i melanesiani delle Nuove Ebridi sono, ancora oggi, con alcune popolazioni dell'Amazzonia, i più primitivi del mondo intero.

Di tutto questo avrei meglio saputo e studiato dopo il mio tentativo di penetrare nell'interno di Pentecôte, ma ne ero già confusamente al corrente al momento del nostro sbarco.

Avevo però anche motivo per rassicurarmi; in fondo, altri viaggi tra popolazioni primitive erano stati conclusi positivamente; ero riuscito a vivere in villaggi remoti da ogni civiltà bianca; avevo potuto vivere con loro giorni *autentici*, nel vero significato della parola. La stessa sorte, con un po' di fortuna, forse mi attendeva anche in Melanesia.

Quando giungemmo al villaggio del «salto» l'intervento del nostro interprete e un congruo dono ci permise d'ottenere il permesso di restare, di abitare tra la gente come se non vi fosse in questo nulla di straordinario, almeno alla superficie. Restammo tre settimane, tra la fine di novembre e l'inizio di dicembre: un periodo buono per il clima, considerato «secco», perché i piovaschi in questo scorcio dell'anno non sono mai più di sei o sette al giorno.

Iniziammo la nostra «ricerca» nelle capanne stesse ove eravamo alloggiati; e non ci volle molto a renderci conto che la struttura di ogni famiglia era complessa: i differenti legami di parentela si contraddistinguevano con una ridda di termini diversi. Comunque il carattere dominante era quello di un'organizzazione familiare di tipo matrilineare. Poi cominciammo a osservare la loro vita quotidiana e gli oggetti della «cultura materiale» che la caratterizzavano.

Il buon *bishlamar* del nostro interprete e un secondo dono ci permettono di organizzare alcune riunioni con i «notabili», dalle quali abbiamo potuto approssimativamente comprendere quanto le nozioni di questa gente sul mondo esterno siano vaghe: non conoscono l'intera isola nella quale abitano; non hanno alcuna idea sulle altre isole di questo arcipelago. Per loro esiste, sì, un grande universo di mare e di terra sul quale si leva ogni giorno il sole, ma è qualcosa di indefinito e poco interessante che nemmeno le vicende della guerra '40-'45 ha fatto uscire dalle nebbie. E questa è la sostanziale differenza che ho sentito fra questi papua e le altre genti del Pacifico, navigatori e marinai tutti, e non solo i polinesiani. A compensare questa mancanza, il loro continuo contatto con la natura li ha resi conoscitori di molti segreti della terra; hanno profonde cognizioni empiriche di scienze naturali, sanno trarre dai frutti, dalle foglie, dai muschi e dalle radici, tutti i vantaggi possibili e medicamenti non di rado efficaci (vedemmo un impiastro di erbe guarire in pochi giorni una brutta infezione).

Un mondo difficile da penetrare (anche se in questi villaggi la nostra presenza sembra sufficientemente sopportata) a causa di quella ben prevedibile, radicata animosità contro i bianchi alimentata dal ricordo delle razzie passate.

Ma non ci scoraggiamo; continuando ad abitare pacificamente tra loro, riusciremo, spero, a trovare la chiave della loro amicizia.

Quella «chiave» ci venne offerta per le cerimonie di un matrimonio tra due *bushmen*, al quale avemmo l'occasione d'assistere.

Vedemmo i maiali con i quali – in numero di undici – lo sposo aveva pagato la sposa. Erano neri e avevano il grugno superiore bucato; da esso uscivano due lunghe e ricurve zanne piegate all'indietro. Questi maiali, ad allevarli, costano anni di fatica perché bisogna avere continua cura di quella dentatura per ricavarne due zanne preziose che bisogna aiutare a crescere così curve: e quando cominciano a esserlo troppo impediscono alla bestia di aprire la bocca. Allora il proprietario deve nutrire il suo animale con infinta pazienza, infilandogli in bocca piccoli bocconi dopo avergli aperto a forza, con le mani, le mascelle. Ma è una pazienza ampiamente ripagata: una volta ricurve, le zanne acquistano una importanza sacra e alla morte del maiale (che viene ucciso durante una lunga e complessa cerimonia) gli uomini se le appendono al collo come amuleti.

«Parte di tradizione sacra» o «componenti di un rito» molto geloso: per questo mi parve di capire che non c'era concesso di fotografare quei maiali neri. Ci saremmo forse riusciti, insistendo; ma ci sforzammo a dimostrare rispetto per quella riservata tradizione e i *bushmen* ne furono sorpresi. Senza che apparentemente nulla cambiasse, da quel momento qualcosa mutò nei nostri rapporti. Quel gesto probabilmente li aveva conquistati e da quel momento furono molto più abbordabili con noi.

Venne un giorno di danze evidentemente rituali e la mia sensazione di amichevole fiducia da parte loro si rafforzò: se c'era permesso assistere a quella festa, di certo avremmo poi potuto assistere alla successiva «prova di coraggio». Le danze, infatti, di chiara evocazione guerriera, erano un preciso preludio alla cerimonia del *kgöl*, come veniva chiamato «il salto» dalla torre di liane; l'essere ammessi alla prima parte del rito poteva voler dire essere ammessi anche alla seconda.

Come un'antica ira che esplode di colpo, le pantomime delle danze di morte, di lotta, di pace, iniziarono all'improvviso e noi vi fummo subito in mezzo.

Gli uomini avevano in mano lunghe aste di bambù. E danzavano (uno, due, tre) intorno a se stessi per trovarsi, a due a due, uno in faccia all'altro e percuotere i bambù con perfetta sincronia, traendone un suono vuoto, solenne *ouverture* primitiva all'apparizione dell'intera tribù in costume di guerra: con lance, pelli, scudi, frecce, maschere. Impiegarono un'ora per uscire dalla boscaglia e arrivare al centro della radura, percorrendo poco più di duecento metri. Quella lentezza aveva la solennità del rito. Poi per più di tre ore narrarono una storia di lotta fra due villaggi e svolsero il loro racconto proprio con la danza.

Fu, inizialmente, la pantomima di una battaglia: lanci di frecce e di giavellotti, danzatori come morti e incitamento di capi lotta; il coro di tutti era sottolineato dal ritmo dei bambù e dal battere dei piedi sulla terra, di ogni uomo e donna presenti in quella piccola valle. Poi d'improvviso, dal lato del monte tagliato da una stretta valle comunicante col mare apparve un danzatore mascherato da «uomo-uccello», il gabbiano della pace, volato dall'oceano sino ai villaggi per fermare lo sterminio. Chiamato dal canto dei bambù l'«uomo-gabbiano» era giunto e danzava tutt'attorno alla radura della festa, al centro della quale i guerrieri come stupiti della sua apparizione avevano sospeso la loro pantomima di lotta e di morte.

I suoi giri erano concentrici, a sfiorare il gruppo dei guerrieri; e chi era toccato da lui, lasciava cadere arco e frecce. Dalle file degli uomini armati, disorganizzate e turbate dal passaggio ripetuto del «gabbiano» si staccarono allora alcuni danzatori: «spiriti della discordia», come diceva il loro stesso costume (foglie secche a indicare la decomposizione, la distruzione). L'«uomo-gabbiano» e i «maligni» si inseguirono veloci, urlando. Poi s'udì un grido acutissimo e vedemmo che l'«uomo-gabbiano» era stato simbolicamente ucciso: gli spiriti della guerra avevano vinto.

Mi chiesi, allora, se la rappresentazione da me vista avesse voluto significare che la gente del villaggio sentiva come propria sorte il dover continuare a lottare per sempre. Oggi, ripensandoci, mi rendo conto dell'errore di voler interpretare la manifestazione di un gruppo primitivo con lo stesso metro che useremmo per spettacoli coreutici o mimici «nostri». Come poter infatti tentare di capire quali simboli suggeriva la seconda parte di quelle danze, quando l'«uomo-gabbiano» morto solo in apparenza rinacque?... Nel silenzio seguito alla sua caduta, alzò all'improvviso la testa, si rimise in ginocchio, mosse le braccia e le allargò come a suggerire un fremito d'ali. I guerrieri ebbero un mormorio, ruppero le ordinate file e si accalcarono in cerchio attorno a lui. Nell'erba, le armi erano oggetti dimenticati; e gli uomini «della discordia» si spogliavano del loro costume. Non c'era più posto per loro; era la pace a dominare, da quel momento.

Fummo certi, a quel punto, che la lunga festa fosse terminata: invece le vuote canne di bambù ripresero con le percussioni il loro ritmo, ed ebbe inizio la «danza dei venti». Un gruppo di uomini a terra simboleggiava foglie abbandonate al centro di una valle e attorno a loro ne apparvero, danzando, altri. Ciascuno rappresentava un vento e si muoveva con un suo ritmo intorno al «gruppo delle foglie». Poi, quando ogni danza singola si fuse in un movimento collettivo e ogni uomo (ogni vento) si mosse insieme, fu come se un ciclone avesse investito l'intera valle. Le «foglie» volarono via e la danza finì così, in un vuoto improvviso e silenzioso.

Era buio quando le canne di bambù smisero il loro ritmo iniziato più di dodici ore prima. Nel silenzio più assoluto sceso su tutti noi, ricordo gli uomini sfiniti a terra: dormivano gli uni sugli altri. E ricordo che, quando spegnemmo le lampade a gas, sperai che non cadesse la solita pioggia notturna: ma non per la paura di finire, come al solito, inzuppati fino al midollo, ma per la certezza che il chiasso di quelle pesanti gocce d'acqua sulle foglie enormi e secche con le quali i *bushmen* s'erano coperti ci avrebbe fatto impazzire.

Come supponevamo, alle sacre danze seguì, a distanza di pochi giorni, la prova di coraggio. Essa si svolge, oltre la foresta, in una radura in pendenza verso l'oceano. Il luogo è simile a un palcoscenico sconfinante nell'immensità del mare davanti all'anfiteatro delle montagne e del cielo. Per ricavare lo spazio libero di quella radura gli uomini hanno bruciato gli alberi; e il sottobosco si è tramutato in una coltre compatta di cenere nera sulla quale sono adagiati, e spiccano per il loro biancore, i tronchi dei grandi alberi caduti. Attorno a essi uomini e donne camminano carichi di lunghe liane tagliate in foresta, portandole verso un albero – completamente spoglio di ogni fronda, ma non bruciato – lasciato in piedi, al centro della spianata.

Per giorni e giorni uomini e donne hanno raccolto le liane in tutta l'isola. Le liane sono indispensabili al *kgöl*, alla tecnica del salto. Scegliendole e raccogliendole il villaggio è entrato in un'eccitazione religiosa e musicale che le grandi danze collettive avevano solo preannunciato.

Sull'unico albero ritto al centro della radura, come una ragnatela, gli uomini «attrezzano» una rozza torre di pali di bambù, di bastoni intrecciati, elastica e disordinata, affastellamento di rami nudi e di liane entro il quale gli uomini salgono, scendono, si muovono in una attività da formicaio che continua sulla cenere della radura, alla base dell'albero. Il fitto polverone sollevato dall'incessante passare e ripassare della gente dell'intero villaggio su quello strato soffice e leggero è cancellato da un acquazzone violento. E quando la pioggia cessa, la cenere è viscida come uno strato di miele.

La mia ansia è al culmine: sto per assistere e per fotografare il salto nel vuoto, il *kgöl* dei *bushmen* di Pentecôte: non solo la «prova di coraggio», ma l'insieme cerimoniale che la precede ed è l'accompagnamento tradizionale della costruzione della torre.

Il «salto» è preceduto infatti da «riti» ininterrotti, per una settimana, che raggiungono il loro culmine alle prime luci dell'alba, nel giorno prescelto per la prova. Il sole è ancora nascosto oltre l'orizzonte quando saliamo – con gli uomini della «prova» – le pendici del vulcano che sovrasta l'isola e con loro arriviamo al cratere dove essi si ingraziano, con un canto, il dio terribile nascosto dal magma rosso in ebollizione sul fondo.

Gli uomini hanno infilato nei capelli una penna (simbolo della loro anima), e per ore hanno camminato attraversando la boscaglia formata dagli arbusti di pandano cresciuti sulla cenere; sono poi sbucati – e noi con loro – nella pianura che circonda il vulcano proprio nel momento in cui il pallido sole di queste isole s'è affacciato all'umido orizzonte.

Una marcia nel silenzio assoluto di un preistorico paesaggio dove la terra, la vegetazione, ogni umore sono stati soffocati dalla coltre di cenere soffiata dal cratere; un piccolo deserto, cupo terreno che rimbomba dei continui brontolii del vulcano. Lentamente lo attraversiamo in lunga fila indiana.

Quando cominciamo la salita al cratere, la cenere eruttata dal vulcano e impalpabile nell'aria, si deposita, sottile, sulla pelle e ci muta in ombre grigie e grigi rende anche i papua; insieme, siamo così – sia loro che noi – dello stesso colore del vulcano. Ma per poco, ché già prima di arrivare in cima al ripido pendio uno scroscio di pioggia ci lava, mente le gocce nel cratere evaporano in una nube densa verso il cielo. Attraverso quella nebbia ci troviamo d'improvviso sul ciglio che pare vivo nei continui tremori del profondo cratere. Alle nostre spalle c'è l'isola e le sue montagne, le foreste e l'oceano.

Prepariamo la macchina da ripresa e filmiamo, mentre i *bushmen* iniziano il canto della preghiera, a gran voce, disordinatamente. Dinanzi a loro e a noi s'apre la voragine fetida, dalla quale salgono fumi irrespirabili, vampe di luce gialla guizzanti dalla lava rovente.

Quando torniamo al villaggio, il sole è allo zenith, sul groviglio della torre, alto già più di trenta metri, gli uomini sono pronti al salto.

Uomini maturi e bambini, vecchi del villaggio e giovani nel pieno delle loro forze sono pronti a misurare coraggio e bravura. Dalla torre salteranno ognuno secondo le proprie possibilità: i bambini e i vecchi da pochi metri d'altezza, i giovani da più in alto; qualcuno dalla cima.

Il nostro marinaio-interprete ha parlato a lungo con i protagonisti della prova e ci spiega che l'intera torre è elastica, a ogni salto ondeggerà, e questo movimento «assorbirà», in un certo senso, lo strappo della liana nell'istante della massima tensione, trattenendo l'uomo per la caviglia. Inoltre, le liane, di per se stesse, sono elastiche e quando si tendono, lo fanno dolcemente: questa loro qualità rende lo sforzo finale del salto sopportabile alle gambe dell'uomo; ma aumenta anche il pericolo della prova, perché se la liana è calcolata di una certa lunghezza e invece nel salto si allunga oltre il previsto, l'uomo può battere contro la terra violentemente e uccidersi. Ma proprio in questo è la bravura dei *bushmen* di Pentecôte: nel calcolo, non solo della lunghezza, ma dell'estensibilità delle liane (e in questo è anche il loro coraggio, perché resta sempre, in definitiva, una buona dose di imponderabilità a rendere rischioso il loro tuffo nel vuoto).

Ogni saltatore è immobile: parte del groviglio vegetale che forma la torre. Sotto di sé ha il vuoto e intorno, sul cerchio della radura, tutte le donne del villaggio. Ogni saltatore è il solo arbitro del proprio futuro, perché un comportamento di coraggio o di paura sarà sufficiente a cambiare poi la sua posizione nell'insieme della comunità. Nella quale ognuno è giudicato e apprezzato, durante la vita quotidiana, a seconda di come affronta la prova del *kgöl*: chi ha paura del salto è «messo da parte», può non trovar moglie se non l'ha, o perderla se l'ha; ed è continuamente posto in imbarazzo dai più coraggiosi.

È magnifica questa torre. È qualcosa ove ognuno può restare sospeso tra cielo e terra, padrone del propio destino fino all'istante del salto. E quell'istante (quella serie d'istanti) è appunto il *kgöl*, prova, per tutti, di confermarsi uomini.

Per primi si gettano i ragazzi dai trampolini più bassi e poi li seguono nel vuoto gli uomini, da tutte le altezze. Finché giunge il momento dei più coraggiosi, che saltano dalla cima.

Ognuno resta, prima del tuffo, immobile per un istante. Un battito delle mani prima di gettarsi nel vuoto (è certo un gesto propiziatorio), poi il corpo del saltatore si lancia nel vuoto, le braccia s'allargano, le donne urlano e l'uomo gira su se stesso, a caposotto, mentre le liane si tendono. L'uomo precipita a terra con tutto il suo peso e quando sembra stia per avvenire un inevitabile impatto, la liana si tende, come frusta all'istante dello schiocco, e anche le gambe si tendono. Il corpo ha uno scatto e miracolosamente immobile, per un attimo, a meno di mezzo metro dal suolo, ricade adagio sulla terra battuta, la testa in basso, le braccia tese.

Ogni saltatore, appena a terra, è inghiottito dall'abbraccio delle donne che corrono a festeggiarlo, senza perdere il ritmo della danza; lo liberano dai nodi della liana che gli legano una caviglia e gli accarezzano i muscoli indolenziti del corpo, tesi dallo strappo finale.

Sulla torre un altro si prepara, guarda in basso.

Batte le mani, chiede coraggio, tutto il coraggio possibile, e salta; cade e scompare a sua volta tra la sua gente e nella foresta. E già salta un altro ancora, un'altra liana si tende, e così via uno dopo l'altro. Tutti volano, pesanti e goffi uccelli senz'ali. Le donne li incitano ritmando gli urli con il silenzio, fino a quando la prova termina.

Sono più di sessanta salti cui assisto, fortunatamente senza incidenti. In certi *kgöl*, si dice, ci furono perfino alcuni morti (in uno nove) e molti feriti.

426

«*Mudman?*» avevo chiesto appena lasciato Goroka ed entrato nella Roka Valley. E dopo qualche giorno senza aver trovato risposta, incontro chi accetta di guidarci: un maestro papua, un ragazzo svelto, nato in una piantagione di caffè dove aveva imparato a leggere e a scrivere. Poi se ne era andato in città, era riuscito a prendere un diploma, ed era infine tornato tra le montagne a insegnare l'alfabeto e i primi rudimenti di cultura ai bambini del suo villaggio. Conosce tutto e tutti nel raggio di molti chilometri, nel vasto territorio dell'intera vallata, anche la sua parte più impervia, oltre il fiume nella zona scoscesa di Roka (vedremo poi quanto questo dato topografico abbia importanza) dove avremmo potuto incontrare i *mudmen*.[1]

Guida e amico, nel verde del bosco guineano come nel groviglio dei pensieri, quasi a confondere ogni traccia ma a ritrovarne di continuo diverse altre; sino al villaggio, alle campagne, alla gente che cercavamo. Quando vi giungiamo siamo accolti senza diffidenza dato che è lui a condurci sino a loro.

Sull'entrata delle capanne sono sedute alcune donne. Il maestro confabula con loro; le donne si allontanano, ritornano, vanno e vengono dalle capanne alle piantagioni di taro nascoste, oltre il villaggio, nel loro groviglio verde degli alberi e del sottobosco. Debbono chiedere ai loro uomini di presentarsi a noi nel loro costume rituale di fango; così ha chiesto la nostra guida. E nell'attesa della loro apparizione, noi prepariamo macchine fotografiche e da ripresa, filtri, esposimetri: il nostro armamentario di sempre.

Qualche maiale corre tra le capanne, e c'è un gran silenzio. E silenziosa è l'apparizione dei *mudmen*.

In un'intermittenza di memoria, quasi un'immagine fissa e ricordo la comparsa, in Africa, in Amazzonia, in India, di altri gruppi primitivi in vesti sacrali o tradizionali o mascherati: i *dogòn* del Mali, i *lamidò* del Camerun, i *bobo* dell'Alto Volta e i *thoda* dell'India meridionale, ovunque la loro apparizione era stata preceduta da fragorose percussioni o suoni a fiato o canto o gridi: di festa come di paura.

Gli «uomini di fango», i *mudmen* della Roka Valley ci vengono

---

[1] Assieme a lui ebbi vicino, in quella spedizione nell'interno, un italiano da tempo stabilitosi tra i papua, Fred Gastaudo; di lui e dei *mudmen* ho scritto nei racconti de *L'avventura e la scoperta*, in questa stessa collana, Mondadori, Milano 1989.

incontro in un silenzio assoluto, muovendosi con passi impercettibili, ognuno come seguendo una propria, personale lentissima danza.

Ecco, li ho trovati – penso – e continuo a fotografarli e filmarli. Ma soprattutto a guardarli.

Ormai certi gesti del mio lavoro, fortunatamente, sono quasi meccanici, e mi sento libero, anche nei momenti di massima tensione, di guardare per poi ricordare.

Guardo i *mudmen*. Sono coperti di fango aderente al loro corpo come una tuta screpolata di gomma. La loro testa è coperta da una grande zucca cava, nella quale sono praticati i fori per gli occhi e per la bocca. La zucca, come il corpo, è coperta di fango, ma è anche decorata; piccoli denti di gatto o di cane segnano la linea della bocca e degli occhi; denti ricurvi di facocero ornano la parte della maschera che rappresenta il naso.

Solo pochissimi – forse lo sciamano o chi un tempo era guerriero – dipingono di colori violenti il fango della loro maschera; in genere le acconciature sono grigie e nere, colore del fango del fiume che scorre vicino al villaggio.

Dopo l'incontro, le modalità per una reciproca maggiore conoscenza; il prezzo, in diplomazia e in denaro, di poter essere «liberi ospiti» di quel villaggio, e potervi organizzare i nostri rapporti. Non è facile, ma non impossibile.

Ecco il nostro primo mattino nel villaggio dei *mudmen*. Mattino di umida aria fredda (siamo oltre i millecinquecento metri). Le famiglie che compongono la comunità hanno dormito come il solito su stuoie di erba all'interno delle capanne, o su piattaforme di legno intrecciato; la cucina viene accesa all'aperto, i fuochi tra sassi, solo quando la nebbia del fiume permette ai primi raggi del sole di aprirsi un varco sino a terra. Anche qui il peso di tutto il lavoro della comunità ricade sulle donne, le quali iniziano prima del sorger del sole ad accendere il fuoco per le cucine e per il resto della giornata poi si occupano delle piccole piantagioni in foresta, dei maiali e dei bambini; lavorano per la famiglia e per la comunità, tessono stuoie e coperture di paglia e, al calar del sole raccolgono legna da ardere per l'indomani.

Gli uomini, in passato, dedicavano la maggior parte del loro tempo a combattere, a cacciare, a lottare; oggi si limitano a costruire le capanne; si occupano delle coltivazioni più lontane e, quando è possibile, vanno a caccia di piccoli animali o di uccelli.

La prima fondamentale osservazione del sistema tribale di lavoro è che, a parte coloro che sono legati alla ritualità magica e adempiono quindi ai compiti relativi – con tutte le implicazioni che essi comportano –, non esistono «specializzati» in alcuna data mansione. Pochi sono più esperti dei loro compagni, né dimostrano desiderio di esserlo. Il lavoro è distribuito egualmente fra tutti. Né il rango, né l'eventuale maggiore ricchezza di un uomo, mi è parso esoneri qualcuno da fatiche quotidiane identiche a quelle del più insignificante membro del gruppo.

Più complesso è il capire quali siano i sentimenti, le credenze, i timori segreti di questa gente; particolarmente qui, dove – più che mai – mi interessa conoscere usi e costumi: l'apparizione mascherata dei *mudmen* m'aveva lasciato con il desiderio di sapere perché e come nasceva quel rito.

Chi ha studiato il problema delle credenze religiose di questi gruppi tribali delle montagne in Nuova Guinea, non ne ha scoperto nessuno il quale creda in un unico Essere Supremo o in un numero precisato di dèi; il rapporto con il mondo ultraterreno piuttosto si traduce per i *bushmen* nel dimostrare rispetto o nel tentare di compiacere o piacere a un certo numero di esseri soprannaturali, antenati di cui il ricordo è vago (alcuni di un tempo tanto remoto per cui non se ne sa più nulla). Di alcuni di questi esseri c'è chi crede di conoscere il luogo di dimora terrestre nelle nebbie di questa o di quella montagna, sotto una certa roccia o in un fiume o in uno stagno. Agli esseri-spiriti viene generalmente attribuita una forma umana, e qui lo studio generale degli specialisti si innesta alla nostra esperienza diretta di «testimoni» nel piccolo mondo tribale dei *mudmen*.

In questo gruppo come in tutto il mondo papua (cfr. pp. 365-373), i vivi credono che gli «spiriti» siano obbligati a reagire a certi riti, in modo da beneficare i credenti (sempre che il rito e il sacrificio siano effettuati secondo la tradizione). Se, dopo i riti in onore degli «spiriti», i campi coltivati non produrranno quanto si sperava non si incolperanno gli spiriti evocati, ma l'incapacità di effettuare il rito secondo la giusta formula.

Questo si innesta, tra i *mudmen* e nel resto del mondo primitivo della Nuova Guinea, sulla tradizionale paura delle forze magiche, sulla convinzione che la morte sia dovuta a stregoneria, malgrado l'eventuale età e lo stato di malattia evidente di un deceduto.

Gli indigeni della Roka Valley – ci dice il nostro maestro-guida – catturano e bolliscono topi «alla morte di un congiunto». Dopodiché, ogni membro del gruppo familiare colpito dalla disgrazia, è obbligato a mangiare quel cibo, e chi ne risente viene «scoperto» come causa del maleficio. È un metodo che fallisce raramente in quanto l'accusato ha generalmente già preso parte a simili procedimenti e non ha mai dubitato della loro efficacia, ed è quindi condizionato e suggestionato al punto *da credere alla verità della prova.*

Al centro del problema è il rapporto magia-suggestione, cioè la passività che può giungere sino al punto, in un individuo colpito da stregoneria, di ammalarsi e anche di morire senza nessuna ragione fisica apparente.

Nelle varie occasioni in cui ci è stato possibile convivere per qualche tempo in un villaggio papua (e questo soggiorno nel villaggio dei *mudmen* è l'ultimo ma non certo il più breve) abbiamo varie volte notato quanto ogni abitante di ogni villaggio viva nel continuo timore che una stregoneria sia organizzata contro di lui; ciascuno evita con scrupolo, conseguentemente, di lasciare in giro unghie, forcine da capelli, o escrementi. Tutte «cose», «tracce» che possono venir usate a suo danno.

In ogni villaggio vi è una persona (generalmente un uomo, ma può trattarsi anche di una donna anziana) alla quale si attribuiscono alte qualità di stregoneria. Nel villaggio di Roka è un uomo a occupare quella posizione di rispetto e di prestigio nella comunità. Conoscendolo e studiandone i rapporti con gli altri membri del gruppo, si comprende che quel «potere» è forte nella misura in cui il beneficiario o la vittima sia a conoscenza della magia, della cura o della maledizione che lo riguarda.

Qui nella Roka Valley chiamano la stregoneria *sanguma* e la considerano tra l'altro come «contagiosa», o meglio, trasmettibile «per contatto» come una infezione della pelle (difficile trovare termini «nostri» per parlare di qualcosa così tipicamente «loro»). Il nostro maestro-guida è stato, di certo, un buon interprete per noi, e non solo nell'aiutarci a parlare e a comprendere il senso di certi discorsi, ma soprattutto spiegandoci queste «credenze», lui che le vede e conosce *dall'interno* (in quanto papua), ma può anche giudicarle *dall'esterno* (in quanto ormai molto occidentalizzato). Un esempio tipico di *sanguma* narrato da lui, ha quindi il valore preciso di una testimonianza davanti alla quale non c'è che da restare sgomenti – sicuri della sua attendibilità – e lasciare agli studiosi di questi problemi il compito di interpretare l'episodio.

Un giorno – ci narra il maestro – un abitante della Roka Valley, il cui figlio frequentava la sua scuola, bussa alla porta della sua abitazione, ai margini del villaggio, e dice di essere vittima di una *sanguma*; aveva passato la notte con una ragazza di un villaggio vicino e, dopo averla lasciata, stava accingendosi a rientrare nel suo territorio quando gli era apparsa la madre della ragazza stessa, dicendogli che la figlia era *sanguma*: «contagiava».

Il dongiovanni papua terrorizzato era perciò venuto dal maestro per chiedergli di essere condotto a Lae, la città più vicina, per essere visitato da un medico; e il maestro cosciente del potere di suggestione della *sanguma* accompagnò immediatamente l'uomo all'ospedale con la sua automobile. Il passeggero, sicuro che la medicina «dell'ospedale» l'avrebbe salvato dal contagio, chiacchierò allegramente durante le sei ore d'auto che separano la Roka Valley da Lae. Poi sembrò perdere conoscenza, tanto che la sua testa si piegò da un lato. All'arrivo all'ospedale, un'infermiera australiana chiese al maestro la causa del male dell'uomo che aveva trasportato. «Stregoneria» rispose questi. «Storie» replicò l'infermiera, con l'atteggiamento tipico del «bianco-medio-civilizzato». Il dottore, invece, che aveva più esperienza in casi del genere, promise di fare il suo possibile ma aggiunse che dubitava di poter salvare il poveretto. Infatti il giovane morì poche ore dopo e non si poté stabilire alcuna ragione fisica del suo decesso.

Giunto in Nuova Guinea, mi ero soprattutto posto il problema di trovare e vedere i *mudmen*; ma, appena dopo averli incontrati, mi sono accorto che il problema più importante era ovviamente un altro: cercar di capire chi sono, perché hanno quelle maschere, quelle armi. Qual è il rapporto con gli altri papua delle montagne (mi stupisce, infatti, che nel villaggio dei *mudmen* ci siano uomini che non indossano quel «costume» e mi stupì, poi, il trovare qualche *mudman* isolato in villaggi lontani e diversi).

A questi primi interrogativi, i discorsi che ascolto e riesco a farmi tradurre sono risposta vaga ma già, in parte, soddisfacente: si copre di fango e si maschera così chi discende da un «ceppo originario» di *mudmen*, un gruppo di uomini che all'origine erano assai pochi. Nel loro villaggio si sono stabilite, col passare delle generazioni, famiglie estranee a quelle originarie; queste nuove famiglie non hanno il diritto di coprirsi di fango. Ed esiste anche il fenomeno inverso: famiglie di *mudmen* sono andate a vivere tra genti diverse, in altri villaggi; questi *mudmen* esuli indossano, in occasione della festa dei loro ospiti, la loro maschera tradizionale di fango.

Queste informazioni sono un primo passo, prime «scoperte»; ma sono anche risultati che rischiano di restare isolati e quindi pressoché inutili, se non riesco a sapere qualcosa di più sull'origine «comune» dei *mudmen*, sia di quelli isolati nel loro villaggio, sia di quelli integrati in altre comunità.

A mettermi sulle tracce è un puro caso.

Quando avevo filmato – appena giunto al loro villaggio – i *mudmen* nei lenti movimenti di quella «danza» con la quale ci avevano accolti, avevo chiesto, tramite l'interprete, se potevo essere accompagnato al fiume Asaro, sulle rive del quale m'era stato detto che i *mudmen* «si truccano», si coprono di fango. Quella mia richiesta aveva avuto un rifiuto secco, ed era anche nata, me ne ero reso conto, una certa agitazione tra tutti i presenti. «Sono offesi» mi aveva spiegato l'interprete «perché il fiume, nel punto dove c'è il fango, è zona sacra, tabù» (dice proprio *tabù*, parola polinesiana che fa evidentemente parte del linguaggio di tutto il Pacifico meridionale). Davanti a quel rifiuto dettato da un motivo magico-religioso, la mia curiosità anziché cancellarsi era, ovviamente, aumentata. Ma in questi casi non può essere né l'insistenza né la fretta ad aiutare il ricercatore; come per un lavoro d'archeologia, occorre scavare piano piano, attenti a non causare frane di sabbia e terriccio (che potrebbero tutto seppellire) e attenti a non colpire con un avventato colpo di piccone un prezioso reperto.

Tra i primitivi, le domande bisogna porle come scavando nella sabbia con le mani: una ogni tanto, ben distanziata, e attenti a quanto accade intorno. A mano a mano che la reciproca conoscenza aumenta, la fiducia e l'amicizia subentrano alla primitiva e giustificata diffidenza.

Tra i *mudmen*, per fortuna, sono rimasto tanto quanto fra i *bushmen* di Pentecôte; e se là riuscii a ottenere di assistere e di filmare il *kgöl* quando ancora era quasi impossibile il solo sperarlo, qui potevo fiduciosamente augurarmi di riuscire a conoscere la storia dei *mudmen*.

Ho passato giorni a ripetermi: il fango fa parte del rito; il fiume dal quale lo traggono è sacro; e le armi (clave, asce, lance, di bambù) sembrano più simboliche che pratiche. Con noncuranza, muto questi miei dubbi in altrettante domande a persone diverse del villaggio in momenti lontani gli uni dagli altri; ed è proprio la serie di risposte che ottengo a comporre a poco a poco la storia dei *mudmen*, come un mosaico. Sono così in grado di conoscere la vicenda della loro origine, in misura e in proporzione che non mi permettono però di discernere tra storia vera o mitizzata leggenda.

I *mudmen* non erano naturalmente tali, un tempo, mi vien detto; erano gente di un villaggio come tanti altri. E come tanti altri furono assaliti da una tribù più forte, che piombò all'improvviso tra le loro capanne, massacrando quanti si opponevano, per rubare viveri e donne. Ma alcuni uomini si salvarono dall'attacco gettandosi nelle acque del fiume, poco lontano dalle capanne; e si nascosero nel fango, per restarvi immobili sino al calare della notte mentre i nemici completavano il saccheggio con riti antropofaghi e danze di trionfo, fermandosi poi a pernottare sul posto.

Appena buio, gli uomini coperti di fango uscirono dal nascondiglio; fecero con bambù e pietre del fiume rozze ma terribili armi.

Strisciarono sino al bivacco di coloro che avevano sterminato i loro vecchi, le loro donne, i loro bambini, e, piombati addosso ai nemici addormentati, li uccisero tutti.

Fu un fatto straordinariamente insolito: per la prima volta, nella tradizione tribale dei papua, gli assalitori erano stati vinti dagli assaliti. Nacquero allora i *mudmen* e la loro fama: uomini salvati dal fango, uomini che dal fango erano usciti come esseri spettrali – bianchi, neri, grigi – e avevano ucciso per vendicare il loro villaggio.

Ancora una volta nella storia dell'uomo (in quella conosciuta e universale, come in quella sconosciuta delle comunità primitive) protagonista di miti ed epopee sembra essere soprattutto la violenza, la morte. Quella morte ritratta, modellata nel fango delle maschere dei *mudmen*, in tutta la sua orrida decomposizione.

Nello scoprire lentamente il *mito d'origine* di questa gente, vengo a sapere che l'apparizione dei *mudmen* è anche un «ritorno dei morti», un'altra vittoria – un altro tentativo di vittoria – sull'evento più temuto: la fine della vita, l'interruzione di un rapporto d'amore, di lavoro, di amicizia.

Gli uomini del fango riappaiono nel villaggio come viventi incarnazioni dei defunti: a loro si offrono cibi, bevande, doni. Tutti sanno chi si nasconde *realmente* sotto la maschera di fango; ma tutti credono egualmente che quella maschera decomposta e orrida rappresenti questo o quel morto *che ritorna* e che bisogna onorare.

Una magia misteriosa toglie all'uomo la vita; un'altra magia gli permette – una volta ogni anno – di riapparire nel mondo dei vivi, Un mistero compensa l'altro nell'equilibrio di un tempo senza tempo, senza dimensione.

Lasciamo i *mudmen* e il loro villaggio, e le foreste e le loro alte montagne con l'aiuto di un elicottero.

Appena siamo in alto e superiamo la cresta scoscesa dei monti sovrastanti le vallate ove ci siamo mossi in jeep e a piedi, intravediamo la linea che si confonde con l'orizzonte lontano: il mare. «Sette sono gli oceani, l'ottavo è la nostra selva» dice un proverbio dei *mogii*, nell'alta valle di Mount Hagen, una gente di montagna che ha conosciuto il mare in un tempo remoto e lo ricorda associandolo all'idea di una immensità insuperabile. Non solo loro, ma tutti i papua dell'interno, anche il più isolato, conservano un antico cordone ombelicale che li lega alla costa, al confine di sabbia e di roccia tra la loro terra e il mare (e come potrebbe essere altrimenti se l'oceano li circonda da ogni lato?). È un rapporto spezzato, dimenticato, il più delle volte temuto. Ma esiste.

Voliamo bassi sul verde della foresta, poi lungo una spiaggia infinita, che corre da Lae verso il Nord. Dalla foresta s'alzano spirali di fumo azzurro a indicare qua e là la presenza di villaggi, tutti a molti chilometri dalla costa. Su questa, i centri abitati non mancano, ma sono in numero nettamente inferiore a quelli dell'interno: una statistica da toccarsi con mano, in un volo di qualche ora a duecento metri di quota.

A terra, con Marvin Hughes, il direttore dei servizi etnografici di Lae, che ci ha accompagnato in questa rapida escursione, parliamo di questo rapporto dei papua con il mare; ed è ascoltandolo che vengo a conoscere i racconti dei «prigionieri venuti dall'oceano».

«Anche se hanno un vero e proprio terrore» mi aveva detto Hughes «i gruppi etnici dei villaggi dell'interno hanno comunque bisogno del mare.»

«Per il sale, immagino...»

«Sì, per il sale ma anche per le conchiglie, preziosa "merce" di scambio, per la loro utilizzazione ornamentale e come monete complementari...»

Camminiamo dove la foresta arriva sino alla spiaggia e un'ombra fresca ci aiuta a parlare e ascoltare senza fatica, anche se siamo in uno dei luoghi forse più caldi e umidi della Terra.

«Accade che per questi scambi siano necessari contatti tra gli uomini che vivono nell'interno e quelli che vengono dal mare.»

«Papua anch'essi?»

«Sì, ma in parte mescolati con gruppi polinesiani abitanti da molte generazioni nelle isole periferiche della Melanesia. In ogni caso, gente profondamente diversa dai loro consimili del *bush*; una differenza che sopravvive persino nelle città ove, evidentemente, le condizioni tribali primitive sono state così profondamente trasformate.»

«Esistono ancora qui, invece...»

«Certo: tutto il mondo papua vive, in questa doppia natura, in questa coesistenza tra l'età della pietra dei villaggi e la città ultramoderna; questo l'avete visto con i vostri occhi.»

Annuisco, e il dialogo riprende là dove l'avevamo interrotto.

«Gli scambi di sale e conchiglie avvengono lungo queste spiagge... senza un rapporto diretto (peraltro difficile per l'impossibilità d'intendersi, dati i linguaggi differenti). È una sorta di scambio, di baratto *muto*.»

«Se ne conoscono esempi anche in Africa...»

«È identico: qui, come laggiù, lo scambio si basa, al contempo, sulla fiducia e la sfiducia più assolute: fiducia perché i due contraenti abbandonano le loro merci a se stesse, senza montar la guardia; ma tornano a riprendersi il frutto del baratto solo quando la controparte se ne è andata, per paura di incontrarla. E in ciò sta la fiducia, cioè la reciproca paura d'esser catturati da un gruppo più forte...»

«Cosa che avviene spesso, credo.»

«Oggi non più, ma un tempo era avvenimento di cronaca comune... In genere erano i *bushmen* a tentar di catturare la gente venuta dal mare, e non solo per impossessarsi del sale e delle conchiglie senza alcuna contropartita, ma anche perché un "prigioniero" del genere era preda preziosa. Era una sorta di ostaggio per divinità diverse e temute; il villaggio lo considerava un sacro e vivente amuleto...»

«Quindi le sue condizioni di prigionia erano buone...»

«Certo, ottime. Fino al giorno in cui, però, ci si accorgeva che certi malanni al villaggio accadevano lo stesso: una epidemia, o la perdita di un raccolto, o l'incendio d'una capanna. In quel caso l'uomo-amuleto appariva d'un tratto non più come un portatore di buona sorte, ma un seminatore di disgrazia. Andava eliminato, e subito. Lo si copriva di fango bianco, il colore del sacrificio e della morte, e veniva ucciso...»

«Usi e costumi superati...»

«Sì e no. Legalmente puniti, certo. Caduti in gran parte in disuso, certo... Ma ancora praticati. Ne abbiamo avuto la prova nel 1969.»

«Un omicidio rituale?»

«Un tentato omicidio... ai danni di un oriundo delle Trobriand, in gran parte di sangue polinesiano. Veniva sulla costa della Guinea, periodicamente, a commerciare.»

«In canoa?»

«In canoa, a vela. Una bella imbarcazione, che però un giorno fu presa da una tempesta improvvisa e naufragò, proprio qui dove siamo ora, a un centinaio di chilometri da Lae...»

«Naufrago e catturato...»

«...fu trascinato in un villaggio alle spalle di questa foresta costiera, oltre gli acquitrini. Gli furono tributati onori e cerimonie, che, naturalmente, lo sconvolsero. Finché venne una epidemia, e la gente cominciò a morire come mosche. Il nostro amico fu allora accusato di esserne la causa...»

«Ma chi ha raccontato tutto questo?»

«Lui stesso: lui che riuscì a fuggire, dopo essere stato cosparso di fango bianco sacrificale e destinato a morire.»

«Fu inseguito?»

«E raggiunto: lo avevano aspettato sulla spiaggia, per impedirgli di raggiungere il mare: temevano evidentemente che uccidendolo così, fuori dall'area sacra del villaggio, a colpi di frecce, avrebbe potuto scatenare ire impensabili, tremende, così si limitarono a formare una gesticolante e minacciosa barriera di guerrieri, per impedirgli di raggiungere il mare, e tentare di catturarlo vivo.»

«E lui?»

«Lui si armò di un sasso e, dicendosi: o vivo o morto (non aveva nulla da perdere), si lanciò disperatamente nel gruppo. Nacque un tumulto che portò i contendenti sino al limite dove le onde lambivano la sabbia. Là il fuggitivo si liberò di uno dei guerrieri che lo stava trattenendo, colpendolo alla testa con la pietra che impugnava. L'uomo cadde riverso. La via del mare era libera. Il fuggitivo prese a correre nell'acqua bassa della laguna, sino al bassofondo della barriera di corallo.»

«E nessuno lo rincorse?»

«Nessuno: erano terrorizzati dal solo contatto con l'acqua di mare. Tanto che lasciarono a terra, senza soccorrerlo, il loro compagno ferito dal colpo di pietra; si dibatteva sulla sabbia, soffocato da ogni onda che si infrangeva sulla riva. Probabilmente è morto affogato.»

«E lui, il fuggitivo?»

«Non ha più messo piede a terra.»

«Come?»

«Ha continuato la sua fuga sulla barriera di corallo...»

Ben sapendo quanto sia impraticabile la superficie di quell'ammasso corallino appena affiorante, caotico, insieme di punte taglienti, ricci pungenti, microscopiche alghe scivolose, sentiero d'incubo nel sogno di una fuga resa impossibile da un terreno ostile, guardo con aria interrogativa il mio narratore.

«Sì, sembra impossibile. Eppure quell'uomo s'è salvato corren-do e camminando, e forse anche riposando stremato, su quella sottile lingua emergente tra oceano e terra. L'ha percorsa per quasi sessanta chilometri: fu trovato esausto da un gruppo di pescatori, che cercavano aragoste per un albergo di Lae.»

Sfuggito alla morte decretata dai *bushmen*, l'uomo del mare s'era salvato correndo sulle acque, come per una magia.

Ho ripensato spesso a queste due diverse umanità primitive a confronto nell'oceano più grande del mondo, l'una che teme e odia l'universo liquido del mare, l'altra che lo ama come motivo di vita, come una continua conquista.

Cercavo parole, paragoni, sintesi per concludere il mio raccon-to, di una così lunga avventura, umana e spirituale, tra questi due opposti eppur complementari poli.

Finché un giorno, alla fine dell'ultimo itinerario melanesiano arrivai a un arcipelago periferico del gruppo delle Salomone, una manciata di isole chiamate Malaita.

«A Malaita devi visitare la laguna di Langa Langa... » mi aveva raccomandato un etnologo francese di Port Vila; e un anno dopo il suo consiglio navigavo proprio in quell'immobile specchio d'acqua, uno dei più vasti bacini salmastri della Melanesia. Appe-na la spiaggia e la costa erano rimaste lontane avevo visto galleg-giare al centro dell'uniforme luce diffusa, ove ci spostavamo in canoa, una flotta di macchie scure; ed era a loro – lo sapevo – che l'amico etnologo pensava quando m'aveva consigliato di visitare Malaita e la sua laguna. Per capire il perché non dovetti attendere molto: a mano a mano che avanzavano, le ombre sospese sull'ac-qua sempre più chiaramente svelavano la loro natura. Dopo una trentina di minuti dacché ci eravamo imbarcati, distinguemmo e capimmo quell'apparizione. Era un arcipelago artificiale, una ve-ra e propria città di capanne galleggianti.

Piccole isole squadrate (da non capir perché, senza saperne la storia), quasi zattere di sasso alla fonda; e, sopra ognuna, una capanna con un albero, talvolta un orto, sovente un piccolo cespu-glio di pandano e papaia, formava un'unità umana a sé stante. L'insieme di diverse centinaia di quegli isolotti-comunità, formava un villaggio nella laguna costruito, sasso madreporico su sasso madreporico, da diciassette generazioni di «uomini di mare» che volevano vivere al sicuro, lontani da eventuali attacchi di popolazioni di terra. Ad alcune miglia dalla costa (e dalle foreste ove i *bushmen* hanno i loro villaggi), al tempo della loro prima fuga dalle coste, questi veneziani del neolitico avevano scoperto al centro del bassofondo, sottili lingue di sabbia affioranti e lì avevano costruito le loro case.

Aumentando le famiglie, queste case, però, non erano state più sufficienti; né c'erano altri brandelli di terra ove edificarne di nuove. E così la Venezia degli antipodi vide i suoi uomini trarre dal fondo della laguna, uno dopo l'altro, massi di corallo e accatastarli a creare nuove superfici emerse su cui costruire sempre nuove case e ricavarne microscopici campi di terra.

Un centro sicuro e felice. Ma non autosufficiente. Ché in ogni caso, quel villaggio sorto sull'acqua aveva bisogno di altri centri abitati sepolti nell'ombra delle foreste. E viceversa: gli uni per commerciare i prodotti della terra, gli altri per commerciare quelli di mare.

E così, in un'isola al centro dell'oceano, due comunità irriducibilmente avversarie per la loro stessa natura (una delle quali aveva addirittura creato una nuova maniera di vivere pur di essere lontana dall'altra) dovevano cercare ogni giorno per sopravvivere la maniera di incontrarsi pacificamente almeno negli istanti di rapidissimi scambi. Per questo motivo Malaita resta nella mia memoria come un luogo-simbolo, in quel suo essere un necessario incontro fra due genti decise reciprocamente a odiarsi e a combattersi per sempre. In quel punto ho capito che nel più duro scontro fra uomo e natura, o fra uomo e uomo, l'oceano non può concedere – per se stesso e per chi lo popola – altra soluzione se non la sua stessa, eterna e insopprimibile: accordarsi comunque, per non essere cancellati, annientati.

Oggi sembra sia l'oceano stesso che corra questo rischio; ma se questo accadesse, vorrà dire che anche noi tutti – genti di terra e genti di mare, come gli abitanti di Malaita – saremo condannati alla stessa fine.

Proprio sulla spiaggia di Malaita, davanti alle acque di Langa-Langa, vedo un uomo del *bush* e uno del villaggio sulla laguna incontrarsi per caso e scambiarsi una lunga occhiata. Cos'è: odio? paura? tentativo di ritrovare una via di fuga o di attacco?; o invece è l'inconscia ricerca (uno negli occhi dell'altro) di una speranza, quella di potersi intendere e aiutare a vicenda?

Al di là delle dune che sono confini della laguna, è l'oceano; l'infrangersi di un'onda più fragorosa di altre mi distrae per un istante; quando volgo di nuovo lo sguardo verso di loro per osservarli, i due papua sono scomparsi: uno nella selva, l'altro verso il mare aperto.

Il saluto dei giganti nella laguna incantata della Baja

La riva occidentale dei Mari del Sud? – L'approdo «che non può esistere» –
Le balene grigie e i loro «piccoli» – Una rete di bolle – I cetonauti e le aree
protette – Novemilaseicento chilometri di migrazioni – «Spiaggiamenti» dei
cetacei e l'ipotesi-mistero dei campi magnetici – Una *nursery* per le balene e i
loro «piccoli» – Il riflesso del Tridente d'oro.

Il mio incontro con «le grigie» del Pacifico lo debbo a una chiacchierata a proposito di questo libro; e di come concluderei, in queste pagine, il racconto dei miei trentacinque anni di viaggi nei Mari del Sud.

Mi trovo a Papeete e di queste pagine, appunto, e «come concluderle» sto parlando con mia moglie Anna e un amico francese, quando lei m'interrompe (è una sua pessima abitudine): «Guarda le bandiere e i porti d'origine di queste barche» mi dice (la sua seconda pessima abitudine, oltre a quella d'interrompere chi parla, è di farlo con un argomento che apparentemente non ha nulla a che vedere con l'oggetto della conversazione di quel momento; poi si scopre che l'interruzione era stata provvidenziale e l'argomento si rivela non solo pertinente, ma utile a portare un discorso vago su una sua conclusione, o a un suo interrogativo molto stimolante).

Siamo sul pontile est del porto di Papeete. In riva all'altro *quai*, le navi della Marina francese sono immense e immobili. Minacciose. Tutti gli altri scafi ormeggiati e ancorati qui, ove siamo noi, appaiono non solo piccoli, al confronto; ma allegri, in quel loro dondolare – innocenti, pacifici – al soffio del *maramù*.

Quasi tutti ostentano il vessillo a stelle e strisce e accanto ai loro nomi – in lettere dipinte, o composte in plastica o in metallo – citano i porti di origine: Los Angeles, San Diego, San Francisco.

«La California è la sponda, l'unica sponda dei Mari del Sud» dice, seguendo il mio sguardo e intuendo quel che penso, Robert

Renalais, skipper di una di queste barche, che ci accompagna nella passeggiata sul molo: «Chi viene qui, nel cuore dei Mari del Sud, o chi parte da qui» aggiunge «arriva *dalla* o si dirige *verso* la California. Solo poche barche vengono dall'Australia, nessuna, che io sappia, dal Giappone. Alcune, ma sono l'eccezione che conferma la regola, arrivano dall'Europa via Panama. Insomma: per chi ancora naviga a vela, l'unica grande rotta per la Polinesia, oggi, è da o per la California».

Immaginando l'Oceano Pacifico come un Mediterraneo di proporzioni dilatate, l'unica costa che rappresenta una vera e propria sponda di questo sconfinato specchio d'acqua è in effetti quella americana. Al nord e al sud a delimitarla sono le due aree polari, che non sono «coste» in senso stretto.

E lungo il suo «lato asiatico» il Pacifico diventa Mar della Cina, Mar del Giappone, Mar del Corallo, e Oceano Indiano molto prima di toccare le rive continentali.

«Un viaggio nei Mari del Sud, oggi...» sorride Anna maliziosamente, tanto da farmi intuire che la sua interruzione alle mie riflessioni sul libro che sto scrivendo ancora una volta non è stata così estemporanea come poteva sembrare. Mi par di comprendere che di «*qualcosa*» vuol convincermi; con il braccio, infatti, indica vero l'est, all'incirca dov'è l'America: «... insomma questo tuo viaggio» continua «io penso che debba concludersi laggiù, oltre l'orizzonte. A quella costa della California dove...».

«E infatti» le dico, tentando di precederla, «noi siamo giunti in Polinesia con un volo diretto da Los Angeles; e da qui ripartiremo con altro volo diretto per Los Angeles. È ovvio che quella che passa per la California è ormai la via più breve tra queste isole e l'Europa...»

«Non mi riferivo a un calcolo di orari e di itinerari aerei» riprende Anna, e intanto Robert Renalais ride «ma intendevo dire che se vuoi veramente concluderlo, il tuo viaggio e il tuo libro, se vuoi essere sino alla fine in sintonia con le esperienze che hai vissuto in Polinesia, in Micronesia e in Melanesia, andando di isola in isola e di approdo in approdo, devi far in maniera di navigare, di gettare l'ancora, laggiù. Là dove "finisce" il Pacifico, all'unica sua sponda: la California. Ma devi arrivare non in un aeroporto della California, ma a un suo approdo sul mare... Isolato, poco conosciuto, deserto...»

Deserta la California? Un approdo isolato? Un ancoraggio «in sintonia» con uno di quelli ove siamo rimasti all'àncora nelle isole? Là dove ci sembrava di essere fuori del tempo? Come alle Trobriand, alle Tuamotu, a Tahaa?

Rimugino questi interrogativi e mi rispondo borbottando fra me: ma stiamo scherzando? Cerchiamo di non immaginare quanto non esiste. Quanto non è certo possibile trovare, lungo la costa californiana. Un approdo deserto!

Un meso dopo galleggio nell'impossibile.

Sono all'àncora in un approdo «che non può esistere»: deserto, luminoso, fuori del tempo. Proprio come un ancoraggio delle isole.

Sono in California (nella Bassa California, per l'esattezza), in una zona ove il Pacifico, anzi i Mari del Sud, hanno all'est quella «sponda» che a ovest, a nord e a sud loro manca. Geograficamente valida e poeticamente in sintonia con l'atmosfera delle isole. Infatti è costa sconfinata e selvaggia, poco popolata dall'uomo e frequentata invece da animali d'ogni specie: un cielo, in acqua, a terra.

C'è una California *yankee*, dove i grattacieli spuntano dappertutto e le *highways* disegnano una ragnatela fittissima. E c'è una California messicana a forma di lunga penisola; da un lato – e alla sua estremità meridionale – gremita di turisti made in Usa; sull'altro suo lato, invece, essendo desolata, ostile all'uomo, è salva, ancora vergine.

A terra e in mare.

E nelle sue lagune, dove appunto, in una di esse, io sono all'àncora.

Assieme ai miei compagni di bordo attendo con pazienza che accanto alla nostra barca si materializzi un'apparizione. Poi metteremo in moto e seguiremo l'ombra o le ombre che prima o poi ci accosteranno: balene grigie che in queste acque vengono a svernare, a partorire, ad allattare. Adulte e neonate: gigantesche alcune, più piccole altre.

«Non vorrai concludere un tuo viaggio nel Pacifico senza incontrare le balene?» mi ero detto lasciando i Mari del Sud, convinto da Anna a cercare in California «un approdo finale» al mio viaggio. E a quel suggerimento avevo aggiunto, da parte mia, l'interrogativo sulle balene appena riferito. Lo rivolgevo a me stesso ed era, ovviamente, un interrogativo retorico, al quale già sapevo come avrei risposto.

È vero: debbo finire le mie peregrinazioni in quest'oceano con un *incontro* con lei: la balena. Con l'essere favoloso, mostruoso che conclude ogni percorso iniziatico. E non v'è dubbio: dieci itinerari in trentacinque anni attraverso le isole del mito sono stati, per me, un lungo, complesso viaggio iniziatico. E al mio ultimo approdo non può attendermi altro essere se non il gigante degli oceani, il «mostro» in senso mitico. Benché dolcissima, mansueta, commovente, è lei «quel» mostro. È la balena grigia con la quale ho appuntamento là dove il 25° parallelo s'insabbia nella costa della Bassa California, dopo aver attraversato tutto il Pacifico, e sfiorato le Roca Alijos, deserte isole che sulle mappe nautiche sono indicate come «ancoraggio pericoloso».

Sulla costa, invece, gli approdi sono difficili da reperire, ma sicuri: una lunga sequela di dune sabbiose delinea e chiude due vastissime lagune, oltre le quali svettano – azzurre per la lontananza – le aride cime rocciose della Sierra.

Prendendo alcune di quelle cime come punti di riferimento, un buon skipper sa come individuare la bocca d'ingresso che porterà la sua barca dall'oceano alle lagune; insomma, le estreme propaggini della Sierra sono quei punti di riferimento ai quali i francesi diedero un nome divenuto poi d'uso internazionale: *les amers*. Indispensabili ai piloti di un tempo, quando cercavano approdo e volevano individuare una via d'acqua sicura, tra le insidie: scogliere o secche o barene nascoste da onde e maree.

Quando si navigava senza lòran e senza radar e senza l'aiuto dei radiofari, quei punti erano di vitale importanza. Tanto, che un grande poeta di spazi, di mare, d'avventura e di mondi ignoti – il francese Saint-John Perse – dedicò loro un intero poema e lo chiamò *Amers*; di tale bellezza che, assieme alle altre sue opere, gli valse il premio Nobel del 1960.

Imboccati e superati i canali che *les amers* lontani ci hanno aiutato a reperire (navighiamo su una barca assai piccola, e quindi *a vista* ovvero come nel passato) dal tumulto delle acque oceaniche, dall'onda lunga e alta e da quelle brevi, sferzanti alzate dal vento, passiamo al riparo delle dune. Nelle lagune ove le acque sono sempre calme e l'ancoraggio è tranquillo.

Così com'è tranquillo «il pascolo» per le balene grigie che in questa baia ogni anno passano circa tre mesi. E in essa sopravvivono nutrendosi di quanto i fondali offrono.

Infatti questi misticeti, ovvero il sottordine di cetacei a cui appartiene la famiglia delle «grigie», *abituées* delle lagune californiane, sono le uniche balene che per nutrirsi arano, per così dire, il fondo del mare con il loro muso. L'operazione consente di sollevare acqua, fango e alghe e permette loro di succhiare e filtrare – con i fanoni – piccoli crostacei e pesci. Gli esperti assicurano che a causa del «vizio» delle balene grigie di frugare nel fondo con il lato destro della bocca, su quel lato i fanoni sono consumati. Particolare che non mi è stato possibile controllare. Così come non sono riuscito a vedere (e tanto meno a fotografare) né qui né in altri mari del mondo la famosa rete di bolle.

«Le magattere» spiega una esperta, Lesley Bow, «usano vari metodi per nutrirsi, ma il più strano è sicuramente quello di nuotare in cerchio sotto un banco di *krill*, e l'aggirano mentre, risalendo lentamente alla superficie, espellono aria che sale sotto forma di bolle. Queste bolle formano una sorta di rete o paratia intorno al *krill*. Che permette alle balene di trovare un buon pasto pronto quando "attraversano" la rete di bolle, e hanno a loro disposizione tutto il *krill* che vi era rimasto come imprigionato.»

Non vedo rete di bolle; ma m'è stato invece facile, in queste lagune californiane quasi a tu per tu con le balene grigie, osservare i cirrìpedi, tipici parassiti dei cetacei, che parassiti non sono.

I cirrìpedi infatti si limitano ad attaccarsi alla pelle delle balene; e così viaggiano e si nutrono. Mangiano piccoli organismi del plancton, e i resti dei pasti delle loro ospiti.

E anche per la loro presenza sul corpo delle «grigie», quando il primo degli attesi «mostri», per vedere i quali sono giunto sino qui, emerge, la sua schiena non mi sembra il lato di un corpo vivo, ma parte di una scogliera. Quel dorso lucido, nero, m'appare come roccia lavica coperta di incrostazioni: ostriche, alghe, ricci.

Sono invece i parassiti (e i non-parassiti) cresciuti sul suo corpo; contrassegni inconfondibili di tutti i giganti del mare. Di loro è tappezzato il corpo di quasi tutti gli esemplari che posso osservare: protuberanze e macchie disposte in naturale disordine e in diversa misura a seconda dell'età. Le balene più vecchie ne son coperte come potrebbe esserlo – di decorazioni – il petto di un generale di qualche repubblica centro-africana; altre – le più giovani – ne sono prive.

José Angel Pacheco è il cetonauta messicano che qui mi guida. Appena il primo esemplare, seguito da un intero branco di giganti, è emerso a breve distanza dalla nostra piccola barca, José manovra in maniera da condurmi sulla scia dei bestioni.

Ora siamo a un passo da loro. Non parliamo, aspettando che risalgano di nuovo in superficie. Poi, nel lungo momento in cui emergono per respirare e il corpo di uno di loro appare più di ogni altro coperto di escrescenze, José ha occasione – indicandomeli – di riportare il discorso sui cirrìpedi e sul fatto che non sono parassiti nel senso scientifico della parola. Lo sono invece – mi spiega – alcuni crostacei capaci d'avvinghiarsi alle balene quando sfiorano il fondo, riuscendo poi a infilarsi nelle pieghe della loro pelle: là s'afferrano con zampette adunche che paiono uncini. «E *letteralmente*» dice Pacheco «si nutrono del tessuto superficiale corporeo delle balene causando piaghe profonde e infette. Tali da provocare grandi sofferenze.»

Per liberarsene, le balene fanno di tutto: si rotolano sul fondo o trovano l'energia per compier balzi fuor d'acqua, nella speranza di uccidere o almeno di staccare le colonie dei parassiti dalla loro pelle, con il contraccolpo prodotto dalla ricaduta delle varie tonnellate del loro corpo quando battono sul pelo dell'acqua dopo il salto fuori dalle onde.

Di questi salti riesco a vederne diversi. Qualcuno ha come palcoscenico proprio lo specchio d'acqua ove galleggia la nostra barca; solida nell'affrontare le onde, ma certamente fragile in rapporto al peso di una balena che, avendo preso male le misure del suo salto, concludesse la sua caduta libera proprio sopra o accanto a noi.

«Niente paura! Quel pericolo non esiste» mi rassicura José Pacheco. «Nella laguna ove ci troviamo e dove studiamo le balene da quasi quindici anni, di queste manifestazioni di potenza, di questi balzi spettacolari, ne abbiamo visti a centinaia in ogni stagione, ma sempre ben calcolati!»

Sono particolarmente impressionanti perché questo gentile «mostro», benché si nutra «solo» di piccoli crostacei raccolti, rastrellati, sul fondo del mare, cresce tanto – e in fretta – da misurare già in giovane età quindici metri di lunghezza e trentatré tonnellate di peso!

Tuffi «al contrario», dal mare verso il cielo che nei mesi dell'inverno, quando le balene sono «di casa» nella Bassa California, hanno due diversi motivi. Oltre a quello di tentare la pulizia esterna del corpo, i «tuffi in cielo» sono «vivaci, eccitate dichiarazioni d'amore di maschio a femmina, o viceversa» mi precisa José, con sorriso malizioso. E mi spiega perché questa laguna ai margini orientali del Pacifico ha una essenziale importanza per la sopravvivenza della balena grigia, la più giovane delle famiglie delle balene, giovane nel senso che con i suoi 100.000 anni d'età, la famiglia delle «grigie» è coetanea dell'uomo, in un certo senso. Forse è per tale motivo – sostiene qualcuno – che «sentiamo» questo cetaceo molto vicino a noi; e d'altra parte, sembrerebbe evidente anche l'inverso e cioè che «esso» dimostra grande attrazione per gli umani. Sono soprattutto le balene grigie a dimostrare curiosità verso di noi, a emergere così spesso accanto alle barche che le seguono. A osservare i «cugini» mammiferi terrestri...

Vastissimi specchi d'acqua, sempre calmi perché protetti da isole frangiflutti, queste lagune sono da sempre luogo privilegiato d'incontro tra i maschi e le femmine della famiglia delle «grigie».

Sono il luogo da loro scelto come habitat ottimale in relazione ai due momenti fondamentali nella loro vita: l'accoppiamento e il parto.

Ai primi rigori dell'inverno artico, a settembre, le balene lasciano le acque oltre il Circolo Polare, il Mare di Bering e di Beaufort. Muovono verso il Sud prima che quelle superfici marine vengano coperte dal ghiaccio del *pack*.

La loro migrazione è il viaggio più lungo compiuto da mammiferi viventi su questo pianeta: 9600 chilometri!

La balena grigia, viaggiando a una velocità di circa otto chilometri all'ora, verso gennaio raggiunge le lagune ove ora mi trovo, e dove mi sposto per osservarle e fotografarle assieme a chi le studia, qui, a ogni loro ritorno.

Questi giganti del mare seguono differenti rotte per raggiungere le più diverse destinazioni ove possano trovare acque tiepide e calme. Alcune di queste rotte sono ignote anche agli specialisti più documentati. Altre sono da tempo conosciute.

«Arrivano al largo della Bassa California verso la fine di novembre a migliaia,» mi racconta José «trovano i canali d'ingresso in laguna senza problemi, e alcune, appena sono al riparo, si cercano e si accoppiano; altre partoriscono e portano a spasso i loro "bebè". Aspettano così il ritorno della primavera per uscir di nuovo in oceano e risalire di nuovo il Pacifico, questa volta in senso contrario: dal sud verso l'Artico.

«Giungono in quelle acque a giugno, quando i ghiacci si sciolgono, il *pack* si spezza, la luce del sole penetra in profondità, "risvegliando" il plancton; e allora tutta la catena biologica marina esce dal suo letargo invernale. Le balene grigie trovano così cibo in abbondanza; tanto che i giovanotti del branco raddoppiano di peso...»

«Torneranno l'anno successivo, ormai liberi dalla tutela della madre» aggiunge Monica Velasquez Ariza, collega di José Pacheco nello studio dei cetacei della California, «e le femmine che giungeranno qui senza un figlio da proteggere e da nutrire, saranno pronte a un nuovo accoppiamento.»

D'un tratto ci troviamo a navigare accanto a un gruppo di «mamme». Quando debbono prender fiato, emergono accanto a noi, senza paura. Vicino alla loro schiena immensa appare quella più piccola del figlio, che naviga letteralmente attaccato a una delle pinne laterali della genitrice. (È un figlio «piccolo» per modo dire: alla nascita già pesa una tonnellata!)

Vedendo apparire sempre più vicini diversi esemplari di «grigie», ho tutto il tempo di notare (e fotografare) alcuni dettagli che rendono questa balena inconfondibile. La sua testa ha un aspetto abbastanza rozzo. Ha peli sulla mascella superiore e invece della pinna dorsale presenta una decina di piccole protuberanze, vicino ai lobi triangolari.

Il colore degli esemplari adulti è di un grigio maculato, con chiazze giallastre di cirrìpedi sulla testa e sul dorso. Due corte pieghe, o solchi, sulla gola, sono molto evidenti, e li noto più volte durante gli «incontri» che si ripetono durante tutto il periodo in cui resto in queste acque.

Dopo aver trascorso tutto il giorno in barca, alla sera alloggio insieme agli altri cetonauti in un accampamento sulla riva.

Un pomeriggio ci rechiamo a vedere quanto resta di una balena grigia *spiaggiata*. L'incidente è avvenuto due settimane addietro; nessuno se ne è accorto; nessuno quindi, ammesso che fosse stato possibile, ha potuto tentare di salvare il gigante finito «in secca».

Osserviamo da lontano – l'odore della decomposizione è barriera insuperabile – il corpo gigantesco. José, quasi intuendo la mia domanda, mi offre, di questo "errore di navigazione" di una balena, l'unica spiegazione che possono dare per ora gli specialisti in cetologia.

«Sugli arenamenti dei cetacei si legge di tutto: sono dovuti a un istinto suicida o alle più diverse malattie, a un "colpo di sonno", come se le balene fossero autisti di camion. Oppure si attribuisce l'incidente a uno "smarrimento di rotta", causato dall'infittirsi delle trasmissioni radio; oppure da "turbamenti" causati da eventi naturali: maremoti, uragani; e anche, ovviamente, all'inquinamento. Nessuna di queste ipotesi, però, è in grado di chiarire in forma soddisfacente il mistero. È evidente, per tutti noi che studiamo il fenomeno» continua Pacheco «che le balene si arenano per errori di navigazione, di casi come questo ora davanti ai nostri occhi ne ho visti ormai a decine. Perché quella bestia ha navigato dritta dritta verso una barriera di sabbia in basso fondale?»

«Gli scienziati del Centro oceanografico di San Diego» aggiunge Monica Velasquez, completando quanto il «suo capo» mi stava dicendo, «si riferiscono al "campo geomagnetico" della terra, ove si evidenziano – loro sostengono – punti elevati e punti bassi, detti "colline" e "valli"; poiché è certo che le balene sono sensibili al magnetismo (e sanno *leggere* questo "campo" proprio come noi leggiamo una mappa geografica) gli incidenti accadono per l'errata valutazione dei "dati magnetici" da parte di una balena.»

«Secondo quanto scrive in proposito la nostra collega Lesley Bow» conclude José «la causa di questa "errata valutazione" si deve al fatto che ogni balena, per interpretare i dati del "campo magnetico", naviga cercando di avere il "campo" più elevato da un lato e quello più basso dall'altro, come facciamo noi quando camminiamo lungo il pendio di una collina, un passo a monte e uno a valle. In oceano, in mare, lungo le coste, in questa stessa laguna può però accadere che le colline e le vallate magnetiche non finiscano lungo il litorale, ma continuino a terra. La balena non se ne accorge, continua a seguire il suo tracciato magnetico, e si trova in secca...»

Monica mi guarda di sottecchi: «Un po' complicato vero?».

«Già...» rispondo.

«Beh, debbo confessare che anch'io non riesco a capire fino in fondo questa teoria; o meglio: la capisco, ma non riesco a farla mia...»

Il soggiorno sulle rive e nelle acque delle lagune occidentali della Bassa California si protrae abbastanza a lungo da permettermi di visitarle in entrambe le «aree» in cui sono suddivise.

Un preciso confine divide infatti questi «pascoli» per cetacei in due settori: in uno, quello più esterno, incrociano sbuffando le coppie che si cercano, si corteggiano e si accoppiano; in quello più interno, dalle acque più calme e calde, pascolano con solenne lentezza le famigliole rette a regime esclusivamente matriarcale.

Le barche degli studiosi possono navigare in entrambi i bacini; non così quelle sulle quali s'imbarcano i curiosi, gli amanti della natura, che sborsano un bel gruzzolo in dollari ad agenzie specializzate per raggiungere le aree lagunari della Bassa California con un volo a bordo di un vetusto DC3 e dopo quattro ore di cammino accidentato tra le rocce della regione, sino a raggiungere le rive lagunari.

Per me e per Andrea che mi assiste in questo ultimo approdo del mio peregrinare nel Pacifico (iniziato prima che lui nascesse!) la situazione è delicata. Possiamo navigare in entrambe le lagune o solo in una?

In effetti non siamo certo «scienziati», ma nemmeno – per la verità! – dei turisti. M'accorgo quant'è difficile esser ammessi dai guardiani del Servizio ecologico messicano nella zona lagunare; quella che definirei la *nursery*, dove incrociano, s'immergono, emergono e si nutrono le gigantesche mamme balene e, non meno imponenti, i loro pargoli. Qui i cetonauti messicani sono restii a concedere permessi di navigazione anche a barche piccole; e questo perché tutta la zona è, dagli anni Settanta in poi, area protetta da legge speciale delle autorità messicane. Un atto coraggioso, che nella Bassa California – ben più che altrove – viene applicato con serietà e impegno.

Comunque, alla conclusione di una lunga, reciproca spiegazione (io «capisco» il loro punto di vista; loro «comprendono» il mio) otteniamo di poter navigare e fotografare anche «tra le mamme».

Nostro accompagnatore (guida ma anche sorvegliante) sarà Monica Velasquez. E così con lei possiamo continuare a intrecciare lunghe chiacchiere sulle «grigie», nei tempi morti che trascorriamo in attesa di una loro «visita».

Essendo Monica una delle più severe guardiane del Parco ecologico creato nelle lagune della Bassa California, il discorso finisce sempre su uno stesso tema: la protezione delle balene.

A questo proposito, ricordando il tempo in cui esse venivano sterminate, Monica Velasquez mi fa notare un comportamento, nei cetacei che avviciniamo, esattamente opposto a quello naturale di ogni animale che vive allo stato selvaggio. Leoni, gazzelle, elefanti, orsi, e quant'altri esseri liberi si vogliano citare, sono estremamente sospettosi verso l'uomo, se non aggressivi (per difesa, quasi sempre). Se li si avvicina per osservarli o fotografarli, bisogna porre la massima attenzione alla direzione del vento, che può portare al «selvatico» l'odore dell'uomo; e occorre star bene attenti a non provocare rumori *inconsueti, estranei*, tali da insospettire e mettere in fuga l'animale che si voglia riprendere da vicino. Qui, tra le balene della Bassa, accade il contrario.

Quando Andrea, instancabile nell'aiutarmi a raccogliere documenti sui nostri incontri in laguna, sostituisce alla macchina fotografica il registratore, per cogliere il suono di una delle tante balene che emergono e «soffiano» accanto a noi, chiediamo al marinaio responsabile della scialuppa su cui siamo imbarcati di spegnere per qualche minuto il motore. Lui esegue ma, anziché farsi meno sospettose per il gran silenzio subentrato al fastidioso ronzio del fuoribordo, e lasciarsi avvicinare più facilmente, le balene che ci circondano spariscono sott'acqua. S'allontanano.

Qualche ora dopo la situazione si ripete: spegniamo una seconda volta il motore, prepariamo registratore e microfono; ma non tardiamo a convenire su una evidenza: contro ogni regola, il rumore del fuoribordo attira le balene, il silenzio sembra spaventarle, e causarne la fuga.

«Non *sembra*, è proprio così...» precisa la nostra accompagnatrice «il silenzio spaventa questi animali. Probabilmente sono rimasti in loro ricordi registrati come esperienze (e quindi sono molle reattive del loro istinto) quelli in cui barche con fiocinatori si avvicinavano di soppiatto a loro e le colpivano con i loro arpioni. Il rumore del fuoribordo, invece, è oggi quello di una barca amica, con la quale si può, per così dire, "fraternizzare".»

L'ipotesi che suggerisce Monica Velasquez è suffragata dalle cronache: la cetonauta ci ricorda che in queste lagune, ove la vita dei grandi cetacei è ora protetta, fino agli anni Quaranta la caccia portava strage. Uccidere le balene grigie non solo era permesso, ma la loro mattanza era sovvenzionata dal Ministero messicano della Pesca. E Monica Velasquez continua: «Solo agli inizi degli anni Settanta sono state emanate le prime limitazioni e poi, di anno in anno, regolamenti di proibizione, e leggi sempre più severe di protezione. Malgrado questo, sino a poco più di una decina di anni fa, nelle lagune della Bassa entravano clandestinamente cacciatori di balene giapponesi. I loro pescherecci d'alto mare, attrezzati a lavorare subito "il pescato", restavano al largo attendendo il frutto della strage compiuta dai loro fiocinatori in laguna; dove, se riuscivano a eludere la scarsa vigilanza della nostra guardia costiera, sterminavano le "grigie" proprio nella loro stagione degli amori e delle nascite. Tanto che anche queste balene, a quel tempo, cominciavano a essere in pericolo d'estinzione».

Ora con leggi più severe anche in campo internazionale e un rafforzato sistema di vigilanza, si calcola che tra le due immense lagune della Bassa California, di «grigie» se ne muovano, come ospiti stagionali fisse, circa tremilacinquecento.

Risultato meritevole di riconoscimenti, quali tutto il mondo ha voluto aggiudicare ai cetonauti della Bassa California. Tra l'altro, anche il Tridente d'Oro, l'ambito premio scientifico ed ecologico, ogni anno proclamato a Ustica, dalla nostra «Accademia delle Scienze del Mare e Sottomarine». Il tridente: simbolo di un'arma che in mare un tempo uccideva. E ora protegge.

Vedo il distintivo del premio sul giaccone a vento che indossa il capogruppo dei cetonauti della Bassa, José Angel Pacheco, la fredda mattina in cui m'accompagna a una pista di terra, ove un DC3 messicano scende ogni tanto a raccogliere o a sbarcare gli eremiti che vanno e vengono da questa zona costiera per studiarne l'habitat. E cercare di proteggerlo.

Il sole batte sulle piccole tre punte d'oro che fanno la loro bella figura sul blu scuro della cerata di José.

Ripenso al giorno in cui avevo proposto, all'«Accademia delle Scienze del Mare e Sottomarine» a Ustica, di attribuire quel riconoscimento a un gruppo sconosciuto di giovani e coraggiosi studiosi decisi a difendere le balene del Pacifico. Ricordo che agisce nella mia memoria come una dissolvenza, un incrocio e sovrapposizione di immagini.

Cancella, dissolve l'immagine di questo oceano della sua costa e delle sue lagune – il paesaggio che ho attorno – e ne compone un'altra. La familiare visione di un gruppo di case bianche sul mare, una piazza, un porto; e le barche di quell'isola mediterranea al largo di Palermo. Là eravamo riuniti per decidere a chi attribuire – quell'anno – il nostro Tridente. Là lo destinammo ai coraggiosi cetonauti di un oceano lontano, i difensori delle «grigie».

A quel ricordo, dimentico il Pacifico e sento, improvviso, un gran desiderio di tornare a casa. Al mio mare.

Indice
dei nomi e dei luoghi

457

Indice generale

«I Mari del Sud
di Folco Quilici»
Collezione Ingrandimenti

Arnoldo Mondadori Editore

Finito di stampare nel mese di novembre 1991
presso la Milanostampa - Farigliano (CN)

Stampato in Italia - Printed in Italy